D0266573

# *Marguerite Patten's*
# 1,000 FAVOURITE RECIPES

FLO

*Marguerite Patten's*

# 1,000 FAVOURITE RECIPES

Bounty Books

First published in Great Britain in 1983 by Marylebone Books

This edition published 2006 by Bounty Books,
a division of Octopus Publishing Group Ltd
2–4 Heron Quays, London E14 4JP



ISBN-13: 978-0-753714-55-3
ISBN-10: 0-753714-55-8

A CIP catalogue record for this book is available
from the British Library

Printed and bound in Spain

# Contents



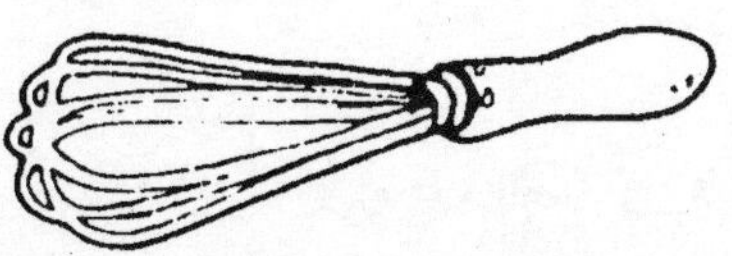

# Introduction

I am delighted to write the introduction to this re-issue of my ***1,000 Favourite Recipes***. When the book was published originally, cooks were loud in their praise and enthusiasm. Comments like, 'I don't know how I managed without it,' were commonplace. The publishers and I have had a very considerable number of requests for the book to be reprinted – and here it is!

All the cookery books I have written have given me pleasure and pride. Some deal with cooking techniques, others reflect the close links between history and food, many are based on changing times and tastes. As the title suggests, ***1,000 Favourite Recipes*** is special, for it contains my timeless choice of well-loved dishes.

People ask, 'How can you test and cook so many dishes?' It is not difficult. For a very long time I gave cookery demonstrations throughout Britain and abroad, cooked on television and discussed foods, cooking and health on radio. Most importantly I have friends and family who share my love of the good food of various countries, so that cooking is not only my job, it is my enjoyment too.

Let me tell you a little about the favourite recipes. As you would imagine these cover appetising dishes for all seasons and occasions; most are based on fresh foods. Nowadays some people would cite lack of time as their reason for cooking less often. Just turn the pages and you will find many recipes that will enable you to produce splendid meals within a short time. Nutritious and interesting cooking need not mean spending hours in the kitchen, nor does it entail spending a fortune on ingredients.

I hope experienced cooks will approve of the inspirational and unusual recipes and that relatively new, and even young, cooks will find the book helpful. At the beginning of each section, or before recipes with special ingredients, there is basic information on choosing, preparing and wise cooking of these. We are urged to include plenty of vegetables and fruits in our meals, and the generous number of recipes using these foods will help achieve this objective. Healthy and delicious meals benefit all members of the family and will win praise for the cook.

Best wishes and enjoy cooking!

Marguerite Patten

# Using the Recipes

Recipes give both metric and Imperial weights and measures. In order to achieve complete success it is important to follow *either* the metric *or* the Imperial figures. Do not confuse the two sets.

When using some recipes for cakes, pastry, etc., you will find I have given less standard metric weights, e.g. in a Victoria sandwich I state 100 g butter or margarine, 110 g caster sugar and 110 g flour with the 2 large eggs. This is to produce the same sized cake that will fit into the same sized tins as when following the Imperial weights, there is more about this on page 351.

**Spoon Measures:** all spoons are a level measurement. Use spoons of standard size.

**Choice of Ingredients:** in some recipes I give a choice of ingredients, e.g. butter or margarine; 2 to 3 onions, etc. The first is *my* personal choice but the recipe can be made with the second ingredient if it is better suited to your requirements or tastes. Sometimes I specify the size of onions or other foods, this is because I feel it important; in other recipes I do not mention the size, for it does not affect the success of the dish.

**Type of Flour:** Some recipes specify a particular type of flour, for this is important. In a recipe where self-raising flour is given you can substitute plain flour with baking powder, see details on page 348. Where recipes simply state 'flour' you can use plain or self-raising flour, although plain flour is correct for coating food and thickening sauces and other liquids.

**Using Herbs:** As fresh herbs give a better flavour to most dishes I generally recommend these; remember chopped fresh herbs can be frozen for winter use. If you need to substitute dried for fresh herbs in a recipe use a maximum of half the quantity, i.e. instead of 2 teaspoons chopped fresh herbs use only 1 teaspoon dried herbs.

**Oven Settings:** I use a variety of cookers when I travel and give demonstrations. This has made me appreciate just how individual ovens vary. All recipes are carefully tested in both electric and gas ovens, but please check the recommended temperature with the knowledge of your particular cooker.

I give the position in which to place the food, where this is important; but if you are the owner of a fan-assisted electric oven you will appreciate that all parts of the oven are of the same heat. It is also advisable to reduce the heat by about 10°C/25°F when using this type of cooker. The timing in recipes assumes the oven has been preheated at the correct setting.

**Freezing:** Nowadays a question I am invariably asked when cooking a particular dish is "Will it freeze?" You will find this symbol ⊛ by dishes that I consider freeze well. Please note the opening remarks in each section though, for although this symbol generally means the cooked dish will freeze there are exceptions. In the case of fish dishes, I prefer to freeze the prepared, but uncooked, dish to avoid over-cooking the fish.

**Servings:** Unless the recipe states to the contrary each dish serves 4 people.

# Hors d'oeuvre and Starters

I thought the best way to introduce my one thousand favourite recipes is in the same way that I so often introduce various friends and acquaintances, by asking them to come to my home for canapés and a drink. Many people say they dislike this form of entertaining, but I do not. It seems to me an excellent way of meeting and talking to lots of people without the interruption of a meal. Obviously there are many times when I would rather entertain friends to a leisurely luncheon, dinner or even a traditional British tea.

So many people enjoy wine today that you might consider serving wine instead of a wide variety of other drinks. It makes it much easier to plan if you just offer people a choice of well-chilled white and/or rosé wines or a good red wine. If it is a special occasion then obviously a sparkling wine is much appreciated. As champagne has become almost unbelievably expensive, check with your wine merchant about the other good sparkling wines that are now available from France, Germany, Italy and Spain.

On the following pages you will find a selection of ideas to serve with drinks ranging from classic Aspic Canapés to modern Dips. Allow about 6 small canapés per person, or rather more if you know your guests have healthy appetites. Each dip given will serve 4 to 6 people but if you are planning to have several different kinds, then obviously they will be enough for more people.

Make all the food you offer with drinks in a form that is easy to handle, as well as delicious to eat. It is not easy to hold a glass, a handbag and delicate pieces of food; each canapé or nibble should be bite-sized.

Do not freeze the Aspic Canapés on page 9 until the jelly is set. Do not freeze any of the savoury dishes that contain hard-boiled eggs and those based upon crisp ingredients, like celery.

Barquettes and Bouchées, page 13 or the tartlets on page 27 should be frozen without a filling. The fillings can be frozen separately. The freezing symbol ⊛ refers to the prepared or cooked dish, many of the dishes can be made with defrosted frozen foods.

# Canapés and Nibbles

The following pages give some of my favourite ideas to serve with drinks. In addition to the recipes in this section, I often cut one or two kinds of quiche into bite-sized pieces. I also find that squares of a hot or cold pizza are a great favourite. Recipes for these dishes are on pages 276 and 279

## Aspic Canapés ⊛

*Aspic Jelly (see page 264) or use packet aspic*
*rye bread or toasted bread*
*ingredients for toppings can include:*
*smoked salmon, prawns, sardines, smoked eel or mackerel or trout*
*cooked asparagus tips, cooked sliced carrots, peas and other vegetables*
*sliced hard-boiled eggs, scrambled eggs, cheese of various kinds*

Make the aspic jelly. You will need about 600 ml/1 pint to coat 36 to 48 small bite-sized canapés. Allow the jelly to cool and become the consistency of a thick syrup. This stage is very important. If the jelly is too thin it soaks into the bread or toast; if too thick it is difficult to spread over the food. The jelly helps to give an attractive appearance to the canapés and it keeps the topping moist.

Put the whole slices of unbuttered bread or toast on to a wire cooling tray with a dish underneath to catch any drips of jelly; these could be gathered up and used. Do not cut the bread or toast into small pieces. Arrange the food on top, suggestions for suitable toppings are given on the left. Completely cover the topping with jelly; this can be spread by dipping a pastry brush in the jelly or by using a palette knife. Leave until firm then cut into small portions with a sharp knife, dipped in hot water.

## Cheese Butter ⊛

*50 g/2 oz butter*
*salt and cayenne pepper*
*50 g/2 oz Cheddar or other hard cheese or 25 g/1 oz Parmesan cheese, very finely grated*

Cream the butter until very soft and light. Beat in the salt, pepper and grated cheese. If storing in the freezer or refrigerator, keep well-covered so that it does not form a hard surface and prevent easy piping or spreading.

VARIATIONS

Soften cream cheese with a few drops of cream or mayonnaise then season well; use instead of Cheese Butter.

⊛ **Anchovy Butter:** Cream the butter with a shake of pepper then add enough anchovy essence to flavour and colour the butter.

## Rich Cheese Pastry ⊛

*225 g/8 oz plain flour*
*salt and cayenne pepper*
*pinch dry mustard powder*
*75g/3 oz butter*
*75 g/3 oz Parmesan cheese, finely grated*
*2 egg yolks*
*a little water*

Sift the flour with the seasonings, rub in the butter, then add the grated cheese. Bind with the egg yolks and just enough water to make a firm rolling consistency. The mixture is very short and inclined to crumble so handle firmly and roll out very firmly too. Use in the recipes below.

VARIATION

⊛ **Economical Cheese Pastry:** Use 75 g/3 oz margarine and 50 g/2 oz grated Cheddar or other cheese. Bind with milk instead of egg yolks. This pastry does not keep as well as the richer version above, so bake and use when fresh, or freeze the cooked biscuits.

## Cheese Butterflies

*Cheese Pastry (see above)*
*Cheese Butter (see page 9)*

Roll out the Cheese Pastry and cut into 3.5 cm/1½ inch rounds; cut half the rounds through the centre to make wings. Bake towards the top of a hot oven (220°C/425°F or Gas Mark 7) for 7 to 10 minutes. Pipe or spread the Cheese Butter on the centre of the rounds, press the halved biscuits into position. Makes about 18.

## Cheese Straws ⊛

*Cheese Pastry (see above)*
GLAZE:
*1 egg white or 1 egg yolk and ½ tablespoon water*

Roll out the Cheese Pastry until about 1.5 cm/¾ inch in thickness and a neat oblong shape. Cut into fingers about 5 mm/¼ inch in width and 5 cm/2 inches in length. Lift carefully on to lightly-greased baking trays; brush either with the egg white (this gives a delicate glaze) or the egg yolk beaten with the water, for a golden colour. Bake towards the top of a hot oven (220°C/425°F or Gas Mark 7) for 7 to 10 minutes. Allow to cool on the baking tray, for the straws are very fragile. Store in an airtight tin or freeze for up to 3 months. Makes 36 to 40.

VARIATIONS

If using the more economical pastry, bake for a slightly longer time in a moderately hot oven (200°C/400°F or Gas Mark 6).

Save some of the pastry, cut into rings and bake and insert 6 or 7 Cheese Straws into each ring to serve.

These straws look most attractive if one end is dipped in mayonnaise and paprika and the other in mayonnaise and chopped parsley. Do this just before serving.

## Carrot and Cheese Balls

*175g/6oz Cheddar cheese, very finely grated*
*2 tablespoons thick mayonnaise*
*50g/2oz carrots, finely grated*
COATING:
*50g/2oz walnuts, finely chopped*

Blend the cheese, mayonnaise and grated carrot together; form into about 30 small balls then roll in the chopped nuts. Chill and put into paper cases or on cocktail sticks.

VARIATION

**Cheese and Ham Balls:** Blend the cheese and mayonnaise with 50g/2oz very finely chopped Parma or ordinary ham. Make sure the mixture is sufficiently soft to roll around 30 stuffed olives. Chill slightly then roll in chopped nuts or finely-crushed potato crisps.

## Celery and Ham Bites

*1 head celery*
*100g/4oz cooked ham, minced or finely chopped*
*2 teaspoons made mustard*
*100g/4oz cream cheese*

Wash and dry the celery; select only the best-looking and most tender sticks. Mix together the ham, mustard and cream cheese. Press the mixture into the cavities in the celery. Cut into about 30 bite-sized pieces.

VARIATION

**Celery and Cheese Bites:** Blend approximately 175g/6oz of any blue cheese with about 3 tablespoons mayonnaise or well-seasoned whipped cream. Press into the celery and top with tiny pieces of red pepper.

## Mustard Cheese Truffles ⊛

*175g/6oz cream cheese*
*175g/6oz Danish blue or other veined cheese*
*1 teaspoon French mustard*
*pinch mustard powder*
COATING:
*50g/2oz desiccated coconut*

Blend together the cheeses and mustards. Divide into 30 portions, roll in balls. Put the coconut on to a flat dish. Coat the small balls in the coconut and chill well. Press a cocktail stick into each ball.

VARIATIONS

Use crushed potato crisps instead of coconut.

⊛ **Sultana Cheese Balls:** Use 175g/6oz cream cheese and 175g/6oz very finely grated Cheddar cheese. Mix 50g/2oz sultanas with 1 tablespoon mayonnaise. Allow to stand for about 30 minutes so the sultanas become softer. Blend with the cheeses, a little pepper and 2 to 3 drops Tabasco sauce. Roll in balls and coat in crushed potato crisps or crushed digestive biscuit crumbs.

# Sandwich Canapés

Attractive tiny sandwiches can be turned into quick canapés. Make sure the bread is very fresh. Either have the open Scandinavian sandwiches or give a new look by rolling the bread around food, as suggested below. Also use slices of white bread then the filling, then brown bread, then more filling, then white bread to cut into ribbon sandwiches.

## Cocktail Smørrebrød ⊛

*bread or biscuits*
*butter*
*lettuce*
*ingredients for toppings can include:*
*smoked salmon, prawns, sardines, cooked vegetables, sliced hard-boiled eggs, cheese*

Use rye, white or brown bread or small biscuits as the base for open sandwiches; be generous with the butter. Top with the lettuce. Choose a range of colourful ingredients as toppings and try to have at least 2 different ingredients on each of the tiny pieces of buttered bread or biscuit. Cocktail Smørrebrød are made just like the larger ones on page 286 but should be finger-sized.

## Rolled Sandwiches ⊛

*fresh sliced bread*
*butter or flavoured butter (see page 9)*
*asparagus tips, smoked salmon or pâté*

If the bread is inclined to be firm and not sufficiently pliable to roll, remove the crust then roll the bread with a rolling pin, exactly as though you were rolling pastry. Spread with butter or with the flavoured butters. Top with asparagus tips, very thin slices of smoked salmon or pâté of some kind and roll firmly. Either serve as small rolls or cut into slices, like a Swiss roll.

## Ribbon Sandwiches ⊛

*white bread and butter*
*fillings (see page 286)*
*brown bread and butter*

Spread the first slice of white bread and butter with a filling, such as pâté, top with buttered brown bread and a different filling, such as cream cheese blended with chopped herbs, then top with a second slice of white bread and butter. Cut the sandwiches into thin fingers to look like pieces of striped ribbon. Ideas for sandwich fillings will be found on page 286.

## Barquettes ⊛

*Shortcrust Pastry, made with 225 g/8 oz flour etc. (see page 291*
*fillings (see method)*

Make the pastry and roll out until very thin. Use to line 30 to 36 cocktail-sized boat-shaped tins. Put a small piece of foil in each to keep them a good shape and 'bake blind' for 8 to 10 minutes, near the top of a moderately hot oven (200°C/400°F or Gas Mark 6). These little cases brown very quickly so check on both the heat and timing with your particular oven. Leave the cases to cool, then fill. Each suggested filling is enough for all the tiny boats. See page 7 for freezing details.

**Anchovy Barquettes:** Lightly scramble 6 eggs with no salt, but pepper to taste, add 50 g/2 oz finely chopped anchovy fillets. Garnish with Anchovy Butter, see page 9.

**Barquettes Dieppoise:** Finely chop 100 g/4 oz peeled prawns, 100 g/4 oz prepared mussels and 50 g/2 oz mushrooms. Bind with thick mayonnaise. Garnish with Cheese Butter, see page 9.

**Chicken Barquettes:** Chop or mince 225 g/8 oz breast of chicken, blend with 3 tablespoons finely chopped red pepper and 3 tablespoons finely chopped green pepper. Bind with mayonnaise.

## Bouchées ⊛

*Puff Pastry, made with 225 g/8 oz flour etc. (see page 292)*
*fillings, (see method)*

Make the pastry and roll out to just over 1.5 cm/¾ inch thickness. Cut into 3.5 cm/1½ inch rounds and place on a baking tray. Using a 1.5 cm/¾ inch cutter, mark a circle in the centre of each round, cutting halfway through the pastry. Bake for about 10 minutes above the centre of a hot oven (230°C/450°F or Gas Mark 8). Check after 5 to 6 minutes and lower the heat if necessary. Remove the lids so that the bouchées are ready to fill. The hot fillings on page 293 can be adapted for these small cases, but make sure the binding sauce is a little thicker.

Each of the following cold fillings is enough for all the pastry cases. (See page 7 for freezing details.)

**Chicken Cream:** Mince 225 g/8 oz cooked chicken breast, blend with 100 g/4 oz cream cheese, a little whipped cream and seasoning or mayonnaise. This can be flavoured with a small amount of chopped herbs or curry paste.

**Prawn and Cucumber:** Blend 225 g/8 oz chopped peeled prawns with about 4 tablespoons peeled and grated cucumber and lemon-flavoured mayonnaise.

**Scrambled egg and Mushroom:** Fry 100 g/4 oz finely chopped mushrooms in 50 g/2 oz butter; add 3 to 4 eggs and lightly scramble.

# Hot Canapés

Cheese is the basis for some of the most delicious hot canapés. In addition to the recipes below, serve warmed quiches cut into small dice and squares of cheese-topped pizzas. The fried fish dishes on pages 76 and 77 make excellent canapés; serve with Tartare sauce in a bowl in the centre of the dish. Fried baby new potatoes can be served in the same way. Fry mushrooms, serve on rounds of well-drained fried bread. The classic savouries, recipes for which start on page 287, also make good canapés. Make sure the portions are bite-sized and the food is not too hot to handle or eat.

## Boulettes de Fromage

*3 egg whites*
*salt and cayenne pepper*
*3 tablespoons grated Parmesan cheese*
*oil for deep frying*

Prepare the meringue mixture just before frying. Whisk the egg whites until very stiff, add the salt, pepper and cheese. Heat the oil in a deep fat fryer to 190°C/375°F, drop small spoonfuls of the meringue mixture into the very hot oil, fry for 1 to 2 minutes. Drain on absorbent kitchen paper. Makes about 15.

VARIATION

**Cheese and Potato Squares:** Coat diced cheese in flour, beaten egg and crushed potato crisps. Fry as above.

## Cheese Aigrettes ⊛

*6 tablespoons water*
*50g/2oz butter*
*75g/3oz plain flour*
*salt and cayenne pepper*
*2 large eggs*
*50g/2oz Parmesan cheese, finely grated*
*oil for deep frying*
GARNISH:
*parsley sprigs*
*grated cheese*

Put the water and butter into a saucepan and heat until the butter has melted. Remove the pan from the heat, add the flour, salt and a very little cayenne pepper. Return to a low heat, stir until the mixture forms a firm dry ball and leaves the sides of the pan clean. Remove from the heat once again and gradually beat in the eggs then add the cheese.

Meanwhile heat the oil to 170°C/340°F. Either drop small teaspoons of the mixture into the hot oil; or put the cheese pastry into a piping bag with a 5mm/¼inch plain pipe attached and squeeze the mixture through this, then cut with a pair of scissors so small portions drop into the hot oil. Fry for 5 minutes until well risen and golden. Drain on absorbent kitchen paper, garnish with the parsley and cheese. Makes about 24.

# Serving Dips

Dips have become popular dishes to serve with drinks or for informal parties. The food not only tastes delicious, but the fun of everyone dipping into the communal bowl adds to the festive atmosphere. Dips are made in minutes so this saves a great deal of time when preparing for a party.

A good dip must be the consistency of thick whipped cream; if too soft the mixture falls off the foods being dipped into the bowl; if too thick and solid, it is virtually impossible to scoop up the dip with the vegetables, biscuits or other foods.

Spoon the dips into bowls and place these on a large tray or dish surrounded with prepared vegetables, such as baby carrots, or sticks of raw carrot, small lengths of cucumber, florets of cauliflower, quartered firm tomatoes, strips of cucumber, radishes, spring onions and long fingers of green and red peppers.

Crisp cocktail biscuits, cooked frankfurter and ordinary sausages, potato crisps, thin fingers of firm cheese can also be included with the various vegatables. Aim to have a colourful array of foods around the dip.

## Avocado Cream Dip ⊛

*2 avocados*
*2 tablespoons lemon juice*
*3 tablespoons mayonnaise*
*1 very small onion or 2 to 3 spring onions, finely chopped*
*2 tablespoons soured cream*
*2 tablespoons double cream*
*salt and pepper*
GARNISH:
*peeled prawns or salted peanuts*

Halve the avocados and remove the stones. Spoon the pulp into a basin; be careful not to break the skins as these will be used for holding the filling. Add the lemon juice at once to prevent avocado discolouring. Mash thoroughly, then blend in all the other ingredients with salt and pepper to taste. Return the mixture to the 4 halved avocado skins and top with prawns or nuts.

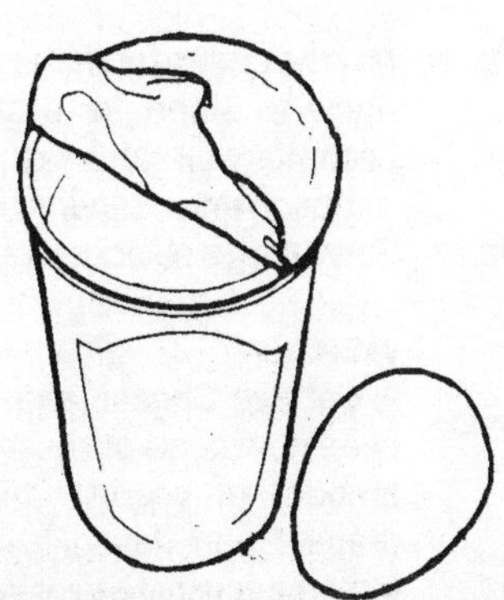

## Blue Cheese Dip ⊛

*175 g/6 oz blue cheese, such as Danish Blue or Stilton*
*2 tablespoons finely chopped onion*
*2 tablespoons finely chopped red pepper*
*2 teaspoons lemon juice*
*approximately 300 ml/½ pint soured cream*
*pepper*

Crumble the cheese into a basin and add the onion and red pepper with the lemon juice. Slowly blend in the soured cream. The exact amount depends upon the freshness of the cheese. If it is very fresh you will not need quite all the amount of cream, whereas if rather stale and dry, you will use the full amount and might even need a little more. Add pepper to taste; salt will not be needed for most people since the cheese has a salty flavour.

Leave the dip to stand for 1 to 2 hours before serving with crudités.

VARIATION

Use a little mayonnaise and fresh cream instead of soured cream.

## Cheese and Mushroom Dip ⊛

*75 g/3 oz butter*
*1 medium onion, chopped*
*175 g/6 oz mushrooms, chopped*
*1 clove garlic, chopped*
*175 g/6 oz cream cheese*
*2 tablespoons lemon juice*
*salt and cayenne pepper*
*2 tablespoons chopped parsley*

Heat the butter in a pan and cook the onion for 2 to 3 minutes. Add the mushrooms and garlic and continue cooking for a further 3 minutes; do not allow to discolour.

Put the mixture into a liquidizer or food processor with the cheese, lemon juice, and salt and pepper to taste and blend to make a smooth purée. Mix in half the parsley. Spoon the dip into a bowl and garnish with the remaining parsley. Serve with biscuits and vegetables.

## Cheese and Corn Dip ⊛

*225 g/8 oz Cheddar or Gouda cheese, finely grated*
*3 tablespoons mayonnaise*
*150 g/5 oz yogurt*
*1 tablespoon Worcestershire sauce*
*175 g/6 oz canned corn*
*1 tablespoon stuffed green olives, sliced*
GARNISH:
*stuffed green olives*

Mix the cheese with the mayonnaise, yogurt and sauce. Allow to stand for a short time so that the cheese becomes well softened. Add the remaining ingredients.

Spoon into a serving bowl and garnish with the olives. Serve with a selection of vegetables and crisps etc.

VARIATION

⊛ **Cottage Cheese and Tuna Dip:** Use sieved cottage cheese instead of the grated cheese and only half the amount of yogurt. Omit the corn, add 225 g/8 oz drained and flaked tuna. Flavour with 1 tablespoon lemon juice instead of Worcestershire sauce.

## Cucumber Mushroom Dip ⊛

*½ medium cucumber, peeled and finely grated*
*50 g/2 oz button mushrooms, thinly sliced*
*1 tablespoon chopped parsley*
*350 g/12 oz cream cheese*
*4 tablespoons single cream*
*1 tablespoon lemon juice*
*few drops Tabasco or chilli sauce*
*1 tablespoon tomato ketchup*
*salt and pepper*

Blend all the ingredients together. Serve with a selection of vegetables, crisps, etc, as detailed on page 15.

VARIATIONS

⊛ **Cucumber and Avocado Dip:** Omit the mushrooms and the tomato ketchup from the above recipe. Blend the pulp from 1 large ripe avocado with the other ingredients. Increase the lemon juice to 2 tablespoons and omit 2 tablespoons single cream.

⊛ **Cucumber and Salmon Dip:** Use sieved cottage cheese instead of cream cheese in the above recipe. Omit the mushrooms and tomato ketchup. As cottage cheese is softer and more moist than cream cheese, use only 2 tablespoons double cream instead of the 4 tablespoons of single cream. Add 175 g/6 oz flaked cooked or canned red salmon to the other ingredients.

## Cottage Cheese and Garlic Dip ⊛

*225 g/8 oz cottage cheese*
*2 tablespoons double cream*
*2 cloves garlic, crushed*
*salt and pepper*

Blend the ingredients together. Cover the dish and leave for 1 hour so that the flavours intermingle.

## Indian Curry Dip ⊛

*25 g/1 oz butter*
*1 small onion, grated*
*1 clove garlic, crushed*
*2 teaspoons curry powder*
*2 tablespoons cornflour*
*300 ml/½ pint chicken stock*
*4 tablespoons tomato ketchup*
*salt and pepper*
*4 tablespoons soured cream*
*cooked chicken, see method*

Heat the butter in a pan, add the onion, garlic and curry powder and fry gently for several minutes, stirring from time to time. Blend the cornflour with the stock and add to the pan with the tomato ketchup. Stir the dip over a low heat until thickened and smooth, then add salt and pepper to taste and soured cream. Keep warm but do not allow to boil. A fondue heater is ideal for this.

Serve with the chicken. The chicken should be cut into neat fingers and dipped into the curry mixture.

## Guacamole ⊛

*1 clove garlic, crushed*
*2 teaspoons very finely chopped onion*
*1 tablespoon mayonnaise*
*2 tablespoons lemon juice*
*2 medium avocados*
*salt and pepper*
*few drops Tabasco sauce*

Blend the garlic, onion, mayonnaise and lemon juice in a basin. Halve the avocados, skin and remove the stones. Add the avocados to the lemon juice mixture immediately so that the flesh does not discolour. Mash with the other ingredients, add salt, pepper and Tabasco sauce to taste.

Serve as a dip. Many people believe that if the avocado stones are put into the bowl until the dip is ready to serve, the flesh does not discolour; however the real secret is to use plenty of lemon juice and cover the bowl until ready to serve. Arrange the bowl on a large tray with a selection of biscuits, crisps and vegetables around. This mixture can be served as a sauce with fish or chicken.

VARIATIONS

Use 1 to 2 tablespoons olive oil in place of mayonnaise.

**Tomato Guacamole:** Concass (skin, halve, de-seed and chop) 2 ripe tomatoes and mash into the recipe above.

## Tomato and Cheese Dip ⊛

*225 g/8 oz ripe tomatoes, skinned*
*225 g/8 oz cream cheese*
*2 tablespoons chopped chives*
*salt and pepper*

Sieve the tomatoes or put into a liquidizer or food processor. Blend with the rest of the ingredients, season well and put into a dish. Serve with raw cauliflower florets and cooked sausages.

VARIATIONS

Use 225 g/8 oz grated cheese with a little cream or yogurt instead of cream cheese.

⊛ **Avocado and Tomato Dip:** Blend the flesh from 1 ripe avocado with the 225 g/8 oz sieved tomatoes; add 100 g/4 oz cream or cottage cheese with the chives and seasoning.

# Tempting Hors d'oeuvre

You will find a considerable number of recipes in this section, for I enjoy both preparing and serving interesting meal starters. I feel a good hors d'oeuvre must fulfil certain important functions. This course should encourage people to feel hungry. Sometimes people are over-tired or just not particularly interested in food. A light, colourful and flavoursome dish at the start of a meal can tempt a jaded palate. If you are normally in the habit of just having a main course and a dessert, there is something festive about introducing a first course to the meal.

When planning an hors d'oeuvre, always consider the main course first. The food served at the beginning of the meal should complement the main dish. If the main dish is rather light, such as one based upon fish, then the hors d'oeuvre can be quite sustaining. A meal starter based upon meat, rice or spaghetti or pastry would be an ideal choice. You will find rice and pasta dishes are not included in the pages that follow, but there are many of these dishes in this book; simply serve a slightly smaller portion.

If your main course is horribly expensive then the hors d'oeuvre can be inexpensive but imaginative.

It is impossible to give general freezing advice for the dishes in this section as they vary in character and the blend of ingredients used. You will however find that the advice given in various chapters and the symbols at the top of each recipe help in deciding what can be prepared and frozen ahead. Generally speaking you should avoid freezing pâtés for too long a period as they lose their moist texture and become dry and unappetising. Freeze for only 3 to 4 weeks. Salad hors d'oeuvre obviously must be freshly made and so should dishes based upon seasonal fruits.

# Fruit Hors d'oeuvre

Fruit makes an excellent start to a meal. What could be more delicious than the luxury of Parma ham with melon or ripe figs or pears? Other less expensive ideas are given below.

## Jamaican Grapefruit

*2 large grapefruit*
*1-2 tablespoons rum*
*2 bananas, sliced*
*1 tablespoon brown sugar*

Halve the grapefruit and remove the segments, discarding any pips. Mix the grapefruit with the rum, bananas and sugar. Spoon back into the grapefruit shells.

## Melon Cocktail

*1 medium honeydew melon*
*1 grapefruit, divided into segments*
*3 canned or fresh pineapple rings, diced*
*2 tablespoons dry sherry*
GARNISH:
*few stoned fresh cherries*
*mint leaves*

Halve the melon and remove the seeds. Either dice the flesh or make into balls with a ball scoop. Mix the melon with the grapefruit segments, pineapple and sherry.

Spoon the mixture into individual glasses and top with the cherries and mint leaves.

VARIATIONS

**Melon and Prawn Cocktail:** Mix the diced melon with 50 to 100g/2 to 4oz peeled prawns. This hors d'oeuvre demands a very delicate dressing, so mix together 2 tablespoons of mayonnaise, 3 tablespoons of soured cream or fresh whipping cream and a little lemon juice with salt and pepper to taste. Spoon the mixture on shredded lettuce in individual glasses.

**Melon and Curried Chicken Hors d'oeuvre:** Blend 3 tablespoons of mayonnaise with 1 teaspoon curry paste. Add 3 tablespoons yogurt and 175g/6oz diced cooked chicken breast together with 25g/1oz cashew nuts. Spoon onto shredded lettuce and top with melon balls.

## Stuffed Pears

*1 tablespoon oil*
*1 tablespoon lemon juice*
*4 small ripe pears*
*100g/4oz cottage cheese, sieved*
*100g/4oz Parma ham, chopped*
*a few lettuce leaves*

Mix the oil and lemon juice. Peel, halve and core the pears and turn in the dressing. Blend the cottage cheese and ham together, spoon into the pear halves and place on lettuce.

# Using Avocados

Avocados have become one of the most popular fruits for an hors d'oeuvre, their flavour is of course a very definite one which I find people either adore or dislike intensely. So always have an alternative such as melon for guests whose tastes you do not know if planning an avocado dish for an hors d'oeuvre.

Avocados must be ripe to be appetising so check carefully when buying them. Do not push the fruit hard at the stalk end; instead, cradle the avocado gently in your hand – it should feel uniformly soft. If a little hard keep in the airing cupboard or somewhere warm, but not too hot, for a day or so.

The simple ways to serve avocados are to split and fill them with a Vinaigrette Dressing, see below, or with shellfish in a Mary Rose Dressing, the recipe for which is on page 25. The fruit discolours very rapidly so have lemon juice or the dressing ready before you cut the avocado and remove the stone. Avocados cannot be frozen as whole fruit, their texture is spoiled, but they can be frozen when made into a dip, see the recipes on pages 15 and 18. You can however keep an avocado in the salad container of the refrigerator for 2 to 3 days to prevent it becoming over-ripe.

## Avocados Vinaigrette

*Vinaigrette Dressing (see page 285)*
*2 large avocados*

Have the Vinaigrette Dressing ready before halving the avocados. Halve and remove the stones, spoon the dressing into the avocados and serve with a teaspoon.

## Avocados Caponata

*1 tablespoon oil*
*1 medium onion, finely chopped*
*2 large tomatoes, skinned, halved and deseeded*
*2 sticks celery, finely chopped*
*1 green pepper, deseeded and finely chopped*
*2 to 3 tablespoons French Dressing (see page 285)*
*2 large avocados*
*4 black or green olives*

Heat the oil in a pan and fry the onion until just soft. Allow to cool and mix with the tomatoes, celery, green pepper and dressing. Halve and stone the avocados just before serving. Top with the onion mixture and the olives.

## Avocados Egyptienne

*3 tablespoons mayonnaise*
*1½ tablespoons lemon juice*
*1 tablespoon tomato purée*
*1-2 teaspoons curry paste or powder*
*2 avocados*
*175g/6oz crabmeat*
GARNISH:
*1 lemon*
*cucumber slices*

Blend together the mayonnaise, ½ tablespoon lemon juice, the tomato purée, curry paste or powder. Halve the avocados, remove the stones and sprinkle with the remaining lemon juice. Blend the crabmeat with the dressing and spoon on top of the avocados.

Cut the lemon into wedges, arrange on each halved avocado and garnish the plates with thinly sliced cucumber.

VARIATION

**Hot Avocados Egyptienne:** Fry a peeled and finely chopped onion in 25g/1oz butter until soft. Blend in 1 to 2 teaspoons curry powder and 1 teaspoon cornflour, cook over a very low heat for 2 to 3 minutes, then blend in 150ml/¼ pint single cream. Season the mixture and blend with 175g/6oz crabmeat. Halve 2 large or 3 smaller avocados, remove the stones and sprinkle with a little lemon juice. Spoon the crabmeat mixture on top of the avocados; put into an ovenproof dish. Heat for about 10 minutes in a moderately hot oven (190°C/375°F or Gas Mark 5).

## Avocados en Cocotte

*3 ripe avocados*
*2 tablespoons lemon juice*
FILLING:
*3 eggs, hard-boiled and chopped*
*75g/3oz cooked ham or salami, finely chopped*
*50g/2oz butter, melted*
*2 tablespoons mayonnaise or double cream*
*3 tablespoons soft breadcrumbs*
*salt and cayenne pepper*
*pinch mustard powder*
TOPPING:
*25g/1oz butter, melted*
*3 tablespoons fresh breadcrumbs*
*3 tablespoons grated cheese*

Mix together all the ingredients for the filling until a soft spreading consistency. Halve the avocados, put into a shallow ovenproof serving dish, cut side uppermost, and top with the lemon juice.

Spoon the filling over the avocado halves and press down firmly. Mix the topping ingredients together and press over the filling. Bake just above the centre of a moderate oven (180°C/350°F or Gas Mark 4) for 15 minutes until the topping is delicately browned. Do not overcook as this will spoil the flavour of the avocados. Serves 6.

## Avocado and Orange Salad

*2 tablespoons salad oil*
*1 tablespoon lemon juice*
*1 tablespoon orange juice*
*salt and pepper*
*2 large oranges*
*2 medium avocados*
*a few lettuce leaves*

Blend together the oil, lemon and orange juice and salt and pepper to taste. Cut away the peel and all the pith from the oranges and cut the fruit into segments. Halve and skin the avocados and put immediately into the dressing. Add the orange segments. Put on to lettuce.

VARIATION

**Avocado and Grapefruit Salad:** Use grapefruit segments instead of orange segments.

## Avocados with Shellfish

*Mary Rose Dressing (see page 25)*
*100g/4oz peeled cooked prawns or other shellfish*
*2 avocados*
*little lemon juice*
GARNISH:
*lemon wedges*
*lettuce*

Make the dressing and blend with the prawns or other shellfish. Halve the avocados, remove the stones, sprinkle with the lemon juice. Top with the shellfish mixture. Garnish with the lemon and lettuce.

VARIATION

**Avocados with Shellfish Mornay:** Make a cheese sauce with 25g/1oz butter, 25g/1oz flour, 150ml/¼pint milk, 4 tablespoons single cream, salt, pepper and 100g/4oz grated cheese. Blend with the shellfish in the above recipe and spoon on to the avocado halves. Put under the grill for 2 to 3 minutes.

## Fried Avocados

*oil for fat for deep frying*
*4 medium avocados*
*1 large egg white*
*25-40g/1-1½oz very fine crisp breadcrumbs*
FILLING:
*75g/3oz butter*
*pinch dry mustard*
*salt and pepper*
*pinch sugar*
*2½ tablespoons lemon juice*
*1 to 2 tablespoons chopped mixed herbs (parsley, chives, tarragon, rosemary)*

Blend the butter for the filling with the seasonings and sugar then gradually beat in 1½tablespoons of the lemon juice and the herbs. Divide into 4 portions and chill for a short time.

Heat the oil or fat in a deep fryer to 190°C/375°F. Halve the avocados, remove the stones and skins. Sprinkle the cut surfaces with a little of the remaining lemon juice. Fill 4 of the avocado halves with the butter mixture, place the other 4 halves over the filling to make the whole avocado shape again. Secure with wooden cocktail sticks. Brush the avocados with the remainder of the lemon juice, then the egg white. Coat in the crisp breadcrumbs and deep-fry for 4 to 5 minutes. Drain on absorbent kitchen paper and serve immediately. Each person should remove his own cocktail sticks.
Note: Never over-cook avocados in this recipe or in any dish where they are being served hot; over-cooking gives the fruit an unpleasant bitter taste.

# Vegetable Hors d'oeuvre

Fresh vegetables can be appreciated more readily if they are served by themselves, rather than with other foods. Globe artichokes and asparagus make some of the most delicious starters to a meal and can be served hot or cold.

When tomatoes and cucumber are at their best, serve them as simple salads topped with a little seasoned oil, vinegar and finely chopped herbs. While the choice of herbs is a matter of personal taste, most French cooks would agree that a tomato salad without basil is sadly lacking in flavour.

## Artichokes Vinaigrette

*4 globe artichokes*
*salt*
*Vinaigrette Dressing (see page 285)*

Trim the stalks from the artichokes, remove any tough outer leaves. Cook in boiling salted water until tender; the time varies from 15 minutes for tiny artichokes to 30 minutes for large ones.

Remove the centre heart (the choke). The tops of the leaves can be trimmed. Cool and fill the centre with vinaigrette dressing before serving or serve hot with melted butter.

VARIATIONS

**Artichokes Tartare:** Fill the artichokes with chopped hard-boiled eggs and Tartare Sauce, see page 100.

**Artichokes with Caviar:** Fill the artichokes with chopped hard-boiled egg yolks and top with caviar (the inexpensive Danish substitute could be used). Garnish with chopped hard-boiled egg whites.

## Asparagus Polonaise

*approximately 1 kg/2 lb fresh asparagus*
*salt*
*75 g/3 oz butter*
*50 g/2 oz fresh breadcrumbs*
*2 hard-boiled eggs, chopped*
*2 tablespoons chopped parsley*

Trim the ends of the asparagus stalks and cook until tender in steadily boiling salted water.

Meanwhile heat the butter, fry the crumbs until crisp then add the eggs and parsley. Spoon the mixture over the asparagus.

VARIATIONS

**Parmesan Asparagus:** Arrange the cooked asparagus on a flameproof dish, top with plenty of melted butter and a thick layer of grated Parmesan cheese. Heat for a few minutes under the grill.

# Fish and Egg Hors d'oeuvre

Most of the dishes in the fish chapter (page 66 to 100) can be served as an hors d'oeuvre. Naturally you will offer slightly smaller portions than when having the dish as a main course. Smoked fish is one of the easiest, as well as most popular starters for a meal. Economical smoked mackerel and trout are now taking the place of luxurious smoked eel and salmon. The accepted accompaniment to both these fish is horseradish cream, but I often serve lightly scrambled egg instead. I was introduced to this pleasant combination some years ago by my sister, who lives in Norway.

Egg dishes with flavour also make a good hors d'oeuvre.

## Prawn Cocktail

*100 to 175g/4 to 6 oz peeled cooked prawns*
*lettuce*
MARY ROSE DRESSING:
*4 tablespoons mayonnaise*
*2 tablespoons double cream*
*2 teaspoons lemon juice*
*2 teaspoons dry sherry*
*few drops Tabasco sauce*
*2 tablespoons fresh tomato purée*
*salt and pepper*
GARNISH:
*lemon slices*
*prawns*

Blend together all the ingredients for the dressing. Add the prawns and allow to marinate in the dressing for at least 1 hour in the refrigerator.

Shred the lettuce very finely and chop into small pieces as it has to be eaten with a teaspoon. Put into 4 individual glasses, top with the prawn mixture. Garnish with the lemon and prawns.

VARIATION

**Piquant Seafood Cocktail:** Make the dressing as above, mix with 3 tablespoons finely chopped celery, 3 tablespoons finely chopped red or green pepper, 75g/3oz peeled prawns, 75g/3oz prepared mussles and 2 to 3 tablespoons flaked crabmeat. Serve on lettuce.

## Crab and Mushroom Ramekins ⊛

*100g/4 oz small button mushrooms*
*40g/1½ oz butter*
*salt and pepper*
*100g/4 oz crabmeat*
*300 ml/½ pint Cheese Sauce (see page 228)*
*25g/1 oz cheese, grated*

Wipe the mushrooms and trim the base of the stalks. Heat the butter in a pan. Cook the mushrooms until just tender. Spoon into 4 individual ovenproof dishes. Season lightly and top with the crabmeat, then the sauce. Sprinkle the grated cheese over the sauce.

Cook towards the top of a moderately hot oven (200°C/400°F or Gas Mark 6) or under a moderate grill, for 10 to 15 minutes or for 3 to 4 minutes in a microwave cooker. Serve with a small spoon and fork.

## Cucumber and Salmon Mousse

*3 tablespoons dry white wine or dry vermouth*
*15 g/½ oz gelatine*
*150 g/5 oz yogurt*
*3 tablespoons thick mayonnaise*
*1 tablespoon lemon juice*
*1 tablespoon tomato purée*
*few drops Tabasco sauce*
*½ medium cucumber, peeled and coarsely grated*
*225 g/8 oz cooked or canned salmon (weight without skin and bones), flaked*
*2 egg whites*

GARNISH:
*lettuce*
*sliced lemon*
*sliced cucumber*
*sliced tomatoes*

Put the wine or vermouth into a heatproof bowl. Sprinkle the gelatine on top. Stand the bowl over a pan of hot, but not boiling, water until the gelatine dissolves. Cool slightly, then add the yogurt, mayonnaise, lemon juice, tomato purée and Tabasco sauce. Stir in the cucumber and fish and leave until lightly set.

Whisk the egg whites until stiff and fold into the mixture. Spoon into 4 to 6 oiled individual moulds or one mould. When firm turn out on to a bed of lettuce. Garnish with slices of lemon, cucumber and tomatoes.

The mixture is firmer with cooked rather than canned salmon. To produce a softer mixture with cooked salmon, add 1 tablespoon extra liquid – either wine, vermouth, fish stock or water.

## Double Salmon Mousse ⊛

*3 tablespoons dry white wine or white vermouth*
*15 g/½ oz gelatine*
*1 tablespoon tomato purée*
*3 tablespoons thick mayonnaise*
*300 ml/½ pint yogurt*
*100 g/4 oz smoked salmon, finely diced*
*350 g/12 oz cooked salmon, flaked*
*salt and pepper*
*2 egg whites*

GARNISH:
*lettuce*
*cucumber slices*
*lemon slices*

Put the wine or vermouth into a heatproof bowl. Sprinkle the gelatine on top and stand over a pan of very hot water until the gelatine has dissolved. Cool slightly then blend in all the other ingredients except the egg whites. (Use salt very sparingly.) Leave the mixture in a cool place until it begins to stiffen.

Whisk the egg whites stiffly, fold into the salmon mixture. Spoon into a lightly oiled 1.2 litre/2 pint basin or mould and allow to set. Turn out and garnish with lettuce, cucumber and lemon slices. Serves 6 to 8 as an hors d'oeuvre.

VARIATION

**Prawn and Crab Mousse:** Omit the cooked and smoked salmon. Use 225 g/8 oz white crabmeat and 175 g/6 oz chopped peeled prawns. Omit tomato purée, and add 1 extra tablespoon mayonnaise to the mixture.

## Smoked Salmon and Spinach Tartlets ⊛

*Shortcrust Pastry, made with 175g/6oz plain flour etc. (see page 291)*

FILLING:
*450g/1 lb spinach*
*salt and pepper*
*25g/1 oz butter*
*25g/1 oz plain flour*
*150ml/¼ pint milk or single cream*

GARNISH:
*50g/2oz smoked salmon*

Make the pastry and roll out very thinly. Using a 6cm/2½ inch cutter, cut out 12 rounds and put into patty tins. Bake blind towards the top of a hot oven (220°C/425°F or Gas Mark 7) for 12 minutes. The tarts should be crisp but pale golden in colour. Lift out of the patty tins and keep hot on an ovenproof dish.

Meanwhile wash the spinach, put into a saucepan with just the water clinging to the leaves. Add a very little salt, cook until tender then drain well and chop or sieve. Heat the butter in a saucepan, stir in the flour, cook for 2 to 3 minutes then gradually add the milk or cream. Continue stirring as the mixture becomes a thick panada (binding sauce). Add the spinach and season to taste. Spoon the hot spinach mixture into the hot pastry cases.

Make 12 small smoked salmon rolls and put on top of the tartlets. Serve at once.

## Sweet and Sour Prawns and Grapefruit

*2 large grapefruit*
*2 tablespoons French Dressing (see page 285)*
*2 teaspoons honey*
*1 teaspoon lemon juice*
*75g/3oz peeled prawns*

Halve the grapefruit and carefully remove the segments of fruit. Do this over a basin so that no juice is wasted. Mix the grapefruit segments and any grapefruit juice with the French Dressing, honey and lemon juice. Add the prawns. Allow to stand for several hours if possible so that the flavours mingle.

Spoon the grapefruit mixture into glasses or into the halved grapefruit skins.

VARIATIONS

**Grapefruit and Crab Cocktail:** Prepare the grapefruit as above but use only 1 tablespoon dressing and 1 teaspoon sugar; omit the honey and lemon juice. Spoon on to a bed of finely shredded lettuce in the grapefruit skins or glasses. Top with a little flaked crabmeat and mayonnaise.

**Grapefruit, Avocado and Prawn Cocktail:** Remove the skin from 1 large or 2 small grapefruit. Cut out the segments of fruit and put into a basin. Peel and halve 1 ripe avocado and cut into neat slices. Mix with the grapefruit, 1 tablespoon French Dressing and 50g/2oz peeled prawns. Spoon on to a bed of lettuce. Do not allow to stand as the avocado has a tendency to darken.

## Egg Mousse

*6 eggs*
*2 tablespoons dry sherry or white wine*
*2 tablespoons water*
*15g/½oz gelatine*
*4 tablespoons mayonnaise*
*½ tablespoon lemon juice*
*150ml/¼pint whipping cream, lightly whipped*
*salt and pepper*
*few drops Tabasco sauce*
GARNISH:
*sliced cucumber*

Hard boil 4 of the eggs; leave to cool then chop the eggs.

Place the sherry or wine and water in a heatproof bowl and sprinkle over the gelatine. Stand the bowl over a saucepan of very hot water until the gelatine dissolves.

Meanwhile separate the remaining 2 eggs and whisk the yolks until thick and creamy. Gradually blend in the warm gelatine mixture. Allow to cool, then mix with the mayonnaise, lemon juice, cream and chopped eggs. Add a little salt, pepper and Tabasco sauce and leave the mixture until beginning to thicken.

Whisk the egg whites until very stiff then fold into the egg mixture. Spoon into 4 to 6 individual dishes and chill until firm. Garnish with cucumber slices.

VARIATIONS

**Watercress and Egg Mousse:** Add 4 tablespoons finely chopped watercress leaves just before adding the egg whites. Omit Tabasco sauce and add a pinch of garlic salt and celery salt.

**Prawn and Egg Mousse:** Use only 3 hard-boiled eggs with 50g/2oz peeled and chopped prawns. Flavour with a little anchovy essence instead of Tabasco.

## Oeufs en Cocotte

*75g/3oz butter*
*2 medium onions, very finely chopped*
*100g/4oz mushrooms, chopped*
*4 eggs*
*150ml/¼pint double cream*
*salt and pepper*
*2 teaspoons Dijon mustard*

Divide the butter between 4 small ovenproof dishes. Heat in a moderate oven (180°C/350°F or Gas Mark 4) for 2 minutes. Add the onions and mushrooms, cover the small dishes with a piece of foil and return to the moderate oven for 7 to 8 minutes, or until the vegetables are soft. Break an egg into each dish. Blend the cream, salt, pepper and mustard together. Spoon over the eggs, return to the oven and cook for 5 minutes or until the eggs are set to your personal taste.

## Oeufs à la Tripe

*50g/2oz butter*
*8 medium onions, sliced*
*1 tablespoon cornflour*
*300ml/½pint milk*
*4 tablespoons double cream*
*salt and pepper*
*6 eggs, hard-boiled and quartered*
GARNISH:
*parsley sprigs*

Heat the butter in a pan and slowly fry the onions until tender and a delicate golden colour.

Blend the cornflour with the milk and cream. Add to the onions and stir well to make a smooth thickened sauce; season to taste. Add the eggs and heat for 1 minute only. Pour into 4 individual shallow dishes and garnish with parsley.

# Making Pâtés

I have given a fairly wide selection of pâtés, including some made with fish as well as various meats and poultry. This is because I, and most of my friends, enjoy making and eating pâté. As well as serving the pâté as an hors d'oeuvre, I often have it for a light lunch. You can cater for a luncheon party just by offering a selection of pâtés with crispbread, French bread or hot toast and butter. Serve with bowls of colourful salads.

## Chicken Liver Pâté ⊛

*75g/3oz butter*
*1 clove garlic, chopped*
*2 small onions, roughly chopped*
*100g/4oz bacon rashers, derinded and roughly chopped*
*350g/12oz chicken livers, roughly chopped*
*4 tablespoons chicken stock*
*2 tablespoons brandy or sherry*
*4 tablespoons double cream*
*2 egg yolks*
*salt and pepper*
GARNISH:
*a few lettuce leaves*
*sliced gherkins*

Heat the butter in a frying pan. Add the garlic, onion and bacon and cook for 3 to 4 minutes. Stir well so that the onions do not change colour. Add the chicken livers and continue cooking for a further 2 minutes only. Mince this mixture or blend in a liquidizer or food processor. Pour the stock into the frying pan, stir well to absorb any juices left, then blend with the liver mixture. Add the remaining ingredients.

Spoon the pâté into a greased 750g/1½lb loaf tin or ovenproof dish. Cover with greased foil. Stand in a bain-marie (a roasting tin filled with enough hot water to come halfway up the loaf tin). Cook in the centre of a moderate oven (160°C/325°F or Gas Mark 3) for 1 hour. Allow to cool in the tin. The pâté is easier to slice if a light weight is placed on top while it cools.

Garnish with lettuce and sliced gherkins. Serve with hot toast and butter.

VARIATIONS

⊛ **Liver and Mushroom Pâté:** Use calves' or lambs' liver in place of the chicken livers. Slice 100g/4oz mushrooms and fry with the liver. When blending the ingredients together use 6 tablespoons cream instead of the 4 tablespoons in the above recipe. Add 1 tablespoon lemon juice with the other ingredients.

⊛ **Country Pâté:** Use 225g/8oz lambs' liver and 225g/8oz pigs' liver in place of the chicken livers. Increase the garlic to 2 cloves. Omit the cream and use 150ml/¼pint good beef stock. The fried liver, onions, bacon and garlic can be put through the coarse plate of a mincer if a less fine pâté is required.

## Liver and Cheese Pâté ⊛

*225 g/8 oz liver sausage or liver pâté*
*225 g/8 oz cream cheese or sieved cottage cheese*
*salt and pepper*
*garlic salt*

Cream together the liver sausage or pâté and cream cheese. Add seasoning and garlic salt to taste.

VARIATIONS

**The above is a basic recipe only; it can be varied by adding a little garlic salt or crushed garlic or you can use sieved cottage cheese in place of cream cheese.**

⊛ **Herb Pâté:** Use the proportions of liver sausage or pâté and cream or cottage cheese above, then beat in 2 tablespoons finely chopped chives, 1 tablespoon chopped parsley, 1 teaspoon chopped lemon thyme, ½ to 1 tablespoon lemon juice.

**Sultana and Nut Pâté:** Soak 50 g/2 oz sultanas in 1 tablespoon lemon juice or dry sherry for 15 minutes, then blend with the liver sausage or pâté and 50 g/2 oz chopped walnuts.

**Watercress and Orange Pâté:** Chop enough watercress leaves to give 5 tablespoons. Halve a large orange, remove the fruit and chop this carefully. Blend the watercress and orange with the liver sausage or pâté and cream or cottage cheese. Use this particular pâté as soon as possible after preparation. Serve with crispbread or wholemeal toast and butter.

## Liver and Bacon Pâté ⊛

*3 bacon rashers*
*75 g/3 oz butter*
*2 medium onions, sliced*
*225 g/8 oz sliced lambs' liver*
*3 tablespoons beef stock*
*3 tablespoons double cream*
*salt and pepper*
*1 teaspoon French mustard*

Cut the rinds off the bacon and reserve; chop the bacon. Heat the butter in a frying pan, add the onions and bacon rinds and fry steadily until the onions are almost cooked. Add the bacon and the liver and fry until tender but do not over-cook.

Lift the onions, bacon and liver out of the pan; discard the bacon rinds. Pour the stock and cream into the frying pan, heat for 1 minute to absorb the meat juices, then add to the liver mixture with salt and pepper to taste and the mustard. Either rub the mixture through a sieve or blend in a liquidizer or food processor. Spoon into a serving dish and leave to cool.

## Sweet and Sour Ham Pâté

*350 g/12 oz cooked lean ham, minced*
*100 g/4 oz butter, melted*
*2 tablespoons chopped parsley*
*6 gherkins, diced*
*4 canned pineapple rings, diced*
*6 black olives, diced*
*2 tablespoons dry sherry (optional)*
*few drops lemon juice*
*salt and pepper*
GARNISH:
*lettuce heart*
*2 canned pineapple rings*
*2 gherkins*

Mix all the pâté ingredients together. The secret of this pâté is to dice the pineapple, gherkins and olives neatly, but not too finely, so you see the contrasting colours. Spoon into a mould and chill well until firm. Turn out and garnish with lettuce heart and small shapes cut from the pineapple rings and gherkins. Serve with brown or wholemeal toast or crispbread.

VARIATION

**Sweet and Sour Duck Pâté:** Mince the flesh from a cooked duck and use instead of the ham. Use only 75 g/3 oz melted butter and add the finely grated rind of 1 orange. Use only 1 tablespoon chopped parsley and add ½ teaspoon chopped fresh sage and ¼ teaspoon chopped tarragon.

## Game Pâté ⊛

*1 plump pheasant or other game bird or 2 smaller birds*
*liver of bird*
*salt and pepper*
*2 tablespoons dry sherry*
*2 tablespoons double cream*
*2 eggs*

Cut all the flesh from the bird. Put the bones into a saucepan with water to cover and simmer for 1 hour, then boil hard until reduced to 4 tablespoons. Strain the stock.

Mince the flesh of the bird with the uncooked liver, blend with the stock and remaining ingredients. Put into a greased ovenproof dish and cover with buttered foil. Stand in a bain-marie (a roasting pan filled with enough hot water to come halfway up the dish). Cook in the centre of a moderate oven (160°C/325°F or Gas Mark 3) for 1¼ hours.

VARIATION

**Chicken Pâté:** Mince the flesh from a small chicken. Omit the stock, in the recipe above, and use an extra 2 tablespoons dry sherry and 2 tablespoons cream. Add 75 g/3 oz diced raw mushrooms.

**Duck and Orange Pâté:** Mince the flesh from a small duck. Simmer the bones with the thinly pared rind of 2 oranges. Use 3 tablespoons of this stock with the other ingredients in the above recipe with 2 tablespoons orange juice.

## Fresh Cod's Roe Pâté ⊛

*450 g/1 lb fresh cod's roe*
*salt and pepper*
*75 g/3 oz butter, melted*
*1 teaspoon anchovy essence*
*2 teaspoons tomato purée*
*garlic salt*
*1 tablespoon lemon juice*
*little double cream*
*1 tablespoon chopped parsley*
*1 teaspoon chopped chives*

Cook the cod's roe in a little salted water until it becomes white – this takes approximately 15 minutes. Drain, skin and mash the roe while warm.

Add the butter, anchovy essence, tomato purèe, a good shake of pepper and garlic salt to taste. Beat the pâté well, then gradually blend in the lemon juice and enough double cream to make a creamy consistency. Beat in the herbs.

Serve with hot toast and butter.

## Smoked Salmon Pâté ⊛

*175 g/6 oz smoked salmon, chopped*
*50 g/2 oz butter, melted*
*1 clove garlic, crushed*
*cayenne pepper to taste*
*5 tablespoons single cream*
*1 to 2 tablespoons lemon juice*

This pâte is not as expensive as it may sound, for many fishmongers will sell the odd pieces of smoked salmon more cheaply and these are excellent. Either blend all the ingredients together and pound hard until smooth, or mince the salmon then mix with the other ingredients. Or blend all the ingredients in a liquidizer or food processor until smooth.

VARIATIONS

⊛ **White Fish Pâté:** Melt 75 g/3 oz butter, blend with 225 g/8 oz finely flaked cooked halibut, turbot or hake. Add salt, pepper and garlic salt to taste together with 4 tablespoons double cream. The pâté can be flavoured with a little anchovy essence, which adds colour as well, or with a little dry sherry or lemon juice, in which case use a little less cream. Add 1 tablespoon chopped fennel leaves, chervil or parsley.

⊛ **Sardine Pâté:** Drain the oil from two 120 g/4½ oz cans sardines in oil, into a basin. Bone the sardines, then add to the oil with 1 crushed clove garlic, 2 tablespoons lemon juice, salt and pepper to taste and 2 tablespoons dry white vermouth. This pâté can be served in hollowed-out lemons, topped with parsley.

⊛ **Smoked Mackerel Pâté:** Flake the flesh from 2 good-sized smoked mackerel. Mix the fish with 1 crushed clove garlic, 225 g/8 oz sieved cottage cheese, shake cayenne pepper, 1 to 2 tablespoons lemon juice (or to personal taste) and 1 to 2 tablespoons finely chopped fennel leaves. If preferred, the mixture can be blended in a liquidizer or food processor, in which case there is no need to sieve the cottage cheese.

## Taramasalata 1 ⊛

*450g/1 lb smoked cod's roe, skinned**
*1 clove garlic crushed*
*75g/3oz butter, softened*
*1 tablespoon lemon juice*
*pepper*
GARNISH:
*lemon wedges*
** The roe weighs appreciably less than 450g/1 lb when skinned*

Mix all the ingredients together. Serve as a sandwich filling or as an hors d'oeuvre with hot toast and butter. Garnish with lemon wedges.

VARIATIONS

For a lighter mixture, add 4 to 5 tablespoons single cream to the mixture.

For a more economical mixture with a less definite flavour, blend in either 25g/1 oz very fine fresh breadcrumbs or 100g/4oz sieved cottage cheese.

## Taramasalata 2 ⊛

*350g/12oz smoked cod's roe*
*1-2 tablespoons lemon juice*
*up to 300ml/½ pint olive oil (use the best quality available)*
*little boiling water*
*1-2 cloves garlic, crushed*
*1-2 tablespoons finely chopped parsley*

The recipe for Taramasalata 1 gives a very strongly-flavoured pâté because the smoked cod's roe is not diluted with other ingredients. In the variations and under Smoked Salmon Pâté, are ways of counteracting the strong taste, if you want a milder pâté. I like the definite and strong taste of the smoked roe, which is why I put it as my first choice. This second recipe however gives a much more subtle flavour and is the pâté you taste more often in a restaurant.

Soak the cod's roe in cold water for 2 to 3 hours before skinning; this makes it much milder in taste. Peel away the skin and mash the roe in a basin or food processor. Beat in the lemon juice, then add the oil gradually; stop when sufficient has been added for your personal taste. Add enough boiling water to make a very light soft mixture, then add the garlic and parsley. Often when buying this pâté, it is bright pink in colour; a few drops of food colouring can be added.

## Tapenade

*canned anchovy fillets with oil from can*
*black olives*
*pepper*

Use the ingredients in proportions to suit your personal taste. Chop the anchovies; stone and chop the olives. Put into a food processor or liquidizer with the pepper to taste and blend until smooth. This highly-flavoured spread is excellent as a cocktail snack, spread on crisp biscuits or diced bread.

Cooked fresh anchovies or sardines could be used with oil, salt and pepper instead of canned fish.

# Beautiful Soups

I am a soup lover. I spend a good deal of my time travelling and often return home late in the evening, rather tired and hungry. On these occasions I enjoy home-made soup almost more than any other dish. It is easily consumed and satisfying, without being over-heavy; it gives me a feeling of warmth and well-being. I hope you share my enjoyment for soups of all kinds.

I think perhaps that many people tend to be a little conservative in their choice of ingredients for a soup. That is a pity, for you can produce an excellent soup from fruit as well as vegetables and from all kinds of fish, meat, poultry, game and cheese. Do not disregard the pleasure of cold, or even iced, soups. These are less usual than the hot varieties, but they are refreshing as well as satisfying.

Most soups freeze well; I would use them within 3 months. You may however find that some thickened soups tend to become rather thinner in consistency after freezing and then defrosting. If that happens all you need to do is to blend 1 or 2 teaspoons cornflour, or a little more flour, with a small amount of cold stock, water or other liquid used in the soup, blend this with the other ingredients and cook gently, stirring well as you reheat the mixture.

When making recipes that contain egg and/or cream and/or wine, you will find it advisable to add these ingredients to the soup after defrosting. If a purée soup has separated during freezing, then sieve or liquidize the mixture when it has defrosted to restore the smooth texture.

Garnishes and accompaniments for soups are on pages 36 and 49.

## Making Stock ⊛

Throughout this book you will find I refer to stock in the various recipes, particularly those used for soups and stews. I always try and make stock from bones and the carcass of poultry. I may not need the stock when first prepared but I freeze this ready for a future occasion.

Stock and similar liquids take up space in the freezer, so it is wise to boil the liquid until it is very concentrated in flavour, then freeze it in ice-making trays. Each little cube can be diluted and used in a recipe.

Brown stock is produced from beef, lamb, duck, goose or game bones. White stock is made from chicken, turkey or veal bones. To darken a stock, heat the bones in a pan until they turn a nutty colour before adding water. You can add 1 or more onions and carrots to the water used to cover the bones, but I avoid doing this as it makes the stock less versatile; you may be making a dish where the flavour of the vegetables is not required.

Cover the bones and add a very little seasoning, plus any herbs you like to use; here again you may prefer to omit these in the basic stock. Simmer for 1 to 2 hours or even longer to extract the maximum amount of flavour. If you have a pressure cooker, use this on HIGH/15 lb pressure and shorten the cooking time by at least 75 per cent.

Do not forget that fish soups and dishes are improved by using fish stock, rather than water. This is made by simmering the bones and skin of white fish in water to cover for about 20 minutes.

When home-made stock is not available use commercial stock cubes. One stock cube to 600 ml/1 pint water should give a good flavour. Strangely enough a chicken stock cube is very good in a fish dish, if you have no fish stock.

# Accompaniments to Soup

Crisply fried croûtons of bread are one of the best accompaniments to soup. Do not add these to the soup until just before serving as they soften very easily. You can, of course, serve them separately so that everyone can help themselves. If you prefer, toast rather than fry the bread, then cut the slices into small dice.

Chopped herbs, yogurt, soured or whipped cream or spoonfuls of cottage cheese make good toppings for most soups, particularly when you need a contrasting colour.

You will find additional garnishes under the Classic Consommés on page 49.

## Fried Croûtons ⊛

*2 to 3 slices bread*
*butter, fat or oil*

Cut the bread into 5 mm/¼ inch dice. Heat the butter, fat or oil and fry the bread until crisp and brown. Drain on absorbent kitchen paper.

## Butter Dumplings

*75 g/3 oz self-raising flour*
*salt and pepper*
*pinch dry mustard powder*
*25 g/1 oz butter*
*milk to mix*

Sift the flour with the salt, pepper and mustard. Cream the butter until soft, add the dry ingredients with enough milk to make a fairly firm rolling consistency. Make into balls the size of a green pea, remember you are using self-raising flour and they will rise a great deal in cooking. If the dumplings are too big they are difficult to eat with a soup spoon.

Drop into the hot soup about 10 minutes before the meal and cook steadily. These are particularly good with clear soups, with meat soups and with vegetable soups, but see the variations below. All dumplings absorb a lot of liquid, so if you are cooking the dumplings in the soup, check on the amount of liquid. However, you can cook dumplings in boiling salted water or stock.

VARIATIONS

**Cheese Dumplings:** Omit the butter and add 25 g/1 oz grated Parmesan cheese; these are excellent with vegetable soups.

**Herb Dumplings:** Use either the Butter or Cheese Dumpling recipe, add 1 tablespoon chopped herbs.

# Vegetable Soups

The following recipes use some of the vegetables that are available during the year. As you will see from the individual recipes, many are given a creamy taste by the addition of cream or a sauce based upon milk. The selection of vegetables will enable you to prepare soups with your favourite vegetables.
If the particular vegetable has good natural thickening qualities, as in the case of Jerusalem artichokes or potatoes, then the amount of thickening used is relatively small; in fact, if you are anxious to avoid using too much flour, or cornflour, it could be omitted completely.
Never over-cook vegetables in a soup, for this spoils both the colour and flavour.

## Cream of Artichoke Soup ⊛

*350g/12oz Jerusalem artichokes*
*1½ tablespoons white vinegar or lemon juice*
*600ml/1pint white stock (from veal or chicken bones)*
*1 medium onion, chopped*
*salt and pepper*
*bouquet garni*
*150ml/¼pint single cream*
GARNISH:
*chopped rosemary, thyme and tarragon*

Scrape the artichokes just before cooking; to prevent the vegetables becoming dark in colour, put into cold water containing 1 tablespoon of the vinegar or lemon juice as each one is scraped.

Pour the stock into a pan with the rest of the vinegar or lemon juice and bring to the boil. Add the artichokes and onion, salt and pepper to taste and bouquet garni. Cover and cook steadily for approximately 25 minutes or until the vegetables are soft. Remove the bouquet garni.

Sieve the soup or blend in a liquidizer or food processor to make a smooth purée. Return the soup to the pan, add the cream and heat. Top with the chopped herbs.

VARIATION

⊛ **Cream of Celeriac Soup:** Peel and dice a large celeriac (celery root). Proceed as recipe above.

## Vegetable Cream Soup ⊛

*350g/12oz mixed root vegetables*
*600ml/1 pint white stock (from chicken bones)*
*1 medium onion, chopped*
*salt and pepper*
*150ml/¼pint single cream*
GARNISH:
*chopped parsley or chervil*

Prepare and cut the vegetables so they will all be cooked at the same time.

Pour the stock into a pan and bring to the boil. Add all the vegetables with salt and pepper to taste. Cover and cook steadily for about 25 minutes or until the vegetables are soft.

Sieve the soup or blend in a liquidizer or food processor to make a smooth purée. Return the soup to the pan, add the cream and heat. Sprinkle with the chopped herbs.

# Cream of Lettuce Soup ⊛

*1 large lettuce*
*2 medium onions, chopped*
*1.2 litres/2 pints chicken stock*
*salt and pepper*
*25 g/1 oz butter or margarine*
*25 g/1 oz flour*
*150 ml/¼ pint milk*
*150 ml/¼ pint single cream*

Wash the lettuce and shred the leaves, reserving just one or two small tender leaves for garnish. Put the shredded lettuce, onion and stock into a saucepan and add a little salt and pepper. Simmer gently for just 15 minutes; over-cooking spoils the colour of the lettuce.

Meanwhile make a sauce in another pan. Heat the butter or margarine, stir in the flour, then gradually blend in the milk and single cream. Bring the sauce to the boil and cook until thickened, stirring well. Mix the sauce with the lettuce mixture and sieve or blend in a liquidizer or food processor to make a smooth purée. Return to the pan and reheat.

Cut the reserved lettuce into tiny shreds and sprinkle over the soup just before serving.

Note: Cooked lettuce is so often over-cooked; this is a delicious soup and an ideal way of using up excess lettuce.

VARIATIONS

**Crême Choisy:** The classic version of the soup above is enriched by whisking 2 well-beaten egg yolks into the hot, but not boiling, purée. Simmer for 2 to 3 minutes only then garnish and serve.

⊛ **Crème Doria:** Use a large peeled and chopped cucumber in place of the lettuce. Follow the recipe above but use all single cream in the sauce. Do not use egg yolks as in the variation above. Garnish with paprika, a little finely shredded cucumber and yogurt.

⊛ **Cream of Asparagus Soup:** Use about 350 g/12 oz fresh asparagus instead of lettuce with 1 small chopped onion and 1 medium chopped leek. It is advisable to remove a few asparagus tips and cook these separately in salted water to serve as a garnish on the soup.

⊛ **Cream of Mushroom Soup:** In order to have a really white looking soup it is a good idea to cook the sauce and the mushrooms separately. Heat 40 g/1½ oz butter in a pan, stir in 40 g/1½ oz flour, stir over a low heat then gradually add 600 ml/1 pint milk. Meanwhile slice 100 to 175 g/4 to 6 oz mushrooms, cook gently in another 40 g/1½ oz butter until soft, add to the sauce with 300 ml/½ pint chicken stock, 150 ml/¼ pint single cream, salt and pepper. Sieve or liquidize if desired.

## Cream of Onion Soup ⊛

*50g/2oz butter or margarine*
*275g/10oz onions, finely chopped*
*600ml/1 pint chicken stock*
*salt and pepper*
*25g/1oz cornflour*
*450ml/¾ pint milk*
*150ml/¼ pint single cream*
*2 egg yolks (optional)*
GARNISH:
*chopped chives or parsley*
*paprika*

Heat the butter or margarine in a good-sized saucepan. Add the onions and cook gently for several minutes – do not allow to brown. Pour in the stock and add a little salt and pepper to taste. Cover the pan and simmer for 15 minutes.

Blend the cornflour with the milk and add to the saucepan. Stir the soup as it comes to the boil and begins to thicken slightly. Cook for several minutes then remove the pan from the heat so that the soup is no longer boiling. Whisk together the cream and egg yolks (if not using the yolks, simply add the cream to the soup. The soup will not be quite as thick, as the egg yolks help to thicken the soup, so you may like to add an extra teaspoon of cornflour).

Whisk the egg yolks and cream into the hot, but not boiling, soup. Return to the heat and simmer gently for 4 to 5 minutes stirring – never allow it to boil. Garnish with the chives or parsley and paprika.

VARIATIONS
Use 50g/2oz flour instead of cornflour; cornflour is easier to incorporate into the hot mixture. 25g/1oz cornflour has the thickening ability of 50g/2oz flour. Sieve or liquidize the soup and serve it as a smooth purée.

## Creamed Spinach Soup ⊛

*50g/2oz butter*
*1 medium onion, finely chopped*
*25g/1oz flour*
*600ml/1 pint milk, or 450ml/¾ pint milk and 150ml/¼ pint single cream*
*salt and pepper*
*350g/12oz spinach*
*little chicken stock or extra milk*
*grated nutmeg*
GARNISH:
*croûtons, see page 36*

Heat the butter in a pan, add the onion and cook until tender but do not allow to discolour. Blend in the flour, then gradually add the milk, or milk and cream. Bring to the boil, and stir to make a smooth thin sauce. Season only very lightly with salt and pepper to taste.

Meanwhile wash and cook the spinach in the water clinging to the leaves. When the spinach is tender, sieve or chop it very finely. Add to the sauce, stir well to blend, then add a little extra stock or milk to make the right consistency. Heat the soup for a few minutes only, adjust the seasoning and flavour with a little grated nutmeg. Top with the croûtons.

## Clear Beetroot Soup ⊛

*3 medium onions, grated*
*1 clove garlic, crushed*
*750 ml/1 ¼ pints chicken stock*
*2 tablespoons chopped chives*
*2 tablespoons chopped parsley*
*225 g/8 oz cooked beetroot, grated*
GARNISH:
*little yogurt*

Simmer the onions and garlic in the stock; add half the chives and parsley. When the onions are almost tender, add the grated beetroot and heat the soup thoroughly. Spoon the yogurt on top and sprinkle with the remaining parsley and chives.

VARIATIONS

⊛ **Cream of Beetroot Soup:** Follow the recipe above but use only 450 ml/¾ pint chicken stock. Heat 40 g/1½ oz butter in a separate pan, stir in 25 g/1 oz flour and cook gently for 2 to 3 minutes, then blend in 300 ml/½ pint milk and 150 ml/¼ pint single cream. Stir as the sauce comes to the boil and thickens. Add the hot beetroot mixture to the hot, but not boiling, sauce and whisk together until well blended. Sprinkle with parsley and serve.

⊛ **Celery and Beetroot Soup:** Follow the recipe above but add the finely chopped heart of a head of celery to the onions and garlic and use beef, rather than chicken stock. Serve with grated cheese.

## Hungarian Mushroom Soup ⊛

*2 rashers fat bacon, derinded and finely chopped*
*175 g/6 oz button mushrooms, thinly sliced*
*25 g/1 oz flour*
*2 teaspoons paprika (sweet type)*
*750 ml/1 ¼ pints chicken stock*
*salt and pepper*
*2 egg yolks*
*4 tablespoons double cream*
GARNISH:
*1-2 tablespoons chopped parsley*

Put the bacon and mushrooms into a pan and fry together. Stir in the flour and paprika and cook gently for 2 to 3 minutes. Gradually blend in the stock. Bring the soup to the boil and stir over a moderate heat until thickened. Add salt and pepper to taste.

Blend the egg yolks and cream together. Whisk in 2 to 3 tablespoons of the very hot, but not boiling, soup, then whisk the mixture into the hot soup in the saucepan and simmer gently, stirring all the time, for 2 to 3 minutes. Serve garnished with the parsley.

VARIATIONS

Use 150 ml/¼ pint sour cream instead of the double cream.

⊛ **Clear Mushroom Soup:** Omit the flour, egg yolks and cream in the recipe above. Use beef stock instead of chicken stock. (Vegetarians can use water and yeast extract.) Add 2 medium grated onions. Simmer the mushrooms and onions in the stock together with 2 tablespoons chopped parsley; season well, Serve topped with more parsley or with yogurt.

## Bortsch ⊛

*1 large raw beetroot, weighing about 450 g/1 lb*
*50 g/2 oz butter*
*2 medium carrots, grated*
*2 medium onions, grated*
*2 sticks celery, finely chopped*
*3 medium tomatoes, skinned and finely chopped*
*1.2 litres/2 pints beef stock*
*2 bay leaves*
*salt and pepper*
*1-2 tablespoons red wine vinegar or lemon juice*
GARNISH:
*yogurt*
*1 small cooked and grated beetroot*

Russian soups are some of the most delicious and these are my favourites:

Peel and grate the raw beetroot; it is important that all the vegetables are of uniform size as this soup is not sieved. The soup is good hot or cold.

If serving hot, heat the butter in a large pan and toss the vegetables in this, then add the rest of the ingredients. Simmer for 1½ hours, then remove the bay leaves. Spoon the yogurt and grated cooked beetroot over the soup.

If serving cold, omit the butter, simply simmer the vegetables and other ingredients in the stock. Chill well. The cold version is rather richer if topped with soured cream or cottage cheese flavoured with a little lemon juice and seasoning, rather than yogurt, then the grated beetroot.

VARIATIONS

⊛ **Jellied Bortsch:** Omit the butter in the recipe above. Cook the soup as in the recipe then sieve or liquidize. Measure the purée and allow 15 g/½ oz gelatine to 1.2 litres/2 pints. Dissolve the gelatine in the hot purée, allow to cool then spoon into chilled soup cups. Garnish with soured cream and finely chopped hard-boiled eggs.

⊛ **Leek and Cabbage Bortsch:** Use only 1 medium-sized raw beetroot; cook the ingredients for approximately 1 hour, then add 3 small finely shredded leeks, about a quarter of a cabbage, finely shredded, and 1 to 2 teaspoons caraway seeds. Cook until the beetroot is tender, then add about 100 g/4 oz neatly diced garlic sausage to the soup. Garnish with chopped parsley.

⊛ **Ukranian Bortsch:** Cook the grated raw beetroot and grated onions in the beef stock, as in the recipe above, but omit the other ingredients, except the seasoning. When the soup is tender, remove from the heat. Blend 300 ml/½ pint double cream, 3 egg yolks and 1 or 2 tablespoons lemon juice (depending upon personal taste) to the hot, but not boiling soup; stir over a low heat until thickened. Serve hot.

⊛ **Cranberry Bortsch:** Use 350 g/12 oz cranberries instead of raw beetroot in the soup. Omit the carrot and tomatoes but add the other vegetables. Increase the sugar to 50 g/2 oz, but this soup should still be sharp in flavour. When cooked, serve either hot or cold topped with soured cream and grated cooked beetroot.

# Root Vegetable Soups

Some of the most popular root vegetables are used in the recipes that follow, but do treat each one as a basic recipe that you can adapt according to the vegetables available; for example, you could use young turnips in place of celeriac in the recipe below; if you want to give more flavour simply add a little chopped celery. Soups depend upon a good balance of flavour, so taste critically as you prepare the ingredients and during cooking. If the result seems to lack flavour then add fresh or dried herbs or a little extra seasoning and flavouring in the form of tomato purée, Worcestershire or soy sauce. Soups made with root vegetables tend to be fairly thick in consistency; ideally the completed soup should be like double cream, so always check before serving and add a little extra liquid if needed.

## Celery Almond Soup ⧆

*1 head celery*
*1 medium onion, diced*
*900 ml/1½ pints beef stock*
*celery salt and pepper*
*150 ml/¼ pint double cream*
*50 g/2 oz blanched almonds*

Cut the celery into small pieces, discarding the tough outer stalks. Put the celery into a pan with the onions, stock, celery salt and pepper to taste. Simmer for 20 minutes or until the celery is tender. Stir in the cream and almonds.

If preferred, sieve or liquidize the soup, then return to the pan and stir in the cream and nuts.

## Celeriac and Tomato Soup ⧆

*450 g/1 lb tomatoes, skinned and finely chopped*
*1 medium onion, finely chopped*
*175 g/6 oz celeriac (celery root), grated*
*1 tablespoon lemon juice*
*1 litre/1¾ pints chicken stock*
*25 g/1 oz long-grain rice*
*1-2 tablespoons tomato purée*
*salt and pepper*

Put the vegetables into a saucepan. Sprinkle over the lemon juice immediately to prevent the celeriac discolouring. Add the stock, rice and half the tomato purée. Simmer the soup for about 20 minutes or until the rice is tender, add salt and pepper and more tomato purée to taste. Serve the soup hot.

VARIATION

⧆ **Celeriac Beet Soup:** Substitute 1 large skinned and diced cooked beetroot for the tomatoes. Omit the rice and tomato purée, but use 225 g/8 oz celeriac. When cooked, top with rounds of bread and grated cheese.

## Carrot and Orange Soup ⊛

*1 large orange*
*2 bacon rashers or several bacon rinds, chopped*
*900 ml/1½ pints water*
*1 onion*
*350 g/12 oz carrots, grated*
*1 tablespoon chopped chives*
*salt and pepper*
GARNISH:
*1 orange*

Pare the rind from the orange, avoiding the bitter white pith. Put the bacon rashers or bacon rinds, water, the orange rind and whole onion into a saucepan. Simmer for 30 minutes, then remove the bacon or bacon rinds, onion and orange rind. Halve the orange, add the juice to the liquid in the pan with the carrots, chives and salt and pepper to taste. Cook for just 5 to 8 minutes so that the carrots retain their pleasant nutty flavour.

Halve the orange for garnish, remove and chop the segments and put into the soup just before serving. This soup is equally good hot or cold.

VARIATION

**Carrot and Tomato Soup:** Omit the orange flavouring in the recipe above, add 4 medium skinned and diced tomatoes to the other ingredients; retain the bacon and onion.

## Potage Parmentier ⊛

*50 g/2 oz butter*
*2 medium leeks, finely chopped*
*2 medium onions, finely chopped*
*450 g/1 lb old potatoes, cut into small dice*
*750 g/1¼ pints ham stock, see method*
*salt (if needed) and pepper*
*milk or single cream (optional)*
*2 tablespoons chopped parsley*

Heat the butter in a saucepan. Toss the vegetables in the butter for several minutes but do not allow to brown. Add the stock and bring to the boil. Cook the soup steadily for about 10 minutes, then add salt, if necessary, and pepper to taste. Continue cooking until the potatoes are soft.

For a perfectly creamy smooth soup, sieve or blend in a liquidizer or food processor. Alternatively, the vegetables can simply be mashed into the soup with a potato masher.

VARIATIONS

A potato soup is a splendid basis for various other flavours; for example, you can add about 50 g/2 oz chopped watercress leaves to the cooked soup or about the same weight of chopped prawns.

⊛ **Potage Dieppoise:** Add about 100 g/4 oz finely diced celeriac or celery heart to the leeks and onions in the above recipe together with the diced potatoes. Use chicken, rather than ham stock for a more delicate flavour. When serving the soup, top each portion with a little cream or small knob of butter, crisp breadcrumbs and parsley.

## French Onion Soup ⊛

*450g/1 lb onions, very thinly sliced*
*500g/2 oz butter or beef dripping*
*1 to 2 cloves garlic, crushed (optional)*
*1.2 litres/2 pints really good beef stock*
*salt and pepper*
TOPPING:
*6 rounds French bread*
*50g/2 oz Gruyère or other good cooking cheese, grated*

Cut the onion slices into smaller pieces to make the soup easier to eat. Heat the butter or dripping in a pan and fry the onions and garlic until tender. Do not over-cook. Add the stock and salt and pepper to taste.

Simmer the soup steadily for about 15 minutes, then adjust the seasoning. Taste this soup critically, for if there is insufficient flavour from the stock, it is disappointing. A little yeast extract gives extra taste but if this is used be sparing with the salt.

Pour the soup into heated soup bowls and top with the French bread and the cheese, then serve. Serves 6.

VARIATION

**French Onion Soup Gratinée:** Spoon the cooked soup into flameproof soup cups (traditional Marmite cups are ideal). Top with the French bread or with rounds of toast and the cheese. Place under the grill until the cheese melts. Do not exceed the recommended amount of cheese; too generous an amount takes too long to melt and becomes stringy.

## Onion Soup Indienne ⊛

*3 large onions, roughly chopped*
*2 large carrots, roughly chopped*
*750ml/1¼ pints lamb stock*
*25g/1 oz chutney*
*1-2 teaspoons curry powder*
*salt and pepper*

Put the ingredients into a saucepan. Simmer for 30 minutes or until the vegetables are tender. Sieve or liquidize the soup and serve hot or cold.

VARIATION

⊛ **Sweet and Sour Carrot Soup:** Use only 2 onions, but increase the carrots to 4. Choose chicken rather than lamb stock. Simmer the vegetables in the stock with only 1 teaspoon curry powder, but 2 tablespoons chutney, 1 tablespoon white wine vinegar or lemon juice, salt and pepper to taste. Sieve or liquidize and return to the pan.

## Leek Soup

*450g/1 lb leeks*
*1.2 litres/2 pints chicken stock*
*25g/1 oz rolled oats*
*salt and pepper*

Cut the leeks into thin slices, use some of the tender part of the green tops as well. Put all the ingredients together in a pan and cook for 20 minutes. Sieve or liquidize the soup and reheat.

VARIATION

For a more definite flavour, omit 1 or 2 leeks and use an onion and clove garlic instead.

## Tomato Soup ⊛

*25 g/1 oz butter or margarine*
*1 medium onion, chopped*
*1 clove garlic, chopped*
*2 bacon rashers, derinded and chopped*
*750 g/1 ½ lb tomatoes, chopped*
*300 ml/½ pint water or chicken or ham stock*
*1 tablespoon tomato purée*
*1 tablespoon chopped basil or pinch dried basil*
*salt and pepper*
*1 teaspoon sugar*
GARNISH:
*1 teaspoon chopped basil*
*1 teaspoon chopped pasley*
*1 teaspoon chopped chives*

Heat the butter or margarine in a saucepan, add the onion, garlic and bacon together with the bacon rinds and fry for several minutes – do not allow to discolour. Add the tomatoes and water or stock with the remaining ingredients.

Cover the pan and simmer gently for 20 minutes; remove the bacon rinds. Sieve the soup or blend in liquidizer or food processor until smooth. Return to the pan and heat through. Serve sprinkled with the herbs.

VARIATIONS

⊛ **Cream of Tomato Soup:** Prepare the tomato soup as above and heat the smooth mixture. Meanwhile, in a second saucepan, heat 25 g/1 oz butter, stir in 25 g/1 oz flour and cook gently for 2 to 3 minutes, then gradually blend in nearly 450 ml/¾ pint of milk or a mixture of milk and single cream. Stir the sauce as it comes to the boil and thickens; season very lightly. Whisk the hot, but not boiling, sauce into the equally hot, but not boiling, tomato soup and serve. This will serve 6 people.

For a slightly stronger flavour either add an extra 1 to 2 tablespoons concentrated tomato purée to the tomato mixture or use a smaller proportion of sauce to the tomato mixture.

⊛ Another way to make a true Cream of Tomato Soup is to thicken the soup by adding a little Beurre Manié, see below, then whisking double cream into the mixture just before serving.

## Beurre Manié

*equal quantities of butter and flour*

In many recipes the term Beurre Manié is used. This mixture of butter and flour is invaluable for thickening the liquid in a soup, as above, or a stew, at the end of the cooking period. This means the consistency of the liquid is easily adjusted.

Cream the butter and work in the flour. Keep the mixture covered in a cool place until required. Add a small mount of the Beurre Manié to the liquid, stir until absorbed then continue like this until the desired thickness. Never try to put in too much of the Beurre Manié at one time; allow each small amount to be absorbed before adding the next.

You need approximately 25 g/1 oz butter and 25 g/1 oz flour to thicken 300 ml/½ pint liquid for a coating consistency, or 600 ml/1 pint liquid for a thin consistency.

# Using Pulses

Peas, beans and lentils, known as the pulses, are excellent ingredients with which to make soups. They are extremely satisfying and an excellent source of protein; they could therefore take the place of a light meal. I find the fact that the soups are particularly delicious in flavour of equal importance to their nutritional value.

## Minestrone Soup

*50-75 g/2-3 oz haricot beans*
*1.2 litres/2 pints chicken stock*
*2 tablespoons oil*
*2 medium onions, finely chopped*
*2 cloves garlic, finely chopped*
*2 bacon rashers, derinded and finely chopped*
*2 sticks celery, finely diced*
*2 medium tomatoes, skinned and chopped*
*2 medium carrots, finely diced*
*salt and pepper*
*50 g/2 oz quick cooking short macaroni*
*175 g/6 oz cabbage heart, finely shredded*

GARNISH:
*chopped parsley*
*grated Parmesan cheese*

Soak the beans overnight in the stock. Heat the oil in a pan and fry the onion, garlic and bacon together for a few minutes. Add the haricot beans with the stock. Bring to the boil and boil for 10 minutes then cover the pan and simmer gently for 1¼ hours.

Add the celery, tomatoes and carrots with salt and pepper to taste and cook for a further 20 minutes; check on the amount of liquid during this time. Add the macaroni and cabbage and cook for a further 10 minutes or until tender. Taste and add extra salt and pepper if desired.

Top the soup with the parsley and a little cheese. Serve with more grated cheese.

VARIATIONS

To save soaking and cooking time, omit the haricot beans and use a can of baked beans. In this case omit about 300 ml/½ pint stock.

**Chicken Broth:** Follow the recipe above but add 100 g/4 oz sweetcorn and 100 g/4 oz peas to the other vegetables. Omit the macaroni but add 175 g/6 oz neatly diced cooked chicken to the cooked soup; heat for 3 to 4 minutes.

## Bean Chowder ⊛

*3 bacon rashers, derinded and chopped*
*2 medium onions, diced*
*3 medium potatoes, diced*
*900 ml/1 ½ pints chicken stock*
*350 g/12 oz tomatoes, skinned and diced*
*1 x 225 g/8 oz can baked beans*
*salt and pepper*
GARNISH:
*little chopped savoury and chopped chives*

Fry the bacon and onions in a pan for 5 minutes. Add the remaining ingredients and cook steadily for 10 to 15 minutes; the potatoes should still be firm. Top the soup with the herbs.

## Lentil Soup ⊛

*225 g/8 oz lentils*
*600 ml/1 pint ham or chicken stock*
*2 medium onions, chopped*
*1 carrot, chopped*
*1 very small dessert apple, peeled and chopped*
*1 clove garlic, crushed*
*bouquet garni*
*salt and pepper*
*1 tablespoon cornflour*
*300 ml/½ pint milk*
*50 g/2 oz butter or margarine*
GARNISH:
*chopped parsley*
*fried croûtons (see page 36)*

Soak the lentils overnight, or for some hours, in the stock. Place in a saucepan with the onions, carrot, apple, garlic, herbs and a little salt and pepper. Simmer the soup steadily for about 1 hour or until the lentils are tender. Either mash with a wooden spoon or sieve or blend in a liquidizer or food processor.

Return the purée to the saucepan. Blend the cornflour with the milk. Stir into the hot purée, add the butter or margarine and heat the soup until thickened. Taste and adjust the seasoning; this soup needs a reasonable amount of pepper. Top with parsley and serve with crisply fried croûtons.

VARIATIONS

You can add 2 skinned and chopped tomatoes to the other ingredients when simmering the lentils. This means you must be very careful when adding the cornflour and milk that the mixture does not boil but only simmers gently. You could, of course, omit the cornflour and milk and simply increase the amount of stock as the soup is reasonably thick with the lentil purée.

⊛ **Dried Pea Soup:** Use split peas in place of the lentils. Add 2 crushed cloves garlic and a little mint in place of the bouquet garni. Garnish with crisply fried pieces of bacon.

**Curried Lentil Soup:** Blend 2 teaspoons curry powder or paste with the other ingredients and cook 1 medium peeled and diced cooking apple with the lentils.

# Using Fruits

A fruit soup may sound a strange beginning to the meal, but many Continental countries provide delicious recipes. I have given a basic recipe using nuts, which you can vary by sustituting cashew, or other nuts for the chestnuts. The apple mixture is another basic recipe, you can substitute sharp flavoured plums, tiny cherry plums or rhubarb.

## Chestnut Soup ⊛

*450 g/1 lb chestnuts*
*50 g/2 oz butter, bacon fat or margarine*
*2 medium onions, finely chopped*
*750 ml/1 ¼ pints ham or chicken stock*
*salt and pepper*
*3-4 tablespoons cream*
GARNISH:
*chopped chives*
*chopped parsley*

Slit the chestnut skins. Put into a pan of cold water and simmer for about 10 minutes, then remove the nuts. Cool the chestnuts slightly so that they can be handled, then remove the outer and inner skins.

Meanwhile, heat the butter, fat or margarine and toss the onions in this for a few minutes. Add the skinned chestnuts, stock, a little salt and pepper and simmer for 30 minutes or until the nuts are soft. Sieve the mixture or blend it until smooth. Return the purée to the saucepan and heat through, adding the cream and any extra seasoning required. Top the soup with the herbs.

VARIATION

⊛ **Bacon and Chestnut Soup:** Simmer the skinned chestnuts in the stock until tender and purée. Fry the onions as in the recipe above with 2 to 3 derinded, chopped bacon rashers. When the onions are tender and the bacon crisp, add the purée. Heat thoroughly and add the cream. Serve with fried croûtons.

## Swedish Apple Soup ⊛

*450 g/1 lb cooking apples*
*1 lemon*
*1.2 litres/2 pints water*
*50 g/2 oz sugar*
*15 g/½ oz arrowroot*
*little ground cinnamon*
*50 g/2 oz seedless raisins*

Chop the apples into small pieces, discarding the core and pips but do not peel as this gives additional flavour. Place the apples in a pan. Pare the zest (yellow part of the rind) from the lemon, add to the apples with most of the water and simmer to make a soft purée.

Rub the mixture through a sieve, removing the pieces of lemon rind. Return the purée to the saucepan with the sugar. Blend the arrowroot with the remaining water, stir into the apple purée and continue stirring until the mixture thickens slightly. Add the cinnamon and raisins to the hot mixture. Leave the soup to cool and serve well chilled; add the lemon juice to taste.

# Meat Soups

The most famous meat soup, although meat is not actually served in the liquid, is a Consommé. Although it takes time to simmer the beef to extract the full flavour, it is time well spent, as the flavour of a good home-made clear Consommé is delicious. In addition to the well-known beef soup, I have included recipes for clear consommés, based upon chicken, duck and game. More sustaining meat, poultry and game soups can form the the basis for a light meal.

## Consommé ⊛

*This is the basis of many interesting hot or cold soups and is invaluable when planning a light first course.*

*750 g/1 ¼ lb shin of beef, cut into small pieces*
*2.25 litres/4 pints well-clarified beef stock (made from beef bones)*
*salt and pepper*
*2 small onions*
*2 small carrots*
*2 bay leaves*
*2 egg whites, lightly whisked*
*shells from the 2 eggs*

Put the meat into a saucepan with the stock, salt, pepper, whole onions and carrots and bay leaves. Cover the pan and simmer gently for 1½ hours. During this time, the liquid will evaporate and become darker in colour and full of flavour. Strain the mixture through several thicknesses of muslin. If it is not sufficiently clear, return to the pan; add the egg whites and the shells and simmer for a further 10 to 20 minutes, until any tiny particles of meat adhere to the egg whites and shells. Strain once again. Serves 6 to 8.

VARIATIONS

Add about 2 tablespoons sherry to each 600 ml/1 pint Consommé.

⊛ **Consommé à la Crême:** Whisk 2 egg yolks, 2 tablespoons dry sherry and 150 ml/¼ pint double cream together. Whisk into the hot, but not boiling, Consommé and simmer for several minutes.

⊛ **Orange Consommé:** Pare the zest from several oranges and simmer with the beef and other ingredients. After straining add 4 to 5 tablespoons fresh, strained orange juice to each 600 ml/1 pint Consommé. Serve cold, garnished with chopped orange.

## Classic Consommés ⊛

*Consommé (see above)*
*garnishes as method*

The garnish gives its name to the soup.

⊛ **Consommé Célestine** garnished with pancakes.

⊛ **Consommé Julienne** garnished with matchsticks of cooked vegetables.

⊛ **Consommé Jardinière** – garnished with diced cooked vegetables.

## Jellied Consommé ⊛

*Ingredients as for Consommé (see page 49)*
*1 knuckle of veal*
FOR THE SOUP CUPS:
*1 egg white, lightly whisked*
*little finely chopped parsley*

Put the ingredients for the Consommé in a saucepan, add the knuckle of veal; this has a high percentage of gelatine. Cook as the recipe for Consommé, strain in the same way. The soup will form a firm jelly when cold.

Either whisk the jelly or cut into small dice and put into well chilled soup cups. These look particularly attractive if the rims are brushed with the egg white, then dipped in the chopped parsley.

VARIATIONS

Omit the knuckle of veal. Measure the hot strained liquid and to each 600 ml/1 pint add 1½ teaspoons gelatine; stir until dissolved in the hot Consommé; allow to set.

⊛ **Iced Consommé:** In order to achieve a better consistency, use the knuckle of veal or gelatine as advised above. Allow the mixture to set lightly, then put into the freezing compartment of the refrigerator or into the freezer. This soup must be served when only lightly frozen, so bring out and keep at room temperature for a time before serving in chilled soup cups. Garnish with wedges of lemon and a little lightly whipped and seasoned cream.

## Game Consommé ⊛

*2.25 litres/4 pints game stock (made by simmering the carcasses of several game birds or venison or hare bones)*
*about 350 g/12 oz shin of beef or game flesh, finely diced*
*100 g/4 oz hare or calves' liver, finely diced*
*1 onion*
*1 small carrot*
*1 small piece of celery, chopped*
*1 bay leaf*
*salt and pepper*
*2 egg whites, lightly whisked*
*shells from 2 eggs*
*red or Madeira wine*

Simmer the stock with the meats, vegetables, bay leaf and salt and pepper for 1½ hours. Strain and clear with the egg whites and shells as described on page 49. Serve the Consommé hot. Add red or Madeira wine to taste. This Consommé is less successful as a jellied or iced soup.

VARIATIONS

⊛ **Chicken Consommé:** Follow the method for Consommé, page 49, but use 2.25 litres/4 pints good chicken stock with vegetables as in above recipe, a sprig of tarragon and rosemary to flavour and 175 g/6 oz diced chicken meat and 225 g/8 oz diced veal instead of the shin of beef. Flavour with a dry white wine. This soup is delicious jellied or iced as described on this page.

⊛ **Duck Consommé:** Follow the method for Consommé, page 49, but use 2.25 litres/4 pints duck stock with the vegetables as in above recipe plus 1 small turnip and a few strips of orange rind. Add a sprig of fresh sage. Use only 225 g/8 oz diced shin of beef with 100 g/4 oz finely diced ox heart. This soup is better served hot, flavoured with red wine.

## Consommé en Croûte ⊛

*900 ml/1 ½ pints canned Consommé or use the recipe on page 49*
*100 g/4 oz frozen puff pastry or use the recipe on page 292*

Pour the soup into 4 ovenproof bowls but do not fill up completely, as the soup has to be topped with the pastry. Roll out the pastry very thinly and cut into 4 rounds the size of the top of the bowls. Lay the pastry rounds on a baking tray and bake towards the top of a hot oven (220°C/425°F or Gas Mark 7) for about 15 minutes. Heat the soup in the bowls, top with the pastry and serve.

## Consommé Casalinga ⊛

*900 ml/1 ½ pints beef Consommé (see page 49)*
*2 tablespoons tomato purée*
*50 g/2 oz mushrooms, thinly sliced*
*40 g/1 ½ oz long-grain rice*
GARNISH:
*2 tablespoons grated Parmesan cheese*
*2 tablespoons chopped parsley*

Bring the Consommé to the boil in a pan. Stir in the tomato purée and mushrooms and simmer for 10 minutes. Add the rice and cook for a further 13 to 15 minutes

Serve the soup topped with cheese and parsley.

VARIATION

⊛ **Chilli Consommé:** Heat 2 tablespoons oil in a pan. Peel, finely dice 2 medium onions and fry in the oil with 100 g/4 oz raw minced beef until both onions and beef are tender; stirring well. Add to the recipe above with a few drops of chilli sauce to taste.

## Consommé Madrilène ⊛

*2 medium tomatoes, skinned, halved and deseeded*
*15 g/½ oz butter*
*2 teaspoons tomato purée*
*1.2 litres/2 pints Consommé (see page 49)*
*salt and pepper*
GARNISH:
*few cooked small noodles*
*1 tablespoon chopped parsley or chervil*

Chop the tomatoes very finely. Heat the butter in a saucepan and cook the tomatoes to make a thick smooth purée. Add the tomato purée (often called tomato paste, from can or tube) then the well-strained Consommé. Heat the soup and add salt and pepper to taste. Top with the noodles and chopped parsley or chervil.

VARIATIONS

Flavour the soup with a little light dry sherry.

⊛ **Speedy Consommé Madrilène:** Blend equal amounts of the well-strained Consommé and tomato juice together. Flavour well with salt, pepper and sherry. Serve hot or cold. This soup and the classic recipe above can be jellied or lightly frozen, see the Consommé recipe on page 50. Omit the noodles in the cold version and top with yogurt or soured cream and chopped herbs.

## Kidney Soup ⊛

*50 g/2 oz butter*
*225 g/8 oz ox kidney, finely chopped*
*2 medium onions, chopped*
*25 g/1 oz flour*
*1.2 litres/2 pints beef stock*
*salt and pepper*
*bouquet garni*
*150 ml/¼ pint red wine*

Heat the butter in a pan and fry the kidney and onions for 5 minutes. Blend in the flour and stir over a low heat for 2 to 3 minutes, then gradually add the stock. Bring to the boil and stir as the mixture thickens slightly. Add salt and pepper to taste and the bouquet garni. Cover the pan and simmer gently for 1¼ to 1½ hours.

Remove the bouquet garni and sieve or liquidize the soup. Return to the saucepan, add the wine and heat through.

VARIATION

⊛ **Luxury Kidney Soup:** Skin and finely dice 6 lambs' kidneys. Cut 2 rashers of derinded back bacon into matchstick pieces. Peel and finely dice 1 medium onion and 1 clove garlic. Thinly slice 50 g/2 oz small button mushrooms. Heat 50 g/2 oz butter in a pan, fry all the above ingredients for 5 minutes, then add 900 ml/1½ pints beef stock, 150 ml/¼ pint red wine, salt and pepper and simmer for 15 minutes. Top with chopped parsley.

## Oxtail Soup ⊛

*Ingredients as Ragoût of Oxtail (see page 107)*
*extra stock or water*
*150 ml/¼ pint dry sherry*

The easiest way to prepare oxtail soup is to cook rather more ragoût than required for the meal. When sufficiently cool to handle, lift the pieces of meat from the thickened gravy and vegetables. Put the gravy and vegetables through a sieve or blend in a liquidizer or food processor until a smooth purée.

Meanwhile cut all the pieces of meat from the bones and dice neatly. Heat the smooth purée soup with sufficient extra stock or water to make a flowing consistency. Add the small pieces of oxtail and the sherry and heat thoroughly.

## Windsor Soup ⊛

*900 ml/1½ pints canned Consommé or use the recipe on page 49*
*2 bay leaves*
*small bunch parsley*
*sprig fresh thyme or pinch dried thyme*
*6 tablespoons Madiera or dry red wine*

GARNISH:

*1 tablespoon chopped parsley*
*few peeled prawns*

Heat the Consommé with the other ingredients. Remove the bay leaves, parsley and thyme sprigs just before serving. Top with the parsley and prawns.

## Mexican Hot Soup ⊛

*2 tablespoons oil*
*2 medium onions, finely diced*
*2 sticks celery, finely chopped*
*1 red pepper, cored, deseeded and finely diced*
*100 g/4 oz raw minced beef*
*a pinch to 1½ teaspoons chilli powder*
*750 ml/1¼ pints beef stock*
*2 tablespoons tomato purée*
*salt and pepper*
*175 g/6 oz canned red kidney beans*
*2 tablespoons chopped parsley*

Heat the oil in a pan and fry the onions, celery and red pepper for 3 to 4 minutes. Mix in the minced beef, then blend in the chilli powder. Add only the minimum amount at this stage, unless you are sure you like a very hot flavour, as the rest can be added during cooking. Blend in the stock and tomato purée, and bring the soup to the boil. Cover and simmer for 20 minutes; add salt, pepper and more chilli powder if desired. Tip in the canned red beans and add the parsley. Heat the soup and serve.

## Spiced Chicken Soup ⊛

*75 g/3 oz butter or chicken fat*
*1 uncooked chicken joint, boned and diced*
*2 medium onions, finely and neatly diced*
*25 g/1 oz flour*
*1 tablespoon curry powder*
*1.2 litres/2 pints chicken stock*
*25 g/1 oz long-grain rice*
*salt and pepper*
*2 dessert apples*
*1 tablespoon lemon juice*

Heat 50 g/2 oz of the butter or fat in a pan. Fry the chicken and onions for several minutes. Stir in the flour and curry powder, then gradually blend in the stock. Bring the mixture to the boil, stirring, then add the rice, a little salt and pepper and simmer for 25 minutes.

When the soup is nearly ready, peel and finely dice the apples. Sprinkle with the lemon juice to keep them a good colour. Heat the remaining butter in another pan and cook the apples gently until soft, but unbroken. Add the apples to the soup and heat for a few minutes then serve.

VARIATION

Add a few sultanas and a little chutney to the soup.

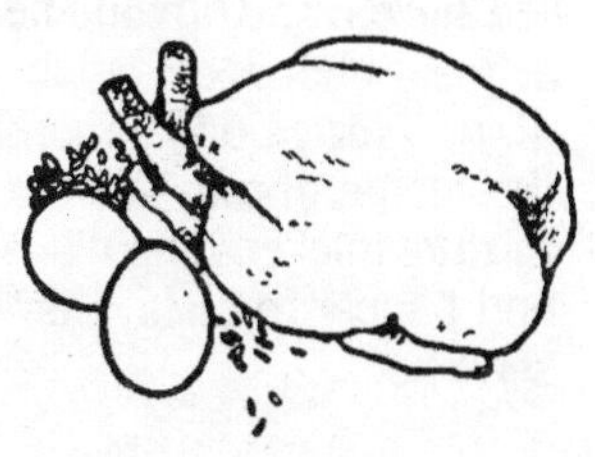

## Gulyas ⊛

*100 g/4 oz beef or veal, finely diced*
*100 g/4 oz lean pork, finely diced*
*2 medium onions, chopped*
*3 medium tomatoes, skinned and chopped*
*900 ml/1 ½ pints beef stock*
*salt and pepper*
*½-1 tablespoon sweet paprika*
*2 medium potatoes*
GARNISH:
*little yogurt*
*chopped parsley*

The Goulash recipe on page 152 is the popular version of this paprika-flavoured mixture, but this soup is equally satisfying and could be the basis of a light meal. It has been recorded that Gulyas or Goulash started as a soup and ended as a stew.

Put the meat, onions, tomatoes and most of the stock into a saucepan and add a little salt and pepper to taste. Bring just to the boil. Blend the paprika with the remaining stock and stir into the pan. Cover the pan and simmer the soup gently for 1 hour, or until the meat is tender.

Meanwhile cut the potatoes into very small dice and keep in cold water so that they do not discolour. When the soup is ready, add the potatoes and cook for a further 15 to 20 minutes until tender. Top each portion of soup with yogurt and parsley.

## Chicken and Asparagus Soup ⊛

*1 x 225 g/8 oz can asparagus*
*225 g/8 oz cooked chicken breast, chopped*
*150 ml/¼ pint single cream*
*600 ml/1 pint chicken stock*
*salt and pepper*

Remove the asparagus from the can and cut off a few tips to use as garnish for the soup. Put the rest of the asparagus, the liquid from the can, the chicken and cream into a liquidizer or food processor and blend until a very smooth purée. Add the stock with salt and pepper to taste. This soup is equally good served hot or cold. Top with the asparagus tips when serving.

VARIATIONS
Use cooked turkey and turkey stock instead of chicken.

⊛ **Speedy Cream of Chicken Soup:** Omit the asparagus in the recipe above. Make sure the chicken stock has plenty of flavour or add 1 chicken stock cube. Increase the amount of chicken very slightly.

⊛ **Chicken and Almond Soup:** Omit the asparagus. Fry a finely choppped onion in 25 g/1 oz butter. Blend 40g/1 ¼ oz ground almonds with the chicken stock in the recipe above. Add to the onion and stir as the mixture thickens slightly; add the chicken, cream, salt and pepper to taste. Sieve or liquidize the soup and serve hot.

## Cock-a-Leekie Soup ⊛

*75g/3oz dried prunes*
*2 small portions shicken breast*
*1.2 litres/2 pints chicken stock*
*salt and pepper*
*4 medium leeks, finely chopped*
*small bunch parsley*
GARNISH:
*chopped parsley*

Soak the prunes in water to cover overnight. Stone and cut the prunes into small pieces. Put the chicken into a saucepan, add the stock and salt and pepper to taste. Cover the pan and simmer for 1 hour, or until the chicken is very tender. Remove the chicken, add the leeks, parsley and prunes to the liquid and cook for 20 minutes.

Meanwhile, dice the chicken very finely, return to the pan and remove the parsley, Heat the soup thoroughly and top with chopped parsley.

VARIATION

The soup can be served topped with grated cheese.

## Game Soup ⊛

*carcass of 1 to 2 pheasants or bones from cooked hare*
*salt and pepper*
*bouquet garni*
*50g/2 oz game dripping or butter*
*2 medium onions, finely and evenly chopped*
*1 carrot, finely and evenly diced*
*2 sticks celery, finely and evenly diced*
*½ small turnip, finely and evenly diced*
*25g/1 oz flour*
*750ml/1¼ pints game stock*
*150ml/¼ pint port or red wine*
*1 tablespoon redcurrant jelly*
GARNISH:
*chopped parsley*

Remove any tiny particles of meat from the carcass or bones and cover the meat so that it does not become over-dry. Break the carcass of each bird into small pieces. Put these, or the hare bones, into a saucepan, add water to cover, salt, pepper and the bouquet garni. Simmer for at least 1 hour, or put into a pressure cooker and cook for at least 30 minutes on HIGH pressure. Strain the stock and measure out 750ml/1¼ pints.

Heat the dripping (obtained from roasting the birds or saddle of hare) or butter in a pan, add the vegetables and cook gently for several minutes. Add the flour, stir into the vegetable mixture then blend in the stock and wine. Bring to the boil, stirring well, and cook until a very thin sauce. Add a little salt and pepper to taste. Cover the pan and simmer for about 20 minutes, add the redcurrant jelly, the meat and heat for a few minutes. Taste and adjust the seasoning. Top with the chopped parsley and serve.

VARIATIONS

The soup can be sieved or put into a liquidizer then reheated.

⊛ **Cream of Game Soup:** Make the stock, fry the vegetables and thicken the soup with the flour, as in the recipe above. Sieve or liquidize then reheat with 150ml/1¼ pint single or double cream, the meat and 50g/2oz flaked almonds.

## Curry Soup ⊛

*50 g/2 oz butter*
*2 large onions, finely chopped*
*1 small dessert apple, peeled and finely chopped*
*½-1 tablespoon curry powder*
*600 ml/1 pint chicken stock*
*25 g/1 oz rice, preferably brown*
*½ tablespoon lemon juice*
*salt and pepper*
*2 egg yolks*
*150 ml/¼ pint single cream*
GARNISH:
*2 tablespoons diced green pepper*
*2 tablespoons diced red pepper*

Heat the butter in a pan, add the onions, apple and curry powder and cook for several minutes.

Pour in the chicken stock, bring to the boil and simmer for 20 minutes. Add the rice, lemon juice and salt and pepper to taste. Cover the pan and simmer gently for 40 minutes.

Blend the egg yolks with the cream; whisk into the soup and simmer for several minutes. Garnish with the diced peppers.

VARIATION

⊛ **Curried Cream Soup:** Chop and fry the 2 onions in the 50 g/2 oz butter, as in the recipe above. Omit the apple. Blend in the ½-1 tablespoon curry powder and add 1 tablespoon cornflour. Cook gently for 2 to 3 minutes, then blend in the 600 ml/1 pint chicken stock, ½ tablespoon lemon juice with salt and pepper to taste. Bring to the boil, stir well until slightly thickened. Cover the pan and simmer for 20 minutes. Blend 2 egg yolks with 150 ml/¼ pint double, not single, cream, as in the above recipe; whisk into the soup and cook for several minutes. Sieve or liquidize if wished and serve hot or cold.

## Mulligatawny Soup ⊛

*50 g/2 oz fat, preferably lamb fat*
*1 large onion, chopped*
*1 small carrot, diced*
*1 small dessert apple, peeled and chopped*
*40 g/1½ oz flour*
*1 tablespoon curry powder*
*900 ml/1½ pints lamb stock*
*salt and pepper*
*1 tablespoon chutney*
*25 g/1 oz sultanas*
*little lemon juice or vinegar*
*pinch sugar*

Heat the fat in a large saucepan, fry the vegetables and apple for several minutes, then blend in the flour and curry powder. Stir over a low heat for 2 to 3 minutes, then gradually add the stock and the rest of the ingredients. Bring to the boil, stir once or twice and simmer for approximately 45 minutes.

Sieve or blend the ingredients in a liquidizer or food processor to make a smooth purée. Taste and adjust the amount of seasoning, lemon juice or vinegar and sugar. The soup should have a pleasant blend of savoury and sweet flavours. Top with crisp croûtons of fried bread or 1 to 2 tablespoons cooked rice.

VARIATION

If you have a little cooked lamb left over this could be added to the other ingredients to make a more satisfying soup.

# Fish Soups

It is surprising how rarely one is offered a fish soup in this country and yet these are an excellent way of using a variety of fish. As you will see from the recipes that follow, a soup makes expensive shellfish serve a number of people for a relatively small outlay.

## Clam Chowder ⊛

*25g/1 oz butter*
*2 bacon rashers, derinded and finely chopped*
*1 medium onion, finely chopped*
*25g/1 oz flour*
*300ml/½ pint fish stock or water*
*300ml/½ pint milk*
*2 medium potatoes cut into 5mm-1 cm/¼ to ½ inch dice*
*salt and pepper*
*350g/12 oz freshly cooked or canned clams, chopped or minced*
*150ml/¼ pint double cream*
*1-2 tablespoons chopped parsley*

Heat the butter and bacon in a saucepan. Add the onion and fry gently for 4 to 5 minutes – do not allow to brown. Stir the flour into the onion mixture, then gradually blend in the stock or water and milk. Bring to the boil and stir over a medium heat until slightly thickened. Add the potatoes and a little salt and pepper. Cover the pan and simmer for 6 to 8 minutes; the potatoes should not become too soft.

Add the clams, cream, half the parsley and heat gently for a further 10 minutes. Adjust the seasoning and top the soup with the remaining parsley. This soup is often served with cream crackers or water biscuits. One or two biscuits can be crumbled and put into each soup bowl before adding the soup.

VARIATIONS

⊛ **Crab or Lobster Chowder:** If using fresh crab or lobster simmer the shell to obtain good fish stock. Omit the bacon in the recipe above; increase the butter to 50g/2 oz. Add 2 tablespoons finely chopped celery and 2 tablespoons finely chopped green pepper to the onion. Flake enough crab or lobster to give 300 to 350g/10 to 12 oz and use the crab or lobster instead of clams.

## Crab Cream ⊛

*1 medium crab*
*300ml/½ pint crab stock*
*300ml/½ pint single cream*
*2 tablespoons tomato purée*
*salt and pepper*
GARNISH:
*chopped fennel or parsley*

Remove the crabmeat from the shell. Wash the shell and simmer in water to cover for 20 minutes, strain the liquid and use 300ml/½ pint for the stock. Flake the fish, blend with the stock, cream, tomato purée, and salt and pepper to taste.

Serve the soup hot or cold, topped with chopped fennel or parsley.

## Lobster Bisque ⊛

*1 medium lobster, preferably hen with coral*
*900ml/1½pints water*
*1 onion, left whole*
*bouquet garni*
*salt and pepper*
*40g/1½oz butter*
*40g/1½oz flour*
*150ml/¼pint double cream*
*2 tablespoons brandy*
GARNISH:
*little double cream*
*2-3 teaspoons chopped fennel leaves*

Remove the flesh and coral from the lobster; wash the shell, crush slightly and put into a saucepan with the water, onion, bouquet garni and a little salt and pepper. Simmer for 30 minutes then strain the stock – it should have reduced to about 600ml/1 pint.

Heat the butter in a pan, stir in the flour, then gradually add the lobster stock. Bring the sauce to the boil and stir until thickened. Pound the lobster flesh until very fine; it could be put into a food processor or liquidizer if desired. Mix the lobster flesh and coral with the sauce. Heat gently, but do not over-cook. Blend the cream and brandy together and whisk into the hot, but not boiling, soup and stir over a low heat for 2 to 3 minutes. Serve the soup topped with a little extra cream and chopped fennel leaves.

VARIATION

⊛ **Crab Bisque:** Use the flesh from a medium-sized crab instead of the lobster. Another method of thickening this crab soup is to omit the flour, just heat the butter, blend in the stock (made from the crushed crab shells), then add about 50g/2oz soft white breadcrumbs with the flaked crabmeat. The colour of Crab Bisque is improved if 2 to 3 teaspoons tomato purée are blended with the stock.

## Partan Bree ⊛

*1 large cooked crab*
*1.2 litres/2 pints chicken stock*
*50g/2 pints chicken stock*
*50g/2 oz long-grain rice*
*150ml/¼pint double cream*
*few drops anchovy essence*
*salt and pepper*

Remove all the flesh from the body and large claws of the crab; carefully discard the stomach bag and the grey fingers. Put the body and large empty claw shells into a saucepan with the stock and simmer for 10 minutes, then strain. The liquid will have absorbed flavour from the shells.

Return the stock to the pan, add the rice and simmer for 15 minutes. Stir in the flaked crabmeat, cream, anchovy essence and salt and pepper to taste. Heat the soup for a few minutes but do not allow to boil rapidly, then serve.

VARIATION

You can use frozen or canned crabmeat, in which case you will not obtain quite as much flavour, as the shell is not simmered with the stock.

## Cream of Salmon Soup ⊛

*900 ml/1 ½ pints milk*
*1 medium onion*
*50 g/2 oz butter*
*40 g/1 ½ oz flour*
*175 g/6 oz cooked or canned salmon (weight without skin and bones)*
*5 tablespoons double cream*
*salt and pepper*
*2 teaspoons lemon juice (optional)*
GARNISH:
*1 tablespoon chopped fennel leaves or parsley*

Heat the milk and onion in a pan, then allow to stand for about 1 hour so that the milk absorbs the onion flavour and becomes cold.

Heat the butter in a pan, stir in the flour and cook over a low heat for 2 to 3 minutes, stirring well. Strain the milk gradually into the butter and flour, discarding the onion. Stir the mixture as the liquid comes to the boil and thickens. Sieve the salmon or flake very finely and blend into the thickened mixture.

Heat the soup gently for a few minutes then add the cream with salt and pepper to taste. A little lemon juice can be whisked into the hot, but not boiling, soup just before serving. Top with the fennel leaves or parsley.

VARIATION

⊛ **Cream of Prawn Soup:** Peel 225 to 350 g/8 to 12 oz prawns. Heat the shells with the milk and onion to give a good flavour then proceed as above. Instead of salt, add a few drops of anchovy essence.

## Salmon Bisque ⊛

*50 g/2 oz butter*
*1 medium onion, chopped*
*40 g/1 ½ oz flour*
*600 ml/1 pint milk*
*150 ml/¼ pint fish or chicken stock*
*225 g/8 oz cooked or canned salmon, flaked*
*salt and pepper*
*150 ml/¼ pint double cream*

Heat the butter in a pan, add the onion and fry for a few minutes – do not allow it to discolour. Stir in the flour, cook for 2 to 3 minutes, then gradually blend in the milk and stock. Bring to the boil and stir well to make a thin sauce. Add the fish, a little salt and pepper and half the cream. Sieve or liquidize the soup to make a very smooth purée. Return to the pan and heat. Whip the remaining cream. Serve each portion of soup topped with whipped cream.

VARIATIONS

⊛ **Salmon Chowder:** Fry a derinded and finely chopped rasher of bacon with the finely chopped onion. Add the other ingredients as in above recipe with 1 peeled and grated carrot and a few cooked peas. Heat together, season well; add 1 teaspoon chopped fennel leaves. Do not sieve or liquidize this version.

⊛ **Tomato and Salmon Bisque:** Use 600 ml/1 pint tomato juice instead of the milk in the recipe above. Omit the cream. Fry 2 skinned, chopped and seeded tomatoes with the onion, add the flour, tomato juice and stock. Make a thin sauce then add the flaked fish, a few cooked peas, season well and include a pinch of cayenne pepper. Garnish with chopped chives.

## Scandinavian Fiskesuppe ⊛

*75 g/3 oz butter or margarine*
*1 medium leek, finely chopped*
*1 medium onion, finely chopped*
*1-2 celery sticks, finely chopped*
*2 medium carrots, grated*
*40 g/1½ oz flour*
*900 ml/1½ pints fish stock*
*salt and cayenne pepper*
*3 tablespoons brown sherry*

Heat the butter or margarine in a saucepan, add the vegetables and cook over a low heat for about 10 minutes; take care they do not discolour. Stir in the flour and cook for 2 to 3 minutes, then gradually add the fish stock. Bring the soup slowly to the boil, stirring all the time, until thickened. Add salt and pepper to taste with the sherry and serve.

VARIATION

⊛ **Brun Fiskesuppe:** Simmer the prepared vegetables in the stock until just tender. Heat 50 g/2 oz butter in a pan, stir in 40 g/1½ oz flour and continue stirring over a low heat until the butter and flour turns a dark brown – take care it does not burn. Gradually add the stock and vegetables; stir well as the mixture heats and thickens. Add the salt, pepper and sherry. This version can also have 2 concassed (skinned, halved, deseeded and finely-chopped) tomatoes added when the liquid has thickened.

# Cheese Soups

One of the most delicious of all special occasion soups is made with our splendid Stilton cheese. The recipe follows on this page, together with various ways to adapt it. Remember the golden rule is that the cheese should not be over-cooked, so prepare the first part of the soup when convenient, add the cheese just before the meal, stir over a low heat to melt, then serve.

## Golden Stilton Soup ⊛

*50 g/2 oz butter*
*1 medium onion, finely chopped*
*25 g/1 oz flour*
*300 ml/½ pint milk*
*450 ml/¾ pint chicken stock*
*175 g/6 oz Stilton cheese, finely diced*
*salt and pepper*
*pinch dry mustard powder*
*4 tablespoons double cream*
*2 medium carrots, grated*
GARNISH:
*fried croûtons*

Heat the butter in a pan, stir in the onion and cook gently for several minutes – do not allow it to discolour. Blend in the flour, then gradually add the milk and stock. Bring to the boil, stir as it thickens, then simmer for 10 minutes.

Add the cheese, seasonings to taste and cream. Stir over a low heat until the cheese has nearly melted, then add the carrot and cook for 2 minutes only, so that the carrot retains its slightly crisp texture. Top the soup with the croûtons just before serving.

VARIATION

⊛ **Celery and Stilton Soup:** Omit the carrot. Use ham or bacon stock in place of chicken stock. Chop several sticks from the heart of the celery and toss in the butter with the onion; it is a good idea to increase the butter to 75 g/3 oz. When the mixture has been simmering for 10 minutes, add the cheese and other ingredients, heat for 1 to 2 minutes only then sieve or liquidize to give a perfectly smooth soup.

⊛ **Stilton Soup:** Omit both the carrot and the celery; simply add Stilton cheese to the mixture. In this soup it is better to use the chicken stock as in the above recipe. Sieve the soup after adding the cheese, return to the pan, then add chopped chives and chopped parsley to garnish.

⊛ **Cheddar Soup:** Follow the recipe above but subsitute Cheddar cheese for Stilton cheese. When adding the cheese, seasonings and cream, add 1 to 2 tablespoons dry sherry. This soup is excellent with the carrots and a few cooked peas as well to give colour and additional flavour.

# Cold Soups

I have included a selection of cold soups, for my friends are now more fond of these. Once everyone seemed to think a soup must be "piping hot", but cold soups are refreshing and satisfying. Do not make them too thick, they should be the consistency of a pouring cream. Chill well before serving.

## Avocado Soup ⊛

*2 ripe avocados*
*2 tablespoons lemon juice*
*600 ml/1 pint chicken stock*
*300 ml/½ pint yogurt*
*salt and pepper*
GARNISH:
*chopped chives*

Halve and skin the avocados and chop the pulp. Put into a liquidizer or food processor with the remaining ingredients and blend to a smooth purée. Chill the soup well and top with chives just before serving.

## Chilled Green Pea Soup ⊛

*1 medium onion, finely chopped*
*225 g/8 oz frozen or shelled peas*
*300 ml/½ pint ham or chicken stock*
*sprig mint*
*salt and pepper*
*150 ml/¼ pint white wine*
*300 ml/½ pint single cream*
GARNISH:
*little chopped chives*

Cook the onion and peas in the stock with the mint and a little salt and pepper for about 10 minutes or until just tender; do not over-cook for you want to retain the attractive colour of the peas.

Either sieve the mixture or blend in a liquidizer or food processor until a very smooth purée. Chill, then add the wine, cream and any extra seasoning required. Top with the chives.

VARIATIONS

If you like a slightly thicker soup, increase the amount of peas slightly, but the recipe above gives an ideal soup for hot weather.

⊛ **Hot Green Pea Soup:** Increase the onions to 2, use all stock, then proceed as the recipe. Return the smooth purée to the saucepan, add the cream. You can be more economical and use 600 ml/1 pint stock and only 150 ml/¼ pint cream or blend the purée with a thin White Sauce, see page 226. When peas are very young, cook some of the tender pea pods with the peas and rub them through a sieve with the peas.

## Cucumber and Yogurt Soup ⊛

*1 small cucumber*
*600 ml/1 pint natural yogurt*
*1-2 teaspoons chopped nuts*
*2 teaspoons chopped parsley*
*4 tablespoons chopped spring onions or chives*
*½-1 tablespoon lemon juice*
*salt and pepper*
GARNISH:
*chopped parsley and chives or chopped walnuts*

Peel and grate or finely chop the cucumber. Mix with the yogurt, nuts and herbs. Add the lemon juice with salt and pepper to taste. Chill the soup well and top with the herbs or nuts. Serve with crisp water biscuits.

VARIATION

⊛ **Cucumber Soup Suprême:** Peel and chop 1 very large or 2 medium cucumbers. Simmer the cucumber in 600 ml/1 pint chicken stock with 1 medium chopped onion and a small sprig of mint. Remove the mint then sieve or liquidize the cucumber. Chill and blend with 300 ml/½ pint single cream and salt and pepper to taste. Top the soup with finely chopped mint and chives. This soup can also be served hot; thicken with Beurre Manié, see page 45.

## Gazpacho ⊛

*750 g/1½ lb ripe tomatoes*
*½ cucumber, peeled and chopped*
*2 onions, chopped*
*2 cloves garlic, chopped*
*2 tablespoons oil*
*1 tablespoon lemon juice or white wine vinegar*
*salt and pepper*
TO SERVE:
*75 g/3 oz fresh bread, neatly diced*
*1 red pepper, cored, deseeded and neatly diced*
*1 green pepper, cored, deseeded and neatly diced*
*½ medium cucumber, peeled and neatly diced*
*2 onions, neatly diced*

Put a jug of water into the refrigerator to become very cold. Skin the tomatoes, unless you intend to sieve them, in which case the skins will be left behind in the sieve. Chop the tomatoes and mix with the chopped cucumber, onions and garlic. Rub the mixture through a sieve, or pound together to make a very smooth mixture, or blend in a liquidizer or food processor until smooth.

Pour the tomato mixture into a large chilled mixing bowl; gradually blend in the oil. Add the lemon juice or vinegar, salt and pepper to taste and enough chilled water to make a flowing consistency. Transfer the soup to a soup tureen or glass serving bowl; chill thoroughly.

Put the diced bread, diced peppers, diced cucumber and diced onion into small individual dishes and arrange around the soup.

VARIATION

⊛ **Malaga Gazpacho:** Make a rich stock by simmering knuckle of veal in water to cover with a chopped onion, 2 chopped cloves garlic, salt and pepper to taste. Strain and chill then blend with 450 g/1 lb skinned diced tomatoes, small peeled diced cucumber and 1 to 2 diced red and/or green peppers. This soup can be made without using oil (ideal for slimmers) or blend in 1 to 2 tablespoons olive oil.

## Guacamole Soup ⊛

*2 medium tomatoes, skinned and chopped*
*about 6 spring onions, chopped*
*½ small red pepper, cored, deseeded and chopped*
*½ small green pepper, cored, deseeded and chopped*
*2 medium avocados, peeled and chopped*
*2 tablespoons lemon juice*
*300 ml/½ pint milk*
*150 ml/¼ pint single cream*
*salt and pepper*

Blend the tomatoes, onions, peppers, avocados and lemon juice in a liquidizer or food processor until a smooth purée. Gradually blend in the milk and cream and add salt and pepper to taste. Serve very cold.

VARIATION

Use yogurt instead of milk.

## Iced Tomato Soup ⊛

*1 medium onion, chopped*
*750 g/1½ lb tomatoes, skinned and chopped*
*2-3 sticks celery, chopped*
*1 small cooked beetroot, skinned and chopped*
*300 ml/½ pint chicken stock*
*300 ml/½ pint dry white wine*
*2 teaspoons lemon juice*
*sprig basil*
*1 bay leaf*
*salt and pepper*

Put the onion, tomatoes, celery and beetroot into a saucepan. Add the stock, wine, lemon juice, herbs and salt and pepper to taste. Simmer steadily for about 20 minutes; do not over-cook. Remove basil sprig and bay leaf. Sieve the mixture or put into a liquidizer or food processor to make a smooth purée. You may find you have some tomato pips left after liquidizing, if you want to remove these then sieve after using the liquidizer.

Taste and add any more seasoning or lemon juice if desired. Freeze lightly then spoon into chilled soup cups.

VARIATION

Make the soup slightly more piquant by adding a few drops Tabasco sauce and a little garlic salt.

## Vichyssoise ⊛

*50g/2oz butter*
*8 medium leeks, chopped*
*2 medium old potatoes, chopped*
*750ml/1¼ pints chicken stock*
*salt and pepper*
*150ml/¼ pint white wine*
*150ml/¼ pint double or whipping cream*
GARNISH:
*2 tablespoons chopped chives*

Heat the butter in a large saucepan. Add the leeks and potatoes and turn in the butter for several minutes; do not allow to brown. Pour in the chicken stock and add a little salt and pepper to taste. Simmer the mixture gently for 20 to 25 minutes until the vegetables are tender; do not over-cook as this will darken the soup. Allow to cool.

Sieve or liquidize the ingredients with the wine and cream to give a velvet-like soup. Chill the soup well and top with the chives.

VARIATIONS

**Apple Vichyssoise:** Cook a large peeled and diced cooking apple with the other ingredients. Proceed as in the recipe above.

When cold add 2 rosy-skinned finely diced apples as garnish. Do not peel the apples (the peel provides a bright colour) and dip the diced apple into lemon juice to prevent browning and preserve colour. Add a little more lemon juice to give a refreshing flavour to the soup.

**Crab Vichyssoise:** Use fish stock, rather than chicken stock if possible. Proceed as in the recipe above. When the mixture is cold, sieve or liquidise with 100 to 175g/4 to 6oz white crabmeat. Add a few drops anchovy essence to give a good flavour and colour, but be sparing with the salt used.

**Mushroom Vichyssoise:** Proceed as in the recipe above, but add 75 g/3 oz finely sliced raw mushrooms and 2 tablespoons diced red pepper as garnish. Raw mushrooms are delicious, but if preferred fry the thin slices of mushrooms in a little oil (butter makes them look cloudy when cold); allow to cool, then add to the cold soup.

## Yogurt and Cheese Soup

*300ml/½ pint yogurt*
*450ml/¾ pint chicken stock*
*175g/6oz Danish Blue cheese*
*1 teaspoon made mustard*
*salt and pepper*
GARNISH:
*1 tablespoon chopped parsley*
*2 teaspoons chopped chives*
*2 teaspoons finely diced red pepper*

Blend all the ingredients in a liquidizer or food processor until quite smooth. Serve the soup well chilled, topped with the parsley, chives and red pepper.

VARIATIONS

Use other cheeses.

This soup can be served hot, but heat without adding the yogurt. Add the yogurt to the hot, but not boiling, soup and heat very gently for a few minutes.

# Fish Dishes

As we live on an island we are fortunate to have a wonderful selection of fish throughout much of the year. This variety should enable us to prepare the most interesting dishes. Unfortunately many people find one or two recipes that please their family or which they find easy to make and then use no other ideas. I feel this is a pity for it precludes many pleasant dishes. Take a look at the selection of fish displayed in a good fishmongers or supermarket, or at the fish market, if you are fortunate enough to live by the coast. There will be white fish, ranging from the humble coley to luxurious sole. When in season there will be a variety of shellfish; you will find recipes in this book using mussels, prawns, scallops, crab and lobster, together with suggestions for serving lesser-known shell as well as other fish.

Changing tastes and conditions determine the kind of fish that becomes popular. Once upon a time mackerel was not readily available because few people had had the opportunity to taste and appreciate this succulent fish; nowadays, as herrings have become less plentiful, mackerel have taken their place as an excellent and economical fish to serve in many ways. Fresh trout is another fish that is seen frequently these days, due to the emergence of trout farms which breed trout of just the right size and quality. The idea of farming fish has been extended to Scottish salmon and this luxury fish is now obtainable throughout the year.

Whatever the kind of fish or recipe you choose, there is one golden rule to follow: do not over-cook fish at any stage in making the dish. Over-cooked fish loses both flavour and moist texture. In quite a few recipes you will find I have omitted the sign that denotes that the complete and cooked fish can be frozen. This is because I feel that freezing and then re-heating the cooked dish will spoil the taste.

Many of the dishes in this section are economical and simple to prepare but you will also find more elaborate dishes for special occasions. Some of these would be equally suitable for an hors d'oeuvre if you serve slightly smaller portions. I serve fish quite frequently in my home for it is one of my favourite foods.

# Cooking White Fish

White fish is incredibly versatile. It can be baked, fried, grilled poached or steamed. You will notice that the word 'boiled' does not appear on this list for boiling is not to be recommended as a method of cooking any fish. I know we often refer to 'boiled fish' but the liquid in which fish is cooked should only simmer gently. Too fast cooking means the outside of the fish is over-cooked before the middle is tender. The term we should use about cooking fish in liquid is 'poaching'.

Here are the basic ways of cooking fish –

**Baking:** Top the fish with butter or add butter and milk or other foods, such as stuffings, bake in the oven, see pages 68 and 69.

**Frying:** Fish can be shallow fried or fried in deep oil or fat. The various coatings and methods of frying are described on pages 75 to 77.

**Grilling:** This method preserves the natural flavour of the fish. Some recipes are on page 78.

**Poaching:** Cook the fish in seasoned water, or in milk or stock or as described under Poached Salmon on page 80. Other recipes are on pages 70 to 74.

**Steaming:** A method which makes fish easily digested, see page 74.

**Freshness of Fish**

White, oily and freshwater fish should all look firm in texture, the eyes and scales or skin of the fish bright. Shellfish should be firm and brightly coloured. To test a lobster's freshness pull out the tail, if it springs back the fish is very fresh; any smell of ammonia is a clear sign of stale fish.

**Freezing Fish Dishes**

I rarely freeze cooked fish dishes, for I find much of the flavour and texture of the fish is lost when the dish has to be reheated. Obviously if serving the dish cold then freezing is quite satisfactory. On the other hand I often prepare a fish dish, then freeze it, ready to cook on other occasion. The freezing symbols shown on the dishes in this chapter indicate those dishes that freeze particularly well. It is a great help to coat fish before freezing, open-freeze, so the coating does not stick to any packaging, then wrap. Freezing helps the coating adhere to the fish.

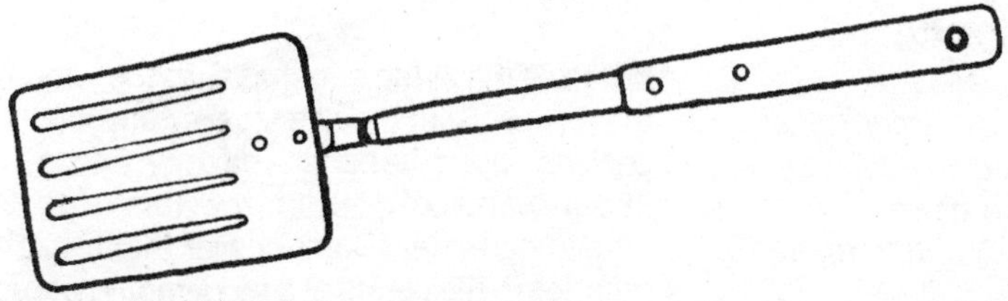

## Baked Fish in Cream ⊛

*4 portions of white fish, eg coley, cod, fresh haddock, hake or halibut*
*25 g/1 oz butter, melted*
*150 ml/¼ pint single cream*
*salt and pepper*
GARNISH:
*lemon wedges*
*parsley sprigs*

Put the fish into an ovenproof dish. Blend the butter and cream and add a little salt and pepper. Pour over the fish. Cover with buttered foil or a lid. If baking thin portions of fish, place above the centre of a moderately hot oven (190°C/375°F or Gas Mark 5) and cook for approximately 20 minutes. If cooking thicker fish portions, place the dish in the centre of the oven and/or reduce the heat to moderate (180°C/350°F or Gas Mark 4) and cook for 25 to 30 minutes. The lid or foil can be removed for the last half of the cooking time, so that the fish colours. Garnish with the lemon and parsley.

VARIATION

⊛ **Baked Fish Normandy:** Bake the fish for half the cooking time, then add 75 g/3 oz peeled prawns, 75 g/3 oz mussels, prepared as page 92 and continue cooking. Instead of cream you can use white wine in this recipe.

## Baked Sole Cécilia

*75 g/3 oz butter, melted*
*4 large or 8 small sole fillets, skinned*
*salt and pepper*
*12 asparagus tips, cooked or canned*
*50 g/2 oz Gruyère cheese, finely grated*

Spoon about 15 g/½ oz butter into a flameproof dish. Fold each fillet in half and put into the dish, add another 40 g/1½ oz butter, salt and pepper to taste. Do not cover the dish as it is better for the fish to become slightly coloured in the oven. Bake just above the centre of a moderately hot oven (190°C/375°F or Gas Mark 5) for 25 minutes, or until tender. Remove from the oven, top with the asparagus tips, the grated cheese and remaining butter. Heat for several minutes under a hot grill, then serve.

**Note:** Always use a flameproof, rather than ovenproof, dish when heating food under the grill.

## Cod Caprice

*4 large bananas*
*1 tablespoon lemon juice*
*2 tablespoons seedless raisins*
*4 thick cod steaks*
*40 g/1½ oz butter, melted*
GARNISH:
*lemon wedges*

Peel and mash the bananas with the lemon juice, add the raisins. Split the fish steaks horizontally to make 4 pockets. Insert the banana mixture. Spoon a little butter into an ovenproof dish, add the stuffed fish, top with the remaining butter. Do not cover the dish. Bake for 30 minutes in the centre of a moderately hot oven (190°C/375°F or Gas Mark 5). Top with the lemon wedges.

## Cod with Mustard ⊛

*50g/2oz butter or margarine*
*1 small onion, finely chopped*
*1 tablespoon French mustard*
*pinch dry mustard powder*
*salt and pepper*
*50g/2oz soft breadcrumbs*
*4 cod steaks*
GARNISH:
*cucumber slices*
*tomato slices*

Heat 40g/1½oz butter or margarine in a frying pan. Cook the onion until soft. Blend with the mustard, salt and pepper and breadcrumbs.

Put the cod into an ovenproof dish, top with the remaining butter then the mustard mixture. Do not cover the dish. Bake in the centre of a moderately hot oven (190°C/375°F or Gas Mark 5) for 30 minutes, or until the topping is golden brown and the fish tender. Add the cucumber and tomato slices for the last few minutes cooking.

## Harvest-time Fish ⊛

*3 bacon rashers*
*50g/2oz butter or margarine*
*2 small onions, cut into thin rings*
*4 medium tomatoes, skinned and thickly sliced*
*2 tablespoons chopped parsley*
*salt and pepper*
*4 portions of white fish*

Derind the bacon, reserving the rinds; chop the rashers. Melt half the butter or margarine in a frying pan with the bacon rinds to give more fat. Add the bacon and onions and fry until the onions are nearly soft. Discard the bacon rinds. Mix the tomatoes and parsley with the onions and bacon and season lightly with salt and pepper.

Spoon half the mixture into an ovenproof dish, top with the fish fillets, the remaining butter and then the last of the bacon mixture. Cover the dish and bake in the centre of a moderately hot oven (190°C/375°F or Gas Mark 5) for 35 minutes.

## Layered Plaice ⊛

*9 plaice fillets, skinned*
*25g/1oz butter, melted*
*1 tablespoon lemon juice*
*salt and pepper*
STUFFING:
*75g/3oz soft breadcrumbs*
*100g/4oz mushrooms, sliced*
*2 tablespoons chopped chives*
*1 teaspoon finely grated lemon rind*
*2 large tomatoes, sliced*
GARNISH:
*lemon slices*

Put 3 plaice fillets into a deep round casserole. Blend the butter, lemon juice and salt and pepper. Brush a little over the fish. Mix the stuffing ingredients together and season well with salt and pepper. Spread half the stuffing over the plaice. Top with another 3 fish, brush these with the butter and lemon mixture, then spread with the remaining stuffing. Top with the last 3 plaice. Cover the dish and bake in the centre of a moderate oven (180°C/350°F or Gas Mark 4) for 35 minutes. Remove the lid after 20 minutes to allow the top layer of fish to brown.

Top with the lemon slices. Cut into wedges to serve. Serves 6.

## Fish Quenelles ⊛

*450 g/1 lb white fish (weight without skin and bones). Use pike, whiting, hake or very young codling – the flesh must be very fine*

SAUCE:

*25 g/1 oz butter*
*25 g/1 oz flour*
*150 ml/¼ pint milk or single cream*
*2 egg yolks*
*salt and pepper*

FOR POACHING AND GARNISH:

*600 ml/1 pint fish stock, see method*
*1-2 tablespoons dry sherry or lemon juice*
*50 g/2 oz butter, melted*
*lemon wedges*
*parsley sprigs*

Dice the raw fish then put through the fine plate of a mincer twice, so that it is very fine. A food processor can be used to chop the fish, but take care it is not processed for too long or the fish will become sticky rather than be made into fine particles.

Heat the butter for the sauce in a pan, stir in the flour and continue stirring over a low heat for 2 to 3 minutes. Gradually blend in the milk or cream and stir over a low heat until a thick binding sauce (known as a panada). Add the fish, egg yolks and salt and pepper to taste. Pound the mixture very well with a wooden spoon or pestle and mortar. Allow the mixture to become quite cold, then form into finger shapes (quenelles) or simply take spoonfuls of the mixture.

Heat the stock with the sherry or lemon juice in a large frying pan; add a little salt and pepper. Add the quenelles and poach for 10 minutes, turning them two or three times so they become evenly cooked. Drain with a perforated spoon. Top with the melted butter and garnish with the lemon and parsley.

VARIATIONS

Serve topped with Hollandaise Sauce instead of butter, see recipe page 234.

Use fresh salmon instead of white fish.

Add a little finely chopped parsley to the quenelle mixture.

⊛ **Quenelles of Chicken or Game:** Use minced breast of young chicken or pheasant or grouse in place of fish. Use half chicken or game stock and half double cream in the quenelle mixture. Poach in chicken or game stock, flavoured with red wine. This can be thickened with a Beurre Manié (see page 45) and then served over the quenelles instead of melted butter.

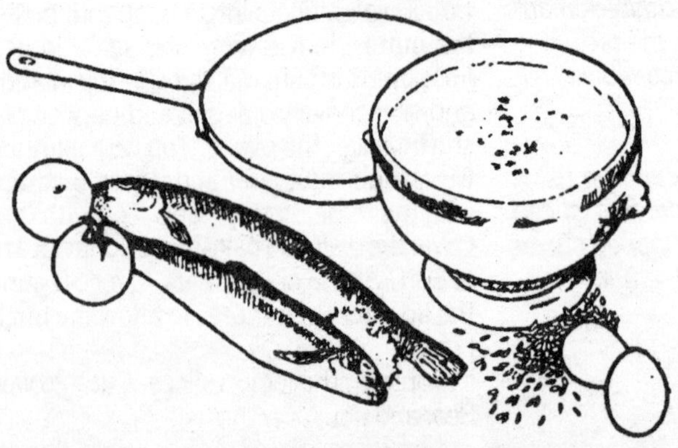

# Adding Flavour to Fish

People sometimes complain that fish dishes lack flavour. The following recipes have been chosen as they include a variety of different ingredients.

## Brill Dugléré ⊛

*4 brill fillets*
*350 g/12 oz tomatoes, skinned and chopped*
*1 small onion, finely chopped*
*150 ml/¼ pint red wine*
*salt and pepper*
*50 g/2 oz butter*
*1 tablespoon flour*
GARNISH:
*lemon wedges*

Place the fish in a dish. Add the tomatoes, onion, wine and salt and pepper. Put half the butter in small pieces over the top of the tomato mixture. Cover the dish. Bake in the centre of a moderately hot oven (190-200°C/375-400°F or Gas Mark 5-6) for 20 to 25 minutes.

Lift the fish from the tomato mixture, place on a hot dish and keep warm. Heat the remaining butter in a saucepan, stir in the flour, then add the tomato mixture and stir until thickened. If you want a very smooth sauce, sieve or liquidize the sauce, but the pieces of tomato and onion add interest to the dish. Garnish with lemon.

VARIATION

Other fish can be cooked in the same way, fresh haddock or thick plaice fillets are excellent.

## Turbot with Sorrel ⊛

*4 turbot portions*
*4-8 canned anchovy fillets*
*pepper*
*150 ml/¼ pint white wine*
*450 g/1 lb sorrel*
*salt*
*150 ml/¼ pint double cream*
*2 egg yolks*

Put the turbot into an ovenproof dish, top with the anchovy fillets, pepper (salt should be unnecessary) and the wine. Cover the dish and cook in the centre of a moderately hot oven (190°C/375°F or Gas Mark 5) for 30 minutes, or until the fish is tender.

Meanwhile wash the sorrel and cook in the water adhering to the leaves, add salt to taste. Strain, chop and return to the pan. Blend the cream with the egg yolks and stir into the sorrel to make a soft purée. Heat gently, without boiling, for a few minutes and put on a serving dish. Lift the turbot and anchovy fillets from the wine and place on the sorrel base and serve.

VARIATION:

⊛ **Turbot Florentine:** Cook spinach instead of sorrel. Blend the chopped spinach with 3 tablespoons of the cream. Strain the wine used in cooking the fish into a saucepan, whisk in the egg yolks and remaining cream, heat and pour over the fish.

## Bouillabaisse

*1 kg/2 to 2¼ lb fish, firm white fish, such as hake or cod. French cooks generally include red mullet and eel; add a more delicate fish such as sole or thick plaice or whiting fillets (this cooks quickly, so could be added after the firmer varieties). Include shell-fish, such as crab or lobster and large peeled prawns*
*2 tablespoons oil*
*2 medium onions or leeks, thinly sliced*
*1-2 cloves garlic, crushed*
*2 large tomatoes, skinned*
*pinch saffron powder or a few saffron strands*
*1 bay leaf*
*parsley sprig*
*salt and pepper*
*150 ml/¼ pint dry white wine*

I humbly admit this is a very simplified version of the famous French recipe, but one that is very possible to make at home. The selection of fish is purely a matter of taste, and buying what is available, but the more varieties you use, the more interesting the dish will be.

Prepare the fish and cut into neat pieces. Remove the meat from shellfish; you could leave the meat in the large claws of crab or lobster, simply crack them and heat with the other fish. They give colour and interest to the completed dish.

Heat the oil in a large saucepan and cook the vegetables for a few minutes. Blend the saffron with a little boiling water; if using saffron strands you can strain the liquid before pouring over the vegetables in the pan. Add all the fish, except any shellfish, to the pan, with sufficient boiling water to cover. Put in the herbs and salt and pepper, then simmer for 10 to 15 minutes. Add the wine and shellfish, simmer for a further 5 to 6 minutes. Remove the herbs. Serve with bread or large pieces of bread fried in oil until crisp and brown.

VARIATION

**Bourride:** Buy a selection of fish, as for the recipe above. Slice several onions, put into a strong saucepan with a sprig of fennel and several fresh herbs too. Pare the rind from 1 or 2 oranges, add to the onions and herbs. Place the fish on top, with water to cover and salt and pepper to taste. Cover the pan and cook for about 15 minutes, or until the fish is tender.

Make the Garlic Mayonnaise (Aioli) see page 236 and blend with 2 egg yolks. When the fish is cooked, whisk 2 to 3 tablespoons of the stock from the saucepan into the mayonnaise. Lift the fish on to a serving dish. Place slices of bread in each deep plate. Put the garlic mayonnaise mixture into a dish. Strain the liquid from the saucepan over the bread. Everyone helps themselves to fish and sauce and has it with the delicious stock and bread.

**Cod Biscayenne:** This dish is often made with morue (salt cod), but is excellent with fresh cod. Peel and slice several onions or shallots; heat 2 tablespoons oil in a casserole, add the onions or shallots and turn in the oil. Add about 750 g/1½ lb cod fillet, then a layer of thinly sliced raw potatoes, then a layer of sliced tomatoes. Season each layer and add 4 tablespoons water. Cover the casserole and cook for 1 hour in a moderate oven (160°C/325°F or Gas Mark 3).

## Sole in Wine Sauce

*4 large or 8 small sole fillets*
*300 ml/½ pint dry white wine*
*salt and pepper*
*Beurre Manié (see page 45)*
GARNISH:
*lemon wedges*
*parsley sprigs*

Although this dish and the recipe below are cooked in the oven, the sole is really poached, for it is cooked gently in liquid. The only reason for cooking in the oven, as opposed to the top of the cooker, is that it is easier to accommodate the shape of the fillets. If more convenient, poach the fish in the liquid given in each recipe on top of the cooker.

Fold the fillets of fish in half and place in an ovenproof dish, add the wine, salt and pepper and cover the dish. Cook gently in the centre of a moderate oven (180°C/350°F or Gas Mark 4) for 25 to 30 minutes until just tender. Lift the sole on to a serving dish. Pour the wine into a saucepan and thicken with Beurre Manié, as described on page 45.

Spoon the sauce over the fish and garnish with lemon and parsley.

VARIATION

**Sole in Cream and Wine Sauce:** Follow the recipe above, but boil the wine until reduced to only 4 tablespoons, add 150 ml/¼ pint double cream and heat gently, then spoon the sauce over the fish.

## Sole Bonne Femme ⊛

*4 large or 8 small sole fillets*
*150 ml/¼ pint white wine*
*salt and pepper*
*75 g/3 oz butter*
*100 g/3 oz mushrooms, sliced*
*25 g/1 oz flour*
*150 ml/¼ pint milk*
*450 g/1 lb cooked potatoes, sieved if possible*
*1 egg yolk*

In this dish the fillets of fish need not be folded; simply put into an ovenproof dish, top with the wine, salt and pepper and cover. As the fish fillets will be thinner, since they are not folded, they can be baked at a slightly higher temperature, ie just above the centre of a moderately hot oven (190°C/375°F or Gas Mark 5) for 20 to 25 minutes.

While the fish is cooking, heat 25 g/1 oz of the butter and fry the mushrooms. In another pan, heat another 25 g/1 oz butter, stir in the flour and cook gently for 2 to 3 minutes. Blend in the milk and stir well as the sauce thickens.

Mash the potatoes with the remaining butter, add the egg yolks and season to taste. Spoon or pipe the potato around the edge of a serving dish and keep hot. Lift the sole into the centre of the dish. Strain the wine into the sauce and stir to blend. If necessary, add a little extra milk to give the sauce a thinner consistency. Do not allow the sauce to boil. Stir in the hot mushrooms then spoon over the fish and serve.

## Sole Mornay ⊛

*4 large sole fillets*
*150 ml/¼ pint white wine*
*salt and pepper*
*25 g/1 oz butter*
*25 g/1 oz flour*
*150 ml/¼ pint milk*
*100 g/4 oz Cheddar or Gruyère cheese, grated*

Follow the directions for cooking the fish and making the sauce in Sole Bonne Femme (page 73) but add 100 g/4 oz grated cheese to the cooked sauce. If preferred the fish could be cooked in fish stock, made by simmering the bones and skin of the fish, rather than white wine, or in 150 ml/¼ pint milk. The combination of wine and cheese in this dish is a very pleasant one.

VARIATION

In this and other recipes expensive sole can be replaced by fillets of plaice or whiting. These fish are less firm in texture, so you will need to reduce the cooking time by several minutes.

## Sole Véronique

*8 small sole fillets, skinned*
*150 ml/¼ pint fish stock (see page 35)*
*150 ml/¼ pint white wine*
*salt and pepper*
*175 g/6 oz white grapes*
*25 g/1 oz butter*
*25 g/1 oz flour*
*150 ml/¼ pint single cream*

Put the sole with the fish stock, white wine, salt and pepper into an ovenproof dish. Peel and deseed half the grapes, add to the fish. Deseed the remaining grapes but do not peel. Cover the dish with buttered foil. Bake in the centre of a moderately hot oven (190°C/375°F or Gas Mark 5) for 25 to 30 minutes.

Meanwhile heat the butter in a saucepan, add the flour and stir over a low heat for 2 to 3 minutes. Blend in the cream and stir as the sauce comes to the boil and becomes thick.

Lift the sole fillets from the liquid on to a hot dish; cover and keep warm. Strain just over 150 ml/¼ pint of the hot fish liquid into the sauce and stir over a low heat to blend. Add seasoning to taste. Spoon the sauce over the sole and top with the remaining grapes.

## Steamed Fish

*4 portions of white fish*
*little butter*
*salt and pepper*
*squeeze lemon juice*
FLAVOURINGS:
*chopped parsley or other herbs*
*cream or milk*
*thinly sliced tomatoes (omit milk if using these)*

Put the fish on to a plate, cover with a little butter, add salt and pepper to taste with a squeeze of lemon juice if desired or other flavourings, see ingredients. Cover with a second plate and cook over a pan of boiling water until the fish is tender.

This is an ideal way to cook fish for an invalid, but it is excellent too if using the fish in dishes, like Fish Cakes, for the fish does not become over-soft or too moist.

# Shallow Frying

The two recipes on this page show how interesting shallow frying can be. The fish is fried without a coating, but most fish to be fried has a coating of flour or egg and breadcrumbs or oatmeal, as in the recipe for herrings on page 84. You can coat the fish then freeze it. Do not defrost before frying. Batter-coated fish is better if deep fried.

## Skate in Black Butter

*4 portions skate*
*2 tablespoons lemon juice*
*salt and pepper*
*100 g/4 oz butter*
*2 teaspoons capers*
*2 tablespoons chopped parsley*
GARNISH:
*lemon wedges*

Skate is a relatively tough fish so it is advisable to simmer it for a short time before frying. Put the fish into a pan with cold water to cover; add 1 tablespoon of the lemon juice and a little salt and pepper. Bring the water to simmering point only and simmer for 5 minutes. Lift the fish from the liquid and drain on absorbent kitchen paper.

Melt half the butter in a frying pan. Add the skate and cook on both sides for 2 to 3 minutes or until tender but unbroken. Remove the fish on to a heated dish. Put the remaining butter into the frying pan and heat steadily until dark brown. This is known as black butter but never allow it to become really black and burned. Add the rest of the lemon juice, the capers and parsley. Heat for a minute. Spoon over the fish. Garnish and serve.

## Sole Meunière

*75-100 g/3-4 oz butter*
*4 large or 8 small sole fillets, skinned, or 4 whole sole, skinned*
*salt and pepper*
*1-2 tablespoons lemon juice or white wine vinegar*
*1-2 tablespoons chopped parsley*
*1-2 teaspoons capers*
GARNISH:
*lemon slices*

Heat 75 g/3 oz butter in a large frying pan. Add the fish and fry until just tender then put on a hot dish. If little butter remains in the pan, add the further 25 g/1 oz. Heat this until it turns deep golden in colour, add the salt and pepper, lemon juice or vinegar, parsley and capers. Spoon over the fish and serve garnished with the lemon slices.

VARIATIONS

This method of cooking is an excellent one for other white fish, fresh trout and scampi.

# Deep Fried White Fish

The favourite way of serving fish in Britain is deep fried and undoubtedly this method of cooking has a lot to recommend it. The coating keeps in the flavour of the fish and the quick cooking ensures it is not over-dried. Adapt the temperature of the oil or fat to the thickness of the fish.

## Isle of Man Seafood Platter ⊛

*8-12 mussels*
*2 large or 4 small sole or plaice fiillets*
*8 small oysters*
*4 large or 8 small scallops*
*small cooked lobster*
*8 large cooked prawns, peeled*
*oil or fat for deep frying*
COATING:
*100g/4oz self-raising flour*
*pinch salt*
*2 eggs, separated*
*150ml/¼ pint milk*
*2 tablespoons water*
GARNISH:
*parsley sprigs*
*lemon slices*

Prepare the mussels (see page 92) and remove from shells. Skin the fillets of fish and cut into narrow strips. Remove the oysters and scallops from their shells; halve large scallops. Remove the lobster from the shell, cut the firm flesh into neat pieces.

Sift the flour and salt together, add the egg yolks, milk, water and beat the batter well. Whisk the egg whites until stiff and fold into batter.

Dip the various fish in the batter. Fry in the hot oil or fat until crisp and golden – remember that the white fish, oysters and scallops are uncooked, whereas the remainder of the fish is pre-cooked and should not be over-heated. Drain on absorbent paper and keep hot.

Wash and dry the parsley then fry for a few seconds only in the hot oil or fat (this makes certain the parsley stays green). Garnish the fish with the crisp parsley and slices of lemon.

VARIATION

⊛ **Fried Fish:** The method above is the way in which portions of white or other popular fish are coated, then fried. The amount of batter given will coat 4 large or 8 smaller portions. White fish should first be coated in a little well-seasoned flour, then with the batter before frying.

Very thin delicate fish fillets are better with a slightly thinner batter, so add 2 to 3 tablespoons extra milk or water to the batter in the above recipe. Fry as above, adjusting the time to the size of the fish.

⊛ **Fritto Misto Mare:** The Italian dish of mixed fried fish is very similar to the recipe above. Include traditional Italian scampi and, if you can obtain octopus, cut it into small pieces, coat and fry with the other fish. Often you will find coated and fried globe artichoke hearts included in the fried fish assortment. Well-drained canned artichoke hearts can be used.

## Goujons of Fish ⊛

*450 g/1 lb white fish – choose thick fillets of plaice, sole, cod, fresh haddock or monkfish*
*oil or fat for deep frying*
COATING:
*salt and pepper*
*little flour*
*1 egg, beaten*
*50-75 g/2-3 oz crisp breadcrumbs*

Skin the fish and cut into narrow ribbons, known as goujons. Coat in seasoned flour and then in beaten egg and crisp breadcrumbs and fry following the instructions on page 76.

VARIATIONS

Instead of coating with egg and breadcrumbs, coat the goujons in batter (see recipes on pages 76, 93 and 96).

**Parmesan Goujons of Fish:** Blend at least 25 g/1 oz finely grated Parmesan cheese with the crisp breadcrumbs or with the batter. This dry cheese is ideal for coating.

## Fried Whitebait ⊛

*1 kg/2 lb whitebait*
*oil or fat for deep frying*
COATING:
*25 g/1 oz flour*
*salt*
*black or cayenne pepper*
GARNISH:
*lemon wedges*
*parsley*

These tiny fish are generally served as an hors d'oeuvre, in which case the amount given would serve 8 people. The fried fish does however make a delicious light main dish, served with a green salad.

If using frozen whitebait, you can fry from the frozen state, but I prefer to allow the fish to defrost sufficiently to dry on absorbent kitchen paper, then dust lightly with the flour, mixed with a little salt and pepper. Heat the oil or fat and fry as the recipe above. Drain on absorbent kitchen paper and garnish with lemon and parsley. Fried parsley (see recipe below) is the correct garnish.

## Fried Parsley

*parsley sprigs*
*oil for frying*

Wash the parsley and dry very thoroughly. Heat the oil to 190°C/375°F and fry the parsley for a few seconds only. It should remain bright green and be extremely crisp.

# Grilling Fish

Always pre-heat the grill before cooking fish. This means the fish cooks rapidly and will not become dry. Thin fillets of fish do not need turning, but thicker portions should be cooked rapidly on either side then grilled more slowly until tender. Always keep fish well basted with melted butter, or margarine or oil during grilling. The fat can be seasoned or flavoured with lemon juice or chopped herbs. You can marinate fish before cooking as described in the recipe on page 86.

Allow sole to soak in well-seasoned milk for about 30 minutes before grilling and be generous with the amount of butter used.

Serve grilled fish with pats of Maître d'hôtel butter (see page 285).

Cheese topped fish: Grill portions of fish, then top with a thick layer of grated cheese, replace under the grill and allow the cheese to melt.

## Fish Brochettes

*450 g/1 lb firm white fish, weight without skin or bones*
*4 rashers long streaky bacon*
*1 green pepper*
*4 very small tomatoes*
MARINADE:
*2 tablespoons oil*
*1 tablespoon lemon juice*
*salt and pepper*
*1 teaspoon tomato purée*
GARNISH:
*lemon wedges*

Fillet of hake, cod or fresh haddock can be used for this dish, or thick fillets of sole or plaice. Cut the fish into about 16 equal-sized pieces. Derind the bacon, cut each rasher into 4 pieces and fold these over. Core and seed the pepper and cut into 16 pieces.

Thread the fish, bacon, pepper and tomatoes on to 4 long metal skewers. Mix together the ingredients for the marinade and pour into a flat dish. Add the skewers and turn several times until the food has absorbed most of the marinade. Cook under a preheated grill or over a barbecue for 8 to 10 minutes. Garnish with lemon wedges. Serve with cooked rice or crusty rolls.

## Grilled Fish with Fennel

*2-3 tablespoons finely chopped fennel leaves*
*75 g/3 oz butter, melted*
*salt and pepper*
*4 portions white fish*

Fennel is one of the best herbs to add to fish. The simpler methods of cooking fish enable the true flavour of the fennel to be appreciated.

Blend the fennel with the butter and salt and pepper. Brush the fish with the flavoured butter and grill as for the Fish Brochettes on this page, allowing 10 to 12 minutes. Turn once or twice and each time baste with the fennel mixture. Serve the fish with the remaining fennel butter.

# Cooking Oily Fish

Oily fish range from the lordly salmon to the humble sprat. Years ago one was inclined to think of herrings as being almost a 'common' fish, but their comparative scarcity today makes them highly prized. The recipes in this section give a wide variety of ideas, many of which can be adapted for other fish.

Frozen oily fish can be used in any dish; the freezing symbol refers to the suitability of freezing the prepared dish.

## Baked Sprats

*1 kg/2 lb fresh sprats*
*salt and pepper*
*little flour*
*25 g/1 oz butter*
GARNISH:
*lemon wedges*

Cut the heads off the fish. Wash and dry the fish, season well and dust with a little flour. Heat the butter in a large roasting tin. Add the sprats and cook above the centre of a moderately hot oven (190°C/375°F or Gas Mark 5) for 10 to 15 minutes. Serve with lemon wedges.

## Salmon Beignets ⊛

*Puff Pastry, made with 150 g/5 oz flour etc. (see page 292) or 300 g/11 oz frozen puff pastry*
*oil or fat for deep frying*
FILLING:
*4 cutlets of fresh salmon, each weighing about 75 g/3 oz, or 6 cutlets weighing 50 g/2 oz*
*salt and pepper*
*little lemon juice*
*1 egg white*
GARNISH:
*lemon slices*
*cucumber slices*

Roll out the pastry until wafer thin. Cut into 4 to 6 large squares – each must be sufficiently large to cover the fish completely. Place a salmon cutlet in the centre of each pastry square. Add a little salt, pepper and lemon juice to the fish. Moisten the edges of pastry with water and fold over the salmon. Seal firmly. Brush the beignets with the unbeaten egg white. Chill for a short time before frying.

Heat the oil or fat to 180°C/350°F (for explanation of testing oil or fat see page 290). Fry the beignets in the oil or fat for 3 to 4 minutes, to brown the pastry lightly, then lower the heat very slightly and fry for a further 3 to 4 minutes for the smaller beignets, and about 5 minutes for the larger ones. By lowering the heat you may be quite certain that the fish is cooked and the pastry not over-cooked. Drain on absorbent kitchen paper and serve hot with Tartare Sauce (see page 100). Garnish with the lemon and cucumber. Serves 4 to 6.

VARIATION

⊛ **Salmon Pasties:** Instead of frying, bake the pastry-coated fish towards the top of a hot oven (220-230°C/425-450°F or Gas Mark 7-8) for 10 minutes, then lower the heat to moderately hot (190°C/375°F or Gas Mark 5) for a further 10 to 15 minutes. This version can be served hot or cold.

# Poached Whole Salmon

*150 ml/¼ pint white wine*
*1 whole salmon*
COURT BOUILLON:
*2-3 carrots, sliced*
*1 onion, sliced*
*1 stick celery, chopped*
*1 bay leaf*
*sprig parsley*
*sprig thyme*
*salt and pepper*
*1.75 litres/3 pints water*

First prepare the court bouillon – the liquid in which the salmon will be cooked. Put the ingredients into a saucepan, cover and simmer for 30 minutes, strain and add the wine. Reheat to boiling point.

Weigh the salmon and calculate the cooking time – allow 10 minutes per 450 g/1 lb for a fish weighing up to 2.75 kg/6 lb, then 6 minutes for each extra 450 g/1 lb over this weight. A whole salmon needs a long container if you are to cook it without spoiling the shape. A fish kettle is ideal, but a very large saucepan or roasting tin can be used. Put an upturned dish into a saucepan or roasting tin to support the fish as it cooks (a fish kettle has a rack). Place the salmon into the container, add the flavoured liquid, cover the kettle or saucepan with the lid or foil. Bring the liquid to simmering point and keep at this temperature throughout the cooking period. Cook the salmon for the calculated time. Skin the salmon while warm and place on a serving dish. Serve hot with Hollandaise Sauce (see page 234) or cold with mayonnaise. A recipe for home-made Mayonnaise is on page 235.

VARIATION

If cooking a very large salmon you will need to increase the amount of court bouillon and wine.

Instead of using court bouillon, the fish can be cooked in water with salt, pepper and lemon juice or white wine or a little white wine vinegar to taste.

**Baked Whole Salmon:** Wrap the whole fish in buttered or oiled foil (see the comments under Poached Salmon Cutlets on page 81), and bake in the centre of a moderate oven (180°C/350°F or Gas Mark 4). Allow 15 minutes per 450 g/1 lb for a fish weighing up to 2.75 kg/6 lb in weight and 10 minutes for each extra 450 g/1 lb over this weight. This is delicious if each portion is topped with a little Anchovy Butter (see page 9).

## Poached Salmon Cutlets

*a little oil*
*4 salmon cutlets, about 2.5 cm/1 inch in thickness*
*salt and pepper*
*little lemon juice*

Cut 4 squares of greaseproof paper. Brush these with oil. Place a salmon cutlet in the centre of each square, add a very little salt and pepper and a squeeze of lemon juice. Tie the paper securely. Put the parcels of fish into a saucepan with sufficient cold water to cover. Bring the water to simmering point – do this fairly slowly. Remove the saucepan from the heat, cover the pan tightly and allow the fish to stand in the water until this becomes cold.

VARIATIONS

**Baked Salmon Cutlets:** Wrap the fish in buttered or oiled foil, season and flavour with a little lemon juice. Bake the fish in moderate oven (180°C/350°F or Gas Mark 4). Allow 20 minutes if serving the fish cold, since it continues to cook a little in the foil parcels as it cools, but 30 minutes if serving the salmon hot. You can of course bake the fish in butter without a covering, in which case reduce the above times by 3 to 4 minutes. Serve with Hollandaise Sauce (see page 234) or melted butter.

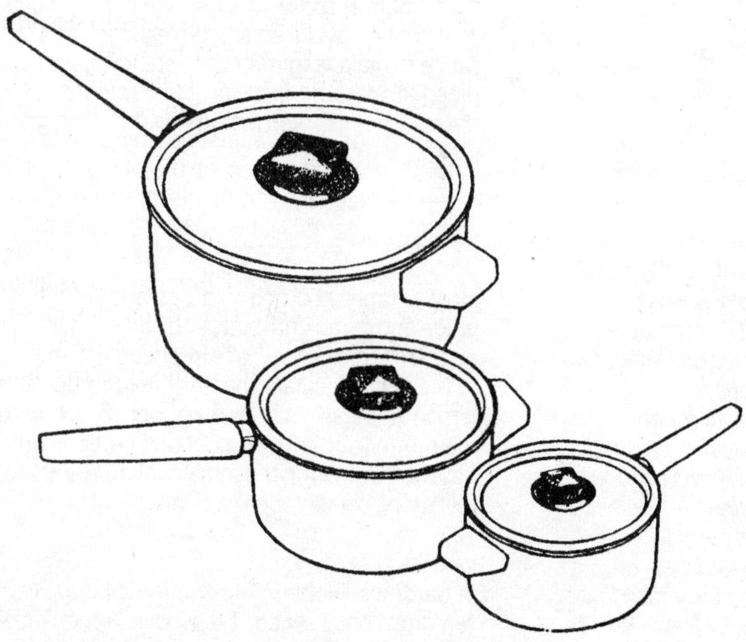

## Salmon Walewska

*4 salmon cutlets*
*100 g/4 oz butter*
*1½ tablespoons lemon juice*
*salt and pepper*
*3 egg yolks*
*approximately 100 g/4 oz lobster meat*
GARNISH:
*lemon slices*
*cucumber slices*

Put the salmon into an ovenproof dish. Melt 25 g/ oz of the butter in a pan; leave the remainder at room temperature to soften. Brush the salmon with the melted butter and sprinkle with ½ teaspoon lemon juice and a little salt and pepper. Cover the dish with foil. Bake in the centre of a moderate oven (180°C/ 350°F or Gas Mark 4) for 25 minutes until just tender – do not over-cook. Lift the fish on to a serving dish.

Meanwhile make the Hollandaise sauce. Put the egg yolks, a little salt and pepper and the remaining lemon juice into a heatproof basin; stand over a pan of hot, but not boiling, water and whisk until thick. Gradually whisk in the rest of the butter then add the diced pieces of lobster; heat for 2 to 3 minutes. Top the salmon with the sauce and garnish with the lemon and cucumber. If using fresh lobster, use some of the small claws for garnish.

VARIATIONS

**Sole Walewska:** Poach 4 large or 8 smaller fillets of sole in white wine, as in the recipes on page 74. Lift the sole from the wine, cover and keep hot on a dish in a cool oven. Meanwhile make the Hollandaise sauce as in the recipe above; boil the white wine left from cooking the sole until it is reduced to 2 tablespoons only, add to the sauce to make a thinner consistency, together with the diced lobster and heat for 2 to 3 minutes. Spoon over the sole; garnish with lemon slices and the small lobster claws.

## Sardines Niçoise ⊛

*1½ tablespoons oil*
*350 g/12 oz tomatoes, skinned deseeded and chopped*
*1 onion, chopped*
*1 clove garlic, crushed*
*2 tablespoons chopped parsley*
*salt and pepper*
*8 fresh sardines*
*2 teaspoons lemon juice*
*few black olives*

Heat 1 tablespoon oil in a pan and fry the tomatoes, onion and garlic until soft. Add half the parsley with salt and pepper to taste. Place in a heated dish.

Meanwhile clean the sardines, sprinkle with the lemon juice and salt and pepper. Brush with the remaining oil and grill for about 6 minutes, or until tender. Lay the sardines on the tomato mixture and top with the rest of the parsley and the olives.

VARIATION

⊛ **Sardines Diable:** Follow the recipe above. Blend a few drops chilli sauce, 1 teaspoon French mustard and 1 tablespoon Worcestershire sauce into the tomato mixture. Omit the olives.

## Trout in Orange Sauce ⊛

*1 onion, sliced*
*450 ml/¾ pint water*
*1 orange*
*salt and pepper*
*4 fresh trout, boned*
*25 g/1 oz butter*
*25 g/1 oz flour*
*150 ml/¼ pint single cream or milk*
GARNISH:
*watercress*
*orange slices*

Put the onion and water into a large deep frying pan. Cut away a few strips of orange zest from the orange. Squeeze the juice and add to the pan with a little salt and pepper. Bring to simmering point and add the trout. Cook gently for 10 to 12 minutes until tender. Lift the fish on to a warm dish; keep hot. Boil the stock until reduced to 150 ml/¼ pint, then strain.

Heat the butter in a saucepan, stir in the flour then gradually blend in the orange-flavoured stock. Bring to the boil, stirring, over a low heat to make a thick sauce. Remove from the heat and blend in the cream or milk. Return the sauce to the heat and stir or whisk until smooth; do not allow to boil. Spoon the sauce over the fish. Garnish with watercress and orange slices.

## Trout Grenoblaise

*4 large fresh trout*
*salt and pepper*
*100 g/4 oz butter*
*50 g/2 oz soft breadcumbs*
*2 lemons*

Clean the trout but do not cut off their heads. Season the fish with salt and pepper. Heat half the butter in a pan and fry the breadcrumbs until crisp. Put on one side and keep hot. Heat the remainder of the butter and cook the fish until tender. Put the fish on a serving dish. Halve the lemons and reserve 4 slices for garnish. Scoop out the pulp from the rest of the fruit. Tip the hot crisp crumbs and lemon pieces over the fish, garnish with the lemon slices.

VARIATION
The above recipe is a change from the more familiar Trout with Almonds, which is often given the same recipe title. Fry 50 g/2 oz blanched, or blanched and flaked almonds, in butter; spoon over the fish.

## Trout Normande ⊛

*4 large fresh trout*
*50 g/2 oz butter, melted*
*salt and pepper*
*1 tablespoon lemon juice*
*1 tablespoon chopped chives*
*1 tablespoon chopped parsley*
*300 ml/½ pint Béchamel Sauce (see page 227)*
*25 g/1 oz soft breadcrumbs*

Remove the heads from the trout. Clean the fish and put into an ovenproof serving dish. Add half the butter, a little salt and pepper, lemon juice and the herbs. Cover the dish and bake in the centre of a moderate oven (180°C/350°F or Gas Mark 4) for 20 minutes.

Remove from the oven, top with the Béchamel Sauce, the breadcrumbs and the remainder of the butter. Return to the top of the oven and heat for 10 minutes.

## Fried Herrings in Oatmeal ⊛

*4 herrings*
*50g/2oz fine or medium oatmeal or rolled oats*
*salt and pepper*
FOR FRYING:
*25-50g/1-2oz fat*
GARNISH:
*lemon wedges*

This traditional Scottish way of cooking herrings is surely the best way of frying them. Clean the fish, remove the heads, dry well. Bone the fish as in the Marinierte Herrings recipe below and flatten. Blend the oatmeal or rolled oats with the salt and pepper and use to coat the fish. Heat the fat in a pan and fry the fish quickly on both sides to brown, then lower the heat and fry gently for a few minutes until tender. Garnish with thick lemon wedges.

## Herrings in Soured Cream ⊛

*50g/2oz butter, melted*
*4 large herrings, filleted*
*salt and pepper*
*150g/¼ pint soured cream*
*2 teaspoons chopped dill or parsley*
*50g/2oz soft breadcrumbs*

Spread half the butter in an ovenproof dish, top with the herring fillets, these should be kept flat if possible. Add a little salt and pepper, the soured cream and herbs. Sprinkle the breadcrumbs over the fish and cream and top with the remaining melted butter. Bake in the centre of a moderately hot oven (190°C/375°F or Gas Mark 5) for 30 minutes.

## Marinierte Herrings

*4 small herrings, 2 of which should have soft roes*
*2 tablespoons water*
*150ml/¼ pint wine vinegar*
*1 tablespoon sugar*
*2 small onions, cut into rings*
*4 lemon slices*
*2 bay leaves*
*1 teaspoon mixed spice*
*6 peppercorns*
*2 tablespoons soured cream*

This is a slightly different way of preparing pickled herrings. If the fishmonger has not filleted the fish, slit the stomachs, cut off the heads and insert the knife into the flesh and open out the fish. Lay the fish, cut side downwards, on a board, run your thumb down the back very firmly. Turn the fish over and the backbone and other bones can be lifted out.

Cut each fish into 2 fillets and put into a container—a deep jar is ideal. Boil together the water, vinegar and sugar; cool slightly. Add the onion to the fish, with the vinegar liquid, lemon, bay leaves, spice and peppercorns. Take the roes from 2 fish and mash with the cream. Add to the other ingredients. If using a basin, stir and cover. Keep for 24 hours then serve the herrings cold with boiled potatoes.

## Herrings au Gratin

*8 small herrings*
*salt and pepper*
*50 g/2 oz butter, melted*
*100 g/4 oz cottage cheese*
*50 g/2 oz Cheddar cheese, grated*
*50 g/2 oz soft breadcrumbs*

Remove the head and intestines from each fish; season well. Blend half the butter with the cottage cheese and a little seasoning. Spoon this mixture into each fish, then place in an ovenproof dish. Bake in the centre of a moderate oven (180°C/350°F or Gas Mark 4) for 10 minutes. Remove from the oven, top with the grated cheese, breadcrumbs and remaining butter. Return to the oven, moving the dish nearer the top for a further 15 minutes.

## Devilled Mackerel ⊛

*4 large mackerel*
*50 g/2 oz butter*
*salt and pepper*
*1 teaspoon curry paste or powder*
*2 teaspoons Worcestershire sauce*
*few drops Tabasco sauce*
*2 tablespoons chopped parsley*

Fillet the mackerel (see Marinierte Herring recipe, page 84). Cream the butter with salt, pepper, curry paste or powder, the sauces and parsley. Spread this flavoured butter over each mackerel fillet. Either grill or bake as in the recipe below. Serve hot or cold.

## Mackerel with Gooseberry Sauce

*4 mackerel*
*salt and pepper*
*25 g/1 oz butter or margarine*
SAUCE:
*225 g/8 oz gooseberries*
*2 tablespoons water*
*25 g/1 oz sugar*

The mackerel can be grilled, fried or baked in the oven. Very little fat is needed as mackerel are very oily fish, but they do need to be well seasoned.

To grill mackerel: Preheat the grill, melt the butter or margarine, brush over the seasoned fish. Grill for about 10 minutes, allow 2 minutes on either side under a high heat, then lower the heat.

To fry mackerel: Melt the butter or margarine in the pan, cook as the timing under grilling.

To bake mackerel: Melt the butter or margarine. Put the seasoned fish in a dish, top with the fat; do not cover. Bake in a moderately hot oven (190°C/375°F or Gas Mark 5) for about 20 minutes.

Meanwhile top and tail the gooseberries. Cook them with the water and sugar – if the gooseberries are very sour, add more sugar to taste but this sauce is better if it is not too sweet. When cooked, the gooseberries can be sieved or liquidized to give a smooth sauce. Serve the sauce and fish hot or cold.

## Mackerel Flamande

*4 large mackerel*
MARINADE:
*300 ml/½ pint slightly sweet cider*
*2 small onions, very finely chopped*
*1 tablespoon oil*
*salt and cayenne pepper*
SAUCE:
*25 g/1 oz butter or margarine*
*25 g/1 oz flour*
*1-2 teaspoons dry mustard powder*
*3 tablespoons double cream*
GARNISH:
*chopped chives*
*chopped parsley*

Cut the heads from the fish and remove the intestines. Any roes can be marinated then cooked with the mackerel. Wash and dry the fish. Mix together all the ingredients for the marinade. Add the fish to the marinade and leave for 2 to 3 hours, turn once or twice if not covered by the liquid. Remove the fish from the marinade, drain for a few minutes then grill as described on page 85. Reserve the marinade.

Heat the butter or margarine in a pan, stir in the flour and mustard and cook gently for 2 to 3 minutes. Add the marinade gradually, blending well, then stir until the sauce has thickened. Remove from the heat so that the liquid is no longer boiling. Whisk in the cream and heat the sauce, without boiling, for 2 minutes. Serve with the grilled mackerel. Sprinkle the herbs over the fish.

VARIATION
The onions will still taste slightly raw so the marinade can be strained into the sauce if preferred.

## Stuffed Mackerel

*4 large mackerel*
*salt and pepper*
*25 g/1 oz butter, melted*
STUFFING:
*50 g/2 oz butter or margarine*
*100 g/4 oz mushrooms, chopped*
*2 large tomatoes, skinned and chopped*
*2 tablespoons chopped parsley*

Slit the mackerel and remove the intestines. Any roes can be put back into the fish under the stuffing. Season the fish with salt and pepper. Blend together the stuffing ingredients and season lightly. Put the stuffing into the fish and place in an ovenproof dish. Top with the melted butter and bake, without covering, in the centre of a moderate oven (180°C/350°F or Gas Mark 4) for 30 to 35 minutes.

VARIATION
**Stuffed Herrings:** Choose 4 large herrings with hard roes. Fry 1 finely chopped onion and the chopped roes in 50 g/2 oz butter, add 2 peeled and diced dessert apples, a little salt and pepper. Put into the fish, bake as above, but for a slightly shorter time.

# Dishes with Shellfish

Here are some of my favourite dishes, based upon a variety of shellfish. Take particular care that the fish is not over-cooked for this makes it horribly tough.

## Seafood Indienne

*50 g/2 oz butter*
*1 medium onion, finely chopped*
*½ small green pepper, deseeded and chopped*
*½ small red pepper, deseeded and chopped*
*2-3 teaspoons curry powder*
*4 tablespoons thick mayonnaise*
*4 tablespoons double cream*
*100 g/4 oz peeled prawns*
*100 g/4 oz prepared mussels (see page 92)*
*100 g/4 oz cooked white fish, flaked*
*salt and pepper*
*175 g/6 oz cooked rice (see page 300)*

Heat the butter in a frying pan and fry the vegetables for 2 to 3 minutes only – they should still be quite firm. Remove the pan from the heat. Add the curry powder, mayonnaise and cream. Return to a very low heat and stir well until blended. Do not overheat this mixture as mayonnaise can curdle. Add the prawns, mussels, fish and salt and pepper. Heat for 2 to 3 minutes only. Serve with cooked rice.

VARIATION

⊛ **Creamed Curry:** Omit the peppers and mayonnaise in the basic recipe above. Heat the butter in a saucepan, fry the onion, add the curry powder with 1 tablespoon cornflour. Cook over a low heat for 2 to 3 minutes, then blend in 300 ml/½ pint milk. Bring the sauce to the boil, stirring well, add salt, pepper and 4 tablespoons double cream. Put in the prawns, mussels and 225 g/8 oz diced cooked white fish. Heat for a few minutes, then serve with cooked rice.

## Crab Mornay ⊛

*25 g/1 oz butter*
*25 g/1 oz flour*
*300 ml/½ pint milk*
*salt and pepper*
*175 g/6 oz Cheddar cheese, grated*
*350 g/12 oz prepared crabmeat*
*50 g/2 oz soft breadcrumbs*
GARNISH:
*chopped parsley*
*lemon slices*

Heat the butter in a saucepan, stir in the flour and cook gently for 2 to 3 minutes. Gradually add the milk, bring the sauce to the boil and stir until thickened. Add salt, pepper and 100 g/4 oz of the grated cheese.

Put the crabmeat in a shallow ovenproof dish, top with the sauce, remaining grated cheese and bread-crumbs. Heat in the centre of a moderate oven (180°C/350°F or Gas Mark 4) for 30 minutes. Garnish with chopped parsley and lemon slices.

VARIATION

**Crab Bonne Femme:** Follow the recipe above but add 100 g/4 oz thinly sliced mushrooms, cooked in 50 g/2 oz butter, and 2 hard-boiled and chopped eggs to the sauce.

## Crab Soufflé Bake

*50g/2oz butter or margarine*
*25g/1oz flour*
*300ml/½pint milk or milk and single cream*
*50g/2oz coarse soft white breadcrumbs*
*75g/3oz Cheddar cheese, grated*
*100g/4oz crabmeat, flaked*
*salt and pepper*
*cayenne pepper*
*3 eggs, separated*

Heat 25g/1oz butter or margarine in pan and stir in the flour. Cook gently over a low heat for 2 to 3 minutes, stirring well, then gradually blend in the milk, or milk and single cream. Bring the sauce to the boil and cook until thickened.

Heat the remaining butter or margarine in another pan and toss the crumbs in this until pale golden and crisp. Add to the sauce, with the cheese, flaked crabmeat and salt and pepper to taste. Beat the egg yolks into the crab mixture. Whisk the whites until stiff, then gently fold into the other ingredients. Spoon into an 18 to 20cm/7 to 8 inch buttered soufflé dish. Bake in the centre of a moderate oven (180°C/350°F or Gas Mark 4) for 35 to 40 minutes. Although the mixture does not rise as dramatically as a classic soufflé, it is still very light so serve the soufflé as soon as baked.

VARIATIONS

**Cheese and Crab Soufflé:** Make the sauce as above, but use only 150ml/¼ pint milk. Omit the crumbs. Add 50g/2oz grated cheese and 100g/4oz flaked crabmeat, and salt and pepper. Separate 4 eggs, beat the yolks into the mixture, then whisk the whites until stiff; fold into the other ingredients. Bake in a moderately hot oven (190°C/375°F or Gas Mark 5) for 25 to 30 minutes.

**Crab Soufflé:** Base this on fish stock made by simmering the crab shell in a little water; strain and reserve 150ml/¼ pint. Make the sauce with 25g/1oz butter, 25g/1oz flour, the crab stock and 4 tablespoons single cream. Add 150-175g/5-6oz crabmeat, then proceed as for the Cheese and Crab Soufflé above.

## Escargots en Croûte

*1 long thin French loaf*
*Garlic Butter (see page 89)*
*16 escargots (snails)*

Cut off the crusty ends from the loaf as these are not suitable for this dish. Cut the rest of the loaf into 16 slices. Make a hollow in the centre of each slice with your thumb, then pull out a little crumb, leaving a distinct indentation. Use above half the Garlic Butter and spread into each cavity. Top with an escargot, then the rest of the butter. Put the filled bread slices on to a flat baking tray.

Preheat the oven for this particular dish, otherwise the bread hardens too much. Bake just above the centre of a hot oven (220-230°C/425-450°F or Gas Mark 7-8) for 4 to 5 minutes. Serve at once.

## Escargots à la Bourguignonne ⊛

*24 escargots with shells, see method*
GARLIC BUTTER:
*100g/4oz butter*
*1-2 cloves garlic, completely crushed*
*1 small shallot, very finely chopped*
*1-2 teaspoons finely chopped parsley*
*salt and pepper*

I travel a great deal, and sometimes after a long journey arrive at a hotel very tired. If escargots (snails) are on the menu, and I know I can eat in solitary state and not offend anyone by the strong smell of garlic, I choose these. They are excellent when you are wanting something piquant in flavour.

Fresh snails are not easy to obtain, but canned are available and you may find frozen snails too. Shells are generally, but not always, supplied so do not discard those you have; wash and dry, for you may need them on a future occasion.

The escargots are ready to heat, so simply blend together all the ingredients for the Garlic Butter. Using half of the butter, insert some into each shell, add the snail, then the rest of the butter, pushing this back into the shell, so that it will not bubble out during cooking. Put the snails into 4 escargotières (dishes with indentations for snails) with the butter side uppermost. It is advisable to moisten the dishes with a very little cold water before using. If these dishes are not available, use a shallow ovenproof dish or 4 individual dishes and pack the filled shells tightly, so they cannot fall during heating. Cook towards the top of a hot oven (230°C/450°F or Gas Mark 8) for about 8 minutes until the butter just starts to melt. Serve at once with lots of French bread.

## Lobster Americaine ⊛

*2 medium lobsters, cooked*
*100g/4oz butter*
*2 small onions, finely chopped*
*6 medium tomatoes, skinned and chopped*
*4 tablespoons white wine*
*salt and pepper*
*2 tablespoons brandy, optional*
GARNISH:
*lemon wedges*

Split the lobsters and remove the meat from the body. Crack the large claws, take out the meat. Clean the shells and polish with olive oil.

Heat the butter in a pan, fry the onions and tomatoes until really tender. Add the wine and lobster meat. Heat thoroughly then add the salt, pepper and brandy to taste. Spoon into the shells and serve as soon as possible. Garnish with lemon and the small claws.

## Lobster Mornay ⊛

*2 medium lobsters*
*300 ml/½ pint Cheese Sauce (see page 228)*
*2 tablespoons double cream*
*2 tablespoons dry sherry*
*25 g/1 oz Gruyère or Cheddar cheese, grated*
GARNISH:
*lemon wedges*
*small lobster claws*

To prepare lobster for a cooked dish: when you split the body always discard the intestinal vein and sac from the head. Remove the flesh, as described in the individual recipes. If you intend to serve the cooked dish in the shells, clean and polish with olive oil.

Split the lobster bodies and crack the large claw. Remove all the flesh. Flake the flesh and blend with the cheese sauce, cream and sherry. Heat gently, but do not allow to boil. Spoon the hot mixture into the four lobster shells or individual flameproof dishes. Top with the grated cheese and heat for 2 to 3 minutes under the grill. Garnish with lemon and the small claws.

## Lobster Newburg

*2 medium lobsters*
*50 g/2 oz butter*
*150 ml/¼ pint milk*
*2 egg yolks*
*150 ml/¼ pint double cream*
*4 tablespoons brandy or sherry*
*salt and pepper*
GARNISH:
*lemon slices*
*small lobster claws*

Split the lobster bodies and crack the large claws. Remove all the flesh. Heat the butter in a saucepan, or better still the top of a double saucepan, over hot water. Add the lobster flesh and turn in the hot butter for 2 to 3 minutes.

Heat the milk in another pan. Blend the egg yolks, cream and hot, but not boiling, milk. Strain over the lobster flesh and cook over a low heat until the sauce begins to thicken, stirring continually. Whisk in the brandy or sherry and salt and pepper to taste. Continue cooking slowly for 4 to 5 minutes. Spoon the hot mixture into the four lobster shells or individual dishes. Garnish with the lemon and small lobster claws.

## Scallops and Bacon ⊛

*8 scallops*
*8 rashers streaky bacon, derinded and halved*
*little lemon juice*

Remove the scallops from their shells and cut each scallop in half. Smooth the bacon with the back of a knife to stretch the rashers and make them more easy to roll up. Sprinkle the scallops with lemon juice, place on the bacon and roll firmly. Thread on to 4 long metal skewers. Grill steadily for about 10 minutes, turn frequently to make sure both bacon and fish are cooked.

## Lobster Thermidor ⊛

*2 medium lobsters*
*300 ml/½ pint Béchamel Sauce (see page 227)*
*4 tablespoons fish stock**
*4 tablespoons white wine*
*½-1 tablespoon French mustard*
*1 shallot, peeled*
*sprig tarragon*
*small bunch chervil or parsley*
*25 g/1 oz Parmesan cheese, grated*
GARNISH:
*small lobster claws*
*parsley*

Split the lobster bodies and crack the large claws. Remove all the flesh. Blend together the sauce, stock, wine and mustard. Add the shallot and herbs. Simmer the sauce over a low heat for 10 minutes, stirring from time to time. Strain the sauce to remove the shallot and herbs. Add the lobster meat to the sauce and heat thoroughly. Spoon the hot mixture into the four lobster shells or individual flameproof dishes. Top with the grated cheese and heat for 2 to 3 minutes under the grill. Garnish with the small claws and parsley.

* To make the fish stock, simmer the discarded pieces of lobster shell in water to cover for 15 minutes, strain and measure the required amount.

## Coquille Saint-Jacques ⊛

*8 large scallops*
*300 ml/½ pint milk*
*salt and pepper*
*65 g/2½ oz butter*
*25 g/1 oz flour*
*2 tablespoons dry white wine or sherry*
*350 g/12 oz cooked potatoes, sieved*
*1 egg yolk*
GARNISH:
*lemon slices*

Remove the scallops from their shells (reserve the shells); if any liquid is in the shells, add this to the milk to give extra flavour. Place the scallops in a saucepan with the milk and a little salt and pepper. Simmer gently for approximately 10 minutes, or until the white part of the fish becomes opaque. Do not over-cook, or the fish will be tough. Lift the scallops from the liquid and cut into slices; leave the orange roes in fairly large pieces.

Heat 40 g/1½ oz butter in a saucepan, stir in the flour and cook gently for 2 to 3 minutes, then add the milk in which the scallops were cooked (if much of this milk has evaporated, make up to 300 ml/½ pint again). Stir the sauce over a low heat until thickened. Return the scallops to the sauce, add the wine or sherry, any more seasoning required and heat gently but do not allow to boil.

While the scallops are being cooked heat the potatoes, add the remaining butter and the egg yolk. Pipe the potato around the scallop shells and place under the grill for a few minutes to brown. Spoon the fish mixture in the centre of each shell and garnish with lemon slices.

# Moules à la Provençale

*1.75 litres/3 pints mussels*
*150 ml/¼ pint dry white wine*
*150 ml/¼/pint water*
*small bunch parsley*
*salt and pepper*
*2 tablespoons oil*
*2 cloves garlic, crushed*
*3 medium onions, chopped*
*4 large tomatoes, skinned and chopped*
*1 tablespoon tomato purée*
*1 tablespoon chopped parsley*

Scrub the mussels well and discard any that do not shut when tapped briskly. Put into a large saucepan with the wine, water, parsley and salt and pepper. Heat steadily for only a few minutes until the shells open. Remove the mussels from the liquid. Strain and reserve the liquid. Remove the mussels from the shells for this particular dish.

Heat the oil in the saucepan, add the garlic and onions and cook for 2 to 3 minutes. Add the tomatoes and cook for a further 2 to 3 minutes – do not overcook. Add the liquid from cooking the mussels, the tomato purée, parsley and a little salt and pepper. Heat well, add the mussels and heat for 2 to 3 minutes only; never over-cook mussels as they become tough. Serve with cooked rice.

VARIATIONS

**Moules Marinière:** Open the mussels as described above but add 1 peeled chopped onion and a little chopped celery to the liquid. When the mussels have opened, strain and reserve the liquid. Pull away one shell so that the mussels are left adhering to the second shell. Discard any beard-like weeds from the shells. Put the mussels back into the saucepan. Pour over the reserved liquid, add 1 tablespoon lemon juice or white wine vinegar for flavour and a little chopped parsley. Heat for 1 to 2 minutes only, then serve. You can add a little cream to the liquid when reheating this, in which case be careful the liquid does not boil as it would curdle.

**Moules à la Crème:** Open the mussels as described above and remove from the shells; reserve the liquid. Strain the liquid and boil until only 3 to 4 tablespoons remain. Make a thick white sauce with 40 g/1½ oz butter, 40 g/1½ oz flour and 450 ml/¾ pint milk. Add 3 to 4 tablespoons cream and the concentrated mussel liquid. Heat the sauce very gently, add the mussels and heat again. Do not allow to boil. Garnish with chopped parsley and serve with cooked rice.

**Mussels with Garlic Butter:** Prepare the mussels, as in the recipe above. Remove from their shells. Put the mussels in small ovenproof dishes and top with Garlic Butter (see page 89). Heat for about 6 minutes in a hot oven. Serve with French bread.

## Camarones Fritos

FISH MIXTURE:
*450 g/1 lb peeled shrimps or small prawns*
*2 tablespoons lemon juice*
*2 tablespoons olive oil*
*salt and pepper*
BATTER:
*100 g/4 oz plain flour*
*pinch salt*
*2 eggs, separated*
*150 ml/¼ pint water*
FOR FRYING:
*oil*

Blend the ingredients for the fish mixture. Leave to stand for at least 1 hour. Mix together the flour and salt. Beat the egg yolks and water into the flour.

Drain the shrimps or prawns and add to the batter. Heat the oil to 170°C/340°F. Whisk the egg whites and fold into the fish and batter mixture. Drop small spoonfuls into the hot oil and fry for 5 minutes or until golden brown.

VARIATION
**Fried Scampi:** This fish is generally sold frozen and uncooked. Defrost sufficiently to handle, coat with a little seasoned flour, then in the batter used for this recipe above. Fry as above. Drain well on absorbent kitchen paper.

## Scampi Provençale ⊛

*450 g/1 lb cooked scampi or large prawns in their shells*
*150 ml/¼ pint water*
*salt and pepper*
*bunch parsley*
*1 tablespoon oil*
*1 clove garlic, crushed*
*2 small onions, chopped*
*4 medium tomatoes, skinned and chopped*
*4 tablespoons-150 ml/¼ pint dry white wine*
*few black olives*
*2 tablespoons chopped parsley*

Peel the scampi or prawns. Put the shells into a saucepan, add the water, a pinch of salt, a shake of pepper and the parsley. Cover the pan and simmer for 10 minutes then strain the liquid. You should have about 3 tablespoons stock; retain this.

Heat the oil in a pan and fry the garlic and onions for 2 to 3 minutes. Add the tomatoes and cook for a further 2 to 3 minutes then add the reserved stock and wine. Use the larger amount of wine if you like a rather moist dish. Add the scampi or prawns, the olives and half the parsley. Heat for a few minutes only and top with remaining parsley. Serve with cooked rice.

VARIATIONS
Scampi is often sold peeled and uncooked. In this case use a little more wine or wine and water. Heat the vegetables for only 1 to 2 minutes in the oil, add the scampi, blend with the vegetables then add the wine and other ingredients and simmer for 6 to 7 minutes or until the fish is tender.

⊛ **Basque Scampi:** Follow the recipe above but increase the oil to 2 tablespoons and fry 1 diced red and 1 diced green pepper with the onions and garlic. Use only 3 tomatoes and 150 ml/¼ pint wine.

# Cooking Smoked Fish

Smoked fish is excellent for most meals. It forms the basis of many interesting hors d'oeuvre, see the first chapter. The recipes that follow would be suitable for breakfast or a light meal. If the smoked fish is rather over salty in flavour, soak for a time in cold water. Two of my favourite smoked fish are given below.

**Arbroath Smokies**

The method of smoking these small young haddock gives a delicious flavour. Cook as poached smoked haddock below, but reduce the time because the flesh is so tender that the minimum of cooking is necessary. You can use the delicate tasting flesh of arbroath smokies in recipes calling for unsmoked fish too.

**Jugged Kippers**

There are many ways of cooking kippers – they can be grilled, fried or baked, but 'jugging' keeps them moist. Put the kippers into a container, cover with boiling water and put on a lid. Leave to stand for 5 minutes, then serve the kippers topped with butter.

## Poached Smoked Haddock

*1 large or 2 smaller smoked haddock*
*water or milk and water*
*50 g/2 oz butter*

A really good smoked haddock makes a delicious light dish, particularly for breakfast. When buying the haddock, avoid any fish that looks dry or dark in colour as this is an indication that it is not entirely fresh and probably over-smoked and very salty. Cut away the fins and tail, divide the haddock into neat pieces. Put into simmering water or milk and water and poach gently for 10 minutes or until just tender. Top with the butter.

VARIATIONS

**Haddock with Poached Egg:** Top each portion with a poached egg.

**Haddock in Cream:** Poach for 3 minutes in water, drain and divide the fish into neat small pieces. Heat 300 ml/½ pint single cream in a frying pan, add a shake of pepper. Put the fish in the cream, cover the frying pan with a lid. Poach gently for another 6 to 7 minutes.

**Fried Smoked Haddock:** Poach the fish for 5 minutes in water, drain and dry well. Fry in hot butter for several minutes. This is better if using small individual smoked haddock or portions of smoked haddock fillets.

# Using Cooked Fish

The recipes that follow use cooked fish in a variety of different ways.

## Fish Cakes ⊛

*50g/2oz butter or margarine*
*25g/1oz flour*
*150ml/¼ pint milk*
*225g/8oz cooked potatoes*
*225g/8oz cooked white fish (see Steamed Fish page 74)*
*salt and pepper*
FLAVOURINGS:
*chopped parsley*
*anchovy essence*
*tomato purée*
*few chopped peeled prawns*
COATING AND FRYING:
*little flour*
*1 egg*
*50g/2oz crisp breadcrumbs*
*50-75g/2-3oz fat or 2 to 3 tablespoons oil*
GARNISH:
*lemon wedges*

Heat 25g/1oz butter or margarine in a saucepan; stir in the flour and cook over a low heat for 2 to 3 minutes. Gradually blend in the milk and stir as the sauce comes to the boil and thickens to become a 'panada' (binding sauce). Mash the potatoes and beat in the remaining butter or margarine. Flake the fish. Blend the potatoes, fish and sauce together and season well. Add any flavouring required, see ingredients. Divide the soft mixture into 8 portions, place on a flat plate and chill for 1 to 2 hours until sufficiently soft to handle. Coat in seasoned flour, then beaten egg and crisp breadcrumbs. Chill again if possible. Heat the fat or oil in a frying pan and fry the fish cakes until crisp and brown on both sides. Drain on absorbent paper and serve with the lemon wedges and any savoury sauce desired.

VARIATIONS
The flavourings suggested can change the taste of these fish cakes, but other fish can be used, some of the most successful being cooked kippers, mackerel, salmon (strangely enough canned salmon gives a better flavour than cooked fresh salmon in this recipe).
Bind the fish and potato with an egg instead of the sauce, this gives a less moist result, which I do not like as much. The process of chilling the fish cakes means you can have a crisp outside and a moist middle to these popular fish cakes.
⊛ **Fish and Rice Croquettes:** Cook the fish and the sauce, add 100g/4oz cooked rice (weight when cooked), 2 tablespoons chopped parsley and 1 teaspoon capers. Form the mixture into finger shapes, coat in seasoned flour, beaten egg and crisp breadcrumbs and deep fry for several minutes.
⊛ **Luxury Croquettes:** Make the sauce as in the above recipe but with single cream not milk. Cook and flake 350g/12oz turbot or halibut or use flaked crabmeat. Add to the sauce and season well with any flavouring desired. Form into 12 small fingers, coat as in the above recipe and fry. Serve with Tartare Sauce (see page 100).

## Crispy Crab Balls

*450 g/1 lb crabmeat (mix light and dark flesh)*
*50 g/2 oz very fine soft breadcrumbs*
*25 g/1 oz butter, melted*
*2 tablespoons double cream or yogurt*
*1 egg yolk*
*salt and pepper*
COATING:
*100 g/4 oz self-raising flour*
*pinch salt*
*1 egg*
*7 tablespoons milk or milk and water*
FOR FRYING:
*oil or fat*

Flake the crabmeat and mix with the other ingredients. Form into about 24 small balls with floured fingers. Season 25 g/1 oz of the flour with salt and pepper, roll the balls in this, then chill for a while.

To make the batter; blend the remaining flour, salt, egg and milk together. Heat the oil or fat to 180°C/350°F (for explanation of testing oil or fat see page 290). Dip the balls into the batter immediately before frying; allow any surplus batter to drip back into the basin. (While you can use a perforated spoon for handling the crabmeat balls, you will coat the small shapes in the batter more evenly if you roll them round in this then hold them above the basin with your fingers.) Fry for 4 to 5 minutes until really crisp. Drain on absorbent paper and serve with the Sweet and Sour Sauce (see page 239).

VARIATION

**Crispy Prawns:** Coat large peeled and cooked prawns with the flour and then the batter; fry for 3 minutes.

**Crispy Fish Balls:** Dice 450 g/1 lb raw white fish (weight without bones and skin). Either put through the fine plate of a mincer or into a food processor until finely chopped; do not over-process as this would make the fish slightly over-sticky. Mix with the basic ingredients as above but make these balls more interesting by moulding the fish around a thin slice of gherkin or piece of peeled prawn or stoned olive. Coat in the seasoned flour and then in the batter. Because the fish is not pre-cooked (as in the case of the crabmeat), fry for 6 to 7 minutes.

## Curried Prawns

*1 tablespoon oil*
*1 medium onion, finely chopped*
*2 teaspoons curry powder*
*1 dessert apple, peeled, cored and diced*
*2-3 sticks celery heart, finely chopped*
*225 g/8 oz peeled prawns*
*½ tablespoon lemon juice*
*3 tablespoons thick mayonnaise*
*1 tablespoon tomato purée*
*300 ml/½ pint single cream*
*salt and pepper*

Heat the oil and cook the onion for 2 to 3 minutes only; it should still be slightly firm. Stir in the curry powder (the amount depends upon personal taste). Blend the apple and celery with the onion and curry powder. Add the prawns and the remaining ingredients and mix well. Chill for 1 hour before serving. Either serve on a bed of shredded lettuce or in a border of Rice Salad (see page 304).

## Crab Tarts

*Shortcrust Pastry, made with 110 g/4 oz flour etc. (see page 291)*
FILLING:
*3 eggs*
*salt and pepper*
*25 g/1 oz butter or margarine*
*2 tablespoons milk or single cream*
*175 g/6 oz fresh, canned or frozen crabmeat, flaked*
*few strips of tomato*
GARNISH:
*lettuce*
*sliced tomatoes*

Make the shortcrust pastry. Roll out thinly and line about 9 to 12 small patty tins. Prick and bake blind in a moderately hot oven (200°C/400°F or Gas Mark 6) for 10 minutes.

Meanwhile beat the eggs with the salt and pepper. Heat the butter or margarine and milk or cream in a saucepan. Add the crabmeat and heat for 1 minute. Pour the beaten eggs into the pan and scramble lightly. Spoon into the hot pastry cases and top with the tomato strips. Serve in a border of lettuce and sliced tomatoes.

## Salmon Cream ⊛

*450 g/1 lb cooked or canned salmon, flaked*
*50 g/2 oz soft white breadcrumbs*
*2 tablespoons fish stock or liquid from the canned fish*
*1 tablespoon lemon juice*
*4 tablespoons double cream*
*3 eggs*
*1 tablespoon chopped fennel leaves or parsley*
*salt and pepper*

Blend the salmon and breadcrumbs with the other ingredients. Put into a well-greased 1 litre/1¾ pint basin. Cover with greased foil. Steam over a pan of hot, but not boiling, water for 1 hour until lightly set. Turn out and serve hot with Hollandaise Sauce (see page 234).

VARIATIONS

⊛ Use cooked white fish instead of salmon. To give a more interesting colour, add a little anchovy essence to the fish stock.

⊛ **Seafood Cream:** Use a mixture of chopped prawns and crabmeat, together with a little cooked white fish instead of salmon.

## Fish Vol-au-vents ⊛

*8 medium vol-au-vents (see page 293)*
*350 g/12 oz cooked or canned fish*
*150 g/¼ pint thick White Sauce (see page 226) or thick mayonnaise*

If serving hot, blend the fish with the hot sauce and put into the hot vol-au-vents just before the meal. If serving cold, add the cold fish to the cold sauce or mayonnaise and put into the cold pastry. By following this procedure you keep the pastry beautifully crisp.

Freeze pastry cases and filling separately.

## Dressed Crab ⊛

*2 medium or 1 large or 4 small cooked crabs*
*salt and pepper*
*little mayonnaise, optional*
GARNISH:
*chopped parsley*
*2 hard-boiled eggs, finely chopped (optional)*

If you intend to serve the crab in its shell it is better to buy smaller ones, so each person can have one crab.

Judge the quality of the crab by the weight. The fish should feel heavy for its size, if surprisingly light then it is of poor quality as it is 'watery'.

The fishmonger may open the crab for you, so the body is easily removed, if not I would wear rubber gloves for the edges of the shell are surprisingly sharp.

First pull away the claws from the body, twist towards you to do this. Ease the rounded front part of the body away from the main shell. Remove the stomach bag from the body, discard this, it MUST NOT be eaten. Take out all the flesh from the body using a teaspoon, discard green fingers that are at the end of the claws or attached to the body (called dead men's fingers).

Now turn your attention to the large shell, also part of the body; you will need to crack this with a light weight so you can remove the flesh. Part of the flesh is white coloured; add this to the flesh from the round part of the body, already removed. The other flesh is darker coloured so should be put into a separate container.

Crack the large claws with a light weight, remove the flesh, add to the white meat.

Wash, dry and polish the shells.

Season the fish very lightly; you can add a small amount of mayonnaise to the light meat if desired. Arrange light and dark meat on the shells, garnish with parsley and hard-boiled eggs.

## Dressed Lobster ⊛

*2 medium or 1 very large or 4 small cooked lobsters*

Judge the quality of lobster by its weight, as described under Dressed Crab, above. The freshness of lobster is discernible by the way the tail springs back, see page 67.

Split the fish, or ask the fishmonger to do this for you. Remove the intestinal vein, that runs down the flesh. Pull away the claws and discard the grey fingers, DO NOT EAT THESE. Remove the sand sac (not always necessary) in the head, discard this. Remove and dice the flesh from the body; crack the large claws and take out the flesh.

If you have bought hen lobster you will have the bright red coral (roe) at the tail end, this is good cold or hot.

Clean the shells and polish with a little oil. Put the lobster flesh back in these. If you have lobster picks simply crack the large claws and allow everyone to remove the flesh themselves.

## Salmon Chaudfroid

*150 ml/¼ pint fish stock (see page 35)*
*15 g/½ oz gelatine*
*350 g/12 oz cooked salmon, (weight without skin and bones)*
*3 tablespoons white wine*
*2 teaspoons lemon juice*
*150 g/¼ pint thick mayonnaise*
*2 hard-boiled eggs, finely chopped*
*salt and pepper*
GARNISH:
*lemon slices*
*cucumber slices*

Put the fish stock, obtained from cooking the salmon, into a saucepan and heat this. Sprinkle the gelatine on top and allow to dissolve. Flake the salmon, add to the warm gelatine mixture; this gives it a pleasantly moist texture, then stir in the wine and lemon juice. Allow the jelly to cool and become syrupy then add the mayonnaise, the chopped eggs and any seasoning required. Oil a 900 ml/1½ pint plain mould or soufflé dish. Spoon in the mixture and allow to set. Turn out and garnish with the lemon and cucumber slices.

VARIATIONS

**Seafood Chaudfroid:** Use only 175 g/6 oz salmon and add 100 g/4 oz peeled and coarsely chopped prawns, 100 g/4 oz flaked white crabmeat and 1 teaspoon finely chopped fennel leaves. The shells of the prawns can be simmered to give a good-flavoured fish stock. Canned salmon can be used in the above recipe or variation. Use the liquid from the can plus water, if necessary, to make the 150 ml/¼ pint fish stock.

**Chicken Chaudfroid:** Use chicken stock in place of fish stock and cooked minced or finely chopped chicken breast in place of salmon. To add more colour and flavour to the mould, blend in a few cooked peas and thinly sliced cooked carrots with the chopped eggs.

## Lax

*tail portion of fresh salmon, weighing 750 g/1½ lb cut into 2 fillets*
PICKLE:
*2-3 tablespoons granulated or caster sugar*
*2 tablespoons salt*
*1 teaspoon black peppercorns, crushed*
*2 tablespoons chopped dill*
*2 tablespoons brandy*

This pickled salmon, known as Lax or Gravad Lax is renowned in Scandinavia. It is served as an alternative to smoked salmon for special occasions. It is not difficult to prepare at home, this is the method I use.

Mix the pickle ingredients together, the amount of sugar can vary slightly according to personal taste, but should not be less than 2 tablespoons. Spoon one third of the pickle evenly on a flat dish, add the first salmon fillet, skin side touching the pickle. Spread the fillet with half the remaining pickle, then add the second fillet, this time with the skin uppermost. Spread with the last of the pickle. Cover the dish with foil and place a light weight on top. Put into the refrigerator and leave for 4 days. Turn the fish every day so that it absorbs the pickles.

To serve the fish cut into thin slices, as smoked salmon. Either serve as an hors d'oeuvre or for a light meal with Dill Mustard Sauce (see page 100).

# Sauces to Serve with Cold Fish

The most famous sauce to accompany cold fish is a Mayonnaise, and recipes for this sauce will be found in the Sauce section on page 235
The following sauces are however particularly suitable for the recipes in this section.

## Dill Mustard Sauce

*2 tablespoons mixed English mustard*
*3 tablespoons sugar*
*1 teaspoon salt*
*shake black pepper*
*2 tablespoons olive oil*
*1 tablespoon white wine vinegar*
*1 tablespoon double cream*
*1-2 tablespoons chopped dill*

Blend all the ingredients together. Serve with Lax (see page 99).

VARIATION
There are many variations of this sauce; some use French mustard instead of the hot English type. You can adjust the proportions of sugar and salt to your personal taste.

## Tartare Sauce 1

*150 ml/¼ pint mayonnaise, (see page 235)*
*2 teaspoons chopped capers*
*2 teaspoons chopped gherkins*
*2 teaspoons chopped parsley*
*½ teaspoon chopped tarragon*
*few drops tarragon vinegar or lemon juice*

There are two ways of making a Tartare Sauce, the first is based upon mayonnaise and the second on Hollandaise Sauce. Both can be served with hot or cold dishes. I like the delicacy of the second recipe with luxury fish dishes. The herb-flavoured Mousseline Sauce is even more delicious.

Blend the mayonnaise with the other ingredients.

VARIATIONS
**Tartare Sauce 2:** Make a Hollandaise Sauce with 3 egg yolks (see page 234). Whisk as the sauce cools, then add the capers and other ingredients as above.
**Mousseline Herb Sauce:** Make the Hollandaise Sauce with 3 egg yolks (see page 234) but only 40 g/1½ oz butter. Whisk as the sauce cools, then fold in 3 tablespoons lightly whipped cream, 1 teaspoon chopped fennel leaves or chopped dill leaves, 1 teaspoon chopped parsley and 1 teaspoon chopped gherkins.

# Meat Dishes

Meat is not only an expensive commodity, but a food which, to most people, is an essential ingredient in the majority of main dishes. It is therefore very important that we learn to judge the quality of meat, buy it wisely and cook it with care.

Really prime cuts of meat, such as sirloin of beef do not require elaborate methods of cooking; when roasted correctly nothing could be better, especially if suitable accompaniments are served with the meat. In these modern days when many of us freeze meat, or buy imported chilled meat, it is important to appreciate that methods of roasting must be adapted and you will find I have considered these facts when giving roasting times and temperatures.

The traditional accompaniments for roast meat immediately follow the recipes, i.e. Yorkshire Pudding and Horseradish Cream with beef, Mint Sauce or Onion Sauce with lamb (or mutton), Apple Sauce and Sage and Onion Stuffing with pork and a rather super gravy to give flavour to veal, the traditional accompaniments being similar to those for chicken or turkey.

Cheaper cuts of meat need more imaginative treatment and this can produce delicious dishes. I am particularly fond of good stews or very savoury meat dishes, so you will find plenty of these in this chapter. I have dealt with each kind of meat separately and ideas for using the cheaper cuts of meat come first in each section.

Raw meat freezes well, so that the majority of dishes in this chapter can be produced from frozen meat. Allow frozen joints to defrost before cooking; chops and steaks can be cooked without first defrosting them. When the meat has to be coated with flour or put in a marinade (as in a stew) then obviously it must defrost completely and be well dried.

The freezing symbol in this chapter is used to denote dishes that can be cooked, then frozen, ready for reheating. In this case do not over-cook the food initially, for you will continue the cooking process when the dish is reheated again. Cooked frozen dishes, based upon meat, should be used within 3 months so they retain their good flavour and texture.

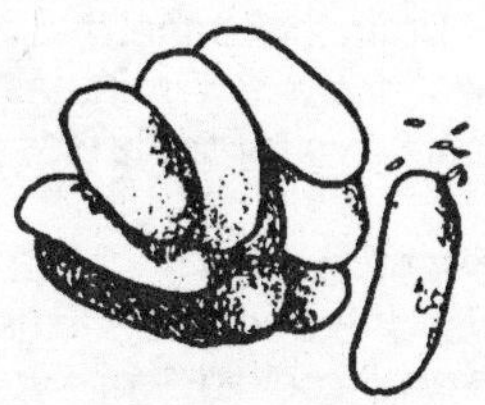

# Cooking Beef

Beef is undoubtedly the favourite meat in most countries and prime quality cuts of beef for roasting or using as steaks are considered, quite rightly, as special occasion foods. Do not despise cheaper cuts of beef, for a really good stew or casserole based upon stewing steak, can be most enjoyable.

This section starts with economical beef dishes and the first recipes use minced beef. When buying ready-minced meat of any kind, check that it looks pleasantly moist and not dry, for that is a sign that it is not fresh. Because minced meat has so many cut surfaces it deteriorates rapidly, so it should be cooked soon after purchase.

Lean beef can be rather dry unless a reasonable amount of fat is used in cooking and stewing steak needs long slow cooking to make it tender, unless using a pressure cooker. Good quality beef should have red-coloured lean meat and firm creamy-white fat.

Dishes made with beef, as well as uncooked beef, freeze well.

## Chilli con Carne ⊛

*50g/2oz fat*
*3 onions, chopped*
*1-2 cloves garlic, crushed*
*450g/1lb stewing steak, minced*
*450ml/¾ pint beef stock*
*1 red pepper, deseeded and diced*
*1-2 teaspoons chilli powder, or to taste*
*4 large tomatoes, skinned and chopped*
*pinch dried cumin*
*salt and pepper*
*1 x 450g/16oz can red kidney beans*

Heat the fat in a pan, add the onions and garlic and cook until a pale golden colour. Add the meat and cook gently for a few minutes, stirring well to separate the small pieces, for minced meat is inclined to form small lumps at this stage. Blend in the stock and the rest of the ingredients, except the canned beans. Unless you know you like the extremely hot flavour of chilli powder, it is better to use only about a quarter of the amount suggested at this stage, for makes vary and it will spoil the dish if it is too hot for your personal taste.

Bring the mixture to boiling point, stir again, cover the pan, lower the heat and simmer for nearly 1 hour. Stir once or twice during this period, taste the mixture and adjust the seasoning and the amount of chilli powder added. If you do add more chilli powder during cooking make sure it is thoroughly mixed in.

Drain the canned beans and add to the meat mixture, heat for a few minutes and serve. This is excellent topped with Tortilla (see page 272).

VARIATION

Use dried red beans. If using these remember they must be well cooked; while you need to simmer the beans to tenderise them they must be kept at boiling point for 10 minutes, to make them quite safe to eat.

## Bolognese Sauce ⊛

*25g/1oz butter*
*1 tablespoon oil*
*50g/2oz mushrooms, finely chopped*
*1 medium onion, finely chopped*
*1 medium carrot, grated*
*1-2 cloves garlic, crushed*
*225-350g/8-12oz raw minced beef*
*300ml/½pint beef stock or water and 1 beef stock cube*
*4 tablespoons tomato purée*
*1 bay leaf*
*1 wineglass red wine or extra stock*
*salt and pepper*

Heat the butter and oil in a pan, add the vegetables and cook gently for 3 to 4 minutes, then add the beef. Blend with the vegetables and stir well until the small particles of meat are separated. Add the rest of the ingredients, bring to simmering point and simmer for 35 to 45 minutes, then remove the lid so the excess liquid evaporates. Stir well as the sauce thickens. This sauce is better if no flour is used as a thickener. Remove the bay leaf before serving.

Although Spaghetti Bolognese is the best known recipe using this mixture of ingredients, it is an essential sauce for many other dishes, see pages 290 and 296. It is worth making a larger amount of sauce and freezing the surplus in small containers. Use within 3 months.

VARIATIONS

Add deseeded and chopped red and/or green pepper.
Vary the proportions of onions, mushrooms and garlic.
Add chopped parsley, chopped oregano and thyme to the sauce.
⊛ **Spaghetti Bolognese:** Cook 225g/8oz spaghetti if serving as a light dish or rather more for hungry people. See comments about cooking spaghetti and other pasta on page 295. Strain the pasta, put on to a hot dish or serving plates, and top with the sauce. Serve with bowls of grated Parmesan or other cheese.

## Minced Collops ⊛

*50g/2oz fat or beef dripping*
*2 medium onions, chopped*
*25g/1oz flour*
*450g/1lb chuck steak, minced*
*scant 300ml/scant ½pint beef stock*
*1 tablespoon mushroom ketchup or tomato purée*
*salt and pepper*
GARNISH:
*triangles of toast*

Heat the fat or dripping, fry the onions steadily until soft, stir in the flour, then add the meat. By adding the flour first you separate the meat particles. Allow the meat to brown lightly. Blend in the stock, stir as the mixture comes to the boil and add the remaining ingredients. Lower the heat, cover the pan and simmer gently for about 30 minutes, stir once or twice. Arrange the toast around the edge of a dish and spoon the meat into the centre.

VARIATIONS

Flavour the meat with curry, add mixed herbs, chopped tomatoes or other diced vegetables, such as carrots.

## Beefburgers

*450g/1 lbn best quality stewing steak or topside of beef or rump steak*
*salt and pepper*
*little fat, see method*

Beefburgers or Hamburgers, whichever name you prefer, use good quality minced beef wisely. This dish has become popular in most countries. Mince the meat yourself if possible or grind it in a food processor. Blend with a little salt and pepper to taste. Form into 4 round cakes. If there is a fair amount of fat in the meat simply grease a heavy frying pan or griddle and heat this; if using very lean meat heat about 25g/1 oz of fat in the pan. Add the Beefburgers, fry for 2 to 3 minutes, turn and cook for the same time on the second side. Serve with vegetables, salad or on toasted soft rolls.

## Beef and Bacon Burgers

*25g/1 oz fat, butter or margarine*
*2-3 rashers streaky bacon, derinded and chopped*
*1 medium onion, grated*
*2 medium potatoes, grated*
*350g/12oz minced raw beef (see Beefburgers above)*
*1 tablespoon chopped parsley*
*salt and pepper*

Heat the fat in a pan; fry the bacon and onion together until tender. Add the rest of the ingredients. Form into 8 flat round cakes and cook as for Beefburgers above. It is important to make smaller flatter burgers in order to cook the onion and potato adequately.

VARIATIONS

**Cheese Burgers:** Top the cooked burgers with sliced cheese and melt under a hot grill.

## Savoury Cutlets ⊛

*50g/2oz fat*
*1 onion, finely chopped*
*25g/1 oz flour*
*150ml/¼ pint beef stock*
*350g/12oz cooked beef, minced*
*50g/2oz soft breadcrumbs*
*mixed herbs to taste*
*salt and pepper*
COATING AND FRYING:
*1 egg*
*50g/2oz crisp breadcrumbs*
*50g/2oz fat*

Over the years I have learned that the word 'rissoles' seems to invite derogatory comments. I do not know why, for well-flavoured rissoles are excellent. Nowadays I generally re-christen this dish as the recipe title given above, to make sure people judge them on flavour and not on a name.

Heat the 50g/2oz fat; fry the onion until soft, add the flour, stir over a low heat for 2 to 3 minutes then blend in the stock. Stir as the mixture comes to the boil and thickens, then add the meat, breadcrumbs, herbs, salt and pepper. Cool and form into 8 small cutlet shapes. Coat in egg and breadcrumbs and fry in the hot fat. Drain on absorbent paper. Serve hot or cold.

## Køttbuller ⊛

*50g/2oz butter*
*1 medium onion, minced or finely chopped*
*50g/2oz soft breadcrumbs*
*150ml/¼pint beef stock*
*4 tablespoons double cream*
*350g/12oz topside beef or chuck steak, finely minced*
*100g/4oz fat pork or bacon rashers, finely minced*
*salt and pepper*
*pinch sugar*
FOR FRYING:
*75g/3oz butter*
*2 tablespoons oil*
SAUCE:
*4 tablespoons water*
*15g/½oz flour*
*150ml/¼pint milk*
*4 tablespoons double cream*

Heat the butter in a good-sized saucepan. Add the onion and fry until tender but do not allow to colour. Meanwhile put the breadcrumbs into a basin, add the cold stock and soak for 15 minutes. Blend with the onion, then add the cream, beef, pork or bacon with salt, pepper and sugar to taste. Form the mixture into 30 to 36 small balls. Do this with two spoons or use one spoon and press the mixture against your hand. Chill the meatballs for a time before frying.

Heat half the butter and half the oil in a good-sized frying pan. Add half the meat balls, fry for 7 to 8 minutes. Remove from the pan and fry the second batch of meat balls in the remaining butter and oil. Keep hot. Add the water to the frying pan. Stir well to absorb any fat remaining in the pan. Blend the flour with the milk and cream. Pour into the frying pan and stir as the sauce thickens. Season well. Coat the meat balls with the sauce.

VARIATION

Add 1 egg and 25g/1oz flour to the meat mixture. This makes less fragile meat balls.

## Beef Shreds

*225-275g/8-10oz topside beef, cut into narrow strips*
*2 teaspoons cornflour*
*2 tablespoons water*
*1 egg white*
*salt and pepper*
*50g/2oz fat*
*225g/8oz bean shoots, fresh or canned*
*75g/3oz canned bamboo shoots, chopped*
*1 small onion, finely shopped*
*1-2 sticks celery, chopped*
*3 tablespoons beef stock*
*2 tablespoons soy sauce*
*1 tablespoon dry sherry*
*2 teaspoons sugar*

Dry the pieces of beef on absorbent paper. Blend the cornflour with the water, the unbeaten egg white, salt and pepper. Coat the beef with this. Heat the fat and fry the meat until it is brown. Meanwhile heat the vegetables in a pan with the stock, soy sauce and sherry. Add the sugar, salt and pepper to taste. Spoon the sauce into a well heated dish and top with the crisply fried steak.

VARIATION

**Beef with Ginger and Onion:** Cut the beef into shreds as described in the recipe above. Marinate in a mixture of 1 tablespoon sherry, 1 tablespoon oil, ½ tablespoon soy sauce and 1 teaspoon sugar. Remove from the marinade, coat and fry as in the recipe above.

In another pan, fry 4 tablespoons chopped spring onions, with 2 tablespoons chopped green ginger (use preserved ginger as a substitute) in 1 tablespoon oil. Blend the fried beef and the fried ginger mixture together. Serve with cooked rice.

## Boeuf à la Bourguignonne ⊛

*3 onions, sliced*
*1 clove garlic, crushed*
*sprig thyme*
*sprig parsley*
*1 bay leaf*
*few strips lemon rinds*
*300 ml/½ pint red Burgundy*
*3 tablespoons oil*
*750 g/1½ lb topside of beef, neatly diced*
*2 thick fat bacon rashers, derinded and chopped*
*salt and pepper*
*25 g/1 oz flour*
*150 ml/¼ pint beef stock*
*100 g/4 oz small mushrooms*
GARNISH:
*lemon wedges*

Prepare a marinade: put 1 sliced onion, the garlic, herbs, lemon rind, wine and 1 tablespoon oil into a dish. Add the beef and marinate for 4 hours, turn once or twice. Heat the remaining oil in a saucepan, fry the 2 onions for several minutes, with the bacon and bacon rinds. Remove the rinds. Lift the meat from the marinade with a perforated spoon (save the wine mixture), coat in seasoned flour, add to the bacon mixture and cook gently for several minutes. Strain the marinade over the beef, add the stock. Stir as the liquid comes to the boil and the sauce thickens. Season to taste, cover the pan and simmer gently for 1½ hours. Add the mushrooms, cook for a further 30 minutes. Garnish with lemon.

VARIATION

⊛ **Beef and Tomato Stew:** Follow recipe above but use 300 ml/½ pint purée of fresh tomatoes instead of the wine. Flavour with chopped basil, pinch allspice, and 2 teaspoons vinegar.

## Carbonnade of Beef ⊛

*500-750 g/1¼-1½ lb stewing steak*
*25 g/1 oz flour*
*salt and pepper*
*1 thick streaky bacon rasher, about 100 g/4 oz in weight*
*50 g/2 oz beef dripping or fat*
*4 large onions, sliced*
*300 ml/½ pint beer*
*150 ml/¼ pint beef stock*
*1-2 teaspoons made English or French mustard*
*1-2 teaspoons brown sugar*
*bouquet garni*

Cut the meat into narrow strips. Blend the flour with a little salt and pepper and coat the meat in the seasoned flour. Cut the rind from the bacon, save this to give flavour to the stew; cut the bacon into thin strips. Heat the dripping or fat in a saucepan together with the bacon rind; fry the onions for 3 to 4 minutes then remove from the pan. Add the steak and bacon and fry together until just golden. Gradually blend in the beer and stock, bring to the boil and stir until thickened. Return the onions to the pan, then add the remaining ingredients. Cover the pan and simmer gently for 2 hours, remove the bacon rind and bouquet garni. This is a fairly thick stew so check halfway through the cooking time to see if there is sufficient liquid in the pan.

Serve with pasta; sauerkraut is the traditional accompaniment, but lightly cooked cabbage could be served instead.

VARIATION

Cook in a covered casserole in a cool oven (150°C/300°F or Gas Mark 2) for 2¼ to 2½ hours.

## Ragoût of Oxtail ⊛

*100g/4oz haricot beans*
*2 medium oxtail, cut into pieces*
*50g/2oz flour*
*salt and pepper*
*50g/2oz dripping or fat*
*2-3 medium onions, sliced*
*4-6 medium carrots, sliced*
*1-2 cloves garlic, crushed*
*1 small turnip, diced*
*2-3 sticks celery, chopped*
*100g/4oz lean bacon cut in one slice (optional)*
*1 x 400g/14oz can tomatoes*
*900ml/1½ pints beef stock*
*2 medium leeks, neatly sliced*
*little red wine (optional)*

Put the beans into a basin, cover with cold water and soak overnight. Remove any excess fat from the oxtail, but do not cut away all the fat, for this helps to give flavour to the dish and the fat can be removed after cooking. Blend the flour with salt and pepper; coat the pieces of oxtail. Heat the dripping or fat and fry the coated oxtail until golden in colour. Remove from the pan, add all the vegetables except the tomatoes and leeks and turn in the dripping or fat for a few minutes. (If using bacon, cut into narrow fingers and fry with the vegetables.) If there is any fat left after cooking the vegetables, spoon it out of the pan. Pour in the tomatoes and stock; return the oxtail to the pan. Bring the liquid to simmering point and check the seasoning. Drain the haricot beans and add to the other ingredients. Cover the pan, bring to the boil and boil for 10 minutes, then simmer gently for about 3½ to 4 hours, until the meat is very tender. The leeks should be put into the stew 20 to 30 minutes before the end of the cooking time.

Note: If you want all the meat to be uniformly tender, it is better to add the large pieces of oxtail first, then add the smaller pieces a little later to the stew. The perfect way to cook oxtail is as above but place it in a dish in the refrigerator after it cools. When quite cold, skim off any fat from the top of the gravy and reheat the ragoût, adding the wine, if using.

## Spanish Beef and Sausage Stew ⊛

*450g/1 lb chuck steak, diced*
*salt and pepper*
*25g/1 oz flour*
*1½ tablespoons oil*
*2 red peppers, deseeded and diced*
*2 medium onions, sliced*
*2 cloves garlic, crushed*
*3 medium tomatoes, sliced*
*300ml/½ pint beef stock*
*150ml/¼ pint red wine*
*450g/1 lb small potatoes, scraped*
*175g/6oz chorizo or garlic sausage, sliced*

Coat the meat in seasoned flour. Heat the oil in a pan, and fry the meat for several minutes. Remove from the pan, add the vegetables, fry for 5 minutes and stir well. Return the meat to the pan and blend in the stock and wine. Stir as the liquid comes to the boil and thickens slightly; add salt and pepper to taste. Cover the pan and simmer gently for 1½ hours. Add the potatoes, continue cooking for 25 to 30 minutes, then put in the chorizo or sausage and heat for 2 to 3 minutes only.

VARIATION

⊛ **Ragoût of Ox-heart:** Use thinly sliced ox-heart instead of steak. Omit the potatoes and sausage in the recipe above, add the grated rind of 2 oranges, 4 tablespoons orange juice, 1 teaspoon chopped sage.

# Braising

The term braised is often used quite wrongly to denote an ordinary stew. When foods, generally meat, poultry or game and occasionally vegetables, are braised, they are cooked on top of a selection of ingredients known as a mirepoix. This means the meat, or other food, is never immersed in liquid; it has therefore a completely different flavour from a stew.

Braised topside, which is given on this page, is a good example of how to braise meat. This method of cooking is ideal for this particular cut of meat because it makes it deliciously moist and tender. The ingredients for the mirepoix can be varied to personal taste, but you must use sufficient weight of vegetables so that the meat, or other food, is not covered with liquid. You can adapt this method of cooking for other foods. As you will see from the recipe below, the cooking time is not very different from the time allowed when roasting in a moderate oven.

## Braised Topside ⊛

*1 kg/2 lb topside*
*50 g/2 oz fat*
MIREPOIX:
*225-350 g/8-12 oz root vegetables, cut into small dice*
*2 sticks celery, chopped*
*2 leeks, thinly sliced*
*2 rashers fat bacon, derinded and chopped*
*2 teaspoons chopped fresh mixed herbs*
*salt and pepper*
*5 tablespoons beef stock or red wine*

Dry the meat well. Heat the fat in a large strong saucepan, fry the meat steadily until golden brown on both sides; remove from the saucepan on to a plate. Pour away any fat left in the pan—this is most important for excess fat would spoil the mirepoix. Add the ingredients for the mirepoix, including the bacon rind. Heat for 5 to 6 minutes until boiling quickly, then place the meat on top of these ingredients, cover the pan and lower the heat. It is essential that the saucepan has a well-fitting lid, otherwise the small amount of liquid will evaporate and allow the food to burn. If the lid does not fit well then put a piece of foil underneath the lid to make a tighter fit. Cook gently for 35 to 40 minutes if you like beef underdone, but add another 10 minutes for well cooked meat. Lift the meat on to a dish. Sieve the mirepoix, after removing the bacon rind, add a little more stock or wine and serve as a delicious sauce with the meat.

VARIATION
Brown the meat in a saucepan as directed above. Put the ingredients for the mirepoix into a casserole, cover and cook for 15 minutes in the centre of a moderate oven (180°C/350°F or Gas Mark 4) then add the browned meat. Cover the casserole and cook for 35 to 45 minutes, depending on how you like beef cooked.

## Boiled Beef ⊛

*1 kg/2¼ lb salted brisket or silverside*
*water to cover*
*about 10 small onions*
*about 10 small carrots*
*1 bay leaf*
*sprig parsley*
*pepper*

The British boiled salted beef and the American New England boiled beef are very similar – succulent beef cooked with a selection of vegetables.

Soak the beef overnight in cold water to cover, strain and discard this water. Put the meat, with fresh water to cover, 2 onions and 2 carrots (these flavour the stock), the herbs and pepper into a large saucepan. Bring to boiling point, lower the heat, cover the pan and simmer gently for 1¼ hours. Add the remaining vegetables after about 45 minutes' cooking time. Serve the meat and vegetables on the dish together.

## Suet Dumplings ⊛

*100 g/4 oz self-raising flour*
*pinch salt*
*50 g/2 oz shredded suet*
*water to bind*

Sift the flour and salt together, add the suet and enough water to make a soft binding consistency. Roll into about 8 small balls with floured hands. Put into the boiling liquid in a meat dish, as above and cook steadily for 15 minutes until well risen.

VARIATIONS

Flavour the mixture with mustard; chopped herbs; diced fried bacon; or use spinach purée instead of water to bind.

## Boiled Ox-tongue ⊛

*1 salted ox-tongue*
*water to cover*
*2 onions*
*2 carrots*
*few strips lemon rind*
*1 bay leaf*
*pepper or few peppercorns*

Cut away all excess fat from the tongue; put into cold water to cover and leave for 12 hours. Drain and discard this water. Put the tongue into a large saucepan with fresh water to cover, add the rest of the ingredients. Bring the liquid to simmering point and simmer gently. Allow 40 minutes per 450 g/1 lb. Test to see if tender as tongues vary considerably in toughness. Cool slightly, then remove from the liquid. Remove the skin and any tiny bones. Serve hot with Madeira Sauce or a Piquant Sauce, see pages 230 and 231.

## Glazed Tongue or Beef ⊛

*1 ox-tongue or joint of beef, cooked as above*
*1½-2 teaspoons gelatine, see method*

Cook the tongue or beef and reserve the stock. Cut the skinned tongue to fit into a round tin (without a loose base) or deep dish; fit the beef into a suitable container. Reduce the stock by boiling briskly – you will need about 300 ml/½ pint. Dissolve 1½ teaspoons gelatine in the stock for tongue but 2 teaspoons for beef. Pour over the meat, put a light weight on top, allow to set.

## Fried Steaks

*Choose fillet, entrecote, porterhouse, rump, sirloin or T-bone steak*
*butter or oil for cooking*

Always be generous with the amount of butter used to cook steaks. Heat the butter or oil, add the steaks. Fry quickly on one side, turn and fry on the second side. Lower the heat slightly and cook to personal taste. If cooking a steak of about 2.5cm/1 inch in thickness, allow about 6 minutes for under-done steaks; about 8 minutes for medium; and about 10 minutes for well-done steaks.

## Steak Diane

*75g/3oz butter*
*1 shallot or small onion, finely chopped*
*2 tablespoons chopped parsley*
*4 minute steaks (thin sirloin or rump steaks)*
*few drops Worcestershire sauce, or to taste*
*2 tablespoons brandy*

Heat the butter in a large frying pan; fry the shallot or onion for 2 to 3 minutes. Sprinkle in the parsley, then add the steaks. Fry for 1 minute, turn and fry for 1 minute on the second side. Sprinkle the Worcestershire sauce over the meat and lift on to a hot dish. Add the brandy to the pan, stir well to absorb any meat juices, ignite if wished, then spoon over the meat.

## Steak Tartare

*450-550g/1-1¼lb fillet steak, freshly minced*
*4 eggs (yolks only used)*
*2 tablespoons capers*
*1 large onion, finely chopped*
*2-3 tablespoons chopped gherkins*
*2 tablespoons chopped parsley*
*salt and pepper*

It is important that the steak is minced just before serving so that it does not dry out. Form the meat into 4 individual rounds on attractive plates. Break the eggs carefully. Pour out the whites (use in one of the recipes on page 363).

Keep each yolk in half an egg shell and put these round or on the meat. Arrange the capers, onions, gherkins and parsley in small mounds round the meat. Serve each plate to the diner; each person will decide if they would like all, or a selection of, the ingredients mixed with the meat.

VARIATIONS

Add a little brandy and/or Worcestershire sauce.

Blend the ingredients together in a bowl. Add salt and pepper to taste then re-form into a neat round on the plate. Serve with salad.

## Grilled Steaks

*Choose fillet, entrecote, porterhouse, rump, sirloin or T-bone steak*
*butter or oil for basting*

Always pre-heat the grill before cooking the meat. Brush the meat with melted butter or with oil before putting under the grill; brush again when you turn the meat and also during cooking,. particularly if you like grilled steaks well cooked. If you are trying to lose weight you must be sparing with the butter or fat, but a little is invaluable for keeping the meat moist. Follow the timings given under Fried Steaks on page 110. Use a high heat to cook one side of the steaks, turn and brush with butter oil, then grill the second side rapidly, lower the heat and cook to personal taste.

## Grilled Tournedos

*4 fillet steaks*
*50-75 g/2-3 oz butter, melted*

Most butchers will prepare tournedos, but if you have to do this yourself it is quite simple. Ask for fillet steaks, about 3-5 cm/1½ inches in thickness. Form each steak into a neat round with the palms of your hands. Secure with fine string.

Brush the tournedos with melted butter. Preheat the grill and cook following the timings on page 110. Tournedos are the basis for many classic dishes and the meat can be fried or grilled.

## Tournedos Africaine

*4 tournedos (see recipe above)*
*75 g/3 oz butter, melted*
*4 small firm bananas*
*little lemon juice*
*horseradish cream*

Cook the tournedos by grilling or frying following the recipe above or on page 110. The butter should be heated in a frying pan if frying or some brushed over the steaks before and during cooking, if cooking under the grill. Peel the bananas, sprinkle with lemon juice. If frying the steaks add the bananas to the pan and cook for 2 to 3 minutes. If grilling the steaks, brush the bananas with melted butter and add to the grill 2 to 3 minutes before the end of the cooking time. Serve the bananas with the steaks and horseradish cream.

## Croûtons for Steaks ⊛

*40-50 g/1½-2 oz butter*
*4 rounds of bread*

It is usual, although not essential, to serve grilled or fried tournedos on rounds of fried bread (croûtons). Heat the butter in a frying pan; fry the bread on one side until golden, turn and fry on the second side. Keep hot and place the cooked steak on top.

## Tournedos Baronne

*Béarnaise Sauce (see page 235 – optional)*
*4 medium tomatoes, skinned, deseeded and chopped*
*salt and pepper*
*4 tournedos*
*100-150 g/4-5 oz butter*
*4 rounds of bread*
*4 medium button mushrooms*

Make the Béarnaise Sauce if serving this. Cook the tomatoes with salt and pepper until a thick purée. Grill or fry the tournedos as described on page 110 and 111; use 50 to 75 g/2 to 3 oz butter for cooking the meat. Heat the remainder of the butter and fry the rounds of bread until brown on both sides. Lift onto a serving dish. Fry the mushrooms in the butter remaining in the pan. Place the tournedos on the fried croûtons of bread, top with the mushrooms and coat with the tomato purée, and Béarnaise Sauce.

## Tournedos Dumas

*150 ml/¼ pint Onion Sauce (see page 229)*
*75-100 g/3-4 oz butter*
*4 rounds of bread*
*4 tournedos*
*40 g/1½ oz Gruyère cheese, finely grated*

Make the Onion Sauce first. Heat half the butter in a pan and fry the rounds of bread; lift on to a hot flameproof dish. Use the remaining butter to grill or fry the meat. Place the steaks on the fried croûtons, top with the Onion Sauce, then the grated cheese. Put under a hot grill for 2 to 3 minutes, then serve.

## Tournedos Pompadour

*4 medium tomatoes, skinned, deseeded and chopped*
*salt and pepper*
*4 tournedos*
*4 very thin gammon slices*
*50-75 g/2-3 oz butter, melted*
*4 medium mushrooms*
*fried croûtons (optional)*

Cook the tomatoes with salt and pepper until a thick purée. Grill the tournedos, and gammon, basting with the melted butter. Grill the mushrooms. These tournedos can be served on fried croûtons, as in the recipe above, but it is not necessary. Top the tournedos with thick tomato purée then the cooked gammon and mushrooms.

## Steak au Poivre

*1-2 teaspoons peppercorns, crushed*
*4 fillet or rump steaks or tournedos*
*salt and pepper*
*75 g/3 oz butter*

Press the peppercorns into each side of the steaks, add salt and pepper to taste. Heat the butter and fry the steaks; following the timings given on page 110.

VARIATION

Cook the steaks, add 4 tablespoons beef stock, 4 tablespoons double cream, 2 teaspoons chopped chervil or parsley and 2 tablespoons brandy to the pan, stir well; heat and spoon over the meat.

## Carpet Bag Steak

*1 kg/2¼ lb rump steak in one piece or topside of beef*
FILLING:
*25 g/1 oz butter*
*8 small oysters or 12 to 16 prepared mussels (see page 92)*
*50 g/2 oz mushrooms, thinly sliced*
*75 g/3 oz soft breadcrumbs*
*2 teaspoons chopped parsley*
*¼ teaspoon grated lemon rind*
*salt and pepper*
*1 egg yolk*

This combination of meat and shellfish is one of the delicious recipes I enjoyed in Australia, where small oysters are so readily available. Heat the butter in a pan, toss the oysters or mussels in this but do not cook. Blend with the rest of the ingredients for the filling.

Make a horizontal cut in the joint of meat to form a good-sized pocket. Insert the filling and skewer or tie so this cannot fall out in cooking. Weigh the joint after stuffing and roast following the timings on page 115. Serves 4 to 5.

Note: If increasing the size of meat then use more filling too.

## Beef Wellington (Boeuf en Croûte)

*1-1.25 kg/2-2½ lb fillet steak, cut in one piece from the thick end of the fillet*
*75 g/3 oz butter*
*225 g/8 oz mushrooms, very finely chopped*
*2 small onions, very finely chopped*
*1 tablespoon chopped parsley*
*salt and pepper*
*Puff Pastry, made with 225 g/8 oz flour etc. (see page 292)*
GLAZE:
*1 egg*
*1 tablespoon water*

Spread the steak with half the butter, roast as beef, page 115, but slightly under-cook; allow to cool. Blend the mushrooms and onions with the remaining butter, parsley and salt. If slightly less finely chopped, cook vegetables in butter until a dry mixture, add parsley and season.

Roll out the pastry until it is a very thin oblong shape, large enough to envelop the meat. Spread with the onion mixture, leaving a border of 1 cm/½ inch without stuffing at the edges. Place the steak in the centre, moisten the edges of the pastry with a little water then fold to cover the meat. Make sure the pastry just overlaps to give a firm join. Seal the ends and the join and turn so this is underneath. Cut leaves and make a pastry rose from the remaining pastry; moisten with a little water and place on the top of the pastry shape.

Lift on to a baking tray. Make 2 or 3 slits in the pastry to allow the steam to escape. Beat the egg with the water and brush over the pastry. Bake in the centre of a hot oven (220°C/425°F or Gas Mark 7) for 35 to 40 minutes, reduce the heat to moderate (180°C/350°F or Gas Mark 4) when the pastry begins to brown. Serve with Red Wine Sauce (see page 232). Serves 6

## Pot Roast of Beef ⊛

*1 kg/2 lb topside of fresh brisket of beef*
*25 g/1 oz fat*
*2-3 fat bacon rashers, derinded and chopped*
*8 medium potatoes*
*8 medium onions*
*8 medium carrots*
*beef stock or water*
*salt and pepper*

Dry the meat so that it will brown well. In a large, deep pan, heat the fat with the bacon rinds, add the beef and turn over a low heat until well browned. Remove the meat and bacon rinds. Add the bacon, fry for 1 minute then add the whole vegetables, with sufficient stock or water to barely cover them, season lightly. Replace the beef in the pan, it should be supported by the bed of vegetables and should not be covered with liquid. Put the lid on the pan, bring the liquid to boiling point, lower the heat and cook steadily for 40 to 50 minutes, depending upon how well done you like beef. Check on the amount of liquid once or twice. Serve the meat with the vegetables and thicken the liquid for gravy.

## Boeuf à la Mode ⊛

*2 kg/4½ lb joint of topside or thick rump*
*100 g/4 oz fat pork (optional)*
*150 ml/¼ pint brandy or extra red wine*
*50 g/2 oz butter*
*1 tablespoon oil*
*12-18 shallots or small onions*
*12 medium carrots*
*450 ml/¾ pint beef stock or water*
*300 ml/½ pint red wine*
*1 calf's foot*
*salt and pepper*

Dry the meat well, this is particularly important if using frozen meat for this purpose. Take the pork and cut it into very narrow strips, put these into a larding needle and thread through the beef. (This process incorporates fat throughout the meat and keeps it moist, but it is not essential.) Pour the brandy or 150 ml/¼ pint red wine into a dish. Place the meat in the brandy or wine for 2 hours, turn once. Heat the butter and oil in a very large strong saucepan. Put in the beef and brown well on all sides, turning frequently, then add the rest of the ingredients. Cover the saucepan and simmer gently for 2½ hours.

Serve the joint with the vegetables, hand the unthickened rather glutinous liquid separately. This is a large joint for 4 people, but this method of cooking beef gives a wonderful flavour to the meat, whether served hot or cold. Any liquid left makes a good basis for a soup.

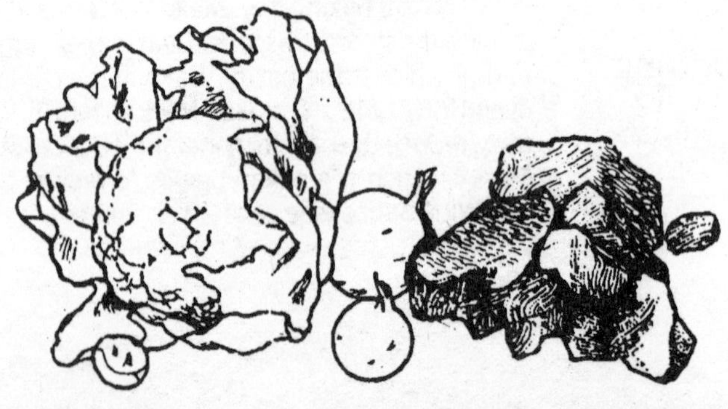

## Roast Beef ⊛

*These joints are suitable for roasting –*

PRIME JOINTS:

*baron (consists of 2 sirloins and part of the rib)*

*fillet*

*rib*

*rib and wing (similar to sirloin, without fillet)*

*sirloin*

CHEAPER JOINTS:

*fresh brisket*

*topside*

WEIGHT TO ALLOW *per person when buying the meat:*

*350 g/12 oz if on bone*

*225-300 g/8-10 oz if boned*

No other meat causes such discussion on how it should be roasted as beef. This is largely because people have such definite ideas on how they like it cooked. It is complicated if there is a difference of opinion in a family, as in mine. I like beef almost raw; my husband likes it well done. The answer – I follow the timing for rare beef then allow an extra 2 to 3 minutes per 450 g/1 lb. My husband carves slices from both sides of the joint. I have the middle.

Beef is a lean meat and if you like to roast in an open tin then you must add a little fat. If you wrap it in foil, use a roaster bag or a covered roasting tin. Fat is not necessary, except when cooking topside.

Prime quality beef which has not been frozen and then defrosted or chilled can be roasted in a moderately hot to hot oven (200-220°C/400-425°F or Gas Mark 6-7). Allow 15 minutes per 450 g/1 lb plus 15 minutes for very rare (under-cooked) beef; 20 minutes per 450 g/1 lb plus 20 minutes for medium cooked beef; 25 minutes per 450 g/1 lb plus 25 minutes for well-cooked beef.

Cheaper cuts of beef, or beef that has been frozen then defrosted or chilled is better roasted in a moderate oven (160-180°C/325-350°F or Gas Mark 3-4). Allow 25 minutes per 450 g/1 lb plus 25 minutes for rare beef; 30 minutes per 450 g/1 lb plus 30 minutes for medium cooked beef and 35 minutes per 450 g/1 lb plus 35 minutes for well-cooked beef.

If using a covered roasting tin or cooking the meat in foil, then allow about 10 to 15 minutes extra cooking time. No extra time is required when using the modern roaster bags.

Beef is generally served with a thin gravy. Traditional accompaniments are given below and on the next page.

## Yorkshire Pudding

*25 g/1 oz fat*

*Batter (see page 289)*

Raise the oven temperature to very hot (230°C/450°F or Gas Mark 8). Heat the fat in a Yorkshire Pudding tin or several deep patty tins. Pour in the batter, bake for 10 minutes at this heat, then reduce to the first temperature given above for cooking the meat. Small Yorkshire Puddings take about 15 minutes cooking time; a large one 25 to 30 minutes.

## Horseradish Cream ⊛

*2 tablespoons grated horseradish*
*1 tablespoon white vinegar or lemon juice*
*1-2 teaspoons sugar*
*150 ml/¼ pint double cream*
*little made mustard to taste*
*salt and pepper*

This is the perfect accompaniment to roast beef. Try and obtain fresh horseradish to make this cream. Mix the horseradish, vinegar or lemon juice, sugar and unwhipped cream and stir briskly to blend; this movement whips the cream. Add a little mustard and salt and pepper as desired.

VARIATION

⊛ **Hot Horseradish Sauce:** Make 300 ml/½ pint White Sauce (see page 226), add 1 tablespoon grated horseradish, 1 tablespoon vinegar, 1 teaspoon sugar and a little made mustard to taste.

## Devilled Beef ⊛

*1.5 kg/3-3½ lb joint beef topside*
MARINADE:
*2 tablespoons oil*
*1 onion, finely chopped*
*1 clove garlic, crushed*
*2 tablespoons Worcestershire sauce*
*2 teaspoons made mustard*
*1 tablespoon tomato ketchup*
*1 tablespoon brown sugar*
*1 tablespoon soy sauce*

Mix together the ingredients for the marinade and put into a deep container. Wipe the joint well, this is particularly important if it has been frozen, then defrosted. Put the joint in the marinade, leave for 2 to 3 hours, turn once. Lift the from the marinade and roast as on page 115. Strain any marinade left into the gravy to give this an interesting flavour.

VARIATION

⊛ **Curried Beef:** Omit the Worcestershire and soy sauce and the tomato ketchup. Blend the other ingredients with 2 tablespoons dry sherry, 2 teaspoons curry paste, pinch ground ginger and 1 tablespoon sweet chutney and cook as above.

## Sherried Beef ⊛

*joint of beef (see page 115)*
SAUCE:
*2 tablespoons beef fat*
*1 medium onion, finely chopped*
*1 clove garlic, crushed*
*2 teaspoons cornflour*
*4 tablespoons brown sherry*
*150 ml/¼ pint beef stock*
*2 tablespoons tomato purée*
*salt and pepper*

Roast the beef following the timings on page 115. Take out of the oven 15 minutes before the end of the cooking time if using the moderately hot to hot temperature, or 25 minutes if using the lower temperature. Pour out all the fat from the roasting tin and reserve. Put 2 tablespoons fat into a pan. Fry the onion and garlic gently until soft. Blend the cornflour with the sherry and stock. Pour into the saucepan, add the tomato purée and salt and pepper. Stir the sauce over a low heat until thickened and smooth. Pour over the beef, return to the oven and complete the cooking.

## Steak and Kidney Pie ⊛

*Flaky Pastry, made with 175 g/6 oz flour, etc. (see page 292)*
FILLING:
*550 g/1 ¼ lb stewing steak, diced*
*175 g/6 oz ox kidney, diced*
*salt and pepper*
*20 g/¾ oz flour*
*50 g/2 oz fat*
*450 ml/¾ pint beef stock or water*
*1 large onion (optional)*
GLAZE:
*1 egg*

Make the pastry as page 292. Coat the meats in seasoned flour. Heat the fat in a pan and fry the meats for about 5 minutes. Blend in the stock or water, bring to the boil and stir over a low heat until slightly thickened. Add the whole onion to the liquid if using this. Cover the pan, simmer gently for 2 hours or until the beef is just tender. Adjust the seasoning. Spoon the meat and a little gravy into 1.2 litre/2 pint pie dish; leave to cool. Remove the onion. Roll out the pastry thinly and cover the pie.

Beat the egg, brush over the pie. Bake in the centre of a hot oven (220°C/425°F or Gas Mark 7) for 20 to 25 minutes until the pastry has risen well, then lower the heat to moderate to moderately hot (180-190°C/ 350-375°F or Gas Mark 4-5) for a further 10 to 15 minutes. Heat the remaining gravy, add a little extra liquid if too thick, then pour into a sauce boat.

VARIATION

⊛ **Steak and Game Pie:** Use 225 g/8 oz diced steak and 1 diced pheasant. Flavour the stock with red wine.

## Steak and Kidney Pudding ⊛

SUET CRUST PASTRY:
*300 g/10 oz flour*
*pinch salt*
*150 g/5 oz shredded suet*
*water to mix*
FILLING:
*750 g/1 ½ lb stewing steak, diced*
*225 g/8 oz ox kidney, diced*
*salt and pepper*
*1 tablespoon flour*
*stock or water*

The amount of pastry given here gives a fairly thick crust, it can be slightly reduced. You can use self-raising flour or plain flour depending on whether you like a puffed crust or thinner one.

Sift the flour and salt. Add the suet and enough water to give a soft rolling consistency. Roll out and use just three-quarters to line a 1.2 to 1.5 litre/2 to 2½ pint lightly greased basin. Blend the meats with the flour, salt and pepper. Put into the pastry lined basin. Add enough stock or water to come about two-thirds up the basin. Roll out the remaining dough into a round sufficiently large to cover the filling. Moisten the edges of the pastry with water, press the pastry lid in position. Cover with greased greaseproof paper and foil. Steam over boiling water for 4½ to 5 hours. If you like extra gravy see the recipe on page 230.

## Musselburgh Pie ⊛

*Flaky Pastry made with 175 g/6 oz flour, etc. (see page 292)*
FILLING:
*450 g/1 lb stewing steak*
*12 oysters or 24 prepared mussels (see page 92)*
*salt and cayenne pepper*
*25 g/1 oz flour*
*2 shallots, finely chopped*
*100 g/4 oz fat bacon, derinded and chopped*
*150 ml/¼ pint beef stock*
GLAZE:
*1 egg*

Make the pastry as page 292. Cut the meat into 24 thin strips; halve the oysters. Roll a strip of steak round each halved oyster or whole mussel. Coat in seasoned flour and put into a 1.2 litre/2 pint pie dish. Add the shallots, bacon and beef stock. Roll out the pastry and cover the pie. Beat the egg and brush over the pastry. Bake in the centre of a hot oven (220°C/425°F or Gas Mark 7) for 25 minutes until the pastry has risen well. Lower the heat to moderate (160°C/325°F or Gas Mark 3) and bake for a further 1¾ to 2 hours. If the pastry is becoming too brown, cover with greaseproof paper. Serve with a thickened gravy.
Note; The Steak and Kidney Pie can be baked as above, instead of the method used in the recipe on page 117.

## Forfar Bridies ⊛

*Flaky Pastry, made with 350 g/12 oz flour, etc. (see page 292)*
FILLING:
*450 g/1 lb topside of beef, or minced stewing steak*
*75 g/3 oz shredded suet or butcher's suet, grated*
*2 medium onions, very finely chopped*
*salt and pepper*

Make the pastry as page 292. Roll out very thinly and cut into 4 large rounds. If using topside beat until very thin and cut into short and narrow strips. Spread half of each round with the suet and onions, top with the meat, salt and pepper. Damp the pastry edges, fold the half without a filling over the meat mixture to enclose this. Seal and flute the edges. Lift on to a baking tray. Bake in a hot oven (220°C/425°F or Gas Mark 7) then lower the heat to moderate (160°C/325°F or Gas Mark 3) for a further 1 hour if using topside of beef or 1¼ hours for stewing steak.
Note: The traditional Bridies were made with a flour and water paste, which becomes horribly hard.

## Cornish Pasties ⊛

*Shortcrust Pastry, made with 350 g/12 oz plain flour, but only 150 g/5 oz fat (see page 291)*
FILLING:
*350-450 g/12 oz-1 lb rump steak*
*2 medium onions*
*2 medium potatoes*
*2 tablespoons beef stock*
*salt and pepper*
GLAZE:
*1 egg*

Make the pastry as page 291, using a little less fat so the pasties can be carried without fear of breaking. Roll out pastry and cut into 4 really large rounds. Cut the meat, onions and potatoes into 5 mm/¼ inch cubes. Mix with the stock, salt and pepper and spoon into the centre of each pastry round. Damp the pastry edges, bring together to form the traditional pasty shape, press firmly and flute. Lift on to a baking tray. Beat the egg and brush over the pasties. Bake in the centre of a hot oven (220°C/425°F or Gas Mark 7) for 20 minutes, then lower the heat to moderate (180°C/350°F or Gas Mark 4) for a further 25 to 30 minutes. Serve hot or cold.

## Beef Cobbler ⊛

*ingredients as Minced Collops (see page 103)*
TOPPING:
*175g/6oz self-raising flour*
*salt and pepper*
*pinch garlic salt*
*pinch cayenne pepper*
*40g/1½oz margarine*
*milk to bind*
GLAZE:
*little milk*

Cook the minced meat mixture following the recipe on page 103. Transfer to a heated casserole. Use a dish that is wide in diameter. If the meat mixture seems a little thin in consistency, remove the lid for the last 10 minutes cooking time. Meanwhile pre-heat the oven to moderately hot (190-200°C/375-400°F or Gas Mark 5-6).

Sift the flour and seasonings, rub in the margarine and add enough milk to make a soft rolling consistency. Roll out to about 1cm/½inch in thickness; cut into 8 rounds. Place these on top of the hot meat, brush with a little milk. Bake for 15 to 20 minutes in the centre of the oven.

## Cheese and Beef Loaf ⊛

*450g/1 lb lean topside, finely minced*
*100g/4oz fat pork or bacon, minced*
*2 medium onions, minced or grated*
*225g/8oz Cheddar or Gruyère cheese, grated*
*4 eggs*
*2 tablespoons chopped parsley*
*salt and pepper*

Mix all the ingredients together. Grease a 1.25kg/2½lb loaf tin or ovenproof casserole. Put in the mixture. Cover with greased foil and stand in a bain-marie (dish of cold water). This prevents the outside of the loaf becoming too dry. Bake in the centre of a moderate oven (180°C/350°F or Gas Mark 4) for 1½ hours. Serve hot with Piquant or Tomato Sauce, see recipes on pages 231 and 233.

VARIATIONS

⊛ **Devilled Beef Loaf:** Omit the cheese; finely chop and fry the 2 medium onions in 25g/1oz fat until soft. Stir in 2 teaspoons curry powder. Add the minced beef and pork and bacon, 100g/4oz soft breadcrumbs, 3 eggs, blend with a pinch cayenne pepper, few drops of Tabasco sauce and 1 teaspoon Worcestershire sauce. Cook as above.

⊛ **Creamy Beef and Ham Loaf:** Heat 25g/1oz butter in a pan, add a finely chopped small onion, cook for 2 to 3 minutes then mix with 450g/1 lb minced chuck steak, 175 g/6 oz minced cooked lean ham, 2 tablespoons chopped parsley, 1 teaspoon made mustard, 1 tablespoon horseradish cream, 1 teaspoon mushroom ketchup, 50 g/2 oz soft breadcrumbs, 150 ml/¼ pint single cream, 2 eggs and salt and pepper to taste. Bake as the recipe above.

# Cooking Lamb

Lamb is a meat that blends well with many different flavours, that is why you can combine the meat with fruit as well as vegetables and herbs. The first recipes in this section give my favourite ideas for pleasant stews and casseroles based on lamb. The more mature mutton could be used instead, in which case allow a slightly longer cooking time.

Young lamb should be pink in colour with creamy-coloured and slightly transparent looking fat. Dishes made with lamb, as well as uncooked lamb, freeze well.

## Bobotie ✳

*75 g/3 oz bread (weight without crusts)*
*450 ml/¾ pint milk*
*50 g/2 oz fat*
*3 medium onions, thinly sliced*
*½-1 tablespoon curry powder*
*450 g/1 lb raw lamb, minced*
*1 teaspoon sugar*
*salt and pepper*
*1 tablespoon vinegar*
*2 eggs*
*25-50 g/2 oz blanched almonds, coarsely chopped*

Put the bread into a basin and add about 150 ml/¼ pint of the milk. Leave to stand for 15 minutes, then mash. Heat the fat in a pan and fry the onions until soft. Blend in the curry powder and cook for a further 1 minute. Mix the curried onions with the meat, sugar, salt, pepper, bread and vinegar. Spoon the mixture into 1.5 litre/ 2½ pint ovenproof dish. Beat the remaining milk with the eggs, add a little salt and pepper. Strain over the meat mixture. Cover the dish and cook in the centre of a moderate oven (160°C/325°F or Gas Mark 3) for 1 hour. Lift the lid towards the end of the cooking time and add the almonds.

VARIATION

This is an excellent way of using up cooked minced meat or poultry. Reduce the cooking time slightly.

## Pilaff of Lamb ✳

*3 tablespoons oil*
*2 large onions, chopped*
*1 clove garlic, crushed*
*175 g/6 oz long grain rice*
*900 ml/1½ pints water*
*salt and pepper*
*pinch turmeric*
*450 g/1 lb cooked lamb, diced*
*3 medium tomatoes, skinned and chopped*
*75 g/3 oz seedless raisins*
*50 g/2 oz pine kernels*
*yogurt or soured cream*

Heat the oil in a large saucepan. Add the onions and garlic and cook for several minutes. Blend the rice with the oil and onions. Add the water, salt and pepper and turmeric. Bring to the boil, lower the heat and cook for 20 minutes. Add the remaining ingredients and continue cooking for a further 20 minutes until the rice is soft and the other foods hot. Keep the lid off the pan at this stage, so the excess liquid evaporates. Check the rice mixture does not stick to the pan as it thickens, stir once or twice.

Serve with yogurt or soured cream separately.

## Lamb Patties ⊛

PATTIES:
*350g/12oz cooked lean lamb, minced*
*50g/2oz soft breadcrumbs*
*3 tablespoons double cream*
*salt and pepper*
*2 teaspoons chopped parsley*
*2 teaspoons chopped chives*
*1 teaspoon chopped mint*
*1 egg yolk*
COATING:
*1 tablespoon flour*
*1 egg white, lightly whisked*
*50g/2oz crisp breadcrumbs*
FOR FRYING:
*50g/2oz butter*

Mix together all the ingredients for the patties. The mixture will be very soft, so divide into 8 portions, put on a flat dish and chill well for at least 1 hour. You then will be able to form the mixture into neat round cakes. Coat in the seasoned flour, egg white and the crisp bread-crumbs. Chill again before frying. Heat the butter in a frying pan and fry the patties for 2 to 3 minutes on either side. Drain on absorbent paper and serve hot or cold.

VARIATION
Use finely minced uncooked lean lamb in the same recipe. In this case fry fairly briskly on either side to brown, then lower the heat and cook more slowly for a further 6 to 7 minutes.

## Lamburgers

*450g/1 lb lean lamb, minced*
*2 tablespoons chopped parsley*
*2 bacon rashers, derinded and minced*
*salt and pepper*
*2-3 tablespoons chutney*
*1 small onion, grated*
*little fat*

Lamb has a different texture and taste from beef and while you can use lamb in exactly the same recipe as the Beefburgers on page 104 I find this mixture of ingredients produces a better flavoured, as well as a more unusual, meat cake. Blend the minced lamb with the parsley, minced bacon, salt and pepper to taste. Form into 8 very flat rounds. Spread half the rounds with the chutney and onion. Put the rest of the rounds on top of the filling. Fry in a greased pan or in a little fat, as described under Beefburgers on page 104.

## Lamb Terrapin ⊛

*450g/1 lb cooked lean lamb*
*1 tablespoon oil*
*1 small onion, diced*
*2 teaspoons lemon juice*
*300ml/½ pint Béchamel Sauce (see page 227)*
*salt and pepper*
*1 teaspoon French mustard*
GARNISH:
*2 hard-boiled eggs*

This is an excellent way of using up left-over lamb; particularly lamb that has been cooked in the Navarin (page 124). Remove any fat and dice the lean part neatly. Heat the oil in a pan, toss the onion in this until just soft; blend with the lamb and the lemon juice. Heat the Béchamel Sauce and add the lamb mixture. Heat without boiling, for a few minutes and add salt, pepper and mustard. Slice or chop the eggs. Arrange the lamb mixture on a hot dish and top with the eggs. Serve with toast.

## Moussaka ⊛

*2 tablespoons oil*
*50 g/2 oz butter*
*2-3 medium onions, thinly sliced*
*4 medium tomatoes, thickly sliced*
*salt and pepper*
*2 medium aubergines, thinly sliced*
*4 medium potatoes, thinly sliced*
SAUCE:
*40 g/1½ oz butter or margarine*
*40 g/1½ oz flour*
*450 ml/¾ pint milk*
*75-100 g/3-4 oz Cheddar or Gruyère cheese, finely grated*
*1 egg*
*little nutmeg, grated*
*450 g/1 lb cooked lamb*
GARNISH:
*chopped parsley*

Heat half the oil and 25 g/1 oz butter in a pan and fry the onions until nearly soft. Add the tomatoes and cook for a further 2 or 3 minutes; season lightly. Heat the remaining oil and butter and cook the aubergines and potatoes until tender; turn several times to prevent the vegetables burning. If you dislike the slightly bitter taste of aubergine skins, peel before slicing or read the advice on page 242.

Heat the butter or margarine for the sauce in a pan and stir in the flour. Cook over a low heat for 2 to 3 minutes then gradually blend in the milk. Stir as the sauce comes to the boil and thickens. Add most of the cheese, the beaten egg and nutmeg: do not heat again.

Mince or finely chop the meat, mix with the onions and tomatoes. Arrange layers of the meat and aubergine mixtures in a casserole, pouring a little sauce over each layer. Top with a layer of aubergines and a good layer of sauce. Add the last of the grated cheese. Bake in the centre of a moderate oven (160°C/325°F or Gas Mark 3) for 1 hour. Top with parsley.

VARIATION
Use uncooked minced lamb or beef and cook for 1½ hours. For a drier result make a sauce with 25 g/1 oz butter or margarine, 25 g/1 oz flour and 300 ml/½ pint milk and use slightly less cheese.

## Lamb and Aubergine Casserole ⊛

*1 tablespoon oil*
*2 medium onions, chopped*
*2 medium aubergines, peeled and diced*
*450 g/1 lb lean lamb, minced (weight without bones)*
*1 x 450 g/16 oz can plum tomatoes*
*salt and pepper*

In this dish the aubergines are peeled so you have a more delicate flavour. Heat the oil, fry the onions for 5 minutes, then mix with the rest of the ingredients. Put into a casserole, cover and cook in the centre of a moderate oven (160°C/325°F or Gas Mark 3) for 1¼ hours.

## Curried Lamb ⊛

*750g/1½lb lamb, diced (weight without bones)*
*1 or 2 tablespoons curry powder*
*pinch ground ginger*
*pinch turmeric*
*2 teaspoons sugar*
*75g/3oz ghee (see note under method)*
*2 medium onions, chopped*
*450ml/¾pint water*
*2 tablespoons desiccated coconut*
*2 tomatoes, skinned and chopped*
*2 tablespoons sultanas*
*salt and pepper*
*2 tablespoons lemon juice*

Sprinkle the lamb with the curry powder, ginger, turmeric and sugar; press well into the meat. Heat the ghee in the saucepan, add the onions and fry gently for 2 to 3 minutes. Add the lamb and fry for 5 minutes, turn several times. Put in the rest of the ingredients, stir to blend. Cover the pan and simmer for 1¼ hours, or until the meat is tender; if necessary lift the lid towards the end of the cooking time so any excess liquid evaporates.

Serve with cooked rice and dishes of sliced bananas (dipped in lemon juice to keep these white); thinly sliced tomatoes and sliced green pepper (discard the core and seeds); small cocktail onions, sliced gherkins; desiccated coconut; sultanas; diced cucumber blended with yogurt and chopped mint; poppadums.

Note: Ghee is butter from which all moisture has been removed, so it is solid fat. To prepare ghee put the butter into a pan, with water to cover, heat only until the butter melts. Allow to cool, then lift the solid fat from the liquid.

VARIATIONS

If you like a generous amount of curry sauce then coat the lamb with 25g/1oz flour as well as the spices. Increase the water to 600ml/1 pint.

Use beef or other meat; adjust the cooking time, stewing beef would need up to 2¼ to 2½ hours cooking, so increase the liquid slightly.

## Ragoût of Mutton ⊛

*1.25kg/2½lb middle or scrag end of neck of mutton, divided into portions*
*2 bacon rashers, derinded and chopped*
*1 mutton kidney, diced*
*8 shallots*
*25g/1oz flour*
*450ml/¾pint chicken stock*
*salt and pepper*
*100g/4oz button mushrooms*

Fry the mutton steadily in a pan until golden. If you dislike too much fat, cut away any excess from the mutton after frying. Spoon the meat into a casserole. Fry the bacon, kidney and shallots in the pan, then add to the mutton. Blend the flour with any fat and meat juices left in the pan and stir in the stock. Continue stirring as the mixture comes to the boil and thickens; season to taste. Pour over the mutton. Cover the casserole and cook in the centre of a cool oven (150°C/300°F or Gas Mark 2) for 2½ hours. Add the mushrooms when the ragoût has cooked for 1½ hours.

VARIATION

Use lamb instead of mutton, allow 1¾ hours cooking time.

## Lamb and Caper Sauce ⊛

*1.25 kg/2½ lb middle neck of lamb, cut into pieces*
*10 medium onions*
*10 medium carrots*
*1.2 litres/2 pints water*
*sprig mint*
*salt and pepper*
CAPER SAUCE:
*40 g/1½ oz butter*
*40 g/1½ oz flour*
*300 ml/½ pint milk*
*150 ml/¼ pint lamb stock, see method*
*2-3 teaspoons capers plus a few drops vinegar*

Put the lamb, 2 onions, 2 carrots, water, mint and salt and pepper into a saucepan. Cover the pan and simmer for 1 hour then add the remaining onions and carrots and continue cooking for a further 30 minutes.

Heat the butter in another pan, stir in the flour and cook for 2 to 3 minutes. Blend in the milk and 50 ml/¼ pint stock from cooking the lamb. Stir as the sauce thickens and season well. Finally add the capers and vinegar from the jar.

Serve the lamb and vegetables with a sauceboat of unthickened stock and another of Caper Sauce.

VARIATION

⊛ **Irish Stew:** Cook the lamb in only 450 ml/¾ pint water with 3 to 4 large sliced onions, salt and pepper to taste. Add 450 g/1 lb thickly sliced potatoes 30 minutes before the end of the cooking time.

## Navarin of Lamb ⊛

*750 g/1½ lb lamb, cut from the leg or shoulder and neatly diced*
*salt and pepper*
*2 teaspoons sugar*
*50 g/2 oz butter*
*25 g/1 oz flour*
*600 ml/1 pint water*
*bouquet garni*
*1 clove garlic, crushed*
*3 tomatoes, skinned and chopped*
*about 750 g/1½ lb young vegetables, see method*

This simple, but delicious, French dish is often called Navarin Printanier because it is prepared in springtime when the vegetables are young and at their best.

Sprinkle the meat with salt, pepper and the sugar. Heat the butter in a large saucepan, add the lamb and cook gently, stirring once or twice, until it is delicately browned; the sugar gives it a faint caramel taste. Blend in the flour, then add the water and stir as the liquid comes to the boil and thickens very slightly. Add the bouquet garni, garlic, tomatoes and any extra seasoning required. Simmer gently for about 45 minutes then add the selection of young vegetables, such as new potatoes, baby carrots, young broad beans, diced young turnips, fresh peas when available. Cover the pan and cook until the meat and vegetables are tender. Check there is sufficient liquid when adding and cooking the vegetables.

VARIATION

Before adding the vegetables, the meat is sometimes lifted from the tomato-flavoured liquid, this is strained to make it clearer then returned to the pan with the half-cooked meat and the selection of vegetables.

## Fricassée of Lamb ⊛

*450 g/1 lb cooked lamb (weight without bones)*
*2 eggs, hard-boiled*
*50 g/2 oz cooked peas*
*2 tablespoons chopped parsley*
*3 tablespoons double cream*
*toast or creamed potatoes*
SAUCE:
*50 g/2 oz butter*
*1 medium onion, finely chopped*
*25 g/1 oz flour*
*150 ml/¼ pint lamb or chicken stock*
*scant 300 ml/scant ½ pint milk*
*salt and pepper*

First make the sauce: heat the butter in a saucepan, add the onion and cook gently for 2 to 3 minutes, blend in the flour, then gradually add the stock and milk. Bring the sauce to the boil, stir until thickened; season to taste.

Cut the lamb in neat pieces, the shape of the cooked meat will determine whether it looks more pleasant sliced or diced. Add to the sauce and heat gently for 5 to 10 minutes; leave the lid off the pan, so the sauce thickens slightly. Chop the egg whites and yolks separately; stir the chopped egg whites into the sauce with the cooked peas, parsley and cream. Heat for a further 2 to 3 minutes then serve in a border of crisp toast or creamed potatoes. Top with the chopped egg yolks.

## Lancashire Hotpot ⊛

*1.25 kg/2½ lb middle or scrag end of neck of lamb*
*salt and pepper*
*2 lambs' kidneys (optional)*
*2-3 carrots (optional), thinly sliced*
*1 small turnip (optional), thinly sliced*
*350 g/12 oz onions, thinly sliced*
*450 g/1 lb potatoes, sliced (weight when peeled)*
*300 ml/½ pint lamb or chicken stock*
*15 g/½ oz butter or margarine*
GARNISH:
*chopped parsley*

Hotpots happen to be a great favourite of mine. The method of cooking seems to retain the maximum flavour of the meat and vegetables. In this recipe I have added both carrots and turnips, as well as kidneys, but many people will say that a 'true' Lancashire Hotpot only consists of potatoes, onions and lamb.

The lamb should be divided into separate chops, if it has not been done by the butcher, do this yourself. Season the meat lightly. Skin the kidneys, remove any fat and gristle and chop finely. Mix the kidneys with the meat and the carrots and turnip with the onions.

Put layers of potato, mixed vegetables and meat in a casserole, beginning and ending with potatoes. Season the stock and pour over the other ingredients. Brush the top layer of potatoes with the melted butter or margarine. Cook in the centre of a cool oven (150°C/300°F or Gas Mark 2) for about 20 minutes without covering the casserole, this makes certain the lid will not stick to the potatoes, then cover and cook for a further 2 hours. You can lift the lid to brown the potatoes for the last 30 minutes. Top with parsley.

VARIATION
⊛ **Irish Hotpot:** Use Guinness instead of stock.

## Rice and Lamb Hotpot ⊛

*4 medium onions, thinly sliced*
*1 celery heart, chopped*
*1 x 425 g/15 oz can plum tomatoes with juice*
*salt and pepper*
*2 teaspoons sugar*
*50 g/2 oz long-grain rice*
*50 g/2 oz sultanas*
*4 large chump or 8 small best end of neck lamb chops*
*1 tablespoon lemon juice*
*celery salt*
*water, see method*
TOPPING:
*100 g/4 oz soft breadcrumbs*
*50 g/2 oz Cheddar cheese, grated*
*50 g/2 oz butter or margarine, melted*

Put half the onions, half the celery and half the well drained tomatoes into a large casserole. (There must be room for the rice to swell in cooking.) Add a little salt, pepper and half the sugar. Sprinkle half the rice over the vegetables, add half the sultanas then place the chops over this layer. Top the meat with the remainder of the rice and sultanas, then the rest of the onions, celery, tomatoes and sugar. Season lightly. Blend the lemon juice, a little celery salt and pepper with the tomato juice and enough water to make 300 ml/½ pint (if the tomato juice is insufficient). Pour over the ingredients in the casserole.

Cover the casserole and bake in the centre of a cool oven (150°C/300°F or Gas Mark 2) for 2 hours. Remove from the oven. Mix the topping ingredients together, sprinkle over the casserole; by this time the rice will have absorbed the liquid so the topping will keep firm. Do not cover. Return to the oven, raise the heat to moderate (180°C/350°F or Gas Mark 4) and cook for a further 30 minutes. Serve with a green vegetable.

## Lamb and Apple Hotpot ⊛

*8 best end of neck lamb chops*
*4 medium potatoes, thinly sliced*
*2 medium onions, thinly sliced*
*2 large dessert apples, peeled and thinly sliced*
*50 g/2 oz seedless raisins*
*150 ml/¼ pint chicken stock*
*150 ml¼ pint apple juice*
*salt and pepper*
*15 g/½ oz butter, melted*

Fry the chops, without additional fat, until golden on both sides. Put half the potatoes, then half the onions and half the apples into a casserole. Top with the meat, raisins and the remaining apple and onion slices. Arrange the rest of the potatoes in a neat design on top. Blend the stock, apple juice and salt and pepper together. Pour into the casserole. Brush the potatoes with the melted butter. Bake in the centre of a moderate oven (160°C/325°F or Gas Mark 3) for 1½ hours. Cover the casserole after the first 40 minutes of cooking time.

## Grilled Lamb

*Choose best end of neck chops or cutlets; chump chops; loin chops or cutlets; slices from the leg (escalopes)*

Lamb chops have a good amount of fat, so extra butter or oil is rarely necessary when grilling. Cutlets have had the fat trimmed away, so always brush the lean meat with a little melted butter or oil before and during cooking. Escalopes need a generous amount of butter. Pre-heat the grill and cook the meat quickly for 2 to 3 minutes on either side; lower the heat and cook more slowly until tender. Chops of about 5 cm/2 inches in thickness take about 15 minutes cooking; cutlets and escalopes a slightly shorter time, but this varies according to the quality of the meat and how well-cooked you like lamb; it can be served 'pink'.

VARIATION

**Fried Lamb:** If chops have a fair amount of fat simply heat gently for 2 minutes; allow the natural fat to flow; then raise the heat and fry quickly on either side to brown. After this reduce the heat and cook more slowly until tender. The timing is as for grilling. Use a reasonable amount of fat with cutlets and escalopes.

## Lamb Mornay

*4 large or 8 small lamb chops or cutlets*

TOPPING:

*75 g/3 oz cream cheese*
*2 tablespoons chopped parsley*
*1 teaspoon chopped rosemary*
*1 teaspoon chopped chives*

Grill the lamb chops or cutlets until just tender. Blend together the ingredients for the topping and spread over the chops. Return to the grill and cook for 2 to 3 minutes only until the topping has melted.

VARIATIONS

Use 75 g/3 oz grated Cheddar cheese with 1 tablespoon double cream to moisten, instead of cream cheese.

**Yogurt Topping:** Blend 150 ml/¼ pint yogurt with 2 tablespoons soft breadcrumbs, 2 tablespoons chopped parsley and 1 teaspoon chopped chives. Spread over the cooked chops and heat for 1 minute.

## Shish Kebab

*450 g/1 lb lamb, from the leg, cut in slices about 2.5 cm/1 inch thick*
*additional ingredients as method*

Dice the meat, thread on to long metal skewers with selected ingredients, such as small mushrooms, small tomatoes, diced red and green pepper, 1 or 2 bay leaves. Flavour a little melted butter or oil with chopped herbs or spices. Brush over the kebabs and grill as above or cook over a barbecue fire. Turn several times and baste well each time you turn the skewers.

## Lamb and Cucumber Sauce

*4 large or 8 small lamb chops or cutlets*
SAUCE:
*25 g/1 oz butter or margarine*
*1 small onion, finely chopped*
*½ small cucumber, peeled and neatly diced*
*150 ml/¼ pint milk or single cream*
*2 tablespoons yogurt*
*salt and pepper*
GARNISH:
*mint leaves*

Heat the butter or margarine, fry the onion and cucumber for a few minutes. Put into a liquidizer or food processor with the rest of the ingredients and make a smooth purée. Heat the sauce in a heatproof bowl over a pan of simmering water or in the top of a double saucepan.

Grill or fry the lamb chops or cutlets and serve with the sauce. Garnish with mint leaves.

VARIATION

**Lamb and Cold Cucumber Sauce:** Blend together ½ small peeled and grated cucumber, 2 tablespoons finely chopped spring onions, 2 teaspoons finely chopped mint and 150 ml/¼ pint soured cream. Add salt, pepper and a pinch of sugar to taste. This sauce can be liquidized or sieved but looks more pleasing with the pieces of cucumber and onion.

## Glazed Mint Chops

*salt and pepper*
*4 large or 8 small lamb chops*
*2-3 tablespoons redcurrant or apple jelly*
*2 teaspoons vinegar*
*1 tablespoon chopped mint*

Season the chops. Grill on both sides until almost cooked. Blend the jelly, vinegar and mint together. Spread over one side of the chops and complete the cooking, with the glazed side uppermost.

## Mustard Chops

*salt and pepper*
*4 large or 8 small lamb chops*
*2 tablespoons French mustard*
*¼ teaspoon dry mustard powder*
*2 teaspoons brown sugar*

Season the chops lightly. Grill for about 3 minutes on either side. Mix the French mustard, mustard powder and sugar together. Spread over one side of the chops and continue cooking with the mustard coated side uppermost.

## Saffron Escalopes

*4 thin escalopes of lamb, cut from the leg*
*2 teaspoons oil*
*salt*
MARINADE:
*good pinch saffron powder or few saffron strands*
*2 teaspoons boiling water*
*150 ml/¼ pint double cream*
*1 tablespoon lemon juice*
*1 small onion, grated*
*1 clove garlic, grated*
*good pinch black pepper*

Dissolve the saffron powder in the water; if using strands, infuse for about 15 minutes then strain and use the liquid. Blend this with the other marinade ingredients, pour into a dish, add the meat. Press the marinade into both sides of the escalopes and leave for some hours before cooking.

Brush the base of the grill pan with the oil and place the escalopes in this. Grill for about 5 minutes on either side, add a light sprinkling of salt just before serving. Any of the marinade ingredients left should be heated for just 1 minute before serving the meat.

VARIATION

**Glazed Escalopes of Lamb:** Marinate 4 escalopes of lamb in a mixture of 2 tablespoons red wine, 1 tablespoon oil, salt, pepper and 1 teaspoon chopped mint for several hours. Drain and fry in 50 g/2 oz hot fat or brush with melted fat or butter and grill until tender. Blend 2 tablespoons redcurrant jelly and 1 teaspoon chopped mint. Spread on one side of the cooked escalopes; heat for 2 minutes under the grill until the jelly melts, then serve.

## Goujons of Lamb

*450 g/1 lb lamb, from the leg, cut into 1 cm/½ inch slices*
COATING AND FRYING:
*salt and pepper*
*1 tablespoon flour*
*1 or 2 eggs*
*50 g/2 oz crisp breadcrumbs*
*oil or fat*

Cut each slice of lamb into narrow ribbons. Coat in the seasoned flour, then the beaten egg and crisp breadcrumbs. Press the crumbs firmly into the small pieces of meat, so they do not fall off in frying. It is always a good idea if you can chill coated goods in the refrigerator for a short time before frying.

Heat the oil or fat to 170°C/345°F (explanation of testing oil or fat is on page 290). Put in the pieces of meat and fry for about 6 minutes until crisp, golden brown and tender. Drain on absorbent paper. Serve with Tartare or Paloise Sauce.

## Preparing Noisettes

*allow 3 best end of neck of lamb chops or 2 to 3 loin chops per person*

Noisettes are quite similar to tournedos of steak in that they are formed from boned meat. Butchers will prepare these, but they are very simple. Cut the bone from the chops, remove all surplus fat, leave a slight margin of fat around the lean. Roll the meat into a neat round and secure with fine string or a skewer. Cook as cutlets.

## Lemon Noisettes

*8 noisettes of lamb*

TOPPING:

*25 g/1 oz butter, melted*
*1 clove garlic, crushed*
*1 teaspoon grated lemon rind*
*2 tablespoons lemon juice*
*75 g/3 oz soft breadcrumbs*
*salt and pepper*

Bake the noisettes of lamb in the centre of a moderately hot oven (190°C/375°F or Gas Mark 5) for 20 minutes.

Meanwhile blend together all the ingredients for the topping. Spread over the meat. Return to the oven and cook for a further 15 to 20 minutes. Do not cover the dish or tin, then the topping becomes pleasantly golden brown.

VARIATION

This topping is also delicious with veal chops.

## Noisettes of Lamb Béarnaise

*Béarnaise Sauce (see page 235)*
*8 lean loin or best end neck of lamb chops, boned*
*4 large slices bread*
*75 g/3 oz butter*

GARNISH:

*watercress*

Make the sauce and keep warm. Form the chops into neat rounds and tie or secure. Cut 8 rounds from the bread. Heat half the butter in a large frying pan. Fry the bread until crisp and golden on both sides; put on a heated dish. Heat the remaining butter and fry the lamb until tender. Put the noisettes on to the bread. Top with the sauce and arrange watercress around each noisette.

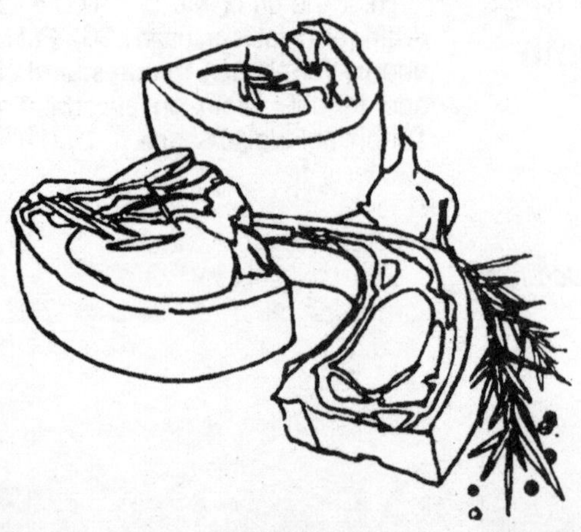

## Lamb in Ginger Cream Sauce ❄

*750 g/1½ lb lean lamb, cut from the leg and diced*
*2-3 teaspoons ground ginger*
*salt and pepper*
*25 g/1 oz butter*
*1 tablespoon oil*
*600 ml/1 pint chicken stock*
*few drops Tabasco sauce*
*25 g/1 oz ground almonds*
*4 tablespoons double cream*
*1-2 teaspoons cornflour (optional)*
GARNISH:
*25 g/1 oz flaked blanched almonds*

Sprinkle the diced lamb with the ground ginger and salt and pepper. Heat the butter and oil in a saucepan, fry the lamb for several minutes, turn over during this period. Reserve 4 tablespoons stock and pour the remainder into the saucepan; add the Tabasco sauce. Cover the saucepan, lower the heat and simmer gently for 45 minutes, or until the lamb is tender. The liquid should have evaporated by this time to just under 300 ml/½ pint; if there seems too much liquid remove the lid towards the end of the cooking time.

Blend the 4 tablespoons stock with the ground almonds and the cream, stir into the liquid in the pan; continue stirring until slightly thickened. Ground almonds do not thicken as much as cornflour or flour, so if you like a thicker sauce, add 1 to 2 teaspoons cornflour to the ground almonds when blending this with the stock. Top with the flaked almonds and serve with cooked rice.

## Mixed Grill

*Choose small chops; sausages; lambs' kidneys; fingers of steak; lambs' or calves' liver; bacon; tomatoes; mushrooms; eggs*
*melted butter*

The skill in producing a perfect mixed grill lies in cooking the foods in the right order, so everything is ready at the same time. You need to start by grilling the chops and sausages, then add the kidneys, then the steak, liver and bacon. Lean foods should be well brushed with melted butter. You can add the tomatoes and mushrooms too or fry these. The eggs are better fried.

## Deep Fried Lamb Chops

*4 lamb chops*
*salt and pepper*
*1 tablespoon flour*
*1 egg*
*50 g/2 oz crisp breadcrumbs*
*oil or fat for frying*

Although coated chops can be shallow fried, they cook better if deep fried. Coat the meat in seasoned flour, then with beaten egg and crisp breadcrumbs. Chill for a short time before frying.

Heat the oil or fat to 170°C/345°F (for an explanation of testing oil or fat see page 290). Fry the chops for about 8 minutes, until brown and tender. Drain on absorbent paper.

## Lamb Stroganoff

*25g/1 oz flour*
*salt and pepper*
*1 teaspoon curry powder*
*½ teaspoon dry mustard powder*
*500g/1 ¼ lb lean boneless lamb (cut from the leg), neatly diced*
*25g/1 oz butter*
*2 tablespoons oil*
*2 onions, sliced*
*100-175g/4-6 oz small button mushrooms*
*300 ml/½ pint pork or beef stock*
*1 tablespoon tomato purée*
*150 ml/¼ pint natural yogurt*
*2 tablespoons brandy or sherry*

Mix together the flour, salt, pepper, curry powder and mustard; coat the meat in this mixture. Heat the butter and oil in a good-sized frying pan, fry the meat and onions for 10 minutes, stirring all the time to prevent the food becoming too dark. Wipe the mushrooms, add to the meat, then stir in the stock and tomato purée. Cook gently for 5 to 6 minutes; add the yogurt and brandy or sherry. Heat without boiling for 5 minutes. Serve with a green salad.

VARIATION

**Beef Stroganoff:** While fillet steak can be used in the recipe above, instead of lamb, it does not produce such a good result as the following recipe.

Cut 450-500g/1-1 ¼ lb fillet steak into neat strips of about 2.5 cm/1 inch in length. Sprinkle with salt and pepper plus a little curry powder, (this is optional). Put on one side for about 1 hour, so the meat absorbs the flavourings. Slice 1 large onion very thinly, then cut each slice into 3 or 4 pieces. Thickly slice 100g/4 oz button mushrooms. Heat 100g/4 oz butter in a large frying pan, fry the onion and mushrooms until tender; add the steak and fry for 2 to 3 minutes only; do not over-cook. Blend in 1 tablespoon flour, then 300 ml/½ pint soured cream, 1 tablespoon tomato purée, ½ teaspoon French mustard. Heat gently and simmer until the steak is cooked to personal taste. Warm 1 to 2 tablespoons brandy, ignite if wished, add to the mixture above.

## Lamb Mornay ✻

*50g/2 oz butter*
*1 small onion, chopped*
*25g/1 oz flour*
*300 ml/½ pint milk*
*150 ml/¼ pint lamb stock*
*450g/1 lb cooked lamb*
*salt and pepper*
*½ teaspoon grated lemon rind*
*150g/5 oz Cheddar cheese, grated*
*3 tomatoes, sliced*
*50g/2 oz soft breadcrumbs*

Heat the butter in a saucepan, fry the onion until soft, stir in the flour and cook gently for 2 to 3 minutes. Blend in the milk and the lamb stock and stir as the sauce comes to the boil and thickens. Slice or dice the cooked lamb, choose whichever shape is suitable for the particular portion of lamb. Add to the sauce, with salt, pepper and the lemon rind. Heat gently but thoroughly. Lastly add 100g/4 oz grated cheese and stir over a low heat until the cheese has melted. Spoon into a heated flame-proof serving dish. Top with the tomato slices, breadcrumbs and remaining cheese. Heat under the grill for a few minutes.

## Roast Lamb ⊛

*These joints are suitable for faster or slower roasting*
*best end of neck (rack)*
*breast*
*leg*
*loin*
*saddle (2 loins)*
*shoulder*
WEIGHT TO ALLOW *per person when buying the meat:*
*350 g/12 oz if on bone*
*225-300 g/8-10 oz if boned*

Lamb joints have a good distribution of fat and lean, so extra fat is not necessary. While some people roast lamb from the frozen state, I have never been happy about this, I let it defrost thoroughly before roasting.

Lamb that has not been frozen and then defrosted or chilled can be roasted in a moderately hot to hot oven (200-220°C/400-425°F or Gas Mark 6-7). Allow 20 minutes per 450 g/1 lb plus 20 minutes, this gives lamb that is well, but not over-cooked. If you like lamb slightly pink, as you have it in France, then reduce the cooking time accordingly.

Lamb that has been frozen and then defrosted or chilled is better roasted in a moderate oven (160-180°C/325-350°F or Gas Mark 3-4).

Allow 35 minutes per 450 g/1 lb plus 35 minutes, or a very slightly shorter time if you like it pink. Mutton, rarely seen today, should be roasted at the lower temperature to give a tender joint.

If using a covered roasting tin or cooking the meat in foil, then allow about 10 to 15 minutes extra cooking time. No extra time is required when using the modern roaster bags.

Lamb is generally served with a thin gravy. Traditional accompaniments are given below.

## Mint Sauce

*a 150 ml/¼ pint measure of mint leaves, loosely packed*
*1-2 tablespoons sugar*
*3-4 tablespoons vinegar*

Chop the leaves with a little sugar on the board, put into a sauce boat. Add the rest of the sugar and the vinegar. While I choose wine vinegar for most purposes I think malt vinegar, white or brown, is better for this sauce. Nowadays most of us use a liquidizer or food processor for preparing this sauce.

Chop the mint leaves and pack in small containers. Freeze for winter use.

## Onion Sauce

*2 medium onions*
*salt and pepper*
*150 ml/¼ pint water*
*300 ml/½ pint White Sauce (see page 226)*

Simmer the onions until tender in the seasoned water. Lift from the water and chop finely on a plate so no juice is wasted. Add the onions and any juice on the plate to the White Sauce and heat.

# To Bone Meat

Most butchers will bone meat for you, if you give them sufficient notice. It is however not a difficult job to do yourself, but it does take time and patience. Use a firm sharp knife. Make a downwards cut until you feel the bone of the joint; turn the knife and gently cut away the meat from the bone or bones. It is particularly successful if you bone shoulder or leg of lamb, for it makes carving so much easier. When the bones have been removed the flesh can be spread out flat, a stuffing spread over it and the meat rolled around the stuffing.

## Apricot Shoulder ⊛

*1 shoulder of lamb*
*Dried Apricot Stuffing (see page 224)*

Bone the lamb as directed above. As shoulder of lamb is considered a difficult joint to carve, boning is of particular value. Insert the stuffing into the cavity made by the removal of the bones. Weigh the joint and roast as the timing on page 133. You will find you can carve neat slices which include both meat and stuffing.

## Crown Roast ⊛

*2 best end of neck or loin of lamb joints (you need a minimum of 12 to 14 chops)*
*Stuffing – for quantities and recipes, see pages 219, 221, 224*

This way of presenting the meat makes it look impressive for a special occasion. The butcher will make the meat into the crown, given a little notice. The chops are formed into a round, the ends of the bones are trimmed like cutlets. Protect the bones with foil, put the stuffing in the centre, weigh and roast as page 133. Decorate with cutlet frills when serving the meat.

## Herb Roasted Lamb ⊛

*1 leg lamb*
COATING:
*50 g/2 oz butter, melted*
*1 teaspoon French mustard*
*1 small onion, finely chopped*
*1 clove garlic, crushed*
*2 tablespoons chopped parsley*
*100 g/4 oz soft breadcrumbs*
*salt and pepper*

Roast the lamb following the timings on page 133. Take out of the oven 25 minutes before the end of the cooking time, if cooking in a moderately hot to hot oven, or 35 minutes if roasting at the lower temperature.

Blend all the ingredients for the coating together. Spread over the lamb. Return to the oven and complete cooking.

## Mutton Pies ⊛

*Shortcrust Pastry made with 350g/12oz flour, etc. (see page 291)*
FILLING:
*350g/12oz cooked mutton, minced or finely diced*
*75g/3oz currants*
*1 tablespoon brown sugar*
*1 large cooking apple, peeled and finely diced*
*25g/1oz soft breadcrumbs*
GLAZE:
*1 egg*

Make the pastry and roll out fairly thinly. Use just over half for the base of the pies. Cut into rounds and line about 8 deep patty tins with the pastry. Mix together all the ingredients for the filling and spoon into the patty tins. Roll out the remaining pastry and cut into rounds to cover the filling. Damp the edges of the pastry, put on the lids and seal firmly. Make a slit on top of each pie for the steam to escape, brush with the beaten egg and bake in the centre of a moderately hot oven (190°C/375°F or Gas Mark 5) for about 30 minutes, until the pastry is crisp and golden brown and the filling hot.

VARIATION

Lamb could be used instead of mutton. If choosing a tender cut, such as leg, you could use uncooked minced meat, but extend the cooking time by 10 minutes.

## Lamb en Croûte

*1 small leg of lamb, boned if possible (see page 134)*
*225g/8oz puff pastry (see page 292)*
*Liver and Mushroom Pâté, (see page 29), or bought pâté of a soft type*
GLAZE:
*1 egg*

Roast the lamb as for the Beef Wellington recipe on page 113, but take out of the oven just before the meat is cooked. Leave to cool. Make the pastry, roll out to an oblong shape sufficiently large to enclose the meat. Spread the pastry with the pâté, place the lamb joint on top, wrap in the pastry and seal well. Beat the egg and water together and brush over the pastry. Follow the cooking instructions for Beef Wellington (page 113).

## Lamb and Tomato Tarts

*9 to 12 baked patty cases*
*175g/6oz cooked lamb, minced*
*175g/6oz soft liver pâté*
*2 tomatoes, chopped*
*salt and pepper*
*9 to 12 tomato slices*
*40g/1½oz Cheddar cheese, grated*

Put the cooked pastry cases on to an ovenproof dish. Blend the lamb, pâté, chopped tomatoes and seasoning. Put into the pastry cases just before heating so the soft filling does not spoil the pastry. Top each tart with a tomato slice and then a layer of grated cheese. Heat towards the top of a moderately hot oven (200°C/400°F or Gas Mark 6) for a few minutes. Serve hot.

# Cooking Pork

It has been said that the only part of a pig that cannot be eaten is its squeak. Pork has such a definite flavour that dishes based upon this meat are full of character; but because pork has a fairly high percentage of natural fat you must be sparing with the amount of additional fat used in cooking. Always cook pork using thoroughly good quality young pork, it should be pale pink in colour, with firm white fat. Dishes made with pork, as well as uncooked pork, freeze well.

## Haslet ⊛

*450g/1 lb bread (weight without crusts)*
*450g/1 lb pork, minced*
*2 onions, finely chopped*
*1-2 teaspoons chopped sage*
*salt and pepper*

Put the bread into a basin, pour cold water over to cover and leave to soak for about 15 minutes, or until just softened. Drain off the liquid, squeeze the bread to make sure it is as dry as possible, them mix with the other ingredients. Wrap in a greased sheet of foil, forming it into a good shape as you do so. Stand on a baking tray and cook in the centre of a moderate oven (180°C/350°F or Gas Mark 4) for 1 hour. Serve hot or cold.

## Nasi Goreng ⊛

*175g/6oz long-grain rice*
*350ml/12fl oz water*
*salt and pepper*
*3 tablespoons oil*
*2 medium onions, finely chopped*
*350g/12oz lean pork, cut into narrow strips*
*175g/6oz pigs' liver, cut into narrow strips*
*50g/2oz sultanas*
*1 tablespoon soy sauce*
*50-75g/2-3oz peeled shrimps or prawns*
OMELETTE:
*2 eggs*
*½ tablespoon water*
*25g/1oz butter*

In order to fry the rice for this dish it must be cooked first. Put the rice and cold water into a saucepan, add the salt. Bring the water to the boil, stir briskly with a fork, cover the saucepan and allow the water to simmer for 15 minutes, or until the rice is tender. At the end of this time, the rice should have absorbed all the liquid. For this particular recipe, you should rinse the rice in cold water, spread it out flat and allow it to dry in the air. Heat half the oil and fry 1 onion until soft then add the rice and turn in the hot oil and onion until pale golden in colour.

While the rice is being fried, prepare the meat mixture. Fry the second onion in the remaining oil, add the pork and liver with a little seasoning; cook until tender. Add the sultanas, soy sauce and shrimps or prawns.

Heat the pork mixture, but do not over-cook, for the shellfish would toughen. Spoon the rice into an attractive dish, top with the meat mixture. Keep hot while making the omelette. Beat the eggs with the water, salt and pepper. Heat the butter in the omelette pan, pour in the eggs, cook until set. Put the omelette over the meat mixture.

## Pork Casserole ⊛

*175g/6oz fine noodles*
*salt and pepper*
*450g/1 lb cooked pork, minced*
*50g/2oz butter or pork fat*
*2 medium onions, chopped*
*3 medium tomatoes, skinned and chopped*
*25g/1 oz flour*
*450ml/¾ pint fat-free pork stock*
*2 tablespoons chopped parsley*

TOPPING:
*75g/3oz fairly coarse soft breadcrumbs*

Cook the noodles in boiling salted water until nearly, but not quite, soft. Strain and mix with the pork. Heat the butter or pork fat in a saucepan, fry the onions until nearly tender, then add the tomatoes and continue cooking for a few minutes. Blend in the flour, then gradually add the pork stock and stir as the mixture comes to the boil and thickens. Add the parsley and season well.

Put the noodle and pork mixture into a casserole, top with the sauce. Cover the casserole and cook in the centre of a moderate oven (180°C/350°F or Gas Mark 4) for 25 minutes. Remove from the oven, take off the lid, sprinkle the breadcrumbs on top. Do not cover the casserole. Replace this in the oven and cook for a further 15 to 20 minutes until the breadcrumbs become golden brown.

## Pork Meat Loaf ⊛

*50g/2oz lentils, cooked (see page 265)*
*25g/1 oz fat*
*1 medium onion, chopped*
*1 small dessert apple, peeled and chopped*
*450g/1 lb lean pork, minced*
*1 teaspoon finely chopped sage*
*salt and pepper*
*4 tablespoons milk*
*2 eggs*

Make sure the lentils are not too damp; they should be cooked until they have absorbed all the liquid. Heat the fat, cook the onion and apple until soft, then blend all the ingredients together. Grease a 1 kg/2 lb loaf tin well, put in the mixture. Cover with greased foil and stand in a tin of cold water (a bain-marie). Bake in the centre of a moderate oven (160°C/325°F or Gas Mark 3) for 1½ hours. Serve hot with vegetables or place a light weight on top of the tin and allow the loaf to cool, then turn out and serve with salad.

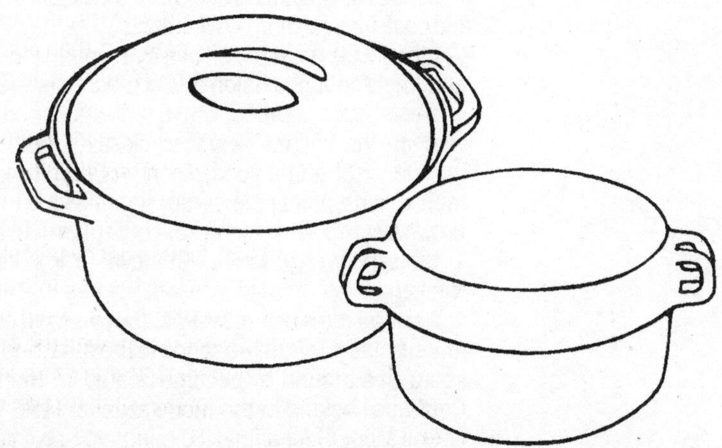

## Curried Spare Ribs

*1.75 kg/4-4¼ lb pork spare ribs*
*1 tablespoon vinegar*
*salt and pepper*
SAUCE:
*2 tablespoons oil*
*450 g/1 lb onions, thinly sliced*
*1 tablespoon curry powder*
*1 teaspoon turmeric*
*3 tablespoons sieved apricot jam*
*1 tablespoon vinegar*
*300 ml/½ pint chicken stock*

Explain to the butcher the kind of dish you are preparing and ask him to cut the spare ribs into neat pieces. Put into a saucepan with cold water to cover. Add the vinegar, salt and pepper. Bring the liquid to simmering point, lower the heat and simmer for 15 minutes; strain and discard the liquid.

Put the spare ribs into a roasting tin and cook in the centre of a hot oven (220°C/425°F or Gas Mark 7) for 15 minutes.

Meanwhile heat the oil in a large frying pan, add the onions and cook gently until nearly tender. Blend in the curry powder and turmeric; cook for 2 to 3 minutes, then stir in the remaining ingredients. Pour over the spare ribs in the roasting tin; lower the heat to moderate (180°C/350°F or Gas Mark 4) and continue to cook for a further 40 minutes. Do not cover the roasting tin. Baste the spare ribs once or twice with the sauce during the cooking period. Serve either as a starter or as a main dish with green salad.

VARIATION

**Barbecued Spare Ribs:** Prepare the spare ribs as the first stage in the recipe above but flavour the liquid in which they are simmered with 1 peeled onion, 1 clove garlic and a pinch of ground ginger. Increase the cooking time to 25 minutes. Strain and reserve 150 ml/¼ pint of the liquid. Dry the spare ribs well for this particular dish as they must be well coated with the sauce and need to become very crisp in the oven. Roast the meat in a hot oven, as indicated above, but increase the roasting time at this stage to 25 minutes. Turn the meat once during this time. Lower the heat to moderate and cook for a further 10 minutes.

Meanwhile, heat the oil in a frying pan; add 1 peeled and finely chopped onion and cook until tender. Blend 1½ teaspoons cornflour with 6 tablespoons brown malt vinegar, the 150 ml/¼ pint stock saved from simmering the meat and a good pinch ground ginger. Add 4 tablespoons pineapple syrup, 1 tablespoon honey or brown sugar, 1 tablespoon apricot or plum jam and ½ to 1 tablespoon soy sauce. Stir over a low heat until thickened.

Remove the roasting tin from the oven and pour away any surplus fat. Add the sauce to the meat and turn the spare ribs around to become coated in the mixture. Continue cooking in the moderate over (180°C/350°F or Gas Mark 4) for a final 10 minutes. Serve any sauce left with the spare ribs.

## Sweet and Sour Spare Ribs

*2 kg/4½ lb spare ribs of pork, cut into portions*
*2 onions, 1 left whole, 1 chopped*
*1 clove garlic*
*ground ginger*
*3 tablespoons oil*
*1½ teaspoons cornflour*
*6 tablespoons brown malt vinegar*
*150 ml/¼ pint pork stock, see method*
*4 tablespoons sweetened pineapple syrup*
*1 tablespoon brown sugar*
*1 tablespoon plum jam*
*1 tablespoon soy sauce*
*salt and pepper*

Ask the butcher for spare ribs of pork with only a limited amount of meat. Put into a saucepan and cover with water. Add the whole onion and whole garlic with a pinch of ground ginger. Simmer for 25 minutes then strain the ribs and dry on absorbent paper. Reserve 150 ml/¼ pint of the stock.

Heat 1 tablespoon of the oil in a pan, add the chopped onion and turn around in the oil. Blend the cornflour and ½ teaspoon ground ginger with the vinegar and the 150 ml/¼ pint of stock. Pour over the onion with the pineapple syrup, sugar, plum jam and soy sauce. Stir over a low heat until thickened, add salt and pepper to taste. Heat remaining oil in a roasting tin and cook the ribs in the centre of a hot oven (220°C/425°F or Gas Mark 7) for 20 minutes. Pour away any surplus oil from the tin, lower the heat to moderate (160°C/325°F or Gas Mark 3) and cook the ribs for 10 minutes. Add the sauce, turn the ribs in this until evenly coated and continue cooking for a further 10 minutes.

## Braised Pork Chops ⊛

*4 large lean pork chops, with rind removed*
MIREPOIX:
*25 g/1 oz fat*
*2 onions, chopped*
*1 leek, chopped*
*2 sticks celery, chopped*
*3 tomatoes, chopped*
*3 tablespoons red wine*
*salt and pepper*

Heat the fat and fry the vegetables for a few minutes, then put into a casserole with the red wine and seasoning. Fry the pork chops until brown on both sides and place over the mirepoix. Cover the casserole tightly and put into the centre of a moderate oven (180°C/350°F or Gas Mark 4). Cook for 1 hour, then remove the lid and move the dish towards the top of the oven; the heat can be slightly raised. Continue cooking for a further 10 to 15 minutes to crisp the top of the chops. Sieve the mirepoix and serve as a sauce.

## Pork Meat Balls ⊛

*ingredients as given in Køttbuller (see page 105) but use all lean pork instead of beef and pork or bacon*

Pork is an ideal meat for meat balls, as it has plenty of flavour, but care must be taken to keep the mixture from being over-rich. Be a little sparing with the butter and oil when frying the meat balls and instead of using milk and cream for the sauce use milk and stock. The variation given on page 105 is also suitable when using pork.

## Grilled Pork

*Choose chump chops; loin chops or cutlets; spare rib chops; slices from the leg (escalopes)*

Grilling is one of the best ways of cooking pork, for the intense heat of a grill enables any excess fat to run away into the grill pan. Remove the rind from the meat, cut the fat at regular intervals to encourage it to crisp. Extra butter or fat is not required when grilling pork chops or cutlets, as even the cutlet has a little natural fat. If you grill slices from the leg (escalopes) of pork, though, you need to baste the meat with a little melted fat before and during cooking.

Pre-heat the grill and cook the meat for about 5 minutes steadily on either side, then lower the heat and cook more slowly. Pork chops about 2.5 cm/1 inch in thickness need about 20 minutes cooking time; cutlets and escalopes slightly less, but pork must be completely cooked and should never be served underdone.

## Pork Escalopes

*slices from the leg of pork*

When veal is not obtainable, you can use very thin slices of lean pork in any recipe where veal escalopes are normally used. Modern methods of breeding pork have produced deliciously tender lean meat. Use nearly, but not quite, as much fat in cooking.

## Crisp Orange Pork

*4 pork chops*

MARINADE:

*150 ml/¼ pint orange juice*
*1 tablespoon oil*
*1 teaspoon chopped parsley*
*1 teaspoon chopped chives*
*¼ teaspoon chopped sage*
*¼ teaspoon chopped tarragon*
*salt and pepper*

TOPPING:

*50 g/2 oz soft breadcrumbs*
*25 g/1 oz butter, melted*
*1 teaspoon grated orange rind*
*1 tablespoon chopped parsley*

Blend together the ingredients for the marinade. Put into a large dish. Remove the rind from the chops, add to the marinade and leave for 2 to 3 hours; turn once or twice. Remove from the liquid; drain and grill until almost, but not quite, tender. This will take 9 to 10 minutes. Brush the meat with any marinade left as it cooks and when turned over during cooking.

Mix together the ingredients for the topping and spread over the surface of each chop. Return to the grill and continue cooking until the topping is crisp and golden and the meat absolutely tender.

VARIATION

The meat can be baked instead of being grilled; allow approximately 25 minutes in an uncovered dish towards the top of a moderately hot oven (200°C/400°F or Gas Mark 6). Turn the meat once during cooking and baste with any marinade left. Top with the crumb mixture and continue cooking for a further 10 minutes.

## Pork Chops in Red Wine Sauce ⊛

*4 pork chops*
*25 g/1 oz fat*
*1 tablespoon flour*
*6 tablespoons red wine*
*6 tablespoons chicken or pork stock*
*2 tablespoons redcurrant jelly*
*¼ teaspoon chopped sage*
*25 g/1 oz blanched almonds*

Cut away the rind from the chops. Heat the fat in a pan and fry the chops on either side until tender. This will take approximately 12 to 15 minutes. Lift the chops on to a heated dish; pour away any surplus fat, but leave just 1 tablespoon in the pan. Blend the flour into this fat, then gradually add the wine, stock and jelly. Stir until the jelly melts and the sauce thickens slightly, then add the sage and almonds. Spoon over the meat and serve.

VARIATION

⊛ **Normandy Chops:** Core, but do not peel, 2 to 3 dessert apples; cut each apple into several thin rings. Use double the amount of fat and fry the apple rings with the chops until the meat and fruit are tender. Arrange the apple rings round the meat. Blend the 1 tablespoon flour with 1 tablespoon of fat left in the pan; gradually blend in either all apple juice or a mixture of apple juice and stock, or use mostly apple juice plus 1 tablespoon Calvados (apple brandy) together with 2 tablespoons redcurrant or apple jelly. The total amount of liquid should be as in the basic recipe. Stir until thickened and smooth. Spoon over the meat and top with chopped chives or parsley.

## Cutlets of Pork à la Charcuterie

*Brown Sauce (see page 230)*
*3 tablespoons white wine*
*50 g/2 oz gherkins, chopped*
*1 teaspoon French mustard*
*salt and pepper*
*8 pork cutlets*
*8 slices black pudding*
*2 small cooking apples, cored and sliced*
*little lard (optional)*
*1 onion, chopped*
*1 clove garlic, chopped*
*1 tablespoon chopped parsley*
*1 tablespoon vinegar*

This classic French dish was named after the French butchers who sell such excellent pork products. The basic recipe consists of the excellent sauce, made as below, served with pork cutlets. Since I have a great fondness for black pudding (from most countries) I have included this; you can of course omit it and the apples.

Make the Brown Sauce, add the wine, gherkins and mustard and keep hot. Season the cutlets and fry in a greased pan until tender; lift on to a hot dish. Add the sliced black pudding and fry in any fat left in the pan together with the thinly sliced apple. Put round the chops. If no fat remains in the pan, add a little lard and fry the onion and garlic until tender. Add this to the sauce mixture with the parsley and vinegar. Serve with the pork chops and black pudding.

## Fried Pork

*Choose: chump chops; loin chops or cutlets; spare rib chops; slices from the leg (escalopes)*

Although pork chops have natural fat, it is advisable to grease the frying pan, for it takes a little time for the fat to flow from the meat. Fry the chops fairly quickly on either side for about 5 minutes then lower the heat and cook more slowly. Chops or cutlets about 2.5 cm/1 inch in thickness take about 20 minutes total cooking time. For frying escalopes see page 140.

## Stuffed Pork Escalopes

*4 slices pork fillet, about 1 cm/½ inch in thickness*
STUFFING:
*25 g/1 oz butter*
*1 small onion, finely chopped*
*2 bacon rashers, derinded and finely chopped*
*50 g/2 oz mushrooms, finely chopped*
*50 g/2 oz soft breadcrumbs*
*2 tablespoons chopped parsley*
*salt and pepper*
COATING AND FRYING:
*25 g/1 oz flour*
*50 g/2 oz butter*
*1 tablespoon oil*
GARNISH:
*4 lemon slices*
*1 tablespoon chopped parsley*

Slit each fillet of pork horizontally to make a good pocket. Heat the 25 g/ oz butter and fry the onion, bacon and mushrooms together until the vegetables are soft. Blend with the other ingredients for the stuffing. Carefully insert into the pockets in the meat.

Blend the flour with a little salt and pepper, coat the meat in this. Heat the 50 g/2 oz butter with the oil in a large frying pan. Fry the pork for 2 to 3 minutes on either side; lower the heat and cook for a further 7 to 8 minutes; turn once during this time. Serve topped with the lemon and parsley.

VARIATION

**Prune and Apple Escalopes:** Peel and grate 1 large cooking apple; blend with 175 g/6 oz cooked, stoned and chopped prunes, a pinch dried sage and salt and pepper to taste. Insert into the pockets of the fillets of pork, as described above. Coat in flour, then beaten egg and crisp breadcrumbs. Fry as above until crisp and golden brown. Drain on absorbent paper. Garnish each portion with a cooked prune and parsley.

## Rice Stuffed Pork

STUFFING:
*25 g/1 oz butter or margarine*
*1 large onion, peeled and chopped*
*2 large tomatoes, skinned chopped*
*1 small green pepper, deseeded and diced*
*50 g/2 oz cooked rice*
*salt and pepper*
*1 teaspoon chopped fresh, or ¼ teaspoon dried, sage*
*4 thick pork chops*
*little butter*

Heat the butter or margarine in a pan and cook the onion until nearly tender. Add the tomatoes and pepper then continue cooking for a further 5 minutes. Stir in the rice, add the salt, pepper and sage.

Split each pork chop horizontally to form a pocket. Fill with the rice mixture, then wrap each chop in buttered foil. Place on a baking tray and cook in the centre of a moderately hot oven (190 to 200°C/375 to 400°F or Gas Mark 5 to 6) for 45 minutes.

## Sweet and Sour Pork Kebabs

*450g/1 lb lean pork, cut into 2.5 cm/1 inch cubes*
*8 very small onions, peeled but left whole*
*2-3 dessert apples, cored but not peeled*
MARINADE:
*150ml/¼ pint orange juice*
*2 teaspoons made mustard*
*50g/2 oz brown sugar*
*2 tablespoons lemon juice*
*1-2 cloves garlic crushed*
*2 tablespoons oil*
*salt and pepper*

Mix together all the ingredients for the marinade. Put into a large dish. Add the diced pork and leave in the marinade for at least 2 hours; turn once or twice.

Simmer the onions for about 10 minutes in salted water; strain and add to the marinade. Cut each apple into about 6 thick wedges. Add to the marinade.

Lift the foods from the marinade and thread on to 4 long metal skewers. Hold over the dish so any liquid drops back into the container. Put under a pre-heated grill and cook for about 12 minutes. Turn once or twice and baste with the marinade each time you turn the skewers. Serve with cooked rice.

VARIATION

**Simple Pork Kebabs:** Dice the pork, as in the basic recipe, put on to skewers with diced red and green pepper – discard the cores and seeds. Add wedges of dessert apple, dipped in lemon juice to maintain the colour. Melt 40g/1½oz butter, add a little salt and pepper and dried sage. Brush the food with the flavoured butter before and during cooking. Grill as above.

## Maiale allo Spiedo

*450g/1 lb lean pork, cut into 2.5cm/1 inch dice*
*225g/8 oz bread (weight without crusts), cut into 2.5cm/1 inch dice*
*225g/8 oz lean gammon, cut into 2.5cm/1 inch dice*
*8 bay leaves*
*salt and pepper*
*little olive oil*

Put the various ingredients on to 4 metal skewers. Season well and brush with olive oil. Pay particular attention to the cubes of bread, for they must get very crisp and brown in cooking.

Either cook under a pre-heated grill, or over a barbecue fire or in the oven. If cooking in the oven, without a rotating spit, suspend the skewers over a tin. The kebabs will take 10 to 15 minutes under the grill or over the barbecue; turn several times and baste with oil. If using the oven allow about 25 minutes in the centre of a moderately hot oven (200°C/400°F or Gas Mark 6). Turn once.

VARIATIONS

Prosciutto is often served instead of gammon; form the thin raw Parma ham into neat rolls. Add small onions to the skewers, par-boil until nearly cooked first.

## Hungarian Style Pork

*350 g/12 oz sauerkraut*
*salt and pepper*
*50 g/2 oz fat*
*3 medium onions, thinly sliced*
*1 small red pepper, deseeded and diced*
*150 ml/¼ pint soured cream*
*4 small pork chops*
*4 rashers bacon, derinded*
*4 pork sausages*

Rinse the sauerkraut in plenty of cold water, then drain well. Cook in a small amount of water with salt and pepper to taste for 25 minutes, then strain. Meanwhile, heat the fat and fry the onions and red pepper for several minutes, blend with the cooked sauerkraut and the soured cream. Put into a wide ovenproof dish, top with the pork chops. Bake towards the top of a moderately hot oven (190°C/375°F or Gas Mark 5) for 25 minutes. If you like pork chops brown and crisp, do not cover the dish during this period, but it is important that the meat covers the sauerkraut layer, otherwise this will dry and burn. If you prefer the meat more moist, cover the dish with a lid or foil.

Remove the dish from the oven, re-arrange the meat, add the bacon and sausages and continue cooking for a further 20 to 25 minutes. Turn the sausages during this time so they brown on all sides.

Note: if the dish is not sufficiently large in size to accommodate all the meats, then cook the sausages separately; it is important to cook the pork and bacon over the vegetables to give these flavour.

## Roast Suckling Pig

*1 suckling pig*
*Sage and Onion Stuffing (see page 145)*
*little fat*
GARNISH:
*1 red apple*
*redcurrant jelly or glacé cherries*
*parsley*

Most countries serve this delicacy for a special celebration. The butcher will clean the young pig throughout and remove all the bones, except those in the legs, which give form to the joint. Fill the pig with stuffing, weigh and roast following the timings on page 145. Keep well basted with hot fat; prick any bubbles that may form in the skin, so this has a smooth surface at the end of the cooking time. When cooked, put a rosy apple in the mouth; redcurrant jelly or glacé cherries in the eyes and garnish with parsley.

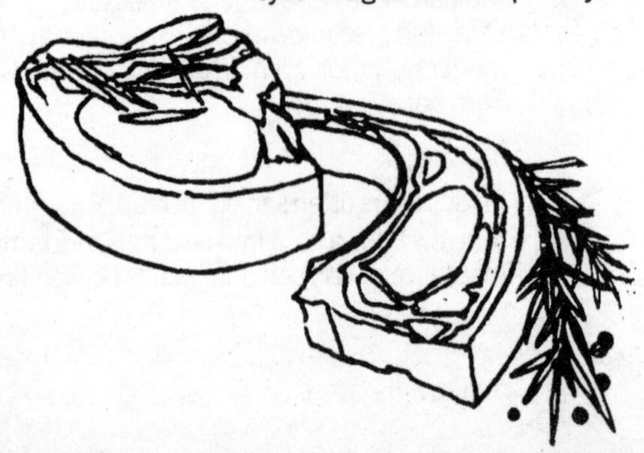

## Roast Pork ⊛

*These joints are suitable for roasting –*
PRIME JOINTS:
*blade bone*
*fillet*
*leg*
*loin*
*spare-rib*
CHEAPER JOINTS:
*belly of pork*
*hand and spring*

*little lard, melted or oil*
*salt (optional)*
WEIGHT TO ALLOW *per person when buying the meat:*
*350 g/12 oz if on bone*
*225-300 g/8-10 oz if boned*

Remove any skin from the meat and score the fat (cut it at regular intervals) if the butcher has not done this. Brush the fat with the lard or oil; sprinkle lightly with a little salt (this is not essential but helps to crisp the fat, by drawing out surplus moisture). If your meat tin has a rack (trivet) stand the meat on this so any surplus fat runs into the meat tin. Do not cover the meat. Roast as timing below.

Pork is a meat that should be well-cooked; never serve it under-cooked. Always defrost thoroughly before roasting.

Prime quality pork which has not been frozen and then defrosted or chilled can be roasted in a moderately hot to hot oven (200-220°C/400-425°F or Gas Mark 6 to 7). Allow 25 minutes per 450 g/1 lb plus 25 minutes over. The heat can be reduced after the first 1 hour. You can of course always use the lower setting below.

Cheaper cuts of pork, or pork which has been frozen then defrosted or chilled is better roasted in a moderate oven (160-180°C/325-350°F or Gas Mark 3 to 4). Allow 40 minutes per 450 g/1 lb plus 40 minutes.

Remember if you are putting the stuffing in the meat you must weigh the joint after stuffing to calculate the total cooking time.

Serve with a thickened gravy. Traditional accompaniments are given below.

## Apple Sauce ⊛

*450 g/1 lb apples, peeled and thinly sliced*
*2 tablespoons water*
*25-50 g/1-2 oz sugar*
*25 g/1 oz butter (optional)*

Simmer the apples with the water, sugar and butter until a soft purée. Sieve or liquidize if wished. There are several interesting variations of this sauce on page 237.

## Sage and Onion Stuffing ⊛

*350 g/12 oz onions*
*salt and pepper*
*50 g/2 oz butter, melted*
*75 g/3 oz soft breadcrumbs*
*2 teaspoons chopped sage*
*1 egg (optional)*

Simmer the onions in a little water with seasoning for 15 minutes, strain and chop. Mix with the rest of the ingredients. Bind with an egg or onion stock (which I prefer), for it gives a lighter stuffing. Use any stock left in the gravy. See another variation on page 219 and baking times page 218.

## Loin of Pork with Prunes ⊛

*175g/6oz dried prunes*
*450ml/¾pint red wine*
*sugar to taste*
*loin of pork*

Soak the prunes overnight in the wine, then simmer gently in a covered saucepan until tender, but not over-soft; add sugar to taste. Roast the pork as page 145. Remove the tin from the oven about 25 minutes before the end of the roasting time; pour out all the surplus fat. Add the prunes and wine and baste the meat with the liquid, then return to the oven and complete the cooking. Use the wine in the gravy to serve with the pork.

## Roast Pork Flamande ⊛

*1.5kg/3lb loin of pork*
*oil or fat, melted*
*salt and pepper*
*750g/1½lb good-sized potatoes*
*1 small red cabbage*
*2 tablespoons red wine vinegar*
*2 cooking apples, thinly sliced*
*100g/4oz sugar*
*450g/1lb small sharp plums*
*4 tablespoons water*

Have the loin of pork boned, but retain both the bones and the skin of the meat. Score the fat and brush with oil or melted fat, as instructions on page 145. Put into the roasting tin and surround with the well seasoned potatoes. Top these with the pork bones and skin and roast as on page 145; use the higher temperature to ensure crisp potatoes.

Meanwhile shred the red cabbage, put into a casserole with the vinegar, salt and pepper. Cover very tightly and cook for 30 minutes in the coolest part of the oven. Add the apples and 25g/1oz sugar and complete the cooking.

Simmer the plums with the water and the rest of the sugar until soft. Serve with the pork and cabbage.

VARIATION
The cabbage could be shredded and cooked in a little salted water with the vinegar to taste: drain and mix with lightly fried sliced apples.

## Pork in Cider ⊛

*joint of pork*
*600ml/1pint sweet cider*

Put the pork into the roasting tin, add the cider; and cover the tin with a lid or with foil. Roast as page 145, but baste several times with cider. You do not get crisp crackling, but a delicious flavour to the meat. Use the cider in the gravy.

## Pork Pie ⊛

*Hot Water Crust Pastry, made with 350g/12oz flour, etc.* *(see page 160)*

FILLING:

*750g/1½lb lean pork, finely diced*

*100g/4oz fat pork, finely diced*

*¼ teaspoon dried sage*

*salt and pepper*

*7 tablespoons pork or white stock*

GLAZE:

*1 egg*

*1 teaspoon gelatine*

Make the pastry as the instructions on page 160. Either line an 18-20cm/7-8inch tin (use one with a loose base) with two-thirds of the pastry or mould this, as described on page 160. Mix together the pork, sage, seasoning and 3 tablespoons stock; put into the pastry. Roll out the remaining pastry and cover the filling, see page 160. Brush with the beaten egg and bake the pie as Veal and Ham Pie on page 160. Allow to become quite cold.

Dissolve the gelatine in the remaining stock, allow this to cool, but not to set, then carefully pour into the pie. Leave until the jelly is firm before cutting the pie.

## Sausages in Apples

*4 large sausages*

*4 large cooking apples, cored*

The sausages can be skinned if desired, press in the centre of each apple, score the skin of the apples to prevent them bursting. Bake in the centre of a moderate oven (180°C/350°F or Gas Mark 4) for 1 hour.

## Toad in the Hole

*25g/1oz fat*

*450g/1lb sausages*

*Pancake Batter* *(see page 289)*

Heat the fat in a good sized tin or ovenproof serving dish. Add the sausages and cook just above the centre of a hot oven (220°C/425°F or Gas Mark 7) for 10 minutes. Pour the batter over the sausages and continue cooking for 30 minutes or until well risen, crisp and brown. Reduce the heat slightly after about 20 minutes.

# Cooking Bacon

Now that many people do not have bacon for breakfast, except perhaps when they are on holiday, I find this food has become a very popular dish for main meals. If grilling bacon, do not pre-heat the grill first; this makes the fat of thick or thin slices or rashers curl and burn before the lean part is cooked. Remember that gammon is not only the most luxurious cut of bacon but the leanest too; the lean part should be brushed with a little melted butter or margarine or an oil mixture, as in a marinade, before and during cooking.

## Grilled Bacon

*Choose: back, gammon, streaky rashers*
*melted butter*

Do not preheat the grill before cooking bacon. Allow 2 to 3 minutes cooking time for thin rashers; about 15 minutes for thick gammon slices. Snip the fat of gammon at regular intervals before grilling or frying to encourage it to crisp and brush the lean part with melted butter before and during cooking.

VARIATION

**Fried Bacon:** Do not preheat the frying pan. Arrange the bacon so the lean of the second rasher is placed over the fat of the first rasher. In this way you prevent the bacon burning or sticking to the pan. When frying gammon melt a little butter or fat in the pan before adding the gammon. Cooking times as for grilling.

## Boiled Bacon

*Choose: collar, forehock or gammon joints*

Follow the directions for Boiled Beef on page 109. Soak cured bacon overnight in cold water to cover but 'green' (mild cure) or sweet-cure bacon does not require soaking. Allow 20 to 25 minutes per 450 g/1 lb plus 20 to 25 minutes over for gammon; 35 to 40 minutes per 450 g/1 lb and 35 to 40 minutes over for collar or forehock.

VARIATON

**Glazed Bacon:** Remove the bacon from the pan 25 to 30 minutes before the end of the cooking time; remove the rind and score the fat. Brush with honey or brown sugar or syrup. This can be mixed with made mustard or spices and fruit juice. Complete the cooking in a moderate oven (180°C/350°F or Gas Mark 4).

## Bacon Casserole ⊛

*750g-1 kg/1½-2 lb collar or forehock of bacon*
*1 bay leaf*
*small bunch parsley*
*12 small carrots*
*12 very small onions*
*pepper*
*little salt, if required*
*few frozen peas*
*little canned sweetcorn*

If the bacon is salt, cover this with cold water and leave to soak overnight or for some hours. Drain and discard this water; sweet-cure or very mild (green) bacon does not need soaking. Put the bacon into a casserole, cover with fresh water, add the herbs. Cover and cook in the centre of a moderate oven (160°C/325°F or Gas Mark 3) for 30 minutes. Add the whole carrots and onions and continue cooking. The pepper could be added then but it is wiser to add the salt just before the end of the cooking time. Cook for a further 50 minutes to 1 hour then add the peas and sweetcorn and complete the cooking for 15 to 30 minutes, depending upon the weight of the bacon. The liquid in this casserole is not generally thickened, but if preferred you could dish up the bacon and vegetables, remove the herbs and then thicken the liquid with cornflour blended with a small amount of dry sherry.

VARIATIONS

Use cider or ginger ale in place of part of the water or instead of water in cooking the bacon.

Choose gammon in place of the cheaper cuts suggested; in this case cook for 30 minutes per 450g/1 lb and 30 minutes over.

## Stuffed Gammon

*4 thick gammon slices, about 1.5cm/¾ inch thick*
*50g/2 oz butter or margarine*

STUFFING:

*2 medium onions, thinly sliced*
*2 sticks celery, finely chopped*
*1 red pepper, deseeded and chopped*
*25g/1 oz breadcrumbs*
*1 tablespoon chopped parsley*
*½ teaspoon chopped sage*
*shake pepper*
*4 cocktail sticks*

Slit the gammon horizontally to make a pocket in each slice. Heat half the butter or margarine and fry the onions for 3 to 4 minutes, then add the celery and pepper. Continue cooking until tender but do not allow to brown. Blend with the rest of the stuffing ingredients. Push the stuffing into each pocket of the gammon, secure each piece with a wooden cocktail stick. Melt the remaining butter or margarine and brush the gammon with half of this. Cook under the grill for 4 to 5 minutes, turn carefully, then brush with the remaining butter or margarine and continue cooking until tender. It will be necessary to reduce the heat after 4 to 5 minutes so that the stuffing is cooked without the gammon over-browning. Remove the cocktail sticks and serve.

## Gammon with Prunes and Cider Sauce ⊛

*175 g/6 oz prunes*
*1.5 kg/3 lb gammon joint*
*1 bay leaf*
*little black pepper*
*450 ml/¾ pint dry cider*
*3 tablespoons brown sugar*
*1 teaspoon mixed spice*
*2 teaspoons cornflour*
*3 tablespoons redcurrant jelly*

Soak the prunes for 12 hours in cold water to cover – do not cook them. Soak the gammon in cold water to cover for the same time, unless mildly cured, ie, green or sweetcure bacon, when soaking for 12 hours is unnecessary. Simply rinse in cold water several times. Put the gammon into a saucepan with cold water to cover, add the bay leaf and pepper. Bring the water to simmering point, then cook for approximately 1¼ hours. Test the gammon at the end of an hour, for wide thinner joints or prime gammon are often tender if you allow 20 minutes per 450 g/1 lb. The bacon should not be over-cooked as it will also be placed in the oven for a short time, which also helps in tenderizing the meat.

Meanwhile drain the prunes, put into a saucepan with 300 ml/½ pint of the cider, 25 g/1 oz of the sugar and the spice. Cover the pan and simmer for about 30 minutes or until the prunes are tender but not over-soft.

Remove the skin from the gammon, score the fat, sprinkle with the remaining sugar and heat for about 10 minutes only, to melt the sugar, in a moderately hot oven (200°C/400°F or Gas Mark 6).

Blend the cornflour with the remaining cider. Add to the prunes and liquid with the redcurrant jelly. Stir over a moderate heat until clear and slightly thickened. Lift the prunes from the hot sauce and arrange around the gammon.

## Marinated Gammon

*4 gammon slices or thick rashers lean back bacon*
MARINADE:
*2 tablespoons honey*
*150 ml/¼ pint sweet cider*
*1 tablespoon white wine vinegar*
*1 clove garlic, crushed*
*1 tablespoon oil*
*shake pepper*

Mix together the ingredients for the marinade. Pour into a shallow dish. Add the gammon or bacon rashers and leave in the mixture for several hours. Turn once or twice. Lift the meat from the marinade, drain and cook over a barbecue fire or under a grill. Brush with any marinade that is left during the cooking period.

VARIATIONS
Add 2 tablespoons finely chopped onion to the mixture. This marinade is excellent with joints of chicken or pork chops.
**Orange Marinated Gammon:** Blend 2 tablespoons oil, 2 teaspoons finely grated orange rind and 4 tablespoons orange juice. Marinate the gammon in this and cook as above.

# Cooking Veal

Veal is less popular in Britain than in many other countries and you may experience difficulty sometimes in obtaining this meat. If you enjoy veal, as I do, then it is worth taking the trouble to find a good supplier.

Veal has virtually no natural fat so be generous in the amount you add to the meat in cooking.

Store veal carefully, as it spoils easily. Good veal should be pale pink in colour and any fat firm and white. It is the meat that I think freezes less well than any other, whether raw or cooked, it seems to lose some of its taste and texture.

## Osso Buco ⊛

*750 g/1½ lb stewing veal, neatly diced*
*salt and pepper*
*25 g/1 oz flour*
*50 g/2 oz butter*
*1 tablespoon oil*
*4-8 small onions*
*4 medium carrots, diced*
*4 tomatoes, skinned and chopped*
*3 sticks celery, chopped*
*bouquet garni*
*grated rind and juice of 1 lemon*
*300 ml/½ pint veal stock*
*300 ml/½ pint white wine or extra veal stock*
*1 tablespoon tomato purée*
GARNISH:
*chopped parsley*

Coat the veal in seasoned flour. Heat the butter and oil in a saucepan and fry the veal for several minutes. Remove from the pan, fry the whole onions, return the meat to the pan with the rest of the ingredients. Stir as the liquid comes to the boil, add any salt and pepper required. Cover the pan, lower the heat and simmer gently for 1½ hours, or until the meat is tender. Remove the bouquet garni. Serve with saffron flavoured rice (see page 300).

VARIATION

The above recipe might be termed an 'easy to eat' version of this well-known Italian dish. The traditional recipe is made with lovely glutinous knuckle of veal, with the meat on the bone. You will of course need at least twice the quantity of meat if using knuckle of veal, but the cooking method is the same. Knuckle is difficult to cut, so ask the butcher to cut it into 5 to 7.5 cm/2 to 3 inch pieces.

## Creamed Veal ⊛

*450 g/1 lb cooked veal*
*Béchamel Sauce (see page 227)*
*4 tablespoons double cream*
*50 g/2 oz butter*
*100 g/4 oz small mushrooms*
*2 tablespoons chopped parsley*

Cut the veal into small neat dice. Blend the sauce, veal and cream together. It is a good idea to heat these in the top of a double saucepan so there is no possibility of the sauce burning or sticking to the pan. Heat the butter in a frying pan, cook the mushrooms until tender, add to the veal mixture with the parsley. Serve with toast or vegetables.

## Goulash ⊛

*750g/1½lb tomatoes, use plum type if possible*
*150ml/¼pint water*
*salt and pepper*
*1 teaspoon sugar*
*500/1¼lb stewing veal, neatly diced*
*1 tablespoon paprika, sweet type*
*50g/2oz fat*
*350g/12oz onions, thinly sliced*
*450g/1 lb potatoes, thickly sliced*
GARNISH:
*yogurt*
*chopped parsley*

First cook the tomatoes with the water, salt, pepper and sugar until a soft purée. Sieve or liquidize if desired, although at this stage it is not important as the tomatoes break up during cooking.

Coat the meat with salt, pepper and paprika. Heat the fat in a pan and fry the meat with the onions – do this carefully for the paprika coating on the meat is easily burned. Blend in the cooked tomato pulp, stir well to mix this with the meat and onions and cover the pan. Simmer gently for 1½ hours or until the meat is becoming tender.

Check carefully that there is sufficient liquid during this cooking period and before proceeding to the next stage, which is to add the potatoes. Put the sliced potatoes into the meat mixture, stir to blend with the rest of the ingredients. This particular version of Goulash is a very thick one, but if you would rather have more liquid, add a little boiling water or stock when putting the potatoes into the pan. Adjust the seasoning, cover the saucepan and cook for a further 20 to 30 minutes. Top with the yogurt and parsley.

VARIATIONS

Use a mixture of meats rather than just one, an admirable blending is to use equal amounts of beef, stewing veal and very lean pork.

## Veal Florentine ⊛

*450g/1 lb spinach*
*salt and pepper*
*pinch grated nutmeg*
*50g/2oz butter*
*50g/2oz flour*
*300ml/½pint milk*
*150ml/¼pint single cream*
*450g/1 lb cooked lean veal, sliced*
*50g/2oz soft breadcrumbs*
*50g/2oz Cheddar cheese, grated*

Wash the spinach and cook in the water clinging to the leaves, add a little salt, pepper and nutmeg. When tender, strain and chop finely.

Heat the butter in a pan, stir in the flour and cook gently for 2 to 3 minutes. Gradually blend in the milk. Bring the sauce gently to the boil, stirring well as you do so. When thickened, blend in the cream and seasoning to taste. Mix 2 to 3 tablespoons with the spinach and put into an ovenproof serving dish. Top with the veal, the rest of the sauce, the breadcrumbs and grated cheese. Cook just above the centre of a moderately hot oven (190°C/375°F or Gas Mark 5) for 25 minutes.

VARIATION

⊛ **Veal in Orange Sauce:** Strangely enough, spinach blends well with the flavour of orange. Use white wine instead of milk and fresh orange juice instead of cream. Omit the cheese from the topping and use just breadcrumbs.

## Veal Olives ⊛

*4 slices veal, cut from the top of the leg (escalopes)*
STUFFING:
*175g/6oz fat bacon, derinded and finely chopped (keep the rinds)*
*75g/3oz soft breadcrumbs*
*grated rind of 1 lemon*
*1 tablespoon lemon juice*
*1 can anchovies, drained and chopped*
*1 egg*
COATING AND FRYING:
*15g/½oz flour*
*salt and pepper*
*1 egg*
*75g/3oz soft, fine breadcrumbs*
*50g/2oz butter*
SAUCE:
*50g/2oz butter*
*100g/4oz button mushrooms, sliced*
*25g/1oz flour*
*450ml/¾pint white stock stock*
*salt and pepper*
*2 tablespoons double cream**
GARNISH:
*lemon slices*

Beat the meat with a rolling pin until very thin. Blend the chopped bacon, breadcrumbs, lemon rind, juice, anchovies and egg. Spread the stuffing over the slices of veal. Roll up firmly, and tie or secure with small cocktail sticks or cotton. Mix the flour with salt and pepper, dust the veal with this; do not exceed the amount given as it should not give a real coating, it just dries the meat. Coat in beaten egg and crumbs.

Fry the bacon rinds in a pan to extract the fat, add the butter and, when hot, turn the veal rolls carefully in this until golden brown. Lift from the pan into an ovenproof baking dish, pour any butter and bacon fat from the pan into the dish. Cook towards the top of a moderate to moderately hot oven (190-200°C/375-400°F or Gas Mark 5-6) for 25 minutes or until the meat is tender.

Meanwhile melt the butter for the sauce in a pan and fry the mushrooms. Stir in the flour and cook for several minutes. Gradually blend in the stock and bring to the boil. Season well and cook until the mushrooms are tender and the sauce thickened. Just before serving, remove the pan from the heat so the sauce is no longer boiling and stir in the cream. Arrange the veal olives on a dish and pour the sauce round. Garnish with lemon slices.

VARIATION

⊛ **Beef Olives:** Slices of topside of beef or good quality stewing steak can be cooked in the same way as veal. The stuffing suggested in this recipe is ideal, but you may prefer to use Sage and Onion Stuffing (see page 145) or any other stuffing in this book. Cook beef for 1½ hours for topside and 2 hours for top-grade stewing steak in a moderate oven (160°C/325°F or Gas Mark 3). Choose beef stock for the sauce; the cream can be omitted.

## Veal Flamande ⊛

*100g/4oz dried apricots*
*100g/4oz dried prunes*
*450ml/¾pint water*
*300ml/½pint rosé wine*
*750g/1½lb stewing veal, neatly diced*
*salt and pepper*
*40g/1½oz flour*
*50g/2oz butter*

Soak the fruits overnight in the water and wine. Coat the veal in the seasoned flour. Heat the butter and fry the veal for several minutes, then put into a casserole. Add the dried fruit and liquid to the pan and heat for several minutes, then stir well to absorb the meat juices. Pour over the veal, cover the casserole and cook in the centre of a moderate oven (160°C/325°F or Gas Mark 3) for 1½hours. Serve the veal with the fruit and sauce.

## Veal in Lemon Sauce ⊛

*750g/1½lb lean veal, diced*
*2 medium onions, sliced*
*2 sticks celery, chopped*
*1 clove garlic*
*1 bay leaf*
*600ml/1 pint chicken stock*
*salt and pepper*
*1 tablespoon chopped parsley*
*25g/1oz butter*
*25g/1oz flour*
*2 egg yolks*
*2 tablespoons lemon juice*
GARNISH:
*parsley*
*lemon slices*

Put the veal, onions, celery, whole garlic clove and bay leaf into a saucepan with the chicken stock. Add salt, pepper and the parsley. Cover the pan and simmer steadily for 1 to 1¼ hours, or until the meat is tender. Lift the meat, onions and celery into a heated dish with a perforated spoon. Strain a generous 300ml/½ pint stock from the liquid used in cooking the veal. Heat the butter in a saucepan and stir in the flour. Cook for 2 to 3 minutes, then gradually blend in the reserved stock. Stir as the sauce comes to the boil and thickens. Remove the pan from the heat, so the sauce is no longer boiling. Whisk the egg yolks and lemon juice together in a basin, add to a little of the hot sauce, blend well then whisk the egg yolk mixture into the sauce in the pan. Stir over a low heat until a coating consistency, taste and add more seasoning if required. Coat the veal with the sauce and garnish with the parsley and lemon. Serve with cooked pasta or rice.

## Veal in Soured Cream ⊛

*750g/1½lb veal fillet, cut into 2.5cm/1 inch cubes*
*salt and pepper*
*1 tablespoon flour*
*50g/2oz butter*
*1 tablespoon oil*
*1 medium onion, thinly sliced*
*175g/6oz small button mushrooms*
*150g/¼ pint veal or chicken stock*
*150ml/¼ pint soured cream*
GARNISH:
*lemon wedges*
*watercress*

Sprinkle the veal with the seasoned flour; this recipe contains little flour and it is better if the amount given is not exceeded. Heat half the butter and half the oil in a frying pan, fry the veal until golden brown. Spoon into a casserole. Add the remaining butter and oil to the pan, heat this and fry the onion and mushrooms gently for 5 minutes; add to the veal. Heat the stock in the frying pan, stir well to absorb any meat juices. Remove from the heat, add the soured cream and pour over the veal. Cover the casserole and cook in the centre of a moderate oven (160°C/325°F or Gas Mark 3) for 1½ hours. Serve with cooked pasta or rice, and garnish with the lemon and watercress.

VARIATION

⊛ **Veal in Paprika Sauce:** Omit the onion; use about 12 to 16 shallots and cook these in the butter and oil until golden before adding the mushrooms. Add to the veal with the mushrooms and a diced canned red pepper. Blend 2 teaspoons sweet-type paprika with the soured cream, mix with the stock. Pour over the veal and cook as above. Garnish with chopped parsley and a diced canned red pepper.

## Grilled Veal

*Choose: loin chops or cutlets; slices from the leg (escalopes)*
*melted butter*

Grilling is a form of cooking that must be carried out carefully when cooking veal, for this meat is so lean that basting with plenty of fat (butter preferably) is essential. Brush the meat with the melted butter before and during cooking. The butter can be flavoured with chopped herbs (rosemary is excellent with veal), salt and pepper.

Pre-heat the grill, cook the meat for 4 to 5 minutes on either side, then lower the heat and cook more slowly until the meat is tender. Chops of about 2.5 cm/1 inch thickness take 18 to 20 minutes, cutlets and escalopes may need a slightly shorter time. Veal must be completely cooked.

VARIATIONS

**Fried Veal:** In my opinion this is a better way of cooking veal, for you can be really lavish with the amount of butter used. Heat 75 to 100g/3 to 4oz butter for 4 chops or cutlets or escalopes. Fry quickly on either side then lower the heat and cook more slowly. The timings are as grilling.

**Veal au Gratin:** Grill or fry the veal. Top with grated cheese, soft breadcrumbs and a little melted butter. Put under the grill for several minutes.

## Veal in Mustard Sauce

*4 veal chops or 4 to 8 cutlets or 4 escalopes, see above*
*75-100g/3-4oz butter*
*1 tablespoon Dijon mustard*
*150ml/¼ pint single cream*
*salt and pepper*
*1-2 teaspoons chopped rosemary*

Fry the veal in plenty of butter until tender. Blend the mustard with the cream and add salt and pepper to taste. Pour the cream mixture over the veal in the pan, add the chopped rosemary and heat for 2 to 3 minutes.

# Escalopes of Veal

These thin slices of meat from the leg are delicious. Use plenty of butter in cooking the meat.

## Wiener Schnitzel

*4 escalopes of veal*
*salt and pepper*
*1 tablespoon flour*
*1 egg*
*50g/2oz crisp breadcrumbs*
*100g/4oz butter*
GARNISH:
*see method*

Flatten and dry the meat, as in the recipe below. Coat in the seasoned flour, beaten egg and crisp breadcrumbs. Heat the butter and fry the escalopes until crisp, brown and tender. The garnish is often a matter of discussion; some people only use lemon slices, other people lemon slices, topped with chopped hard-boiled egg, parsley and anchovy fillet.

## Veal Escalopes Meunière

*4 thin slices fillet of veal*
*75-100g/3-4oz butter*
*1 tablespoon lemon juice*
*2 teaspons capers*
*1-2 tablespoons chopped parsley*
*salt and pepper*
GARNISH:
*lemon wedges*

Flatten the veal with a damp rolling pin or by rolling the meat over greaseproof paper; this saves harming the fibres of the tender meat. Dry the meat well on absorbent paper. Heat the butter in a large frying pan, put in the meat and cook fairly rapidly on either side for 2 to 3 minutes or until it has changed colour very slightly. Lower the heat and cook more slowly for 8 to 10 minutes or until tender. Lift the meat onto a heated serving dish. If all the butter in the pan has been absorbed by the meat, heat another 25 to 50g/1 to 2oz before adding the rest of the ingredients. Stir the lemon juice, capers, parsley and salt and pepper into the butter. Heat until it darkens slightly, spoon over the meat and garnish with lemon wedges.

VARIATIONS

Use escalopes (thin slices from the breast) of chicken or turkey.

**Veal Escalopes in Orange and Walnut Sauce:** Fry the escalopes in the butter as in the recipe above. When nearly cooked, add 1 to 2 teaspoons finely grated orange rind, 150ml/¼pint orange juice, 50g/2oz coarsely chopped walnuts and salt and pepper to taste. Spoon over the meat as it finishes cooking. Serve garnished with orange slices and watercress.

## Escalopes Chasseur ⊛

*75g/3oz butter*
*1-2 cloves garlic, crushed*
*2 medium onions, chopped*
*50g/2oz mushrooms, sliced*
*4 large tomatoes, skinned, deseeded and chopped*
*150ml/¼pint white stock*
*150ml/¼pint white wine*
*salt and pepper*
*1 tablespoon oil*
*4 escalopes of veal or turkey breast*

Heat half the butter in a saucepan. Fry the garlic and onions for several minutes. Add the mushrooms, tomatoes, stock and white wine with a little salt and pepper. Cover the pan and simmer gently for 10 minutes. Lift the lid at the end of this time and continue simmering for 5 to 10 minutes so the excess liquid evaporates.

Meanwhile heat the remaining butter and oil in a large frying pan. Fry the veal or turkey escalopes until tender. Lift on to a hot serving dish. Top with the Chasseur Sauce.

VARIATION

⊛ **Escalopes Niçoise:** Omit the mushrooms in the recipe above. Stir 1 tablespoon tomato purée into the vegetable mixture. Add 2 tablespoons sliced black olives and 1 tablespoon chopped parsley just before serving.

## Veal Cordon Bleu

*4 escalopes of veal*
*4 thin slices cooked ham*
*4 thin slices Gruyère or Cheddar cheese*
COATING AND FRYING:
*little flour*
*salt and pepper*
*1 egg*
*50g/2oz fine soft or crisp breadcrumbs*
*50g/2oz butter*
*2 tablespoons oil*
GARNISH:
*lemon wedges*
*watercress or parsley*

Beat the veal with a dampened rolling pin until very thin and about twice the size of the ham and the cheese. Place the ham and cheese over the veal so that they cover only half the meat. Fold the uncovered veal over the ham and cheese to form a sandwich. Season the flour with salt and pepper. Coat the veal with the flour, then the beaten egg and breadcrumbs. (In view of the relatively long cooking time, soft breadcrumbs are advisable.)

Heat the butter and oil in a large frying pan. Fry the veal on either side for approximately 4 minutes or until crisp and golden brown. Lower the heat and cook for a further 6 to 7 minutes. Lift on to a heated dish and garnish with lemon and watercress or parsley. The Spiced Tomato Sauce (see page 233) is an excellent accompaniment.

## Blanquette of Veal ⊛

*100 g/4 oz butter*
*4 escalopes of veal*
*25 g/1 oz flour*
*300 ml/½ pint veal or chicken stock*
*salt and pepper*
*150 ml/¼ pint double cream*
*2 egg yolks*
*1 tablespoon lemon juice*
GARNISH:
*lemon slices*
*parsley*

Although this dish is frequently made with stewing veal, my version has escalopes of veal, so it is ideal for a special occasion.

Heat the butter and fry the escalopes until tender; lift into a heated serving dish and cover so that the meat does not dry. Blend the flour into the butter remaining in the frying pan, stir well, then gradually blend in the stock. Stir or whisk as the sauce comes to the boil and thickens, season well, then remove from the heat. Blend the cream, egg yolks and lemon juice together and whisk into the hot, but not boiling, sauce. Return to a very low heat and simmer for 2 to 3 minutes. Pour over the veal. Garnish with lemon and parsley.

VARIATION

For a more economical version of this recipe, dice 750 g/1½ lb stewing veal and simmer it in well seasoned stock until tender. Make a sauce with 40 g/1½ oz butter, 40 g/1½ oz flour, 150 ml/¼ pint milk and 150 ml/¼ pint single cream. Add the well drained veal and only about 150 ml/¼ pint of the stock. Heat gently. Whisk the yolks of 2 eggs with 1 tablespoon lemon juice, add to the hot, but not boiling, mixture; simmer gently for 2 to 3 minutes.

## Veal à la Sevillana

*150 g/4 oz butter*
*4 escalopes of veal*
*150 ml/¼ pint veal stock*
*salt and pepper*
*4 tablespoons bitter type orange marmalade*
*lemon juice*

Heat the butter in a pan and fry the escalopes until tender. Lift on to a heated serving dish. Stir the stock, salt and pepper into the fat remaining in the pan, then add the marmalade and heat for a few minutes. Stir in enough lemon juice to give a definite sharpness in flavour. Spoon over the escalopes.

## Veal in Tomato Sauce ⊛

*75 g/3 oz butter*
*4 escalopes of veal*
*1 small onion, finely chopped*
*1 clove garlic, crushed*
*350 g/12 oz tomatoes, skinned and chopped*
*150 ml/¼ pint veal stock*
*salt and pepper*

Heat the butter in a pan and cook the escalopes on either side until golden brown; slightly undercook the meat. Lift from the frying pan. Add the onion, garlic, tomatoes and stock to the pan, with seasoning to taste. Simmer until a soft purée, then return the meat to the pan and complete the cooking. Turn the meat over several times so that it absorbs the sauce.

## Roast Veal ⊛

*These joints are all suitable for faster or slower roasting:*
*best end of neck*
*breast*
*fillet*
*leg*
*loin*

*fat belly of pork or fat bacon or butter*
WEIGHT TO ALLOW *per person when buying the meat:*
*350g/12oz if on bone*
*225-300g/8-10oz if boned*

Veal is a particularly lean meat and it is very important that it is kept well basted or moistened during cooking. The best way to keep the meat moist is to buy fat belly or pork or fat bacon; cut this into very narrow strips, put the strips in a larding needle and thread through the joint – you then have an excellent distribution of fat and lean. If this is not possible, use a generous amount of butter or fat bacon on the joint. A covered roasting tin, foil or a roaster bag is ideal for keeping veal moist. If using foil or a covered roasting tin then allow 10 to 15 minutes extra cooking time. No extra time is required when using modern roaster bags.

Veal which has not been frozen and then defrosted or chilled can be roasted in a moderately hot to hot oven (200-220°C/400-425°F or Gas Mark 6-7). Allow 25 minutes per 450 g/1 lb plus 25 minutes.

Veal which has been frozen then defrosted or chilled is better roasted in a moderate oven (160-180°C/325-350°F or Gas Mark 3-4). Allow 40 minutes per 450 g/1 lb plus 40 minutes.

Veal is generally served with a thickened gravy. Traditional accompaniments are as Roast Chicken (see pages 184 to 186).

## Bacon Rolls

*4 to 6 rashers streaky bacon*

Derind the bacon and halve the rashers. Stretch with the back of a knife – this increases the length of the bacon rashers and also makes them easier to roll up. Form into rolls, thread several on a metal skewer; do not pack too tightly. Cook in the oven at one of the temperatures given above. Allow about 10 minutes at the higher temperature or 15 to 20 minutes at the lower setting.

## Port Wine Gravy ⊛

*3 tablespoons veal fat*
*25g/1oz flour*
*300ml/½ pint veal stock*
*150ml/¼ pint port wine*
*2 teaspoons Dijon mustard*
*salt and pepper*

Pour away all the fat from the roasting tin, except for 3 tablespoons. Blend in the flour and cook over a low heat until the 'roux' turns golden brown. Gradually blend in the stock, wine, mustard and seasoning. Stir as the gravy comes to the boil and thickens.

# Raised Pies

Home-made raised pies really are very unlike the mass produced type you buy. The pastry should be beautifully crisp and the filling richly moist. The reason the pies are called 'raised' is that the pastry should be moulded into a shape, rather than being placed in a tin. The recipe for Veal and Ham Pie on this page describes two methods of handling the pastry dough.

Pies of this kind are ideal to serve cold with salads. In addition to the recipe on this page you will find other dishes on pages 161 and 162 that present meat in an appetising guise for hot weather fare.

## Hot Water Crust Pastry ⊛

*350 g/12 oz plain flour*
*¼ teaspoon salt*
*110 g/4 oz lard*
*150 ml/¼ pint milk or water*
*1 egg yolk (optional)*

Sift the flour and salt into a warm dish. Put the lard and milk or water into a saucepan and heat until the lard melts. Pour the melted liquid on to the flour and mix with a knife. Add the egg yolk (this makes the pastry a better colour and flavour). Gather the dough together with your fingers; knead lightly and use.

## Veal and Ham Pie ⊛

*Hot Water Crust Pastry, made with 350 g/12 oz flour, etc. (see recipe above)*

FILLING:
*500 g/1¼ lb veal, finely diced*
*175 g/6 oz ham, finely diced*
*salt and pepper*
*1 teaspoon grated lemon rind*
*2 eggs, hard-boiled*
*7 tablespoons veal stock*

GLAZE:
*1 egg*
*1 teaspoon gelatine*

To raise the pastry, take about two-thirds of the dough; keep the rest in a warm place so that it does not harden. Mould (raise) the dough into a good shape; once you could buy special moulds, but nowadays I put a large greased jar on the dough and mould this around the jar rather like a potter moulds clay. If preferred, grease an 18 to 20 cm/7 to 8 inch cake tin (use one with a loose base). Line the tin with two-thirds of the pastry.

Mix the meats, seasoning and lemon rind together. Put half into the pastry, top with the eggs, then the rest of the filling and 3 tablespoons of the stock. Roll out the remaining pastry into a round; damp the edges and place over the filling, seal the edges. Make a slit on the pastry lid and decorate the top with pastry leaves and a rose shape. Brush with beaten egg and bake in the centre of a moderate oven (180°C/350°F or Gas Mark 4) for 2¼ hours. Allow to cool. Dissolve the gelatine in the remaining hot stock, cool but do not allow to set. Pour through the slit in the pastry lid. Leaving the filling to set before serving.

## Beef Loaf ⊛

*300 ml/½ pint clear beef stock or consommé*
*15 g/½ oz gelatine*
*2 tablespoons dry sherry*
*4 tablespoons tomato juice*
*pinch of curry powder*
*350 g/12 oz lean cooked beef, minced*
*4 tablespoons grated raw carrot*
*1 tablespoon chopped parsley*
*salt and pepper*

Heat the stock or consommé. Sprinkle the gelatine over the hot, but not boiling, liquid and allow to dissolve. Add the sherry, tomato juice and curry powder. Stir the minced beef into the warm gelatine mixture (the heated liquid softens the meat and makes it more moist). Leave until cold then add the carrot, parsley and salt and pepper to taste. Spoon into a 1 litre/1¾ pint oiled loaf tin or mould. Leave until set, then turn out on to a bed of salad.

VARIATIONS

⊛ **Yogurt Beef Mould:** Use only 150 ml/¼ pint beef stock or consommé. Follow the recipe above but blend 150 ml/¼ pint yogurt into the meat mixture with the carrot and parsley. Add 1 teaspoon capers and 25 g/1 oz thinly sliced raw mushrooms.

⊛ **Chicken Loaf:** Use cooked chicken in place of beef in the above recipe or variation with yogurt. (Other meat or a mixture of meats, poultry and game can be used instead of beef.)

## Beef Mould

*300 ml/½ pint beef stock, well strained*
*15 g/½ oz gelatine*
*450 g/1 lb cooked roast beef, minced*
*300 ml/½ pint tomato juice*
*2 eggs, hard-boiled and chopped*
*salt and pepper*
*mixed salad, to serve*

Heat the stock and dissolve the gelatine in this. Add the beef to the hot liquid and leave until cool. Stir in the tomato juice, chopped eggs and salt and pepper to taste. Put into an oiled 1.2 litre/2 pint mould and leave until firm. Turn out on to a bed of mixed salad and serve.

VARIATIONS

Add a generous amount of mustard to the stock or blend a little Worcestershire sauce and/or Tabasco sauce and/or curry paste with the stock. Do not exceed the liquid amount in the recipe.

**Veal and Ham Mould:** Use 350 g/12 oz cooked veal and 175 g/6 oz cooked ham. The meat can be minced or neatly, and finely, diced. You can use tomato juice as in the Beef Mould or substitute veal stock, flavoured with a little lemon juice. If you have boiled veal bones for some time in water to cover, you should have extracted a lot of natural setting quality, so you can reduce the amount of gelatine to 1 teaspoon.

## Ham Mousse ⊛

*5 tablespoons white wine*
*15 g/½ oz galatine*
*300 ml/½ pint yogurt*
*2 tablespoons mayonnaise*
*1 tablespoon tomato purée*
*1 tablespoon lemon juice*
*few drops Tabasco sauce*
*450 g/1 lb cooked ham, minced*
*2 egg whites*
GARNISH:
*lettuce*
*cucumber slices*
*lemon slices*
*few grapes*

Put the wine into a large heatproof bowl and sprinkle the gelatine on top. Stand over a saucepan of boiling water until the gelatine has dissolved, then stir briskly. Add the yogurt, mayonnaise, tomato purée, lemon juice, Tabasco sauce and the ham. Allow the mixture to stiffen slightly. Put the egg whites into a bowl and whisk until stiff. Fold into the ham mixture. Oil a 1 litre/1¾ pint mould, spoon the mousse into this and leave until firm. Turn the mousse out on to a bed of lettuce and garnish with the cucumber, lemon and grapes.

## Aspic Meat Mould ⊛

*600 ml/1 pint aspic jelly, made as the recipe on page 264 or a packet of aspic jelly crystals with 600 ml/1 pint water*
*few cooked carrots, sliced*
*few cooked green peas*
*225 g/8 oz lean ham, minced*
*225 g/8 oz lean cooked veal, minced*

Make the aspic jelly following the recipe on page 264, or use a packet of jelly crystals with 600 ml/1 pint water. Dissolve as the instructions on the packet.

Pour 2 to 3 tablespoons jelly into an oiled 1.2 litre/2 pint mould. Arrange a layer of sliced cooked carrots and green peas in the jelly. Leave to set. Blend the minced meats with the remaining jelly and allow to cool, but not set, then spoon carefully over the clear layer at the base of the mould. Leave until firm, then turn out. To turn out any mould, wrap a tea cloth, dipped in hot water and wrung out, around the outside of the mould. Hold the tea cloth in position for a few seconds then invert the mould on to a damp serving dish. It should drop out at once. The purpose of damping the serving dish is to allow you to slide the mould into position. Serve with salad.

# Cooking Offal

In America offal is known as 'variety meats', which makes these excellent cuts of meat sound rather more interesting. The method of cooking depends of course on the particular meat, but here are some of the ways I cook liver, kidney and other variety meats. These are highly perishable so store carefully before and after cooking. Cooked dishes or the uncooked meats keep well and retain their flavour when frozen.

## Calves' Brains in Black Butter

*450 g/1 lb calves' brains*
*100 g/4 oz butter*
*1-2 tablespoons lemon juice*
*2 teaspoons capers*
*2 tablespoons chopped parsley*
GARNISH:
*lemon wedges*
*parsley*

Put the brains to soak in cold water for an hour. Drain well and dry on absorbent paper. Heat half the butter in a frying pan and cook the brains steadily for 10 to 15 minutes until they become white and opaque. Remove to a hot dish. Add the remaining butter to the pan and cook until dark brown. This is known as black butter but never allow it to become really black and burned. Stir in the lemon juice to taste, capers and parsley. Heat thoroughly and spoon over the brains. Garnish and serve.

## Kidneys Turbigo ✱

*8 lambs' kidneys*
*salt and pepper*
*15 g/½ oz flour*
*75 g/3 oz butter*
*100 g/4 oz button mushrooms*
*8 small sausages or frankfurters*
*150 ml/¼ pint chicken stock*
*4 tablespoons red or port wine*
*½-1 teaspoon made mustard*
GARNISH:
*chopped parsley*

Halve and skin the kidneys and cut away any excess fat. Coat them in the seasoned flour. Heat 50 g/2 oz of the butter in a pan. Fry the kidneys for 10 minutes or until tender then remove from the pan on to a dish. Keep hot. Add the remaining butter to the pan and fry the mushrooms and sausages until tender. Arrange on the dish with the kidneys. Pour the stock and wine into the pan, and stir well to absorb any fat that remains. Cook until slightly thickened then add salt, pepper and mustard to taste. Spoon over the kidney mixture and top with the parsley.

## Madeira Kidneys ⊛

*12 lambs' kidneys*
*salt and pepper*
*15g/½oz flour*
*50g/2oz butter*
*150ml/¼pint Madeira wine*
*150ml/¼pint chicken stock*
*450g/1 lb spinach*

Halve and skin the kidneys, cut away any excess fat and coat in the seasoned flour. Heat the butter and fry the kidneys for 4 to 5 minutes, then blend in the Madeira and stock. Stir as the sauce comes to the boil and begins to thicken. Lower the heat, cover the pan and simmer for 10 to 12 minutes so the sauce thickens.

Meanwhile cook the spinach, drain and season. Place in a heated serving dish. Top with the kidneys and the sauce.

## Liver Croquettes ⊛

*50g/2oz butter or margarine or fat*
*2 medium onions, chopped*
*25g/1 oz flour*
*150ml/¼pint milk*
*50g/2oz soft breadcrumbs*
*½ teaspoon chopped fresh, or pinch dried, sage*
*½ teaspoon chopped fresh, or pinch dried, thyme*
*1 teaspoon finely grated lemon rind*
*350g/12oz calves' or lambs' liver, minced or finely chopped*
*salt and pepper*

COATING AND FRYING:
*little seasoned flour*
*1 egg*
*50g/2oz crisp breadcrumbs*
*25g/1 oz fat or 2 to 3 tablespoons oil*

GARNISH:
*lemon wedges*
*parsley*

Heat the butter, margarine or fat in a saucepan and fry the onions until soft. Stir in the flour and cook for 2 to 3 minutes, then gradually blend in the milk. Bring to the boil, stirring all the time, as this is a thick binding sauce. Add the breadcrumbs, herbs, lemon rind, liver and salt and pepper. Cool the mixture and divide into 8 portions. Chill for 1 hour to make it easier to handle the mixture. Form into finger shapes. Coat with seasoned flour, egg and breadcrumbs. It is advisable to chill the croquettes again, if time permits, before frying.

Heat the fat or oil in a frying pan and fry the croquettes steadily for about 8 minutes until crisp and golden brown. Do not overcook. Drain on absorbent paper; garnish with lemon and parsley. Serve with Tomato or Brown Sauce (see pages 233 and 230).

VARIATIONS

These can be pre-fried if preferred.

⊛ **Liver Quenelles:** Prepare the liver mixture as above but do not coat. Poach in 300 to 450ml/½ to ¾pint hot chicken or beef stock for 8 to 10 minutes. Drain, keep hot and coat with Brown Sauce (see page 230). Use the stock in which the quenelles were poached in the sauce.

Note: When using liver in recipes such as these, remember that the liver will be spoiled if it is over-cooked; as the liver is minced or finely diced it cooks very speedily.

## Liver Lyonnaise Style

*4 medium onions, sliced*
*450g/1 lb calves' or lambs' liver, sliced*
*salt and pepper*
*15g/½ oz flour*
*100g/4 oz butter or dripping*
*4 tablespoons beef stock*
*squeeze lemon juice*
GARNISH:
*Duchesse Potatoes (see page 251*

Separate the onions into rings. Coat the liver in seasoned flour. Heat half the butter or dripping in a frying pan and fry the onions until tender but still pale in colour. Lift on to a heated dish and keep hot. Heat the remaining butter or dripping and fry the liver until just tender; turn once. Do not overcook as this makes the meat tough. Lift on to the dish with the onions. Pour the stock into the pan and add the lemon juice. Stir well to absorb any juices in the pan, heat for 2 to 3 minutes then spoon over the liver. Spoon or pipe the potatoes around the edge of the dish.

VARIATION

**Liver in Orange Sauce:** Omit the onions in the recipe above. Grate the zest from 1 large orange, and add to the flour used to coat the liver. Fry the liver in hot butter as above. Lift on to a hot dish. Stir 4 tablespoons orange juice and 4 tablespoons beef stock into the pan. Add 1 teaspoon brown sugar. Heat for 2 to 3 minutes then spoon over the liver.

## Liver Soufflé

*25g/1 oz butter or margarine*
*25g/1 oz flour*
*150ml/¼ pint milk*
*2 tablespoons double cream*
*100-175g/4-6 oz raw calves' or lambs' liver, minced*
*3 eggs, separated*
*salt and pepper*
*1 egg white*

Heat the butter or margarine in a good-sized saucepan, stir in the flour and cook for 2 to 3 minutes, then gradually blend in the milk and cream. Bring the sauce to the boil, stirring all the time until thickened. Add the liver, then the egg yolks and salt and pepper to taste. Whisk the egg white until it just stands in peaks; do not over-whisk. Fold into the liver mixture. Spoon into an 18cm/7 inch greased soufflé dish. Bake in the centre of a moderate to moderately hot oven (180-190°C/350-375°F or Gas Mark 4-5) for 30 to 35 minutes.

VARIATIONS

Use tomato juice or purée instead of the milk and cream.

Flavour the mixture with chopped chives, cooked onion or chopped parsley. Do not use much onion as this will make the mixture heavy.

## Liver and Bacon

*450 g/1 lb calves' or lambs' liver, cut into thin slices*
*salt and pepper*
*little flour*
*8 bacon rashers, derinded*
*extra butter or fat if necessary*

It was not until I began cooking that I realised there was no reason to dislike fried liver. Often I had been given it when overcooked, which of course made it tough, dry and not very pleasant. Liver should be pleasantly moist and juicy, but this does necessitate careful timing in cooking. You may like to coat the slices of liver with a light dusting of seasoned flour, personally I do not do this, as I think it hardens the outside. I just season the liver. I first fry the bacon and push it to one side in the pan, or keep it hot on a dish. I then check the fat content in the frying pan; liver needs a good amount of fat; the amount given assumes the bacon was reasonably fat. You can of course always fry the bacon rinds too, and remove these from the pan when you have extracted all the fat or add extra fat. Fry the seasoned liver for 2 to 3 minutes only, then serve. That is the way I like it, so that it is pink in the middle.

VARIATIONS

If you sprinkle the liver with a little sugar. it develops a delicious caramel-like taste, which endears it to many people.

Add a little orange juice to the pan after cooking the liver and bacon; heat and spoon over the liver.

**Black Pudding and Bacon:** This is one of the best breakfast dishes. Slice the black pudding, fry the bacon, then rings of cooking apples; keep hot while you fry the black pudding until firm on the outside. Serve at once, for like liver it should not be kept waiting; this can cause hardening.

## Fried Sweetbreads

*450 g/1 lb calves' or lambs' sweetbreads*
*salt and pepper*
*300 ml/½ pint stock*
COATING AND FRYING:
*25 g/1 oz flour*
*1-2 eggs*
*50-75 g/2-3 oz crisp breadcrumbs*
*50-75 g/2-3 oz butter*
*4-8 bacon rashers, derinded*

Soak and blanch the sweetbreads as in the recipe on page 167. Put into the well seasoned stock and simmer for 30 minutes. Remove from the stock, cool sufficiently to handle then remove any gristle. Cool and coat in the well seasoned flour, then beaten egg and breadcrumbs. Press the breadcrumbs very firmly into the small pieces of sweetbread. Chill for a short time if possible before frying. Heat the butter in a frying pan and fry the sweetbreads steadily for about 5 minutes, turning them several times, so they brown evenly; add the bacon rashers towards the end of the cooking time.

## Sweetbreads Princesse ⊛

*675g/1½ calves' or lambs' sweetbreads*
*25g/1oz flour*
*salt and pepper*
*25g/1oz butter or margarine*
*2-3 bacon rashers, derinded and diced*
*450ml/¾ pint chicken stock*
*1 egg yolk*
*3 tablespoons double cream*
*1 tablespoon dry sherry*
GARNISH:
*fried croûtons (see page 36)*

Wash the sweetbreads well, then allow to soak in cold water for 1 hour. Put into a pan of cold water, bring this to boiling point then strain the sweetbreads and discard the water. This is known as blanching. Cut away any gristle and skin from the sweetbreads and divide into equal sized pieces. Mix the flour with a little salt and pepper and use to coat the sweetbreads. Heat the butter or margarine, add the bacon together with the coated sweetbreads and fry for 3 to 4 minutes or until golden in colour. Stir in the stock and continue stirring as the liquid comes to the boil and becomes a smooth thin sauce. Cover the pan and simmer for 20 to 25 minutes or until the sweetbreads are tender. Lift the lid towards the end of the cooking time to allow the sauce to thicken.

Blend the egg yolk, cream and sherry together in a basin. Remove the saucepan from the heat so the mixture is not boiling. Whisk a little of the hot sauce from the pan on to the egg mixture then blend this with the sweetbreads and sauce. Return the pan to the heat, simmer for a few minutes, then spoon on to a hot serving dish. Garnish with the crisp croûtons immediately before serving.

## Spiced Tripe

*1kg/2lb dressed tripe*
*50g/2oz butter or fat*
*2 large onions, sliced*
*2 large tomatoes, skinned and sliced*
*25g/1oz flour*
*1 teaspoon paprika*
*1 teaspoon mustard powder*
*½ teaspoon ground nutmeg*
*450ml/¾ pint beef stock*
*2 teaspoons brown malt vinegar*
*salt and pepper*
GARNISH:
*fried croûtons (see page 36)*

Cut the tripe into fairly large squares. Put into a pan of cold water, bring the water to the boil and discard this. This process is known as blanching the tripe and helps to give it a good flavour. Drain the tripe well.

Heat the butter or fat in a large saucepan, add the tripe and fry gently for a few minutes. Add the onions and tomatoes and cook for a further 5 minutes. Blend the flour with the paprika, mustard powder and nutmeg. Stir into the fried ingredients and cook gently for 2 to 3 minutes, stirring all the time. Gradually blend in the stock, stirring as the sauce comes to the boil and thickens. Add the vinegar and salt and pepper to taste. Cover the saucepan and simmer for 1 hour. Top with the croûtons just before serving.

## Tripe and Onions ⊛

*1 kg/2 lb dressed tripe*
*450 g/1 lb onions, thickly sliced*
*450 ml/¾ pint milk*
*salt and pepper*
*150 ml/¼ pint chicken stock or water*
*1½ tablespoons cornflour*
*50 g/2 oz butter*
GARNISH:
*chopped parsley*
*paprika*

Some people look quite pale when you discuss cooking tripe; often I find they have never tasted it, but are confident they would hate it. Personally I enjoy tripe from time to time and I vary the method of cooking, as you will see from the four quite different dishes included on this and the previous page.

Cut the tripe into fairly large squares and blanch it, as explained on page 167. Put the tripe and onions into a pan with 300 ml/½ pint milk, salt and pepper to taste and the stock or water. Simmer gently for 45 minutes, or until tender. Blend the remaining milk and cornflour, add to the pan with the butter and stir until thickened and creamy. Top with chopped parsley and paprika.

## Flaki ⊛

*1 kg/2 lb dressed tripe*
*50 g/2 oz butter*
*50 g/2 oz flour*
*750 ml/1¼ pints brown stock*
*2 medium carrots, sliced*
*2 medium onions, sliced*
*2 celery sticks, chopped*
*bouquet garni*
*pinch ground ginger*
*few cloves*
*salt and cayenne pepper*
GARNISH:
*chopped marjoram*
*Gruyère cheese, grated*

Cut the tripe into narrow fingers and blanch it as explained on page 167. Heat the butter in a pan, stir in the flour and cook over a very gentle heat until golden brown. Blend in the stock, stir as the sauce comes to the boil and thickens. Add the rest of the ingredients, except the garnish. Stir in the tripe. Cover the pan, lower the heat and cook very gently for 1¾ to 2 hours.

Top the cooked stew with chopped marjoram and the grated cheese.

VARIATION

⊛ **Tripe à la Mode de Caen:** This recipe is often given as 'tripes', for ideally you should have the four kinds, honeycomb, belly, reed and psalterium. Cut the tripe into large squares; blanch as described on page 167. Ask the butcher for a calf's foot, cut into pieces, or an ox foot, if available. All the bones should be removed if possible. Put 2 sliced carrots, 2 large sliced onions and 2 large sliced leeks in the bottom of a casserole, add 2 crushed cloves garlic, salt, pepper and a bouquet garni of herbs. Top with the tripe and the calf's or ox foot. Blend 300 ml/½ pint cider, 300 ml/½ pint water and 3 tablespoons Calvados (the apple liqueur). Pour over the other ingredients, cover the casserole tightly and cook in a cool oven (140°C/275°F or Gas Mark 1) for 5 to 6 hours.

# Poultry Dishes

Times have changed a great deal and poultry, chicken and turkey in particular, are now a relatively economical choice for main dishes. The modern methods of rearing chickens mean you can purchase exactly the size required, from tiny individual-sized spring chicken (poussin) to large family-sized capon. You can also obtain the parts that are ideal for a particular dish, i.e., all breast meat or all leg joints. This is a great advantage for small families or one person. The recipes on pages 178 to 183 are ideal for single portions.

I hope you are able to buy turkey joints too, for these make a pleasant change when you do not require a whole turkey. The recipes on pages 198 to 200 give a selection of recipes I have enjoyed creating based upon cuts of turkey plus ideas to use cooked left-over turkey. Many of the ideas are equally successful with chicken.

Nowadays ducks are bred to give a better proportion of lean meat and ideas for serving duck, a great favourite in my home and with my guests, are on pages 203 to 206. Geese are less easy to obtain than ducks; if available try the recipes on pages 207 and 208.

ALWAYS completely defrost frozen birds before roasting or cooking whole. In some instances joints or small portions of poultry and game can be cooked from the frozen state—in other recipes it is advisable to defrost the flesh first. The recipes state which procedure to follow.

Most cooked dishes made with poultry freeze extremely well. Use within 3 months. Never over-cook poultry in a dish to be frozen or served freshly cooked, for the food ceases to be enjoyable if the poultry flesh is not succulent.

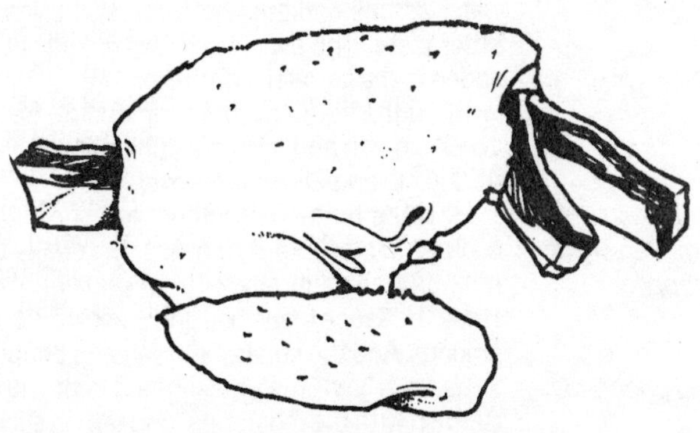

# Cooking Chicken

Select the right kind of chicken for each dish, i.e. young frying (or broiler) birds for frying or grilling and any form of speedy cooking. Never over-cook chicken, as it dries very easily and keep it well basted with fat during cooking. The first recipes are for stews and casseroles using chicken.

# Quality of Chickens

Older boiling fowls are not readily available these days; most birds are young and easily tenderized. A boiling fowl, while taking longer to cook, has an excellent flavour and is suitable for dishes, such as 'Boiled Chicken' or any of the casserole dishes. The cooking times though, assume you are using a younger bird so allow at least twice the time if cooking a boiling fowl. When buying chicken you can tell if the bird is young; the wishbone should be pliable. A boiling fowl tends to be creamy-yellow in colour, due to the amount of fat on the bones; the wishbone will be rigid.

In some recipes I have specified the weight of the chicken (after draining and trussing) for it has to be in proportion to the other ingredients used; in other recipes, such as below, I have not done so, since the cooking time is calculated easily.

## Boiled Chicken ⊛

*1 large chicken with giblets*
*salt and pepper*
*sprig parsley*
*sprig thyme*
*2 medium onions*
*2 medium carrots*
SAUCE:
*50 g/2 oz butter*
*50 g/2 oz flour*
*300 ml/½ pint milk*
*300 ml/½ pint chicken stock*
*3 tablespoons chopped parsley*
GARNISH:
*1 can red peppers, chopped*
*lemon slices*

Put the bird into a pan with cold water to cover. Add the seasoning, parsley, thyme, onions and carrots. The giblets can be added, but avoid cooking the liver in the water as this darkens the stock and gives it a slightly bitter taste. The liver could be cooked separately and added to the garnish if desired.

Bring the liquid to simmering point, lower the heat, cover the pan and cook steadily. Allow 20 minutes per 450 g/1 lb and 20 minutes over.

Heat the butter in another pan, stir in the flour and cook gently for 2 to 3 minutes. Gradually blend in the milk and chicken stock (from cooking the chicken). Bring the sauce to the boil and cook until thickened and smooth. Add the parsley and salt and pepper to taste.

Carve or joint the chicken and coat with the sauce. Garnish with the red pepper and lemon slices.

Serve with cooked rice or pasta. Serves 6.

## Chicken Blanquette ⊛

*1 large chicken with giblets*
*salt and pepper*
*sprig parsley*
*sprig thyme*
*13 small onions*
*13 small carrots*
SAUCE:
*50g/2oz butter*
*50g/2oz flour*
*150ml/¼pint milk*
*150ml/¼pint single cream*
*300ml/½pint chicken stock*
*2 egg yolks*
GARNISH:
*chopped parsley*

Cook the chicken as on the previous page; put 1 whole onion and 1 whole carrot in the pan with the chicken at the start of the cooking period. Add the remaining carrots and onions about 35 minutes before the bird is cooked, so they can be served around it. When the chicken is cooked, strain off 300ml/½ pint stock. Carve the chicken neatly, put on to a hot dish with the whole vegetables.

Heat the butter in a pan, stir in the flour and cook slowly for 2 to 3 minutes. Gradually blend in the milk, cream and most of the 300ml/½pint stock. Stir as the sauce comes to the boil and thickens; season well. Blend the egg yolks with the remaining stock, whisk into the sauce and cook gently, without boiling, for several minutes. Spoon the sauce over the chicken, garnish with chopped parsley. Serves 6.

VARIATION

⊛ **Devon Chicken:** Cook the chicken and vegetables in dry cider instead of water. Thicken 600ml/1 pint stock with Beurre Manié (see page 45). Whisk 3 tablespoons double cream into the hot, but not boiling, sauce. Serve with jacket potatoes.

## Chicken Suprême ⊛

*4 cooked chicken breasts*
*25g/1 oz butter*
*25g/1 oz flour*
*300ml/½pint chicken stock*
*150ml/¼pint milk*
*salt and pepper*
*2 egg yolks*
*3 tablespoons double cream*
*1-2 tablespoons dry sherry*
GARNISH:
*2 eggs, hard-boiled and chopped*
*paprika*
*chopped parsley*

Skin the chicken breasts. Heat the butter in a large pan, stir in the flour and cook for 2 to 3 minutes over a low heat. Gradually add the stock and milk. Stir as the sauce comes to the boil and begins to thicken; it should not be too thick at this stage. Season lightly.

Beat the egg yolks, cream and sherry together. Pour a little hot sauce over the egg yolk mixture, whisking hard as you do so, then return to the saucepan. Place the chicken breasts into the sauce. Lower the heat so there is no possibility of the sauce reaching boiling point and simmer for 10 minutes; do not cover the pan. Stir several times during this period. Serve the chicken and sauce topped with the eggs, paprika and parsley. Cooked rice is the ideal accompaniment.

## Greek Cinnamon Chicken ⊛

*2 cloves garlic, crushed*
*salt and pepper*
*4 chicken joints*
*1 tablespoon olive oil*
*1 teaspoon ground cinnamon*
*8 medium tomatoes, thinly sliced*
*100g/4oz black olives, chopped*
*2 oranges, thinly sliced*
*1 lemon, thinly sliced*
*150ml/¼ pint dry white wine*

Press the garlic, salt and pepper into the chicken joints. Blend the oil with the ground cinnamon and brush the chicken with this, using all the oil. Place the chicken in a casserole. Top with the sliced tomatoes and olives. Remove all the pips from the sliced oranges and lemons. Place over the tomatoes and olives, add the wine. Cover the dish and cook in the centre of a moderate oven (180°C/350°F or Gas Mark 4) for 1¼ hours. Serve with pasta.

## Chicken Curry ⊛

*50g/2oz ghee (see page 123)*
*2 medium onions, chopped*
*2 cloves garlic, chopped*
*1 tablespoon curry powder*
*1 teaspoon curry paste*
*1 tablespoon cornflour*
*4 chicken portions*
*300ml/½ pint chicken stock*
*25g/1oz desiccated coconut*
*25g/1oz sultanas*
*salt and pepper*

COCONUT MILK:

*150ml/¼ pint boiling water*
*100g/4oz fresh grated coconut, or desiccated coconut*

First make the coconut milk: pour the boiling water over the coconut; leave for 2 hours, strain and use the liquid in the mixture below.

Heat the ghee and fry the onions and garlic for 3 to 4 minutes. Stir in the curry powder, curry paste and cornflour and continue cooking for 2 minutes. Add the chicken joints and turn in the onion and spice mixture until well coated. Add the coconut milk, stock, coconut, sultanas and salt and pepper to taste. Cover the pan tightly and simmer gently for 1 hour. This dish is nicer if cooked one day, cooled and kept in the refrigerator, then reheated the next day. Serve with cooked rice, chutney and the accompaniments suggested on page 123.

VARIATION

⊛ **Creamed Chicken Curry:** Make the coconut milk, as the recipe above. Heat the ghee and fry the onions (omit the garlic) for 3 to 4 minutes. Stir in the curry powder (omit the curry paste). Coat 4 chicken portions with 25g/1oz seasoned flour and 1 teaspoon sweet paprika. Add to the onion and curry mixture, turn over a low heat, then gradually blend in 300ml/½ pint chicken stock, 300ml/½ pint single cream, the coconut milk, 50g/2oz cashew nuts and 1 chopped canned red pepper. Stir as the sauce comes to the boil and thickens. Lower the heat, cover the pan and simmer for 1 hour. Serve with cooked rice.

## Coq au Vin ⊛

*50g/2oz butter*
*1 tablespoon oil*
*100g/4oz bacon, cut in 1 rasher, derinded and diced*
*100g/4oz button mushrooms*
*12 small shallots or onions*
*1-2 cloves garlic, crushed*
*1 x 2kg/4lb cock bird*
*25g/1oz flour*
*600ml/1 pint red wine*
*salt and pepper*

This can be one of my least favourite recipes if a poor quality chicken and indifferent wine is used. You need a plump bird and reasonable quality wine. French cooks say there is a distinct improvement if you choose a bird to match the title, i.e. a cock, not a hen.

Heat the butter and oil in a large pan, add the bacon and vegetables and cook gently until they colour slightly; remove from the pan with a perforated spoon, leaving as much fat as possible behind. Put in the chicken, heat steadily in the fat, turning round as required. The bird should be golden coloured. Lift from the pan. Blend in the flour, cook gently for 2 to 3 minutes, then gradually add the wine. Stir as the sauce comes to the boil and add salt and pepper to taste. Replace the chicken, bacon and vegetables. Cover the pan and simmer gently for 45 minutes to 1 hour. Serves 6.

VARIATION

⊛ **Chicken Chasseur:** Omit both the bacon and garlic in the recipe above; but add sliced shallots or onions and mushrooms, together with 4 skinned tomatoes. Fry the vegetables in the butter and oil. Add 4 chicken portions; turn in the vegetable mixture until golden. Remove from the pan. Blend in 25g/1oz flour, then add 150ml/¼pint dry sherry and 450ml/¾pint chicken stock. Bring to the boil, stir over a low heat until thickened, then replace the chicken and vegetables. Season the sauce, cover the pan and simmer for 40 minutes.

## Normandy Chicken ⊛

*2 medium onions, sliced*
*2 carrots, sliced*
*2-3 stick celery, chopped*
*1 x 1.5kg/3lb chicken with giblets*
*salt and pepper*
*25g/1oz butter*
*2 tablespoons lemon juice*
*300ml/½pint dry cider*
*4 tablespoons double cream*
*2 egg yolks*

Put the vegetables into a deep casserole. Add the chicken and season lightly. Spread with the butter and sprinkle with the lemon juice. Add the cider and cover the casserole. Cook in the centre of a moderate oven (160°C/325°F or Gas Mark 3) for 1¾ hours.

Meanwhile simmer the giblets in a little water to give stock. Lift the chicken on to a hot dish. Sieve or liquidize the vegetables with the liquid from the casserole. Add sufficient strained chicken stock from the giblets to make a coating consistency. Pour into a saucepan, bring to simmering point. Whisk the cream and egg yolks. Add to the hot, but not boiling, sauce. Stir over a very low heat for 5 to 6 minutes. Carve or joint the chicken. Coat with the sauce.

## Catalan Chicken ⊛

*6 chicken portions*
*25 g/1 oz flour*
*salt and pepper*
*3 tablespoons oil*
*2 medium onions, sliced*
*2 cloves garlic, chopped*
*1 green pepper, deseeded and cut into rings*
*4 medium tomatoes, skinned and thickly sliced*
*300 ml/½ pint chicken stock*
*4 tablespoons dry sherry*
*2 tablespoons chopped parsley*

Dry the chicken portions on absorbent kitchen paper; coat in the flour, seasoned with a generous amount of salt and pepper. Heat the oil in a large pan, fry the chicken portions until golden coloured, then put into a casserole. Add the vegetables to any oil remaining in the pan and cook for 5 minutes. Spoon over the chicken. Pour the stock and sherry into the frying pan, stir well to absorb any oil and juices remaining in the pan and add a little salt and pepper, if desired. Pour over the chicken and vegetables. Cover the casserole and cook in the centre of a moderate oven (180°C/350°F or Gas Mark 4) for 1 hour. Add the parsley to the sauce about 5 minutes before the end of the cooking time. Serve with rice, pasta or boiled potatoes and a crisp green salad. Serves 6.

## Lemon Chicken ⊛

*1 lemon, halved*
*1 x 2 kg/4½ lb chicken*
*12 small onions, peeled*
*2-3 sticks celery, chopped*
*12 small carrots, peeled*
*1 bay leaf*
*salt and pepper*
*water, see method*
SAUCE:
*300 ml/½ pint stock (see method)*
*50 g/2 oz butter*
*50-100 g/2-4 oz very small mushrooms*
*2 egg yolks*
*4 tablespoons dry sherry*
*4 tablespoons double cream*
*50 g/2 oz blanched almonds*

Squeeze the lemon juice over the chicken; remove any pips from the lemon and place the halved fruit inside the bird. Put the vegetables into a deep casserole with the bay leaf and a little salt and pepper. Place the chicken on the vegetables, pour water around the chicken to within 2.5 cm/1 inch of the top of the casserole. Cover and cook in the centre of a slow oven (150°C/300°F or Gas Mark 2) for 2 hours. Lift the chicken and vegetables on to a heated dish and keep hot. Carve or joint the chicken just before serving.

Strain off 300 ml/½ pint stock from the casserole, bring to boiling point. Heat the butter and fry the mushrooms. Whisk the egg yolks, sherry, cream and the very hot stock together. Cook over a low heat until a coating consistency. Add the fried mushrooms and almonds. Coat the chicken with this sauce. Cooked rice is an ideal accompaniment.

VARIATION

⊛ **Chicken Brawn:** Flavour the chicken with lemon, as the recipe above. Put into a casserole with the giblets, 2 pigs' trotters, fresh herbs, water to cover and seasoning. Cover and cook as above, then remove all the meat from the chicken, giblets and trotters; dice neatly and put into a basin. Boil the stock until 300 ml/½ pint; strain over the meats; allow to set.

## Spezzatino of Chicken Italiana ⊛

*4 chicken portions*
*50g/2oz butter or margarine*
*4 onions, finely chopped*
*450g/1 lb tomatoes, skinned, deseeded and chopped*
*1 tablespoon tomato purée*
*1.2 litres/2 pints chicken stock*
*1 teaspoon chopped fresh, or ½ teaspoon dried, mixed herbs*
*100g/4 oz long-grain rice*
*salt and pepper*
GARNISH:
*parsley sprigs*

Dry the chicken portions on absorbent paper. Heat the butter or margarine in a large saucepan and fry the chicken until golden. Add the onions, tomatoes, tomato purée and stock to the chicken portions. Bring to the boil, add the herbs, rice with salt and pepper to taste. Simmer for 5 to 10 minutes only then spoon into a pre-heated casserole. Bake in the centre of a moderate oven (180°C/350°F or Gas Mark 4) for approximately 30 to 40 minutes until the rice and chicken are tender. Do not cover the dish, stir once or twice. Top with sprigs of parsley.

VARIATIONS

⊛ **Chicken Risotto:** Cut the meat from the chicken portions in the recipe above. Use only 225g/8oz tomatoes. Fry the chicken in the butter or margarine. Add the onions and tomatoes and cook gently for 2 to 3 minutes then add 225g/8oz medium-grain rice (if unavailable use long grain rice). Turn the rice in the chicken mixture, then add 750ml/1¼pints chicken stock, 1 tablespoon tomato purée, salt and pepper to taste. Simmer steadily for 25 minutes or until the chicken and rice are tender and the excess liquid absorbed. Top with chopped parsley and grated cheese.

⊛ **Chicken Liver Risotto:** Omit the chicken and use 225 to 350g/8 to 12oz chicken livers. Fry these for 1 to 2 minutes only in 75g/3oz butter, remove from the pan. Fry 4 chopped onions, 100g/4oz sliced mushrooms in the butter remaining in the pan. Add 225g/8oz medium or long grain rice, turn in the vegetable mixture, then add 750ml/1¼pints chicken stock and salt and pepper. Simmer for 25 minutes, return the livers to the pan with 25g/1oz sultanas. Simmer for a further 10 minutes, or until the rice and livers are tender and the excess liquid is absorbed. Top with grated cheese.

⊛ **Pilau of Chicken:** Fry 1 medium chopped onion and 50g/2oz pine kernels in 50g/2oz butter for 2 to 3 minutes. Add 225g/8oz medium or long grain rice, turn in the onion mixture. Pour in 600ml/1 pint chicken stock, stir well, add salt and pepper to taste then simmer gently for 20 minutes, or until the rice is nearly tender. Add 350g/12oz neatly diced cooked chicken, 2 large skinned and diced tomatoes, 50g/2oz sultanas and heat for a further 10 minutes.

## Djaja Mammra ⊛

*75 g/3 oz semolina, cooked in muslin (see method)*
*50 g/2 oz blanched almonds, chopped*
*75 g/3 oz butter*
*100 g/4 oz raisins*
**Ras el Hanout*
*pinch salt*
*1 large chicken*
*pinch powdered ginger*
*1-2 onions*
*pinch saffron*
*little extra salt*

The semolina used in this dish is very coarse (ask for semolina for cous-cous), almost like a small rice grain. It should be tied in muslin, allowing room for it to swell in cooking, put in a steamer over a pan of boiling water and cooked for about 25 minutes until tender.

Mix the almonds with the semolina, 25 g/1 oz butter, raisins and the Ras el Hanout to taste. Add salt to taste and put this stuffing into the chicken; tie or skewer very firmly. Put the chicken into a pan with only enough water to half cover. Add the other ingredients, including the remaining butter. Boil steadily in a covered pan for about 1 hour, lift off the lid and finish cooking in an open pan so that the water evaporates, leaving only the butter and chicken fat in the base of the pan. Turn the chicken in the butter over a steady heat until brown. Serve the chicken with stuffing and any buttery sauce left in the pan. Serves 4 to 6.

***Ras el Hanout:** This is a traditional Moorish spice which has an almost unbelievable number of ingredients, including mixed spice, cinnamon, pimento, black pepper, ginger, etc. It is very hot. When not available make a substitute by blending a little curry powder, ginger, pepper and mixed spice together.

## Chicken Stew ⊛

*1 x 1.5 kg/3 lb chicken*
*salt and pepper*
*bouquet garni*
*8 medium onions*
*8 medium carrots*
*8 medium potatoes*
*50 g/2 oz butter*
*50 g/2 oz flour*
*450 ml/¾ pint chicken stock*
*150 ml/¼ pint milk*

Put the chicken into a large saucepan with water to cover, salt, pepper and the bouquet garni. Cover the pan, bring to the boil, then simmer gently for 15 minutes. Add the vegetables and simmer for a further 45 minutes or until the chicken and vegetables are tender. Heat the butter in another pan, stir in the flour and cook gently for 2 to 3 minutes. Gradually blend in 450 ml/¾ pint stock from cooking the chicken and the milk. Stir as the sauce comes to the boil and thickens. Season well. Serve with the chicken and vegetables.

## Chicken Hotpot ⊛

*1 x 1.5 kg/3 lb chicken*
*salt and pepper*
*750 g/1 ½ lb potatoes (weight when peeled), thinly sliced*
*350 g/12 oz onions, thinly sliced*
*350 g 12 oz tomatoes, thinly sliced*
*2 tablespoons chopped parsley*
*1 teaspoon chopped rosemary*
*15 g/½ oz butter or margarine*

Slice the meat from the chicken. Put the bones into a pan with water and salt and pepper. Simmer for about 1 hour to give 300 ml/½ pint stock.

Put half the potatoes, onions and tomatoes into a casserole and season well. Top with the sliced chicken, chopped herbs, stock, salt and pepper. Add the remaining tomatoes, onions, and finally the rest of the sliced potatoes. Top with the butter or margarine. Cook in the centre of a moderate oven (160°C/325°F or Gas Mark 3) for 30 minutes. Cover the casserole and continue cooking for a further 1 hour. Remove the lid for the final 20 minutes, so that the potatoes can brown. Serves 6.

## Sweet and Sour Chicken ⊛

*1 x 1.5 kg/3 lb chicken or 4 chicken joints*
*salt and pepper*
*4 tablespoons dry white wine*
*1 tablespoon sweet sherry*
*2 tablespoons oil*
*1 tablespoon vinegar*
*3 teaspoons cornflour*
*1 tablespoon soy sauce*
*1 tablespoon caster sugar*
*4 tablespoons redcurrant jelly*
*2-3 sticks celery, finely chopped*
*¼ cucumber, peeled and diced*

Cut the flesh away from the chicken bones. Put the bones into a saucepan, cover with water and season lightly. Simmer for 1 hour to give good stock; strain off 300 ml/½ pint for the sauce. Cut the chicken flesh into neat strips. Blend a little salt and pepper with the wine and sherry. Pour into a deep dish, add the chicken flesh and marinate for 3 to 4 hours. At the end of this time, remove the chicken from the dish and reserve the marinade. Heat the oil and fry the chicken until tender and golden in colour; keep warm. Meanwhile prepare the sauce. Blend the vinegar and stock with the cornflour. Put into a saucepan. Add the wine marinade, the soy sauce, sugar and redcurrant jelly. Stir over a moderate heat until thickened and smooth. Add the celery, cucumber and cooked chicken. Heat for 2 to 3 minutes only. Serve with rice.

VARIATION

**Chicken in Pineapple:** Cut the chicken in strips; make 300 ml/½ pint stock, as the recipe above. Coat the chicken in 25 g/1 oz seasoned flour, fry until brown and tender in 3 tablespoons oil. Meanwhile blend 25 g/1 oz cornflour with the chicken stock, 300 ml/½ pint sweetened canned pineapple syrup and 1 tablespoon lemon juice. Cook until thickened and clear. Add 8 to 10 chopped pineapple rings and about 12 cocktail onions. Serve the sauce with the chicken.

## Deep-fried Chicken

*4 chicken portions*
*salt and pepper*
*1 tablespoon flour*
*oil or fat for frying*
COATING:
*75 g/3 oz flour*
*pinch salt*
*1 egg*
*150 ml/¼ pint milk and water*
*1 tablespoon oil*

Allow frozen chicken portions to defrost. Skin if wished and coat in the seasoned flour. Make the batter coating by blending all the ingredients together and coat the chicken. Heat a pan of deep oil or fat to 170°C/340°F (explanation of testing oil or fat on page 290). Fry the chicken steadily for about 10 minutes or until tender; drain on absorbent paper. Serve with shallow fried tomatoes and mushrooms.

Note: the speed of frying chicken portions is not the same as for Chicken Kiev (page 180), for in that recipe you have to cook the outside very rapidly, to keep the butter from bursting through the coating.

VARIATION

**Spiced Chicken:** Add 1 tablespoon chopped mixed herbs, a pinch grated nutmeg, 1 teaspoon tomato purée and pinch cayenne pepper to the batter; use only ½ tablespoon oil (this helps to give a crisp batter).

## Fried Chicken

*4 chicken portions*
*1 tablespoon oil*
*50 g/2 oz butter*
*salt and pepper*

If frying the chicken without a coating, there is no need to allow frozen chicken portions to defrost. Heat the oil and butter in a large frying pan. Put in the chicken and fry steadily for about 5 minutes, turning once or twice; by this time frozen chicken will begin to defrost. Raise the heat and fry until golden coloured, then lower the heat once again and cook until tender. Sprinkle a little salt and pepper over the chicken when nearly cooked. Young frying chicken portions take about 15 minutes.

## Crisp-coated Chicken

*4 chicken portions*
*salt and pepper*
*1 tablespoon flour*
*1 egg*
*50 g/2 oz crisp breadcrumbs*
FOR FRYING:
*1 tablespoon oil*
*50 g/2 oz butter*

Allow frozen chicken portions to defrost. Skin if wished and dry well. Coat in the seasoned flour, beaten egg and crisp breadcrumbs. Heat the oil and butter and fry as above. Drain on absorbent paper.

VARIATION

**Parmesan Chicken:** Blend 25 g/1 oz grated Parmesan cheese with the breadcrumbs.

## Chicken in Calvados

*1 tablespoon lemon juice*
*4 dessert apples, cored and thickly sliced*
*4 chicken breasts*
*salt and pepper*
*25 g/1 oz flour*
*75 g/3 oz butter*
*3 tablespoons Calvados*
*150 ml/¼ pint chicken stock*
*5 tablespoons double cream*

Sprinkle the lemon juice over the apple slices so they do not discolour. Skin and coat the chicken in the seasoned flour. Heat half the butter in a large frying pan. Cook the apples slowly, turning several times until just tender. Lift on to a plate and keep hot. Heat the rest of the butter, fry the chicken joints until pale golden on either side and almost tender. Add the Calvados, stock and cream. Stir well as the mixture heats and thickens. Simmer for several minutes but DO NOT ALLOW TO BOIL. Serve the chicken and sauce topped with apple slices.

VARIATIONS

Omit the Calvados, use apple juice instead.

**Gammon in Whiskey:** Use slices of uncooked gammon instead of chicken. Coat this with only 15 g/½ oz flour mixed with a shake of pepper. Fry the apple slices and gammon as above then add 3 tablespoons Irish whiskey, 150 ml/¼ pint single cream but no stock. Heat as above.

## Chicken Maryland

*4 joints young frying chicken*
*4 small bananas*
*1 x 325 g/11½ oz can sweetcorn*
*oil for frying*
COATING:
*25 g/1 oz flour*
*salt and pepper*
*1 egg*
*50 g/2 oz crisp breadcrumbs*
FRITTER BATTER:
*100 g/4 oz flour*
*pinch salt*
*1 egg*
*150 ml/¼ pint milk*
GARNISH:
*watercress*

Dry the chicken joints well; if frozen they must be allowed to defrost completely so that the coating will adhere to the flesh. Blend the flour with a little salt and pepper; coat the chicken in half the seasoned flour, then in the beaten egg and crisp breadcrumbs. Peel the bananas, halve if wished, and coat with the remaining flour.

Blend together the ingredients for the batter and add the well drained sweetcorn.

Heat the oil in a deep pan to 170°C/340°F (for explanation of testing oil see page 290). Fry the chicken for 10 minutes in the hot oil then add spoonfuls of the sweetcorn fritter mixture. Continue frying the chicken and fritters for about 5 minutes; remove from the oil and drain on absorbent paper. Add the bananas and cook for 1 minute only. Arrange the fried foods on a heated dish and garnish with the watercress.

Note: For many people this dish consists of too many fried foods, in which case fry the chicken and bananas, as in the recipe and serve sweetcorn as a vegetable.

## Chicken Kiev

*100g/4oz butter*
*4 good sized chicken breasts*
*oil or fat for frying*
COATING:
*salt and pepper*
*25g/1oz flour*
*1 egg*
*50g/2oz fine soft breadcrumbs*
GARNISH:
*watercress*

Cut the butter into 4 portions and chill or freeze these until very hard. Bone the chicken breasts or ask the butcher to do this for you. Frozen chicken joints must be defrosted first. If the joints include the wings you can retain the wing tip bones. Flatten the chicken flesh with a rolling pin. Place a pat of butter on each chicken portion; fold in the sides of the flesh to encase the butter and then roll up firmly to form a neat shape. If the wing-tip bones are retained these should, of course, be outside the roll.

Coat the chicken in seasoned flour, beaten egg and crumbs. Chill for an hour before frying. Heat the oil or fat to 190°C/375°F (explanation of testing oil or fat on page 290). Fry the chicken for 2 minutes then lower heat slightly and continue cooking for a further 4 to 5 minutes. Drain on absorbent paper and garnish with watercress.

VARIATION

**Piquant Chicken Kiev:** Use very small boned whole spring chickens instead of chicken breasts.

Fry 2 tablespoons finely chopped green pepper, 1 finely chopped onion, 1 crushed clove garlic and 50g/2oz sliced mushrooms in 50g/2oz butter. Drain well and blend with just 50g/2oz butter and 1 tablespoon chopped parsley. Season well. Divide into 4 portions. Chill, then proceed as above.

## Chicken in Lemon and Anchovy

*4 chicken portions*
*salt and pepper*
*3 tablespoons lemon juice*
*75g/3oz butter*
*2 tablespoons chopped parsley*
*small can anchovy fillets*

Skin the chicken portions and sprinkle with salt, pepper and half the lemon juice. Leave to stand for 1 hour, so the flesh absorbs the flavourings. Heat the butter in a frying pan and fry the chicken steadily until tender and golden in colour. Remove on to a hot dish. Add the rest of the lemon juice, the parsley and anchovy fillets, with any oil from the can. Heat for 1 minute then spoon over the chicken.

VARIATION

**Chicken Niçoise:** Fry the chicken as above and remove from the pan. Heat 2 tablespoons oil and fry 2 chopped onions, 2 crushed cloves garlic, 3 skinned chopped tomatoes and seasoning; spoon over the chicken. Garnish with black olives.

## Chicken Roman Style ⊛

*2 medium onions, thinly sliced*
*3 tablespoons oil*
*25 g/1 oz butter*
*6 joints young frying chicken*
*200 ml/⅓ pint white wine*
*3 tablespoons tomato purée*
*2-3 sage leaves or pinch dried sage*
*50 g/2 oz plain chocolate*
*salt and pepper*
*50 g/2 oz cooked ham*
GARNISH:
*50 g/2 oz blanched almonds*
*few potato crisps*

Separate the onions into rings. Heat half the oil in a very large frying pan and fry the onions until just tender; do not allow to brown. Lift out of the frying pan on to a plate. Heat the rest of the oil and the butter in the frying pan, add the chicken joints and fry steadily until nearly tender. Blend the wine and tomato purée, pour into the pan and add the sage, chocolate, salt and pepper to taste. Stir over a low heat until the chocolate has melted. Cut the ham into narrow strips. Return the onions to the pan, add the ham and heat for 2 to 3 minutes. Remove the sage leaves. Spoon the chicken and sauce on to a hot serving dish and top with the almonds. Add the potato crisps at the very last minute so they retain their crispness. Serves 6.

VARIATION

⊛ **Lamb Roman Style:** Substitute 8 boned and rolled lamb cutlets for the chicken. Use red instead of white wine. As lamb has more natural fat than chicken, use only 2 tablespoons oil. Increase the onions to 3. Allow 2 cutlets per person.

## Fried Lemon Chicken

*4 portions young frying chicken*
*salt and pepper*
*50 g/2 oz flour*
*75 g/3 oz butter*
*1 tablespoon oil*
*300 ml/½ pint chicken stock*
*2 tablespoons lemon juice*
*3 tablespoons double cream*
*2 egg yolks*
GARNISH:
*25 g/1 oz blanched almonds*
*2 tablespoons chopped parsley*

Dry the chicken portions well. Blend a little salt and pepper with half the flour and coat the chicken in this. Heat 50 g/2 oz of the butter and the oil in a large frying pan. Fry the chicken joints until golden in colour and tender – this takes 12 to 15 minutes.

Meanwhile heat the remaining butter in a saucepan, stir in the remaining flour and cook for 2 to 3 minutes. Blend in the stock and lemon juice, bring the liquid to the boil then stir until thickened. Allow to simmer for 5 minutes, stirring now and again. The sauce will then be a good coating consistency. Take the pan off the heat when the chicken is ready to dish up. Whisk together the cream and egg yolks and whisk into the hot, but not boiling sauce. Do not reheat. Pour the sauce round the chicken joints and top with the almonds and parsley.

## Chicken in Vermouth

*4 tablespoons oil*
*12 very small onions*
*2 cloves garlic*
*4 chicken portions*
*25 g/1 oz flour*
*1 teaspoon paprika*
*150 ml/¼ pint white vermouth*
*300 ml/½ pint chicken stock*
*2 tablespoons tomato purée*
*salt and pepper*
*4 tablespoons yogurt*

Heat the oil in a large saucepan, fry the whole onions and garlic for 5 minutes, or until the onions are pale brown. Remove from the pan and discard the garlic. Add the chicken portions to the oil remaining in the saucepan and fry for 5 to 6 minutes, or until golden in colour. Remove from the pan. Blend the flour and paprika with any oil left in the saucepan, then gradually add the vermouth, stock and tomato purée, stirring well as you do so. Continue to stir as the sauce comes to the boil and thickens and add salt and pepper to taste. Return the onions and chicken to the saucepan. Put on a lid and simmer gently for 40 minutes or until the chicken is tender. Lift the chicken and onions on to a heated serving dish. Add the yogurt to the sauce, but do not stir vigorously, for the sauce looks more interesting with a slightly streaky effect. Spoon over the chicken and serve with cooked rice or pasta.

## Barbecued Chicken

*1 whole chicken or 4-6 chicken joints*
BARBECUE SAUCE:
*1 teaspoon made mustard*
*2 tablespoons tomato ketchup*
*1 tablespoon mushroom ketchup*
*3 tablespoons Worcestershire sauce*
*few drops Tabasco sauce*
*2 tablespoons oil*
*2 tablespoons tomato purée*
*salt and pepper*
*2 tablespoons brown sugar*

Chicken is one of the most popular foods for a barbecue. You can cook the whole chicken, allow the same time as when roasting at the higher temperature given on page 184. If cooking chicken joints, allow the same time as when grilling, see page 183.

Always baste the chicken or the joints with seasoned oil or butter before and during cooking and turn several times.

You can however baste the chicken with the highly spiced sauce given in this recipe. Simply mix the ingredients together.

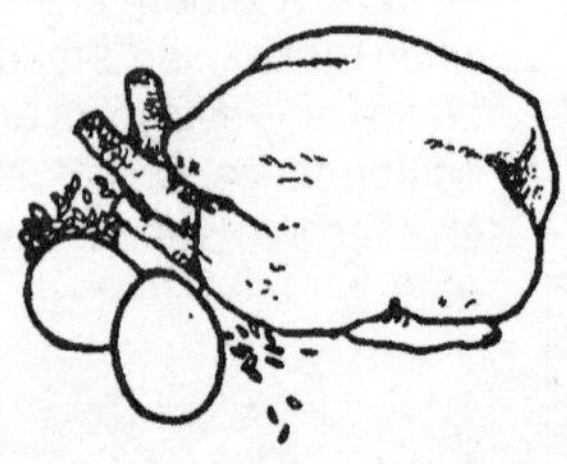

## Grilled Chicken

*4 chicken portions*
*salt and pepper*
*2 tablespoons oil or 50 g/2 oz butter, melted*

There is no need to defrost frozen chicken portions for grilling, unless flavouring with herbs and spices, as in the recipes below, or adding some kind of topping. Brush the chicken with seasoned oil or melted butter before and during cooking. Preheat the grill, for it spoils young chicken to be cooked too slowly.

Cook rapidly for 2 to 3 minutes, until the chicken begins to brown. Lower the heat and cook more slowly. Young chicken portions will take from 10 to 15 minutes cooking.

VARIATIONS

**Chicken au Gratin:** Grill the chicken until almost tender. Top with 50 g/2 oz soft breadcrumbs, 50 g/2 oz grated cheese and 25 g/1 oz melted butter, grill for 2 to 3 minutes.

**Pizza Chicken:** Grill the chicken until almost tender. Fry 1 chopped onion and 3 chopped tomatoes in 2 tablespoons oil, add salt and pepper and pinch dried oregano. Top the chicken portions with this mixture then with 25 g/1 oz grated cheese, 8 anchovy fillets; heat for 2 minutes.

## Spatchcock of Chicken

*2 poussin (spring chickens)*
*50 g/2 oz butter, melted*
*squeeze lemon juice*
*salt and pepper*
GARNISH:
*4 tomatoes, halved*
*watercress*

Split the chickens down the back so the birds can be flattened. Place on the grid of the grill pan, skinside uppermost. Mix the butter, lemon juice and a little salt and pepper. Brush the chickens with the flavoured butter and grill for 10 to 15 minutes (according to size) until tender. Add the halved tomatoes to the grill pan 3 to 4 minutes before the end of the cooking time. Arrange the chickens and tomatoes on a hot dish and garnish with watercress. Serves 2.

VARIATIONS:

**Chicken Italienne:** Blend 1 teaspoon chopped sage, pinch ground ginger, 2 tablespoons chopped parsley and ½ teaspoon chopped rosemary with the seasoned butter in the recipe above; then add the lemon juice to taste.

**Orange Spatchcock:** Grate the zest from 2 large oranges. Blend with the seasoned butter. Add 1 tablespoon orange juice in addition to the squeeze of lemon juice. Cook as above. Garnish with segments of fresh orange and watercress.

## Roast Chicken and Turkey ⊛

*There is a high percentage of bone in poultry, so the amounts allowed per person may seem high; obviously this quantity can be reduced*

WEIGHT TO ALLOW *per person when buying the bird:*

*450g/1 lb per person for turkey, but since the bones of chicken are smaller you can allow rather less*

These birds are very lean and great care must be taken that they do not become dry, so cover well with fat. It is a good idea to roast turkey and large chickens with the breasts turned downwards for the first half of the roasting time; this means any fat runs down and keeps the breast moist. After this, turn the bird so the breast is uppermost and will become pleasantly brown. A covered roasting tin, if sufficiently large, is excellent for cooking these birds. I do not wrap them completely in foil, but rather just put foil loosely over the bird until towards the end of the cooking period. You can use a roaster bag. Always calculate the total roasting time after stuffing the birds.

Chickens and turkeys which have not been frozen and then defrosted or chilled can be roasted in a moderately hot to hot oven (200-220°C/400-425°F or Gas Mark 6-7).

Allow 15 minutes per 450 g/1 lb plus 15 minutes. If cooking a large turkey, follow this timing up to 5.5 kg/12 lb then allow an extra 12 minutes per additional 450 g/1 lb.

Chickens and turkeys which have been frozen then defrosted or chilled are better roasted in a moderate oven (160-180°C/325-350°F or Gas Mark 3-4). Allow 22 to 25 minutes per 450 g/1 lb plus 22 to 25 minutes. Chicken and turkey are generally served with a thickened gravy.

Note: It is essential that frozen poultry is COMPLETELY defrosted before roasting.

## Bread Sauce ⊛

*few cloves (optional)*
*1 small onion*
*300 ml/½ pint milk*
*50 g/2 oz soft breadcrumbs*
*salt and pepper*
*40 g/1½ oz butter*
*2 tablespoons double cream (optional)*

Press the cloves into the peeled onion and put in a pan with the milk. Bring the milk to the boil, remove from the heat and add the breadcrumbs, salt, pepper and butter. Cover and leave in a warm place to infuse. Add the cream and reheat just before the meal. Stir briskly before serving; remove the onion. It is wiser to cook bread sauce in the top of a double saucepan or basin over hot water so there is no fear of it burning. This richer than standard recipe for this sauce, which blends so well with chicken, turkey, veal and game birds, is delicious.

# Accompaniments to Roast Chicken and Turkey

Bread Sauce (see page 184) has always been a traditional accompaniment to roast chicken and turkey. Over the years, however, Cranberry Sauce, recipe below, has become increasingly popular. At Christmas time, or when you are cooking for quite a number of people, you could serve both sauces. Bacon rolls and cooked sausages complement the delicate flavour of chicken and turkey. Make the bacon rolls (see Roast Veal recipe, page 159), add to the roasting tin together with sausages, so they are cooked by the time the poultry is ready to serve. Use both the Chestnut Stuffing (see below) and Thyme and Parsley Stuffing (page 186) in good-sized birds.

Roast veal is served with the same accompaniments as chicken and turkey.

## Cranberry Sauce ⊛

*150 ml/¼ pint water*
*150 g/5 oz sugar or to taste*
*450 g/1 lb cranberries*
*3 tablespoons redcurrant jelly*

Put the water and sugar into a saucepan and stir until the sugar has dissolved. Add the cranberries and cover the saucepan with a lid, as the berries tend to 'explode' as they start to cook. Cook gently until nearly tender, this takes about 8 minutes. Add the redcurrant jelly and stir over a low heat until the jelly has dissolved. Serve hot or cold. Serves 6 to 8.

VARIATIONS

Use orange juice in place of water; or use red or port wine in place of the water.

## Chestnut Stuffing ⊛

*450 g/1 lb chestnuts*
*150 ml/¼ pint chicken stock*
*salt and pepper*
*50 g/2 oz butter, melted*
*100 g/4 oz bacon, derinded and finely chopped*

Slit the chestnuts skins and simmer in water for 10 minutes. Peel while warm and return to the pan. Add the stock and simmer gently for 15 minutes, then mash, sieve or liquidize. Mix with the other ingredients. Put into the body of the chicken or turkey before cooking. Spoon out to serve. Serves 6 to 8.

## Giblet Stuffing ⊛

*giblets of chicken or turkey*
*salt and pepper*
*ingredients as Thyme and Parsley Stuffing (page 186)*

Cook the giblets, without the liver, in seasoned water. The stock produced makes a good gravy. Chop the cooked giblets and the uncooked liver very finely and mix with the other stuffing ingredients. This makes a pleasant alternative to Thyme and Parsley Stuffing but children may find the flavour too strong.

## Thyme and Parsley Stuffing ⊛

*100 g/4 oz soft breadcrumbs*
*50 g/2 oz shredded suet or butter, melted*
*2 tablespoons chopped parsley*
*1 teaspoon chopped thyme*
*1 teaspoon grated lemon rind*
*1 tablespoon lemon juice*
*salt and pepper*
*1 egg*

Mix all the ingredients together. Put into the neck end of the chicken or turkey; bring down the skin to cover. Secure with a small skewer or wooden cocktail sticks. This stuffing can be carved in neat slices.

## Forcemeat Stuffing ⊛

*450 g/1 lb sausagemeat*
*2-3 tablespoons chopped mixed fresh herbs*
*1 egg*

Blend the sausagemeat, herbs and egg together. Use instead of sausages or as an alternative to Chestnut Stuffing.

VARIATION

⊛ **Chestnut and Sausage Stuffing:** Mix the stuffing above with the ingredients for Chestnut Stuffing (see page 185). This makes an excellent and economical mixture for a large bird.

## Chicken Pot Roast

*50 g/2 oz chicken fat or other fat*
*1 chicken, about 1.5 kg/3 lb in weight*
*6-8 large potatoes*
*6 large onions*
*6 large carrots*
*4 large leeks, cut into 5 cm/2 inch lengths*
*150 ml/¼ pint chicken stock*
*150 ml/¼ pint white wine*
*salt and pepper*
*2 teaspoons chopped rosemary*

Heat the fat in a very large saucepan. Add the chicken and brown thoroughly all over. Lift the chicken from the saucepan and pour away all the fat. Add the potatoes, onions, carrots and leeks with the stock, white wine, salt, pepper and rosemary. Replace the chicken in the saucepan. Cover the saucepan with a tightly-fitting lid. Bring the liquid just to simmering, adjust the heat so there is no fear of it boiling rapidly and evaporating. Cook for 1¼ hours and check once or twice that you have enough liquid. Lift the chicken and vegetables from the pan. The vegetables can be served with the dish or used in a soup the next day. Use the liquid in the saucepan as the basis for gravy.

## Chicken in Cream and Lemon ⊛

*50 g/2 oz butter, melted*
*salt and pepper*
*1 teaspoon grated lemon rind*
*1 medium chicken*
*150 ml/¼ pint soured cream*
*1 tablespoon lemon juice*

Blend the butter with salt, pepper and lemon rind. Brush over the chicken and roast as page 184. Take the chicken out of the oven 10 minutes before the end of the cooking time, if using the hotter temperature, but 15 minutes before the end of the cooking time, if roasting at the lower heat. Blend the soured cream and lemon juice with salt and pepper to taste. Pour away all the surplus fat from the roasting tin. Cover the bird with the soured cream mixture, return to the oven and complete the cooking.

## Cider Chicken ⊛

*25 g/1 oz butter, melted*
*300 ml/½ pint dry cider*
*salt and pepper*
*1 x 1.5 kg/3 lb chicken*
*4 dessert apples*
*4 medium onions*

Blend the butter, cider and salt and pepper. Put the chicken with the cored, but not peeled apples and whole onions in the roasting tin. Spoon the cider mixture over the bird. Cover the tin and roast as page 184. Baste several times with the cider liquid. Serve the chicken with the apples and onions and use the cider liquid to make the gravy.

## Glazed Chicken ⊛

*1 medium chicken*
*50 g/2 oz butter, melted*
*2 tablespoons honey*
*2 teaspoons Dijon mustard*
*2 teaspoons lemon juice*
*salt and pepper*

Brush the chicken with the melted butter and roast as page 184. Take the bird out of the oven 10 minutes before the end of the roasting time, if using the hotter temperature, but 15 minutes before the end of the cooking time, if roasting at the lower heat. Blend the honey, mustard, lemon juice and seasoning together. Pour out the excess fat from the roasting tin. Cover the bird with the honey mixture, return to the oven and complete the cooking.

## Rosemary Chicken ⊛

*75 g/3 oz butter*
*2½ tablespoons chopped rosemary*
*1 medium chicken*
*3 medium potatoes*
*salt and pepper*

Melt 50 g/2 oz of the butter, blend with 2 tablespoons chopped rosemary and brush over the chicken. Put the whole peeled potatoes inside the bird. Weigh and roast as page 184. When cooked, spoon the potatoes from inside the bird, mash with the remainder of the butter and the rest of the rosemary. Season well and serve as an accompaniment to the chicken.

## Terrine of Chicken ⊛

*1 large chicken, about 2.25 kg/5 lb in weight*
*1 onion*
*1 bay leaf*
*sprig fresh thyme*
*salt and pepper*
*50 g/2 oz soft breadcrumbs*
*4 tablespoons chicken stock (see method)*
*4 tablespoons double cream*
*1 tablespoon chopped parsley*
*2 egg yolks*

COATING:

*600 ml/1 pint packet aspic jelly or use the recipe on page 264.*

Carefully cut the raw breast meat from the chicken into neat thick slices. Cover well so the lean meat does not dry. Cut all the remaining flesh from the chicken and either mince this or chop finely in a food processor.

Put the chicken bones with the onion, herbs and a little salt and pepper into a saucepan. Add water to cover, put a lid on the pan and simmer gently for 1 to 1½ hours. Strain the liquid very carefully and put 4 tablespoons on one side for the terrine. Save 600 ml/1 pint to make the jelly. Any stock remaining should be kept in a cold place or frozen to use in a soup or stew.

Cut the thick slices of chicken into thinner slices (the reason for slicing thickly initially is to keep the flesh more moist). Mix the minced chicken flesh with the breadcrumbs, the reserved 4 tablespoons stock, cream, chopped parsley and egg yolks. Add a little salt and pepper. Put a quarter of the minced chicken mixture into a terrine mould or an oval or round buttered 1.2-1.5 litre/2-2½ pint casserole. Add a layer of sliced breast meat, another layer of minced meat, more sliced breast, another layer of minced meat, then a final layer of the sliced breast and a topping of minced meat. Cover the dish with buttered foil and stand in a bain marie of cold water. Bake in the centre of a moderate oven (160°C/325°F or Gas Mark 3) for 1½ hours. Cool in the baking dish then turn out carefully.

Dissolve the aspic jelly in the reserved 600 ml/1 pint chicken stock. Allow this to cool and thicken slightly. Place the terrine on a dish, brush about half the thick jelly over the shape and leave to set. Allow the remaining jelly to become firm, whisk with a fork and spoon round the terrine. Serve with salad.

VARIATIONS

Mince about 225 g/8 oz cooked tongue, ham or lean uncooked pork or veal with the chicken. Blend the minced chicken meat with 225 g/8 oz pork sausage-meat. Add 50 g/2 oz chopped blanched almonds.

⊛ **Terrine of Duck:** Prepare the large duck as the recipe above but add 1 teaspoon finely chopped fresh sage to the minced mixture, together with 2 very finely chopped onions, which should be cooked gently in 25 g/1 oz butter. When making the stock from the duck bones, allow this to become cold and remove any fat from the top. Additional flavour is given to this terrine if the juice and thinly pared orange zest of 1 to 2 oranges are added to the duck bones when making the stock.

# Using Cooked Chicken

## Chicken and Pineapple Bake

*225g/8oz cooked green beans*
*450g/1 lb cooked chicken, diced*
*50g/2oz blanched almonds, flaked*
*450ml/¾ pint White Sauce (see page 226)*
*1 x 225g/8oz can pineapple rings*
*1-2 small packets potato crisps*

Mix together the beans and chicken. Put into a shallow ovenproof serving dish. Add the almonds and sauce. Cover with a lid or foil and bake in the centre of a moderate oven (180°C/350°F or Gas Mark 4) for 20 minutes. Meanwhile drain the pineapple rings. Remove the foil or cover from the casserole, top with the pineapple rings and potato crisps. Do not replace the covering. Return to the oven for a further 5 minutes, then serve.

VARIATION

⊛ **Chicken and Cheese Bake:** Omit the pineapple rings. Put layers of cooked chicken, sliced cheese and beans in the casserole. Top with the almonds and sauce. Heat as the recipe above. Remove the lid, top with thickly sliced tomatoes and potato crisps. Heat for 5 minutes.

## Curried Chicken ⊛

*225g/8oz cooked chicken breast*
*75g/3oz canned water chestnuts*
*75g/3oz canned bamboo shoots*
*2 tablespoons oil*
*2 medium onions, finely chopped*
*50g/2oz blanched almonds, coarsely chopped*
*2 teaspoons curry powder*
*1 tablespoon soy sauce*

Cut the chicken, water chestnuts and bamboo shoots into neat, even-sized strips about 1 cm/½ inch in width. Heat the oil in a large frying pan and fry the onions with the almonds for several minutes unitl pale golden in colour. Blend in the curry powder then add all the ingredients and heat thoroughly; stir well to prevent the mixture burning. Serve with boiled or Pineapple Rice, page 191.

VARIATION

This dish is extremely good when served cold. Proceed as above, cool and blend with a little thick mayonnaise. Serve on lettuce.

## Chicken and Cheese Fritters

*100 g/4 oz flour*
*salt and pepper*
*1 egg*
*5 tablespoons milk*
*225 g/8 oz cooked chicken, minced*
*75 g/3 oz Cheddar or Gruyère cheese, grated*
FOR FRYING:
*75 g/3 oz butter*
*1 tablespoon oil*

Blend together the flour, salt and pepper to taste, egg and milk. Add the chicken and cheese. Mix well. Heat together the butter and oil. Put about 8 spoonfuls of the chicken mixture into the pan. Cook steadily for 2 to 3 minutes, turn and cook on the second side for the same time, then lower the heat and cook for a further 2 to 3 minutes. Drain on absorbent paper. Serve hot or cold with salad. Serves 2 as a main meal, 4 as a snack.

VARIATION

⊛ **Chicken Pancakes:** Cook 8 to 12 small pancakes (see page 289). Make a sauce with 25 g/1 oz butter or chicken fat, 25 g/1 oz flour, 150 ml/¼ pint milk, 150 ml/¼ pint chicken stock and 2 tablespoons double cream. Add 350 g/12 oz cooked diced chicken, heat and blend with 50 g/2 oz sliced fried mushrooms. Fill the pancakes with the chicken mixture, roll up and serve.

## Pancake Piroshki

*Pancake Batter (see page 289)*
FILLING:
*50 g/2 oz cooked long-grain rice*
*225 g/8 oz cooked chicken, finely minced*
*2 hard-boiled eggs, chopped*
*225 g/8 oz cooked spinach, finely chopped or sieved*
*salt and pepper*
*1 egg*
COATING:
*2 eggs*
*1 tablespoon water*
*50-75 g/2-3 oz crisp breadcrumbs*
*oil or fat for frying*

Make the batter and cook 12 small thin pancakes. Blend together the ingredients for the filling and divide the mixture between the pancakes. Fold in the edges to envelop the filling and roll up very firmly. Beat the eggs for the coating with the water, dip the pancakes in this mixture, then coat with the breadcrumbs. Secure the pancake rolls with wooden cocktail sticks.

Heat the oil or fat to 170°C/345°F (for explanation of testing oil and fat, see page 290), put in the pancakes and fry steadily for 5 minutes. Drain on absorbent paper, remove the cocktail sticks and serve hot. These make a delicious hors d'oeuvre or main dish served with more cooked spinach.

VARIATION

**Cheese and Mushroom Piroshki:** Use 225 g/8 oz sieved cottage or cream cheese instead of the minced chicken and 100 g/4 oz finely chopped cooked mushrooms in place of the hard-boiled eggs. This version can be prepared and frozen, whereas the basic recipe is unsuitable for freezing as it contains hard-boiled eggs.

## Devilled Chicken ⊛

*100g/4oz butter or margarine*
*2 tablespoons chutney*
*1 teaspoon mustard powder*
*pinch cayenne pepper*
*salt and garlic salt*
*1 small cooked chicken*
*75g/3oz soft breadcrumbs*

Cream 75g/3oz of the butter or margarine, add the chutney, mustard powder, cayenne pepper, a little salt and the garlic salt to taste. Cut the chicken into neat joints – 2 or 4 leg joints, 2 or 4 breast joints. Spread the chutney mixture over one side of the joints and place these in an ovenproof dish. Top with the breadcrumbs. Melt the remaining butter or margarine and pour round the chicken joints. Do not cover the dish. Bake above the centre of a moderately hot oven (200°C/400°F or Gas Mark 6) for 25 to 30 minutes. Serve with Pineapple Rice below or Saffron Rice (see page 300).

## Pineapple Rice ⊛

*50g/2oz butter or margarine*
*1 medium onion, chopped*
*3 sticks celery, chopped*
*150ml/¼pint water*
*300ml/½pint pineapple juice*
*1 teaspoon grated orange rind*
*175g/6oz long-grain rice*
*salt and pepper*
*1 tablespoon chopped parsley*
*½ teaspoon chopped thyme*

Heat the butter or margarine, add the onion and cook for 2 to 3 minutes. Add the celery and continue cooking for 2 to 3 minutes; do not allow the vegetables to brown. Add the water, pineapple juice, orange rind and the rice. Bring to the boil, add salt and pepper, and stir briskly, then cover the pan. Lower the heat and simmer for about 15 minutes. When the rice is cooked, add the chopped parsley and thyme.

## Chicken and Ham Mousse ⊛

*3 tablespoons white wine, dry cider or chicken stock*
*15 g/½ oz gelatine*
*2 tablespoons thick mayonnaise*
*1½ tablespoons tomato purée*
*1 teaspoon made mustard*
*salt and pepper*
*150 ml/¼ pint yogurt*
*225 g/8 oz chicken breast, minced or finely chopped*
*100g/4 oz lean ham, minced or finely chopped*
*150 ml/¼ pint double cream, whipped*
*2 egg whites*
GARNISH:
*lettuce*
*cooked sweetcorn*
*cooked peas*

Put the wine, cider or stock into a fairly large basin and sprinkle the gelatine on top of the liquid. Stand over a saucepan of very hot water until dissolved, then add the mayonnaise, tomato purée, mustard, a little salt and pepper, the yogurt and then the chicken and ham. Leave in a cool place until the mixture begins to stiffen slightly, then blend in the whipped cream. Whisk the egg whites until stiff and fold into the other ingredients. Taste the mixture and add more seasoning if required. Spoon into a straight-sided 1.2 litre/2 pint oiled mould. Leave until set, then turn out onto a bed of shredded lettuce. Garnish with the sweetcorn and peas.

VARIATION

⊛ **Chicken and Asparagus Mousse:** Omit the tomato purée and yogurt. Use 350 g/12 oz cooked chicken and omt the ham. Make 10 tablespoons thick asparagus purée by sieving or liquidizing cooked or canned asparagus. Do not use any of the liquid from cooking the vegetable or from the can in the purée. Add the asparagus purée to the other ingredients before folding in the whipped cream and whisked egg whites. Garnish with asparagus tips, sliced hard-boiled eggs and lettuce heart.

## Curried Chicken Cream ⊛

*1 tablespoon oil*
*1 medium onion, finely chopped*
*2 teaspoons curry paste or powder*
*3 tablespoons mayonnaise*
*150 ml/¼ pint single cream*
*1 tablespoon desiccated coconut*
*1 tablespoon chopped gherkins*
*1 tablespoon chutney*
*salt and pepper*
*pinch sugar*
*450 g/lb cooked chicken, diced*

Heat the oil and fry the onion for 2 to 3 minutes, then cool. Mix together all the ingredients, except the chicken. If the chutney has large lumps, these should be finely chopped. Add the chicken. Allow to stand for 1 hour. Serve with Spanish Rice Salad (see page 304).

## Curried Avocado and Chicken Salad

*4 medium avocados*
*lettuce*
DRESSING:
*4 tablespoons mayonnaise*
*1-2 teaspoons curry paste or powder*
*2 tablespoons double or single cream*
*1½-2 tablespoons lemon juice*
FILLING:
*225 g/8 oz cooked chicken, finely chopped*
*1 canned red pepper, finely chopped*
*1-2 sticks celery, finely chopped*
*1 small dessert apple, peeled and finely chopped*

Mix together all the ingredients for the dressing, except 1 tablespoon lemon juice. Skin and halve the avocados and remove the stones. Sprinkle with the remaining lemon juice. Put the avocados on a bed of crisp lettuce and top with the chicken mixture, made by blending the ingredients together.

VARIATION

**Curried Avocado and Shellfish Salad:** Omit the apple from the recipe above and substitute 4 tablespoons neatly diced cucumber. Use 100 /4 oz peeled prawns, 100 g/4 oz flaked crabmeat plus a few prepared mussels if available instead of the chicken. Flavour the sauce with a little more lemon juice if desired.

## Chicken and Mushroom Salad

*300 g/11 oz cooked chicken, preferably breast meat, diced*
*100 g/4 oz button mushrooms, sliced*
*1 small green pepper, deseeded and diced*
DRESSING:
*3 tablespoons mayonnaise*
*1 tablespoon lemon juice*
*2 tablespoons double cream*
*salt and pepper*
GARNISH:
*1 lettuce*
*tomato slices*

Mix together the mayonnaise, lemon juice and cream with a little salt and pepper. Blend all the ingredients together. Allow to stand for 1 hour. Serve on a bed of lettuce and garnish with the tomato slices.

VARIATIONS

**Chicken, Mushroom and Pineapple Salad:** Omit the green pepper in the recipe above and substitute 3 to 4 diced pineapple rings instead.

**Chicken Rice Salad:** Cook 75 g/3 oz long-grain rice, drain if necessary. Blend with the mayonnaise, lemon juice and cream, as in the recipe above, while the rice is hot, then add 2 tablespoons chopped parsley and 1 teaspoon chopped rosemary. Allow to cool. Blend with 350 g/12 oz diced cooked chicken, 2 skinned diced tomatoes, 100 g/4 oz cooked peas and 2 grated raw carrots.

# Chicken Salads

Cold chicken is universally popular but can become somewhat monotonous if always served the same way. The suggestions below give chicken a very new look.

## Coronation Chicken

*1 cooked chicken, about 1.5 kg/3½ lb in weight (it is better to steam rather than roast the chicken to give a more moist flavour and a paler colour)*

DRESSING:

*150 ml/¼ pint mayonnaise*
*1-2 teaspoons curry paste*
*150 ml/¼ pint soured cream*
*1-2 tablespoons fruit chutney, such as mango, peach or apple, sieved or chopped to make it very smooth*

GARNISH

*1-2 lettuce, finely shredded*
*6 tomatoes, thinly sliced*

Blend together the mayonnaise, curry paste, soured cream and chutney. Cut the chicken into neat small pieces, blend with the dressing and leave for an hour for the various flavours to blend. Serve in a border of shredded lettuce and sliced tomatoes. Serves 6.

VARIATIONS

**Avocado and Grapefruit Chicken:** The dressing can be made with the curry paste and chutney if desired, but there is sufficient flavour in the dish if these are omitted. Blend together the mayonnaise, soured cream and 1 tablespoon salad oil. Peel and neatly dice the flesh from 2 avocados and the segments from 2 grapefruit, add to the dressing, together with the chicken and 2 tablespoons seedless raisins.

**Chicken Montmorency:** Include the chutney but omit the curry paste. Blend the chicken mixture with 175 g/6 oz stoned black cherries, 50 g/2 oz cashew nuts. Add about 175 g/6 oz neatly diced pineapple just before serving. The pineapple can be put in with the other ingredients, but its acidity is inclined to make the chicken over-soft with standing for 1 hour.

**Crispy Chicken Salad:** Omit the chutney but use just 1 teaspoon curry paste. Use yogurt instead of soured cream to make a light dressing. Blend the mayonnaise, yogurt and curry paste together, add the prepared chicken and leave for 1 hour. Core, but do not peel, 2 dessert apples and cut into neat dice. Finely chop a small celery heart and chop enough spring onions to give 3 tablespoons. Add these ingredients to the chicken mixture, together with 1 deseeded and neatly diced red pepper. Put on the lettuce and serve as soon as possible. Top with coarsely chopped walnuts or other nuts.

**Tarragon Chicken Salad:** Omit the curry paste and chutney. Blend the mayonnaise with 1 tablespoon lemon juice, 1 tablespoon finely chopped tarragon and 1 tablespoon finely chopped chives or spring onions.

## Country Chicken Pie ⊛

*Flaky Pastry, made with 225 g/8 oz flour, etc. (see page 292)*
*1 egg*
FILLING:
*1 x 2 kg/4½ lb chicken*
*salt and pepper*
*450 ml/¾ pint chicken stock (see method)*
*50 g/2 oz butter*
*4 lean bacon rashers, derinded and chopped*
*2 medium onions, sliced*
*3 medium carrots, sliced*
*25 g/1 oz flour*
*1 tablespoon chopped parsley*

Make the pastry and chill while preparing the filling. Bone the chicken and cut the meat in small pieces. Put the bones and giblets (except the liver) into a pan and cover with water. Add salt and pepper to taste and simmer for about 1 hour, strain then boil the liquid very hard until only about 450 ml/¾ pint stock remains.

Heat the butter in a pan, add the bacon and vegetables and cook gently for a few minutes. Remove from the pan. Coat the chicken with the flour, mixed with salt, pepper and parsley. Turn in any fat remaining in the pan, then put into a 1.5 litre/2½ pint pie dish, add the vegetables and bacon and about 150 ml/¼ pint of the chicken stock. Roll out the pastry and use to cover the filling. Make a slit on top for any steam to escape during cooking. Decorate with leaves and a rose of pastry. Beat the egg and brush over the pastry. Bake in the centre of a hot oven (220°C/425°F or Gas Mark 7) for 25 minutes, then reduce the heat to moderate (160-180°C/325-350°F or Gas Mark 3-4) and cook for a further 1¼ hours.

Heat the remaining stock in a pan, thicken with Beurre Manié, if desired (see page 45) or serve as thin gravy with the pie. Serves 6.

VARIATIONS

⊛ **Chicken, Liver and Steak Pie:** Dice the uncooked liver of the chicken and 175 g/6 oz lean tender rump steak, mix with the diced chicken (you could use a slightly smaller bird). Omit the carrots and add 100 g/4 oz small button mushrooms to the filling.

⊛ **Creamy Chicken and Leek Pie:** Omit the onions and carrots and use 3 medium leeks instead. Slice these and cook in the butter, as the recipe above. Add 150 ml/¼ pint single cream to the filling, instead of the chicken stock. You can add 2 to 3 sliced frankfurters to the filling for a more piquant flavour.

⊛ **Chicken and Ham Pie:** Follow the recipe for the Veal and Ham Pie on page 160, using hot water crust pastry. Use the meat from a 1.75 g/4 lb chicken with 175 g/6 oz diced lean ham instead of the filling given on page 160. Simmer the chicken bones in water to cover and use the same quantity of stock and gelatine as in the recipe.

# Cooking Guinea Fowl

I always regret the fact that guinea fowl is not as plentiful here, as in France, for it can be very delicious. It is a versatile bird, as it can be treated like chicken or a game bird. Remember it is very dry fleshed, so keep it well basted during cooking. Pot roasting (see page 186), is a good method of cooking guinea fowl.

## Guinea Fowl Véronique ⊛

*2 small guinea fowl*
*salt and pepper*
*75 g/3 oz butter, softened*
*225 g/8 oz grapes, deseeded*
*100 g/4 oz cream cheese*
*150 ml/¼ pint double cream*
*300 ml/½ pint guinea fowl stock (see method)*

Put the giblets of the guinea fowl into a pan with a little salt and pepper and water to cover. Simmer for 1 hour to obtain good stock, strain then boil briskly until reduced to only 300 ml/½ pint; reserve the stock. Blend the butter with a little salt and pepper and spread over the birds. Mix half the grapes with the cheese, season lightly, put inside the birds. Roast following the timings on page 184; use the hotter temperature for very young birds and the lower setting if they are older or are defrosted frozen birds.

About 10 minutes before the end of the cooking time, lift the birds from the tin. Pour out all the fat except 1 tablespoon, blend this with the cream and the reserved stock. Return the birds to the roasting tin and spoon the creamy liquid over them. Complete the cooking, basting once or twice. Dish up the guinea fowl. Pour the liquid into a saucepan and boil hard for several minutes to make a slightly thickened liquid. Add the remaining grapes and heat for 2 minutes. Carve the birds, arrange on a dish with the cheese and grape stuffing. Serve the creamy grape sauce separately.

VARIATION

⊛ **Normandy Pintade:** Blend the cream cheese with 2 peeled and neatly diced dessert apples, 1 tablespoon Calvados and a little seasoning. Put inside the birds, cook as above. When nearly cooked, blend the cream with another 2 tablespoons Calvados and 150 ml/¼ pint guinea fowl stock. Proceed as above. Meanwhile core, but do not peel, 2 or 3 dessert apples. Cut into rings and fry in a little butter. Carve or joint the guinea fowl. Put on a dish, with spoonfuls of the stuffing. Coat with the sauce and garnish with the apple rings.

# Cooking Turkey

Do not regard turkey as a 'once a year' food, just for Christmas time. We can buy fresh and frozen birds throughout the year. In many stores you can obtain turkey portions and these are ideal for small families or to make just one dish. Whether cooking whole turkey or turkey portions you must keep the flesh well moistened with fat.

## Turkey Casserole ⊛

*1 x 3.5 kg/8 lb turkey, oven-ready weight*
*salt and pepper*
*40 g/1 ½ oz flour*
*1 tablespoon oil*
*50 g/2 oz butter*
*16-20 shallots*
*100 g/4 oz bacon, cut in 1 thick rasher, derinded*
*750 ml/1 ¼ pints turkey stock*
*2 teaspoons grated orange rind*
*4 tablespoons orange juice*
GARNISH:
*orange slices*
*watercress*

Carefully cut the meat from the bones, or joint the bird to give 10 joints, i.e 2 drumsticks, 2 portions from each thick thigh and 2 portions from each breast and wing. Put any bones and the giblets into a pan, cover with water, season well and simmer to give 750 ml/1 ¼ pints stock. Strain and reserve the stock. Coat the turkey meat in well-seasoned flour. Heat the oil and butter in a pan and fry the turkey until golden, then put into a large casserole. Turn the whole shallots in the fat that remains in the pan, add to the casserole. Fry the bacon for 2 to 3 minutes and add to the turkey. Blend the reserved stock, orange rind and juice with any fat that is left in the pan; stir well to absorb all the flavour of the fried foods, season generously and pour over the turkey. Cover the casserole and cook in the centre of a cool oven (150°C/ 300°F or Gas Mark 2) for 2 hours. Garnish the turkey with orange slices and watercress. Serves 8 to 10.

VARIATIONS

If the sauce tends to be a little thinner than you would like, heat in a pan and thicken with Beurre Manié (see page 45). Use small onions instead of shallots.

⊛ **Turkey en Daube:** Joint the turkey as described above. Put into a marinade made by blending together 3 tablespoons red wine, 2 tablespoons oil, 2 crushed cloves garlic, 1 teaspoon grated orange rind. Turn the meat several times in the mixture and leave for 1 hour. Meanwhile simmer the giblets and any bones to give 450 ml/¾ pint stock. Place the turkey and marinade into a large casserole with the stock, 3 sliced onions, 6 sliced carrots, the well seasoned strained stock and 175 g/6 oz diced bacon. Cook as the recipe above.

## Stuffed Leg of Turkey ⊛

*1 uncooked turkey leg, weighing about 1 kg/2 to 2¼ lb*

STUFFING:

*50 g/2 oz butter*
*3 bacon rashers, derinded and chopped*
*2 onions, finely chopped*
*2 tablespoons chopped parsley*
*100 g/4 oz soft breadcrumbs, preferably brown*
*1 egg*
*salt and pepper*

Slit the turkey leg and gently cut away the meat from the bones. Lift out the bones and use these as the basis for stock for gravy to serve with the dish.

Heat 25 g/1 oz of the butter in a frying pan, add the bacon and onions and fry for a few minutes. Add the parsley, breadcrumbs, egg and salt and pepper to taste. Press the stuffing into the cavity left after removing the bones and tie or skewer to prevent the stuffing coming out in cooking. Weigh the turkey leg after stuffing. Melt the remaining butter, brush over the turkey and roast at either of the temperatures given on page 184.

VARIATION

⊛ **Cream Cheese and Pepper Turkey Leg:** Prepare the turkey leg as above. Meanwhile put a small green and a small red pepper into boiling salted water and simmer for 3 minutes. Remove from the water, drain and chop the peppers, discarding the cores and seeds. Blend with 225 g/8 oz cream cheese, 2 tablespoons chopped parsley and season well. Put the stuffing into the boned leg of turkey and cook as above.

## Crunchy Drumsticks

*4 turkey drumsticks*
*salt and pepper*
*50 g/2 oz butter, softened*
*50 g/2 oz potato crisps, crushed*

If using frozen drumsticks, allow to defrost and dry well. Blend seasoning with the butter. Put the drumsticks into an ovenproof dish and spread with the seasoned butter. Roast as above, but take out of the oven about 15 minutes before the end of the cooking time and press the crushed crisps around the drumsticks. Return to the oven and complete the cooking.

## Curried Turkey Drumsticks ⊛

*4 turkey drumsticks*
*50 g/2 oz butter, softened*
*2 teaspoons curry powder*
*1 teaspoon lemon juice*
*2 teaspoons desiccated coconut*
*salt and pepper*

If using frozen drumsticks, allow to defrost then dry well. Blend together the butter and the other ingredients. Put the drumsticks in an ovenproof dish and spread with the butter mixture. Bake in the centre of a moderately hot oven, (190°C/375°F or Gas Mark 5) for 40 to 50 minutes or until tender. Serve with cooked rice and chutney.

## Turkey Escalopes Holstein

*4 thin slices uncooked turkey breast*
*salt and pepper*
*1 tablespoon flour*
*100 g/4 oz butter*
*4 eggs*

Flatten the thin turkey slices with a damp rolling pin, then coat in seasoned flour. Heat 75 g/3 oz butter and fry the escalopes of turkey gently on both sides until tender; this takes about 10 minutes. Lift on to a hot dish. Heat the rest of the butter in the frying pan and fry the eggs. Serve the turkey escalopes topped with the fried eggs.

VARIATIONS

Serve turkey escalopes in any of the ways suggested for these thin slices of meat, see pages 129, 140, 156, 157.

## Turkey Escalopes Caprice

*4 thin slices uncooked turkey breast*
*salt and pepper*
*1 tablespoon flour*
*100 g/4 oz butter*
*2 tablespoons lemon juice*
*4 small bananas*

Flatten the turkey slices with a damp rolling pin, then coat in seasoned flour. Heat 75 g/3 oz butter in a large frying pan and fry the escalopes until tender. Lift on to a hot dish. Add the remaining butter and lemon juice to the pan, heat together, then add the peeled bananas. Cook for 3 to 4 minutes, spoon the lemon and butter sauce over the escalopes and top with the bananas.

## Nutty Goujons of Turkey

*450 g/1 lb uncooked turkey breast*
*2 medium onions*
*100 g/4 oz button mushrooms*
*75 g/3 oz butter*
*100 g/4 oz salted peanuts*

Cut the turkey meat into thin strips. Cut the onions into rings, then divide the rings to make small strips. Cut the mushrooms into thin slices. Heat the butter in a large frying pan. Fry the onions for 2 to 3 minutes but do not allow to colour. Add the turkey and fry steadily for about 8 to 10 minutes, until nearly tender. Add the mushrooms and continue frying for several minutes. Finally add the peanuts and heat. Serve with cooked rice.

## Turkey Kebabs

*450-500 g/1-1¼ lb uncooked turkey breast*
*3 teaspoons chopped mixed herbs*
*50 g/2 oz butter, melted*
*salt and pepper*

Cut the turkey breast into neat dice. Blend the herbs with the butter and seasoning. Put the turkey breast onto 4 metal skewers and brush with the flavoured butter. Grill steadily for about 10 minutes, or until tender; turn several times. Serve with cooked rice and mixed vegetables.

# Using Cooked Turkey

Any of the recipes based upon cooked chicken are equally successful if cooked turkey is substituted, see pages 189 to 194. The dishes on this and the next page make delicious use of the pieces of turkey left after roasting the bird.

## Turkey à la King ⊛

*50 g/2 oz turkey fat or butter*
*1 small onion, finely chopped*
*50-100 g/2-4 oz button mushrooms*
*25 g/1 oz flour*
*300 ml/½ pint milk*
*150 ml/¼ pint turkey stock*
*450 g/1 lb cooked turkey meat, diced*
*100 g/4 oz cooked or canned corn*
*3 tablespoons double cream*
*salt and pepper*
GARNISH:
*1 canned red pepper, finely chopped*
*1 tablespoon chopped parsley*

Heat the fat or butter in a saucepan, add the vegetables and cook for 5 minutes, then stir in the flour. Stir over a low heat for 2 to 3 minutes, then gradually blend in the milk and turkey stock. Bring the liquid to the boil and continue stirring until a smooth sauce. Add the diced turkey, corn, cream and salt and pepper. If possible, allow the mixture to stand for a while so the flavours blend together. Reheat gently for about 7 to 8 minutes. Garnish with red pepper and parsley. Serve with cooked rice, pasta or new potatoes.

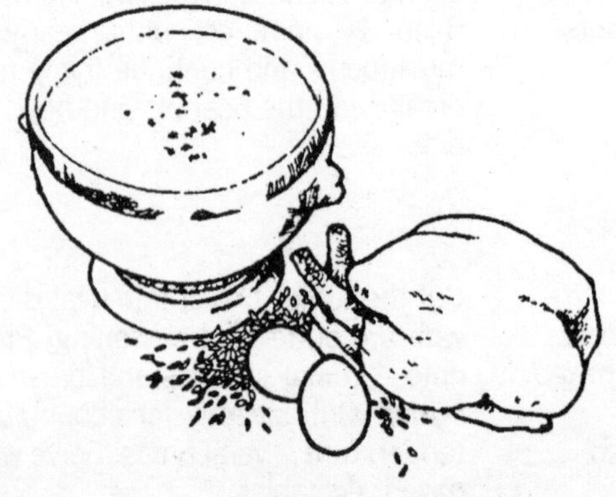

## Turkey and Macaroni Pie ⊛

*75 g/3 oz macaroni*
*salt and pepper*
*40 g/1 ½ oz butter or margarine*
*40 g/1 ½ oz flour*
*450 ml/1 ¾ pint milk*
*225 g/8 oz cooked turkey, finely diced*
*100 g/4 oz Cheddar cheese, grated*
TOPPING:
*50 g/2 oz Cheddar cheese, grated*
*40 g/1 ½ oz soft breadcrumbs*
*25 g/1 oz butter, melted*
GARNISH:
*6 tomato slices*

Put the macaroni into 1.2 litres/2 pints boiling salted water and cook until just tender; drain. Heat the butter or margarine in a saucepan, stir in the flour, and gradually blend in the milk. Stir as the sauce comes to the boil and thickens. Season well. Add the turkey, cheese and macaroni. Mix well. Spoon into an ovenproof dish, top with the grated cheese, breadcrumbs, then the melted butter. Bake in the centre of a moderately hot oven (190°C/375°F or Gas Mark 5) for 35 minutes. Garnish with the sliced tomatoes and return to the oven for a few minutes to heat the tomatoes.

VARIATION

**Farmhouse Turkey:** Cook the macaroni as the recipe above; drain well. Meanwhile slice 2 medium onions; skin and slice 4 large tomatoes. Heat 50 g/2 oz turkey fat or butter and fry the onions until tender, then add the tomatoes and heat for 2 to 3 minutes. Stir in the hot macaroni, 2 tablespoons chopped parsley, 225 g/8 oz finely diced cooked turkey and 3 beaten eggs. Season the mixture well and stir over a low heat until the eggs are just set. Serve with crusty rolls.

## Turkey Stuffed Tomatoes

*4 very large tomatoes*
*25 g/1 oz turkey fat*
*1 medium onion, chopped*
*2 teaspoons chopped parsley*
*50 g/2 oz soft breadcrumbs*
*175 g/6 oz cooked turkey, finely chopped*
*pinch grated nutmeg*
*1 egg*
*salt and pepper*

Halve the tomatoes, scoop out the centre pulp and chop this finely. Heat the turkey fat and fry the tomato pulp with the onion and blend with the remaining ingredients. Spoon into the tomato cases. Put into a greased ovenproof dish and bake towards the top of a moderately hot oven (190°C/375°F or Gas Mark 5) for 10 to 15 minutes.

## Turkey with Prunes and Apples ⊛

*225g/8oz dried prunes*
*600ml/1 pint water*
*4 tablespoons red wine*
*25g/1oz sugar*
*3 large dessert apples*
*100g/4oz butter, melted*
*1 x 4.5kg/10lb turkey, oven-ready weight*
*salt and pepper*
*40g/1½ flour*
*600ml/1 pint turkey stock (see method)*
*2 tablespoons redcurrant jelly*

Put the prunes in a bowl, add the water, red wine and sugar and leave overnight. Drain the prunes, reserving the liquid, and remove the stones.

Peel, core and thinly slice the apples, mix with the prunes and 25g/1oz butter. Put inside the turkey. Brush the bird with the remaining butter and roast at one of the temperatures on page 184. Meanwhile simmer the giblets in water to cover with a little salt and pepper to make good stock. Spoon 3 tablespoons turkey dripping into a pan and stir in the flour. Cook for 2 to 3 minutes and blend in 600ml/1 pint well strained turkey stock, the liquid from soaking the prunes and the redcurrant jelly. Stir as the sauce comes to the boil and thickens. Season to taste. Serve with the turkey and the fruit stuffing. Serves about 10.

VARIATION

⊛ **Almond Stuffed Turkey:** Cook 75g/3oz long-grain rice in 300ml/½pint seasoned turkey stock until tender and until the stock is absorbed. Chop 2 medium onions, fry in 50g/2oz butter or turkey fat, add 100g/4oz blanched and coarsely chopped almonds, the cooked rice, 75g/3oz seedless raisins, salt, pepper and 1 teaspoon ground cinnamon. Put the stuffing inside the turkey. Melt 50/2oz butter, add ½ to 1 teaspoon ground cinnamon, brush over the bird and roast as page 184.

## Parslied Turkey ⊛

*1 x 4.5kg/10lb turkey, oven-ready weight*
*50g/2oz butter, melted*
STUFFING:
*50g/2oz butter, softened*
*175g/6oz mushrooms, finely chopped*
*1 teaspoon chopped rosemary*
*8 tablespoons chopped parsley*
*2 tablespoons chopped chives*
*salt and pepper*

Insert your forefinger under the skin of a turkey breast and loosen this to make a 'pocket' for the stuffing. Blend all the ingredients for the stuffing together, spread over the turkey flesh, under the skin. At first this seems quite difficult to do, but if you work patiently you will soon get a smooth layer of the mushroom and parsley mixture covering the whole of the breast; take great care not to break the skin, for the mixture would then ooze out during cooking. Brush the bird with the melted butter and roast at one of the temperatures on page 184. Serves about 10.

# Cooking Duck

Duck may not be as economical as chicken, due to the fact it has a less plump breast, but it makes a delicious change. While roasted duck is probable the favourite meal for most people there are other interesting ways of using this flavoursome bird.

## Duckling à la Bordelaise ⊛

*2 young duckling with giblets*
*50 g/2 oz butter or fat*
*600 ml/1 pint giblet stock (see method)*
*50 g/2 oz flour*
*1 wine glass brandy*
*12 very small onions or shallots*

STUFFING:
*duckling livers, finely chopped*
*1 large onion, finely chopped*
*1-2 cloves garlic, crushed*
*2 tablespoons chopped parsley*
*2 tablespoons soft breadcrumbs*
*3 tablespoons green olives, stoned and chopped*
*2 eggs*
*salt and pepper*
*pinch ground cinnamon*
*½ teaspoon chopped fresh sage or pinch dry sage*

GARNISH:
*orange slices*
*watercress*
*green olives*

This is a very old way of cooking duckling; roasting and casseroling are combined and the sauce is ready to serve with the duck.

First simmer the giblets, but not the livers, in water to give 600 ml/1 pint of stock. Strain carefully. (If you wish to make rather more stuffing you can chop the cooked meat from the neck and stomach very finely and add to the other ingredients.) Check there is no green bile from the gall bladders with the livers, then mix them with the other stuffing ingredients. Put the stuffing into the ducklings and secure with skewers.

Heat the butter or fat in a roasting tin or very large casserole. turn the ducklings in this until well coated, roast in a moderately hot oven (200°C/400°F or Gas Mark 6) for approximately ½ hour; do not cover. Lift the tin or casserole out of the oven, put the ducklings on to a dish and pour away the surplus fat leaving just 2 tablespoons behind. Blend the 600 ml/1 pint of giblet stock with the flour and cook in a saucepan until thickened. Add the brandy and approximately 12 very tiny onions or shallots (if you cannot get these, use cocktail onions).

Put the ducklings back into the tin or casserole and pour the sauce round, not over, the birds. Stir to absorb the 2 tablespoons fat. Cover and cook in the centre of a moderate oven (180°C/350°F or Gas Mark 4) for about 1 hour. Lift the ducks onto a hot dish, strain the sauce into a sauceboat, garnish with orange slices, watercress and olives. Serve with an Orange Salad (see page 287).

VARIATION
Make a more substantial stuffing by adding 75 g/3 oz soft breadcrumbs to the other ingredients.

## Salmis of Duck ⊛

*1 large duck*
*450 g/1 lb chestnuts, skinned*
*75 g/3 oz butter or margarine*
*2 rashers bacon, derinded and chopped*
*100 g/4 oz soft breadcrumbs*
*salt and pepper*
*50 g/2 oz small button mushrooms*
*12 tiny onions or shallots*
*25 g/1 oz flour*
*450 ml/¾ pint duck giblet stock*
*2 tablespoons port wine*

Follow the directions for roasting the duck on page 205 but remove the bird from the oven before it is quite cooked. Drain well to remove all surplus fat.

Chop, mince or liquidize half the chestnuts. Melt 25 g/1 oz of the butter or margarine and mix with the bacon, breadcrumbs, salt and pepper and chopped chestnuts. Put into the partially cooked duck. Place this in a deep casserole. Heat the remaining butter or margarine in a saucepan and fry the mushrooms, onions and whole chestnuts for a few minutes; spoon into the casserole. Blend the flour with any fat remaining in the saucepan and stir in the stock and wine. Bring slowly to the boil and cook until a smooth, fairly thin sauce; stir well and season to taste. Pour the sauce around the duck. Cover the casserole and cook for 1 hour in the centre of a moderate oven (160-180°C/ 325-250°F or Gas Mark 3-4). Lift the duck and vegetables on to a heated serving dish. Carve or joint the duck and serve topped with stuffing. Keep hot while you boil the sauce from the casserole very hard in an uncovered saucepan for about 10 minutes until reduced to about 300 ml/½ pint. Serve with the duck.

VARIATIONS

Use the well strained duck fat from the roasting tin instead of butter or margarine.

⊛ **Salmis of Pheasant:** This is an excellent method of cooking rather tougher game birds, as well as tender ones. You need 2 small pheasants with the quantities of chestnuts and sauce given in the recipe above. If you know the birds are old, then spread with butter and roast for 15 minutes only, just to brown the outside. Cool, after roasting, sufficiently to handle then continue as the recipe above; cook for 2 hours in a cool to moderate oven (150°-160°C/300-325°F or Gas Mark 2-3).

If the birds are young, then cook as page 213 but allow only 40 minutes roasting time. Proceed as for the Salmis of Duck recipe above, but allow just 45 minutes only in the casserole. Add 2 tablespoons redcurrant jelly to the ingredients for the sauce and 2 tablespoons glacé cherries.

⊛ **Salmis of Turkey:** Roast the turkey until almost tender, then proceed as for the duck. If cooking a large turkey you will need to use double the ingredients for the stuffing and the sauce.

## Roast Duck and Goose ⊛

*no fat is required when cooking fresh birds; use a little melted butter for defrosted frozen birds*

WEIGHT TO ALLOW *when buying the bird:*

*550-675g/1¼-1½lb, or one small duckling to serve 2 people or one plump duckling would give 3 or4 smaller portions*

Often people complain that ducks and geese are ultra-fat. That is because they have not allowed the fat to run away. Never cover these birds when roasting, if possible stand on a rack in the roasting tin, so the fat runs away into the tin. Roast as recommended below. After the birds have been cooking for 30 minutes, if using the hotter oven, or 40 minutes, if using the lower heat, prick the skin lightly. You will see the excess fat spurting out. Do this at 30 minute intervals during roasting. Insert a fine skewer or fork very delicately for if you prick too deeply the fat runs *into* the flesh, not *out* of it. Although there is so much fat on these birds, I do rub well dried defrosted birds with a very little melted butter before roasting.

Ducks and geese which have not been frozen and then defrosted or chilled can be roasted in a moderately hot to hot oven (200-220°C/400-425°F or Gas Mark 6-7). Allow 15 minutes per 450g/1 lb plus 15 minutes.

Ducks and geese which have been frozen then defrosted or chilled are better roasted in a moderate oven (160-180°C/325-350°F or Gas Mark 3-4). Allow 22 to 25 minutes per 450g/1 lb plus 22 to 25 minutes.

Note: It is essential that frozen poultry is COMPLETELY defrosted before roasting.

Duck and goose are generally served with a thickened gravy. The traditional accompaniments are those served with pork, i.e. Apple Sauce and Sage and Onion Stuffing (see page 145) but nowadays Orange Sauce or other fruit sauces are more popular; see below and page 206.

## Black Cherry Sauce

*1 tablespoon duck fat*
*1 teaspoon arrowroot*
*150ml/¼pint rosé wine*
*3 tablespoons cherry brandy*
*5 tablespoons duck giblet stock*
*225g/8oz black cherries, stoned*

Pour the duck fat into a saucepan. Blend the arrowroot with the other ingredients, add to the fat, then stir over a low heat until thickened.

VARIATION

Use the syrup from canned cherries instead of wine.

## Duckling Americaine

*1 duckling, sufficient for 4 portions, roasted as page 205 until nearly, but not quite, cooked*
*1 tablespoon French mustard*
*40 g/1½ oz butter, melted*
*2 teaspoons Worcestershire sauce*

Cut the duck down the middle, then remove both leg joints to make 4 portions. Blend the French mustard with the butter and Worcestershire sauce. If the duck is inclined to be rather fat, then it is advisable to remove the skin, take away the excess fat and replace the skin or grill the duck without skin. Brush the skin side (or side where the skin was removed) with the butter mixture and cook under a pre-heated grill until very hot. Serve with a Tomato Sauce (see page 233).

VARIATION

⊛ **Duckling à la Mode:** Roast the duckling until tender then divide into 4 portions as described above. Peel and thinly slice 3 medium onions; heat 2 tablespoons of duck fat (from the roasting tin) in a large frying pan and fry the onions until tender. Add the portions of duckling and fry until well heated.

Stir 1 teaspoon chopped fresh sage or a pinch of dried sage into 150 ml/¼ pint red wine, heat for 2 to 3 minutes, then serve.

## Duckling Bigarade ⊛

*1 large or 2 smaller duckling*
ORANGE SAUCE:
*2 medium oranges*
*150 ml/¼ pint water*
*2 teaspoons arrowroot*
*300 ml/½ pint duck stock (see method)*
*2 teaspoons sugar*
*salt and pepper*

Roast the duckling in the way described on page 205. Remove from the tin when cooked and keep hot. Spoon 1 tablespoon strained fat out of the roasting tin.

Cut away the peel from the oranges, discarding any bitter white pith. Cut the orange 'zest' into matchstick pieces and simmer for 10 minutes in the water. Blend the arrowroot with the very well strained duck stock, add to the orange peel, together with the juice of the oranges and the duck fat. Stir over a low heat until thickened and clear, add the sugar, salt and pepper to taste.

VARIATION

⊛ **Orange Sauce No 2:** This dark rich sauce is based on using a bitter Seville orange with Espagnole Sauce. Make the Espagnole Sauce (see page 231). Remove the peel from the orange and cut the 'zest' into matchsticks, as described above. Simmer in 150 ml/¼ pint water for 10 minutes. Blend the Espagnole Sauce with the orange peel and any liquid left in the pan, add the orange juice, 2 tablespoons red wine and simmer for a few minutes.

# Cooking Goose

Once upon a time, goose was probably more plentiful, and popular than turkey. Sadly this is no longer the case and goose is difficult to obtain. From that comment you will gather that I am particularly fond of this bird. A few recipes follow which I hope you will try when goose is available.

## Cassoulet ⊛

*225 g/8 oz haricot beans*
*2 cloves garlic, finely chopped*
*bouquet garni*
*salt and pepper*
*3 tablespoons goose fat*
*1 thick streaky bacon rasher, weighing about 175 g/6 oz, derinded and neatly diced (keep the rinds)*
*3 medium onions, sliced*
*4 medium tomatoes, skinned and sliced*
*300 ml/½ pint goose giblet stock*
*225 g/8 oz garlic sausage, sliced*
*225-350 g/8-12 oz cooked goose, diced*
*75 g/3 oz soft breadcrumbs*

Cover the beans with cold water and soak overnight. Next day put the beans with the water in which they were soaked into a saucepan; add 1 chopped garlic clove, the bouquet garni, a little salt and pepper. Boil for 10 minutes, then simmer gently for nearly 2 hours or until tender; by this time the water should almost all have been absorbed; if not drain the beans.

Heat the goose fat in a large saucepan, add the bacon, bacon rind and onions, with the remaining garlic and fry until the onions are nearly tender. Add in the tomatoes and continue cooking for a further 5 to 10 minutes. Pour in the stock, stir to blend with the vegetables and bacon; discard the bacon rind. Add the garlic sausage, beans and goose and heat thoroughly. Spoon into a casserole and top with the breadcrumbs but do not cover the dish. Bake just above the centre of a moderately hot oven (190°C/375°F or Gas Mark 5) for 30 minutes until the topping is crisp and brown.

## Devilled Goose

*1 goose, prepared as page 205*
*4 tablespoons brown malt vinegar*
*1 teaspoon curry paste*
*2 teaspoons made mustard*
*salt and cayenne pepper*
*1-2 teaspoons Worcestershire sauce*

Prepare the goose for roasting and add any stuffing required. Roast the goose as directed on page 205 but take out of the oven 45 minutes before the end of the cooking time. Lift the bird on to a large dish and pour out all the fat from the tin. Blend the vinegar with the other ingredients. Return the goose to the tin, pour the vinegar mixture over the bird. Return to the oven and continue roasting, but baste the goose several times with the vinegar liquid.

When making the gravy from the giblet stock add some of the vinegar liquid, the amount depending upon personal taste.

## Goose with Olives ⊛

*1 goose*
*3 tablespoons goose fat*
*4 medium onions, cut into neat rings*
*225 g/8 oz small mushrooms, halved*
*150 ml/¼ pint goose giblet stock*
*4 tablespoons red wine*
*1 teaspoon chopped fresh sage or pinch dried sage*
*salt and pepper*
*about 20 stuffed green olives*

Roast the goose as described on page 205. The bird could be stuffed for this dish, but in view of the fact it will be cut up before serving, it is better to cook the stuffing in a separate dish. Cook the olive mixture below towards the end of the roasting time.

Heat the fat (from the roasting tin) in a good-sized frying pan. Add the onions and mushrooms and fry gently for 3 to 4 minutes. Add the giblet stock, wine, sage and a little salt and pepper; simmer gently until the vegetables are tender, but do not allow them to become a purée. Add the halved olives. Keep this mixture hot, while slicing the hot cooked goose. If the bird is large you may only require the flesh from the breast and wings, in which case the legs could be saved for another meal.

Cut the flesh into neat pieces. Arrange the olive mixture in the centre of the dish with the neatly sliced goose round.

## Goose Normandy ⊛

*3-4 dessert apples (that also cook well)*
*2 tablespoons goose fat*
*3 medium onions, cut into neat rings*
*4 tablespoons Calvados or apple juice*
*salt and pepper*
*cooked goose legs*

Core, but do not peel, the apples and cut into fairly thick rings. Heat the goose fat in a roasting tin, add the onion and apple rings with the Calvados or apple juice and a little salt and pepper. Cover the tin and cook in a moderately hot oven (190°C/375°F or Gas Mark 5) for 40 minutes. Add the goose legs and continue cooking, without covering the tin, for a further 25 to 30 minutes, or until the goose legs are hot.

# Dishes with Game

Fortunately my family are as fond of game as I am, so I serve it whenever it is available and at a reasonable price. As game birds are a luxury for most town dwellers I generally invite friends for a meal, so the quantities given for some recipes are sufficient for 6 to 8 people.

Young birds are at their best when roasted with traditional accompaniments. You will find details on page 213. Do not despise older game birds, for they are delicious in stews and casseroles, there are some recipes for these on pages 210 to 211.

I have included a second game pie, there is one under Steak and Kidney Pie on page 117 for I find this is one of the most popular winter time dishes. It makes a good main course for a buffet party if you make sure that all the flesh is neatly diced.

Rabbit may sound humble game fare, but is infinitely versatile and can be used in many dishes suggested for chicken. My favourite game, apart from game birds, is undoubtedly hare. The old-fashioned Jugged Hare is really one of the most delicious of dishes based upon this particular food. If you feel that the quantity given is too large for a smaller family, why not make Jugged Hare from the legs of the hare and roast the back (known as the Saddle of Hare) and serve this as suggested on page 214.

There seems to be slightly more venison these days, if you have never tried this meat I think you will find it most enjoyable.

Game freezes extremely well; always hang to your personal taste before freezing. Use within about 9 months. Game Pudding, like other similar puddings can be frozen before cooking or after cooking for 2 to 3 hours. Never cook completely otherwise the filling will be over-cooked when the pudding is reheated. The casseroles and pies with game also freeze well.

Any stock left from simmering game bones makes the basis for an excellent soup, see page 55.

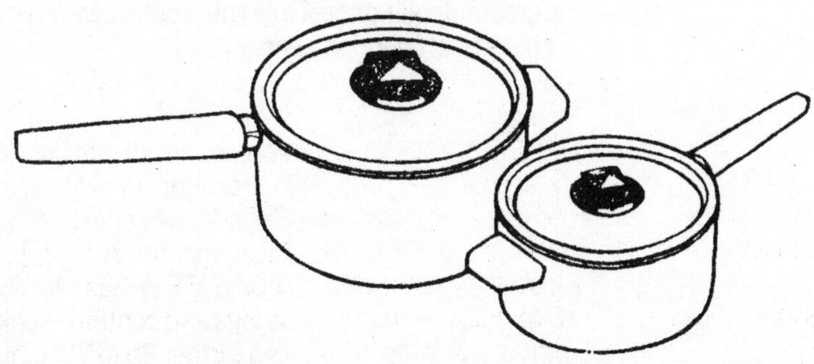

# Ragoût of Pigeons ⊛

*4 plump pigeons*
*1 thick streaky bacon rasher, about 100g/4oz in weight*
*50g/2oz fat*
*8-12 small onions*
*8 small carrots*
*100g/4oz button mushrooms*
*25g/1oz flour*
*450ml/¾ pint chicken stock*
*150ml/¼ pint red wine*
*salt and pepper*
GARNISH:
*Forcemeat Balls (see page 215)*
*fried croûtons (see page 211)*

Wash and dry the pigeons. Derind the bacon and save the rind to add flavour to the sauce. Cut the bacon into narrow strips. Heat the fat and bacon rind in a large saucepan, fry the pigeons until golden in colour and turn several times during this period. Remove from the pan, add the bacon and fry for 2 to 3 minutes. Put the pigeons, bacon and bacon rind into a casserole. Fry the onions, carrots and mushrooms for 2 to 3 minutes in the fat remaining in the saucepan; add to the casserole. Put the flour into the saucepan, stir well to absorb any fat and meat juices, then gradually blend in the stock and wine. Stir as the sauce comes to the boil and thickens slightly. Add salt and pepper to taste. Pour over the pigeons and vegetables, cover the casserole and cook in the centre of a cool oven (150°C/300°F or Gas Mark 2) for 2 hours. Remove the bacon rind. Garnish with the Forcemeat Balls and the croûtons, see pages 215 and 211. Serve with redcurrant jelly.

VARIATIONS

⊛ **Mock Duck Ragoût:** Use 1kg/1½lb ox heart instead of the 4 pigeons. Omit 4 tablespoons stock and substitute 4 tablespoons orange juice. Add 1 teaspoon finely grated orange rind and a pinch of dried sage to the sauce. While you can use chicken stock, beef stock is better for this strongly flavoured offal. There is a definite similarity in the flavour of the heart to duck when cooked in this way.

⊛ **Ragoût of Rabbit:** Cut the flesh from a medium rabbit into fairly large pieces; if preferred buy 2 small rabbits and joint these. Prepare as in the above recipe, but omit the mushrooms and instead add 225g/8oz peeled and neatly diced celeriac (celery root). Omit the red wine and use milk or single cream instead. Garnish the creamy looking casserole with cooked green peas or beans or finely chopped parsley.

## Pigeon Casserole

*8 good-sized pigeons*
*25g/1 oz flour*
*salt and pepper*
*pinch cayenne pepper*
*50g/2 oz butter or beef dripping*
*2 onions, chopped*
*100g/4 oz button mushrooms*
*450 ml/¾ pint beef stock*
*150 ml/¼ pint double cream*
*2 hard-boiled eggs*
FRIED CROÛTONS:
*2-3 slices bread*
*50g/2 oz butter or 2 tablespoons oil*

Coat the pigeons in flour and plenty of seasoning. Heat the butter or dripping in a large pan and fry the birds, then the onions and mushrooms for several minutes; put into a large casserole. Heat the stock in the pan, stir well to absorb any juices and pour over the pigeons. Cover the casserole and cook in the centre of a cool oven (150°C/300°F or Gas Mark 2) for 2 hours. Stir in the cream just before the end of the cooking time. Garnish with the sliced eggs and croûtons, made by dicing and frying the bread in the butter or oil.

VARIATION

⊛ **Venison Casserole:** Use 750g/1½ lb diced venison. Marinate in 300 ml/½ pint red wine for 3 hours, drain; proceed as the recipe above. Use the wine with only 300 ml/½ pint stock and omit the cream and eggs. Heat the wine and stock in the pan with 2 teapoons Dijon mustard and 2 tablespoons redcurrant jelly.

## Pheasant Casserole ⊛

*2 small pheasants*
*450 ml/¾ pint stock (see method)*
*salt and pepper*
*bouquet garni*
*25g/1 oz flour*
*50g/2 oz butter*
*4 thick back bacon rashers, derinded and chopped*
*100g/4 oz small button mushrooms*
*225g/8 oz chestnuts, peeled*
GARNISH:
*croûtons of fried bread (see above)*

Cut each pheasant into 4 portions – 2 leg joints and 2 breast joints. Put the giblets and rest of the pheasant carcass into a pan and cover with water. Add salt, pepper and a bouquet garni. Simmer for about 1 hour, strain and measure out 450 ml/¾ pint of the stock and reserve. Any stock left could be used in a soup.

Coat the pheasant joints in seasoned flour. Heat the butter in a large saucepan. Fry the bacon and mushrooms for 2 to 3 minutes. Remove from the pan and put into a casserole. Place the coated pheasant joints in the fat remaining in the saucepan, fry until golden brown then put into the casserole together with the chestnuts. Pour the reserved stock into the saucepan; stir well to absorb any juices left then spoon over the food in the casserole. Cover tightly. If the pheasants are young and tender, cook in the centre of a moderate oven (180°C/350°F or Gas Mark 4) for 1¼ hours. If these are older birds, allow 2 hours at 160°C/325°F or Gas Mark 3. Top with the croûtons just before serving.

VARIATION

Use a little less stock and add red or port wine instead.

## Partridge with Black Cherries ⊛

*2 large or 4 small young partridge*
*75 g/3 oz butter*
*1 teaspoon chopped thyme*
*salt and pepper*
*1 x 425 g/15 oz can black cherries*
*2 teaspoons arrowroot*
*4 tablespoons cherry brandy*
GARNISH:
*watercress*

Wipe the partridges. Blend the butter with the thyme and a little salt and pepper. Put half the flavoured butter inside the birds and spread the remainder over the breasts. Roast in the centre of a moderately hot oven (200°C/400°F or Gas Mark 6) for 45 to 50 minutes or until almost tender. Remove the birds from the roasting tin, pour out and reserve the dripping. Return the birds to the tin, spoon 4 tablespoons syrup from the cherries over the birds; continue cooking for a further 10 minutes. Save the liquid in the tin.

Meanwhile, blend the remaining cherry syrup with the arrowroot and 2 tablespoons strained dripping. Tip into a saucepan and stir over a low heat until thickened. Add the liquid from the roasting tin, the cherries and cherry brandy and simmer for 5 minutes. Halve the birds and arrange on a hot dish. Top with the sauce and garnish with watercress.

## Pheasants in Calvados ⊛

*2 young pheasants*
*75 g/3 oz cream cheese*
*100 g/4 oz grapes, deseeded, halved and skinned*
*50 g/2 oz butter*
*generous 150 ml/¼ pint Calvados*
*35 g/1¼ oz flour*
*300 ml/½ pint stock (from simmering pheasant giblets)*
*150 ml/¼ pint double cream*
*salt and pepper*
GARNISH:
*100 g/4 oz deseeded grapes*
*watercress*

Stuff the pheasants with the cream cheese and the grapes. Heat the butter in a roasting tin; turn the pheasants until coated then roast in a moderately hot oven (200°C/400°F or Gas Mark 6) for 30 minutes. Leave 2 tablespoons butter in the roasting tin, pour away any excess. Add the Calvados, cover the tin loosely with foil but do not wrap the birds tightly. Lower the heat slightly, cook for 30 minutes or until the birds are just tender; do not over-cook. Lift the pheasants on to a heated dish and keep warm; cover to prevent drying.

Strain the liquid from the roasting tin into a saucepan. Blend the flour and stock and add to the pan, stir until thickened, then simmer for 5 minutes. Add the cream and cook without boiling for 5 minutes. Season well. Carve or joint the pheasants then coat with the sauce. Garnish with the grapes and watercress. Serves 6 to 8.

## Roast Game Birds ⊛

*The variety of birds suitable for roasting are given in the method*

FOR ROASTING:
*butter or fat*
*bacon*
*toast (see method)*

WEIGHT TO ALLOW *when buying the bird:*
*a plump pheasant will give 4 small portions*
*a small grouse, mallard, plover gives 2 medium portions or 1 large portion*
*small birds – allow 1 bird per person*

It is only possible to roast young game birds, when older they are better cooked in a casserole. Game birds are very lean and they need plenty of butter or bacon over the flesh when roasting.

The method and timing for roasting larger game birds, such as pheasant and grouse (the most popular and most easily available) is the same as for chicken and turkey. Plover, golden plover, ptarmigan, are roasted in the same way and so is capercailzie (wild turkey). Mallard (a wild duck) is cooked as duck.

The small birds, such as quail, ortolan, partridge, pigeon, snipe or widgeon, teal (small wild ducks) and woodcock would need a total cooking time of 25 to 30 minutes in a moderately hot to hot oven (200-220°C/400-425°F or Gas Mark 6-7); add 5 to 10 minutes if wrapped in foil or put into a covered roasting tin; no longer in a roaster bag.

While most birds are drawn before roasting and the giblets used to make gravy, it is better not to draw ortolan or woodcock as the intestines are particularly delicious. Put a piece of toast under these birds (also any other small birds if desired) to catch the meat juices as the birds cook in the oven.

Serve the birds with the accompaniments suggested on this page.

## Accompaniments to Roast Game Birds

Serve with thickened gravy or the special sauce on page 159 and with Bread Sauce (page 184) or redcurrant jelly.

Other accompaniments are –

**Fried Crumbs:** Make fairly coarse breadcrumbs (nicer than fine ones). Fry until golden brown in hot butter or fat; turn several times. Drain on absorbent paper.

**Game Chips:** Cut peeled potatoes into wafer-thin slices (a food processor is wonderful for this). Deep fry for several minutes in very hot oil or fat. Drain on absorbent paper, then serve.

Note: No one wants to do this frying at the last minute, especially if you are entertaining guests, so I fry both the crumbs and potatoes earlier in the day, spread them out on flat baking trays, lined with absorbent paper and heat in the oven for 1 to 2 minutes. Beware as they easily scorch.

## Roast Venison ⊛

*joint of venison about 1.5 kg/3 lb in weight*
*fat or butter*
MARINADE:
*300 ml/½ pint red wine*
*2 tablespoons red wine vinegar*
*½ teaspoon crushed peppercorns*
*2 teaspoons Dijon mustard*
*1 bay leaf*
*1 clove garlic, crushed*
*3 tablespoons oil*
*2 leeks, thinly sliced*

Dry the meat well. Mix together the ingredients for the marinade and pour into a deep casserole. Add the meat and leave to marinate for at least 2 days in the refrigerator. Turn once or twice a day. Lift the meat from the marinade, strain this and save and add some of this liquid to the gravy, the amount depends entirely upon personal taste.

Put the venison into a roasting tin. Spread with a plentiful amount of fat or butter, for it is a dry flesh, although the marinade tenderizes, flavours and moistens the flesh. Roast as for the timing for veal on page 159. Serve with the same accompaniments as veal or pork or roast game birds.

VARIATION

**Grilled Venison:** Tender venison steaks can be grilled. They need basting well with oil or melted butter or you could marinate them, as suggested above, then cook under the grill. Timing as for Grilled Veal (see page 155).

## Civet of Hare ⊛

*1 young hare, jointed and with blood and liver*
*300 ml/½ pint stock (see method)*
*50 g/2 oz butter*
*225 g/8 oz fat pork, diced*
*18 small pickling onions*
*25 g/1 oz flour*
*300 ml/½ pint red wine or extra stock (see method)*
*salt and pepper*
*100 g/4 oz button mushrooms*
*150 ml/¼ pint double cream*
MARINADE:
*2 tablespoons oil*
*4 tablespoons brandy or red wine*
*salt and pepper*
GARNISH:
*fried croûtons (see page 211)*
*maçedoine vegetables (see page 249*

Blend the ingredients for marinade and pour into a shallow dish. Add the joints of hare and leave in the marinade for 2 hours; turn once or twice. Meanwhile simmer the hare liver in well seasoned water until tender; strain then mash or sieve. Reserve 300 ml/½ pint of the stock for the sauce (if omitting the red wine, reserve 600 ml/1 pint stock).

Melt the butter in a large pan, fry the pork and then the whole onions until golden; remove from the pan. Blend the flour into any fat remaining in the pan, then slowly stir in the stock and wine (or all stock). Put in the hare, plus any marinade not absorbed, the pork, salt and pepper to taste. Cover the pan and simmer for 1 hour. Add the onions and mushrooms and continue cooking for a further 30 minutes or until the hare is tender. Blend the blood of the hare, the cream and liver and stir into the hot, but not boiling, sauce; heat gently for a further 10 minutes.

Serve in a border of croûtons and vegetable maçedoine. Serves 6 to 8.

## Jugged Hare ⊛

*1 hare, jointed with blood and liver*
*900 ml/1 ½ pints water*
*2 tablespoons vinegar*
*salt and pepper*
*50 g/2 oz flour*
*75 g/3 oz dripping or cooking fat*
*2 medium onions, sliced*
*2 medium carrots, sliced*
*150 ml/¼ pint red or port wine*
*2 tablespoons redcurrant jelly*
GARNISH:
*Forcemeat Balls, see method*
*croûtons of fried bread (see page 211)*

Put the blood of the hare on one side. Place the liver in a pan with the water. Cover the pan and simmer for ¾ hour, or until the liver is tender. Strain the liquid, add more water to make 900 ml/1½ pints once again. Meanwhile soak the hare for 1 hour in cold water with the vinegar. Drain and dry on absorbent paper. Coat the joints of hare with half the seasoned flour. Heat the dripping or fat in a large saucepan. Fry the hare until just golden. Remove from the pan then fry the onions and carrots for a few minutes. Lift these out of the saucepan. Stir in the remaining flour and blend in the 900 ml/1½ pints stock. Bring the sauce to the boil, add the wine, blood of the hare and redcurrant jelly. Sieve or mash the liver, stir into the sauce and season well. The liver adds a delicious flavour and texture to this sauce. Replace the hare in the sauce with the onions and carrots. Simmer for 2½ to 3 hours. Top with the forcemeat balls and croûtons. Serve with redcurrant jelly.

⊛ **Forcemeat Balls:** Make the Parsley and Thyme Stuffing (see page 186) but make it sufficiently stiff to roll into small balls. Bake on a flat tin in a moderate oven (180°C/350°F or Gas Mark 4) for about 30 minutes. Arrange on the Jugged Hare just before serving.

VARIATION

Transfer the hare, sauce and vegetables to a casserole. Cover and cook for 3 hours in the centre of a cool oven (150°C/300°F or Gas Mark 2).

## Roast Hare ⊛

*1 young hare (leveret), or roast just the saddle (back of the hare) and use the legs in Jugged Hare above or Civet of Hare (see page 214)*
*100-225 g/4-8 oz fat bacon rashers*
*Apple Sauce (see page 145)*
*Sage and Onion Stuffing, (see page 145)*

A hare that is to be roasted must be young; (this is known as a leveret) and the flesh is pale, rather the colour of rabbit flesh. Cover the hare with the bacon and roast as chicken (see page 184). You can remove the bacon towards the end of the cooking time so that the flesh browns and looks inviting. Simmer the liver to give stock for gravy.

Serve with the same accompaniments as roast pork.

VARIATION

⊛ **Mustard Rabbit:** Cover a young rabbit with butter blended with a little English or French mustard. Roast as chicken (page 184) then cut into joints. Heat 300 ml/½ pint double cream with 1 tablespoon fat from the tin and a squeeze lemon juice, pour over the rabbit.

## Game Pudding ⊛

*2 small or 1 large pheasant or grouse, or equivalent in pigeons or other game bird(s)*
*bouquet garni*
*salt and pepper*
*25 g/1 oz flour*
*100 g/4 oz chicken livers, diced*
*225 g/8 oz bacon cut in 2 slices, derinded*
*2 medium onions, sliced*
*Suet Crust Pastry, made with 300 g/10 oz flour, etc. (see page 117)*

Dice the flesh from the bird(s). Put the bones and giblets, except the liver(s) into a pan, cover with water, add the bouquet garni and salt and pepper. Cover the pan and simmer gently for 1 hour. Strain the stock and use for the pudding and gravy. Season the flour and coat the diced game and chicken livers. Mix with the bacon and onions.

Make the suet crust pastry and roll out thinly. Grease a 1.8 litre/3 pint pudding basin. Use nearly two-thirds of the pastry to line the basin. Put in the game mixture. Add enough stock to come halfway up the filling. Moisten the edges of the pastry; roll out the remaining pastry dough to a neat round to cover the basin. Seal the edges. Cover with greased greaseproof paper and then with foil. Steam over boiling water for 3 to 4 hours.

Make a gravy with the remaining stock; it could be flavoured with a little port wine. Serves 6 to 8.

## Game Pie

*Flaky Pastry, made with 225 g/8 oz flour, etc. (see page 292)*

FILLING:
*2 young pheasants or grouse, or 4 young pigeons*
*bouquet garni*
*salt and pepper*
*1 tablespoon flour*
*50 g/2 oz fat*
*2 medium onions, diced*
*100 g/4 oz small button mushrooms*
*4 rashers lean bacon, derinded*
*3 hard-boiled eggs, sliced*
*generous 150 ml/¼ pint game stock (see method)*

GLAZE:
*1 egg*
*1 tablespoon water*

Make the pastry so that it has time to rest. Meanwhile dice the flesh from the birds. Put the bones into a saucepan, add water to cover, the bouquet garni and salt and pepper. Cover the pan and simmer for 1 hour.

Blend a little salt and pepper with the flour, coat the game with this then fry in the hot fat for a few minutes. Spoon into a 1.5 to 1.8 litre/2½ to 3 pint pie dish. Fry the vegetables and bacon in the pan for several minutes, add to the game and top with the sliced eggs. Pour the 150 ml/¼ pint game stock into the same pan; stir to absorb any flour left and add to the other ingredients in the pie dish. Allow the mixture to cool. Retain the remaining stock for gravy.

Roll out the pastry and cover the pie. Cut a small slit in the centre to allow steam to escape. Decorate with leaves and a rose of pastry. Beat the egg and water and brush over the pastry.

Bake in the centre of a very hot oven (230°C/450°F or Gas Mark 8) for 10 to 15 minutes then lower the heat to moderate (160°C/325°F or Gas Mark 3) for a further 1¼ hours. Cover the pastry with greaseproof paper or foil if becoming too brown. Serve hot with gravy. Serves 6 to 8.

## Bastilla

FILLING:
*75 g/3 oz butter*
*2 plump pigeons*
*450 ml/¾ pint chicken stock or water*
*1 medium onion, finely chopped*
*pinch ground ginger*
*pinch ground coriander*
*pinch saffron powder*
*1 teaspoon chopped parsley*
*½ teaspoon chopped mint*
*½ small chilli (hot) pepper, finely chopped*
*salt and pepper*
*3 eggs, beaten*
*1 x 375 g/13 oz packet frozen puff pastry or home-made pastry made with 175 g/6 oz flour etc. (see page 292)*
SUGAR MIXTURE:
*50 g/2 oz sugar*
*50 g/2 oz blanched almonds, finely chopped*
*¼ teaspoon ground cinnamon*

To make the filling: heat 50 g/2 oz of the butter in a large saucepan, turn the pigeons in this until pleasantly brown, then add the stock or water, onion, spices, saffron herbs and the chilli pepper. Season the mixture well. Cover the pan and simmer steadily for 1 hour, or until the pigeons are tender. Cool sufficientlfy to handle; cut away all the meat from the bones of the pigeons then chop this very finely. Add 5 tablespoons of the pigeon stock (this need not be strained) to the beaten eggs. Heat the remaining butter in a small pan, pour in the eggs and stock, stir gently over a low heat until lightly scrambled.

Roll out the pastry until wafer thin; cut into 12 large rounds (cut round a saucer or small tea plate if you do not possess a sufficiently large cutter). Put 4 rounds on to a baking tray. Divide the pigeon mixture and scrambled eggs into 8 portions.

Mix together the sugar, blanched almonds and the ground cinnamon. Sprinkle the rounds of pastry on the baking tray with an eighth of this, top with a portion of pigeon and egg; top with another round of pastry, more sugar mixture, another portion of pigeon and egg. Top with rounds of pastry. Seal the edges of the 3 layers very firmly together. Bake in the centre of a very hot oven (230°C/450°F or Gas Mark 8) for 15 minutes; by this time the pastry should be rising well. Lower the heat to moderately hot (190-200°C/375-400°F or Gas Mark 5-6) and cook for a further 25 to 30 minutes. Serve hot as a substantial main dish or hors d'oeuvre. The stock left from cooking the pigeons can be used in a stew or soup.

## Rabbit Pie ⊛

*Shortcrust Pastry, made with 225 g/8 oz flour, etc. (see page 291)*
*1 medium rabbit, jointed*
*salt and pepper*
*25 g/1 oz flour*
*100 g/4 oz fat pork, diced*
*4 medium leeks, sliced*
*300 ml/½ pint milk*
*3 teaspoons chopped parsley*
GLAZE:
*1 egg*

Make the pastry. Roll the rabbit in the seasoned flour. Fry the pork in a pan until golden then remove. Turn the coated rabbit in the fat remaining in the pan. Put the rabbit, pork and leeks into a 1.5 to 1.8 litre/2½ to 3 pint pie dish. Heat the milk in the pan, stir to absorb all juices and any flour left, season well and add the parsley. Spoon over the rabbit, making sure the pie dish is sufficiently deep so the milk does not boil out.

Roll out the pastry and cover the filling. Make a slit on top to allow the steam to escape, decorate with pastry leaves and a rose. Brush with beaten egg. Bake as the pie on page 216, but use a slightly cooler oven as you are using shortcrust pastry.

# Stuffings and Sauces

This chapter covers many of my favourite recipes, for I am a great lover of the foods that help to flavour main dishes. I have already given the well-known and traditional accompaniments to roast meats, poultry and game; in each case these follow the particular meat or bird. To many people these are the perfect partners; obviously they have been developed over years to complement the particular food, but I must confess that I like variety in food and I delight in trying a new stuffing or sauce.

For easy reference I have listed stuffings based on herbs, on vegetables, on fruits and on meat or fish in that order, so you may find a recipe to match the ingredients you have available. In every case the recipe details the kind of food with which the stuffing blends best. In many cases the stuffing is cooked with the meat, poultry or fish. If you prefer to cook the stuffing separately then cover the dish so the mixture does not become over-dry. Most stuffings require approximately 45 minutes to 1 hour in moderate to moderately hot oven.

Stuffings freeze exceptionally well; pack the cooked or uncooked mixture in family sized containers and use within 3 months.

A basic white or brown sauce is frequently an essential part of a dish. Take time and trouble to achieve a perfect blending of flavours and a good texture. The simple sauces begin on page 226. A general mistake made by many people is to under-cook a sauce, this results in the mixture tasting of flour, or cornflour. Allow adequate time to simmer the sauce after it has thickened, then taste it critically, adjust the seasoning and/or flavouring and cook for a longer period if necessary.

Sauces can be frozen, although I feel that simple basic sauces are better freshly made. Frequently a sauce becomes over-thin in consistency when it is frozen; this can be remedied by allowing the sauce to simmer until it returns to its original texture or by adding extra thickening. The easiest way to incorporate extra thickening is to top each batch of about 600 ml/1 pint sauce with 3 teaspoons flour or 1½ teaspoons cornflour. As the sauce is reheated, stir well to blend in and cook the extra flour or cornflour.

## Basil and Tomato Stuffing ⊛

*3 tablespoons chopped basil*
*4 large tomatoes, skinned and chopped*
*1 teaspoon grated lemon rind*
*1 tablespoon lemon juice*
*50 g/2 oz butter, melted*
*75 g/3 oz soft breadcrumbs*
*1 egg*
*salt and pepper*

Blend all the ingredients together and season well.

This stuffing is excellent in fish, poultry or as a stuffing in vegetables; particularly in red or green peppers. If cooking in a separate dish, follow the instructions on page 218.

VARIATIONS

⊛ **Fennel Stuffing:** Substitute 3 tablespoons chopped fennel leaves for the basil; use only 2 tomatoes and 50 g/2 oz breadcrumbs. Add 4 tablespoons chopped fennel root to the mixture, with the remaining ingredients in the recipe above. Serve with fish.

⊛ **Mint Stuffing:** Substitute 2 tablespoons chopped mint for the basil. Omit the tomatoes and add 4 tablespoons finely diced or grated cucumber. Increase the lemon juice to 2 tablespoons and blend with the rest of the ingredients in the recipe above. Serve with lamb.

⊛ **Parsley and Oatmeal Stuffing:** Blend 4 tablespoons chopped parsley with 75 g/3 oz rolled oats. Omit the basil and breadcrumbs, but use 2 large skinned and chopped tomatoes. Blend with the remaining ingredients in the recipe above, but add 2 tablespoons milk or stock to give a softer mixture. Serve with poultry or veal.

⊛ **Sage and Celery Stuffing:** Use 2 to 3 tablespoons finely chopped sage instead of the basil. Omit the breadcrumbs in the recipe above, but use the remaining ingredients, together with approximately 175 g/6 oz finely chopped celery and 1 tablespoon chopped celery leaves. Serve with poultry, fish or meat.

## Sage and Apple Stuffing ⊛

*350 g/12 oz cooking apples (weight after peeling and coring), grated*
*2 tablespoons chopped sage*
*50 g/2 oz soft wholemeal breadcrumbs*
*50 g/2 oz butter, melted*
*50 g/2 oz sultanas*
*salt and pepper*

Blend all the ingredients together and season well. If cooking in a separate dish, follow the instructions on page 218. Serve with pork, duck or goose or with cooked sausages.

VARIATION

⊛ **Sage, Prune and Apple Stuffing:** Soak 100 g/4 oz prunes in water to cover for 12 hours; strain and chop the fruit. Use instead of sultanas.

## Thyme and Lemon Stuffing ⊛

*75 g/3 oz butter*
*100 g/4 oz soft coarse breadcrumbs*
*3 teaspoons chopped thyme*
*2 teaspoons grated lemon rind*
*3 tablespoons lemon juice*
*1 egg*
*salt and pepper*

Heat the butter in a pan and fry the breadcrumbs until crisp. Blend with the remaining ingredients. Serve with fish, chicken, turkey or veal.

VARIATION

⊛ **Thyme and Rice Stuffing:** Substitute 100 g/4 oz cooked rice for the breadcrumbs. Heat the butter and toss the rice in this until golden in colour. Mix with the other ingredients.

## Celery Stuffing ⊛

*50 g/2 oz butter or margarine*
*1 large onion, finely chopped*
*175 g/6 oz celery, finely chopped*
*100 g/4 oz soft breadcrumbs*
*1 tablespoon chopped parsley*
*½ teaspoon chopped thyme*
*1 teaspoon grated lemon rind*
*1 tablespoon lemon juice*
*1 egg*
*salt and pepper*

Heat the butter or margarine in a pan and fry the onion and celery gently for about 15 minutes; do not allow to become brown in colour. Add the rest of the ingredients.

Serve with any poultry or veal or with fish.

VARIATIONS

⊛ **Corn and Celery Stuffing:** Omit the onion and breadcrumbs, fry the celery in the butter or margarine for 5 minutes only, so it still remains slightly firm. Blend with 175 g/6 oz drained canned corn, 1 chopped canned red pepper and the remaining ingredients in the above recipe. Serve with fish or lamb.

⊛ **Celery and Ham Stuffing:** Fry the onion and celery in the butter or margarine as the above recipe, then blend with 100 g/4 oz chopped lean ham, 50 g/2 oz soft breadcrumbs, 1 small peeled and diced apple, ½ teaspoon chopped sage and the remainder of the ingredients in the above recipe. Serve with pork, duck or lamb.

⊛ **Rice, Celery and Pepper Stuffing:** Fry the onion and celery in the hot butter or margarine, as in the above recipe, then add 175 g/6 oz cooked brown or white rice, 2 chopped red peppers (discard the cores and seeds), 2 tablespoon chopped parsley, 50 g/2 oz sultanas or seedless raisins, grated rind and juice 1 large lemon, grated rind and juice 1 large orange, 1 egg, salt and pepper to taste. Serve with chicken, turkey, duck or goose.

⊛ **Garlic and Celery Stuffing:** Peel and chop 2 to 3 cloves garlic, toss in 75 g/3 oz butter or margarine, then blend with the ingredients in the above recipe. Serve with lamb.

## Corn and Orange Stuffing ⊛

*1 medium onion, finely chopped*
*175g/6oz soft white breadcrumbs*
*50g/2oz walnuts, chopped*
*2 teaspoons grated orange rind*
*2 tablespoons orange juice*
*50g/2oz seedless raisins*
*175g/6oz canned or cooked sweetcorn*
*25g/1oz butter, melted*
*1 egg yolk*
*salt and pepper*

Mix all the ingredients together. This stuffing is excellent with chicken or turkey. It is equally good hot or cold. If baking in a separate dish, rather than putting it into the body of the bird, use the whole egg to mix and add another 25g/1oz melted butter to give a more moist texture. Cover tightly and cook for 45 minutes to 1 hour, depending upon oven temperature used for poultry.

VARIATIONS

⊛ **Corn and Ham Stuffing:** Omit the orange rind and juice. Add 100g/4oz finely chopped cooked ham, 2 tablespoons chopped parsley, 4 tablespoons finely chopped celery. Add 1 tablespoon lemon juice and 1 tablespoon milk to the other ingredients.

⊛ **Savoury Corn Stuffing:** Use only 100g/4oz sweetcorn and 100g/4oz breadcrumbs. Add the finely diced uncooked liver from the chicken or turkey with 2 tablespoons chopped parsley.

Serve either of these stuffings with chicken, turkey or veal.

## Green Pea Stuffing ⊛

*75g/3oz butter*
*1 large onion, finely chopped*
*100g/4oz coarse soft breadcrumbs*
*175g/6oz cooked green peas*
*1 teaspoon chopped mint*
*1 egg*
*salt and pepper*

Heat half the butter in a pan and fry the onion until soft. Remove the onion, heat the remaining butter in the pan then fry the breadcrumbs until crisp and golden. Blend with the remainder of the ingredients.

This stuffing is excellent if baked in an uncovered dish, so you get a brown crust on top of the mixture. Allow about 40 minutes in a moderate oven. Serve with pork.

VARIATION

⊛ **Lentil Stuffing:** Heat 40g/1½oz margarine in a pan; fry 1 finely chopped onion and 1 diced cooking apple until soft, then blend with 225g/8oz cooked lentils (these should be a firm purée), 1 teaspoon chopped sage, 2 tablespoons chopped parsley, 1 egg, salt and pepper to taste. Cook as directed under Green Pea Stuffing, but cover the dish. Serve with pork or duck or vegetable dishes.

## Mushroom Stuffing ⊛

*50 g/2 oz butter or margarine*
*1 medium onion, chopped*
*100 g/4 oz mushrooms*
*2 large tomatoes, skinned and chopped*
*2 tablespoons chopped parsley*
*salt and pepper*

Heat the butter or margarine and fry the onion and mushrooms for several minutes. Blend with the remaining ingredients.

This stuffing is excellent put into boned trout or other fish before cooking.

## Potato Stuffing ⊛

*225 g/8 oz cooked potatoes*
*100 g/4 oz celery, chopped*
*100 g/4 oz carrots, grated*
*2 tablespoons chopped parsley*
*50 g/2 oz butter or margarine, melted*
*1 teaspoon grated lemon rind*
*salt and pepper*

Mash the potatoes and blend with the celery, carrots, parsley and the remainder of the ingredients.

This stuffing is delicious if put into the body of chicken, guinea fowl or pheasant, before cooking.

VARIATION

⊛ **Potato and Green Olive Stuffing:** Omit the carrots and lemon rind in the stuffing recipe above. Add 50 g/2 oz sliced green olives, 1 egg and 1 teaspoon chopped sage.

Put into the body of a duck and goose before cooking.

## Tomato and Cucumber Stuffing ⊛

*50 g/2 oz butter or margarine*
*1 small onion, chopped*
*100 g/4 oz cucumber, peeled and grated*
*225 g/8 oz tomatoes, skinned and chopped*
*100 g/4 oz soft breadcrumbs*
*1 tablespoon chopped parsley*
*salt and pepper*

Heat the butter or margarine in a pan and fry the onion and cucumber until soft; do not allow to colour. Blend with the remaining ingredients.

This is an ideal stuffing for white fish. Put into boned fish or on top of individual cutlets or portions of fish before cooking. Do not cover, for the stuffing is sufficiently moist to prevent it drying during cooking.

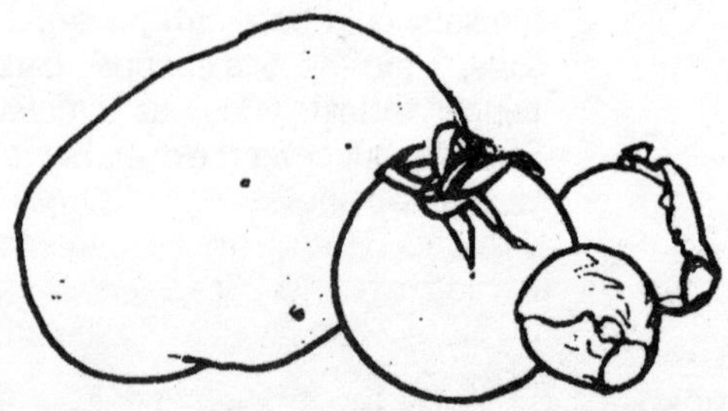

## Apple and Onion Stuffing ⊛

*1 medium onion, finely chopped*
*350 g/12 oz cooking apples (weight when peeled), grated*
*75 g/3 oz soft breadcrumbs*
*½-1 teaspoon grated nutmeg*
*½ teaspoon ground cinnamon*
*50 g/2 oz butter or margarine, melted*
*salt and pepper*

Mix all the ingredients together and allow to stand for a short time so the apple moistens the breadcrumbs. If cooking in a separate dish, cover and follow the directions on page 218. Serve with pork, duck, goose or sausages.

VARIATION

⊛ **Apple and Raisin Stuffing:** Omit the onion from the recipe above. Put 100 g/4 oz seedless raisins into a dish, moisten with 1 tablespoon lemon juice and 50 g/2 oz melted butter or margarine; leave for 30 minutes. Add the breadcrumbs, as in the recipe above, with 2 tablespoons chopped parsley and either 1 teaspoon chopped sage or chopped mint. Season well.

Serve with pork, duck, goose, sausages or with lamb.

## Cranberry Relish

*75 g/3 oz long-grain rice*
*salt*
*600 ml/1 pint water*
*150 ml/¼ pint sweet white wine*
*350 g/12 oz cranberries*
*1 large orange*
*100 g/4 oz mincemeat*
*3-4 canned pineapple rings, finely chopped*
*175 g/6 oz sugar*
*100 g/4 oz walnuts, chopped*

Cook the rice in the salted water until soft. Drain well and add to the wine while the rice is still warm so it absorbs the liquid; allow to cool. Chop or mince the cranberries. Peel the orange and remove all the flesh. Chop or mince the orange and blend with the rice and cranberries. Add the mincemeat, pineapple, sugar and nuts and leave for several hours. This relish can be served without cooking, but it can be put into a dish, covered tightly and cooked for just 40 minutes in a moderate oven.

Serve with turkey, chicken or any game birds.

## Orange Rice Stuffing

*50 g/2 oz butter or margarine*
*75 g/3 oz long-grain rice*
*1 small onion, grated*
*300 ml/½ pint water*
*salt and pepper*
*3 medium oranges*

Heat the butter or margarine in a pan, add the rice and onion and turn in the fat for several minutes. Add the water, a little salt and bring to the boil. Stir briskly, lower the heat and simmer for 10 minutes. Grate the rind from 2 oranges and add to the rice. Simmer, uncovered, for a further 10 minutes until, the rice is soft and the liquid absorbed. Remove the segments from 3 oranges, chop and add to the rice. Season well.

This is delicious put into the body of a duck before cooking.

## Dried Apricot Stuffing ⊛

*100 g/4 oz dried apricots, cut into small pieces*
*4 tablespoons boiling water*
*25 g/1 oz butter or margarine*
*1 large onion, chopped*
*100 g/4 oz soft breadcrumbs*
*2 tablespoons chopped parsley*
*1 teaspoon chopped fresh, or ¼ teaspoon dried, thyme*
*1 egg*
*salt and pepper*

Put the apricots into a basin. Add the water and leave for 1 hour. Heat the butter or margarine in a pan, add the onion and cook until soft. Blend with the breadcrumbs, herbs, apricots (and any liquid left from soaking these), the egg, salt and pepper to taste.

This stuffing is excellent with lamb, pork or duck.

VARIATION

⊛ **Apricot and Raisin Stuffing:** Use 225 g/8 oz drained canned or cooked apricot halves; slice these and add to the breadcrumbs, parsley, thyme, egg and melted butter or margarine in the recipe above. Stir in 50 g/2 oz seedless raisins, 1 teaspoon grated lemon rind, 1 tablespoon lemon juice and 2 tablespoons of the sweetened syrup in which the apricots were canned or cooked.

This stuffing is equally good with lamb, pork or duck.

## Pineapple Stuffing ⊛

*100 g/4 oz sultanas*
*4 tablespoons syrup from canned pineapple*
*2 teaspoons grated lemon rind*
*2 tablespoons lemon juice*
*25 g/1 oz brown sugar*
*8 canned pineapple rings finely chopped*
*75 g/3 oz soft breadcrumbs, preferably brown*
*25 g/1 oz butter, melted*

Put the sultanas into a dish, add the pineapple syrup, lemon rind and juice and leave to stand for 30 minutes. Add the rest of the ingredients and blend well.

If cooking this in a separate container as described on page 218, cover very well, for this sweet stuffing tends to burn easily. It is particularly good if put into the body of a chicken before cooking. Serve with chicken, turkey or duck.

VARIATION

⊛ **Prune Stuffing:** Use about 225 g/8 oz canned or cooked prunes. Cut the cooked prunes into pieces, blend with 100 g/4 oz soft brown breadcrumbs, 1 tablespoon lemon juice, 2 tablespoons syrup from canned or cooked fruit, 1 teaspoon mixed spice, 2 tablespoons chopped parsley, 25 g/1 oz melted butter, 50 g/2 oz chopped walnuts, salt and pepper. Allow to stand for at least 30 minutes, then cook as the recommendations in the recipe above and those on page 218.

Serve with duck or pork or with roast beef.

## Prune and Apple Stuffing ⊛

*350 g/12 oz cooked prunes*
*450 g/1 lb cooking apples*
*2 teaspoons chopped sage*
*salt and pepper*

Stone and halve the prunes; peel and dice the apples. Mix with the sage and seasoning. Put inside a goose before cooking.

## Oatmeal Stuffing ⊛

*4 rashers fat bacon, derinded and chopped, (reserve the rinds)*
*100 g/4 oz rolled oats*
*2 medium onions, finely chopped*
*2 tablespoons chopped parsley*
*½ teaspoon dried mixed herbs*
*2 large tomatoes, skinned and chopped*
*6 tablespoons lamb, pork or duck stock*
*salt and pepper*

Fry the bacon and bacon rinds in a pan, then remove. Add the rolled oats, turn in the bacon fat remaining in the pan and blend with the bacon and rest of the ingredients. This stuffing will seem very moist before cooking, but the rolled oats will expand; if too dry the stuffing is spoiled.

This stuffing is better put into the meat or poultry before these are cooked, rather than being cooked in a separate container. Serve with lamb, pork or duck.

VARIATION

**Fried Crumb Stuffing:** Omit the rolled oats, tomatoes and stock from the recipe above. Make 175 g/6 oz fairly coarse breadcrumbs. Fry the bacon with the onions until both are cooked; do not allow to brown. Remove from the pan, add 25 g/1 oz fat, heat and fry the breadcrumbs in the pan until crisp and brown. Mix with the bacon, onions, parsley and herbs. Season the mixture, heat for a few minutes in an uncovered dish.

Serve with veal, chicken or turkey.

## Sausage and Bacon Stuffing ⊛

*450 g/1 lb pork sausagemeat*
*4-6 bacon rashers, finely chopped*
*3 tablespoons chopped parsley*
*1 egg*

Blend all the ingredients together. The mixture can be put inside the meat or bird before roasting, or it can be baked in a separate dish, as described on page 218. The dish should be covered to give a soft stuffing or left uncovered for a crisp-topped mixture. If preferred, roll in balls and bake for about 25 minutes in a moderately hot oven.

Serve with veal, chicken or turkey.

# Sauces Based on a Roux

A 'roux' is the name given to the mixture of fat (generally butter or margarine) and flour which thickens many basic and classic sauces.

The stages of making this sauce are simply:

**1** Heat the butter or margarine in a pan; it is advisable to choose one with a flat base, so the 'roux' cannot burn.

**2** Add the flour, this should be done with the pan off the heat, blend the flour with the melted fat, then return the pan to the heat and cook gently for 2 to 3 minutes, this ensures that the flour is cooked and therefore there is less chance of the sauce forming lumps, due to uncooked flour.

**3** Remove the pan from the heat once again. Add the cold liquid (often milk) slowly to the 'roux', stirring carefully as you do so, put back over the heat and continue stirring as the sauce comes to the boil and thickens. Or add all the cold liquid, allow this to come to the boil and whisk very briskly as the sauce thickens.

**4** Whichever method is used, in point 3, it is essential that the sauce cooks gently and slowly for several minutes. Add salt and pepper to taste or other flavourings, as described in the particular recipe.

### Basic Proportions

A coating sauce is generally made with 25 g/1 oz fat, 25 g/1 oz plain flour and 300 ml/½ pint liquid. A thin sauce is made with the same amounts of fat and flour, but 600 ml/1 pint liquid. A very thick sauce (generally called 'a binding sauce' or 'a panada') is made with the same amounts of fat and flour but only 150 ml/¼ pint liquid.

### VARIATIONS

Instead of 25 g/1 oz flour you can use 15 g/½ oz cornflour.

Instead of using the method described above you can blend the flour with the liquid, pour this into the saucepan, add the fat, then stir over a low heat as the sauce comes to the boil and thickens. This is called the 'blending method of making a sauce'.

## White Sauce ⊛

*25 g/1 oz butter or margarine*
*25 g/1 oz flour*
*300 ml/½ pint milk*
*salt and pepper*

Heat the butter or margarine in the pan, stir in the flour, cook for 2 to 3 minutes, as described above, then blend in the milk. Stir as the sauce comes to the boil, and continue stirring until thickened. Season to taste.

# Based on White Sauce

These sauces are all based upon the method described on page 226 and the proportions of fat, flour and milk used in White Sauce, also on page 226, or on the more interesting Béchamel Sauce, given below.

## Béchamel Sauce ⊛

*300 ml/½ pint milk plus a little extra, see method*
*1 small onion, halved*
*1 small carrot*
*1 stick celery, chopped*
*1 spring parsley*
*few white peppercorns*
*25 g/1 oz butter*
*25 g/1 oz flour*
*salt and pepper*

This sauce has more piquancy than White Sauce, due to the fact that the milk is infused with the various other ingredients. Pour the 300 ml/½ pint milk into the pan, add the onion, carrot, celery, parsley and peppercorns. Bring the milk just to boiling point, stir well so you blend the other ingredients with the milk. Cover the pan, remove from the heat and allow to stand for about 1 hour. Strain the milk into a jug, add more milk if necessary to make the 300 ml/½ pint again. Proceed as for White Sauce on page 226.

## Anchovy Sauce ⊛

*White or Béchamel Sauce (see page 226 or above)*
*1-2 teaspoons anchovy essence*
*1-2 teaspoons lemon juice (optional)*

Make the basic sauce, but be very sparing with salt, as anchovies are highly salted. Blend in the anchovy essence plus a little lemon juice if desired. The juice is an asset if serving the sauce with fish; never add lemon juice to a boiling sauce, for this could cause it to curdle, i.e. separate. Serve with fish or egg dishes.

VARIATIONS

Use 2 to 3 sieved anchovies instead of the essence.

**Italian Anchovy Sauce:** This is my version of this sauce, often served with lamb or veal as well as fish. Heat 50 g/2 oz butter in a pan, fry 1 crushed clove garlic, blend in 2 tablespoons chopped parsley, 1 teaspoon chopped fresh basil. Open a small can of anchovies in oil, drain and chop the anchovy fiillets. Mix with the ingredients above, season to taste and spoon on to the meat or fish. To make a more economical sauce, blend 25 g/1 oz flour with 300 ml/½ pint milk, stir into the mixture; allow to come to the boil and thicken, taste and adjust the seasoning.

## Caper Sauce ⊛

*White or Béchamel Sauce (see pages 226 and 227 but use 150 ml/¼ pint milk and 150 ml/¼ pint stock, see method)*
*2-3 teaspoons capers*
*little vinegar from jar*

Make the sauce as in the basic recipe, but use half lamb stock, if serving this sauce with boiled lamb, or fish stock, if serving it with a fish dish. When the sauce has thickened, remove from the heat so it is no longer boiling, add the capers (these could be chopped if preferred) and the vinegar from the jar.

This sauce is excellent with any form of cooked lamb or with cooked white fish or grilled mackerel or trout.

## Cheese Sauce ⊛

*White Sauce (see page 226)*
*50-100 g/2-4 oz cheese, grated*
*little made mustard (optional)*
*shake cayenne pepper (optional)*

Make the White Sauce and when the sauce has thickened, add the cheese; do not cook after adding the cheese as over-cooked cheese becomes tough. Add the mustard and cayenne pepper if desired.

Note: Always use a good cooking cheese, such as Cheddar, Gruyère, Parmesan or Dutch Gouda. If adding cheese to a Béchamel Sauce the correct name is Mornay Sauce.

## Egg Sauce

*2 hard-boiled eggs*
*White or Béchamel Sauce (see pages 226 and 227)*

Shell and chop the eggs, add to the sauce and heat for 2 to 3 minutes only.

Serve with fish or chicken or vegetable dishes.

## Mushroom Sauce ⊛

*25 g/1 oz butter*
*50-75 g/2-3 oz mushrooms, thinly sliced*
*White or Béchamel Sauce (see pages 226 and 227)*

Heat the butter and fry the mushrooms until just tender. Add the mushrooms to the hot sauce.

Serve with fish or chicken or any savoury dish.

## Mustard Sauce ⊛

*White or Béchamel Sauce (see pages 226 and 227)*
*1-3 teaspoons mustard*
*1 teaspoon vinegar*

Make the sauce. Blend the mustard with the vinegar and add to the hot, but not boiling, sauce.

Serve with fish, egg or meat dishes. If preferred use half milk and half stock in the sauce.

## Prawn Sauce ⊛

*175 g/6 oz unpeeled prawns or 50-75 g/2-3 oz peeled prawns*
*White or Béchamel Sauce (see pages 226 and 227 and see method)*
*1 tablespoon lemon juice*

If using prawns in their shells, peel and gently simmer the shells in water to cover for 15 minutes, strain and use this liquid instead of all milk in the White or Béchamel Sauce. Chop the prawns into small pieces and add to the thickened sauce. Heat for 2 minutes only as over-cooking toughens the shellfish. Add the lemon juice.

Serve with fish or in pancakes or omelettes.

## Onion Sauce ⊛

*2 medium onions, finely chopped*
*salt and pepper*
*150 ml/¼ pint water*
*White Sauce (see page 226 but use only just over 150 ml/¼ pint milk)*

Put the onions into the salted water, cover the pan and simmer steadily until the onions are tender. Meanwhile make the White Sauce. Add the onions and liquid to the sauce and stir well to blend.

Serve with meat dishes.

VARIATION

⊛ **Sauce Soubise:** Cook the onions in the water as in the recipe above. Remove from the liquid and sieve or put into a liquidizer or food processor to give a smooth purée. Make the Béchamel Sauce (see page 227) but use slightly less milk than usual. Add the onion purée and 2 to 3 tablespoons double cream.

Serve with meat dishes or with grilled fish.

## Parsley Sauce ⊛

*White or Béchamel Sauce (see pages 226 and 227)*
*2-3 tablespoons finely chopped parsley*
*pinch grated nutmeg (optional)*

Make the sauce and when thickened, add the chopped parsley. For a mellow flavour, simmer the parsley in the sauce for several minutes. Add the nutmeg.

VARIATIONS

This sauce can be made with half milk and half stock, depending upon the dish with which it is served.

Serve with cooked vegetables, meat (especially boiled ham or bacon) and with fish or egg dishes.

⊛ **Maîte d'hotel Sauce:** Use rather less milk in the sauce and add a little double cream; stir in the parsley. Remove from the heat and add 1 tablespoon lemon juice. This sauce can also be made with half milk and half stock, according to the dish with which it is to be served.

# Based on Brown Sauce

A sauce made with a good brown stock is the basis of a number of recipes. The technique of making a brown sauce is exactly the same as that described on page 226, except that the flour should be allowed to darken in cooking. As gravy is very similar to a simple brown sauce you will find it given on this page.

## Brown Sauce ⊛

*25 g/1 oz dripping or fat*
*25 g/1 oz flour*
*300 ml/½ pint stock*
*salt and pepper*

Heat the dripping or fat in a pan and stir in the flour. Stir over a low heat as the 'roux' darkens slightly; do not allow to become too brown, or it will spoil the taste of the sauce. Gradually blend in the stock, stirring the sauce as it comes to the boil and thickens; season to taste.

Serve with meat, poultry or savoury dishes.

VARIATIONS

⊛ **Richer Brown Sauce:** Heat 50 g/2 oz dripping or fat in a pan and fry 1 finely chopped onion, 1 chopped carrot, 1 chopped stick celery until soft; stir in the flour, proceed as the recipe above. Either strain the sauce or sieve or liquidize. This gives a thicker consistency, which should be diluted with extra stock if required. Serve with meat, poultry or savoury dishes.

⊛ **Thin Gravy:** Pour away all the fat from the roasting tin except 1 good tablespoon (do not remove any tiny pieces of meat or poultry or stuffing). Blend in 1 tablespoon flour, cook gently for 2 to 3 minutes, then gradually add 300 ml/½ pint meat or poultry stock or liquid from cooking the vegetables. Stir as the sauce comes to the boil and thickens slightly. Add seasonings or flavourings to taste. You can add a little mushroom or tomato ketchup, a dash of soy or Worcestershire sauce, garlic or celery salt. Strain before serving.

⊛ **Thickened Gravy:** Use 20-25 g/¾-1 oz flour with the same amount of fat and liquid.

If more convenient, spoon the dripping and any pieces of meat into a saucepan and make the gravy in that.

⊛ **Madeira Sauce:** Make the Richer Brown Sauce as above, or the Espagnole Sauce on page 231. Sieve and reheat with about 150 ml/¼ pint Madeira wine. Simmer gently for about 10 minutes.

Serve with meat; it is especially good with tongue and ham.

## Espagnole Sauce ⊛

*50 g/2 oz fat or dripping*
*1 medium onion, chopped*
*1 medium tomato, chopped*
*25 g/1 oz mushrooms, chopped*
*1 stick celery, chopped*
*1 bacon rasher, derinded and chopped*
*25 g/1 oz flour*
*generous 300 ml/generous ½ pint brown stock*
*sprig parsley*
*1 bay leaf*
*1 tablespoon tomato purée*
*salt and pepper*
*2 tablespoons dry sherry*

Espagnole Sauce is the basis of many other interesting sauces. Heat the fat or dripping and fry the vegetables and bacon for 5 minutes. Blend in the flour and stir over a low heat for 2 to 3 minutes. Gradually add the stock. Stir as the sauce comes to the boil and thickens. Add the herbs, tomato purée and seasoning; cover the pan and simmer for at least 30 minutes. Either sieve or liquidize the ingredients then return to the pan with the sherry and reheat.

Serve with savoury dishes.

VARIATION

Instead of sieving the sauce; strain, discard the solid ingredients and serve as a thinner sauce.

## Chasseur Sauce ⊛

*Richer Brown Sauce or Espagnole Sauce (see page 230 or above)*
*25 g/1 oz butter*
*50 g/2 oz mushrooms, sliced*
*2 onions, sliced*
*2 tomatoes, sliced*
*2 tablespoons brandy or sherry*

Make the sauce, strain and return to the pan. Heat the butter, fry the mushrooms, onions and tomatoes and add to the basic sauce with the brandy or sherry.

Serve with meat or poultry.

VARIATION

⊛ **Lyonnaise Sauce:** Make the Espagnole Sauce, strain and return to the pan. Heat 40 g/1½ oz butter and fry 2 large thinly sliced onions until golden and tender. Add to the sauce. Serve with pork, duck or sausages.

## Piquant Sauce ⊛

*2 tablespoons meat dripping*
*1 medium onion, finely chopped*
*25 g/1 oz flour*
*150 ml/¼ pint red wine*
*150 ml/¼ pint stock*
*2 teaspoons Worcestershire sauce*
*juices from cooking meat (see method)*
*2 tablespoons redcurrant jelly*

Heat the meat dripping in a saucepan, add the onion and fry gently for 5 minutes. Stir in the flour, cook for 2 to 3 minutes then gradually stir in the wine, stock, Worcestershire sauce and any meat juices from roasting the meat. Add the redcurrant jelly. Bring to the boil, stirring all the time. Cover the pan and simmer gently for 10 minutes. This sauce blends well with beef or pork.

## Poivrade Sauce ⊛

*10 black peppercorns, crushed*
*1 small onion, chopped*
*6 tablespoons red wine vinegar*
*6 tablespoons red wine*
*Espagnole Sauce (see page 231)*

Put the peppercorns, onion, vinegar and red wine into a pan, simmer until reduced to about 4 tablespoons. Make the Espagnole Sauce and strain or sieve, depending upon whether you prefer a thinner or thicker mixture. Strain the peppercorn mixture into the sauce and reheat.

Serve with game, particularly good with venison.

## Red Wine Sauce ⊛

*2-3 mushrooms*
*1 small onion*
*bouquet garni*
*few peppercorns*
*450 ml/¾ pint beef stock*
*50 g/2 oz butter*
*50 g/2 oz flour*
*300 ml/½ pint red wine*
*salt and pepper*

Put the mushrooms and onion into a pan with the bouquet garni, peppercorns and stock. Bring to the boil and simmer for 5 minutes; remove from the heat. Allow to stand for several hours so the stock absorbs the flavour of the vegetables and herbs. Strain and retain the stock (it should be just over 300 ml/½ pint by this time).

Heat the butter in a saucepan and stir in the flour. Cook for several minutes, then gradually blend in the stock and wine. Stir or whisk the sauce over a low heat until a coating consistency; add salt and pepper to taste.

Serve with meat (particularly beef) or game. This is excellent with Beef Wellington (see page 113).

## Barbecue Sauce ⊛

*2 tablespoons oil*
*1 large onion, chopped*
*2 cloves garlic, chopped*
*1 x 400 g/14 oz can plum tomatoes*
*2 tablespoons sweet pickle (see method)*
*1 tablespoon cider or white wine vinegar*
*1 tablespoon brown sugar*
*2 tablespoons tomato ketchup*
*2 teaspoons French mustard*
*1 teaspoon Worcestershire sauce*
*salt and pepper*

Heat the oil in a strong saucepan and cook the onion and garlic over the barbecue fire or on top of the cooker until soft; do not allow to brown. Blend in all the remaining ingredients, stirring well to break up the tomatoes and the sweet pickle if this is rather lumpy. Stir over the barbecue or on top of the cooker until slightly thickened and very hot. Pull to one side of the barbecue while cooking the other foods.

Serve with any barbecued foods; the sauce can be used for basting the foods as they cook over the barbecue.

## Tomato Sauce ⊛

*40 g/1 ½ oz butter or margarine*
*1 small onion, chopped*
*½ small apple, chopped*
*450 g/1 lb tomatoes, skinned and chopped*
*2 teaspoons cornflour*
*150 ml/¼ pint ham stock or water*
*1 teaspoon brown sugar*
*salt and pepper*

Heat the butter or margarine in a pan and fry the onion, apple and tomatoes until a soft purée. Sieve then return to the pan. Blend the cornflour with the stock or water, add to the tomato purée with the sugar, salt and pepper and stir as the sauce comes to the boil and thickens.

Serve with any savoury dish.

VARIATION

Add a little concentrated tomato purée, Worcestershire sauce or soy sauce or fry 1 to 2 bacon rashers with the onion.

## Sherried Tomato Sauce ⊛

*40 g/1 ½ oz butter or margarine*
*2 medium onions, finely chopped*
*3 large tomatoes, skinned and chopped*
*25 g/1 oz flour*
*300 ml/½ pint chicken stock or water*
*salt and pepper*
*4 tablespoons dry sherry*

Heat the butter or margarine in a saucepan, add the onions and fry for several minutes – do not allow to brown. Add the tomatoes and cook for a further 2 to 3 minutes, then blend in the flour and the stock or water. Bring slowly to the boil, stirring all the time and cook until thickened. Rub through a sieve or liquidize the mixture to give a smooth sauce; return to the saucepan and reheat. Add the salt, pepper and sherry and heat until a coating consistency.

Serve with any savoury dish.

## Sanfayna ⊛

*3 tablespoons olive oil*
*4 large tomatoes, skinned and chopped*
*2 medium onions, chopped*
*2 red peppers, deseeded and chopped*
*1 courgette, thinly sliced*
*1 clove garlic, crushed*
*50-100 g/2-4 oz mushrooms, chopped*
*salt and pepper*

Heat the oil in a large saucepan or deep frying pan. Add all the ingredients and season well. Cook steadily until a thick purée. Serve as a sauce with meat, poultry or fish.

VARIATIONS

Use canned plum tomatoes and canned red peppers.

Omit the courgette and add chopped green pepper instead.

⊛ **Herb Sanfayna Sauce:** Increase the garlic to 2 to 3 cloves; add 2 tablespoons chopped parsley, 1 teaspoon chopped rosemary, 1 teaspoon chopped tarragon.

Serve with vegetarian dishes as well as those suggested above.

# Sauces Based on Eggs

In the sauces that follow, eggs or egg yolks are used to thicken the mixture. Flour or cornflour is not required. Be careful when heating the mixture that the eggs are not subjected to undue heat, for this could harden the egg yolks, or make the sauce separate (curdle).

## Hollandaise Sauce ⊛

*2 egg yolks*
*1 tablespoon lemon juice or white wine vinegar*
*salt and pepper*
*pinch cayenne pepper*
*100 g/4 oz unsalted butter, slightly warmed.*

Put the egg yolks, lemon juice or vinegar and seasonings into a heatproof basin or the top of a double saucepan. Stand over hot, but not boiling, water and whisk until thick and creamy. Gradually whisk in the butter. Never add the butter too quickly as this can cause the sauce to curdle. The butter can stand at room temperature to soften but should never be allowed to become oily when mixing the sauce by hand, as in this method. When the sauce is thickened it is ready to serve. Serve with vegetables, poached or grilled fish.

VARIATIONS

⊛ **Economical Hollandaise Sauce:** Use only 50g/2oz butter.

⊛ **Mousseline Savoury Sauce:** Use only 25 g/1 oz butter. Allow the sauce to cool then add 4 to 5 tablespoons of whipped cream and a little grated nutmeg. This is excellent with vegetables.

⊛ **Paloise Sauce:** Make the Hollandaise Sauce as the recipe above then add 2 to 3 teaspoons freshly chopped mint. This is excellent with lamb.

## Hollandaise Sauce (Liquidizer Method)

*Ingredients as in recipe above*

Heat the butter to boiling point – take care it does not overheat and discolour. Put the egg yolks, seasonings and lemon juice or vinegar into the liquidizer goblet or food processor bowl. Put on the lid and switch on for a few seconds. Leave the motor running and add the boiling butter in a slow steady stream through the hole in the lid of the liquidizer or feed tube of the food processor.

## Béarnaise Sauce ⊛

*2 tablespoons white wine vinegar*
*1 shallot, finely chopped*
*1 spring tarragon or pinch dried tarragon*
*1 sprig thyme or pinch dried thyme*
*1 bay leaf*
*2 egg yolks*
*100 g/4 oz unsalted butter, slightly warmed*
*salt and pepper*
*1 teaspoon chopped chervil or parsley*
*½ teaspoon chopped tarragon*

Put the vinegar into a small saucepan. Add the shallot and the sprigs of tarragon and thyme or dried herbs and the bay leaf. Bring the vinegar to boiling point and boil until reduced by half. Remove from the heat and leave for 1 hour then strain. Put the egg yolks into a heatproof basin or the top of a double saucepan. Stand over hot, but not boiling, water. Add the strained vinegar and whisk until thick and creamy. Gradually whisk in the butter with salt and pepper to taste. Finally add the chopped fresh herbs. Keep the sauce over warm water until ready to serve, whisking from time to time. Serve on steak or with meat.

VARIATIONS

Make in a liquidizer or food processor as described under Hollandaise Sauce (see page 234).

Use only 50 g/2 oz butter for a less rich sauce.

⊛ **Choron Sauce:** Add up to 1 tablespoon tomato purée to the thickened sauce.

## Mayonnaise

*2 eggs yolks*
*up to 300 ml/½ pint oil (I use half best quality olive oil and half corn oil)*
*salt and pepper*
*½ teaspoon mustard powder*
*½ teaspoon caster sugar*
*up to 2 tablespoons lemon juice*
*1 tablespoon boiling water*

Make sure the basin you use is dry and free from grease. Ensure that the egg yolks and oil are both at room temperature before making the sauce.

Put the egg yolks with a pinch salt, shake of pepper, the mustard, sugar and half the lemon juice into the basin. Beat to blend, then gradually beat in the oil, drop by drop with a wooden spoon. When the sauce starts to thicken, the oil can be added a little more rapidly. The more oil used, the thicker the sauce will become. Finally whisk in the remaining lemon juice and water.

VARIATIONS

The type of mustard and oil used are my personal preference, but can be changed as desired, e.g. use Dijon mustard and all olive oil. Use half lemon juice and half white wine vinegar.

**Liquidizer Mayonnaise:** You can use whole eggs when using a liquidizer or food processor. Put the eggs or egg yolks into the goblet or bowl. Add the seasonings and sugar. Switch on for a few seconds, then add the oil slowly with the machine in operation. Finally add the lemon juice and water. Where you have a choice of setting, use the medium speed throughout the process.

## Mayonnaise Verte

*1-2 tablespoons of each of the following: parsley, tarragon, chives, spinach or watercress*
*2 tablespoons boiled water, ingredients and method as liquidizer method of making mayonnaise*

Put the parsley, tarragon, chives, spinach or watercress leaves into a basin and add the boiling water. Leave for 5 minutes, drain and add to the mayonnaise in the liquidizer or food processor, switch on until finely chopped and blended with the mayonnaise.

Serve with any cold salad.

VARIATIONS

**Aioli Sauce:** Blend 2 to 3 crushed cloves garlic with the basic mayonnaise, or soak 2 tablespoons fine soft breadcrumbs in 3 tablespoons warm milk until a purée, blend with the mayonnaise then add the garlic.

**Fennel Mayonnaise:** Add 2 to 3 tablespoons chopped fennel leaves to the mayonnaise. Serve with fish.

## Rémoulade Sauce

*2 eggs, hard-boiled*
*1 egg yolk*
*½-1 tablespoon French mustard*
*salt and pepper*
*up to 300 ml/½ pint olive oil*
*1-2 tablespoons lemon juice*

Halve the cooked eggs and remove the yolks. Cream the egg yolks until smooth with the uncooked egg yolk, mustard, salt and pepper. (The hard-boiled egg whites can be chopped and added to a salad.) Gradually incorporate the oil, as the recipe for Mayonnaise (see page 235). Finally add the lemon juice. Serve with any salad or blend with shredded celeriac and serve as an hors d'oeuvre.

## Avgolemono Sauce

*4 egg yolks or 2 whole eggs*
*salt and pepper*
*4 tablespoons lemon juice*

Put the egg yolks or whole eggs with a little salt and pepper into a heatproof basin over hot water. Whisk until thick and creamy then gradually whisk in the lemon juice. Serve with fish.

VARIATION:

**Chicken Avgolemono Sauce:** Proceed as above, then gradually whisk in from 150 to 300 ml/¼ to ½ pint very well-flavoured chicken stock. The consistency depends upon personal taste. Continue whisking over heat until well thickened.

**Avgolemono Soup:** Simmer 40 g/1½ oz long-grain rice in 900 ml/1½ pints well-flavoured chicken stock until just tender. Meanwhile prepare the sauce as above. Whisk the sauce into the rice and stock and serve.

## Cider Apple Sauce ⊛

*350g/12oz cooking apples (weight when peeled), thinly sliced*
*150ml/¼ pint sweet cider*
*25g/1oz butter*
*2 tablespoons sugar*
*2 tablespoons sultanas*

Put the apples, cider, butter and sugar into a saucepan. Simmer until a thick pulp. Mash with a wooden spoon or sieve or liquidize; add the sultanas, reheat or serve cold. This is softer than the usual Apple Sauce (see page 145).

Serve with duck, goose, pork or cooked bacon.

VARIATIONS

⊛ **Spiced Apple Raisin Sauce:** Simmer the apples in 3 tablespoons water with 1 tablespoon lemon juice, 2 tablespoons moist brown sugar and 1 teaspoon mixed spice. When cooked add 50g/2oz seedless raisins.

Serve with savoury dishes, as above, or with ice cream.

⊛ **Orange and Apple Sauce:** Grate the rinds from 2 large oranges, put into a saucepan with 2 tablespoons orange juice, 1 teaspoon lemon juice, 2 tablespoons water and 50g/2oz caster sugar. Stir until the sugar has dissolved then add 350g/12oz sliced dessert apples and poach gently until tender.

Serve with savoury dishes as above recipe.

## Cumberland Sauce ⊛

*1 large orange*
*1 lemon*
*150ml/¼ pint water*
*1 teaspoon arrowroot or cornflour*
*3 tablespoon port wine*
*4-6 tablespoons redcurrant jelly*
*1-2 teaspoons made mustard*
*salt and pepper*

Peel the orange then cut away all the white pith and leave just the top orange part (called the zest). Cut this into matchstick strips. Squeeze out the juice from the orange and lemon. Put the orange rind and water into a saucepan. Cover the pan and simmer gently for 10 minutes. Blend the arrowroot or cornflour with the fruit juices. Add to the pan with the wine and redcurrant jelly. Stir over a low heat until thickened and clear. Add the mustard, salt and pepper to taste. Excellent with pâté, boiled bacon or ham.

## Morello Cherry Sauce ⊛

*150ml/¼ pint water*
*2 tablespoons port wine or red wine*
*50-75g/2-3oz sugar*
*3 tablespoons redcurrant jelly*
*350g/12oz Morello cherries, stoned*

Put the water, wine, sugar and redcurrent jelly into a good-sized saucepan. Stir over a low heat until the sugar and jelly have dissolved. Add the cherries and poach until tender. Serve hot or cold. This sauce is excellent with duck, goose, boiled or baked ham.

## Pineapple Mustard Sauce ✳

*1 x 200 g/7 oz can pineapple rings with syrup from the can*
*1 teaspoon arrowroot*
*1-2 teaspoons French mustard*
*1 tablespoon lemon juice or white wine vinegar*
*1 tablespoon honey*
*salt and pepper*

Drain the pineapple, reserving the syrup, and chop finely. Blend the arrowroot and mustard with the reserved syrup. Put into a saucepan, add the lemon juice or vinegar, honey and salt and pepper. Stir over a low heat until thickened and clear. Add the chopped pineapple but do not cook the sauce after adding this. Serve cold with pork as a change from Apple Sauce, or with bacon. It is also surprisingly good with chicken and veal.

VARIATION

✳ **Sweet Pineapple Sauce:** Follow the recipe above but omit the mustard. Use the lemon juice but do not substitute vinegar. Increase the honey to 2 tablespoons or use caster sugar instead. This is a good sauce to serve with plain yogurt or ice cream.

## Prune Sauce ✳

*175 g/6 oz dried prunes*
*300 ml/½ pint red wine, water or stock*
*25 g/1 oz sugar*
*25 g/1 oz blanched almonds*

Put the prunes into a dish and top with the wine, water or stock; you can use a little wine and stock but the total liquid amount should be 300 ml/½ pint. Leave the prunes to soak overnight or for several hours. Put into a saucepan, add the sugar, cover the pan and simmer gently until tender. Remove the stones, then sieve the fruit with the liquid or put into a liquidiser or food processor until a smooth, thick purée. Top with the nuts. This sauce blends well with pork or bacon.

VARIATION

✳ **Prune and Redcurrant Sauce:** Follow the recipe above but omit the almonds. Use wine or water in which to soak and cook the prunes. Return the smooth purée to the saucepan, add 2 to 3 tablespoons redcurrant jelly. Blend 1 teaspoon arrowroot with 150 ml/¼ pint of extra red wine or water and add to the prune mixture. Stir over a low heat until thickened and clear. This is also excellent with pork or bacon and can be used to serve with cooked ham.

✳ **Spiced Prune Sauce:** Soak the prunes in 300 ml/½ pint well-strained cold tea, to which is added ½ teaspoon grated nutmeg and ½ teaspoon ground cinnamon. Cook as the recipe above, but use brown sugar. Serve with pork.

## Savoury Orange Sauce ⊛

*300 ml/½ pint stock (see method)*
*2 large oranges*
*1 ½ teaspoons arrowroot*
*1 ½ teaspoons lemon juice*
*50 g/2 oz plain or bitter chocolate*
*salt and pepper*
*2 tablespoons orange curaçao*

Simmer the giblets of the duck or goose in water to cover for 1 hour. Strain very thoroughly and boil until reduced to 300 ml/½ pint clear strongly-flavoured stock. Cut the zest from both oranges and cut into thin matchstick strips. Put into the stock and leave to soak for 15 to 30 minutes. Cover the saucepan and simmer gently for 15 minutes. Halve the oranges, squeeze out the juice and blend with the arrowroot, pour into the pan containing the orange rind. Add the rest of the ingredients and stir over a low heat until smooth and thickened.

Serve with duck or goose.

## Sweet and Sour Sauce

*1 tablespoon cornflour*
*150 ml/¼ pint orange juice*
*150 ml/¼ pint chicken stock*
*2 tablespoons honey*
*1-2 tablespoons lemon juice*
*12 very small cocktail onions*
*2 tablespoons diced gherkins*
*salt and pepper*

Blend the cornflour with the orange juice and stock. Put into a saucepan with the honey and lemon juice; stir over a low heat until thickened, clear and smooth. Add the onions, gherkins and salt and pepper just before serving.

VARIATIONS

Vary the kind of stock, according to the food with which the sauce is to be served, i.e., if serving with fish use fish stock; if this is not available chicken stock is a good alternative.

**Pineapple Sweet and Sour Sauce:** Use pineapple juice or syrup from canned pineapple instead of orange juice. Add 3 to 4 tablespoons neatly diced pineapple with the onions, gherkins and seasoning.

**Crunchy Sweet and Sour Sauce:** Follow the above recipe, add 2 tablespoons diced celery, 2 tablespoons diced green pepper and 2 tablespoons diced red pepper with the onions. Omit the gherkins.

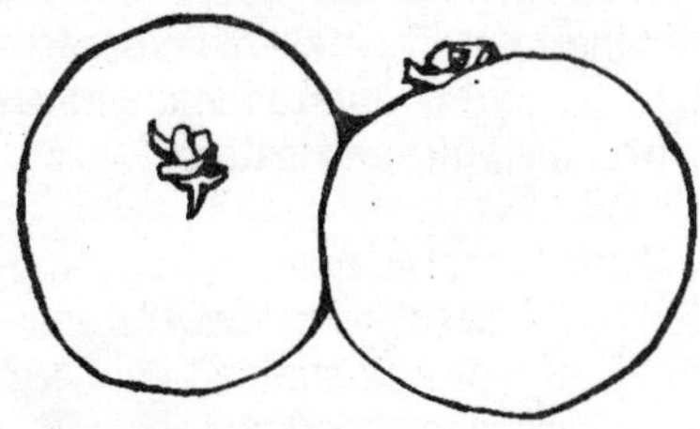

# Vegetables and Salads

It has not been easy to select my favourite recipes for this chapter as I am one of the people who enjoy virtually every kind of vegetable, providing it is cooked carefully, and I find interesting salads a delight.

The recipes I have chosen are those based upon vegetables that have become so much more plentiful in the shops these days, but which are still somewhat unfamiliar to many cooks (I mean aubergines, courgettes and peppers). I have also included a few unusual ways of serving everyday vegetables, such as carrots, cauliflower and mushrooms. I could not omit fried potatoes, for there is no doubt that whether these are called 'chips', 'French fried', or just 'frites' they are popular in many parts of the world, but it is surprising how few people seem to know the secret of perfect frying. I hope the recipe on page 252 will be helpful.

It has been a great encouragement to people like myself, who write and talk about cookery, to find that over the years the majority of people have learned to appreciate the importance of cooking vegetables lightly, so they retain their flavour, texture and nutrient value. It is for this reason that only a small number of vegetable dishes in this section are marked with the freezing symbol ⊛ since these are the only ones I consider taste almost as good after freezing and reheating as they do when freshly cooked. You can, of course, substitute frozen vegetables for fresh in many of the recipes.

Salad recipes begin on page 254; you will find I have included quite an amount of fresh fruit with the vegetables, as the fruit not only adds colour and interest to the dish, but can be an economical replacement for salad vegetables at certain times of the year.

Some of the salad recipes are sufficiently sustaining to be served as a light main dish, or an hors d'oeuvre. In other recipes I have indicated the dishes with which I feel the salad combines best. There are many occasions when a salad can be served with hot meat, fish or poultry, as an alternative to a cooked vegetable to give a pleasing contrast in temperature and texture.

## Aubergines Tingira ⊛

*4 medium aubergines*
*salt and cayenne pepper*
*350 g/12 oz cooked or corned beef, minced or flaked*
*3 bacon rashers, derinded and minced*
*1-2 cloves garlic, crushed*
*100 g/4 oz soft breadcrumbs*
*2 tablespoons tomato purée*
*1 egg*
TOPPING:
*50 g/2 oz butter*
*50 g/2 oz soft breadcrumbs*
GARNISH:
*chopped parsley*

Score the skins of the aubergines, sprinkle with a little salt and leave standing for about 30 minutes (the salt draws out the bitter flavour from the skins). Obviously if you do not dislike the flavour, then this step is unnecessary. Personally I feel it does detract from the taste I enjoy. Rinse the aubergines in cold water, dry and halve lengthways. Scoop out most of the centre pulp, chop this finely and mix with the beef, bacon, garlic, breadcrumbs, tomato purée and egg. Season well. Spoon into the aubergine cases.

Heat the butter in a pan and fry the 50 g/2 oz breadcrumbs until crisp and golden brown. Sprinkle over the tops of the stuffed aubergines. Bake in the centre of a moderate oven (180°C/350°F or Gas Mark 4) for 30 minutes. Garnish with parsley.

## Aubergine and Tomato Bake ⊛

*2 large aubergines, cut into 1 cm/½ inch slices*
*salt and pepper*
*6 large tomatoes, cut into 1 cm/½ inch slices*
*50 g/2 oz soft breadcrumbs*
*50 g/2 oz butter*

Put the aubergines into boiling salted water and cook for 5 minutes, drain and allow to dry. This step hastens cooking and means the tomato slices remain fairly firm when the dish is baked.

Put layers of aubergines and tomatoes into an ovenproof serving dish, seasoning each layer lightly.

Fry the breadcrumbs in the butter, as described in the recipe above and sprinkle over the vegetables. Bake in the centre of a moderately hot oven (200°C/400°F or Gas Mark 6) for 20 to 25 minutes. Serve as a light dish or with cooked meat, fish or poultry.

## Fried Aubergines

*allow 1 small or ½ large aubergine per person*
*salt and pepper*
*flour*
FOR FRYING:
*butter or oil or fat*

If you do not like the bitter flavour of the skins, prepare the aubergines as described in the first recipe on this page. Cut into 1 cm/½ inch slices. Mix a little salt and pepper with the flour and coat the aubergine slices well. Either shallow fry in hot butter or oil or deep fry in hot oil or fat until crisp and brown on the outside and tender inside. This takes from 4 to 6 minutes. Drain on absorbent paper and serve.

## Stuffed Aubergines ⊛

*2 large or 4 small aubergines*
*½ tablespoon olive oil*
*salt and pepper*
STUFFING:
*75 g/3 oz soft breadcrumbs*
*100 g/4 oz cooked ham, chopped*
*2 hard-boiled eggs, chopped*
*2 large tomatoes, skinned and chopped*
*50 g/2 oz Cheddar cheese, grated*
TOPPING:
*50 g/2 oz Cheddar cheese, grated*
*25 g/1 oz crisp breadcrumbs*

If you wish to avoid the bitter taste of aubergine skins, follow the first recipe on page 241. Halve the aubergines lengthways, score the cut surface, brush with oil and season lightly. Put into an oiled ovenproof dish, cover and cook in the centre of a moderately hot oven (200°C/400°F or Gas Mark 6) for 20 minutes. Scoop out the soft centres and blend with the stuffing ingredients. Return the stuffing to the aubergine skins, add the topping and bake for a further 15 to 20 minutes. Serve with Cheese Sauce (see page 228).

VARIATION

⊛ **Little Slippers:** Prepare and bake the aubergines as above. Chop 2 medium onions and 1 to 2 cloves garlic. Skin and chop 3 large tomatoes. Heat 2 tablespoons oil and fry the vegetables until soft. Blend with the soft centres of the aubergines. Add 225 g/8 oz minced cooked meat (preferably lamb), salt, pepper and cayenne pepper. Spoon into the aubergine cases. Heat 50 g/2 oz butter in a pan, turn 50 g/2 oz soft breadcrumbs in this; spoon over the filling. Bake as above.

## Carrot Cheesecake ⊛

BISCUIT CRUST:
*175 g/6 oz digestive biscuits, crushed*
*50 g/2 oz butter, melted*
FILLING:
*150 ml/¼ pint very finely grated carrots (do not pack the measure too tightly with the carrots)*
*450 g/1 lb cottage cheese, sieved*
*4 tablespoons double cream*
*2 eggs*
*salt and pepper*

Lightly grease a 20 cm/8 inch cake tin with a loose base. Blend the biscuit crumbs and butter and press into the base of the cake tin. Blend together the ingredients for the filling and spoon over the biscuit-crumb base. Cook in the centre of a cool oven (150°C/300°F or Gas Mark 2) for approximately 1 hour until just firm to the touch. When cold, remove from the tin. Serve with a green salad.

VARIATIONS

⊛ **Sweet Carrot Cheesecake:** Omit the salt and pepper, add 50 to 75 g/2 to 3 oz caster sugar to the other ingredients, together with 1 tablespoon lemon juice and 50 g/2 oz seedless raisins. Use only 3 tablespoons cream. When quite cold, top with lightly whipped cream.

**Carrots Gratinée:** Slice and cook the carrots in the usual way; drain and pack into an ovenproof dish. Top the hot carrots with a layer of cream cheese, then grated cheese, crisp breadcrumbs and a little melted butter. Heat for a short time under the grill until the topping is brown.

## Turkish Beans

*450g/1 lb French or other green beans*
*salt and pepper*
*2 tablespoons olive oil*
*2 cloves garlic, crushed*
*2 medium onions, sliced*
*1 green pepper, cored, seeded and diced*
*3 large tomatoes, skinned and sliced*
*2 tablespoons chopped parsley*

Prepare and cook the beans in salted water, strain thoroughly. Meanwhile heat the oil in a pan and fry the garlic, onions, pepper and tomatoes until just tender. Blend with the beans and chopped parsley; season well.

VARIATION

**Beans Arabic Style:** Heat the grated rind of 1 orange, 2 tablespoons orange juice, 1 tablespoon honey and 2 tablespoons flaked almonds in 25g/1 oz melted butter. Cook the beans in the usual way, drain thoroughly, then heat for 1 to 2 minutes in the honey and orange mixture.

## Orange Beetroot

*8 tiny cooked beetroot, skinned*
*1 teaspoon grated orange rind*
*4-6 tablespoons orange juice*
*2 tablespoons white malt vinegar*
*1 teaspoon arrowroot*
*25g/1 oz sugar*

Put the beetroot into a dish. Blend the remaining ingredients together. Pour into a saucepan, stir until slightly thickened and clear. Pour over the beetroot. Serve cold. This is excellent with cooked beef or pork.

VARIATIONS

Heat the beetroot in the sauce.

**Ginger Beetroot:** Omit the orange juice and rind and use ginger beer instead. Thicken the sauce, season well. Pour over the beetroot or heat the beetroot in the sauce.

## Cabbage in Sour Cream

*1 cabbage, finely shredded*
*salt and pepper*
*40g/1 ½ oz butter*
*150 ml/¼ pint soured cream*
*1 teaspoon caraway seeds*

Put the cabbage into boiling salted water and cook for 1 to 2 minutes only; the cabbage should still be crisp. Drain thoroughly. Heat the butter, add the cabbage and remaining ingredients and cook for 2 to 3 minutes.

## Prawn Stuffed Cauliflower

*1 medium cauliflower*
*salt and pepper*
FILLING:
*25 g/1 oz butter*
*25 g/1 oz flour*
*200 ml/⅓ pint milk*
*175 g/6 oz Cheddar cheese, grated*
*100 g/4 oz peeled prawns*
*2 tablespoons chopped gherkins*
*1 teaspoon capers*
GARNISH:
*tomato slices*
*chopped chives*
*chopped parsley*

Trim the cauliflower and cook whole in boiling seasoned water until just tender – do not overcook. Scoop out the centre, and chop this finely. Heat the butter in a pan, stir in the flour then gradually blend in the milk. Bring the sauce to the boil and stir until thickened. Add a little salt and pepper, 100 g/4 oz of the grated cheese, the prawns, gherkins, capers and chopped cauliflower. Spoon into the centre of the cauliflower. Top with the remaining grated cheese. Put into an ovenproof dish and cook in a moderately hot oven (200°C/400°F or Gas Mark 6) for 10 to 15 minutes. Arrange the sliced tomatoes around the cauliflower and top with the chives and parsley.

VARIATION

**Stuffed Cauliflower Polonaise:** Cook the cauliflower as above. Prepare a thick White Sauce (omit the cheese) from the above recipe; add 2 tablespoons chopped parsley, 3 hard-boiled and chopped eggs, the chopped cauliflower centre. Spoon into the cauliflower, top with crisp breadcrumbs and melted butter. Heat as above.

## Cauliflower Stifado

*1 medium cauliflower*
*2 tablespoons oil*
*2 tiny pickling onions, peeled but left whole*
*2 cloves garlic, peeled but left whole*
*1 tablespoon tomato purée*
*1 tablespoon white vinegar*
*450 ml/¾ pint water*
*1 teaspoon chopped rosemary*
*1 teaspoon chopped parsley*
*1 bay leaf*
*salt and pepper*

Divide the cauliflower into neat florets. Heat the oil in a saucepan, add the onions and garlic and fry until golden brown. Blend the tomato purée, vinegar and water with the onions and oil in the pan; add the herbs, salt and pepper. Cover the pan and simmer gently for 20 minutes, or until the onions are soft; lift the lid towards the end of the cooking period so very little liquid remains in the pan.

Meanwhile put the cauliflower into a small amount of boiling salted water and cook until nearly tender. Strain and add to the onion mixture. Simmer for 5 minutes then remove the bay leaf and garlic and serve. This is excellent with all meals.

VARIATIONS

**Cauliflower Amandine:** Divide a cauliflower into florets. Cook in boiling salted water until tender, then drain. Meanwhile heat 50 g/2 oz butter, fry 25 to 50 g/1 to 2 oz blanched flaked almonds until golden. Add to the cauliflower and serve.

Brussels sprouts, broccoli, carrots can all be served in the same way.

## Creamed Celeriac ⊛

*1 large or 2 small celeriac roots, peeled and thinly sliced*
*2-3 teaspoons lemon juice*
*salt and pepper*
*150 ml/¼ pint double cream*
*40 g/1½ oz butter, melted*

Put the sliced celeriac into lemon flavoured water when prepared so that it keeps a good colour. Add a few drops of lemon juice to boiling salted water and cook the celeriac for 10 to 15 minutes until just tender. Drain thoroughly. Pack the celeriac in layers in an ovenproof dish, adding a little cream, melted butter and seasoning to each layer. Top with cream and melted butter. Cook in the centre of a moderately hot oven (190°C/375°F or Gas Mark 5) for 25 minutes until slightly golden on top.

VARIATIONS

⊛ **Celeriac au Gratin:** Prepare celeriac as above, but add grated cheese to the cream and melted butter. Top with cream, breadcrumbs and grated cheese. Bake as above.

**Celeriac Purée:** Mash cooked celeriac with butter, a little cream, chopped parsley and seasoning. This is excellent with poultry or game.

## Chicory and Ham ⊛

*8 small heads chicory*
*salt and pepper*
*300 ml/½ pint Cheese Sauce (see page 228)*
*8 thin slices cooked ham*

To make sure there is no confusion about chicory, I am referring to the white vegetables, for in many countries this is known as endive, while the curly lettuce is called chicory. Trim the ends from each head, cook in a little well seasoned water for 6 to 8 minutes only – overcooking makes the vegetable bitter. Meanwhile make the sauce. Drain the chicory, wrap each head in ham, put into a flameproof dish, top with the sauce and heat for a few minutes under the grill.

## Courgettes Frittata ⊛

*50 g/2 oz butter*
*1 medium onion, chopped*
*350 g/12 oz courgettes, thinly sliced*
*salt and pepper*
*4 to 6 eggs*
*4 tablespoons single cream*
*few drops Tabasco sauce*
*3 tablespoons chopped parsley*

Heat the butter and fry the onion and courgettes together until tender; season well. Spoon into an ovenproof dish. Beat the eggs with the cream, Tabasco, half the parsley and seasoning. Pour over the courgette mixture. Cook just above the centre of a moderately hot oven (200°C/400°F or Gas Mark 6) for 15 to 20 minutes. Top with the remaining parsley and serve.

## Dolmas ⊛

*about 30 young vine leaves*
FILLING:
*2 tablespoons oil*
*1 large onion, finely chopped*
*50 g/2 oz long grain rice*
*150 ml/¼ pint beef stock*
*225 g/8 oz raw good-quality beef, minced*
*¼ teaspoon chopped mint*
*pinch ground cinnamon*
*50-75 g/2-3 oz pine kernels*
*salt and pepper*
*approximately 150 ml/¼ pint white wine*

Fill a bowl with very hot water, add the vine leaves and leave for just a minute; remove and spread flat. This tenderizes the leaves so they can be rolled. Heat the oil, add the onion and fry for several minutes, then stir in the rice and turn in the onion mixture until well coated. Add the beef stock, cover the pan and simmer for 10 minutes. Lift the lid towards the end of the cooking time so that the excess liquid evaporates. The rice will not be completely tender, but that is correct as if it is completely cooked, it becomes too soft in the vine leaves. Blend in the raw beef, mint, cinnamon and pine kernels. Blend in the raw beef, mint, cinnamon and pine kernels. Season to taste. Divide the mixture between the vine leaves; fold in the ends, then roll up to make finger shapes. Tightly pack the filled leaves in a shallow saucepan or deep frying pan so they cannot become unrolled during cooking. Add the wine to the pan – this should cover the leaves completely and will do so if the leaves are sufficiently tightly packed. However, if the tops of the leaves are left dry, add more wine or water just to cover. Put on a lid or cover the pan with foil. Cook over a very low heat for 25 to 30 minutes; remove the lid or foil towards the end of the cooking time (the leaves and filling will be cooked) so that any excess liquid evaporates. Serve cold as an hors d'oeuvre, or as a light main dish.

VARIATION

⊛ **Stuffed Cabbage Leaves:** Take 8 good sized, but tender cabbage leaves; put into boiling salted water for just 1 minute, remove and lay flat. The short cooking time makes it easier to roll them. Prepare the stuffing as in the recipe above, or the recipes on pages 241 and 242. Either cook as the recipe for Dolmas or bake as the timing given in the recipes for Aubergines.

## Stuffed Courgettes

*6 to 8 courgettes*
*stuffing (see method)*

If the courgettes are fairly thick, halve lengthways, remove and chop the centre part and blend with the stuffing as given in the Dolmas recipe above or the aubergine recipes on pages 241 or 242. If the courgettes are rather thin, it is better to cut each vegetable into about 4 portions, remove the centre, leaving a ring of peel and pulp, chop the centre and add it to the stuffing. Bake the courgettes as the timing on pages 241 or 242 or cook in a saucepan, as for the Dolmas.

## Leeks à la Grecque

*8 leeks*
*3 tablespoons olive oil*
*4 tomatoes (preferably plum type), skinned and sliced*
*2 tablespoons lemon juice*
*150 ml/¼ pint water*
*salt and pepper*
*1 teaspoon sugar*
*few black olives*

Cut the leeks into 3.5 cm/1½ inch pieces; discard any tough green part. Heat the oil and cook the tomatoes for 2 to 3 minutes, add the lemon juice, leeks, and water. Bring to the boil, add salt, pepper and sugar and cook for about 5 minutes in a covered pan. Remove the lid and continue cooking until the leeks are tender, but not too soft, and the excess liquid has evaporated; add the olives. Chill well and serve as a separate course.

VARIATIONS

Add chopped parsley and sliced lemons as a garnish to the cold leeks.

Increase the water to 450 ml/¾ pint, add 50 g/2 oz long grain rice when the tomatoes, leeks and liquid have come to the boil, then cook the leeks until tender. Remove the leeks from the pan and finish cooking the rice, then add to the leeks. Chill well.

⊛ **Mushrooms à la Grecque:** Put 2 finely chopped onions, 225 g/8 oz skinned and chopped tomatoes and 225 g/8 oz whole small firm mushrooms into 3 tablespoons hot olive oil, cook gently for 5 minutes. Add 2 tablespoons lemon juice, a little chopped thyme, salt and pepper to taste. Cook gently until the mushrooms are just soft. Chil well before serving.

## Sweet and Sour Lettuce

*1 large or 2 smaller lettuces, shredded*
DRESSING:
*4-5 bacon rashers, derinded and chopped*
*1 small onion, chopped*
*1 egg*
*25 g/1 oz sugar, preferably brown*
*salt and pepper*
*4 tablespoons malt or wine vinegar*
*1½ tablespoons water*

Put the lettuce into a salad bowl. Fry the bacon until crisp. Add the onion to the bacon together with the remaining ingredients. Bring just to boiling point but do not attempt to soften the onion. Pour the mixture over the lettuce and serve immediately.

VARIATIONS

This sauce can be served over sliced and cooked Florence fennel or cooked cauliflower or broccoli.

Lettuce can be cooked and served as cabbage, it makes an excellent cooked vegetable; shred it finely and cook for a very short time, or follow the recipe for cooking cabbage on page 243. The leaves of lettuce could be used instead of vine leaves in Dolmas (see page 246).

## Seafood Mushrooms

*12-18 large flat mushrooms*
*75 g/3 oz butter or margarine*
*3 eggs*
*2 tablespoons single cream*
*salt and pepper*
*75 g/3 oz peeled prawns*
*2 teaspoons chopped parsley*

Wipe the mushrooms, remove the stalks and chop these finely. Heat 25 g/1 oz butter or margarine in a pan and cook the mushroom caps until tender. Put onto an ovenproof dish and keep hot while preparing the topping. Beat the eggs with the cream, salt and pepper. Add the prawns and parsley. Heat the remaining butter, fry the mushroom stalks for 2 to 3 minutes then pour in the egg mixture and cook over a low heat. Stir from time to time until lightly set. Spoon onto the flat dark side of the mushrooms and serve at once.

## Piquant Mushrooms

PÂTÉ:
*25 g/1 oz butter*
*1 medium onion, finely chopped*
*225 g/8 oz chicken, finely minced*
*50 g/2 oz sausagemeat*
*1 tablespoon chopped parsley*
*2 tablespoons red wine, sherry or red vermouth*
*salt and pepper*
*24 even-sized medium mushrooms*
COATING AND FRYING:
*25 g/1 oz flour*
*2 eggs*
*50 g/2 oz fine crisp breadcrumbs*
GARNISH:
*watercress*

Heat the butter and fry the onion until soft. Blend the onion with the other pâté ingredients to form a soft pâté. Remove the stalks from the mushrooms (these can be added to a soup or stew – a suitable recipe is the Salmis, see page 204). Wipe the mushroom caps – there is no need to skin them as the skin adds flavour and prevents them breaking in this recipe. Spread one-twelth of the pâté on the dark side of one mushroom. Top with a second mushroom so that the dark side is next to the pâté. Continue like this until all the pâté and mushrooms are used.

Season the flour, coat the mushrooms in this, then in the beaten egg and crisp breadcrumbs. Chill if possible before frying. Either heat enough oil or fat in a frying pan to give a depth of at least 1.5 cm/¾ inch, or use deep fat or oil. The oil or fat should be heated to a temperature of 185°C/365°F; this is very hot and a cube of day-old bread dropped into the fat should start to change colour within a few seconds. Fry the mushrooms for 3 to 4 minutes only; drain on absorbent paper and serve. Garnish with watercress.

VARIATION

**Cheese Stuffed Mushrooms:** Sandwich the mushroom caps with finely chopped parsley mixed with cream cheese, canned red pepper and chopped capers. Fry as above.

## Mushrooms in White Wine ⊛

*75 g/3 oz butter*
*2 medium onions, finely chopped*
*1-2 cloves garlic, crushed*
*450 g/1 lb small button mushrooms*
*150 ml/¼ pint white wine*
*1-2 tablespoons lemon juice*
*salt and pepper*
*1 tablespoon chopped parsley*

Heat the butter in a frying pan, fry the onions and garlic for 2 to 3 minutes, then add the mushrooms. Turn the mushrooms in the butter and onion mixture, then add the rest of the ingredients and simmer gently for 10 minutes. At the end of this time the liquid will have evaporated, leaving the mushrooms moist and well-flavoured. Serve as an hors d'oeuvre with brown bread and butter or as an accompaniment to main dishes.

VARIATION

**Paprika Mushrooms:** Fry the onions and garlic as in the recipe above. Add the mushrooms and cook for 2 to 3 minutes, then add 150 ml/¼ pint white wine and simmer for 10 minutes. Blend 1 to 2 teaspoons paprika with 150 ml/¼ pint soured cream, stir into the ingredients in the frying pan, with the salt, pepper and 2 teaspoons chopped tarragon. Heat thoroughly, but do not allow to boil.

## Macedoine of Vegetables ⊛

*450 g/1 lb mixed root vegetables, cut into 5 mm to 1 cm/¼ to ½ inch dice*
*100 g/4 oz shelled peas*
*100 g/4 oz green beans, neatly diced*
*salt*

GARNISH:
*little melted butter*
*chopped parsley*

Put the vegetables into a small amount of boiling salted water and cook steadily until tender. Strain and toss in the butter and parsley.

VARIATION

**Russian Salad:** Cook the vegetables as above, strain well and toss in thick mayonnaise while still warm. When cold blend with plenty of chopped parsley. The authentic Russian Salad includes neatly diced cooked tongue and hard-boiled eggs.

## Mushrooms au Gratin ⊛

*350 g/12 oz small button mushrooms*
*50 g/2 oz butter*
*squeeze lemon juice*
*salt and pepper*
*4 tablespoons double cream*
*75 g/3 oz Bel Paese, Gruyère or Cheddar cheese, grated*

Wipe the mushrooms. Heat the butter and fry the mushrooms until tender. Squeeze a little lemon juice over the mushrooms and add a little salt and pepper to taste. Spoon into 4 individual heated flameproof dishes. Top with the double cream and cheese and heat for a few minutes under the grill. Serve with hot toast.

## Stuffed Peppers ✱

*4 green peppers*
*salt and pepper*
*50 g/2 oz butter*
*2 medium onions, finely chopped*
*100 g/4 oz bacon, derinded and chopped*
*few anchovy fillets, chopped*
*½ teaspoon chopped oregano*
*75 g/3 oz cooked rice, preferably brown*
*50 g/2 oz pine kernels*
*1 tablespoon chopped black olives*

GARNISH:
*black olives*
*anchovy fillets*

Cut a slice from the top of each green pepper; chop these slices finely; core and deseed the peppers. Blanch the pepper cases for 5 minutes in boiling salted water and drain.

Heat the butter in a pan, add the onions and bacon, cook gently for a few minutes. Add the chopped pepper, anchovy fillets, oregano, rice, pine kernels, olives, with salt and pepper to taste. Spoon the mixture into the pepper cases and put into a greased casserole. Cook in a moderate oven (180°C/350°F or Gas Mark 4) for 30 to 35 minutes. Garnish with the olives and anchovy fillets. Serve with Tomato Sauce (see page 233).

VARIATION

**Cheese Stuffed Peppers:** Prepare the pepper cases as above but do not cook. Blend 225 g/8 oz cream cheese, 100 g/4 oz grated cheese, the chopped pepper, 2 tablespoons chopped parsley, 2 tablespoons mayonnaise, 1 tablespoon capers. Put into the pepper cases. Chill then slice. Serve on lettuce.

## Savoury Stuffed Peppers ✱

*2 green peppers, halved and deseeded*
*2 red peppers, halved and deseeded*
*salt and pepper*

STUFFING:
*50 g/2 oz cooked rice*
*50 g/2 oz Cheddar cheese, grated*
*50 g/2 oz butter, melted*
*225 g/8 oz cooked meat, minced*
*25 g/1 oz sultanas*
*2 tablespoons chopped parsley*
*1 teaspoon Worcestershire sauce*
*1 egg*

TOPPING:
*2-3 tablespoons crisp breadcrumbs*
*3 tablespoons grated cheese*

Put the halved peppers into boiling salted water and blanch by boiling for 5 minutes only. Drain well. Blend together all the ingredients for the stuffing and put into the halved peppers. Place in an ovenproof dish. Top each halved pepper with the crisp breadcrumbs and the cheese. Cook in the centre of a moderate oven (180°C/350°F or Gas Mark 4) for 25 to 30 minutes. Serve with Sherried Tomato Sauce (see page 233).

## Pommes Anna ⊛

*450 g/1 lb potatoes, very thinly sliced*
*salt and pepper*
*100 g/4 oz butter, melted*

Arrange a layer of potatoes in the base of a well-greased 15 cm/6 inch cake tin or ovenproof soufflé dish. Season the melted butter. Brush the layer of potatoes with a generous amount of the seasoned butter. Continue filling the tin or dish with potatoes and use all the butter. Cook in the centre of a moderate oven (160°-180°C/325°-350°F or Gas Mark 3-4) for 1¼ hours. Turn out and cut in slices like a cake.

VARIATION
Cook the potatoes in an attractive ovenproof serving dish; do not turn out.

## Duchesse Potatoes ⊛

*750 g-1 kg/1½-2 lb cooked potatoes, sieved or mashed*
*50-75 g/2-3 oz butter*
*2-3 egg yolks*
*salt and pepper*

Blend the ingredients together; pipe into fancy shapes on a greased baking tray or flat ovenproof dish. Brown in the oven.
Note: Do not add any milk to the potatoes or they will lose their shape when re-heating.

## Lyonnaise Potatoes

*450 g/1 lb potatoes, weight when peeled*
*salt*
*50 g/2 oz butter*
*225 g/8 oz onions, weight when peeled, thinly sliced*
GARNISH:
*chopped parsley*

Cook the potatoes in salted water until nearly, but not quite cooked; cool then slice. Heat the butter and fry the sliced onions for several minutes, add the potatoes and continue cooking together until tender. Top with parsley.

VARIATION
**Sauté Potatoes:** Fry sliced cooked or partially cooked potatoes in hot fat or butter.

## Jacket Potatoes

*4 large old potatoes*
*15 g/½ oz butter (optional)*
TOPPINGS:
*butter or cottage cheese or soured cream and chopped parsley*

Wash and dry the potatoes well; prick with a fork. Rub the outside with a little butter if you like a really crisp skin. Bake in a moderately hot oven (190-200°C/375-400°C, or Gas Mark 5-6) for about 1 hour or a longer period in a cooler oven. Cut a cross on top of each potato then top with knobs of butter or cottage cheese or soured cream and chopped parsley.

## Potato Chips

*450g/1 lb potatoes, cut into chip shapes*
*oil or fat for frying*

Most modern food processors have an attachment for cutting potatoes into chip shapes; generally the shape is thinner than the normal British chip, it is like those served in France. Always dry the potatoes well before frying.

The secret of good fried potatoes is to fry them twice. Heat the oil or fat to approximately 170°C/340°F. Always heat the frying basket so the uncooked potatoes will not stick to this. To test the temperature without a thermometer, drop in one chip, this should rise to the top of the hot oil or fat and there should be rapid bubbling around the chip. Half-fill the frying basket with potatoes, lower into the oil or fat and fry steadily until tender, but still pale in colour. The time varies between 4 to 6 minutes, depending on the thickness of the chips. Remove from the pan; fry the next batch and continue like this. Reheat the oil or fat until very hot, i.e. 190°C/375°F; replace the potatoes and fry for 1 to 2 minutes, or until crisp and brown. Drain over the pan for a few seconds then on absorbent paper and serve as soon as possible after cooking.

VARIATIONS

**Allumette Potatoes:** Cut the potatoes into matchstick shapes. Fry at 190°C/375°F for 2 to 3 minutes. Drain.

Wafer thin slices of potato, as Game Chips (page 213) are fried in the same way without an initial frying.

Frozen potato chips should be fried as directed.

**Soufflé Potatoes:** Slice the potatoes, fry as for chips but allow them to become absolutely cold before the second frying. You will find they puff up on the outside; although some types of potatoes (the waxy textured type) puff better than others.

**Parisienne Potatoes:** Cut the potatoes into small balls with a vegetable scoop. Fry as Potato Chips or roast in hot oil in the oven until crisp and golden brown.

Thinly sliced raw Jerusalem artichokes can be fried in any of the ways suggested for potatoes.

**Fried Onions:** Peel onions, cut into slices and separate these into rings. Either coat in a little milk then in seasoned flour or in a thin batter (see page 253). Fry in shallow fat, or deep oil or fat as for potatoes. These do not need two stages of frying.

## Scalloped Tomatoes and Courgettes ⊛

*750 g/1 ½ lb tomatoes, skinned and thickly sliced*
*450 g/1 lb courgettes, thinly sliced*
*salt and pepper*
*3 tablespoons chopped onions*
TOPPING
*50 g/2 oz butter, melted*
*50 g/2 oz soft breadcrumbs*

Arrange the tomatoes and courgettes in layers in an ovenproof serving dish, beginning and ending with tomatoes. Season each layer and flavour with the chopped onions. Blend the butter and breadcrumbs and sprinkle over the top layer of tomatoes. Cook in the centre of a moderate oven (180°C/350°F or Gas Mark 4) for 35 minutes.

VARIATION

⊛ **Ratatouille:** This is one of the most versatile vegetable dishes I know. It freezes perfectly, can be served hot or cold, as an hors d'oeuvre or as an accompaniment to main dishes. Please do not over-cook the vegetables to a 'mush', each vegetable should retain its appearance and firm texture. Heat 2 to 4 tablespoons olive oil (or any first class cooking oil) in a pan; the amount depends upon personal taste. Add 2 to 4 crushed cloves garlic, 3 medium chopped onions, 450 to 750 g/1 to 1½ lb skinned and sliced tomatoes; cook until the tomato juice begins to flow. Add 450 g/1 lb sliced or diced courgettes and 2 medium aubergines, cut into slices or diced as the courgettes. Season well, cover the pan and cook steadily until nearly tender, then add 2 to 3 tablespoons chopped parsley and finish cooking.

You can add diced red or green pepper(s), sliced mushrooms and a little tomato purée (from a tube or can) for extra flavour.

## Vegetable Fritters

*approximately 450 g/1 lb vegetables (see method)*
*salt and pepper*
*25 g/1 oz flour*
FRITTER BATTER:
*75 g/3 oz flour*
*1 egg*
*150 ml/¼ pint milk and water*
*2 teaspoons oil*
FOR FRYING:
*oil or fat*

This is an excellent way of serving many vegetables. I like to half-cook florets of cauliflower or Brussels sprouts (but they must still be firm). Do not cook onion rings, sliced Jerusalem artichokes, sliced aubergines or courgettes. Season the flour and dust the prepared vegetables with this so that the batter will adhere to the surface better. Mix together the ingredients for the batter. Heat the oil or fat to 170°C/340°F if frying uncooked vegetables, or have it a little hotter for partially cooked ones. Coat the vegetables in the batter and deep fry for several minutes. Drain on absorbent paper and serve.

## Carrot and Apple Pyramids

*3 large carrots, grated*
*2 tablespoons chopped nuts*
*225 g/8 oz cottage cheese*
*1 tablespoon chopped parsley*
*4 tablespoons mayonnaise*
*salt and pepper*
*2 dessert apples, cored and thickly sliced*
*lettuce*
*1 tablespoon lemon juice*

Blend the carrots with the nuts, cheese, parsley, half the mayonnaise, salt and pepper to taste. Arrange the apple slices on the lettuce and immediately sprinkle with the lemon juice, spread with the remaining mayonnaise. Top with pyramids made from the carrot mixture.

## Savoury Cauliflower Salad

*1 cauliflower*
*salt and pepper*
*2 tablespoons oil*
*2 cloves garlic, crushed*
*2 tablespoons chopped spring onions*
*1 red pepper, cored, deseeded and chopped*
*1 tablespoon wine vinegar*

Divide the cauliflower into florets. Cook in well seasoned boiling water until nearly tender, then strain. Meanwhile heat the oil in a pan, add the garlic, onions and red pepper. Cook for 2 to 3 minutes, add the vinegar then blend with the warm cauliflower. Allow to cool then serve as part of a mixed salad or by itself.

This is excellent with meat, poultry or cheese.

## Cauliflower Cheese Salad

*1 small cauliflower*
*1 tablespoon salad oil*
*1 tablespoon lemon juice*
*salt and pepper*
*3 tablespoons mayonnaise*
*100 g/4 oz Cheddar cheese, diced*
*100 g/4 oz blue cheese, diced*
*watercress*
*2 tablespoons chopped red pepper*

Divide the cauliflower into small florets. Blend the oil, lemon juice, salt and pepper with the mayonnaise. Add the raw cauliflower, mix well then stir in the cheeses. Spoon on to a bed of watercress. Top with the red pepper and serve as a light supper dish.

VARIATIONS

The cauliflower can be lightly cooked as in the recipe above.

**Cauliflower and Parmesan Bites:** Coat small raw cauliflower florets in thick mayonnaise then roll in a mixture of grated Parmesan cheese and very finely chopped parsley. Serve as part of a mixed salad or as a cocktail snack.

## Stuffed Cucumber Salad

*1 thick cucumber*
*salt and pepper*
*1 tablespoon lemon juice or white wine vinegar*
*1 lettuce, shredded*
*little mayonnaise*
FILLING:
*2 eggs, hard-boiled and chopped*
*2 tomatoes, skinned and chopped*
*225 g/8 oz cottage cheese*
*1 tablespoon chopped parsley*
*1 tablespoon chopped chives*

Cut the cucumber in half lengthways, then cut each half into 5 cm/2 inch pieces. These pieces can be peeled if desired. Scoop the centre out of each portion, chop this finely and put into a basin. Sprinkle the cucumber with salt, pepper, lemon juice or vinegar and leave to stand for an hour so that the pieces of cucumber become well-seasoned. Mix the eggs, tomatoes, chopped cucumber, cheese and herbs together and season well. Spoon into the cucumber boats. Serve on a bed of lettuce and top with mayonnaise.

VARIATIONS

**Piquant Cucumber:** Omit the eggs and tomatoes from the recipe above. Add 2 tablespoons finely chopped green pepper, 3 tablespoons chopped spring onions, 1 crushed clove garlic, few drops Tabasco sauce, 1 teaspoon Dijon mustard and 2 tablespoon thick mayonnaise.

## Lettuce and Cheese Dolmas

*8 large tender lettuce leaves*
*2 tablespoons thick mayonnaise*
FILLING:
*1 clove garlic, crushed*
*1 tablespoon chopped parsley*
*1 teaspoon chopped chives*
*½ teaspoon chopped rosemary*
*½ teaspoon chopped tarragon*
*3 large tomatoes, skinned and finely chopped*
*2 tablespoons chopped spring onions*
*300 g/11 oz cream or curd cheese*
*salt and pepper*

Blend together the ingredients for the filling. Divide the filling between the lettuce leaves, top with a little mayonnaise and roll the leaves around the filling. Secure with cocktail sticks until ready to serve. This makes an interesting hors d'oeuvre, light supper or picnic dish.

VARIATIONS

**Egg and Caviar Dolmas:** Hard-boil, shell and chop 4 eggs, mix with 2 tablespoons mayonnaise, 2 tablespoons chopped spring onions, 1 tablespoon chopped gherkins, 1 tablespoon chopped parsley and 50 g/2 oz finely chopped prawns. Season lightly. Put on the 8 lettuce leaves and top with a little inexpensive Danish caviar. Although these can be rolled for a picnic dish, the mixture looks attractive on the open lettuce leaves.

**Rice and Prawn Dolmas:** Blend 75 g/3 oz chopped prawns, 50 g/2 oz cooked rice, 175 g/6 oz sieved cottage cheese, 2 teaspoons chopped fennel, 2 tablespoons mayonnaise, 1 tablespoon lemon juice, salt and pepper to taste. Put on lettuce as in the recipe above.

## Hot Potato Salad

*450-550g/1-1¼lb small new potatoes*
*salt and pepper*
*sprig mint*
DRESSING:
*150ml/¼pint double cream*
*2 tablespoons lemon juice or white wine vinegar*
*2 tablespoons chopped parsley*
*1-2 teaspoons capers*
GARNISH:
*2 tablespoons chopped parsley*
*paprika*

Cook the potatoes in well-seasoned boiling water until just tender. Add the mint for flavour. Meanwhile blend together the ingredients for the dressing. Drain the potatoes. Tip the potatoes into the dressing and turn once or twice, then spoon into a heated serving dish. Top with the parsley and a generous amount of paprika. Serve immediately – the contrast between the hot potatoes and cold dressing is delicious.

VARIATIONS

Add the hot potatoes to the dressing, then leave to cool.

**Potato and Cucumber Salad:** Dice 12 hot cooked new potatoes, blend with ½ small peeled and diced cucumber, 3 tablespoons diced green pepper, 1 crushed clove garlic, 2 tablespoons chopped spring onions and the dressing above, allow to cool then top with chopped parsley.

## Potato Salad

*450g/1 lb new or old potatoes, cooked and diced*
DRESSING:
*1 tablespoon salad oil*
*1 tablespoon white wine or malt vinegar*
*4 tablespoons mayonnaise*
*2 tablespoons chopped parsley*
*2 tablespoons grated onion*
GARNISH:
*chopped parsley*
*chopped chives*

A potato salad is much better if made when the potatoes are hot. They will be firmer if cooked in their skins, then peeled or scraped after cooking. Mix together all the other ingredients, then add the diced potatoes. Turn gently in the dressing. Put into a dish and chill well. Top with the parsley and chives just before serving.

VARIATIONS

Add diced gherkins and/or capers. Mix chopped celery or dessert apple with the potato salad when it is cold.

**Creamy Potato Salad:** Use only 2 tablespoons mayonnaise and blend this with 2 tablespoons double or whipping cream. Use only 2 teaspoons salad oil and 1 tablespoon lemon juice in place of the vinegar.

## Yogurt Salad

*450g/1 lb mixed root vegetables, diced*
*salt and pepper*
*150ml/¼pint yogurt*
*ingredients as dressing in Potato Salad (see above)*

Cook the vegetables in well seasoned boiling water until just tender; drain thoroughly. Blend the yogurt with the dressing; add to the hot vegetables and allow to cool.

## Banana Sweetcorn Salad

*4 tablespoons yogurt*
*1 tablespoon lemon juice*
*175 g/6 oz canned sweetcorn*
*4 large firm bananas*
*lettuce*

Put the yogurt and lemon juice into a basin; add the sweetcorn. Peel the bananas, cut into thick slices, add to the other ingredients. Serve on a bed of lettuce. This blends well with cold fish, cold chicken or turkey.

## Melon Salad

*1 small honeydew melon*
*4 tablespoons French Dressing (see page 285)*
*2 dessert apples, peeled and diced*
*4 sticks celery, neatly diced*
*50 g/2 oz walnuts, chopped*
*2 tablespoons mayonnaise*
*lettuce*

Halve the melon, scoop out and discard the seeds. Scoop out the pulp and dice neatly or remove with a vegetable scoop, making small balls of the fruit pulp. Put the prepared melon pulp into a basin, add the French Dressing, apples and celery. Leave for about 1 hour, then add the chopped nuts and mayonnaise. Spoon back into the melon skins or on to a bed of lettuce. This is delicious with veal or cold shellfish.

## Minted Grape Salad

*3 oranges*
*¼ cucumber, thinly sliced*
*225 g/8 oz grapes, deseeded*
*1 lettuce heart*
*1 tablespoon lemon juice*
*1 tablespoon chopped mint*
*salt and pepper*
*pinch sugar*

Cut away the rind from 2 oranges, then cut out neat segments of fruit and discard all pips and skin. Mix with the cucumber and grapes. Arrange the lettuce leaves in a bowl and top with the grape mixture. Halve the remaining orange, squeeze out the juice and blend with the lemon juice, mint, salt, pepper and sugar. Spoon over the grape mixture. Serve with lamb or fish or as an hors d'oeuvre.

## Pineapple Cheese Salad

*4 fresh pineapple rings*
*175 g/6 oz Cheddar cheese, diced*
*50 g/2 oz Cheddar cheese, grated*
*3 tablespoons mayonnaise*
*3 tablespoons chopped watercress*

Remove the peel and the centre hard core from the rings of pineapple; this is done with the help of an apple corer. Cut the fruit into neat pieces and mix with the diced cheese and then with the grated cheese and mayonnaise. Finally add the chopped watercress. Serve as a light main dish or with hard-boiled eggs.

# Pineapple and Apple Coleslaw

*3 tablespoons French Dressing (see page 285)*
*3 tablespoons mayonnaise*
*2 dessert apples, peeled and diced*
*4 fresh or canned pineapple rings, diced*
*½ small white cabbage heart, finely shredded*

GARNISH:
*2 tablespoons chopped walnuts*

Blend the French dressing and mayonnaise together. Put the apples into the dressing to prevent discoloration. Add the pineapple and cabbage to the apple mixture. Spoon into a salad bowl and top with chopped walnuts.

VARIATIONS

**Golden Coleslaw:** Blend the French Dressing and mayonnaise, as in the recipe above. Shred ½ small white cabbage heart, blend with 3 medium grated carrots, the diced fruit from 2 oranges and the dressing.

**Spiced Coleslaw:** Blend the French Dressing and mayonnaise, as in the recipe above with 1 tablespoon French mustard, a few drops Worcestershire sauce and a pinch of cayenne pepper. Shred ½ small white cabbage heart, blend with the dressing, 2 to 3 tablespoons diced gherkins, 2 teaspoons capers, 3 tablespoons finely chopped celery and 3 tablespoons chopped spring onions.

# Orange Rice Salad

*600 ml/1 pint water*
*½ teaspoon salt*
*50 g/2 oz long-grain rice*

DRESSING:
*1 small onion, grated*
*1 clove garlic, crushed*
*2 tablespoons salad oil*
*2 tablespoons lemon juice*
*1 teaspoon brown sugar*
*½ teaspoon tomato purée*
*100 g/4 oz peeled prawns*
*50 g/2 oz button mushrooms, thinly sliced*
*4 large oranges*
*1 slice pineapple, diced*

GARNISH:
*parsley*
*lettuce*

Bring the water to the boil, add the salt and rice. Cook for 15 minutes then strain. Blend the onion, garlic, oil, lemon juice, brown sugar and tomato purée. Mix the rice with this dressing and add the prawns and raw mushrooms. Allow to stand for a while.

Cut a slice from each orange and scoop out the flesh; discard the skin and pips. Keep the orange cases intact. Mix the orange and diced pineapple with the rice mixture. Spoon into the orange cases. Garnish with parsley and lettuce.

VARIATION

**Pepper and Rice Salad:** Cook 100 g/4 oz long-grain rice as in the recipe above. Strain and blend with 2 tablespoons mayonnaise, 1 tablespoon salad oil, 1 tablespoon lemon juice, 2 tablespoons chopped chives. Leave to cool, then add 1 finely diced green pepper, 1 finely diced red pepper, 3 tablespoons chopped spring onions and a little chopped parsley.

## Stuffed Pears

*3 ripe dessert pears*
*100g/4oz cream cheese*
*2 tablespoons chopped olives*
*2 tablespoons chopped walnuts*
*1 tablespoon chopped parsley*
*lettuce*

DRESSING:
*1 teaspoon French mustard*
*3 tablespoons oil*
*2 tablespoons lemon juice or white wine vinegar*
*pinch sugar*
*salt and pepper*

GARNISH
*watercress*

Blend the ingredients for the dressing and pour into a shallow dish. Peel, halve and core the pears. Marinate in the dressing for at least 15 minutes, turning once or twice. Blend the cheese, olives, walnuts and parsley. Lift the pears out of the dressing. Put the pears on to the lettuce, fill with the cheese mixture and garnish with watercress. Serves 6.

## Summer Salad

*350g/12oz mixed black, red and white currants*
*175g/6oz dessert cherries, stoned*
*1 lettuce, shredded*

DRESSING:
*2 tablespoons mayonnaise*
*2 tablespoons yogurt*
*1 tablespoon lemon juice*
*salt and pepper*
*sugar to taste*

Mix together the ingredients for the dressing, add the fruits and marinate for 1 hour. Spoon on to the lettuce.

Serve with cold pork, duck or cheese.

VARIATION

**Carrot and Apple Salad:** Mix 225g/8oz grated carrots, 2 to 3 diced dessert apples and the dressing above. Spoon on to the lettuce and watercress, top with chopped nuts and chopped chives. Serve as an hors d'oeuvre.

## Waldorf Salad

*4 dessert apples, peeled and diced*
*4-5 tablespoons French Dressing (see page 285)*
*small head celery, neatly diced*
*75g/3oz dried or fresh walnuts, chopped*
*2-3 tablespoons mayonnaise*
*lettuce*

Blend together the apples and dressing (this keeps them a good colour), then the celery and walnuts. Toss in the mayonnaise just before serving. Put on to a bed of lettuce. Serve by itself or with cold meats or duck.

VARIATION

**Apple and Watercress Salad:** Prepare the apples, as in the recipe above, blend with the French Dressing, add 4 to 5 tablespoons coarsely chopped watercress leaves, 1 teaspoon finely chopped tarragon, 100g/4oz deseeded but not skinned black grapes and 50g/2oz coarsely chopped cashew nuts. This salad is delicious as a starter or served with cold lamb or chicken. A little mayonnaise can be added to the salad, but do not make it too rich.

## Caesar Salad

*50 g/2 oz butter*
*2 large slices bread, cut into small dice*
*1 clove garlic, halved or crushed (see method)*
*1 lettuce, shredded*
*3 medium tomatoes, sliced*
*¼ medium cucumber, sliced*
*3 hard-boiled eggs, sliced*
*5 tablespoons mayonnaise*
*100 g/4 oz Cheddar cheese, grated*
*1 can anchovy fillets*

Heat the butter in a frying pan and fry the diced bread until crisp and golden; drain on absorbent paper. Either rub the halved garlic around the inside of the salad bowl or crush and blend with the mayonnaise for a stronger flavour. Put the lettuce into the salad bowl, add the sliced tomatoes, cucumber and eggs. Top with the mayonnaise, cheese and well-drained anchovy fillets. Scatter the croûtons over the top just before serving.

## Smoked Mackerel and Potato Salad

*150 ml/¼ pint yogurt*
*2 tablespoons horseradish cream*
*1 tablespoon lemon juice*
*¼ medium cucumber, peeled and neatly diced*
*1-2 tablespoons chopped fennel leaves*
*salt and pepper*
*450 g/1 lb new potatoes, freshly cooked*
*lettuce*
*3-4 smoked mackerel fillets*
GARNISH:
*lemon wedges*

Blend the yogurt with the horseradish cream and lemon juice. Add the cucumber, fennel leaves and salt and pepper to taste. If the potatoes are very small, leave them whole; if larger, dice or halve neatly and put into the dressing. If this can be done while they are hot it produces a better-flavoured salad. When cold, put on to a bed of lettuce and arrange narrow strips of smoked mackerel all round the salad. Garnish with the lemon.

VARIATION

**Continental Potato Salad:** The dressing used for this makes a delicious change. Cook the potatoes and meanwhile prepare the dressing. Blend 150 ml/¼ pint soured cream, 2 tablespoons salad oil, 1 to 2 tablespoons red wine vinegar or lemon juice, 1 to 2 teaspoons French or Dijon mustard and 2 teaspoons capers. Turn the hot potatoes in this mixture and top with chopped chervil or parsley.

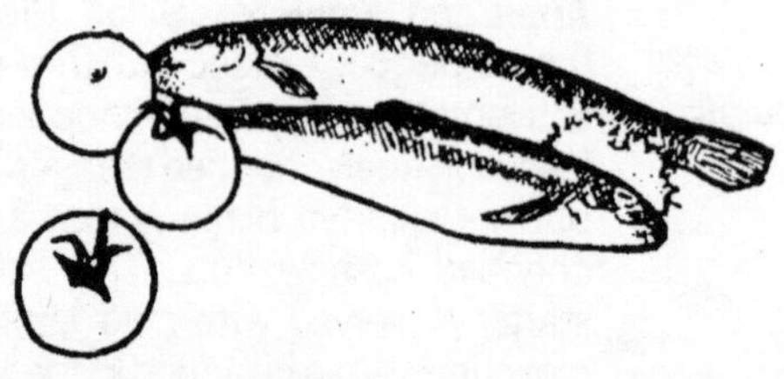

## Chicken Chaudfroid

*4-6 portions cooked chicken*
CHAUDFROID SAUCE:
*300 ml ½ pint aspic (see page 264)*
*150 ml/¼ pint Béchamel Sauce or Mayonnaise (see pages 227 and 235)*
GARNISH:
*red pepper, gherkins, etc. (see method)*

Make the aspic and allow it to become cold and stiffen very slightly, then blend with the sauce or mayonnaise. Place the chicken portions on a wire tray, with a dish underneath to catch any drips from the sauce. Brush or spread the chicken with some of the sauce, allow to stiffen slightly, then spread with a second coating. Make small shapes with red pepper, gherkins, sliced radishes and place these on the coating before it becomes quite firm.

Serve with green or mixed salads.

VARIATIONS
If the weather is hot, dissolve an extra ½ to 1 teaspoon gelatine in the aspic jelly.

If coating game, use a little stock as well as milk in the Béchamel Sauce.

## Sillsalat

*1 peeled cooked beetroot, diced*
*1 dessert apple, cored and diced*
*2 tablespoons white wine vinegar*
*4 cooked potatoes, diced*
*175 g/6 oz cooked meat, diced*
*150 ml/¼ pint mayonnaise*
*2 teaspoons capers*
*1-2 tablespoons orange juice*
*2 rollmop herrings, flaked*
*2 gherkins, thinly sliced*
*salt and pepper*
GARNISH:
*lettuce*
*chopped dill*
*3 hard-boiled eggs*

Put the beetroot and apple into the vinegar, leave for a short time, then blend with all the other ingredients. Taste and season well. Spoon into a good-sized basin or mould and leave for 1 to 2 hours, so the mixture has time to form a neat shape. Turn out on to a dish, garnish with the lettuce and the dill. Quarter the eggs and arrange around the mould.

VARIATION
This mixture of meat and fish is famous in Scandinavia. You may however like to adapt it for a fish mould.

**Herring Salad:** Grill 3 large herrings, bone and cut into small pieces. Blend with 4 tablespoons mayonnaise, 1 to 2 tablespoons horseradish cream. Add the beetroot, apple, potatoes, vinegar, capers and gherkins, then proceed as in the recipe above. This salad can be garnished with a few anchovy fillets as well as the lettuce, dill and eggs.

# Moulded Salads

It makes a pleasant change to serve salad ingredients in the form of a mould. This can be produced by using a flavoured jelly, as in the second recipe on this page or an aspic flavoured jelly as page 264 or by blending various ingredients with sufficient mayonnaise to give a mixture that is sufficiently soft to form a pleasing shape, as in the first recipe.

## Moulded Cauliflower Salad

*1 small cauliflower*
*salt and pepper*
*4 tablespoons mayonnaise*
*2 hard-boiled eggs, chopped*
*2 tablespoons chopped chives*
*1 teaspoon chopped tarragon*
GARNISH:
*1 lettuce, shredded*
*sliced tomatoes*
*sliced cucumber*

Divide the cauliflower into small florets. Cook in a little boiling salted water until only just tender; do not overcook. Strain and blend with the mayonnaise and other ingredients while still warm. Put into a basin and leave until cold. Turn out on to a bed of shredded lettuce and arrange rings of tomato and cucumber around. Serve as a light snack or with cooked meat, fish, poultry or cheese.

## Moulded Golden Salad

*1 packet lemon flavoured jelly*
*scant 450 ml/¾ pint boiling water*
*2 teaspoons white wine vinegar or lemon juice*
*salt and pepper*
*150 ml/¼ pint orange juice*
*1 large orange*
*3 medium carrots, finely grated*
GARNISH:
*lettuce*
*mayonnaise*

Dissolve the jelly in the very hot water; be a little sparing with the amount as the orange segments will also provide extra liquid. Add the vinegar or lemon juice, salt and pepper. Allow to cool then add the orange juice. Cut out the segments of the orange, chop fairly finely, add to the jelly with the grated carrots. Put into a lightly-oiled 1 litre/1¾ pint basin or mould. Leave until set. Turn out on to a bed of lettuce and top with a little mayonnaise. This is excellent with cold duck or pork.

VARIATION

**Moulded Cucumber Salad:** Dissolve the lemon jelly in 450 ml/¾ pint very hot water, add 1 tablespoon white wine vinegar. Allow to cool. Cut ½ large unpeeled cucumber into wafer-thin slices. Add to the jelly together with salt and pepper to taste. Put into a mould and set as above.

## Grape and Cucumber Ring

*450 ml/¾ pint water, less 2 tablespoons*
*15 g/½ oz gelatine*
*2 teaspoons white wine vinegar*
*2 teaspoons lemon juice*
*sprig mint*
*small bunch parsley*
*sprig thyme*
*sprig sage*
*salt and pepper*
*100 g/4 oz cucumber, peeled and very thinly sliced*
*100 g/4 oz grapes, deseeded and halved but not skinned*

GARNISH:
*watercress*
*lettuce*

Heat 150 ml/¼ pint of the water in a saucepan; sprinkle the gelatine on top of the water and stir to dissolve. Add the vinegar and lemon juice to the liquid and put on one side. Meanwhile put all the herbs into the remaining water, bring to boiling point, reduce the heat and simmer for 5 minutes. Strain this liquid onto the gelatine mixture, add salt and pepper, then allow it to become cold and the consistency of a thick syrup. Add the cucumber and grapes. Oil a 900 ml/1½ pint ring mould and spoon in the cucumber jelly. Leave until firm then unmould on to a large serving dish. Garnish with the watercress and lettuce. This is delicious with cold lamb or chicken or fish.

VARIATION

Use a lemon-flavoured dessert jelly instead of the gelatine. Infuse the water for the jelly in the same way as the above recipe and also include both the vinegar and lemon juice to sharpen the flavour.

## Savoury Tomato Mould

JELLY:
*600 ml/1 pint tomato juice*
*15 g/½ oz gelatine*
*2 tablespoons finely chopped spring onions or chives*
*few drops Tabasco sauce*
*salt and pepper*
*celery salt*

HAM LAYER:
*100 g/4 oz cooked ham, finely chopped or minced*
*100 g/4 oz cream cheese*
*2 tablespoons thick mayonnaise*
*1 tablespoon chopped spring onions or chives*
*1-2 tablespoons chopped watercress leaves*

GARNISH:
*watercress*
*lettuce*

Heat 150 ml/¼ pint of the tomato juice, sprinkle the gelatine on top and stir to dissolve; cool and add the rest of the ingredients for the jelly. Allow to become cold then pour one-third into a lightly-oiled 1.2 litre/2 pint mould or loaf tin. Leave until set, but keep the remaining jelly at room temperature, so it remains a liquid.

Blend together all the ingredients for the ham layer. Spread half of this over the set tomato mixture. Top with half the remaining jelly. Let this set then cover with the last of the ham and a final layer of tomato jelly. Leave until quite firm, then unmould and garnish with watercress and lettuce.

VARIATIONS

Use 100 g/4 oz grated cheese instead of the ham or use finely chopped peeled prawns instead of the ham.

**Tomato and Aspic Mould:** Use a packet of aspic jelly instead of the plain gelatine. Dissolve this in 150 ml/¼ pint tomato juice, then add 450 ml/¾ pint well strained stock. Do not add seasonings as aspic jelly is highly seasoned.

## Home-made Aspic

*900 ml/1½ pints beef, chicken or fish stock*
*2 tablespoons lemon juice*
*3 tablespoons wine or wine vinegar (see method)*
*3 tablespoons sherry (see method)*

Clear the stock carefully, as advised under Consommé (see page 49). Blend the lemon juice, wine or wine vinegar and sherry with the stock; season to taste. Use red wine or red wine vinegar and brown sherry for meat or game moulds and white wine or white wine vinegar and light sherry with chicken and moulds made with the breast of game birds.

If making a fish aspic then you can use all white wine and omit the sherry.

The amount of gelatine used to liquid depends a great deal on the other ingredients in the recipe, but when making a clear aspic to coat food or blend with dry textured foods, such as breast of chicken, then you can allow 600 ml/1 pint of the aspic liquid, prepared as above to 15 g/½ oz gelatine. Plain gelatine should be used.

## Aspic Mould

*1 packet aspic jelly with 600 ml/1 pint water or stock, or*
*600 ml/1 pint aspic liquid, prepared as above, with 15 g/½ oz gelatine*
*75 g/3 oz cooked carrots, sliced*
*100 g/4 oz cooked peas*
*2 hard-boiled eggs, neatly sliced*
*175 g/6 oz cooked chicken breast, neatly diced*
*50 g/2 oz ham (cooked in one slice), neatly diced*
*lettuce*

Dissolve the aspic jelly in the very hot liquid as instructed on the packet, or heat the home-made aspic liquid, sprinkle the gelatine on top and stir to dissolve. Pour enough of the jelly liquid into an oiled 1.2 litre/ 2 pint mould to give a depth of about 5 mm/¼ inch. Allow this to set but make sure the rest of the aspic jelly is kept at room temperature so that it remains a cold liquid.

Dip some of the carrot slices into the liquid jelly, arrange neatly on the set jelly layer, then spoon a few peas in the centre and a few egg slices. Spoon about 2 tablespoons liquid jelly carefully over the food, being careful not to dislodge it. Allow to set, then dip half the chicken and half the ham in liquid jelly, put on to the vegetable and egg layer and cover with 2 to 3 tablespoons cold liquid jelly. Continue like this until all the jelly and food is used. Save enough jelly for a final covering of the food. It takes time to set layers of food like this, but it does look more professional and with the help of a freezer or freezing compartment of the refrigerator, each layer sets quickly. Turn out on to a bed of lettuce.

VARIATION

**Vegetarian Aspic:** Use vegetable stock with a little tomato juice and sherry as the liquid in which to set a selection of vegetables.

# Especially for Vegetarians

Many of the recipes given on the previous pages can be included in a vegetarian diet, but always remember that adequate protein must be served with, or as part of, the dish. The two recipes on this page are great favourites of mine, although I am not a vegetarian.
The chapters that follow on Egg and Cheese and Pasta and Rice dishes also contain a number of recipes suitable for vegetarians.

## Rice and Peanut Dolmas

FILLING:
*2 tablespoons oil*
*2 cloves garlic, finely chopped*
*2 medium onions, finely chopped*
*50 g/2 oz long-grain rice*
*12 tablespoons water*
*salt and pepper*
*75 g/3 oz peanuts*
*50 g/2 oz sultanas*
*little grated nutmeg*
*12 large tender cabbage leaves*
*1 tablespoon lemon juice*
*300 ml/½ pint tomato juice*

Heat the oil in a saucepan, toss the garlic and onions in the oil for several minutes, then add the uncooked rice and blend with the onions and garlic. Add the water, salt and pepper to taste and simmer gently for 10 minutes. Stir once or twice and cover the pan. At the end of this time, the liquid should be almost absorbed, but the rice will not be quite cooked. Stir in the nuts, sultanas and grated nutmeg to taste.

Meanwhile blanch the cabbage leaves in a little boiling salted water for 2 minutes only. Drain and spread out flat. Put a little rice stuffing in the centre of each leaf and roll firmly. Rinse out the saucepan. Arrange the cabbage rolls in the pan, top with the lemon and tomato juices, salt and pepper to taste. Cover the pan and cook for 45 minutes over a gentle heat. Serve the cabbage rolls with the unthickened liquid, or, if preferred, thicken this with a little Beurre Manié (see page 45).

## Lentil Roast ⊛

*225 g/8 oz lentils*
*50 g/2 oz vegetarian fat*
*2 medium onions, chopped*
*2 large tomatoes, skinned and chopped*
*1 small apple, peeled and chopped*
*50 g/2 oz soft breadcrumbs*
*1 teaspoon chopped sage*
*1 egg*
*salt and pepper*

Soak the lentils in cold water to cover for 12 hours, then simmer in the same water for about 1 hour, or until the lentils are tender and all the liquid has been absorbed. Meanwhile heat the fat and fry the onions, tomatoes and apples until just soft. Blend with the lentils and the remainder of the ingredients. Put into a well-greased 1 kg/2 lb loaf tin and cover with greased foil (unless you want a very crisp topping). Cook in the centre of a moderate oven (180°C/350°F or Gas Mark 4) for 50 to 60 minutes, until firm to the touch. Turn out and serve with fresh tomato purée.

# Egg and Cheese Dishes

It was Thomas Moore, writing about 150 years ago, in 'The Fudge Family in Paris', who said:-

'Yet, who can help loving the land that has taught us
Six hundred and eighty-five ways to dress eggs?'

While the French have created wonderful recipes based upon eggs, every country has its favourite ways of serving this important and versatile food. The recipes that follow are ideal for light or main meals.

The chapter starts with a selection of recipes based upon simple methods of cooking eggs, together with omelettes and savoury soufflés. For some reason many people feel both these dishes are difficult to make; they are really very simple when you appreciate their techniques. When making an omelette you must wait for the eggs to set on the base of the pan, before you start to 'work' them. Omelettes are on pages 271 to 273. I always point out to people that a soufflé is basically three things only – a sauce or purée, flavouring, and eggs. Never over-cook a soufflé by leaving it in the oven for too long a period or by using too low a temperature; do not keep it waiting before serving. You can, however, prepare the soufflé mixture and keep it waiting for up to 1 hour before it is cooked. It is essential however to cover the filled soufflé dish with an upturned basin to exclude all the air; recipes are on page 274 with a cold cheese soufflé on page 275.

While dishes made with cooked eggs cannot be frozen, for the eggs become tough and inedible, you can freeze savoury egg tarts, quiches and pizzas very successfully for up to 3 months. A selection of recipes for these popular dishes will be found on pages 270 and 275 to 280.

Eggs and cheese are two of my favourite foods and these are combined in many dishes. There is an almost bewildering array of cheeses from which to choose today, if you go to a good supermarket or cheese specialist. I have indicated in most recipes which cheese I would prefer, but you can certainly substitute your own favourite, provided it is of the type that will produce a similar texture when cooked.

Modern entertaining is often less formal than in past years and fondues of various kinds are ideal for these occasions. You will find the classic Fondue, with less usual recipes, on pages 280 and 282.

Cheese freezes well, if you have any left over, but allow it to stand at room temperature for some time after thawing, so the full flavour will develop. I would only freeze cheese for several weeks if possible, so the original flavour and texture is not lost.

## Spanish Baked Eggs

*3 tablespoons oil*
*2 cloves garlic, chopped*
*1 large onion, finely chopped*
*2 red peppers, cored, deseeded and finely diced*
*225 g/8 oz tomatoes, skinned and finely diced*
*100 g/4 oz chorizo (Spanish garlic sausage), diced*
*3 medium cooked potatoes, finely diced*
*salt and pepper*
*4 eggs*

Heat the oil and fry the garlic and onion until nearly soft. Add most of the pepper and tomatoes and continue cooking for a few minutes. Mix with the sausage, potatoes and a little salt and pepper. Spoon the mixture into a shallow ovenproof serving dish. Make 4 hollows in the mixture and break an egg into each. Cook towards the top of a moderately hot oven (200°C/400°F or Gas Mark 6) for 5 minutes, then top the eggs with the remaining diced red pepper. Return to the oven for a further 5 minutes, or until the eggs are set to personal taste.

VARIATIONS

Allow 8 eggs if serving this as a dish for a main meal.

**Oeufs Provençal:** Omit the chorizo and potatoes in the recipe above; increase the tomatoes to 750 g/1½ lb. Add a little chopped marjoram or basil and olives to the cooked tomato mixture. Cook as above.

## Stuffed Tomatoes

*4 very large tomatoes*
*1 tablespoon finely chopped mixed herbs (basil, chives, parsley, sage and thyme)*
*salt and pepper*
*4 eggs*
*25 g/1 oz butter, melted*

Cut a thin slice from each tomato at the end opposite the stalk, you will find the tomatoes stand upright better. Scoop out the centre pulp, chop this and blend with all the herbs and a little seasoning. Spoon half the flavoured pulp back into the tomato cases, then break an egg into each tomato, season and top with most of the butter. Spoon the remaining herb-flavoured pulp on to the tomato slices. Cook in a greased and covered dish in the centre of a moderately hot oven (190°C/375°F or Gas Mark 5) for about 15 minutes until the eggs are set to your personal taste.

VARIATIONS

**Stuffed Potatoes:** Bake jacket potatoes (see page 251). Halve very large potatoes, or cut a slice from medium-sized potatoes, scoop out the pulp and mash this with salt, pepper, butter and a little cream, or cream cheese. Spoon the pulp back into the potato cases, making a flan shape. Break an egg into each cavity, top with melted butter and a little seasoning. You can add a spoonful of cream and grated cheese too if desired. Bake as for tomatoes in the recipe above.

## Devilled Eggs

*8 eggs, hard-boiled*
*50 g/2 oz butter*
*1 small onion, finely chopped*
*1 teaspoon curry powder*
*1 teaspoon Worcestershire sauce*
*salt and pepper*
*25 g/1 oz salted peanuts*

Halve the eggs, remove the yolks and mash or sieve. Heat the butter in a pan and cook the onion until soft. Add the curry powder, Worcestershire sauce, then the egg yolks. Season to taste. Spoon the mixture into the egg whites and top with the chopped nuts. Serve with salad or crisp toast.

VARIATIONS

There are many ways to stuff eggs; mix the yolks with softened butter or mayonnaise and grated cheese; mashed sardines, finely chopped smoked salmon or other smoked fish or chopped shellfish or ham or chicken.

## Curried Eggs and Prawns

*50 g/2 oz butter or margarine*
*1 medium onion, finely chopped*
*25 g/1 oz flour*
*1 tablespoon curry powder*
*450 ml/¾ pint milk*
*4 eggs, hard-boiled*
*100 g/4 oz peeled prawns*
*salt and pepper*

Heat the butter or margarine in a pan, cook the onion until soft, then stir in the flour and curry powder. Continue cooking for 2 to 3 minutes, stirring all the time, then blend in the milk. Bring to the boil and cook until thickened and smooth, stirring well all the time. Add the eggs and prawns, season to taste. Try to let the ingredients stand for an hour before reheating so the curry sauce blends with the other ingredients. Serve in a border of cooked rice, chutney and some of the other accompaniments to curry, described on page 123.

VARIATION

Use 300 ml/½ pint milk and 150 ml/¼ pint single cream for a richer sauce.

## Luxury Scotch Eggs

*4 large or 6 smaller eggs, hard-boiled*
*100g/4oz cream cheese*
*salt and pepper*
*450g/1 lb sausagemeat*
COATING AND FRYING:
*1-2 tablespoons flour*
*1-2 eggs*
*50g/2oz crisp breadcrumbs*
*oil, fat or butter*

I must confess I find the usual Scotch Egg dry and dull, but this simple variation makes the egg more moist. Halve the eggs lengthways, remove the yolks, mash and blend with the cheese and seasoning. Spoon this mixture back into the white cases; press the filled halves together again. Divide the sausagemeat into 4 or 6 portions and flatten on a lightly floured board. Wrap around the eggs, cover completely and seal firmly. Roll into good shapes, then coat with seasoned flour, beaten egg and breadcrumbs. It is essential to coat the Scotch Eggs well, so the sausagemeat keeps it shape.

Either deep fry in hot oil or fat for a good 10 minutes or shallow fry in hot fat or butter for about 15 minutes; turning several times. Drain on absorbent paper. Serve hot or cold.

VARIATIONS

The egg yolks can be flavoured with a little softened butter or mayonnaise and curry powder or curry paste or chopped mixed herbs instead of the cream cheese.

## Egg Cutlets

*25g/1oz butter or margarine*
*25g/1oz flour*
*150ml/¼ pint milk*
*6 eggs, hard-boiled, and finely chopped*
*50g/2oz soft breadcrumbs*
*1 tablespoon chopped parsley*
*1-2 teaspoons chopped chives*
*salt and pepper*
COATING AND FRYING:
*25g/1oz flour*
*1 egg*
*50g/2oz crisp breadcrumbs*
*50g/2oz butter or fat*

Heat the butter or margarine in a pan, stir in the flour and cook over a low heat for 2 to 3 minutes. Gradually blend in the milk and stir as the mixture comes to the boil and forms a thick panada (binding sauce). Add the eggs, breadcrumbs, parsley, chives and salt and pepper to taste. Divide the mixture into 4 large or 8 smaller portions; allow to cool and stiffen slightly, then form into neat cutlet shapes. Coat in seasoned flour, beaten egg and crisp breadcrumbs.

Heat the butter or fat and fry the cutlets for 2 to 3 minutes on either side; drain on absorbent paper and serve hot or cold.

VARIATIONS

Use tomato juice instead of milk; flavour the thick white sauce with a little curry powder; add Worcestershire or soy sauce; add 50g/2oz grated cheese. Substitute 100g/4oz finely chopped cooked ham for 50g/2oz breadcrumbs.

**Savoury Egg Cutlets:** Use 50g/2oz butter or margarine and fry 1 crushed clove garlic, 2 medium peeled and finely chopped onions and 2 medium skinned and chopped tomatoes in this before adding the flour.

## Scrambled Eggs

*4 eggs*
*2 tablespoons single cream or top of the milk*
*salt and pepper*
*40 g/1½ oz butter*

Everyone I know thinks their own scrambled eggs are the best they ever tasted. I share that belief. I find the secret is not to over-beat the eggs and certainly not to stir too much when cooking over a very low heat.

Blend the eggs with the cream or milk, salt and pepper. Heat the butter in a strong saucepan, add the egg mixture, then cook gently over a very low heat until the consistency of a thick cream. Stir very lightly as the mixture cooks. Serve at once on crisp buttered toast. Serves 2.

VARIATION

**Scrambled Eggs and Smoked Salmon:** One of the quickest and most luxurious of light dishes. Cut 50 g/2 oz smoked salmon into narrow strips. Blend most of these with the half-cooked egg mixture and continue cooking. Top with the remaining smoked salmon when serving the eggs.

A microwave is excellent for cooking scrambled eggs.

## Pipérade

*50 g/2 oz butter or margarine*
*1 small onion, finely chopped*
*2 medium tomatoes, skinned and chopped*
*1 small green pepper, cored, deseeded and chopped*
*4 eggs*
*salt and pepper*
*1 tablespoon chopped parsley*

Heat the butter or margarine in a saucepan. Add the vegetables and cook until soft. Beat the eggs with the salt, pepper and parsley. Pour into the vegetable mixture; scramble lightly, as instructions above.

VARIATIONS

⊛ **Pipérade Tart:** Make and bake a flan blind as in the Quiche (see page 276) but allow a slightly longer cooking time as this filling cooks quickly. Prepare and cook the vegetables, as in the recipe above. Add 6 eggs, salt, pepper and parsley; mix well, but do not cook. Spoon into the pastry case, top with a little grated cheese and put in the centre of a cool to moderate oven (150-160°C/300-325°F or Gas Mark 2-3) for about 15 minutes. Serve hot or cold.

**Bacon and Sweetcorn Scramble:** Derind and chop 4 bacon rashers; skin and chop 2 to 3 medium tomatoes. Heat 50 g/2 oz butter, add the bacon and tomatoes and cook until soft. Blend 6 eggs, salt, pepper, 1 tablespoon chopped parsley and 100 g/4 oz cooked sweetcorn. Pour into the bacon mixture. Scramble as first recipe.

## Poached Eggs au Gratin

*Cheese Sauce (see page 228)*
*4 eggs*
*salt*
*50g/2oz cheese, grated*
*50g/2oz crisp breadcrumbs*
*25g/1oz butter, melted*

Make the sauce before cooking the eggs. Poach the eggs in boiling salted water until just set. Lift from the water; drain well and put into a shallow flameproof dish. Top with the sauce, grated cheese, breadcrumbs and melted butter. Put under the grill for 2 to 3 minutes, until the topping is brown. Serve at once.

VARIATIONS

Use boiled and shelled eggs instead of poached eggs. Place the eggs on a bed of cooked vegetables, as in Florentine Eggs (see page 28).

## Zuppa Pavese

*50g/2oz butter*
*4 small slices bread*
*600ml/1 pint Consommé, (see pages 49 and 50)*
*1 tablespoon tomato purée*
*4 eggs*
*50g/2oz cheese, grated*
*2 tablespoons chopped parsley*

Although this is termed a soup, it is really a light meal in a dish. Heat the butter and fry the bread until crisp and brown on either side. Put into 4 soup plates and keep hot. Heat the consommé with the tomato purée in a shallow saucepan or frying pan. Break the eggs into this and poach until just set. Lift out with a fish slice or perforated spoon and put onto the fried bread. Spoon the consommé over the eggs, add the cheese and parsley and serve at once.

## Swedish Baked Omelette

*25g/1oz butter*
*6 eggs*
*6 tablespoons double cream*
*salt and pepper*

Heat the butter in a shallow ovenproof serving dish. Beat the eggs with the cream, salt and pepper. Add to the hot butter and cook near the top of a moderately hot oven (200°C/400°F or Gas Mark 6) for 10 to 15 minutes.

VARIATIONS

Flavourings such as herbs etc. suggested on page 272 can be added to the eggs. The fillings given on that page can be heated and spooned on to the cooked omelette before serving or heated in the ovenproof dish before the egg mixture is added. If heating the flavourings in the dish, cover this to prevent the food becoming dry.

## Herb Omelette

*4 eggs*
*salt and pepper*
*1 tablespoon water*
*1-2 tablespoons finely chopped herbs (chives, parsley, thyme)*
*40-50 g/1 ½-2 oz butter*

The simple flavouring of fresh herbs allows one to enjoy the full flavour of the eggs. If, like me, you prefer an omelette really soft in the centre, time the cooking carefully and serve immediately after cooking. For this French type of omelette simply mix the yolks and whites, do not beat hard, add salt, pepper, water (to give a lighter texture), then the herbs. Heat the butter in a 15 to 18 cm/6 to 7 inch omelette pan (a larger pan with this quantity of eggs gives too thin an omelette).

If using the larger amount of butter, add a little to the eggs (this gives a richer taste). Pour the eggs into the hot butter, wait ½ minute, or until set on the bottom, then tilt the pan and, with the help of a fork or palette knife, push the top liquid egg to the sides of the pan. Continue 'working' the omelette in this way until set to personal taste; fold or roll away from the handle and tip onto a hot dish. Serves 2.

VARIATIONS

**Flavourings:** Add hot chopped cooked onions, mushrooms or other vegetables, as in the Spanish Omelette below. Add finely chopped cooked ham, chicken or smoked fish; add grated cheese (these foods need not be hot).

**Fillings:** Make quite sure the filling is cooked and ready before cooking the omelette. Cook the omelette, spoon the filling in the centre; fold or roll.

Some good fillings are: grated or cream or cottage cheese; thick cheese sauce, fried bacon and tomatoes; cooked vegetable purée or vegetables in a thick cheese or other sauce: fish, meat or poultry in a creamy sauce.

## Spanish Omelette

*2 tablespoons oil*
*2 onions, thinly sliced*
*2 large cooked potatoes, cut into 5 mm/¼ inch dice*
*25 g/1 oz butter*
*6 eggs*
*salt and pepper*
*2 tablespoons water*

Heat the oil in a large omelette pan and cook the onions until nearly tender, add the potatoes and heat thoroughly, then add the butter to the pan. Beat the eggs with the salt, pepper and water. Pour over the vegetables. Cook as the basic omelette on this page, but serve flat.

VARIATIONS

Other vegetables, fish or meat can be heated in the oil but the above simple Spanish omelette is authentic and delicious.

## Ham and Cheese Soufflé Omelette

*8 eggs*
*salt and pepper*
*3 tablespoon water*
*40g/1½oz butter*
FILLING:
*75g/3oz cheese, grated*
*75g/3oz ham, finely chopped*
GARNISH:
*parsley*

Separate the egg yolks from the whites. Put the whites into a mixing bowl and whisk until they almost hold their shape. Blend the yolks with the salt, pepper and water. Fold in the egg whites. Heat the butter in a large omelette or frying pan, pour in the egg mixture and cook fairly quickly for about 1 minute. Transfer the pan to a pre-heated grill with the heat set to medium and cook until just firm. Fill the omelette with the cheese and ham, fold and slide onto a serving dish. Garnish with parsley and serve at once.

VARIATION

**Cheese and Haddock Omelette:** Blend 40g/1½oz grated Parmesan cheese with the egg yolks in the recipe above. Cook the omelette, fill with smoked haddock, blended with thick cream. Fold the omelette and top with cheese.

## Salmon Pancake Soufflé

*12 cooked pancakes (see page 289 and method)*
FILLING:
*25g/1oz butter, melted*
*3 eggs*
*225g/8oz cooked or canned salmon*
*2 teaspoons lemon juice*
*2 tablespoons double cream*
*salt and pepper*
*1 teaspoon French mustard*

Make the pancakes the right size to fit into a deep soufflé or ovenproof serving dish. Brush the dish with the butter. Separate the eggs. Put the yolks into a basin and whisk until thick and frothy. Flake the salmon and fold into the egg yolks, then add the lemon juice, double cream, salt, pepper and French mustard. Whisk the whites until stiff and fold into the other ingredients. Put the first pancake into the dish, top with a little salmon mixture. Continue like this until all the pancakes and soufflé mixture are used. Finish with a fairly thick layer of the soufflé mixture. If the pancakes are still hot, cook in the centre of a moderately hot oven (190-200°C/375-400°F or Gas Mark 5-6) for 25 minutes. If the pancakes have become cold, allow 35 to 40 minutes at a slightly lower heat.

VARIATIONS

Use finely minced cooked chicken or ham or a mixture of meats in the filling instead of salmon.

Used flaked crabmeat, chopped prawns or other cooked fish in the filling instead of salmon

## Cheese Soufflé

*25 g/1 oz butter*
*25 g/1 oz flour*
*150 ml/¼ pint milk*
*3 tablespoons cream or extra milk*
*100-150 g/4-5 oz Cheddar cheese grated*
*3 eggs*
*salt and pepper*
*little mustard*
*1 egg white*

A cheese soufflé makes an excellent light luncheon dish or an enjoyable savoury at the end of a meal.

Heat the butter in a good-sized saucepan, stir in the flour and cook over a gentle heat for 2 to 3 minutes, then add the milk and cream. Stir as the mixture comes to the boil and thickens. Remove the saucepan from the heat, add the grated cheese. Separate the eggs, stir the yolks into the cheese mixture together with any seasonings required. Whisk all the egg whites until they just stand in peaks, fold gently, but thoroughly, into the rest of the ingredients. Spoon into a 15 to 18 cm/6 to 7 inch greased soufflé dish and cook in the centre of a moderately hot oven (190°C/375°F or Gas Mark 5) for approximately 30 to 35 minutes or until well risen and golden brown. Serve at once.

VARIATIONS

If the egg yolks are omitted, the flavour is less good but the soufflé does not sink as rapidly. Other cheese may be used instead of Cheddar.

**Cheese and Haddock Soufflé:** Make the sauce as in the basic recipe above, with 150 ml/¼ pint milk, add 2 tablespoons fish stock, 3 tablespoons double cream, 100 g/4 oz cooked flaked smoked haddock and 40 g/1½ oz grated Parmesan cheese. Continue and bake as above.

**Salmon Soufflé:** Use 40 g/1½ oz butter with 25 g/1 oz flour, 150 ml/¼ pint single cream and 4 tablespoons fish stock (if using fresh salmon) or liquid from the can (if using canned fish), to make the sauce. Add 175 g/6 oz flaked cooked or canned salmon, then continue and bake as the above recipe. For special occasions serve with the same sauce as Salmon Walewska (see page 82).

Smoked salmon can be used instead of cooked or canned salmon. In this case, flavour the sauce with a little lemon juice; use 100 g/4 oz chopped smoked salmon. Serve with wedges of lemon as an hors d'oeuvre.

**Spinach Soufflé:** Prepare 220 ml/7½ fl oz smooth spinach purée from lightly cooked fresh or frozen spinach, add 4 tablespoons double cream and a shake of cayenne pepper. Make the sauce as in the above recipe, using the creamed spinach as the liquid. Continue and bake as the Cheese Soufflé. This is delicious served with melted butter, flavoured with chopped anchovy fillets or anchovy essence.

## Camembert Soufflé

*25g/1 oz butter*
*25g/1 oz flour*
*300 ml/½ pint milk*
*75g/3 oz Camembert (weight with rind removed)*
*25g/1 oz Parmesan cheese, finely grated*
*2 tablespoons water*
*2 teaspoons gelatine*
*2 teaspoons tomato purée*
*½ teaspoon Dijon mustard*
*salt and cayenne pepper*
*2 eggs*
*1 egg white*
GARNISH:
*wafer thin cucumber slices*

Prepare a 13 cm/5 inch soufflé dish, as described on page 341 by tying a band of buttered paper round the dish so it stands above the rim. Make a coating sauce with the butter, flour and milk. Add the cheeses to the hot sauce and, stir over a low heat until melted. Meanwhile put the water into a heatproof basin, sprinkle the gelatine on the top, do not stir, but stand over a saucepan of boiling water until dissolved. Blend the hot gelatine liquid with the hot cheese sauce, together with the tomato purée, mustard, salt and pepper. Separate the 2 eggs and whisk the yolks into the sauce. Allow the mixture to become quite cold and stiffen slightly.

Whisk the egg whites until stiff, fold into the sauce. Spoon into the soufflé dish and leave until firm, then remove the band of paper. Top with cucumber slices.

## Spanish Onion Tart

SHORTCRUST PASTRY:
*225g/8 oz plain flour*
*pinch salt*
*110g/4 oz butter or margarine*
*1 teaspoon lemon juice (optional)*
*water to mix*
FILLING:
*450g/1 lb onions, finely chopped*
*175g/6 oz bacon, derinded and chopped*
*2 eggs, beaten*
*150 ml/¼ pint milk*
*salt and pepper*

First make the pastry. Sift the flour and salt into a mixing bowl, rub in the fat, then mix in the lemon juice and cold water. Roll out and line a 23 cm/9 inch flan dish. Fry the onions and bacon together until soft, but not brown – no extra fat should be necessary. Allow to cool, then blend in the eggs and milk. Season to taste. Pour into the uncooked pastry case. Cook in the centre of a hot oven (220°C/425°F or Gas Mark 7) for 15 to 20 minutes, then lower the heat to moderate (180°C/350°F or Gas Mark 4) for a further 15 to 20 minutes or until the pastry is crisp and the filling set. Serve hot or cold.

VARIATION
Add 50 to 75 g/2 to 3 oz grated cheese to the filling. The amount of pastry allowed here is a generous one, which makes the tart easy to carry for a picnic. If preferred use pastry made with 175 g/6 oz flour etc.

# Making a Quiche

These flans, filled with savoury custard and other interesting ingredients, have become an accepted part of our menus. I find quiches are equally suitable to serve as an hors d/oeuvre or as the main dish for a light lunch or supper. They are ideal for buffet or picnic meals and a delicious nibble, if cut into small neat squares, to serve with drinks. As quiches freeze perfectly for up to 3 months, they are an excellent standby in the freezer. The result of freezing is particularly good if single cream is used instead of milk.

The suggested flan size is given in each recipe, but check not only the diameter but also the depth of the container in which you plan to bake the quiche. It is important that the flan dish, tin or ring is at least 3.5 cm/1 ½ inches in depth to accommodate the amount of filling given. If your container is more shallow then use one wider in diameter.

## Quiche Lorraine ⊛

*shortcrust pastry made with 175 g/6 oz plain flour, etc. (see page 291)*

FILLING:

*4 bacon rashers, derinded and chopped*
*2 egg yolks*
*2 eggs*
*450 ml/¾ pint milk or single cream, or use half milk and half cream*
*salt and pepper*
*100 g/4 oz Gruyère cheese, grated (optional)*

Roll out the pastry and line a 23 cm/9 inch flan tin or ring. Bake blind, as described on page 322 in the centre of a moderately hot oven (200°C/400°F or Gas Mark 6) for 15 minutes or until set and golden.

Meanwhile grill or fry the bacon and put into the flan case. Beat together the yolks and whole eggs. Warm the milk or cream, add to the eggs and season well. It is a fact that the original Quiche Lorraine did not include cheese, but I add at least 100 g/4 oz to the custard. Pour carefully over the bacon; do not add all the custard if the flan seems to be over-filled.

Cook the flan in a cool oven (150°C/300°F or Gas Mark 2) for 15 minutes, then add the remaining custard (the level will have sunk in baking). Cook for a further 30 minutes or until firm. Serve hot or cold.

VARIATIONS

⊛ **Quiche Provençal:** Line the bottom of the lightly cooked flan with wafer-thin pancakes (to prevent base becoming soft). Cover with a layer of lightly cooked onions, crushed garlic and tomatoes, then the cheese custard mixture. Bake as in the above recipe.

⊛ **Seafood Quiche:** Use a mixture of cooked shell and white fish instead of bacon.

⊛ **Spinach Quiche:** Blend about 175 g/6 oz cooked spinach with the custard and cheese. Bake as in the above recipe.

Other vegetables, such as cooked mushrooms can be used.

## Cheddar Soufflé Quiche

CHEESE PASTRY:
*175g/6oz plain flour*
*salt and pepper*
*pinch dry mustard*
*50g/2oz butter or margarine*
*50g/2oz Cheddar cheese, finely grated*
*1 egg yolk*
*water to bind*
FILLING:
*50g/2oz butter or margarine*
*50g/2oz flour*
*300ml/½ pint milk*
*2 eggs*
*100g/4oz Cheddar cheese, finely grated*
*1 egg white*

Sift the flour with the seasonings, rub in the butter or margarine, add the cheese, egg yolks and sufficient water to make a firm rolling consistency. Roll out and line a 20-23cm/8-9 inch flan dish, tin or ring on an upturned baking tray. Bake blind in the centre of a moderately hot oven (190-200°C/375-400°F or Gas Mark 5-6) for 15 minutes, or until firm but pale in colour.

Meanwhile make a thick binding sauce (panada) with the remaining butter or margarine, flour and milk; remove the pan from the heat. Separate the 2 eggs, beat the egg yolks, grated cheese and a little salt and pepper into the sauce. Whisk the 3 egg whites until stiff, fold into the sauce ingredients. Spoon into the partially-baked pastry, return to the oven for a further 20 minutes or until both filling and pastry are firm. Serve at once.

VARIATION

**Cheddar Potato Quiche:** Omit the butter, flour and milk used to make the sauce in the filling above. Cook and sieve 100g/4oz potatoes (weight when cooked); gradually blend in 4 tablespoons single cream, salt, pepper and 1 tablespoon chopped parsley, 2 egg yolks, 100g/4oz finely grated Cheddar cheese. Finally fold in 3 stiffly whisked egg whites. Spoon into the partially-baked flan case and continue cooking as in the above recipe.

## Tortilla Quiche ⊛

*Cheese Pastry (see recipe above)*
FILLING:
*2 tablespoons oil*
*2 medium potatoes, cut into 1cm/½ inch dice*
*2 medium onions, cut into 5mm/¼ inch dice*
*1 red pepper, cored, deseeded and diced*
*2 eggs or 3 egg yolks*
*300ml/½ pint single cream or milk*
*100g/4oz Cheddar cheese, finely grated*
*salt and pepper*

Make and lightly bake the pastry flan, as in the recipe above. Heat the oil in a frying pan, add the diced potatoes and onions and cook steadily for 5 to 6 minutes, then add the red pepper and continue to cook until tender. Spoon into the pastry case. Blend the eggs or egg yolks with the cream or milk, cheese and a little salt and pepper. Spoon over the vegetables. Return the flan to the oven, lowering the heat to 150°C/300°F or Gas Mark 2 and cook for 45 minutes, or until the filling is firm. Serve hot or cold.

## Onion Cheese Flan ⊛

*shortcrust pastry made with 175g/6oz flour (see page 291)*
FILLING:
*50g/2oz butter*
*350g/12oz onions, thinly sliced*
*225g/8oz Gruyère or Cheddar cheese, grated*
*3 egg yolks or 2 eggs*
*4 tablespoons milk or single cream*
*1 teaspoon chopped savory*
*1 teaspoon chopped chives*
*salt and pepper*

Roll out the pastry and line a 20cm/8 inch flan dish or tin. Bake blind in the centre of a moderately hot oven (200°C/400°F or Gas Mark 6) for 15 minutes or until set but still very pale in colour.

Heat the butter and fry the onions until very soft. Spoon the onions into the partially cooked flan and top with the cheese. Blend the egg yolks or whole eggs with the milk or cream, herbs, salt and pepper to taste. Pour over the onions and cheese. Return to the oven, lowering the heat to cool to moderate (150-160°C/300-325°F or Gas Mark 2-3) for a further 30 minutes or until the filling is firm and the pastry crisp. Serve hot or cold.

## Salé ⊛

*shortcrust pastry made with 175g/6oz flour etc. (see page 291)*
FILLING:
*25g/1 oz butter*
*25g/1 oz flour*
*300ml/½ pint milk*
*4 tablespoons double or whipping cream*
*3 eggs*
*175g/6oz Gruyère cheese, grated*
*salt and pepper*
*pinch grated nutmeg*

Roll out the pastry until fairly thin and line a 23cm/9 inch flan dish, tin or flan ring (this must be at least 2.5cm/1 inch deep). Heat the butter, stir in the flour and cook for 2 to 3 minutes over a low heat. Gradually blend in the milk. Stir the sauce as it comes to the boil and thickens. Remove from the heat. Whisk the cream and eggs together then add to the sauce with the remaining ingredients. Pour carefully into the uncooked pastry case. Cook in the centre of a moderately hot oven (200°C/400°F or Gas Mark 6) for 20 to 25 minutes, then lower the heat to moderate (160°C/325°F or Gas Mark 3) for a further 20 minutes or until the filling is quite firm. Serve hot.

## Cheese Gâteau ⊛

*50g/2oz butter*
*225g/8oz mushrooms, thinly sliced*
*8 to 12 large pancakes (see page 289)*
*600ml/1 pint Cheese Sauce, (see page 228, coating consistency)*
*50g/2oz Cheddar cheese, grated*

Heat half the butter and toss the mushrooms in this, do not over-cook as they soften in the oven. Put the first pancake on to an ovenproof serving dish, top with some of the sauce, then a few mushroom slices; continue like this, ending with a plain pancake. Top with the grated cheese. Melt the remaining butter and spoon over the cheese. Cook in the centre of a moderately hot oven (200°C/400°F or Gas Mark 6) for about 20 minutes. Cut into slices and serve as you would a cake.

## Pizza Neapolitan ⊛

DOUGH:
*220 ml/7½ fl oz water*
*15 g/½ oz fresh yeast or*
*7 g/¼ oz dried yeast with*
*1 teaspoon sugar*
*350 g/12 oz strong plain flour*
*salt and pepper*
*1 tablespoon olive oil*
TOPPING:
*1 tablespoon oil*
*1 kg/2 lb tomatoes, skinned and chopped*
*2 medium onions, finely chopped*
*1-2 cloves garlic, crushed*
*1-2 teaspoons chopped fresh oregano or ¼ teaspoon dried oregano*
*225 g/8 oz Mozzarella or Bel Paese cheese, grated*
*small can anchovy fillets*
*8-12 black olives*

Heat the water until just tepid – it should be blood heat. If using fresh yeast, cream this then add the water. If using dried yeast, add the sugar to the water, sprinkle the dried yeast on top and leave for about 10 minutes; stir to blend, then use as fresh yeast.

Sift the flour, salt and pepper together; add the 1 tablespoon of oil and the yeast liquid. Knead the dough until smooth, cover as described on page 371 and leave to prove in a warm place for 1 to 1½ hours, or until double the original size.

Heat the oil and fry the vegetables until a soft thick purée; make sure all surplus liquid has evaporated. Add seasoning and the oregano.

Put the proven dough on to a floured board and knock back, then roll out to a 25 cm/10 inch round or square. Put on to a lightly greased baking tray and cover with the tomato mixture. Add the grated cheese. Put into a warm place once again for the final proving – this will take about 25 to 30 minutes. Cook just above the centre of a hot oven (220°C/425°F or Gas Mark 7) for 15 to 20 minutes. Remove the pizza from the oven after about 10 minutes and quickly add the anchovy fillets and olives. You could also add a little extra grated cheese if desired. Adding the anchovy fillets and olives during cooking keeps them moist.

VARIATIONS

⊛ **Bacon Pizza:** Prepare the base of the pizza and cover with the tomato topping as above. Brush the tomato mixture with a very little oil so it does not dry. Allow to prove then bake for 10 minutes, as directed above. Remove from the oven, top with thin slices of Cheddar cheese and a lattice of strips of streaky bacon instead of the grated cheese, anchovy fillets and olives. Return to the oven and continue cooking. Garnish with tomato slices.

⊛ **Pizza Fruits de Mer:** Cover the dough with the tomato mixture and about 50 g/2 oz grated cheese; bake for 10 minutes, as in the above recipe, then top with peeled prawns and mussels as well as the anchovy fillets. Sprinkle a few capers over the tomato mixture, top with more cheese and return to the oven to complete the baking. Garnish with lemon and tomato slices.

⊛ **Pizza Paysanne:** Cover the dough with the tomato mixture and with lightly cooked button mushrooms, top with the grated cheese and bake for 15 to 20 minutes.

# Making a Fondue

On this page you will find the classic Swiss recipe, together with ways in which it can be adapted. Fondues enable you to plan informal entertaining with the minimum of effort. Use an earthenware Fondue pot for cheese mixtures if possible as this does not become as hot as the metal pot. The metal fondue pan must however be used in heating oil for a meat fondue.

Always check that the fondue heater is placed well away from curtains and cannot be knocked over by people. If it is being put onto a polished surface protect this with heat-resisting mats.

## Cheese Fondue

*15g/½oz butter*
*1 clove garlic, halved*
*1 teaspoon cornflour*
*300ml/½ pint white wine*
*225g/8oz Gruyère cheese, grated*
*225g/8oz Emmenthal cheese, grated*
*salt and pepper*
*bread or toast, cut into squares*

This classic dish can be served as a dip as well as being an excellent main dish. Rub the inside of a ceramic fondue pot with the butter, then the garlic. Blend the cornflour with the wine, add to the pot with the cheeses, salt and pepper. Place on the fondue heater and stir from time to time until the cheese melts, or put onto an ordinary cooker, melt over a low heat, then transfer to the fondue heater. It is essential the cheese mixture does not become over-heated. Arrange the bread or toast around the fondue pot; everyone spears a piece with a fondue fork and dips it into the creamy mixture.

VARIATIONS

Instead of bread or toast spear large cooked prawns or small button mushrooms or other vegetable on to the fondue forks.

Use Cheddar or other good cooking cheese instead of Gruyère and Emmenthal with dry cider instead of white wine.

## Fonduta

*2 teaspoons cornflour*
*salt and pepper*
*150ml/¼ pint milk*
*150ml/¼ pint single cream*
*1 teaspoon French mustard*
*4 egg yolks*
*450g/1 lb Gruyère cheese, finely grated*
GARNISH:
*chopped parsley*
*diced canned red pepper*

Blend the cornflour with a little salt and pepper; add the milk and half the cream. Pour into a saucepan and stir until thickened and smooth. At this stage the mixture can be transferred to the fondue pot if preferred. Mix the remaining cream with the mustard and egg yolks, stir into the hot, but not boiling sauce, together with the cheese. Heat until the cheese melts. Top with the parsley and pepper. Serve in the same way as the Cheese Fondue above.

## Fried Camembert

*about 225 g/8 oz Camembert cheese (weight when rind is removed)*

COATING AND FRYING:

*1 tablespoon flour*
*1 egg, beaten*
*50 g/2 oz crisp breadcrumbs*
*oil or fat*

Cut the cheese into 4 neat portions. Coat with flour, then with egg and crumbs. It is a good idea to chill the coated cheese as this helps the coating to adhere. Heat the oil or fat to 190°C/375°F. This is very hot, but the coating must crisp and brown within 1 to 2 minutes, so the cheese does not melt sufficiently to break through the coating. If testing the fat with a cube of day-old bread, the bread should turn golden within seconds.

Lower the cheese into the hot oil or fat and fry for 1 to 2 minutes; drain on absorbent paper and serve. This is a simple, but very versatile dish. It can be eaten with a salad, but it is nicest with a sharp sauce, such as Apple Sauce, Gooseberry Sauce or Cranberry Sauce (see pages 145, 85 and 185). When serving in this way, the cheese can be served as an unusual hors d'oeuvre or even as a dessert.

VARIATIONS

Other creamy cheeses can be served in the same way.

Cubes of hard cheese can be coated and fried; they are very pleasant as a canapé.

## Iced Camembert ⊛

*Camembert cheese*

Cut the Camembert cheese into neat pieces, put into the freezing compartment of the refrigerator or into the freezer for about 30 minutes only. Serve with cheese biscuits and grapes.

VARIATIONS

Brie or other creamy cheese could be used instead of Camembert.

Cut away the rind from the Camembert cheese, put the cheese into a basin. Gradually beat in a little double cream until the mixture stands up in peaks. Add a shake of pepper if desired. Freeze as above. Never allow the cheese to become too hard, it should be like ice cream.

## Cheese en Surprise

*8-12 large very thin slices of bread*
*100 g/4 oz butter*
*75 g/3 oz Cheddar cheese, finely grated*
*25 g/1 oz walnuts, chopped*
*25 g/1 oz sultanas*

Roll each slice of bread with a rolling pin to make it thinner and less rigid; remove the crusts. Cream half the butter and mix with the cheese, walnuts and sultanas. Spread over the bread. Roll up tightly and secure the rolls with wooden cocktail sticks if necessary. Melt the remaining butter and brush over the rolls. Chill for a short time, while preheating the oven to moderately hot (190°C/375°F or Gas Mark 5). Bake the rolls for 8 minutes or until crisp and brown.

## Welsh Rarebit

*25g/1 oz butter*
*25g/1 oz flour*
*5 tablespoons milk*
*4 tablespoons ale*
*salt and pepper*
*2 teaspoons made English mustard*
*225-350g/8-12 oz Double Gloucester or Cheddar cheese, grated*
*4-6 slices bread*
*little butter*
GARNISH
*parsley*

If you want a quick, but very delicious snack or savoury at the end of a meal, do remember the traditional Welsh Rabbit – or Rarebit.

Heat the butter in a pan, stir in the flour and cook over a low heat for 2 to 3 minutes, then gradually blend in the milk and ale. Stir as the mixture comes to the boil and make a thick sauce, add a very little salt, good shake of pepper and the mustard. Remove from the heat, add the cheese, but do not cook again.

Meanwhile toast and butter the bread, spread with the rarebit mixture; keep it away from the edges of the toast as this is a moist mixture and does spread in heating. Put under a preheated grill and cook for 2 to 3 minutes until golden. Cut each slice in half if serving as an after-dinner savoury. Top with parsley. Serves 4 to 6, or 8 to 12 as a savoury.

VARIATIONS

If you do not want the bother of making a sauce, then cream 50g/2oz butter, add 350g/12oz grated cheese, salt, pepper, 2 teaspoons made mustard and 2 tablespoons ale. Spread over the toast as in the recipe above. An egg yolk can be added if desired.

**York Rarebit:** Put slices of lean ham on the toast, top with the rarebit mixture and grill.

**Buck Rarebit:** Top the cooked rarebit with poached eggs.

⊠ **Welsh Rarebit Fondue:** The first recipe makes an excellent Fondue. Double the amounts, make the sauce, add the cheese, then transfer to a fondue pot and place over a fondue heater.

## Croque Monsieur

*8 slices of bread*
*little butter*
*4 slices Gruyère or other cheese*
*4 slices cooked ham*
*1 egg*
*2 tablespoons milk*
FOR FRYING:
*50g/2 oz butter*

Spread the bread with a little butter, then make 4 sandwiches with the cheese and ham; cut these into quarters or halves if desired. Beat the egg with the milk. Dip the sandwiches in this quickly to moisten. Heat the butter and fry the sandwiches on either side until crisp and brown. Serve at once.

VARIATIONS

**Cheese in a Carriage:** Coat the sandwiches with beaten egg and breadcrumbs and deep fry.

## Cheese Rings

*225 g/8 oz self-raising flour*
*salt and pepper*
*pinch mustard powder*
*25 g/1 oz butter or margarine*
*50 g/2 oz Cheddar cheese, finely grated*
*1 egg*
*milk to mix*
FOR FRYING
*oil or fat*

Sift together the flour with the seasonings. Rub in the butter or margarine and add the grated cheese. Bind with the egg and enough milk to make a soft rolling consistency. Roll out until about 2 cm/¾ inch in thickness, cut into eight or ten 5 to 7.5 cm/2 to 3 inch rings.

Heat the oil or fat to 175°C/345°F (explanation of testing oil or fat on page 290). Fry the rings for 6 to 7 minutes until well risen, crisp and brown. Drain on absorbent paper. Serve hot or cold.

## Cheese Soufflé Tarts

*shortcrust pastry made with 100 g/4 oz flour, etc. (see page 291)*
FILLING:
*3 large eggs*
*75 g/3 oz Cheshire cheese, grated*
*salt and cayenne pepper*

Roll out the pastry until very thin; this is important, as the pastry must be cooked by the time the light filling is set. Cut into rounds to fit 9 to 12 shallow patty tins. Beat the eggs, there is no need to separate the white from the yolks; add the cheese, salt and pepper. Spoon the mixture into the uncooked pastry cases. Cook in the centre of a moderately hot to hot oven (200–220°C/400-425°F or Gas Mark 6-7) for 15 minutes by which time the filling will have risen and become firm and golden. Serve hot or cold; the filling tends to sink when cold.

VARIATIONS
Add 50 g/2 oz finely cooked mushrooms to the cheese.
**Cheese and Parma Ham Tarts:** Make the pastry as above, line the patty tins, prick the bottom of the pastry and bake the tartlets without a filling for about 12 to 15 minutes. Allow to cool. Blend 175 g/6 oz cream cheese with 50 g/2 oz finely diced Parma ham, salt and pepper to taste and 2 tablespoons whipped cream. Spoon into the tartlet cases and garnish with a twist of cucumber.

Smoked salmon could be substituted for Parma ham.

# Snacks and Savouries

There are many occasions when a light, but sustaining, snack or savoury dish can take the place of a complete meal. There are light snacks under Salads and Egg and Cheese Dishes and more recipes are given in this chapter. The dishes that follow are based upon bread, pancakes, pastry, pasta and rice. These foods are all easily obtainable and adaptable.

I have started the chapter with a favourite dish of mine. I refer to the selection of vegetables given the French name of Crudités. While each vegetable can be beautifully prepared and cut into small pieces I like to present a bowl of perfect vegetables, together with the dressing, so that everyone can cut off just the amount they require.

As my sister and her family live in Norway, I have grown to appreciate the convenience of serving open sandwiches for a meal. These look so inviting and one can put a really generous amount of foods on the bread, in which case the sandwiches must be served with a knife and fork. It is not difficult to take open sandwiches as part of a packed meal; keep the topping fairly flat and cover each sandwich with a square of waxed or greaseproof paper instead of bread and butter.

Ordinary sandwiches can be prepared, packed and frozen if desired. Do not freeze sandwiches with a filling of salad ingredients, cooked eggs or fillings blended with mayonnaise. Wrap the sandwiches carefully and use within 3 months or a shorter time if using salted fillings, such as smoked ham or smoked fish.

Toasted sandwiches or foods served on hot toast are always popular. The recipes on pages 287 and 288 are equally suitable for after-dinner savouries, in which case serve small portions.

I enjoy pancakes filled with savoury or sweet ingredients as a quick snack; you will find details about freezing these on page 289. Many different pastries have been used throughout this book; pages 291 to 294 cover the technique of making and using the most usual kinds of pastry.

Both pasta and rice can be combined with a variety of different foods; some of the recipes I enjoy making, and eating, are given on pages 295 to 304.

## Les Crudités

*raw Brussels sprouts, red or green cabbage, cauliflower, cucumber, fennel, lettuce, green and red peppers, radishes, spring onions, tomatoes*

Wash the vegetables and cut away any parts that cannot be eaten. Arrange in a large bowl. Provide everyone with a sharp knife, bowl of dressing, a finger bowl and napkin. Cut off bite-size pieces of the vegetables desired and dip in the dressing.

To make a more substantial meal, include cold hard-boiled eggs and Jacket Potatoes cooked as page 251. The eggs should be left in their shells, so they do not become dry. Serve with one of the dressings below.

VARIATIONS

Prepare small portions of each vegetable and arrange on a flat dish.

**Vegetable Platter:** Cook a selection of vegetables, serve with Cheese Sauce (see page 228) or top with Maître d'hotel Butter, below.

## French Dressing

*½-1 teaspoon made English or French mustard*
*salt and pepper*
*pinch sugar*
*150 ml/¼ pint salad or olive oil*
*4 tablespoons lemon juice*

This recipe gives the standard proportions of oil and lemon juice, but these can be adapted to personal taste.

Blend the mustard, salt, pepper and sugar with the oil and gradually blend in the lemon juice. The ingredients can be mixed in a liquidizer or food processor.

You can make larger amounts and keep the dressing in a screw-topped jar. Shake before use.

VARIATIONS

Add a little crushed garlic and 1 to 2 teaspoons freshly chopped mixed herbs.

**Vinaigrette Dressing:** Follow the proportions above but use white or red wine vinegar.

**Anchovy Dressing:** Make the French or Vinaigrette Dressing and blend in a little anchovy essence or 1 or 2 finely chopped canned anchovy fillets. This dressing blends well with vegetables.

## Maître d'hôtel Butter ⊛

*100 g/4 oz butter*
*salt and pepper*
*squeeze lemon juice*
*2-3 tablespoons chopped parsley*

Cream the butter and add all the other ingredients. Cut the butter into neat rounds or pats and chill.

Top hot meat, fish or vegetables with the chilled butter pats.

## Smørrebrød

*white, brown or rye bread*
*butter*
TOPPINGS:
*see method*

Cut the bread into thin slices, spread with butter then lettuce if the toppings are moist, to prevent these soaking into the bread.

Remember real Scandinavian open sandwiches are a delight to look at so plan pleasing contrasts in colour as well as texture.

Some of the toppings I enjoy are:

1) Well-drained Bismarck herring with potato salad and diced beetroot. Top with chopped dill.
2) Portions of smoked salmon or mackerel, topped with horseradish cream with scrambled egg.
3) Prawns topped with thick mayonnaise, sliced hard-boiled egg, twists of lemon and cucumber.
4) Fried fillets of fish with Tartare or Remoulade Sauce (see pages 100 and 236), cucumber slices and orange segments.
5) Liver pâté, topped with crisp bacon and a little Cumberland or Cranberry Sauce (see pages 237 and 185).
6) Sliced cooked pork with cooked prunes and apple slices, topped with mayonnaise.
7) Sliced cooked beef with mustard pickle, beetroot and potato salad.
8) Steak Tartare (see page 110).
9) Selection of sliced cheeses with grapes and orange segments.

## Sandwiches ⊛

*various kinds of bread*
*butter or margarine*
FILLINGS:
*see method*
⊛ *See remarks on freezing sandwiches (page 284)*

Modern sliced bread makes sandwich cutting much easier; if you have to cut thin slices of bread warm the bread knife. Hard butter or margarine can be softened by blending it with a few drops of warm milk (this also makes the fat go further).

Some of the ingredients given above could be adapted for ordinary sandwiches.

Fish fillings can be prepared with canned or cooked fish of various kinds. Blend this with mayonnaise or scrambled egg, shredded lettuce, diced cucumber or cress.

Meat, poultry and game is more moist if blended with a little mustard or curry flavoured mayonnaise.

Cheese of various kinds can be blended with nuts, fruit, crisp bacon and mayonnaise.

Eggs can be soft or hard-boiled, scrambled and blended with salad ingredients.

# A New Look to Sandwiches

Rolled sandwiches are made by using fresh bread, cut very thinly. Remove the crusts and roll the bread, as though it were pastry, spread with butter or margarine, then the filling and roll.

Three-decker sandwiches are made by using two slices of white or brown bread and one slice of a contrasting bread, with two fillings; choose those that blend well together.

Toasted sandwiches are easily made today with modern sandwich toasters; you can, however, make the sandwiches then toast these on either side under a preheated grill, set to moderate. The sandwiches can be brushed with a little melted butter to give a crisper result.

Snacks on toast make excellent light meals or after-dinner savouries, see this page and 288.

## Orange Salad

*4-6 oranges*
*1 lettuce*
*1 bunch watercress*
*Vinaigrette Dressing (see page 285)*

Cut away the pith and peel from the oranges, cut the fruit into neat segments and discard the skin and pips. Put the prepared lettuce and watercress on flat plates, top with the fruit and dressing.

This is an ideal salad to serve with a Ploughmans' lunch. To prepare this, serve crusty French bread or rolls or slices of fresh bread with plenty of butter and a selection of cheeses. Pickles or chutneys are the usual accompaniments, but oranges give essential vitamins.

## Angels on Horseback

*4 rashers bacon, derinded and halved*
*8 small oysters*
*squeeze lemon juice*
*shake pepper*
*4 slices bread*
*little butter*
GARNISH
*paprika*

Stretch each piece of bacon with the back of a knife. Flavour the oysters with the lemon juice and pepper. Roll the bacon around the oysters and secure with wooden cocktail sticks if necessary. Cook under a moderate grill until the bacon is crisp. Toast and butter the bread and put the bacon and oysters on to the toast. Top with paprika.

VARIATIONS

Use large mussels prepared as page 92 instead of oysters.

**Devils on Horseback:** Use large cooked prunes instead of oysters. The stones can be removed and the cavity filled with liver pâté.

## Bengal Toasts

*50g/2oz butter*
*25g/1oz flour*
*1-2 teaspoons curry powder*
*150ml/¼ pint milk*
*2 tablespoons double cream*
*2 tablespoons smooth chutney*
*175g/6oz cooked ham, minced or finely chopped*
*salt and pepper*
*4 slices bread*
*4 tablespoons grated cheese*
GARNISH:
*strips of tomato or red pepper*
*chopped parsley*

Heat 25g/1oz butter in a pan, stir in the flour and curry powder and cook for 2 to 3 minutes, then add the milk and cream, stir as this comes to the boil and becomes very thick. Add the chutney, ham, salt and pepper. Toast the bread, spread with the remaining butter, then the ham mixture. Top with the cheese and put under a preheated grill for 2 to 3 minutes. Top with tomato or red pepper and parsley.

VARIATION

**Devilled Shrimps:** Make the curry-flavoured sauce, as in the recipe above. Add the cream, but omit the chutney. Add approximately 225g/8oz peeled shrimps, a few drops Tabasco sauce and soy sauce, heat gently. Serve hot on hot buttered toast, as the above recipe, but omit the cheese topping.

## Helford Angels

*little lemon juice*
*8 oysters or 16 mussels (prepared as page 92)*
*cayenne pepper*
*8 thin small slices bread*
*50g/2oz butter*

Sprinkle lemon juice over the oysters or mussels and add a shake of cayenne pepper. Cut the crusts from the bread and roll the slices to make them more pliable (see page 287). Spread with half the butter. Put one oyster or 2 mussels on each slice of buttered bread, roll up firmly and secure with wooden cocktail sticks. Put on to a flat baking tray.

Melt the remaining butter, brush over the rolls and bake above the centre of a moderately hot oven (200°C/400°F or Gas Mark 6) for 5 to 6 minutes. Serve at once.

## Scotch Woodcock

*4 slices buttered toast*
*4 scrambled eggs (see page 270)*
*8 canned anchovy fillets*

Prepare the toast before cooking the eggs. Top the toast with the eggs. Split the anchovy fillets lengthways, arrange in a lattice design on top of the eggs. Serve at once.

## Pancake Batter

*100 g/4 oz plain flour (see method*)*
*pinch salt*
*1 egg*
*scant 300 ml/½ pint milk, or milk and water (see method**)*

*Plain flour gives a better batter for both pancakes and Yorkshire Pudding; it is possible to use strong flour (the type sold for bread-making) when preparing the batter for a Yorkshire Pudding.

**In order to achieve the correct consistency use only 270 ml liquid for 100 g is a scant 4 oz flour.

Sift the flour and salt together, add the egg and enough liquid to make a sticky mixture, beat well, then gradually whisk in the remaining liquid.

Keep in a cool place until ready to use and always whisk the batter just before using it as the flour tends to sink a little.

VARIATIONS

**Richer Batter:** Use 2 eggs and reduce the liquid by 2 tablespoons.

Add 1 tablespoon oil or melted butter to the batter when making pancakes; this gives a crisper result and is an additional aid in preventing the pancakes sticking to the pan; also the cooked pancakes freeze better. Do not add this to the batter for a Yorkshire Pudding or Toad in the Hole, (pages 115 and 147).

## Pancakes ⊛

*Pancake Batter (see above)*
*little oil or fat (see method)*

Prepare the batter. If you have a pan, which is used just for omelettes and pancakes, use only enough oil or fat to give a greasy surface over the base of the pan when cooking the first one or two pancakes. After that you should be able to cook pancakes without additional oil or fat.

Either transfer the batter to a jug, or I keep it in the bowl and use a spoon which, when filled, gives me exactly the right amount of batter for a wafer-thin pancake. Heat the greased pan until a *faint* haze is seen. Pour or spoon a little batter into the pan, *immediately* tilt this, so the batter coats the base. Cook steadily for 1½ to 2 minutes (if cooked, the pancake moves easily in the pan). Toss or turn and cook on the second side. Make the rest of the pancakes. The batter gives 12 to 16 thin pancakes. depending on the size of the pan. Keep cooked pancakes hot on an uncovered dish in a low oven or over a pan of hot water.

⊛ **To freeze:** separate with squares of oiled waxed or greaseproof paper, then pack in foil or a freezer polythene box. Use within 3 months.

# Fillings for Pancakes

Throughout this book you will find pancakes used in both savoury and sweet dishes. In addition to those recipes, remember you can turn pancakes into quick snacks with some of the following fillings. Make the pancakes as the recipe on page 289.

**Savoury fillings:**

Cheese sauce; cooked fish or meat in a thick savoury sauce or tomato purée; cottage or cream cheese; fried mushrooms; fried tomatoes with bacon.

**Sweet fillings:**

Cream or cottage cheese with sweetened fruit purée; ice cream (this must be put into the hot pancakes just before serving) topped with Hot Chocolate Sauce (see page 346); jam, lemon or orange curd; segments of fresh orange (serve the pancakes with a hot marmalade sauce).

**Deep Fried Pancakes**

Pancakes look very interesting if they are filled and fried. Use about two-thirds of the batter to make the pancakes. Put in the savoury or sweet fillings, seal the ends of the pancakes firmly before rolling so no filling can fall out. Heat the pan of deep oil or fat to 170°C/340°F. Dip the rolled pancakes into the remaining batter; put into the hot oil or fat and fry for 2 to 3 minutes. Drain on absorbent paper and serve.

# Testing Oil or Fat

It is important that oil or fat is preheated to the correct temperature for frying the food. Advice on this is given in various recipes. If the oil or fat is too cool, the food is over-greasy; if too hot, the food becomes over-brown on the outside before it is cooked in the centre. Modern electric fryers have a temperature control which makes frying very easy or you can use a thermometer to test the temperature when heating oil or fat in a pan on top of the cooker.

To test without a thermometer, use a cube of day-old bread (if the bread is too fresh it takes longer to brown). If the bread turns golden within 10 seconds the oil or fat is ultra-hot and must be cooled slightly. If it turns golden within about 30 seconds then the temperature is approximately 190°C/375°F and suitable for the second frying of potatoes, see page 252 or any food that is small and needs very quick frying. If the bread turns golden within 45 seconds the temperature is nearer 185°C/365°F; if it takes nearly 1 minute then the oil or fat is about 170°C/340°F.

# Making Good Pastry

There is a belief you are either born a good pastrycook or you are not, and if you cannot make pastry at this moment you never can, or will, achieve a good result. That is quite wrong. Good pastry depends upon using correct basic proportions, learning to handle the ingredients carefully, plus the correct cooking time and temperature which naturally varies with the kind of pastry and the particular recipe.

**Proportions of Fat in Pastry:** the method of incorporating the fat into flour is one way of determining the texture of the pastry. The amount of fat used determines the richness of the pastry. While there may be slight adjustments for special recipes remember:

Shortcrust Pastry* and Suet Crust Pastry – use half fat to flour. Flaky Pastry and Rough Puff Pastry – use three-quarters of the amount of fat to flour. Puff Pastry – use equal quantities of fat and flour.

* Use just under half fat if transporting Cornish Pasties (see page 118).

## Shortcrust Pastry ❄

*225g/8oz flour, preferably plain*
*pinch salt*
*110g/4oz fat, either butter or margarine or a mixture of butter or margarine and cooking fat or lard*
*cold water to bind*

Sift the flour and salt into a mixing bowl; cut the selected fat into small pieces and drop into the flour. You will note that I have given a less usual metric conversion for 4oz; this is because shortcrust pastry should have double the amount of flour to fat. You could, of course, use 200g flour with 100g fat, but that would not produce quite as much pastry as when following the imperial weights. Rub the fat into the flour with the tips of your fingers, lifting the mixture high above the bowl, so it remains cool and does not become over-sticky. Stop immediately the mixture looks like fine breadcrumbs. Add the cold water slowly and gradually until you have just enough to bind the mixture together and leave the mixing bowl clean. You can use a knife at the beginning of the process but you must use your fingertips to judge the consistency of the dough. Knead together very gently then use as in the recipe.

VARIATIONS

For Cheese Pastry see page 10.

**Economical Sweet Shortcrust:** Add just 25g/1oz caster or sifted icing sugar to the above ingredients. Use an egg yolk with water to bind.

**Nut Pastry:** Add 50g/2oz finely chopped walnuts and 50g/2oz sifted icing sugar to the basic ingredients. Use 1 or 2 egg yolks to bind with a very little water.

## Flaky Pastry ⊛

*225 g/8 oz plain flour*
*pinch salt*
*175 g/6 oz fat, this can be all butter or one-third butter and two-thirds cooking fat*
*cold water to bind*

Make the pastry ahead so it can stand. Sift the flour and salt into a mixing bowl. Divide the fat into 3 parts. Rub the first part into the flour until the mixture looks like fine breadcrumbs, then add enough water to make an elastic dough.

Roll out to an oblong shape. Divide the second part of the fat into small pieces and place these at regular intervals over the top two-thirds of the dough; leave the bottom third without any fat. Take the two corners of this dough and bring over the middle part of the dough, at this stage the pastry looks like an open envelope. Bring down the top third of the dough, so enclosing the 'envelope'. Turn the pastry at right angles, seal each end of the shape. Rib the pastry, as described under Puff Pastry below, then gently, but firmly, roll out to an oblong again.

Repeat the above procedure with the remaining fat, fold as described above, turn at right angles, seal the ends, rib the pastry. Cover and leave in a cool place.

Give the final rolling and folding, cover and chill again if possible, before using the pastry. Flaky pastry should have 3 rollings and 3 foldings. Use as in individual recipes.

VARIATION

⊛ **Rough Puff Pastry:** Use the proportions given above, but cut all the fat into the flour, blend with cold water to make an elastic dough, then proceed as Puff Pastry, giving the dough 5 rollings and 5 foldings.

## Puff Pastry ⊛

*225 g/8 oz plain flour*
*pinch salt*
*squeeze lemon juice*
*cold water to bind*
*225 g/8 oz butter, preferably unsalted*

Make the pastry well ahead so it has time to stand. Sift the flour and salt and mix to an elastic dough with the lemon juice and water. Roll out to an oblong shape; place the butter in the centre. Bring up the bottom to cover one-third of the dough, then bring down the top one-third, so enclosing the butter. Turn the pastry at right angles, seal each end of the shape. Rib (i.e. depress the pastry at intervals with the rolling pin), roll out gently but firmly to make an oblong once again. Fold the pastry in three, turn at right angles, seal the ends and rib as before. Give a total of 7 rollings and 7 foldings. You will need to cover the pastry and put it in the refrigerator between the rollings. Covering the pastry ensures that it does not harden on the outside. Roll out the pastry and use as individual recipe.

## Vol-au-Vents ⊛

*Puff Pastry, made with 225g/8oz flour, etc. (see page 292)*

GLAZE

*1 egg or 1 egg white with a little caster sugar (see method)*

Roll out the pastry until 1.5cm/¾inch in thickness; cut into 12 rounds about 6 to 7.5cm/2½ to 3 inches in diameter. Put on to a slightly damp baking tray. Take a 3.5cm/1½inch cutter, press halfway through the pastry. Brush the rim of the pastry with beaten egg for savoury vol-au-vents and with lightly whisked egg white and a sprinkling of caster sugar for sweet cases. Flake the sides of the rounds so the pastry rises well. Chill before cooking. Bake just above the centre of a hot oven (230°C/450°F or Gas Mark 8) for about 10 minutes or until the cases have risen. Lower the heat slightly and cook for a further 3 to 4 minutes or until firm. With the tip of a knife lift out the centres of the cases (these can be used as 'lids' over the filling). If necessary, return the cases to the oven for a few minutes to dry out.

If serving hot, put the hot filling into the hot pastry and serve at once. If serving cold, make sure that both filling and pastry are quite cold before they are combined.

Savoury Fillings: Diced cooked fish, ham, chicken or cooked vegetables in a thick sauce or mayonnaise or as Pastry Horns, below.

Sweet Fillings: As Pastry Horns, below.

⊛ Vol-au-Vent cases and Pastry Horns can be frozen when uncooked or cooked. Freeze pastry and fillings separately.

## Pastry Horns ⊛

*Puff Pastry (see recipe on page 292, using half quantities)*

GLAZE:

*1 egg white*

*little caster sugar for sweet horns*

FILLING:

*savoury and sweet ingredients as given in method*

Roll out the pastry until wafer thin. Cut about 2.5cm/1 inch wide strips; be careful not to stretch the pastry. Lightly grease cream horn tins on the outsides. Wind the pastry around the 8 to 10 tins (depending upon the size), starting from the base and allowing the edges to slightly overlap. Brush with egg white and sprinkle with a very little sugar if using a sweet filling.

Bake just above the centre of a hot oven (230°C/450°F, Gas Mark 8) for 10 to 12 minutes. Cool, then remove from the tins and fill just before serving.

Savoury Fillings: cream cheese with chopped parsley and red pepper; fillings as Vol-au-Vents, above; scrambled egg with prawns or chopped smoked salmon.

Sweet Fillings: Jam or thick fruit purée with whipped cream; sieved and sweetened cottage cheese with diced fruit.

## Mille Feuilles ⊛

*Puff or Rough Puff Pastry (see page 292)*
FILLINGS:
*sweet or savoury (see method)*

Roll out the pastry until about the thickness of a coin; cut into two equal sized oblong shapes or rounds or into smaller fingers (make sure you have an even number as they will be sandwiched together). Put on to slightly damp baking tins. Flake the sides and bake in a hot oven as for Vol-au-Vents (see page 293). When cold, trim the edges so the layers are seen.

Savoury Mille Feuilles: Although less usual than a sweet pastry, these are delicious. Sandwich the two layers together with well seasoned cream cheese or finely grated cheese blended with whipped cream.

Sweet Mille Feuilles:Sandwich the layers together with jam and whipped cream or Crème Pâtissière, page 359. Either dust the top with sieved icing sugar or coat the top with glacé icing, made as page 352.

## Sausage Rolls ⊛

*Flaky Pastry made with 225g/8oz flour, etc. (see page 292)*
*450g/1 lb sausagemeat*
GLAZE:
*1 egg*
*2 teaspoons water*

Roll out the pastry until it is very thin. Cut into long strips; if making cocktail bite-sized rolls these should be about 3.5 to 5cm/1½ to 2 inches in width; for larger sausage rolls about 7.5 to 10cm/3 to 4 inches in width. Roll the sausagemeat into long rolls of under half the width of the pastry. Place on the pastry strips. Damp the edges of the pastry and fold to enclose the sausagemeat. Seal and flake the edges, then cut into desired lengths. The quantities above should give about 36 tiny sausage rolls or 12 to 18 medium sized rolls. Make 2 slits on top with kitchen scissors, put on to a flat baking tray. Beat the egg with the water. Brush over the pastry and bake in the centre of hot oven (220°C/425°F or Gas Mark 7) for a good 10 minutes until the pastry rises, then lower the heat slightly for a further 5 to 10 minutes.

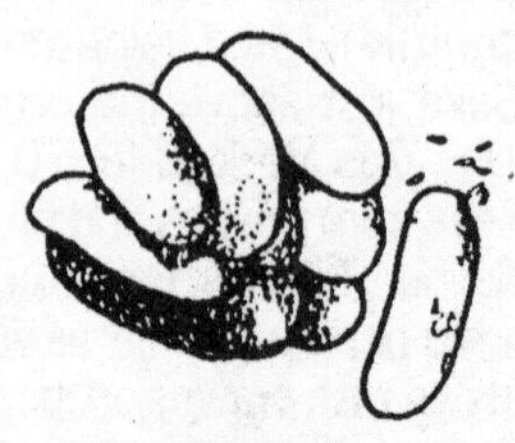

# Cooking Pasta

Various forms of pasta are available and they enable the cook to make a variety of interesting dishes. Whichever shape you may choose it is important that the pasta is not over-cooked. The Italians have a very descriptive word for the ideal pasta, it should be cooked until *'al dente'*, which means it is not over-soft, but pleasantly firm to bite.

Always use sufficient water for cooking pasta; i.e. a minimum of 1.2 litres/2 pints for each 100 g/4 oz uncooked pasta. Bring the water to the boil, add salt to taste, put in the pasta; do this steadily, rather than all at once. Allow the food to boil for a few minutes, then lift to separate with two spoons. This stage is particularly important with long-type pasta, such as spaghetti. Do not cover the pan while cooking the pasta, otherwise the water will boil over. When the pasta is cooked, strain and use, as in the recipes. You can rinse pasta to remove any surface starch, but I feel this is not necessary, unless using it for a salad, as page 304. Never over-cook pasta if freezing the cooked dish.

## Spaghetti with Tuna Sauce ⊛

*225 g/8 oz spaghetti*
*salt and pepper*
*1 x 225 g/8 oz can tuna in oil*
*1 can sardines in oil*
*2 tablespoons oil*
*1 small onion, chopped*
*2 cloves garlic, crushed*
*450 g/1 lb tomatoes, skinned and chopped*
*2 tablespoons chopped parsley*
*75 g/3 oz Parmesan cheese, grated*

Cook the spaghetti in boiling salted water until just *al dente* (cooked but firm), then strain. Meanwhile open the two cans of fish and pour any oil into a large frying pan. Add the 2 tablespoons of oil, heat this and fry the onion and garlic for 2 to 3 minutes. Add the tomatoes, lower the heat and continue to cook gently until the tomatoes are a fairly soft purée. Add salt and pepper to taste, then the flaked tuna fish. Heat for 1 minute, add the strained spaghetti, turn this in the tuna mixture. Add the sardines and parsley and heat for a few minutes, then stir in half the cheese. Serve topped with the remaining cheese.

VARIATION

⊛ **Spaghetti alla Marinara:** Cook the spaghetti as above. Omit the garlic but fry 1 large chopped onion, 2 derinded and chopped bacon rashers and 100 g/4 oz sliced mushrooms in 2 tablespoons of oil for 3 minutes. Add 450 g/1 lb skinned sliced tomatoes and cook until tender. Blend in the contents of a 50g/2 oz can of anchovy fillets and 100 g/4 oz peeled prawns or flaked canned tuna together with the strained spaghetti and 2 tablespoons chopped parsley. Heat thoroughly then serve topped with grated cheese.

## Spaghetti alla Carbonara ⊛

*225 g/8 oz spaghetti*
*salt and pepper*
*100 g/4 oz bacon, derinded and diced*
*4 eggs or egg yolks only*
*3 tablespoons cream*
*75 g/3 oz Parmesan cheese, grated*

Cook the spaghetti in boiling salted water until *al dente*, then strain. Meanwhile fry the bacon until crisp. Blend the eggs or egg yolks, cream, half the cheese and salt and pepper. Return the spaghetti to the saucepan with the hot bacon, add the egg mixture, stir over the heat for about 2 minutes. Serve with the remaining cheese.

## Lasagne al Forno ⊛

*Bolognese Sauce (see page 103)*
*300 ml/½ pint Cheese Sauce (see page 228)*
*175-225 g/6-8 oz lasagne*
*salt*
*25-50 g/1-2 oz Gruyère or Cheddar cheese, grated*

Prepare both the sauces. Cook the lasagne in boiling salted water until just tender. Some cooks recommend using the lasagne without pre-cooking but unless you have a brand of pasta for which this is recommended, I find the result less pleasing. Drain the lasagne after cooking; it is a good idea to drape the long ribbons of pasta over a saucepan for a short time so that all excess moisture evaporates. Put a layer of lasagne, then one of meat sauce, then a little cheese sauce in an ovenproof dish. Continue like this ending with a layer of cheese sauce and the grated cheese. Heat in a moderate oven (180°C/350°F or Gas Mark 4) for approximately 30 minutes.

VARIATIONS

Use 450 ml/¾ pint Cheese sauce for a more moist dish.

⊛ **Lasagne alla Napoletana:** Omit the sauce but use layers of cheese instead. The best combination is to use 100 g/4 oz cream cheese (preferably Italian Ricotta), 100 to 175 g/4 to 6 oz thinly sliced Mozzarella or Gruyère cheese and 50 g/2 oz grated Parmesan cheese. The dish should be topped with some of the Parmesan cheese before baking in the oven.

⊛ **Lasagne with Shellfish:** Make 450 ml/¾ pint White Sauce as page 226 (use a little fish stock as well as milk if possible). Add 175 g/6 oz flaked cooked crabmeat, 100 g/4 oz peeled prawns. Use instead of the Bolognese Sauce. Follow the method for Lasagne alla Napoletana, put layers of the fish sauce and mixed cheeses with the pasta.

Instead of fish use 225 g/8 oz diced cooked chicken and 50 g/2 oz sliced cooked mushrooms.

Lasagne verde (spinach flavoured lasagne) is excellent in any of the dishes on this page.

## Cannelloni alla Romana ⊛

*12-16 cannelloni tubes*
*salt and pepper*
FILLING:
*50 g/2 oz butter*
*1 medium onion, finely chopped*
*1 medium carrot, finely chopped*
*25 g/1 oz mushrooms finely chopped*
*225 g/8 oz tomatoes, skinned, seeded and chopped*
*225 g/8 oz lean beef, finely minced*
*50 g/2 oz Parma ham or bacon, finely minced*
*1 tablespoon flour*
*4 tablespoons white wine*
*2 tablespoons chopped parsley*
TOPPING:
*Bologneses Sauce (see page 103)*
*50 g/2 oz Parmesan cheese, grated*
*25 g/1 oz butter, melted*

Cook the cannelloni in boiling salted water until tender, then strain and cool. Heat the butter for the filling, cook the onion, carrot and mushrooms for several minutes; add the tomatoes and cook for another 2 minutes. Coat the beef and ham or bacon with the flour, add to the vegetable mixture, then blend in the wine. Stir over a low heat for 5 minutes; add the parsley and seasoning to taste. Carefully spoon the filling into the cannelloni tubes, place in an ovenproof dish.

Cover with the Bolognese Sauce, cheese and butter. Cook in the centre of a moderate oven (180°C/350°F or Gas Mark 4) for 30 to 35 minutes.

VARIATIONS

It is possible to buy cannelloni that does not need precooking. When using this type, increase the baking time by 10 minutes and make the sauce you use contain 25 per cent more liquid than usual as uncooked pasta absorbs more liquid.

Squares of home-made pasta or cooked pancakes could be used instead.

⊛ **Cannelloni Florentine:** Make 750 ml/1¼ pints Cheese Sauce (see page 228). Take out 300 ml/½ pint, blend with 300 ml/½ pint smooth cooked spinach purée, plus an extra 50 g/2 oz grated cheese. Insert into the cannelloni; this could be done by putting the mixture into a piping bag and using a plain 1.5 cm/¾ inch pipe or with a teaspoon. Put a little cheese sauce at the bottom of the dish, add the filled cannelloni; top with the remaining cheese and a layer of fine breadcrumbs. Bake as the recipe above.

## Home-made Pasta

*450 g/1 lb strong or plain flour*
*¼ teaspoon salt*
*4 egg yolks*
*little milk*

Sift together the flour and salt, work in the egg yolks and milk to bind. Knead until smooth; cover the bowl and allow to stand for at least 30 minutes. Knead again, roll out very thinly and cut into the desired shapes; allow to dry in the air for some time, then use.

You can make a firmer pasta with just 1 whole egg plus 2 teaspoons oil. Home-made pasta is better cooked steadily, rather than rapidly. It must be remembered that commercially made pasta comes from durum wheat, (a hard wheat that keeps its shape in cooking) whereas home-made pasta gives a softer egg noodle.

# Easy Ways to Serve Pasta

Pasta makes an excellent accompaniment to meat or fish as well as a light snack or hors d'oeuvre. One of the easiest ways of serving pasta is to toss it in plenty of melted butter, plus chopped parsley, or other fresh herbs, then top it with plenty of grated cheese.

The pasta can be served with an interesting sauce, Tomato Sauce is the most usual accompaniment and either of the two recipes on page 233 would be ideal

Cheese, Mushroom, Mustard, Prawn, Onion, Barbecue or Espagnole Sauce would make a pleasant change, see pages 228 to 231. The Mustard and Cheese Sauce blends well with cooked egg noodles, spaghetti or other cooked pasta.

## Mushroom Noodles ⊛

*225g/8oz egg noodles*
*salt and pepper*
SAUCE:
*25g/1oz butter*
*100g/4oz small mushrooms, thinly sliced*
*100g/4oz cream cheese*
*150ml/¼pint yogurt*
*few drops Tabasco sauce*

Cook the noodles in boiling salted water, strain and top with the sauce, made as follows

Heat the butter in a saucepan, fry the mushrooms gently until tender; transfer to a heatproof basin or top of a double saucepan. Stand over a pan of hot water, add the remaining ingredients and heat together. Stir well to blend and season to taste. Serve the noodles topped with the sauce.

VARIATION

**Fried Noodles:** Cook the thin Chinese-type noodles for 3 minutes only; drain and dry in the air, then fry in hot oil until crisp and brown. Serve with savoury dishes.

## Macaroni Cheese ⊛

*75g/3oz macaroni*
*salt*
*450ml/¾pint Cheese Sauce (see page 228)*
TOPPING:
*50g/2oz cheese, grated*
*25-50g/1-2oz soft breadcrumbs*
*25g/1oz butter, melted*

Cook the macaroni in boiling salted water until *al dente*. Modern short-type macaroni is cooked within about 7 minutes; strain and blend with the sauce. Put into a 1.2 litre/2 pint pie or ovenproof dish. Top with the grated cheese, breadcrumbs (the amount depends upon whether you like a rather thick crisp topping) and the melted butter. Cook in the centre of a moderate oven (180°C/350°F or Gas Mark 4) for 35 minutes.

## Gnocchi alla Romana ⊛

*600 ml/1 pint milk*
*salt and pepper*
*175 g/6 oz fine semolina*
*50 g/2 oz butter*
*75 g/3 oz Parmesan cheese, grated*
*1 egg yolk*
GARNISH:
*chopped parsley*

Bring the milk to the boil, add salt, pepper and the semolina. Stir briskly as you add the semolina to make sure the mixture is smooth. Stir and cook over a low heat for 5 to 6 minutes until the mixture thickens. Remove from the heat and add half the butter, 25 g/1 oz of the grated cheese and the egg yolk. Return to the heat, stir for 1 to 2 minutes then turn the mixture out on to a large lightly oiled plate. Press until only 5 mm/¼ inch in thickness, allow to cool, then cut into small rounds. Put these into a buttered ovenproof dish, top with the remaining cheese. Melt the rest of the butter, spoon over the cheese and cook just above the centre of a hot oven (220°C/425°F or Gas Mark 7) for 15 minutes. Garnish with parsley.

VARIATION
**Subrics de Semoule:** Cook the semolina in chicken stock instead of milk. Add salt, pepper, a little grated nutmeg, 2 egg yolks, 50 g/2 oz grated Parmesan cheese. 50 to 75 g/2 to 3 oz finely chopped cooked ham can also be added. Press out the semolina mixture as above. When cold, cut into small rounds or form into small balls. Roll in dry semolina. Fry in a mixture of 2 tablespoons oil and 50 g/2 oz butter until golden brown. Serve with grated cheese.

## Potato Gnocchi

*450 g/1 lb old potatoes, cooked*
*salt and pepper*
*175 g/6 oz plain flour*
*1 egg yolk*
*15 g/½ oz butter, melted*

Sieve the potatoes, mix with the other ingredients. Form into small balls; cook steadily in boiling salted water for 10 minutes. Drain and serve with grated cheese and Tomato Sauce (see page 233).

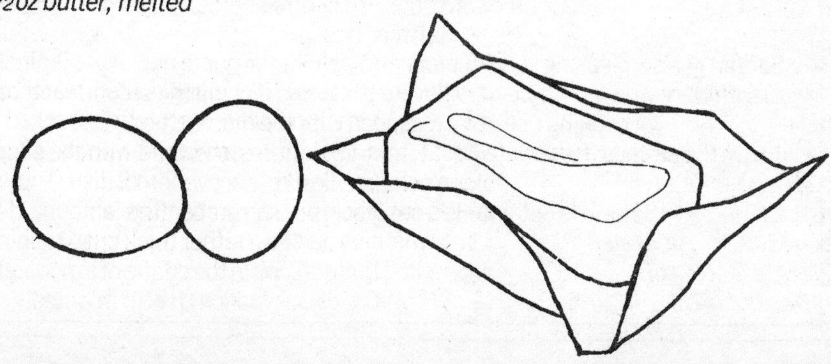

# Cooking Rice

In order to achieve the best results choose rice correctly. For savoury dishes you need long-grain rice, for puddings short (or round) rice and for risottos a medium grain rice, which gives the correct kind of sticky consistency. Medium grain rice is not easy to obtain so you may need to substitute the long grain type.

There are many ways in which rice can be cooked. One of the most popular methods is to put the rice into a large amount of boiling salted water and boil it until just tender. Rice, like pasta, should not be over-cooked, it should have a nutty texture. If using this method rinse the rice after cooking. Strain the cooked rice through a fine sieve, then pour boiling water over the grains; shake dry and serve. If time permits, you can rinse in cold water, then put the rice on a flat dish and dry and reheat it in a very cool oven.

The second method is accurate and easy. You will need to rinse the rice. To obtain the correct proportion of liquid to rice, you can measure or weigh the rice and proceed as follows:

To each 25 g/1 oz ordinary long grain rice you need 60 ml/2 fl oz cold water and a little salt to taste, or use a measure – 1 cup of rice and 2 cups of water. Put the rice and water and salt into a pan. Bring the liquid to the boil, stir with a fork, cover the pan, lower the heat and simmer for 15 minutes, by which time the liquid should have been absorbed and the rice grains tender. Fluff up with a fork.

If using par-boiled rice, allow 75 ml/2½ fl oz water to each 25 g/1 oz rice or 1 cup rice and 2½ cups of water, simmer for 20 minutes.

Brown rice is becoming increasingly popular. Use 120 ml/4 fl oz water to each 25 g/1 oz brown rice or 1 cup rice and 4 cups of water, cook for 35 minutes, or as packet instructions.

If intending to keep rice hot after cooking, add 1 tablespoon of olive or other good quality oil to the water in which the rice is cooked. Keep cooked rice covered well to prevent it becoming dry.

Cooked rice freezes well for several months. In order to separate the grains, freeze lightly, fork the rice, then continue freezing.

To flavour rice: The liquid used in cooking long-grain rice can be stock or water flavoured with chopped or dried herbs.

**Saffron Rice**

Saffron gives a pleasing yellow colour and a slight flavour to rice. A good pinch of saffron powder is sufficient to flavour the liquid if using the second method of cooking rice or ½ teaspoon with the first method.

Leave the strands in the water for at least 15 minutes, then strain and use the golden coloured liquid.

Saffron is obtainable from grocers or some chemists.

## Risotto with Scampi ⊛

*2 tablespoons oil*
*1 small onion, chopped*
*2 cloves garlic, crushed*
*225 g/8 oz large cooked prawns or scampi, peeled*
*150 ml/¼ pint white wine*
*salt and pepper*
RISOTTO:
*50 g/2 oz butter*
*225 g/8 oz medium grain rice*
*600 ml/1 pint fish or chicken stock*
GARNISH:
*few unpeeled prawns*
*chopped fennel leaves or chopped parsley*
*grated Parmesan cheese*

Heat the oil in a pan, fry the onion and garlic for several minutes, add the prawns or scampi and white wine. Simmer for a few minutes only, then add salt and pepper to taste. Heat the butter in a pan, add the rice and stir until it has absorbed the butter. Add the stock together with salt and pepper to taste. Cook for approximately 15 minutes, or until the rice is nearly tender. Blend in three-quarters of the scampi mixture and heat for a further few minutes. Garnish with the unpeeled prawns, the remaining scampi mixture, fennel or parsley. Top with grated Parmesan cheese and serve extra grated cheese.

VARIATION

⊛ **Risotto with Chicken and Peas:** Heat 50 g/2 oz butter and 2 tablespoons oil in a pan and fry 2 chopped onions and 1 chopped clove garlic with 225 g/8 oz uncooked chopped chicken until just golden. Add 225 g/8 oz medium or long-grain rice, blend with the onion and chicken mixture, then pour in 600 ml/1 pint chicken stock, with salt and pepper to taste. Cook for approximately 10 minutes. Add 100 g/4 oz frozen peas and continue cooking for a further 5 to 10 minutes. Stir in 25 g/1 oz butter before serving. Top with grated Parmesan cheese and chopped parsley.

## Risotto alla Finanziera ⊛

*75 g/3 oz butter*
*175 g/6 oz calves' liver, diced*
*2 medium onions, chopped*
*1 red pepper, deseeded and chopped*
*225 g/8 oz medium grain rice*
*900 ml/1½ pints chicken stock*
*salt and pepper*
TO SERVE:
*grated cheese*

Heat the butter, toss the liver in this for 1 minute only; remove from the pan. Add the onions and red pepper and fry gently for 3 minutes. Add the rice and turn in the butter mixture until coated. Pour in the chicken stock, season to taste and cook steadily for 15 minutes. Return the liver to the pan, stir to blend and cook for a further 5 to 10 minutes or until the liver is tender and the liquid has been absorbed. Serve with grated cheese.

There are other risottos on page 175; extra vegetables can be added to any risotto if desired.

## Rice Suppli

*600 ml/1 pint chicken stock*
*salt and pepper*
*1 small onion, finely chopped*
*100 g/4 oz short-grain rice*
FILLING:
*75 g/3 oz Cheddar cheese, grated*
*75 g/3 oz cooked ham, finely chopped or minced*
*1 tablespoon chopped parsley*
*1 egg yolk*
COATING AND FRYING:
*25 g/1 oz flour*
*1 egg*
*50 g/2 oz crisp breadcrumbs*
*oil*
GARNISH:
*watercress*
*sliced tomatoes*

Bring the chicken stock to the boil with the salt, pepper and onion. Add the rice and stir with a fork. Cover the pan and simmer for 13 to 15 minutes or until a very thick mixture. Stir several times to prevent the rice burning or cook in a double saucepan for a little longer.

Mix together the cheese, ham, parsley and egg yolk.

Allow the rice to cool until it can be handled. Divide into about 15 to 18 small portions, flatten and top with a little filling then form the rice into balls to enclose the filling. Blend the flour and seasoning, coat the rice balls in the seasoned flour, beaten egg and crisp breadcrumbs. Heat the oil to 175°C/345°F (explanation of testing oil, see page 290). Deep fry the rice balls for 4 to 5 minutes. Drain on absorbent paper and serve at once. Garnish with watercress and tomato slices.

VARIATIONS
Use minced liver and bacon for the filling or other savoury ingredients.
Blend 25 g/1 oz finely grated Parmesan cheese with the cooked rice.
Bake the balls instead of frying them. Oil and preheat a flat baking tray for 5 minutes. Place the Suppli on to the hot tray and bake towards the top of a hot oven (220°C/425°F or Gas Mark 7) for 10 to 12 minutes.

## Fried Rice

*225 g/8 oz long-grain rice*
*salt*
*2 tablespoons oil*

Cook the rice by one of the methods given on page 300; take particular care that the rice is not over-cooked. Strain and allow to dry. It is a good idea if the rice is cooked at least 12 hours before frying.

Heat the oil in a pan, add the rice and turn in the oil, then fry steadily until golden coloured.

VARIATION
**Chinese Fried Rice:** Toss the rice in the oil, as method above, then add 3 to 4 tablespoons coarsely chopped spring onions, continue frying for 2 to 3 minutes. Add 2 eggs, beaten with a few drops of soy sauce and seasoning; stir over a low heat until the egg mixture coats the rice. Serve at once.

## Paella ⊛

*3 tablespoons oil*
*1 x 1 kg/2 lb chicken, cut into 4 joints*
*1 onion, chopped*
*1 clove garlic, chopped*
*750-900 ml/1 ¼-1 ½ pints chicken stock*
*225 g/8 oz long-grain rice*
*pinch saffron powder*
*2 medium tomatoes, skinned and chopped*
*1 red pepper, cored, deseeded and neatly diced*
*salt and pepper*
*12 large peeled prawns*
*12-18 prepared mussels, (see page 92, leave on half the shells)*
*100 g/4 oz frozen peas*
GARNISH:
*chopped parsley*

Heat the oil in a very large frying pan (the word paella means cooked and served in a pan). Fry the chicken joints until golden then remove from the pan. Add the onion and garlic and fry for 3 to 4 minutes only. Pour in half the chicken stock and stir well. Return the chicken joints to the pan; simmer for 10 to 15 minutes over a very low heat. Do not cover the pan. Add the rice, turn in the mixture to separate the grains. Blend the saffron powder with about 300 ml/½ pint of the remaining stock, pour over the ingredients in the pan. Add the tomatoes, red pepper, salt and pepper to taste. Simmer gently for about 10 minutes, or until the rice is beginning to become tender. Check on the liquid; if necessary add the rest of the stock. Put in the prawns, mussels and peas and continue to cook for the final 5 to 6 minutes. At the end of the time, the rice and all the other ingredients should be tender; the mixture should be pleasantly moist with no excess liquid in the pan. Top with parsley and serve.

VARIATION
Use fresh peas instead of frozen and add with the red pepper and tomatoes.

## Kedgeree ⊛

*175 g/6 oz medium or long-grain rice*
*salt and pepper*
*50 g/2 oz butter*
*2-3 tablespoons double cream*
*255 g/8 oz cooked smoked haddock, flaked*
*2 eggs, hard-boiled*

Cook the rice by one of the methods on page 300; do not over-salt the water. Drain, but do not rinse in water, as a slightly sticky texture is good for this dish. Heat the butter and cream and add the rice and fish. Heat gently. Chop the whites and yolks of the eggs separately, add the whites to the fish mixture, season to taste. Spoon into a neat shape on a hot dish and top with the chopped hard-boiled egg yolks.

VARIATIONS
To give more flavour, add fried onion rings together with chopped parsley and lemon juice.

The proportions of rice and fish can be altered.

Although haddock is the best fish to choose, other varieties can be substituted.

## Spanish Rice Salad

*100 g/4 oz long-grain rice*
*salt and pepper*
*2 cloves garlic, crushed*
*6 tablespoons mayonnaise*
*1 Spanish onion, finely diced*
*1 red pepper, cored, deseeded and neatly diced*
*1 green pepper, cored, deseeded and neatly diced*
*12 stuffed olives, sliced*
*3 tomatoes, skinned and sliced*
*1 lettuce, shredded*

Cook the rice in salted water by one of the methods described on page 300, rinse in boiling water, then drain well. Blend the hot rice with the garlic, mayonnaise and onion; allow to cool then add the peppers, olives and tomatoes, season well. Put on to a bed of lettuce.

VARIATIONS

**Curried Rice Salad:** Cook the rice, as in the recipe above, rinse and drain well. Omit the garlic, but blend the mayonnaise with 1 to 2 teaspoons curry paste, add to the hot rice, together with 2 tablespoons sultanas, 1 tablespoon desiccated coconut. Allow to cool, then add 2 tablespoons chopped spring onions, 1 deseeded and diced green pepper and 225 g/8 oz flaked cooked fish or cooked diced chicken breast or diced lean lamb or beef.

**Rice and Vegetable Salad:** Cook the rice, as in the above recipe, rinse and drain well. Cook about 350 g/12 oz diced mixed root vegetables, strain; blend with the warm rice, chopped parsley and chives to taste and mayonnaise to bind. Serve cold.

## Cheese and Pasta Salad

*100 g/4 oz pasta shells or short-cut macaroni*
*salt*
*1 teaspoon French mustard*
*5 tablespoons mayonnaise*
*100 g/4 oz Cheddar cheese, diced*
*100 g/4 oz Stilton cheese, diced*
*2 tablespoons chopped spring onions or chives*
*3 tablespoons chopped watercress leaves*
*½ tablespoon lemon juice*
*1 or 2 dessert apples, peeled and diced*
GARNISH:
*1 bunch watercress*

Cook the pasta in salted water as page 295; rinse in boiling water, then drain well. Blend together the mustard, mayonnaise and hot pasta, allow to cool, then mix with the rest of the ingredients. Spoon on to a dish and garnish with sprigs of watercress.

VARIATION

**Seafood Salad:** This can be made with cooked rice or pasta. Use the amount given in either recipe on this page, remember cooked rice or pasta is 2½ to 3 times as heavy as when uncooked. Rinse and drain, then blend with 6 tablespoons mayonnaise, then with approximately 100 g/4 oz peeled prawns, 100 g/4 oz mussels prepared as page 92, 100 g/4 oz flaked cooked white fish; season well. Allow to cool, then add 100 g/4 oz peeled diced cucumber, 2 skinned diced tomatoes and lemon juice to taste.

# Puddings and Desserts

This section includes some classic recipes, but also a variety of original puddings and desserts, for I find that even the most conservative of my friends appreciate dishes that are a little out of the ordinary when it comes to the sweet course.

In most cases the recipes are based upon a basic principle of cookery, so I have grouped them together and given brief hints on the correct method of mixing and cooking to ensure success with every recipe.

I am not a little amused when visitors from abroad obviously have the idea that we serve only 'stodgy' steamed puddings in this country. That, of course, is far from the true facts; we have a wealth of traditional puddings that are not steamed. In any case, there is nothing 'stodgy' about a feather-light sponge pudding, topped with golden syrup or home-made jam, or a fruit pudding made with wafer-thin suet crust pastry and filled with seasonal fruit (see page 306). A Christmas Pudding is certainly a rich pudding, but should never be over-heavy. This recipe is a well-loved one, for I had the pleasure of demonstrating it for two consecutive years on BBC television and I think it is probably one of the best known of all recipes for this important traditional dish. In my travels in various countries I meet people who say 'I always make *your* Christmas Pudding'.

I am a great lover of fruit, as you will appreciate when you see how many of the recipes in this section are based upon fruit. Try to avoid over-cooking it, so you retain all the good flavour and texture of freshly picked fruit.

Puddings and desserts need not be elaborate to be good, some of the simplest recipes are the best. As the contents vary appreciably I have given advice on freezing in sub-headings. Most desserts freeze well, which is a great asset to busy cooks, for you can prepare a batch beforehand and freeze the surplus, ready to serve when you are extra rushed.

You will notice in some cases where cream is given among the ingredients I give 'whipping' cream as my first choice. This is not only because it is more economical than double cream, but because I find I get a better texture to the dessert with the slightly less rich cream.

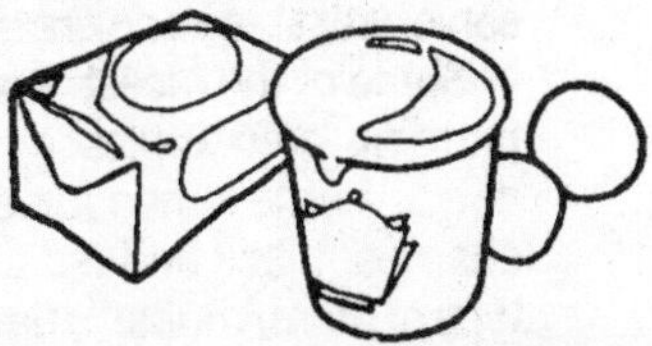

# Steamed Puddings

The recipes that require steaming vary a great deal. In those recipes where self-raising flour is used, it is important to allow the pudding to cook fairly rapidly for the first half of the cooking period so the mixture rises and becomes light. After this time the heat can be slightly reduced, although the water must boil at all times. In the case of the Christmas Pudding, on page 308 the water can boil steadily, rather than rapidly. If using a proper steamer make quite sure there is adequate water in the saucepan under the steamer. If you do not have a steamer then put the basin on an up-turned heat-resisting saucer or patty tin, so it is raised above the base of the pan and make sure the level of the water is not so high that it boils into the pudding. Check the water levels periodically and always fill up with boiling water.

The puddings based upon egg custards, which begin on page 311 need to be cooked over, or in, hot but not boiling, water.

If you make a thick wide and long band of foil and put this under the container it is easy to remove the basin or other heatproof dish from the steamer or saucepan. The foil band can be dried and used on several occasions.

**Using plain flour**

If you prefer to use plain flour in recipes where self-raising flour is given, add 2 teaspoons baking powder to each 225 g/8 oz flour; remember these should be absolutely level teaspoons. Sift with the flour.

Steamed puddings can be prepared then frozen or cooked and frozen. Use within 3 months. For advice on freezing egg custards, see page 332.

## Fruit Pudding ⊛

SUET CRUST PASTRY:
*225 g/8 oz flour, preferably self-raising*
*pinch salt*
*110 g/4 oz shredded suet*
*water to mix*
FILLING:
*450 g/1 lb fruit (weight when prepared), sliced or cut into convenient-sized pieces*
*50-75 g/2-3 oz sugar*
*liquid (see method)*

Before making the pastry read the comments on page 117 about the choice of flour when making suet puddings. Roll out the pastry and use approximately three-quarters to line a 1.2 litre/2 pint basin.

Put in the fruit, add the sugar plus any liquid required. This is not necessary if you have soft berry fruit, but you require 2 to 3 tablespoons with hard fruit such as sliced cooking apples. Cover the fruit with the remaining pastry, greased greaseproof paper and foil. Steam over boiling water for 2½ hours. Turn out and serve with sugar and cream.

Some of the nicest combinations of flavours for this pudding are: apples and blackberries; apples with dates, a little lemon juice with the water; apricots and cherries; black and red currants with raspberries; any type of plum; rhubarb, flavoured with chopped candied orange peel and orange juice.

## Toffee Apple Pudding ⊛

*Suet Crust Pastry made with 225g/8oz flour etc. (see page 306)*

COATING:

*25g/1 oz butter, softened*

*50g/2oz demerara sugar*

FILLING:

*450g/1 lb cooking apples (weight when peeled), thinly sliced*

*2 tablespoons golden syrup*

*2 tablespoons sultanas*

*1 tablespoon lemon juice*

*1 tablespoon water*

Make the pastry and roll it out thinly. Before filling the 1.2 litre/2 pint basin, spread the bottom and sides of this with the butter, then coat with the sugar. Line the basin with approximately three-quarters of the dough and put in the filling ingredients mixed together. Cover with the rest of the pastry dough, greased greaseproof paper and foil. Steam over boiling water for 2½ hours, then turn out.

The suet crust will be covered with a golden toffee-like coating. Serve with cream.

## Snowdon Pudding ⊛

*75g/3oz soft breadcrumbs*

*25g/1 oz flour*

*50g/2oz suet, finely chopped or shredded*

*75g/3oz light brown or caster sugar*

*grated rind of 1 lemon*
*1 orange*

*2 tablespoons lemon or orange marmalade*

*1 egg*

*100g/4oz seedless raisins*

*50g/2oz glacé cherries, halved*

*15g/½oz butter*

Mix together the breadcrumbs, flour, suet, sugar, grated fruit rind, marmalade, egg, half the raisins and half the cherries. Grease a 1 litre/1¾ pint basin with the butter. Press the remaining raisins and cherries on the base of this. Spoon the breadcrumb mixture into the basin and cover well with greased greaseproof paper and foil. Steam for 1½ to 2 hours over steadily, not rapidly, boiling water. Serve with hot custard or Marmalade Sauce (see page 346).

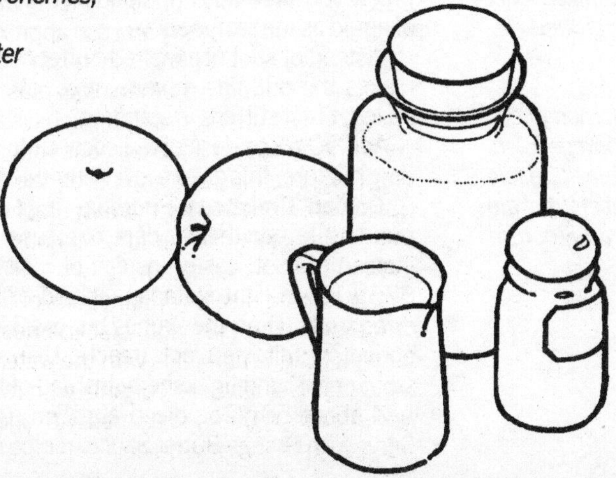

## Christmas Pudding ⊛

*225g/8oz fine soft breadcrumbs*
*110g/4oz flour, preferably plain*
*225g/8oz shredded suet, or see under variations*
*225g/8oz moist brown sugar*
*450g/1 lb seedless or stoned and chopped raisins*
*225g/8oz sultanas*
*225g/8oz currants*
*110g/4oz dried apricots*, finely chopped*
*50g/2oz dried prunes*, stoned and finely chopped*
*225g/8oz mixed candied peel, chopped*
*110g/4oz glacé cherries*, chopped*
*110g/4oz cooking apple, (weight when peeled), grated*
*110g/4oz carrots (weight when peeled), grated*
*110g/4oz blanched almonds, chopped*
*1 teaspoon grated lemon rind**
*1 teaspoon grated orange rind**
*½-1 teaspoon ground nutmeg*
*1-2 teaspoons mixed spice*
*½-1 teaspoon ground cinnamon*
*4 large eggs*
*1 tablespoon lemon juice**
*1 tablespoon orange juice**
*1 tablespoon black treacle*
*150ml/¼ pint stout or ale*
*1 wineglass brandy or rum*

I make a fairly large amount of the Christmas Pudding mixture for I like to offer it to visitors from abroad who have heard of, but never tasted, our traditional pudding. It is important to allow this recipe to mature for at least six weeks.

To give virtually the same amount I have 'rounded off' metric amounts to correspond with the Imperial.

Mix all the ingredients together. I like to leave the uncooked pudding mixture standing overnight, so that the flavours blend better. It also allows all members of the family to stir the mixture and wish.

Grease four 1.5 litre/2½ pint or two 2.5 litre/4½ pint basins; put in the mixture. Cover well with greased greaseproof paper and foil. A Christmas pudding does not rise in the same way as a light sponge pudding, but it swells in cooking, so never fill the basins too full. If you press the mixture down firmly you can cut neater slices of the cooked pudding, but my recipe gives a crumbly pudding rather than a solid one.

Steam each pudding for 6 to 8 hours depending upon the size; take off the damp covers at once; cool the puddings, then put on dry covers. Store in a cool dry place. On Christmas morning steam for another 2 to 3 hours. Serve with Brandy Butter, recipe on the next page.

VARIATIONS

The pudding above has a lovely subtle flavour, but if you want a simpler recipe just omit those ingredients marked with an asterisk. Because you will then omit a little liquid, add another 2 tablespoons ale or stout unless you like a very firm pudding then use the amount of liquid as the recipe above.

Instead of suet use melted butter or margarine; this makes the pudding mixture appear very liquid when mixed, but it stiffens in standing.

Add 50g/2oz desiccated coconut to the basic pudding mixture, this gives a lovely 'nutty' taste.

⊛ **Golden Christmas Pudding:** If you like a pretty pudding rather than a dark one, use melted butter instead of suet, caster instead of moist brown sugar, 675g/1½lb light sultanas instead of the mixture of dried fruits. Omit the prunes but use 175g/6oz diced apricots; omit the black treacle. Use milk instead of stout or ale, and light sherry instead of brandy or rum. Add about 50g/2oz diced angelica. Cook as above. Serve with Orange Butter Sauce, recipe next page.

## Brandy Butter

*100g/4oz butter, preferably unsalted*
*175g/6oz icing sugar, sieved*
*3-4 tablespoons brandy*
DECORATION:
*few glacé or Maraschino cherries*
*angelica and/or blanched almonds*

Cream the butter very well until soft, then add the sugar and beat again until the mixture is very white. Gradually beat in the brandy. Either spoon or pipe into an attractive shape in the serving dish. Decorate with small pieces of the cherries, and angelica and/or nuts. Make this a day or so before it is being served so it becomes very hard; it is better not to freeze it, for freezing destroys some of the brandy flavour.

This is the perfect accompaniment to Christmas Pudding and is also excellent with mince pies. It is often known as Hard Sauce.

VARIATIONS

Add a very little grated orange rind to the creamed mixture.

**Rum Butter:** Substitute demerara sugar for icing sugar and rum for brandy. This is the other traditional accompaniment to Christmas Pudding.

**Orange Butter Sauce:** Pare several strips of the very top rind from 1 large or 2 small oranges. Make quite certain you have just the zest and there is no white pith. Chop this zest very finely. Cream the butter and icing sugar as Brandy Butter, above, and add the orange rind. Gradually beat in 2 tablespoons orange juice or curaçao. Chill as Brandy Butter.

## Collegiate Pudding ⊛

*100g/4oz soft breadcrumbs*
*50g/2oz sultanas*
*50g/2oz currants*
*50g/2oz caster sugar*
*½ teaspoon baking powder*
*75g/3oz suet, finely chopped or shredded*
*pinch grated nutmeg*
*pinch ground cloves*
*pinch ground cinnamon*
*2 eggs*

Mix together all the dry ingredients. Beat the eggs and blend with the other ingredients. Spoon into a well-greased 1 litre/1¾ pint basin. Cover and steam for 1¼ to 1½ hours. In this pudding, which does not contain flour, the water should boil steadily, rather than rapidly. Serve with one of the sauces on page 346.

VARIATIONS

For a more substantial pudding add 50g/2oz flour with 3 tablespoons milk or orange juice.

⊛ **Orange Sultana Pudding:** Follow the above recipe or the variation above. Omit the currants and spices, add 100 g/4 oz sultanas together with 1 tablespoon finely grated orange rind and 3 tablespoons orange marmalade.

## Golden Cap Pudding ⊛

SPONGE:
*110 g/4 oz butter or margarine*
*110 g/4 oz caster sugar*
*2 large eggs*
*110 g/4 oz self-raising flour*
TOPPING:
*3 tablespoons golden syrup*

Cream together the butter or margarine, and the sugar until soft and light. Gradually beat in the eggs. Sift the flour and fold into the creamed mixture. Grease a 900 ml to 1.2 litre/1½ to 2 pint basin, put the syrup at the bottom, cover with the light sponge, greased greaseproof paper and foil. Steam for 1¼ to 1½ hours over boiling water, turn out and serve with more heated syrup or a Syrup and Lemon Sauce (see page 346).

VARIATIONS

⊛ **Economical Sponge Pudding:** The above gives a very light sponge, but as the mixture is eaten when freshly cooked you can economize quite appreciably, e.g. use the same weight of fat and sugar and the same number of eggs with 157 g/6 oz self-raising flour plus 3 tablespoons milk (or other liquid), see below.

You can use half the amount of fat and sugar to flour, i.e. in the basic recipe just 50 g/2 oz fat and 50 g/2 oz sugar with the 2 eggs and amount of flour given, in which case you need to add 2 tablespoons liquid.

⊛ **Blackcap Pudding:** Use blackcurrant jam instead of golden syrup and serve the pudding with Jam Sauce. (see page 346).

Various jams give their name to the pudding, i.e. Redcap Pudding if red jam is used.

⊛ **Fruit Pudding:** Add up to 175 g/6 oz dried fruit to the Economical Sponge, above, see the comments about heavy ingredients falling in a light mixture under Ginger Pudding below. You can add glacé cherries instead of dried fruit.

⊛ **Ginger Pudding:** Add 1 to 2 teaspoons ground ginger to the flour and add 50 g/2 oz finely diced crystallized ginger to the other ingredients. It is advisable to use the more economical recipe as the basic sponge is so light the diced ginger tends to fall to the bottom of the mixture; this does not affect the flavour in any way.

⊛ **Lemon Sponge Pudding:** Cream the finely grated rind of 1 or 2 lemons with the fat and sugar. Use only small eggs in the basic sponge and add 2 tablespoons lemon juice. Serve with Lemon Sauce, or you can put lemon marmalade or lemon curd at the bottom of the basin. Orange rind and juice can be used instead of lemon rind and juice.

⊛ **Chocolate Sponge Pudding:** Omit 15 g/½ oz flour and use the same amount of cocoa powder or omit 25 g/1 oz flour and use the same amount of chocolate powder. Serve with Chocolate Sauce (see page 346).

## Apricot Pudding

*100g/4oz dried apricots, diced*
*150ml/¼ pint water*
*450ml/¾ pint milk*
*1 medium macaroon biscuit, crumbled*
*50g/2oz fine cake crumbs*
*4 egg yolks or 2 egg yolks and 2 eggs*
*50g/2oz caster sugar*

Put the diced apricots into a basin. Heat the water, pour over the fruit and allow to stand for 3 to 4 hours. Strain; if any liquid remains this can be incorporated into the sauce. Heat most of the milk, add the macaroon, cake crumbs and apricots. Whisk the egg yolks, or yolks and whole eggs, with the sugar, add the remainder of the milk. Stir or strain into the apricot mixture, then mix thoroughly. Cook as for Cabinet Pudding, below. Turn out and serve hot with Lemon or Apricot Jam Sauce (see recipes on page 346).

VARIATION

Put a layer of well-soaked halved dried apricots at the bottom of the basin together with blanched almonds.

## Cabinet Pudding

*100g/4oz bread (weight without crusts), neatly diced*
*600ml/1 pint milk*
*few drops vanilla essence*
*4 eggs yolks or 2 egg yolks and 2 eggs*
*50g/2oz caster sugar*
*15g/½oz butter*
*100g/4oz mixed dried fruit*

Put the bread into a basin. Warm most of the milk with the vanilla and pour over the bread; leave for 15 minutes. Whisk the egg yolks or yolks and whole eggs, with the sugar; add the remainder of the milk. Stir or strain into the bread mixture, then mix thoroughly.

Spread the butter over the base and sides of a 1.2 litre/2 pint basin. Press the dried fruit over the butter. Spoon the pudding mixture into the basin, taking care not to dislodge the fruit. Cover the basin with greased greaseproof paper and foil and steam over simmering, but not boiling, water for 1½ to 1¾ hours or until firm to the touch. Turn out and serve hot with cream.

## Mocha Pudding

*25g/1oz sweetened chocolate powder*
*200ml/⅓ pint strong coffee*
*200ml/⅓ pint milk*
*50g/2oz fine cake crumbs*
*4 egg yolks or 2 eggs and 2 egg yolks*
*50g/2oz caster sugar*

Heat the chocolate powder with the coffee and most of the milk. Stir the cake crumbs into the hot mixture in the saucepan and leave for 5 minutes. Whisk the egg yolks, or yolks and whole eggs, with the sugar; add the remainder of the milk. Stir or strain into the coffee mixture, then mix thoroughly. Grease a 1.2 litre/2 pint basin, pour in the mixture and cook as for Cabinet Pudding above. Turn and serve hot with a Chocolate or Coffee sauce (see recipes on page 346).

VARIATION

Use 15g/½oz cocoa powder instead of chocolate powder.

## Bread and Butter Pudding

*2 large slices bread and butter*
*50-75 g/2-3 oz sultanas or other dried fruit*
*25 g/1 oz candied peel, chopped (optional)*
*3 large eggs or 4 egg yolks*
*50 g/2 oz sugar*
*600 ml/1 pint milk*
*little grated nutmeg (optional)*

Although it is a baked, rather than a steamed pudding, I have grouped Bread and Butter Pudding with the more glamorous dish below. A really good Bread and Butter Pudding with a thick layer of egg custard happens to be one of my favourite puddings; it is equally good hot or cold. You can, of course, make less custard to give a more solid and economical pudding.

Cut the bread and butter into triangles. You can remove the crusts, but I like the crispness these give to the pudding. Arrange in a 1.2 litre/2 pint pie dish. Add the fruit and peel, if using this. Beat the eggs or egg yolks with the sugar; warm the milk and pour over the beaten eggs, mix well, then pour over the bread and butter mixture. Leave for at least 15 minutes before cooking if possible. Top with the grated nutmeg. Cook in the centre of a cool oven (150°C/300°F or Gas Mark 2) for 1¼ hours.

VARIATION

If you like a crisp topping, add a little extra sugar to the pudding after about 45 minutes' cooking.

## Viennoise Pudding ❋

CARAMEL:
*75 g/3 oz granulated or caster sugar*
*3 tablespoons water*

PUDDING:
*300 ml/½ pint milk*
*300 ml/½ pint single cream*
*100 g/4 oz bread (weight without crusts), diced*
*50 g/2 oz glacé cherries, quartered*
*25 g/1 oz candied peel, chopped*
*50 g/2 oz blanched almonds or walnuts, chopped*
*4 egg yolks or 2 egg yolks and 2 whole eggs*
*40 g/1½ oz caster sugar*
*2 tablespoons sherry*

To make the caramel: put the sugar and water into a strong saucepan. Stir over a moderate heat until the sugar has dissolved, then boil steadily without stirring until a dark golden brown caramel. Remove from the heat, so that the sugar mixture does not become too brown and taste burned. Allow to cool, then add the milk. Stir over a low heat, until the milk absorbs the caramel. Do not allow the mixture to boil as it will curdle. Add the cream to the hot mixture, then allow to stand for 30 minutes. Add the cherries, peel and nuts. Whisk the egg yolks or yolks and whole eggs with the sugar and sherry. Stir or strain into the bread mixture, then mix thoroughly. Grease a 1.2 litre/2 pint basin or a soufflé dish, pour in the mixture and cover. Steam over simmering, but not boiling, water for approximately 2½ hours or bake in a bain marie in a cool oven (150°C/300°F or Gas Mark 2). Turn out and serve hot with cream or ice cream.

# Making Fritters

Fruit fritters make a delicious dessert; the fruit can be varied throughout the year, for you can substitute canned fruit, when fresh fruit is not available. Always drain canned fruit well and dry it on absorbent paper before coating. It is advisable to coat all fruit with a light dusting of flour before dipping it into the batter.

It is important to fry fruit fritters correctly, so they are beautifully crisp on the outside. While shallow oil or fat can be used, it is better to select deep oil or fat. The ideal temperature is between 170 and 175°C/340 to 350°F. Use the higher setting for canned fruit fritters or those in which the fruit cooks quickly, but the lower setting when cooking apple or pear fritters. Advice on testing oil or fat is given on page 290.

Always drain the fried fritters on absorbent paper before dusting them with sugar.

Advice on making pancakes is on page 289.

## Banana Fritters

*4 large or 8 small bananas*
*little flour*
FRITTER BATTER:
*100 g/4 oz flour*
*pinch salt*
*1 egg*
*150 ml/¼ pint milk*
*4 tablespoons water*
*1 tablespoon oil or melted butter*
FOR FRYING:
*deep or shallow oil or fat*

Mix together all the ingredients for the batter and pour into a shallow dish. Heat the oil or fat to 175°C/345°F if using a deep fryer, or test as instructions given on this page. Peel the bananas and dust with a very little flour – this makes sure the batter adheres to the mixture. Large bananas can be halved to make them easier to serve. Coat in the batter and fry for about 4 minutes until crisp and golden brown. If using shallow fat turn after browning first side. Drain on absorbent paper. Banana Fritters can be dusted with sugar or served with a hot Lemon or Apricot Jam Sauce (see page 346).

VARIATIONS

**Dutch Fritter Batter:** Omit the egg, milk and water in the batter above and use 200 ml/⅓ pint (12 tablespoons) beer instead.

**Apple Fritters:** Peel and core the cooking apples then cut into slices just under 1 cm/½ inch in thickness. If too thick it is difficult to cook the fruit before the batter over-browns. You can add 1 teaspoon mixed spice to the batter. Use a slightly lower temperature or reduce the heat as soon as the batter starts to brown. Cook for about 6 minutes.

**Pineapple Fritters:** Drain canned pineapple rings, dry well with absorbent paper, then coat with flour and batter. Fry as Apple Fritters.

## Poor Knight's Fritters

*8 slices bread, crusts removed*
*little butter*
*little jam*
*1 egg*
*150 ml/¼ pint milk*
*few drops vanilla essence*
*50 g/2 oz caster sugar*
FRYING:
*50 g/2 oz butter*

Make sandwiches of the bread, butter and jam and cut into neat, even-sized fingers. Beat the egg with the milk, vanilla and 25 g/1 oz of the sugar. Dip the sandwiches into the egg mixture for a few seconds, until moistened, but not over-moist. Heat the butter in a frying pan and fry the sandwiches until crisp and golden brown on both sides. Top with the remaining sugar and serve.

VARIATIONS

**Butterscotch Fritters:** Make the sandwiches as above; apricot jam blends with the butterscotch coating. Dip into the egg mixture and fry. Top with a sauce made by heating together 40 g/1½ oz butter, 40 g/1½ oz brown sugar and 2 tablespoons golden syrup.

**Fruit Fritters:** Leftover slices of fruit cake or Christmas Pudding can be fried as above or use mincemeat as the filling in the sandwiches. Make a thicker batter of 1 egg, 3 tablespoons milk or sherry and 25 g/1 oz sugar. Fry in the hot butter. Serve topped with brown sugar.

## Strawberry Croûtes

*225 g/8 oz strawberries*
*little sugar*
*3 tablespoons redcurrant jelly*
*4 tablespoons water*
*40 g/1½ oz butter*
*4 slices bread, crusts removed*

Put the fruit on to a plate and sprinkle with a little sugar if you have a sweet tooth. Put the jelly and water into a pan, stirring until the jelly has dissolved. Keep slightly warm. Heat the butter in a frying pan. Fry the bread on both sides until crisp and golden. Sprinkle with sugar. Put on to plates. Top with the fruit and redcurrant sauce. Serve at once.

## Apple Curd Pancakes ⊛

FILLING:
*300 ml/½ pint thick apple purée*
*25 g/1 oz butter*
*grated rind and juice of 1 lemon*
*1 egg yolk*
*50 g/2 oz caster sugar*
*8 to 12 cooked pancakes, (see page 289 or below)*
TOPPING:
*2 tablespoons caster sugar*
*4 tablespoons lemon juice*

Put the apple purée, butter, lemon rind and juice into a strong saucepan. Heat gently, stirring from time to time until a thick mixture. Remove from the heat, beat in the egg yolk and sugar. Return to a low heat and keep warm, without boiling. Fill the hot cooked pancakes with the apple mixture; fold or roll and put on to a heated serving dish. Top with sugar and lemon juice.

## Crêpes Suzette ⊛

BATTER:
*100 g/4 oz plain flour*
*pinch salt*
*2 eggs*
*250 ml/scant ½ pint milk and water*
*½ tablespoon oil or melted butter*
FOR FRYING:
*oil, fat or butter*
FILLING:
*100 g/4 oz butter*
*75-100 g/3-4 oz caster or icing sugar*
*grated rind of 2 oranges or 3 tangerines*
*1 tablespoon Curaçao*
SAUCE:
*25 g/1 oz butter*
*50 g/2 oz caster sugar*
*150 ml/¼ pint orange or tangerine juice*
*2-3 tablespoons Curaçao*

Blend together the ingredients for the pancake batter; adding the oil or butter just before cooking. Heat enough oil, fat or butter in the pancake pan to give a shiny look; do not use too much. Pour in sufficient batter to give a paper-thin coating. Cook steadily for 2 minutes or until set, toss or turn and cook on the second side. Remove from the pan. Continue in this manner; if you have a good pan you should need little, if any oil, fat or butter after cooking the first one or two pancakes. This batter will make about 12 pancakes.

Cream the butter for the filling until soft and light, then gradually add the caster or sifted icing sugar and the fruit rind. Beat in the Curaçao. Spread the pancakes with this mixture and fold into four. Heat the butter and sugar in a large frying pan until a golden colour; do not allow to become too dark. Add the fruit juice and blend with the sugar mixture. Put in the pancakes and heat gently; do not allow the sauce to boil for this spoils the shape of the pancakes. Add the Curaçao, warm thoroughly and serve. The Curaçao should be warmed in a metal spoon and ignited before adding to the sauce.

## Ginger Nut Pancakes ⊛

BATTER:
*50g/2oz gingernut biscuits, crushed*
*50g/2oz flour, preferably plain*
*2 eggs*
*250ml/8fl oz (½ pint less 2 tablespoons) milk*
FOR FRYING AND TOPPING:
*oil or fat*
*caster sugar*
FILLING:
*300ml/½pint thick sweetened apple purée*
*50g/2oz finely chopped crystallized ginger*
*50g/2oz coarsely chopped walnuts*

Blend together the ingredients for the batter. Heat a very little oil or fat in a pan and cook the first pancake; continue like this until all the pancakes are cooked. Keep hot (as the information given on page 289).

Meanwhile heat the apple purée, add the ginger and nuts. Fill the pancakes, roll and put on to a heated dish. Top with the sugar.

## Orange Hazelnut Omelette

*6 eggs*
*pinch salt*
*3 teaspoons sugar*
*1 teaspoon grated orange rind*
*2 tablespoons single cream*
*50g/2oz butter*
FILLING:
*3-4 oranges*
*50g/2oz hazelnuts, finely chopped*

Beat the eggs with the salt, sugar, orange rind and cream. Prepare the filling before cooking the omelette. Cut the segments from the oranges, discard the pips, skin and any pith. Mix the orange with the nuts.

Heat the butter in a large omelette pan, pour in the eggs and cook as directed on page 272. When the eggs are set to personal taste, add the filling, fold the omelette and serve.

VARIATIONS
Make 3 or 4 individual omelettes.
Separate the egg yolks from the whites and cook as a Soufflé Omelette (see page 273).

# Baked Puddings

I have started this section with the kind of pancakes rarely seen nowadays, a pity, for these are so delicious and easy to make with modern heat-resisting saucers or patty tins. I follow that with a rather special rice pudding; there is another of my pet rice pudding recipes on page 340.

This section continues with hot soufflés; these make a truly impressive ending to a meal, then various kinds of pies, flans and cheesecakes.

## Saucer Pancakes

*50/2 oz butter*
*75 g/3 oz caster sugar*
*2 eggs*
*50 g/2 oz rice flour or plain flour*
*200 ml/7½ fl oz milk*
*1 teaspoon finely grated lemon rind*
*fruit purée or jam*

Cream the butter and 50 g/2 oz sugar until soft and light. Separate the eggs and beat the yolk into the creamed mixture. Add the flour, then gradually beat in the milk and lemon rind. Whisk the egg whites until stiff and fold into the batter just before cooking.

Grease and heat about 12 ovenproof saucers or patty tins in a preheated hot oven (230°C/450°F or Gas Mark 8). Spoon the fluffy batter into the saucers or tins and bake just above the centre of the oven for 10 to 12 minutes or until the pancakes are firm. Reduce the heat to moderately hot (200°C/400°F or Gas Mark 6) if the pancakes are getting too brown after 5 to 6 minutes. Put the remaining sugar on a plate. Turn the pancakes out on to the sugar, coat with this, then serve with the hot fruit purée or jam.

## Rice Pudding with Almonds

*40 g/1½ oz short-grain rice*
*450 ml/¾ pint milk*
*½ teaspoon vanilla essence*
*50 g/2 oz sugar*
*25 g/1 oz butter*
*3 eggs*
*3 tablespoons double cream*
*3 tablespoons blanched almonds, chopped and browned*

Cook the rice in the milk with the vanilla essence, sugar and butter until soft, creamy and firm. Use a good-sized saucepan or the top of a double saucepan for this purpose. Cool slightly.

Separate the yolks from the whites of the eggs. Blend the egg yolks with the cream, then stir into the rice pudding with the almonds. Whisk the egg whites until stiff, fold into the mixture. Spoon into an 18 cm/7 inch buttered soufflé dish. Bake in the centre of a moderate oven (160°C/325°F or Gas Mark 3) for approximately 35 minutes or until well risen and firm. Serve hot with fruit purée or Jam Sauce (see page 346).

## Pineapple Soufflé Pudding

*50 g/2 oz butter or margarine*
*50 g/2 oz caster sugar*
*2 large eggs*
*200 ml/⅓ pint pineapple juice*
*50 g/2 oz self-raising flour*

Cream together the butter or margarine and sugar. Separate the eggs and beat the yolks into the creamed mixture. Gradually beat in the pineapple juice. You may well find the mixture curdles slightly, but this does not matter in this particular recipe. Sift the flour; whisk the egg whites until very stiff. Fold the flour, then the egg whites into the pineapple mixture. Spoon into a 1 litre/1¾ pint pie dish; stand this in a bain-marié (dish of cold water). Bake in the centre of a slow to moderate oven (150-160°C/300-325°F or Gas Mark 2-3) for 45 minutes until just firm to the touch. Serve hot. This pudding separates into two layers. The top is like a soufflé and the bottom a sauce.

VARIATIONS

**Orange Soufflé Pudding:** Use fresh or canned orange juice instead of pineapple juice. Add 1 to 2 teaspoons of finely grated orange rind to the flour. Top with segments of orange just before serving.

**Lemon Soufflé Pudding:** Use 6 tablespoons lemon juice and 6 tablespoons water. Add 1 to 2 teaspoons finely grated lemon rind to the flour. Increase the sugar to 75 g/3 oz.

## Brandy Soufflé

*about 12 sponge finger biscuits*
*6 tablespoons brandy or curaçao*
*100 g/4 oz glacé cherries, chopped*
*25 g/1 oz butter*
*25 g/1 oz flour*
*150 ml/¼ pint milk*
*150 ml/¼ pint single cream*
*50 g/2 oz caster sugar*
*3 eggs*
*1 egg white*

Arrange the sponge finger biscuits in the bottom of a 15 to 18 cm/6 to 7 inch soufflé dish; add 3 tablespoons brandy or curaçao and the cherries. Heat the butter in a large saucepan. Stir in the flour and cook gently for several minutes. Gradually blend in the milk and cream. Bring the sauce slowly to the boil, stirring all the time, and cook until thickened. Add the sugar and the remainder of the brandy or curaçao. Separate the eggs and beat the yolks into the sauce. Whisk the 4 egg whites until stiff and fold into the egg yolk mixture. Spoon over the sponge fingers. Bake in a moderate oven (180°C/350°F or Gas Mark 4) for approxiamately 35 to 40 minutes in a moderate oven. Serve at once.

VARIATION

Use other liqueurs instead of brandy.

## Crème de Menthe Soufflé

*1 tablespoon cornflour*
*150ml/¼pint milk*
*4 tablespoons single cream*
*25g/1 oz butter*
*50g/2oz sugar*
*2 tablespoons crème de menthe*
*3 eggs*
*1 egg white*
DECORATION:
*icing sugar*

Blend the cornflour with the milk and cream and pour into a good-sized saucepan. Add the butter and sugar and bring the mixture to the boil, stirring all the time. Continue to stir as the mixture thickens over a low heat. Remove from the heat and add the liqueur. Separate the eggs and beat the yolks into the thickened mixture. Whisk the whites until they stand up in peaks; do not over-beat. Fold into the other ingredients. Butter a 15cm/6 inch soufflé dish, spoon in the soufflé mixture. Bake in the centre of a moderate oven (180°C/350°F or Gas Mark 4) for 25 minutes or until well risen. Sieve icing sugar over the top and serve at once.

This is a very moist soufflé, bake a little longer for a firmer texture.

VARIATIONS

**Vanilla Soufflé:** Use ½ teaspoon vanilla essence instead of the crème de menthe in the recipe above.

**Hot Apricot Soufflé:** Use smooth apricot purée instead of the milk and cream in the recipe above.

## Rothschild Soufflé

*65g/2½oz butter*
*75g/3oz caster sugar*
*1 tablespoon cornflour*
*150ml/¼pint milk or single cream*
*few drops vanilla essence*
*2 tablespoons sweet sherry*
*2 tablespoons chopped glacé cherries*
*2 tablespoons sultanas*
*2 tablespoons chopped blanched almonds*
*1 tablespoon chopped angelica*
*3 large eggs*
*1 egg white*

Grease the inside of a 15 to 18cm/6 to 7 inch soufflé dish with 15g/½oz of the butter. Sprinkle with 25g/1oz of the sugar. Blend the cornflour with the cold milk or cream and pour into a saucepan. Add the remaining butter and stir over a very low heat until thickened. Add the rest of the sugar, then the vanilla essence. Remove from the heat and, when the sauce is no longer boiling, whisk in the sherry, then the cherries, sultanas, almonds and angelica. Separate the eggs and beat the yolks into the mixture. Whisk the 4 egg whites until they stand in peaks—do not make them too stiff and dry. Fold gently and carefully into the soufflé mixture. Spoon into the prepared dish and bake in the centre of a moderately hot oven (190°C/375°F or Gas Mark 5) for approximately 30 minutes. This souflé is nicer if slightly moist in the centre.

## Apfel Strudel ⊛

STRUDEL DOUGH:
*225 g/8 oz plain flour*
*pinch salt*
*1 egg yolk*
*1 tablespoon melted butter or oil*
*approximately 150 ml/¼ pint warm water*
FILLING:
*50 g/2 oz breadcrumbs*
*100 g/4 oz butter, melted*
*750 g/1½ lb cooking apples, peeled, cored and thinly sliced*
*50 g/2 oz currants*
*50 g/2 oz stoned or seedless raisins*
*50 g/2 oz caster sugar*
*1-2 teaspoons ground cinnamon*
*grated rind of ½ lemon*
DECORATION:
*icing sugar*

Sift together the flour and salt. Stir in the egg yolk, melted butter or oil and sufficient warm water to make a soft dough. Knead on a warm floured board. When smooth, cover with a warm cloth and bowl and leave to stand for approximately 15 minutes.

To make the filling: fry the crumbs in half the melted butter until crisp. Carefully mix the apples with the rest of the ingredients except the remaining butter. Cover the table with a clean cloth. Sprinkle with flour, place the dough in the middle and roll out as thinly as possible with a floured rolling pin. Gently pull the dough from the middle, using mainly the balls of the thumbs. It should be pulled out thinly enough to read through, but this takes time and practice. Spread the apple mixture over the dough to within 1 cm/½ inch of the edges. Roll up like a Swiss roll. Lift on to a baking tray and curve into a horseshoe shape if necessary to fit the tray. Use some of the remaining melted butter to brush over the uncooked strudel. Bake in the centre of a hot oven (220°C/425°F or Gas Mark 7) for 20 minutes. Reduce the heat to moderate (180°C/350°F or Gas Mark 4) and continue baking for 30 minutes. Brush with the rest of the butter at least twice during baking. Top with the sifted icing sugar. Cut into slices and serve hot or cold with whipped cream.

VARIATIONS
You can add chopped nuts to the apples.
Sliced plums could be substituted for apples.

## Gilacgi ⊛

*100 g/4 oz flour, preferably plain*
*100 g/4 oz fine semolina*
*50 g/2 oz caster sugar*
*100 g/4 oz butter, melted*
FILLING:
*150 ml/¼ pint boiling water*
*225 g/8 oz dates (weight when stoned), chopped*
*1 tablespoon honey*
*1 tablespoon lemon juice*
*½ teaspoon ground cinnamon*
*50 g/2 oz walnuts or blanched almonds, chopped*

Pour the water over the dates for the filling, blend with the rest of the filling ingredients and leave to stand for 15 minutes. Mix the flour, semolina and sugar and add the melted butter. Spoon half the semolina mixture into a greased shallow 20 cm/8 inch ovenproof dish. Add the date mixture and spread evenly over the crumbly base, being careful not to dislodge any crumbs. Add the remainder of the semolina mixture, flatten with a palette knife. Bake in the centre of a moderately hot oven (190°C/375°F or Gas Mark 5) for about 45 minutes; reduce the heat to moderate after 20 minutes if the mixture is becoming too brown. This dessert is delicious hot or cold.

## French Apple Tart

PASTRY:
*85 g/3 oz butter or margarine*
*40 g/1 ½ oz caster sugar*
*175 g/6 oz plain flour*
*1 egg yolk*
*water to bind*
FILLING:
*450 ml/¾ pint thick sweetened apple purée*
*3 dessert apples, peeled and thinly and evenly sliced*
*little sugar*

Cream the butter or margarine with the sugar. Work in the flour, egg yolk and enough water to bind. Roll out and line a 23 cm/9 inch flan tin or dish. Bake blind in the centre of a moderately hot oven (190-200°C/375-400°F or Gas Mark 5-6) for about 15 minutes or until firm but uncoloured. Fill with the hot apple purée.

Arrange the apple slices neatly over the purée. Sprinkle with the sugar. Return to the oven, reducing the heat to moderate (160°C/325°F or Gas Mark 3), for about 30 minutes or until the pastry is golden and the apple slices are tender. Serve hot or cold.

VARIATIONS
Glaze the top of the tart with sieved apricot jam.
**French Fruit Flan:** Make and bake the pastry, as in the basic recipe above, but cook this completely. Allow to cool. Fill the flan with Crème Pâtissière, made as page 359 then top with about 350 g/12 oz fresh strawberries or dessert cherries.

Heat 4 tablespoons redcurrant jelly with 1 tablespoons lemon juice or water, cool slightly, then brush over the fruit and allow to set.

## German Apple Tart

PASTRY:
*as French Apple Tart, above*
FILLING:
*50 g/2 oz butter or margarine*
*450 ml/¾ pint thick unsweetened apple purée*
*2 eggs*
*4 tablespoons single cream*
*25-50 g/1-2 oz chopped blanched almonds*
*50 g/2 oz caster sugar*
*2 teaspoons grated lemon rind*
TOPPING:
*caster sugar*

Make the pastry and line a 20 cm/8 inch flan dish or tin; this must be at least 3.5 cm/1½ inches in depth. Bake blind, see recipe for French Apple Tart above.

Melt the butter or margarine, mix with the rest of the filling ingredients. Spoon into the pastry case. Return to the oven, reduce the heat to moderate (160°C/325°F or Gas Mark 3) for 40 minutes or until the filling is firm. Sprinkle with the sugar and serve hot or cold.

VARIATIONS
Do not use apple purée but about 350 g/12 oz very thinly sliced cooking apples instead.
**Spiced German Tart:** Omit the lemon rind and use 1 teaspoon mixed spice instead.

# Orange and Lemon Flan

PASTRY:
*150g/5oz plain flour*
*25g/1oz cornflour*
*100g/4oz butter or margarine*
*1 teaspoon grated lemon rind*
*25g/1oz caster sugar*
*1 egg yolk*
FILLING:
*25g/1oz cornflour*
*300ml/½ pint orange juice*
*1 tablespoon lemon juice*
*50g/2oz caster sugar*
*150ml/¼ pint double cream, lightly whipped*
DECORATION:
*segments of fresh orange*

Sift together the flour and cornflour. Cream the butter or margarine with the lemon rind and sugar; add the flour mixture and egg yolk and knead lightly. Add sufficient water to make a rolling consistency. Roll out and line a 20cm/8inch flan dish, tin or ring on an upturned baking tray. Bake blind in the centre of a moderately hot oven (190°C/375°F or Gas Mark 5) for 20 to 25 minutes until quite firm. Make certain the flan does not become over-brown; if necessary lower the heat slightly. Allow to cool.

Blend the cornflour with the orange and lemon juice. Pour into a saucepan, add the sugar and stir over a low heat until thickened. Leave the mixture in the saucepan until quite cold, then blend in the whipped cream. Spoon into the flan case and top with the orange slices.

VARIATIONS

**Three-fruit Flan:** Make and bake the flan case as above. Meanwhile peel and slice 350g/12oz cooking apples. Put into a saucepan with ½ teaspoon grated lemon rind, ½ teaspoon grated orange rind, 1 tablespoon lemon juice, 2 tablespoons orange juice and 50 to 75g/2 to 3oz sugar. Cook slowly until a smooth, thick purée. Leave to cool, then fold in 150ml/¼pint lightly whipped cream. Spoon into the flan. Decorate with orange segments.

**Fruit Flans:** The pastry above is an excellent choice, you can use all flour instead of flour and cornflour. Bake blind, as note below. If using ripe fruit arrange this in the pastry, top with a glaze, see French Fruit Flan, page 321. If using fruit that needs cooking, poach in about 300ml/½pint sweetened syrup until tender, but unbroken; drain, cool and fill the flan. To glaze: blend 150ml/¼pint syrup with 1 teaspoon arrowroot, stir over a low heat until thickened and clear. Cool slightly, then brush or spread over the fruit. 1 or 2 tablespoons redcurrant jelly or sieved apricot jam could be heated with the glaze.

*To bake blind*: Roll out the pastry to fit a flan ring or dish. Either put a piece of greased greaseproof paper over the pastry with the greased side touching the dough and top with crusts of bread or dried beans, or use a thick round of foil. Bake for 15 minutes, remove the paper or foil and continue cooking. In this way the flan remains a good shape.

## Australian Pineapple Pie

*100g/4 oz flour*
*50g/2 oz cornflour*
*75g/3 oz butter*
*75g/3 oz caster sugar*
*2 egg yolks*
*little milk, see method*
FILLING:
*small can pineapple rings*
*2 cooking apples*
*2 bananas*
*1-2 tablespoons lemon juice*
ICING:
*100g/4 oz icing sugar*
*1 tablespoon lemon juice*
*1 tablespoon pineapple syrup*

Sift together the flour and cornflour and rub in the butter. Add 50g/2 oz sugar, the egg yolks and enough milk to make a firm rolling consistency. Divide in half and roll out one portion to fit an 18 to 20 cm/7 to 8 inch flan dish. (Cook in the serving dish as the pastry must be very thin.) Drain the pineapple well and chop the fruit finely. Peel and grate the apples. Slice the bananas and sprinkle with lemon juice. Put the mixed fruit over the bottom round of pastry; add the 25g/1 oz sugar. Roll out the second portion of pastry to fit the dish. Damp the edges of the bottom pastry, put on the top layer, seal the edges and bake just above the centre of a moderately hot oven (200°C/400°F or Gas Mark 6) for 10 minutes, then reduce the heat to moderate (180°C/350°F or Gas Mark 4) for a further 20 minutes. Leave to cool.

Blend the sifted icing sugar, lemon juice and pineapple syrup and spread over the top pastry. Leave for 2 to 3 hours to set.

## Apple Flapjack Crumble ⊛

*450g/1 lb cooking apples, peeled and sliced*
*2-3 tablespoons water*
*50g/2 oz sugar*
CRUMBLE:
*50g/2 oz butter or margarine*
*50g/2 oz brown sugar*
*1 tablespoon golden syrup*
*100g/4 oz rolled oats*

Put the apples into a 1.2 litre/2 pint pie dish with the water and sugar. Cover with foil and bake in the centre of a moderate oven (160°C/325°F or Gas Mark 3) for 20 minutes.

Meanwhile melt the butter or margarine, sugar and syrup in a saucepan. Add the rolled oats. Remove the dish from the oven, take off the foil and sprinkle the flapjack mixture over the partially cooked apples. Smooth flat with the back of a metal spoon. Return to the oven and continue cooking for a further 35 minutes. Serve hot with cream, custard or ice cream.

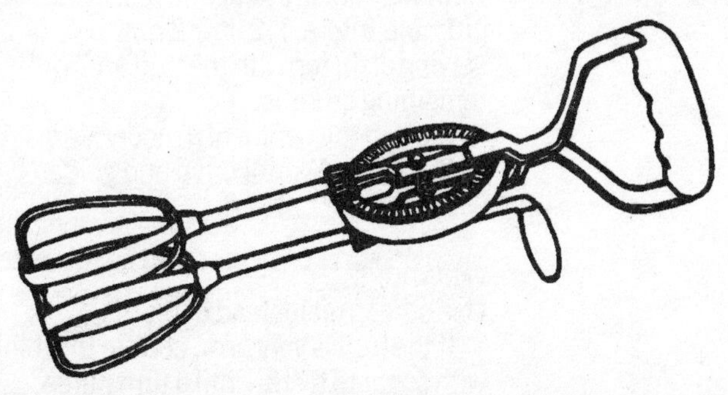

## Rhubarb and Orange Crumble

*450 g/1 lb rhubarb, cut into 2.5 cm/1 inch lengths*
*2 large oranges*
*75 g/3 oz sugar*
CRUMBLE:
*175 g/6 oz flour, plain or self-raising*
*75 g/3 oz butter or margarine*
*100-150 g/4-5 oz sugar*

Put the rhubarb into a 1.2 litre/2 pint pie dish. Grate the zest (orange part of rind) from both oranges. Sprinkle half over the rhubarb and reserve the remainder. Add the 75 g/3 oz sugar to the fruit. If using tender forced rhubarb do not pre-cook before adding the crumble. If using less delicate garden rhubarb, cover the dish with foil and cook in the centre of a moderate oven (180°C/350°F or Gas Mark 4) for 10 to 15 minutes. Add 2 tablespoons of water with this less tender fruit.

Meanwhile cut the oranges into neat segments; discarding pith and skin. Put the orange segments on the rhubarb. Mix the remaining orange rind with the flour. Rub in the butter or margarine and add the sugar. Sprinkle the crumble over the fruit. Bake in the centre of a moderate oven (180°C/350°F or Gas Mark 4) for approximately 35 to 40 minutes until the topping is golden brown. Serve hot or cold with cream, custard or ice cream.

VARIATIONS
Use other fruits instead of rhubarb.
**Coconut Crumble:** Add 25 to 50 g/1 to 2 oz desiccated coconut to the flour mixture.

## Plum Charlotte

*175 g/6 oz bread (weight without crusts)*
*75 g/3 oz butter*
*75 g/3 oz sugar, preferably demerara*
*450 g/1 lb ripe, but firm, plums, halved*
*sugar to taste*

Make the bread into coarse breadcrumbs; do this with your fingers by pulling the bread. I prefer this to slices of bread or fine breadcrumbs for this dessert. Heat the butter in a frying pan, add the breadcrumbs and turn in the butter, do this away from the heat. Return to a low heat and cook gently until the crumbs are golden brown. Remove from the heat and mix in the sugar. Put half the crumble into a 1.2 litre/2 pint pie, or other ovenproof serving dish, top with the fruit and a little sugar, then the remaining crumbs.

Bake in the centre of a moderate oven (180°C/350°F or Gas Mark 4) until crisp and golden brown. Serve hot with cream or custard.

VARIATIONS
Use other fruit instead of plums.

If the fruit is very firm, cook in the minimum of water, with sugar to taste, until a firm purée.

# Making Cheesecakes

I have chosen several of my favourite recipes. Cheesecakes have become so popular during the last years and there are so many different ways of making these that they should never be boring.

If baking a cheesecake, always allow it to cool in the oven with the heat turned off as this prevents any possibility of the delicate mixture wrinkling when it comes into contact with the air. This means that you should be careful not to over-cook the mixture for obviously it continues to cook, although only slightly, in the heat retained in the oven.

Cheesecakes freeze wonderfully well; open-freeze then wrap and use within 3 months.

## Apple Cheesecake ⊛

BISCUIT BASE:
*100 g/4 oz digestive biscuits, crushed*
*50 g/2 oz butter, melted*
*25 g/1 oz caster sugar*
FILLING:
*50 g/2 oz butter*
*75 g/3 oz caster sugar*
*350 g/12 oz cottage cheese, sieved*
*150 ml/¼ pint thick unsweetened apple purée*
*1 teaspoon grated lemon rind*
*3 eggs*
*1 tablespoon cornflour*
*50 g/2 oz sultanas*

Grease the base and sides of a 20 cm/8 inch loose-bottomed cake tin. Mix together the biscuit crumbs, butter and sugar. Press over the base of the cake tin.

Cream the butter and sugar for the filling. Add the cottage cheese, apple purée and lemon rind and beat well. Gradually beat in the eggs and add the cornflour and sultanas. Spoon the filling over the crumb base. Cook in the centre of a cool oven (150°C/300°F or Gas Mark 2) for 1¼ hours until firm to the touch. Allow to cool then remove from the tin. To do this, loosen the sides of the mixture with a palette knife, push the cheesecake up from the base of the tin, then slide the palette knife under the crumb mixture to remove from the metal base of the cake tin.

VARIATIONS

Top with whipped cream and well drained poached apple slices, or raw apple sliced and dipped in lemon juice. Glaze with sieved apricot jam.

⊛ **Vanilla Cheesecake:** Follow the proportions for the Apple Cheesecake, above but use 450 g/1 lb cream or curd cheese instead of the cottage cheese and ½ to 1 teaspoon vanilla essence instead of lemon rind. Add 4 tablespoons double cream and omit the apple purée.

## Orange Cheesecake ⊛

BISCUIT BASE:
*175 g/6 oz digestive biscuits*
*50 g/2 oz butter*
*1 tablespoon honey*
*grated rind 2 oranges*
*50 g/2 oz caster sugar*
FILLING:
*50 g/2 oz butter*
*grated rind 1 orange*
*75 g/3 oz caster sugar*
*2 eggs*
*25 g/1 oz cornflour*
*350 g/12 oz cottage cheese*
*2 tablespoons orange juice*
DECORATION:
*little icing sugar*
*small can mandarin oranges*

Crush the biscuits until most of them are very fine crumbs but keep some of the crumbs a little coarser to make a interesting texture. Cream the butter, honey, orange rind and sugar and add all the crumbs. Use this mixture to line the base and sides of an 18 to 20 cm/7 to 8 inch loose-bottomed cake tin.

To make the filling: cream the butter, orange rind and sugar together. Separate the eggs. Add the egg yolks, cornflour, cottage cheese (this can be sieved if wished but it is not essential) and orange juice. Whisk the egg whites until stiff and fold into the cheese mixture. Spoon into the biscuit case and cook in a cool oven (150°C/300°F or Gas Mark 2) for about 1¼ hours until firm to the touch. Allow to cool in the oven with the heat turned off; this stops the cake sinking. Remove from the cake tin (see Apple Cheesecake recipe on page 325). Sift the icing sugar over the top ot the cheesecake and decorate with well-drained mandarin orange segments.

## Orange Apricot Cheesecake ⊛

BISCUIT BASE:
*175 g/6 oz digestive biscuits, crushed*
*50 g/2 oz butter, melted*
*25 g/1 oz caster sugar*
*grated rind 2 oranges*
FILLING:
*225 g/8 oz can apricot halves*
*50 g/2 oz butter*
*75 g/3 oz caster sugar*
*grated rind 2 oranges*
*2 eggs*
*450 g/1 lb cream or curd cheese*
*2 tablespoons orange juice*
DECORATION:
*150 ml/¼ pint whipping cream, lightly whipped*
*few apricot halves*
*angelica, cut into leaves*

Blend together the biscuit crumbs, melted butter, sugar and orange rind. Press over the base only of a greased 20 cm/8 inch loose-bottomed cake tin.

Drain the apricot halves very well and cut into neat slices. Cream the butter, sugar and orange rind for the filling. Beat in the eggs, then add the cheese, orange juice and the sliced apricots. Spoon over the crumb base. Cook in the centre of a cool oven (150°C/300°F or Gas Mark 2) for 1¼ hours until firm to the touch. Allow to cool then remove from the tin, see Apple Cheesecake recipe on page 325.

When quite cold, decorate with the cream, apricots and angelica.

VARIATION

**Lemon and Apricot Cheesecake:** Use the grated rind of 1 lemon only in the filling and in the biscuit-crumb crust but use 2 tablespoons lemon juice in the filling.

# Fruit Desserts

Although fruit is used in many desserts in this book, the following recipes are for very simple dishes in which fruit is the main ingredient. These recipes should be freshly prepared.

## Almond Apples

*4 large cooking apples, cored*
FILLING AND COATING:
*100 g/4 oz caster sugar*
*50 g/2 oz ground almonds*
*2 tablespoons soft sponge cake crumbs*
*1 tablespoon brandy*
*few drops almond essence*
*2 large eggs*

Slit the skins of the apples. Put into a baking dish and cook in the centre of a moderate oven (180°C/350°F or Gas Mark 4) for just 30 minutes. Meanwhile blend together 50 g/2 oz of the sugar with the ground almonds, sponge crumbs, brandy and almond essence. Separate the eggs and add the egg yolks to the ground almond mixture. Press the filling in the centre of each partially-cooked apple. Return to the oven and continue cooking for a further 20 to 25 minutes until cooked. Remove from the oven and lift away the skins.

Whisk the egg whites until very stiff and fold in the remaining sugar. Spoon the meringue over the apples. Put back into the oven, but reduce the heat to cool (140°C/275°F or Gas Mark 1) and leave for a further 25 to 30 minutes until the meringue is pale golden in colour. Serve with ice cream.

## Pommes Alice

*50 g/2 oz sugar*
*300 ml/½ pint water*
*4 medium cooking apples, peeled and halved*
CUSTARD:
*2 eggs*
*25 g/1 oz sugar*
*150 ml/¼ pint milk*
*few drops vanilla essence*
FILLING AND TOPPING:
*50 g/2 oz chopped candied peel*
*25 g/1 oz brown sugar*
*25-50 g/1-2 oz blanched and flaked almonds*

Blend together the ingredients for the custard and cook in the top of a double saucepan or in a heatproof basin over hot, but not boiling, water until sufficiently thick to coat the back of a wooden spoon.

Heat the sugar and water in a deep frying pan and poach the halved apples until just tender – do not overcook. Lift the fruit from the liquid and put into an ovenproof dish with the cut side uppermost. Fill the centres with the candied peel.

Pour the hot custard around and over the apples. Top this with the sugar and almonds and place under a grill for 2 to 3 minutes until brown.

Note: Any syrup left from poaching the apples can be saved and used in a fruit salad.

## Birds' Nest Pudding

*600ml/1 pint milk*
*25-40g/1-1½oz sugar*
*40g/1½oz short-grain rice*
*few drops vanilla essence*
*4 small cooking apples, peeled and cored*
*2-3 tablespoons bramble jelly*

Put the milk, sugar, rice and vanilla into a strong saucepan. Cook gently until nearly tender and stir from time to time (you may prefer to cook the mixture in the top of a double saucepan over boiling water). Place the apples in a large pie dish or ovenproof serving dish and fill the centres with the bramble jelly. Pour the rice pudding around the apples. Cook in a cool oven (150°C/300°F or Gas Mark 2) for 45 minutes to 1 hour.

VARIATION

**Apricot Pudding:** Slice 225g/8oz dried apricots; soak then cook until tender and strain. Put the fruit into a dish, cover with the rice pudding, half-cooked as above. Complete the cooking process as for recipe above.

## Butterscotch Apples

*50g/2oz butter*
*50g/2oz light brown sugar*
*4 medium cooking apples*
*8 glacé cherries*

Melt the butter and sugar in a heatproof bowl over hot water. Core, then peel and halve the apples horizontally. Put into an ovenproof serving dish. Top with the butter mixture and cover the dish. Cook in the centre of a moderate oven (160°C/325°F or Gas Mark 3) for about 40 minutes. Check after about 30 minutes, as apples vary considerably in the speed with which they are cooked. Top each halved apple with a glacé cherry.

VARIATIONS

**Stuffed Baked Apples:** Core the apples, do not peel but score the skin round the centre of the fruit. This prevents the apples bursting. Put into an ovenproof dish, press the filling in the centre; do not use more filling than can be pressed down into the centre hole. Some of my favourite fillings are:

a) Apricot jam with finely chopped almonds or rather soft marzipan.
b) Bramble jelly or mashed blackberries and sugar.
c) Mincemeat or sultanas mixed with a little brown sugar and a small knob of butter.

The cooking time depends upon the type and size of the apples. Medium-sized good cooking apples take about 40 to 45 minutes in the centre of a moderate oven (180°C/350°F or Gas Mark 4).

## Blushing Peaches ⊛

*3 tablespoons redcurrant jelly*
*150 ml/¼ pint rosé wine*
*25 g/1 oz caster sugar*
*4 large ripe peaches*
*25 g/1 oz flaked blanched almonds*

Heat together the redcurrant jelly, wine and sugar in a large deep frying pan or a shallow saucepan. Skin and halve the peaches and remove the stones. Put the fruit into the wine mixture immediately so the flesh does not discolour. Turn the fruit in the sauce and cook gently for a few minutes until it absorbs most of the sauce. Spoon into a serving dish and top with flaked almonds. Serve hot or cold with cream.

VARIATIONS

⊛ **Pears in Red Wine:** Use pears instead of peaches. If the pears are ripe, follow the recipe above but use red instead of rosé wine. Add 1 tablespoon lemon juice and increase the amount of sugar to 50-75 g/2-3 oz. If the pears are hard, add 300 ml/½ pint water to the other ingredients. Simmer the pears gently for about 45 minutes. Cover the pan for the first 30 minutes, but turn the pears in the liquid several times. Lift the lid after this period so the liquid can thicken. If the liquid is still too thin when the fruit is tender, remove the pears and boil the liquid rapidly until the desired consistency.

⊛ **Gingered Pears:** Use 3 tablespoons apricot jam and 300 ml/½ pint ginger ale instead of redcurrant jelly and wine. Put the pears in the hot liquid and cook as above. 50 g/2 oz diced preserved or crystallized ginger can be added towards the end of the cooking period. This dessert is delicious served hot with vanilla ice cream.

## Caramelled Tangerines

*12 small seedless tangerines, peeled*
*peel of 3 to 4 tangerines*
*300 ml/½ pint water*
*75 g/3 oz granulated, caster or loaf sugar*

Put the fruit into a serving dish. Take the peel kept from the tangerines and scrape away all the white pith. Cut the top zest into very narrow strips. Put into the water and simmer for 15 minutes; reduce the liquid to 150 ml/¼ pint. Measure out 3 tablespoons of this liquid and put into a strong pan with the sugar. Stir until the sugar has dissolved then boil steadily to a golden caramel. Blend with the liquid left in the pan and the peel and pour over the tangerines; allow to cool.

Oranges can be prepared in the same way.

VARIATION

Oranges can be prepared in the same way.

## Flummery

*300 ml/½ pint single cream*
*1 piece of cinnamon stick, about 3.5 cm/1½ inches long*
*1 teaspoon very finely grated orange rind*
*75 g/3 oz caster sugar*
*50 g/2 oz blanched almonds, finely chopped*
*2 tablespoons brandy*
*2 teaspoons gelatine*
*4 tablespoons sweet white wine*
*150 ml/¼ pint double cream, lightly whipped*
*50 g/2 oz blanched flaked almonds, browned*

Put the single cream, cinnamon stick and orange rind into a saucepan and heat slowly until nearly at boiling point. Stir in half the sugar and all the chopped almonds. Put the brandy in a heatproof basin, add the gelatine and dissolve over a pan of very hot water. Cool slightly then blend with the cream mixture. Strain, then add the remaining sugar and wine. Allow the mixture to set until like a thick syrup then fold in the whipped cream. Spoon into individual glasses and top with the browned almonds.

*To brown almonds:* Spread almonds on a flat tray and cook in a moderate oven (160°C/325°F or Gas Mark 3) until pale golden brown. If preferred brown under the grill.

## Syllabub

*75 g/3 oz loaf sugar*
*2 lemons*
*2 tablespoons brandy*
*2 tablespoons sweet sherry*
*450 ml/¾ pint whipping cream, lightly whipped*

DECORATION:
*crystallized violet or rose petals or fresh fruit, cut into small pieces*

Rub the loaf sugar over the lemons until all the top yellow zest is removed. Put the loaf sugar into a basin and crush with a wooden spoon. Halve the lemons and squeeze out 2 tablespoons juice. Add 1 tablespoon juice to the sugar and stir until the sugar has dissolved. Gradually beat the brandy, sherry and another 1 tablespoon of lemon juice into the lightly whipped cream; do this gradually so there is no possibility of the cream curdling. Blend with the sweetened lemon juice. Spoon into glasses then chill. Top with the crystallized petals or fresh fruit.

**Note:** Whipping cream is better than double cream in this recipe for it is lighter.

VARIATION

**Wine Syllabub:** Omit the brandy and sherry and use 5 tablespoons white wine; omit the lemon rind and just use 3 tablespoons lemon juice and 50 g/2 oz sugar. Double cream should be used in this recipe.

## Fruit Foule

*450 ml/¾ pint thick fruit purée, sweetened*
*450 ml/¾ pint thick custard, sweetened*

This easy dessert, generally called 'Fruit Fool', is made by blending smooth fruit purée and custard together then chilling the mixture. It is nicer if some whipped cream is used instead of all custard.

## Parsonage Standby

*25g/1 oz caster sugar*
*300 ml/½ pint whipping cream, lightly whipped*
*8 small sweet biscuits*
*4 tablespoons fruit juice*
*6 tablespoons lingonberry jam*

Add the sugar to the cream. Put the biscuits into 4 sundae glasses and moisten with the fruit juice. Add a thick layer of the jam and finally top with the whipped cream. Chill well.

**Note:** Lingonberry jam is a speciality of Scandinavia where I tasted this recipe; it has a very definite flavour but morello cherry jam or home-made apricot jam could be used instead. Do not use over-sweet jam.

## Surprise Oranges

*300 ml/½ pint yogurt*
*75g/3 oz plain chocolate, chopped*
*25g/1 oz walnuts, chopped*
*4 large oranges*

Blend together the yogurt, chopped chocolate and the walnuts. Cut a slice from each orange, carefully scoop out the pulp and discard any pith and pips. Chop the orange pulp and put back into the orange cases. Top with the yogurt mixture. Chill well before serving.

VARIATION

**Orange Alaska:** Cut a slice from the oranges, scoop out the pulp as described above and return to the orange cases. Fill the oranges with very firm ice cream. Whisk the whites of 2 eggs, fold in 50 to 75 g/2 to 3 oz caster sugar. Pile on top of the ice cream. Heat for 3 minutes only in a very hot oven (230°C/450°F or Gas Mark 8). Serve at once.

## Marsala Cream

*450 ml/¾ pint double cream, lightly whipped*
*50g/2 oz icing sugar, sieved*
*3 tablespoons lemon juice*
*2 tablespoons Marsala*
DECORATION:
*fresh or glacé fruits*

Blend together the cream and icing sugar. Gradually beat the lemon juice and Marsala into the sweetened cream. Spoon into glasses, chill well and top with the fruit.

VARIATIONS

**Sherry Cream:** Use sweet sherry in place of Marsala.
**Orange Cream:** Use orange juice in place of Marsala.

## Zabaglione

*3 egg yolks*
*75g/3 oz caster sugar*
*3 tablespoons Marsala or any sweet Madeira wine*

Put the egg yolks and sugar into a heatproof basin and whisk over a pan of hot water until thick and creamy. Gradually whisk in the wine. Serve warm by itself with sponge finger biscuits or over dessert fruit.

# Egg Custards

Desserts based upon egg custards may sound rather ordinary but, when made perfectly, they are delicious. If you use at least 50 per cent cream in the dish, the dessert can be frozen for up to 2 months. A high percentage of egg yolks, rather than all whole eggs, makes a creamier and richer custard. The left-over whites can be used in meringues and soufflés. By beating the egg yolks, or whole eggs, and sugar before adding the liquid you may well avoid having to strain the custard.

It is essential that egg custard mixtures are not cooked too rapidly for excess heat will cause the mixture to curdle.

## Oeufs à la Neige

*3 eggs*
*600 ml/1 pint milk*
*100 g/4 oz caster sugar*
*few drops vanilla essence*

Separate the yolks from the whites of the eggs. Pour 2 tablespoons of the cold milk over the egg yolks to prevent a hard skin forming. Whisk the egg whites until stiff and fold in 75 g/3 oz of the sugar. Bring the milk with the remaining sugar and vanilla essence just to boiling point in a large frying pan. Drop 8 spoonfuls of the meringue mixture on to the milk and poach for 2 minutes. Turn with a fish slice or large perforated spoon and poach for 2 minutes on the second side. Lift the cooked meringue on to a sieve to drain over a plate. Strain the milk from the frying pan on to the egg yolks and beat well. Cook in the top of a double saucepan or basin over hot, but not boiling, water until a coating custard. Stir or whisk while cooking. Pour into a serving dish. Cool and top with the meringue.

## Floating Islands Trifle

*4 trifle sponge cakes*
*little jam*
*ingredients as Oeufs à la Neige (see above)*
*2 tablespoons sweet sherry*
*150 ml/¼ pint double cream, lightly whipped*
*4 glacé cherries, halved*

Split the sponge cakes, then sandwich together again with the jam and put into the serving dish. Poach the meringues and make the custard as in the recipe above. Whisk the sherry into the warm custard and pour this over the sponge cakes. Allow to cool, then top with the whipped cream, the meringues and the halved glacé cherries.

**Note:** Floating Islands is the other name for Oeufs à la Neige.

## Crème Renversée ⊛

CARAMEL:
*75g/3oz granulated or caster sugar*
*4 tablespoons water*
CUSTARD:
*5 egg yolks or 2 eggs and 3 egg yolks*
*25g/1oz caster sugar*
*300ml/½ pint milk*
*few drops vanilla essence*
*300ml/½ pint single or double cream*

Put the sugar and 3 tablespoons of the water into a strong saucepan. Stir over a moderate heat until the sugar has dissolved, then boil without stirring to a golden caramel. Add the remaining tablespoon of water and stir into the hot caramel. This makes sure none of the sauce is wasted. Warm an 18cm/7 inch soufflé dish, or cake tin without a loose base, or mould. Hold this with a cloth, pour in the hot caramel and turn until the base and sides are coated; leave until fairly set before adding the custard.

Beat the egg yolks or whole eggs and yolks with the sugar. Warm the milk with the vanilla essence and whisk into the eggs. Add the cold cream. Strain or pour the mixture into the dish or mould. Cover and steam over simmering, but not boiling, water for 1¼ hours. Or allow a little longer time in a bain marie in a cool oven (140-150°C/275-300°F or Gas Mark 1-2) until firm. There is no need to cover the container when baking the custard. Cool slightly then invert onto a serving dish. Serve well chilled.

VARIATION
**Caramel Custard:** Use all milk in the custard.

## Caramel Cream Brûlée ⊛

CARAMEL:
*75g/3oz granulated or caster sugar*
*3 tablespoons water*
CUSTARD:
*300ml/½ pint milk*
*4 egg yolks or 2 eggs and 2 egg yolks*
*40g/1½oz caster sugar*
*300ml/½ pint double cream*
TOPPING:
*50g/2oz demerara sugar*

Make the caramel, as in Crème Renversée above, cool slightly. Add the milk and heat slowly until the milk has absorbed the caramel. Beat the eggs and sugar, add the cream and then the caramel liquid. Strain into an 18 to 20cm/7 to 8 inch buttered soufflé dish. Cook as Crème Renversée, above, then allow to cool.

Top with the sugar and place under a grill, with the heat fairly low. Grill for 2 to 3 minutes or until the sugar has melted and become crisp.

VARIATIONS
The desserts above and below can be topped with flaked blanched almonds and then with the sugar and browned.
⊛ **Crème Brûlée:** Make the caramel-flavoured custard only as under Caramel Cream Brûlée, but use all cream. Allow the custard to cool, top with the sugar and brown as in the recipe above.

## Sherry Trifle

*4-6 trifle sponge cakes*
*3-4 tablespoons jam (apricot or raspberry are particularly suitable)*
*4-6 tablespoons sweet sherry (the best quality possible)*
*25-50 g/1-2 oz blanched almonds*
*about 12 ratafia biscuits (see page 364)*

CUSTARD:
*3 egg yolks*
*25-50 g/1-2 oz sugar*
*600 ml/1 pint milk*
*vanilla pod or few drops vanilla essence*

DECORATION:
*150-300 ml/¼-½ pint double or whipping cream, lightly whipped*
*few glacé cherries*
*angelica*

Split the sponge cakes and sandwich together again with the jam. Put into the serving dish or individual dishes. Sprinkle the sherry over the sponge cakes, so they are evenly moistened. Coarsley chop half the almonds and sprinkle over the sponges with the ratafia biscuits.

Meanwhile whisk the egg yolks with the sugar. Warm the milk, pour over the egg mixture and add the vanilla pod or essence. Cook the custard in the top of a double saucepan or basin over hot, but not boiling, water until sufficiently thick to coat the back of a wooden spoon. Remove the vanilla pod. Pour the hot custard slowly over the sponge cakes; cover immediately with a plate or foil to exclude the air, this is particularly important when using custard powder, see below. Allow the trifle to become quite cold. Top with a layer of the cream, then use the remaining cream to pipe around the trifle. Halve the cherries, cut the angelica into leaves or narrow strips and arrange on the cream. Any almonds left can be browned under the grill and used as decoration. Serves 6 to 8.

VARIATIONS

Make a thick custard sauce with custard powder, sugar and milk instead of egg yolks.

Top the sponge cakes with well-drained sliced canned pears or peaches; use sweetened berry fruit such as raspberries; use a little fruit syrup and less sherry to moisten the sponge cakes.

Top the sponge cakes with a fruit-flavoured jelly; allow to cool and set then add the cold custard.

Dilute the sherry with a syrup made by boiling 3 tablespoons water and 25 g/1 oz sugar together for 2 or 3 minutes.

# Making Jellied Desserts

I have given quite a number of cold desserts, based upon gelatine, for I find most people appreciate the fact that these can be made ahead and they form a deliciously light course at the end of the meal.

If the dish contains approximately 50% cream it will freeze well, but always allow the mixture to set completely before freezing. I do not like freezing cold soufflés, for I feel they lose their delicacy.

Dissolving gelatine: If the recipe contains a high percentage of liquid heat this, shake the required amount of gelatine on top of the liquid, then allow to dissolve. If you are dissolving gelatine in only a very small amount of liquid put this into a basin and stand the basin over a pan of very hot water. Sprinkle the gelatine on top of the liquid, leave until virtually dissolved then stir. If you stir vigorously before the gelatine has dissolved you push this to the sides of the pan where it becomes hard.

Incorporating cream: In most of the recipes that follow whipped cream is added. Never over-whip this, otherwise it is almost impossible to blend with the light jelly mixture. Allow the jelly to stiffen until the consistency of a thick syrup before adding whipped cream or whisked egg whites.

## Port Wine Jelly

*1 lemon*
*450 ml/¾ pint water*
*50 g/2 oz caster sugar*
*15 g/½ oz gelatine*
*approximately 300 ml/½ pint port wine (see method)*

DECORATION:
*150 ml/¼ pint double cream, lightly whipped*
*1 tablespoon caster sugar*
*1 tablespoon port wine (optional)*
*few grapes, deseeded*

Pare the yellow rind from the lemon. Put into a pan with the water and simmer for 10 minutes. Dissolve the sugar and then the gelatine in the hot liquid. Strain and measure and add port wine to make 600 ml/1 pint liquid. Pour into a mould and leave to set. Wrap a damp hot tea cloth around the mould for a few seconds to loosen the jelly, then turn it out on to a serving dish.

Blend the cream, sugar and port wine, if using. Spoon or pipe on top of the jelly and decorate with the grapes.

VARIATIONS

**Fresh Lemon Jelly:** Follow the method above, but use 6 tablespoons fresh lemon juice instead of port wine, add water to make 600 ml/1 pint. Sweeten to taste.

**Fresh Orange Jelly:** Use 600 ml/1 pint fresh orange juice, dissolve the gelatine in 3 tablespoons of heated juice, in a basin over hot water, add the rest of the cold juice.

## Port Wine and Raisin Jelly

*450ml/¾pint water*
*50g/2oz caster sugar*
*15g/½oz gelatine*
*100g/4oz seedless raisins*
*5 tablespoons port wine*
*2 tablespoons lemon juice*
DECORATION:
*150ml/¼pint whipping cream, lightly whipped*
*25g/1oz seedless raisins*
*25g/1oz blanched almonds*

Heat the water and sugar together, stirring until the sugar has dissolved. Sprinkle the gelatine on to the hot syrup and allow to dissolve. Add the raisins to the hot liquid and leave until cold, then stir in the port wine and lemon juice. Allow the jelly to cool and become slightly syrupy, stir briskly to distribute the raisins then pour into a rinsed 600 to 900ml/1 to 1½pint mould. When the jelly is firm, turn out on to a serving dish and top with the cream, more raisins and the almonds.

**Note:** In order to pipe cream on jellies, blot the jelly with a little absorbent paper first – this makes the cream adhere rather better.

VARIATION

**Port Wine and Fruit Cream:** Use only 300ml/½pint water in which to dissolve the sugar and then the gelatine. Add 50g/2oz seedless raisins and 50g/2oz sultanas to the hot liquid; allow to cool, then add 150ml/¼pint port wine, 50g/2oz quartered glacé cherries and 25g/1oz chopped almonds. Put the jelly on one side until slightly syrupy, then fold in 150ml/¼pint lightly whipped whipping or double cream. Proceed as the recipe above, but decorate with glacé cherries rather than raisins.

## Pineapple and Orange Snow

*1 x 439g/15oz can pineapple rings*
*2 large oranges*
*150ml/¼pint orange juice*
*15g/½oz gelatine*
*2 egg whites*
*25g/1oz caster sugar*
DECORATION:
*whipped cream*
*orange segments*

Drain the syrup from the canned pineapple. Chop the fruit very finely. Grate the top rind (zest) from 1 orange and blend with the chopped pineapple. Cut away the pith and skin from both oranges, leaving just the segments of fruit. Put these on one side for decoration. Measure the syrup from the pineapple – you need 300ml/½pint. If insufficient, use a little water or extra orange juice. Heat the pineapple syrup and dissolve the gelatine. Allow to cool, then add the orange juice and chopped pineapple and leave until beginning to set.

Whisk the egg whites until stiff; add the sugar, then fold into the pineapple mixture. Spoon into 4 glasses. When quite firm, top with the whipped cream and orange segments.

VARIATION

Use canned apricots instead of pineapple.

## Orange Bavarian Cream ⊛

*150 ml/¼ pint plus 3 tablespoons water*
*15 g/½ oz gelatine*
*50 g/2 oz caster sugar*
*300 ml/½ pint orange juice*
*1 tablespoon lemon juice*
*150 ml/¼ pint double cream, lightly whipped*
DECORATION:
*fresh orange segments*

Put the 3 tablespoons water into a heatproof basin and sprinkle the gelatine on top. Stand over a pan of very hot water until the gelatine has dissolved. Meanwhile heat the remaining water and sugar together, stirring until the sugar has dissolved. Blend the dissolved gelatine with this syrup, cool and add the fresh orange and lemon juice. Allow the jelly to become the consistency of a thick syrup, then fold in the cream. Spoon into a serving dish or individual glasses and leave to set. Top with the orange segments.

VARIATIONS
Use all orange juice in place of water and orange juice.
⊛ **Orange Mousse:** Use only 5 tablespoons water. Dissolve the gelatine in this. Meanwhile, separate the whites from the yolks of 2 large eggs. Beat the yolks with the 50 g/2 oz sugar until thick and creamy, whisk the hot gelatine liquid gradually on to the beaten egg yolks, then add the orange and lemon juice. Allow to cool and stiffen slightly, then fold in the whipped cream and finally the 2 stiffly whisked egg whites. Put into a large serving dish or individual glasses, decorate with more whipped cream and finely chopped pistachio nuts.
⊛ **Raspberry Bavarian Cream:** Use 300 ml/½ pint sieved raspberry purée in place of orange juice. As this is thicker than orange juice, increase the water by 1 tablespoon. You can also omit the lemon juice and add water instead.

## Orange and Lemon Mousse ⊛

*15 g/½ oz gelatine*
*1 tablespoon lemon juice*
*300 ml/½ pint orange juice*
*50 g/2 oz caster sugar*
*150 g/¼ pint double cream, lightly whipped*
*2 egg whites*
DECORATION:
*orange slices*

Dissolve the gelatine in the lemon juice with 2 tablespoons orange juice over a pan of hot water. Stir in the sugar while the mixture is warm. Cool and blend with the rest of the cold orange juice. Allow the mixture to stiffen slightly, then fold in the cream. Whisk the egg whites until stiff and fold into the mixture. Spoon into a serving dish. Top with orange slices and chill before serving.

VARIATION
**Chocolate Mousse:** Melt 225 g/8 oz plain chocolate with 1 tablespoon brandy or water over hot water, add 4 egg yolks and whisk until thick and creamy, cool then fold in the 4 stiffly whisked egg whites. Spoon into 4 to 6 glasses and allow to set. Gelatine is not necessary.

## Pineapple Cheese Mousse ⊛

*1 x 425g/15oz can pineapple rings*
*water or water and lemon juice (see method)*
*15g/½oz gelatine*
*175g/6oz cream cheese*
*150ml/¼pint double cream, lightly whipped*
*25g/1oz caster sugar (optional)*
*2 egg whites*
DECORATION:
*few angelica leaves*
*few glacé cherries, halved*

Drain the syrup from the canned pineapple. Measure the syrup and add sufficient water (or water with 1 tablespoon lemon juice) to make 300ml/½pint. Heat the syrup and dissolve the gelatine; allow to cool and begin to stiffen slightly. Meanwhile chop most of the pineapple; reserving 1 or 2 rings for decorating the mousse. Blend the chopped pineapple, cheese and whipped cream into the gelatine mixture. Taste and add the sugar if necessary but this should have a refreshing, rather than over-sweet taste. Whisk the egg whites until they stand in peaks and fold into the other ingredients. Spoon into a rinsed mould and leave to set. Turn out and decorate with the pineapple, angelica and glacé cherries.

VARIATIONS
Use 225g/8oz sieved cottage cheese in place of cream cheese.
⊛ **Apricot Cheese Mousse:** Canned apricots could be used instead of pineapple. In this case purée most of the well drained fruit by rubbing through a sieve or putting it into a liquidizer or food processor. Use 300ml/½pint apricot purée, 1 tablespoon lemon juice and only 150ml/¼pint syrup from the can. This is a softer mousse and it is advisable to serve it in glasses rather than making a mould.

## Strawberry and Kiwi Cream

*1 packet strawberry jelly*
*150ml/¼pint hot water*
*450g/1 lb small strawberries*
*175g/6oz cottage cheese, sieved*
*150ml/¼pint double cream, lightly whipped*
*25g/1oz caster sugar (optional)*
*2 kiwi fruit, skinned and sliced*

Dissolve a quarter of the jelly in the hot water; allow this to cool but not to set. Liquidize or sieve enough strawberries to give 300ml/½pint purée. Heat this purée, add the remaining jelly and stir until dissolved. Allow to cool, then blend in the cheese, cream and sugar if you feel this is needed, but do not over-sweeten. Spoon into a serving dish. Allow to stiffen slightly then arrange the remaining strawberries and the kiwi fruit on top. Spoon the liquid jelly over the fruit. Leave until set.

## Spanish Coconut Cream

*3 eggs*
*50g/2oz caster sugar*
*few drops vanilla essence*
*450ml/¾ pint milk*
*4 tablespoons water or pineapple syrup*
*15g/½ oz gelatine*
*50-75g/2-3oz desiccated coconut*
*150g/5oz canned pineapple rings, well drained and finely chopped*
*150ml/¼ pint double cream, lightly whipped*

Separate the eggs. Beat the yolks with the sugar and vanilla essence, then add the milk. Stand the heatproof basin over a pan of hot, but not boiling, water and cook gently, stirring frequently until the custard sauce coats the back of a wooden spoon. Put the water or pineapple syrup into another basin and sprinkle the gelatine on top. Stand this over the hot water until the gelatine has thoroughly dissolved. Stir the gelatine into the hot egg custard sauce with the coconut. Allow the coconut mixture to cool and become syrupy, then add the pineapple and cream. Put on one side again to slightly stiffen. Whisk the 3 egg whites until stiff and fold into the coconut mixture. Spoon into glasses. Serves 6.

VARIATION

When fresh coconut is available, grate the white flesh and use instead of the desiccated coconut. As this is more moist, use only 3 tablespoons water with the gelatine.

**Note:** Do not use fresh pineapple. Uncooked pineapple destroys the setting quality of gelatine. If you want to use fresh pineapple in any recipe containing gelatine, you must first simmer this in sugar and water until like canned fruit.

## Pears Sauternes

*8 canned pear halves*
*300ml/½ pint pear syrup*
*15g/½ oz gelatine*
*25g/1oz caster sugar*
*300ml/½ pint Sauternes or other sweet white wine*
*few drops red food colouring*

DECORATION:

*150ml/¼ pint whipping cream, lightly whipped*
*25g/1oz flaked almonds, browned*
*few maraschino cherries*

Put the pears into a wide serving dish. Heat the pear syrup and dissolve the gelatine in this; add the sugar and the wine. Tint the syrup a pale delicate pink with the colouring, pour over the pears and allow to set. Top with the whipped cream, browned flaked almonds and cherries.

VARIATIONS

Use a little less pear syrup and blend 1 tablespoon of maraschino liqueur with the wine; this gives a delicate pink colour as well as flavour.

**Peaches in Curaçao:** Use just under 300ml/½ pint Sauternes, add 2 tablespoons Curaçao. Use canned peaches and peach syrup instead of the pears.

## Empress Rice ⊛

*40 g/1½ oz short-grain rice*
*750 ml/1¼ pints milk*
*¼ teaspoon vanilla essence*
*50 g/2 oz caster sugar*
*2 eggs*
*15 g/½ oz gelatine*
*2 tablespoons sherry*
*2 tablespoons apricot jam, sieved*
*2 tablespoons chopped glacé cherries*
*1 tablespoon chopped angelica*
*150 ml/¼ pint double cream, whipped*

DECORATION:
*glacé cherries, halved*
*angelica, cut into leaves*

Cook the rice in 450 ml/¾ pint of the milk with the vanilla essence and 25 g/1 oz of the sugar, until soft, creamy and firm in texture. Use the top of a double saucepan to prevent any possibility of the rice sticking to the pan or burning.

Make a custard sauce with the eggs, the remaining 300 ml/½ pint milk and 25 g/1 oz sugar, see page 339.

Meanwhile dissolve the gelatine in the sherry, add to the hot custard and blend thoroughly. Stir the custard into the rice pudding with the apricot jam, chopped glacé cherries and angelica. Allow the mixture to cool. Fold half the whipped cream into the custard-rice mixture and spoon into a large serving dish or 6 individual glasses. Leave to set. Decorate with the remaining cream, glacé cherries and angelica. Serves 6.

## Coffee Raisin Cheesecake ⊛

BISCUIT BASE:
*50 g/2 oz butter*
*175 g/6 oz digestive biscuits, crushed*
*25 g/1 oz caster sugar*

FILLING:
*100 g/4 oz seedless raisins*
*3 tablespoons Tia Maria*
*150 ml/¼ pint coffee (drinking strength)*
*75 g/3 oz soft light brown sugar*
*15 g/½ oz gelatine*
*450 g/1 lb cream cheese*
*150 ml/¼ pint double cream, lightly whipped*

DECORATION:
*2-3 tablespoons chopped walnuts*
*little extra whipped cream*

Melt the butter and mix with the biscuit crumbs and sugar. Put on one side. Place the raisins in a dish with the coffee liqueur and leave for 1 hour. Heat the coffee and add the brown sugar. Sprinkle over the gelatine and stir until dissolved. Allow to cool, then gradually blend with the cream cheese. Take half the raisins out of the liqueur and reserve for decoration. Stir the remaining raisins and any Tia Maria not absorbed by the fruit into the cream cheese mixture. Allow to stiffen slightly, then fold in the cream. Spoon into a 23 cm/9 inch loose-bottomed cake tin. Sprinkle the biscuit crumb mixture on top. Leave until set then invert on to a serving dish. Top with the remaining raisins, the chopped nuts and whipped cream. Serves 6 to 8.

# Cold Soufflés

The soufflés that follow provide some of the most delicious desserts. While the jellied mixture can be put into an attractive serving dish or individual sundae glasses, it looks much more interesting if it is prepared in the traditional manner.

To prepare a soufflé dish: always select a size that will allow the mixture to stand well above the rim. Fold a sheet of greaseproof paper to make a firm band, the circumference of the soufflé dish. Spread part of this with a little melted butter. Tie the band round the soufflé dish so the buttered portion stands above the rim of the dish. This is to support the jellied mixture as it sets. When the soufflé is firm remove the paper. To do this ease away from the jellied mixture. A warm flat-bladed knife enables you to do this without harming the light soufflé.

## Mocha Soufflé

*150 ml/¼ pint strong coffee*
*15 g/½ oz gelatine*
*3 eggs*
*50 g/2 oz caster sugar*
*75 g/3 oz plain chocolate*
*few drops vanilla essence*
*300 ml/½ pint double cream, whipped*

Heat the coffee in a pan. Sprinkle the gelatine on the very hot, but not boiling, coffee and stir until dissolved; allow to cool. Separate the eggs. Put the egg yolks, half the sugar, the chocolate and vanilla essence into a heatproof basin. Stand over a pan of hot, but not boiling, water. Stir briskly until the chocolate has melted and the mixture is light in texture. Gradually stir in the coffee and gelatine liquid. Allow to cool and set to the consistency of a thick syrup then fold in nearly all the whipped cream. Whisk the egg whites until stiff and fold in the remaining sugar. Fold this mixture into the coffee mixture. Spoon into a 15 cm/6 inch prepared soufflé dish (see above). Leave until quite firm. Remove the buttered paper from around the mixture. Decorate with the remaining whipped cream.

VARIATIONS

**Chocolate Soufflé:** Use 150 ml/¼ pint water instead of coffee in the recipe above.

**Mocha Nut Soufflé:** Blend 50 g/2 oz finely chopped nuts into the mixture before adding the cream and egg whites. Press finely chopped nuts against the sides of the soufflé after removing the buttered paper. Decorate the top of the soufflé with whipped cream and halved or chopped walnuts or flaked almonds.

## Lemon Soufflé

*3 eggs*
*75 g/3 oz loaf sugar*
*2 lemons*
*300 ml/½ pint milk*
*15 g/½ oz gelatine*
*150 ml/¼ pint double cream, lightly whipped*

DECORATION:
*little whipped cream*
*crystallized rose or violet petals*

Separate the eggs and put the yolks into a basin. Rub the loaf sugar over the lemons until the sugar absorbs the oil and the flavour. Add the lemon-flavoured sugar to the egg yolks. Stir over a pan of hot, but not boiling water, until the sugar has melted. Add the milk and cook until a thick coating custard.

Halve the lemons, squeeze out 4 tablespoons juice and put into a heatproof basin. Sprinkle the gelatine on top and dissolve the gelatine over a pan of hot water. Blend the dissolved gelatine and lemon juice with the warm custard. Allow the mixture to cool and begin to stiffen.

Whisk the egg whites until stiff. Fold the whipped cream and then the egg whites into the jellied custard. Spoon into a 15 cm/6 inch soufflé dish, prepared as on page 341. Chill until firm. Remove the paper band and decorate the top of the soufflé with the whipped cream and crystallized petals.

VARIATION

Use oranges instead of lemons. Since the flavour is less definite use 150 ml/¼ pint orange juice and only 200 ml/⅓ pint milk in the custard.

## Orange Chiffon Pie ⊛

BISCUIT BASE:
*175 g/6 oz digestive biscuits, crushed*
*50 g/2 oz butter, melted*
*50 g/2 oz caster sugar*

FILLING:
*200 ml/7½ fl oz orange juice*
*15 g/½ oz gelatine*
*2 eggs*
*50 g/2 oz sugar*
*150 ml/¼ pint double cream, lightly whipped*

DECORATION:
*segments of 2 oranges*
*angelica, cut into leaves*

Blend the biscuit crumbs, butter and sugar. Press into a 20 cm/8 inch flan dish and chill. Put 4 tablespoons of the orange juice into a heatproof basin, add the gelatine and dissolve over a pan of hot water. Separate the eggs. Whisk the yolks and sugar over hot water until thick and creamy. Whisk in the dissolved gelatine mixture, then the remaining orange juice. Allow the mixture to cool and begin to stiffen. Whisk the egg whites until very stiff. Fold the cream and then the egg whites into the partially-set jelly. Spoon into the biscuit crust and leave until firm. Decorate with orange segments and angelica.

VARIATIONS

⊛ **Lemon Chiffon Pie:** Use 6 tablespoons lemon juice and 6 tablespoons water instead of all orange juice. Increase the sugar in the filling to 100 g/4 oz. Decorate with whipped cream.

⊛ **Coffee Walnut Chiffon Pie:** Use 200 ml/⅓ pint strong coffee instead of orange juice, add 50 g/2 oz chopped walnuts. Increase the sugar to 75 g/3 oz. Decorate with whipped cream and halved walnuts.

# Iced Desserts

Good home-made iced desserts depend upon quick freezing, which is easy in these days, when modern refrigerators with the 3-star markings have a very cold freezing compartment, or where a freezer will be used. There is no need to adjust the cold control on a freezer when freezing ice cream, sorbets or iced desserts as the normal storage setting is quite efficient for this purpose. I do set the control on a refrigerator to the coldest position about 30 minutes before freezing, then return it to the normal setting for storing the dessert.

When making ice cream, use recipes that give a light texture but contain a sufficient proportion of fat, in the form of cream. Sorbets are given a light texture by the use of whisked egg whites. I like to add a little gelatine to the mixture if I am storing the sorbet for any length of time for it helps to produce a better texture.

Use ice cream and sorbets within 3 months. If the recipe contains marshmallows I find it better to use it within 4 to 6 weeks.

## Vanilla Ice Cream ⊛

*2 eggs*
*50 g/2 oz icing sugar, sieved*
*¼-½ teaspoon vanilla essence*
*300 ml/½ pint double or whipping cream*

Whisk the eggs, sugar and vanilla until thick and creamy (see Whisked Sponges, page 360). Whip the cream in another bowl until it stands in peaks; do not over-whip. Fold the cream into the whisked egg mixture, spoon into a container and freeze. Do not whisk during freezing.

VARIATIONS

⊛ **Vanilla Ice Cream 2:** Whip the cream, add the sugar and essence. Freeze lightly, then fold in 2 stiffly whisked egg whites and continue freezing. Full cream evaporated milk can be whisked and used instead of cream.

⊛ **Brown Bread Ice Cream:** Crisp 75 g/3 oz fine brown bread crumbs in the oven, cool; blend with other ingredients when lightly frozen.

⊛ **Chocolate Ice Cream:** Either sift 40 g/1½ oz chocolate powder with the sugar in either recipe or melt 50 to 75 g/2 to 3 oz plain chocolate, cool and blend with the other ingredients when lightly frozen.

⊛ **Coffee Ice Cream:** Dissolve 1½ teaspoons instant coffee powder in 2 tablespoons hot milk, cool and blend with the other ingredients when lightly frozen.

⊛ **Fruit Ice Cream:** Use double cream, omit vanilla essence. Prepare either Vanilla Ice Cream recipe, freeze lightly; blend in 200 ml/7½ fl oz lightly sweetened fruit purée.

## Lemon and Avocado Ice Cream ⊛

*2 tablespoons lemon juice*
*2 teaspoons finely grated lemon rind*
*2 avocados*
*75 g/3 oz icing sugar*
*300 ml/½ pint whipping or double cream, lightly whipped*

Put the lemon juice and rind into a basin. Halve the avocados and remove the stones and skin. Mash the pulp with the lemon juice and rind. Do this immediately after skinning so the fruit does not darken. Sift the icing sugar into the avocado mixture then blend this with the whipped cream and freeze.

VARIATION

⊛ **Lemon and Cheese Cream:** Use 175 g/6 oz cream cheese and only 150 ml/¼ pint whipped cream instead of all whipped cream. This is an interesting basis for either a sweet ice cream (in which case use icing sugar as the recipe above), or you can season the mixture well, then add a few drops of Tabasco sauce. Freeze this and serve on shredded lettuce as an unusual hors d'oeuvre.

## Marshmallow Ice Cream ⊛

*200 g/7 oz marshmallows*
*150 ml/¼ pint rosé wine*
*300 ml/½ pint double cream, lightly whipped*
*25 g/1 oz icing sugar, sieved*

Cut the marshmallows into neat pieces with damp kitchen scissors. Put the wine and two-thirds of the marshmallows into a strong saucepan and heat gently until the marshmallows have melted; allow to become quite cold. Blend the cream, sugar, marshmallow mixture and remaining diced marshmallows. Spoon into a container and freeze.

VARIATIONS

⊛ **Cherry and Almond Mallow:** Dice and melt the marshmallows in wine as above, add 50 g/2 oz chopped Maraschino cherries, 50 g/2 oz chopped blanched almonds and 1 to 2 chopped macaroon biscuits. Blend with 300 ml/½ pint whipped cream and 25 g/1 oz sieved icing sugar. Freeze.

⊛ **Raisin and Cherry Ice Cream:** Chop 25 g/1 oz angelica and 50 g/2 oz glacé cherries and soak in 2 tablespoons sweet sherry or orange juice with 50 g/2 oz seedless raisins. Melt the marshmallows in milk instead of wine. Cool and blend with the cherry mixture then with 300 ml/½ pint whipped double cream. Freeze.

⊛ **Strawberry Mallow:** Dice and melt 175 g/6 oz marshmallows in 200 ml/7½ fl oz (12 tablespoons) hot fresh strawberry purée. Allow to cool. Blend with 300 ml/½ pint whipped cream and 25 g/1 oz sieved icing sugar. Freeze.

## Raspberry Sorbet ⊛

*water (see method)*
*50 g/2 oz sugar or to taste, or use sugar substitute for slimmers*
*1 teaspoon gelatine*
*450 g/1 lb raspberries*
*1 tablespoon lemon juice (optional)*
*2-3 egg whites*

Heat 150 ml/¼ pint water with the sugar, stir well, then add the gelatine and allow to dissolve; cool this mixture.

Rub the raspberries through a nylon sieve and add the gelatine liquid. If necessary, add more water to make 600 ml/1 pint together with the lemon juice if you like a sharper flavour. Pour into a container and freeze lightly. Whisk the egg whites until very stiff, fold into the half-frozen mixture, then continue freezing.

VARIATIONS

Use other fruit purées; some of the most refreshing are apple (tint the sorbet a delicate pink); apricot; black or red currant; cherry (use cooked Morello cherries); damson; fig; gooseberry; loganberry; mango; melon (use either honeydew or water melon purée, add a generous amount of lemon juice and/or ground ginger, this makes an excellent hors d'oeuvre as well as a dessert); plum; quince; strawberry.

⊛ **Lemon Sorbet:** Pare just the top zest from 2 large lemons and simmer in 600 ml/1 pint water for 5 minutes. Dissolve 50 to 75 g/2 to 3 oz sugar in this with 1 teaspoon gelatine. Allow to cool, strain and add the lemon juice. Freeze lightly, then fold in 2 stiffly whisked egg whites and continue freezing. Orange, grapefruit or other citrus fruit could be used.

## Frosted Coffee Gâteau ⊛

*75 g/3 oz butter, softened*
*3 large eggs*
*150 g/5 oz caster sugar*
*3 teaspoons instant coffee powder*
*3 tablespoons boiling water*
*225 g/8 oz sponge finger biscuits*
*50 g/2 oz walnuts*
DECORATION:
*150 ml/¼ pint whipping or double cream*
*few halved walnuts*

Take the butter out of the refrigerator and leave in a warm place. Whisk the eggs and sugar in a heatproof bowl over a pan of very hot water until thick and creamy. Gradually whisk in the butter. Remove from the heat. Dissolve the coffee in the boiling water and whisk into the egg mixture. Allow to cool.

Crumble the sponge biscuits into fine crumbs. Chop the nuts. Blend the biscuits and nuts with the coffee mixture. Line a 750 g/1½ to 2 lb loaf tin with waxed paper. Spoon in the mixture and freeze until firm. Turn out. Whip the cream until it just stands in peaks. Spoon over the top of the coffee gâteau. Decorate with the halved walnuts.

## Chocolate Sauce

*225g/8oz plain chocolate*
*15g/½oz butter or a few drops olive oil*
*3 tablespoons water, milk or cream*

Break the chocolate into pieces and put into a heatproof basin with the other ingredients. Melt over a pan of hot but not boiling water or in a microwave cooker. Serve hot. If serving this sauce cold, add another tablespoon liquid.

VARIATIONS

Use brandy or orange juice as the liquid.

**Economical Chocolate Sauce:** Put 4 tablespoons water, 50g/2oz caster sugar, 2 tablespoons golden syrup, 25g/1oz butter or margarine and 25g/1oz cocoa powder or 50g/2oz chocolate powder into a basin. Heat over a pan of boiling water until a smooth mixture, stir well before serving.

**Chocolate and Coffee Sauce:** Use 4 tablespoons very strong coffee in either Chocolate Sauce recipe above instead of water.

## Lemon and Apricot Jam Sauce

*6 tablespoons water*
*grated rind of 1 lemon*
*1 teaspoon arrowroot*
*3 tablespoons lemon juice*
*6 tablespoons apricot jam*
*1 tablespoon sugar*

Put the water and lemon rind into a pan, simmer for 5 minutes and strain if wished. Blend the arrowroot with the lemon juice and add to the pan with the other ingredients. Stir over a low heat until thick and clear.

VARIATIONS

**Jam Sauce:** Omit the lemon juice and rind. Use 225g/8oz jam, proceed as above.

**Syrup and Lemon Sauce:** Follow the basic recipe above, but substitute golden syrup for jam.

**Marmalade Sauce:** Use marmalade instead of jam.

## Mock Maple Syrup

*4 tablespoons brown sugar*
*4 tablespoons golden syrup*

Blend the sugar and syrup together. This mixture has the flavour of the true maple syrup.

## Sabayon Sauce

*3 egg yolks*
*75g/3oz caster sugar*
*4 tablespoons white wine*
*1-2 tablespoons rum*

Put the egg yolks and sugar into a heatproof basin over a pan of hot but not boiling water, then whisk until thick and creamy. Gradually whisk in the white wine and rum. Serve this sauce hot or cold over fruit, the most suitable being dessert pears or peaches.

# Ice Cream Sundaes

The sauces below and on page 346 enable you to prepare a number of interesting ice cream desserts, here are some of the nicest.

**Banana Splits:** Halve bananas and sprinkle with lemon juice to preserve their colour. Top with ice cream and either the Melba or Berry Cream Sauce (see recipes below).

**Coupe Jacques:** Make a fresh fruit salad or use a mixture of fresh and canned fruit, spoon into sundae glasses and top with either Melba or Berry Cream Sauce (see recipes below).

**Fruit Melbas:** Choose fresh fruit wherever possible, such as raspberries, strawberries, skinned and halved peaches, or use canned fruit. Make or buy the ice cream, put into dishes and top with the fruit and Melba Sauce (see recipe below). Decorate with lightly whipped cream if desired.

**Poires Belle Hélène:** Top ice cream with halved dessert or canned pears and Chocolate Sauce (see page 346).

## Melba Sauce ⊛

*225 g/8 oz fresh or frozen raspberries*
*1 teaspoon arrowroot or cornflour*
*3 tablespoons water*
*3 tablespoons redcurrant jelly*
*50 g/2 oz caster sugar*

Put the raspberries into a saucepan and crush with a wooden spoon. Blend the arrowroot or cornflour with the water and add to the raspberries with the jelly and sugar. Stir over a low heat until the jelly has melted and the mixture has thickened and cleared. Either beat hard to make sure the raspberries have become a soft purée, sieve or liquidize. Cool and serve over ice cream in the recipes above.

VARIATION

Use 1 tablespoon brandy in the recipe above or white wine in place of water.

## Berry Cream Sauce ⊛

*175 g/6 oz raspberries*
*175 g/6 oz strawberries*
*1 teaspoon gelatine*
*50 g/2 oz sugar*
*150 ml/¼ pint double cream, lightly whipped*

Sieve or liquidize the fruit. Put 4 tablespoons of the purée into a saucepan, add the gelatine and sugar and stir over a low heat until both have dissolved. Allow to cool and become a slightly stiffened mixture, then fold in the cream. Serve over ice cream as a change from Melba Sauce.

# Good Baking

In this part of the book there are some of my favourite recipes. Many people say that 'old-fashioned' tea-time is no longer appreciated. I find that to be quite untrue. Admittedly I only serve this occasionally, for like most people I am busy and a cup of tea and a biscuit generally suffice. But when I entertain friends, particularly those who come from abroad and have heard of our wonderful tea-times in Britain, I enjoy preparing tiny sandwiches, scones or home-made bread with home-made preserves, followed by a selection of cakes.

A freezer makes it worthwhile baking, for you can cook more than is needed for the occasion and freeze the remainder. Cakes and scones keep well for 3 months and I feel that gâteaux and light sponges seem to taste even better after they have been frozen. Open-freeze, so you do not spoil the delicate texture or decorations, then wrap or pack in a freezer quality polythene box; unwrap before thawing.

I mentioned the popularity of 'my' Christmas Pudding, I think the Christmas Cake, given on page 356 is even more well-known. I demonstrated this particular recipe several times on BBC television and even now, many years later, still find it is one of the most popular of my recipes. A question I often am asked about this, and other rich cakes, is why I stress that plain flour should be used? This is because raising agent in such a rich mixture causes the cake to rise too much and the heavy weight of fruit to fall.

Many years ago I had the pleasure of working in Australia and while I was there I learned how to make the special fondant-type icing which is used to such good effect. Use it instead of royal icing for coating a cake in minutes or to mould flowers of such delicacy that you feel they are real. This fondant icing is given on page 359.

There is a great revival in home-baking of bread and I know most people find this an enjoyable task. It is better to buy the special bread-making flour, known as 'strong flour' for this purpose. The yeast dough rises better and you produce a better texture. If fresh yeast is difficult to obtain, use dried yeast and the results will still be excellent.

**Using Plain Flour**

If you prefer to use plain flour with baking powder instead of self-raising flour you need 2 level teaspoons baking powder to each 225g/8oz plain flour, unless stated to the contrary.

## Rock Buns ⊛

*225g/8oz self-raising flour*
*½-1 teaspoon mixed spice*
*150g/5oz butter or margarine*
*150g/5oz caster or granulated sugar*
*100-150g/4-5oz mixed dried fruit*
*25-50g/1-2oz mixed candied peel, chopped*
*1 egg*
*milk to bind*
TOPPING:
*1 tablespoon caster or demerara sugar*

It may seem strange to give such plain cakes as being a favourite, but when these are eaten fresh they are delicious. You will notice I give rather more fat and sugar than in the usual recipe, in consequence the buns do not keep such a good shape, but they taste infinitely better.

Sift the flour and spice, rub in the butter or margarine, add the sugar, fruit, peel and egg. Mix well then add just enough milk to make a sticky consistency. Spoon on to well greased baking trays, leaving space for the mixture to spread – this mixture will make 12 buns. Sprinkle with the caster or demerara sugar and bake above the centre of a hot oven (220°C/425°F or Gas Mark 7) for approximately 12 minutes. Cool for 5 minutes on the baking trays as these cakes are rather fragile when hot, then lift on to a wire cooling tray.

## Welsh Cakes ⊛

*225g/8oz self-raising flour*
*pinch mixed spice*
*75g/3oz butter or margarine*
*100g/4oz caster sugar*
*75g/3oz currants*
*1 egg*
*milk to bind*
TOPPING:
*25g/1oz caster sugar*

Anyone who has tasted these crisp little cakes, which are baked on a griddle, knows they are delicious. They must be eaten when freshly made, although they do freeze well.

Sift the flour and spice and rub in the butter or margarine. Add the sugar, currants, egg and enough milk to make a firm rolling consistency. Roll out to 5mm/¼ inch thickness and cut into small rounds.

Grease and heat the griddle – to test if it is the right heat, shake a little flour on the plate; it should turn brown within 1 minute. Put the cakes on to the griddle, cook for 2 to 3 minutes or until golden brown on the bottom, turn and cook for the same time on the second side. Remove from the heat when firm to the touch, cool and sprinkle with the sugar.

# Creamed Mixtures

It is always important to cream the margarine or butter and sugar well; do not melt the fat. If the fat is melted, it is almost impossible to incorporate air into the mixture. If the fat is very hard, warm the mixing bowl.

Beat the eggs gradually into the creamed mixture; if done too quickly the mixture curdles. A little flour can be added if there is a sign that the mixture is curdling and this will rectify the condition, if not too severe. A badly curdled mixture never produces as good a sponge or cake.

Sift the flour and incorporate it into the above ingredients carefully and gently. Over-beating in cakes made by this method produces a poor texture.

Do use the right position in the oven, as well as the correct temperature and of course preheating the oven is important when baking cakes. As ovens do vary a little, check that the average setting, as given in the recipes in this book, is the one recommended by the manufacturer of your particular cooker.

## Madeleines ⊛

*110g/4oz butter or margarine*
*110g/4oz caster sugar*
*2 eggs*
*110g/4oz self-raising flour*
COATING AND TOPPING:
*3-4 tablespoons raspberry jam*
*4 tablespoons desiccated coconut*
*6-8 glacé cherries*
*angelica, cut into 24 to 32 leaves*

Cream together the butter or margarine and sugar until soft and light. Gradually beat in the eggs. Sift the flour and fold into the creamed mixture. Grease and flour 12 to 16 dariole moulds (castle pudding tins). Spoon the soft mixture into the tins – these should be no more than three-quarters filled. Stand on a flat baking tray and bake just above the centre of a moderately hot oven (200°C/400°F or Gas Mark 6) for approximately 12 to 15 minutes or until firm to the touch. Turn out and allow to cool. The top of each cake may need cutting flat if it has risen unevenly as this becomes the base.

Warm the jam but do not allow to become too hot. Insert a fine skewer into the first cake so your fingers do not get sticky. Coat the top and sides of the cake with jam – it is easier to do this with a pastry brush than a knife. Put the coconut on to a plate and roll the jam-coated cake in this. Stand upright and press half a glacé cherry and two angelica leaves on the top of the cake. Continue like this until all the cakes are coated.

**Note:** Do not be confused with the French Madeleines. These are sponges, baked as page 360.

## Victoria Sandwich ⊛

*175 g/6 oz butter or margarine*
*175 g/6 oz caster sugar*
*3 large eggs*
*175 g/6 oz self-raising flour*

Cream together the butter or margarine and sugar until soft and light. Gradually beat in the eggs (see the comments about the mixture curdling on the previous page). Sift the flour and fold gently and carefully into the creamed mixture. If the eggs are large, you should have a slow dropping consistency. If the eggs are small, add a few drops of water. Divide the mixture between two 18 to 19 cm/7 to 7½ inch greased and floured or lined sandwich tins. Bake just above the centre of a moderate to moderately hot oven (180-190°C/350-375°F or Gas Mark 4-5) for 18 minutes or until firm to the touch. Turn out and allow to cool.

To fill a Victoria Sandwich: Fill with jam or with jam and whipped cream or with dessert fruit and whipped cream or with one of the butter icings on the next page. Top with sifted icing or caster sugar or with Glacé Icing, see the next page.

VARIATIONS

Bake in one 18 to 19 cm/7 to 7½ cake tin for about 55 minutes or a 20 cm/8 inch cake tin for about 45 minutes.

Use 2 eggs and 110 g of fat, sugar and flour for a 15 to 16.5 cm/6 to 6½ inch sandwich and bake for about 15 minutes.

⊛ **Chocolate Sponge:** Omit 25 g/1 oz flour and substitute 25 g/1 oz cocoa powder. Fill with Chocolate Butter Icing and top with melted chocolate or Chocolate Glacé Icing (see page 352).

⊛ **Coffee Sponge:** Use 3 small eggs, blend with 1½ tablespoons coffee essence or with 1½ teaspoons instant coffee blended with 1½ tablespoons hot water. Fill with Coffee Butter Icing and top with Coffee Glacé Icing (see page 352).

⊛ **Lemon Sponge:** Cream 1 to 2 teaspoons finely grated lemon rind with the butter or margarine and sugar. Use 3 small eggs and 1½ tablespoons lemon juice. Fill with lemon curd or with Lemon Butter Icing and top with Lemon Glacé Icing (see page 352).

⊛ **Fruit Shortcake:** Use only 150 g/5 oz butter or margarine and sugar with 2 eggs and 175 g/6 oz self-raising flour. Put into the greased and floured sandwich tins. Bake in a moderate oven (160-180°C/325-350°F or Gas Mark 3-4) for 20 minutes until firm. Cool slightly in the tins, turn out and cool. Fill and top with fruit and whipped cream. Freeze without filling.

# Icings for Sponges

These soft icings are ideal for the Victoria Sandwich mixture or the lighter type sponge on page 360.

## Vanilla Butter Icing ⊛

*50 g/2 oz butter*
*75 g/3 oz icing sugar, sifted*
*few drops vanilla essence*

Cream together the ingredients until soft and light. This gives a good layer of filling in a sponge of the size given on page 351.

VARIATIONS

⊛ **Chocolate Butter Icing:** Use only 50 g/2 oz icing sugar and 25 g/1 oz chocolate powder.

⊛ **Coffee Butter Icing:** Dissolve 1 teaspoon instant coffee powder in ½ tablespoon hot water; cool and add to the creamed ingredients. If too soft, add a little extra icing sugar; omit the vanilla essence.

⊛ **Lemon Butter Icing:** Use 100 g/4 oz icing sugar. Cream with the butter and 1 tablespoon lemon juice. A little very finely grated lemon rind can be added too.

## Glacé or Water Icing ⊛

*225 g/8 oz icing sugar*
*approximately 2½ teaspoons water or other liquid, see method*

Although you can sift the icing sugar, I find that if I moisten it with the liquid given in the recipe, then allow it to stand, the soft lumps do come out within minutes. If the lumps in the icing sugar are very hard, then you must sift it. Blend the icing sugar and liquid together. This is a soft icing which is generally used to coat soft cakes and biscuits. You cannot use it for piping, except for writing in icing or any design with lines.

This amount of icing would give a generous topping on a 18 cm/7 inch sponge or a thinner layer on the top of a 20 to 23 cm/8 to 9 inch sponge or the top and sides of a 15 cm/6 inch sponge. This icing never hardens; it does set, of course, but with keeping tends to crack.

VARIATIONS

⊛ **Chocolate Glacé Icing:** Blend a little chocolate or cocoa powder with the icing sugar.

⊛ **Coffee Glacé Icing:** Mix the icing with strong coffee.

⊛ **Lemon Glacé Icing:** Mix the icing with lemon juice.

## Rich Dark Chocolate Cake ⊛

*100g/4oz butter or margarine*
*225g/8oz moist brown sugar*
*100g/4oz plain chocolate, melted*
*2 large eggs*
*200g/7oz self-raising flour, or plain flour and 1½ teaspoons baking powder*
*½ teaspoon ground cinnamon*
*150ml/¼ pint soured cream*
*3 tablespoons strong coffee*

Line a 20 to 23cm/8 to 9 inch cake tin with greased greaseproof paper. Cream together the butter or margarine and sugar, add the melted chocolate and gradually beat in the eggs. Sift the self-raising flour, or plain flour and baking powder, with the ground cinnamon. Blend into the creamed mixture with the soured cream and coffee. Spoon into the cake tin and bake in the centre of a moderate oven (180°C/350°F or Gas Mark 4) for 1 to 1¼ hours or until firm to the touch. Lower the heat slightly after 30 minutes. Cool in the tin for 5 minutes, then turn out carefully and leave to cool on a wire rack.

VARIATION

Both cakes on this page can be topped with chocolate. Melt 175 to 225g/6 to 8oz plain chocolate with 15g/½oz butter, cool, then spread over the top of the cake.

## Mocha Cake ⊛

*100g/4oz golden syrup*
*100g/4oz soft light brown sugar*
*100g/4oz butter or margarine*
*200g/7oz self-raising flour*
*25g/1oz cocoa*
*1 teaspoon bicarbonate of soda*
*1 egg*
*140ml/scant ¼ pint (7 tablespoons) strong coffee*

Put the syrup, sugar and butter or margarine into a strong saucepan and melt over a low heat. Sift together the flour, cocoa and bicarbonate of soda. Add to the melted mixture, mix well, then beat in the egg and the coffee. Line the base of an 18cm/7 inch cake tin with a round of greaseproof paper and grease the tin. Spoon in the mixture. Bake in the centre of a moderate oven (160-180°C/325-350°F or Gas Mark 3-4) for 1 hour until firm to the touch. Cool for a few minutes in the tin then turn out on to a wire cooling tray.

VARIATIONS

Use a microwave cooker and line the base of a 20cm/8 inch ovenproof glass or ceramic soufflé dish with greaseproof paper. Allow approximately 10 minutes cooking time on the setting recommended for simmering or about 8 minutes on maximum setting. The top will look slightly moist, but the cake will set perfectly as it cools.

⊛ **Moist Chocolate Cake:** Use milk instead of coffee for mixing the cake.

## Madeira Cake ⊛

*175g/6oz butter*
*200g/7oz caster sugar*
*3 large eggs*
*225g/8oz plain flour*
*1 teaspoon baking powder*
*3 tablespoons milk*
GLAZE:
*1 tablespoon caster sugar*
*large thin slices of candied lemon peel*

Cream together the butter and sugar. Gradually beat in the eggs. Sift the flour with the baking powder and fold into the creamed mixutre with the milk. Put into a greased and floured 18cm/7 inch cake tin and sprinkle over the sugar. Bake in the centre of a moderate oven (160°C/325°F or Gas Mark 3) for approximately 1¼ hours but remove the cake carefully after 45 minutes and put the peel on top. You can put it on at the beginning of the cooking period, but it tends to become over-dry.

VARIATIONS

⊛ **Cherry Cake:** Halve and flour 100g/4oz glacé cherries or rinse these and dry well (this prevents them dropping in the cake). Use only 2 tablespoons milk and omit the peel.

⊛ **Genoa Cake:** Add 225 to 300g/8 to 10oz mixed dried fruit, 50g/2oz chopped candied peel, 50g/2oz chopped glacé cherries to the cake. Use 2 tablespoons milk. Bake for an extra 15 minutes.

## Dundee Cake ⊛

*175g/6oz butter or margarine*
*175g/6oz caster sugar*
*3 large eggs*
*225g/8oz plain flour with 1 teaspoon baking powder, or use half plain and half self-raising flour*
*25g/1oz ground almonds*
*2 tablespoons dry sherry or milk*
*50g/2oz glacé cherries, chopped*
*50g/2oz candied peel, chopped*
*450g/1lb mixed dried fruit*
TOPPING:
*25-50g/1-2oz blanched almonds*
*little egg white (see method)*

Cream together the butter or margarine and sugar until soft and light. Gradually beat in the eggs; save a little egg white for glazing the top of the cake. Sift the flour and baking powder or the two flours together. The amount of raising agent in the recipe gives a cake that rises well but has an absolutely flat top. Fold the flour and ground almonds into the creamed mixture, then add the sherry or milk, cherries, peel and dried fruit. Grease and flour or line a 20cm/8 inch cake tin. Spoon in the mixture and smooth over the top. Arrange the almonds on top and brush with the leftover egg white. Bake in the centre of a moderate oven (160°C/325°F or Gas Mark 3) for 30 minutes then lower the heat to 150°C/300°F or Gas Mark 2 for a further 1½ hours or until the cake has shrunk away from the sides of the tin and is firm to the touch. Leave to cool for 5 minutes in the cake tin, then carefully turn out on to a wire cooling tray.

This cake keeps for some weeks in an airtight tin; try to allow at least 2 to 3 days before cutting.

VARIATION

Bake in an 18cm/7 inch cake tin for a total of 2¼ hours instead of the 2 hours in the recipe above, i.e., bake for 1¾ hours at the lower setting.

## Simnel Cake ⊛

*Ingredients for marzipan (see page 357)*

CAKE:

*175 g/6 oz butter*

*175 g/6 oz caster or moist brown sugar*

*3 eggs*

*225 g/8 oz plain flour with 1½ level teaspoons baking powder, or 100 g/4 oz plain and 100 g/4 oz self-raising flour*

*1 teaspoon mixed spice*

*2 tablespoons milk or sherry*

*450 g/1 lb mixed dried fruit*

*50 g/2 oz glacé cherries, chopped*

*50 g/2 oz blanched almonds, chopped*

*50 g/2 oz candied peel, chopped*

GLAZE:

*1-2 egg whites*

Make the marzipan (see page 357). Use just under half to make a round of 20 cm/8 inches in diameter. Keep the remainder of the marzipan covered so that it does not dry. Cream the butter and sugar together and gradually beat in the eggs. Sift the flour or flours with the spice. Stir into the creamed mixture then add the milk or sherry and the dried fruit, cherries, almonds and peel. Grease and flour a 20 cm/8 inch cake tin or line with greased greaseproof paper. Put in half the cake mixture then the round of marzipan then the rest of the cake mixture. Bake in the centre of a moderate oven (160°C/325°F or Gas Mark 3) for approximately 2½ hours. Reduce the heat slightly after 1½ hours so the top of the cake is not too brown. Allow the cake to cool for a while before removing from the tin. Brush the top of the cake with a little of the egg white. Form the rest of the marzipan into a 20 cm/8 inch round plus 12 round balls for the edge of the cake, put on top of the cake and brush with more egg white to glaze. Either brown under a very low grill or for a short time in the oven. Tie some pretty ribbon round the cake and top with chickens or other suitable Easter cake decorations.

**Using Leftover Marzipan**

A little marzipan may be left after decorating a Simnel or Christmas cake. Use this to stuff stoned dessert dates or glacé cherries or tint the marzipan and form it into small fruit shapes. Allow these to dry in the air then coat them with caster or a little sifted icing sugar. Cut the marzipan into small shapes, top with pieces of cherry or nut or sandwich halves of galcé cherries or walnuts with marzipan. You can coat marzipan shapes with melted chocolate. All these make good petits fours.

Marzipan makes a delicious filling for cored cooking apples. Prepare and bake as on page 328.

## Christmas Cake ⊛

*350g/12oz plain flour*
*1 teaspoon ground cinnamon*
*1 teaspoon mixed spice*
*110g/4oz candied peel, chopped*
*900g/2lb mixed dried fruit, preferably 450g/1lb currants, 225g/8oz sultanas, 225g/8oz seedless raisins*
*50-100g/2-4oz blanched almonds chopped*
*110g/4oz glacé cherries, chopped*
*4 large eggs*
*4 tablespoons milk, sherry, brandy or rum*
*finely grated rind 1 lemon*
*finely grated rind 1 orange (optional)*
*225g/8oz butter or best quality margarine*
*225g/8oz sugar, preferably dark moist brown sugar*
*1* level *tablespoon black treacle or golden syrup*

This is a rich Christmas cake that should be made at least one month before Christmas. It gives the right amount of ingredients for a 23cm/9inch round or 20cm/8inch square cake. Prepare the tin carefully. Line the bottom of the tin with a double round of brown paper and cover this with a double thickness of lightly greased greaseproof paper. Line the sides of the tin with greased greaseproof paper. Tie a deep band of brown paper around the outside of the tin.

Sift together all the dry ingredients. Mix together the peel, fruit, almonds and cherries (if these are slightly sticky then flour lightly). Blend the eggs with the milk, sherry, brandy or rum. Cream together the lemon and orange rinds with the butter or margarine, sugar and treacle or golden syrup until soft. Do not over-beat as this type of cake does not need as much beating as light cakes. Gradually blend in the egg mixture and sifted dry ingredients. Stir in all the fruit. Put the mixture into the tin, smooth flat on top, then press with *slightly* damp knuckles as this helps to keep the cake moist on top and flat.

Bake in the centre of a moderate oven (160°C/325°F or Gas Mark 3) for about 1½ hours, then lower the oven to cool (140-150°C/275-300°F or Gas Mark 1-2). Baking times for rich fruit cakes like this vary considerably according to your particular oven, so test it carefully.

To test the cake: first press firmly on top, there should be no impression, check to see if the cake has shrunk away from the sides of the tin. If it has, remove from the oven, listen carefully. A rich fruit cake that is not quite cooked gives a definite humming noise, in which case return it to the oven. Cool the cake in the baking tin, then turn out carefully, wrap in foil if wished, but store in an airtight tin.

This cake is given a very moist texture if you prick it once or twice before icing and pour several tablespoons of sherry, brandy or rum into the cake. Use a steel knitting needle or fine skewer, make a number of small holes on top of the cake and spoon the sherry or brandy or rum over this. If wished, turn the cake upside down and do the same thing. Wrap tightly in foil and store in a cool, dry place. If you do not wish to moisten the cake during storage do not worry, for it is still very rich and delicious.

# Decorating Christmas Cakes

The cake should have risen to be flat on top but if it is slightly domed, turn it upside down, or remove a thin slice. After this, brush away any loose crumbs and coat with sieved apricot jam or lightly whisked egg white.

You need a marzipan coating if using the American Frosting or Royal Icing on the next page; if by chance you do not like this icing then you must put one coating of Royal Icing over the cake, allow this to dry then put your chosen icing over the top. However, the Australian Icing (often called a Fondant Icing) on page 359 can be put on to a cake without marzipan, although to most people this almond-flavoured paste is one of the delights of a rich cake.

Roll out the marzipan, cut a round or square for the top of the cake, then a band to go around the outside. If you work quickly you can put the frosting or icing on immediately. If however you have kneaded and handled the marzipan a good deal, allow it to dry for 48 hours, brush with a little whisked egg white to act as a seal, then put on the icing.

## Marzipan ⊛

*110g/4oz icing sugar*
*110g/4oz caster sugar*
*225g/8oz ground almonds*
*few drops almond essence*
*2 egg yolks*
*extra icing or caster sugar*
*Note: you should use equal amounts of sugar and ground almonds, necessitating the less usual metric conversion above*

Blend the icing sugar with the other ingredients. It is a good idea to add the second egg yolk rather slowly, since ground almonds vary a great deal. If they are very fresh and moist they absorb far less egg yolk. The mixture should be like a soft dough that you can gather up in your hands. Roll out on a board sprinkled with a little sifted icing or caster sugar. You might even find that if the ground almonds are stale and dry you need more egg yolks than given.

It is very important that this icing is not overhandled otherwise the oil from the ground almonds seeps through the icing and spoils the colour.

The amount given would be sufficient for a generous layer on the top only of a 20cm/8inch square or 23cm/9inch round cake, such as the Christmas Cake on page 356.

*To coat the top and sides of the cake with marzipan use 175g/6oz icing sugar, 175g/6oz caster sugar 350g/12oz ground almonds, almond essence and 3 egg yolks.

VARIATION

***Marzipan for Simnel Cake:** to give two layers of marzipan for a 20cm/8inch Simnel Cake use the amount given above for coating the top and sides of the cake.

## American Frosting

*350 g/12 oz granulated or caster sugar*
*150 ml/¼ pint water*
*2 eggs whites*
*pinch cream of tartar or few drops lemon juice*

Put the sugar and water into a strong saucepan, stir until the sugar has dissolved then allow the syrup to boil rapidly until it reaches 114.4°C/238°F on a sugar thermometer i.e., the soft ball stage, see below. While the sugar is boiling and before it has reached the required temperature, you should whisk the egg whites until stiff.

Beat the sugar mixture in the saucepan until it turns slightly cloudy, then gradually beat into the egg whites. When all the syrup has been incorporated, beat in the cream of tartar or lemon juice. The icing should be sufficiently stiff to spread easily or to sweep up in peaks. It can be used on soft sponges or instead of Royal Icing on a Christmas cake.

The amount given is enough to coat the top and sides of a 23 cm/9 inch cake, with a thin layer only. For a thicker layer increase the ingredients by 50 per cent.

**To test for soft ball stage:** Drop a small amount of the sugar mixture into cold water; if it can be rolled into a soft ball, it has reached the right temperature.

## Royal Icing ⊛

*450 g/1 lb icing sugar*
*1 tablespoon lemon juice*
*2 egg whites*
*1 teaspoon glycerine (see method)*

Sift the icing sugar with extra care for this recipe, for you cannot achieve a smooth coating with tiny lumps and you could not use the icing for piping. Blend with the other ingredients. The glycerine is not essential but it does help to keep the icing softer.

Beat only until smooth and shiny. Over-beating by hand or electric mixer creates air bubbles, which spoil the coating and make piping difficult. Keep Royal Icing covered with damp absorbent paper or a cloth until ready to use as it hardens very rapidly.

This amount of icing would be sufficient for a moderately thick layer on the top only of a 20 cm/8 inch square or 23 cm/9 inch round cake, such as the Christmas Cake on page 356, with a little left over for piping.

To coat the top and sides of the cake with Royal Icing, use double the ingredients given; this allows for a modest amount of piping.

Royal icing is rarely flavoured but it can be tinted as desired.

## Australian Icing ✳

*15 g/1½ oz gelatine*
*3 tablespoons lemon juice or water*
*100 g/4 oz liquid glucose*
*3 teaspoons glycerine*
*900 g/2 lb icing sugar, plus extra icing sugar for kneading the mixture*

Put the gelatine and lemon juice or water into a small container. Stand this in a saucepan of boiling water until the mixture softens and the gelatine dissolves. Put the glucose and glycerine into a large saucepan, heat very gently and add the gelatine mixture then continue heating until blended. If you wish to colour the icing, it is better to add this to the glycerine mixture before incorporating the icing sugar.

Remove the saucepan from the heat, sift the icing sugar into the saucepan. Mix very well with a wooden spoon and then with your hands until well blended and reasonably smooth.

Sprinkle a large pastry board with sifted icing sugar, add the large lump of icing and continue to knead until it is free from cracks and very smooth. Dust a rolling pin with more sifted icing sugar and roll out the icing to the required size. The amount given here is sufficient for a fairly thick coating on an 18 to 20 cm/7 to 8 inch cake, with a little left for moulding.

When the cake is well covered, smooth the icing with the palm of your hand; the more you handle this icing the shinier it becomes. The cake can be finished by piping in the usual way.

Always keep any icing left in a polythene bag so it does not harden. When ready to use this remove from the bag, knead well then mould it into flowers or other shapes.

Pipe a little Royal Icing onto the back of the flowers and stick on the cake.

This icing never hardens in the way that Royal Icing does.

## Crème Pâtissière ✳

*1 tablespoon cornflour*
*150 ml/¼ pint milk*
*½-1 tablespoon caster sugar*
*few drops vanilla essence*
*2 egg yolks*
*150 ml/¼ pint double cream, lightly whipped*

Blend the cornflour with the milk, add most of the sugar (the sweetness does depend upon the dish with which this is being used). Put into a pan with the vanilla and stir over a low heat until thickened. Remove from the heat. Whisk the egg yolks and beat into the hot, but not boiling, mixture. Return the pan to a very low heat and cook gently, stirring continually, for 2 to 3 minutes; do not allow to boil. Cover the mixture and allow to cool, stirring from time to time to prevent a skin forming. Blend with the whipped cream and adjust the amount of sugar used.

# Whisked Sponges

This type of sponge is so often looked upon as being difficult to make. It is a mixture that must be handled with care, but when once you have found the secret of success it really is wonderfully quick and simple. The hard work of whisking the eggs and sugar is made so much easier with the help of an electric mixer.

The important steps to success are:

a) Whisking the eggs and sugar until really thick – you should be able to see the trail of the whisk in the mixture. Many people believe it is easier to whisk over a pan of hot, but not boiling, water. Personally I find I get a better result by not using hot water. If you are whisking by hand, rather than with an electric mixer, then you will achieve a lighter result if you use a balloon, rather than a rotary, whisk.

b) Sifting the flour at least once; if you leave this on a plate in the warmth of the kitchen for a short time you lighten it.

c) Folding the flour gently and carefully into the light fluffy egg mixture.

## Sponge Cake ⊛

*Ingredients as Swiss Roll (see page 361)*

FILLING:

*150 ml/¼ pint double cream, firmly whipped*

*jam or fresh fruit*

TOPPING:

*little caster sugar*

Prepare the sponge as given above and in the recipe for Swiss Roll on page 361. This mixture is inclined to stick to the tins, so either line them with greased greaseproof paper or grease and flour the tins. It is a wise precaution to grease even non-stick tins. For 3 eggs etc. you need two 18 to 19 cm/7 to 7½ inch tins. Bake above the centre of a moderately hot oven (190°C/375°F or Gas Mark 5) for about 12 minutes or until firm to a gentle touch. Turn out on to sugared paper and sandwich together with the cream and jam or fresh fruit, such as strawberries or raspberries or well drained canned or fresh peach slices. Top with sugar.

VARIATIONS

Bake in one 18 to 19 cm/7 to 7½ inch tin for about 35 minutes at a moderate heat (160°C/325°F or Gas Mark 3).

⊛ **Sponge Fingers:** The 3 eggs will give about 18 to 24 small sponge fingers. Grease and flour the special tins and bake as above, the sponge mixture can be topped with a little caster sugar before baking.

The French type of Madeleines are different from those given on page 350; they are delicate sponge fingers, baked in rather wide shaped tins as above, then coated with a generous amount of sifted icing sugar after baking.

## Swiss Roll ⊛

*85 g/3 oz flour, see note below**
*3 large eggs*
*110 g/4 oz caster sugar*
FILLING:
*6-8 tablespoons jam*
**As the eggs and sugar are beaten so vigorously in this type of sponge, they provide the light texture so you can use plain flour without a raising agent. If however you are making this sponge for the first time, you may feel happier to use self-raising flour.*

Preheat the oven well for this sponge. Set it to moderately hot (190°C/375°F or Gas Mark 5). Line a large Swiss roll tin, approximately 23 x 33 cm/9 x 13 inches, with greaseproof paper, grease lightly. Sift the flour, keep in a warm place.

Whisk the eggs and sugar until thick. Fold the flour into the whisked eggs and sugar as page 360. Pour into the tin and bake for 9 to 10 minutes above the centre of the oven or until firm to the touch. Meanwhile warm, but do not over-heat, the jam. Sprinkle caster sugar over a sheet of greaseproof paper. Turn the cooked sponge onto the sugared paper; strip away the greaseproof paper. Spread with the warmed jam and roll up firmly.

VARIATIONS
Lemon curd or thick fruit purée can be used as a filling.
⊛ **Bûche de Noel:** Prepare 2 or 3 times the amount of Chocolate Butter Icing below or the amount of Chestnut Filling in the Vacherin on page 365. Bake the Swiss Roll, roll around greaseproof paper, cool, then fill roll again and coat with the chocolate or chestnut mixture, shake sifted icing sugar on top, decorate with holly and a robin.
⊛ **Chocolate Swiss Roll:** Omit 15 g/½ oz flour and use 15 g/½ oz cocoa powder instead or omit 25 g/1 oz flour and use 25 g/1 oz chocolate powder. Sift the cocoa or chocolate powder with the flour; bake as above, spread with apricot jam and roll. For a richer cake put greaseproof paper over the sponge, roll and allow to cool. When cold unwrap, fill with apricot jam and 150 ml/¼ pint whipped double cream, then roll up again.

The filled roll can be coated with more whipped cream or with about 225 g/8 oz melted plain chocolate or with butter icing made by creaming 75 g/3 oz butter, 75 g/3 oz icing sugar sifted with 25 g/1 oz cocoa powder or blended with 50 g/2 oz melted chocolate.
⊛ **Fruit Cream Roll:** Roll the sponge around greaseproof paper as recipe above, unroll, fill with whipped cream and fruit. Roll up again and coat with whipped cream.
**Swiss Alaska:** Make the Swiss Roll, fill with crushed fruit and ice cream, coat with a meringue made with 3 stiffly whisked egg whites and 75 to 175 g/3 to 6 oz sugar (depending upon personal taste). Put into a hot oven (230°C/450°F or Gas Mark 8) for 3 to 5 minutes.

## Black Forest Roulade ⊛

*6 large eggs*
*225g/8oz caster sugar*
*50g/2oz cocoa powder*
*little extra sugar*
FILLING:
*1 x 425g/15oz can black cherries, stoned*
*1 tablespoon arrowroot or cornflour*
*2 tablespoons redcurrant jelly*
*25g/1oz caster sugar*
*50g/2oz plain chocolate*
*150ml/¼pint double cream, whipped*
DECORATION:
*150ml/¼pint double cream, whipped*
*50g/2oz plain chocolate*

Line a 33 x 21cm/13 x 8½inch Swiss roll tin with greased greaseproof paper or silicone paper. Separate the eggs. Put the yolks and the 225g/8oz sugar into a large bowl and whisk until thick and creamy. Sift the cocoa and fold into the egg yolks. Finally whisk the whites until these stand in peaks and fold into the chocolate mixture. Spread this evenly into the lined tin. Bake just above the centre of a moderate oven (180°C/350°F or Gas Mark 4) for 15 to 20 minutes until firm to the touch. Turn on to sugared greaseproof paper. Top with another sheet of greaseproof paper. Roll up as described on page 361, allow to cool.

Meanwhile strain the juice from the cherries and blend with the arrowroot or cornflour. Tip into a saucepan and add the jelly and sugar. Stir over a low heat until thickened and clear. Stir in about three-quarters of the cherries. Melt the 50g/2oz chocolate over a pan of hot water. Cool but do not allow to set again. Fold into 150ml/¼pint whipped cream. Unroll the sponge and remove the paper. Spread with the chocolate cream, then the cherry mixture and re-roll. Decorate with the cream and cherries. Grate the 50g/2oz chocolate and sprinkle over the roll.

VARIATION
**Black Forest Gâteau:** Make the Chocolate Sponge or Cake as pages 351 or 353; fill and coat as above.

## Nut Roulade ⊛

*3 eggs*
*100g/4oz caster sugar*
*few drops vanilla essence*
*75g/3oz hazelnuts, very finely chopped or ground (skinned or unskinned as desired*)*
COATING:
*little caster sugar*
FILLING AND TOPPING:
*150-300ml/¼-½pint double cream, whipped*
*few hazelnuts*
**see Gâteau Ganache (page 364) for details*

Whisk the eggs and sugar with the vanilla essence until thick, see under Whisked Sponges (page 360). Fold in the nuts carefully. Put into the prepared tin, bake and test as for Swiss Roll (page 361).

Turn out on to sugared paper, roll up with the paper inside and allow to cool. When quite cold, unroll and fill with some of the cream; roll up again without the paper and decorate with the remainder of the cream and whole nuts.

Do not be disappointed that this mixture does not rise, as when using flour.

VARIATION
Use ground almonds instead of hazelnuts. Ground almonds are more moist, than hazelnuts, so should be dried for a few minutes in a cool oven before using.

## Meringues

*2 egg whites*
*110*g/4 oz sugar, either all caster or half caster and half sieved icing sugar*
**generous 100 g to ensure meringues stay crisp*

Whisk the egg whites until very stiff; do not over-beat otherwise they become dry and crumbly. There are three ways of adding the sugar, i.e. gradually beat in half the amount then fold in the remainder or gradually fold in all the sugar, this produces a rather soft type meringue. The third method is to gradually beat in all the sugar, this works well with a mixer set to low speed and it produces a very firm meringue.

Lightly oil baking trays or greaseproof paper on the trays. If using silicone (non-stick) trays or paper, do not oil. Either spoon or pipe the meringue mixture on to the trays or paper. Two egg whites makes 8 to 10 large shapes; 24 small rounds or finger shapes or about 48 small meringues, suitable for petits four.

Bake at the coolest temperature in the oven, this varies a little with individual cookers but should be 90 to 110°C/200 to 225°F or Gas Mark 0 to ¼. Allow from 1¼ to 2½ to 3 hours, depending upon the size. Test to see if cooked by trying to lift them from the tray or paper; if ready they come away quite easily. Cool and store in an airtight tin.

VARIATIONS

Blend a few drops vanilla, or other essence, with the egg whites.

**Chocolate Meringues:** Sift 1 tablespoon chocolate powder with the sugar, add a few drops vanilla essence too.

**Coffee Meringues:** Sift ½ to 1 teaspoon instant coffee powder with the sugar.

## Almond Meringues

*40 g/1½ oz blanched almonds, finely chopped*
*Ingredients as for Meringue recipe (see above)*

It is essential to make sure the blanched and chopped nuts are well dried, so spread out on a flat tray a little while before making the meringues and leave in a warm place. Blend the nuts with the sugar and proceed as Meringues above.

VARIATIONS

Use chopped dried walnuts or hazelnuts instead.

Do not add nuts to the sugar but sprinkle gently over the egg whites when on the trays before baking.

**Coconut Meringues:** Add 40 g/1½ oz desiccated coconut instead of the almonds. This could be toasted first in a low oven, then allowed to cool.

## Gâteau Ganache ⊛

*4 egg whites*
*250 g/9 oz caster sugar*
*125 g/4½ oz ground hazelnuts**
*1 teaspoon malt vinegar*
*few drops vanilla essence*
FILLING AND DECORATION:
*1-2 tablespoons rum or brandy*
*150 ml/¼ pint double cream, whipped*
CHOCOLATE SAUCE:
*100 g/4 oz plain chocolate*
*300 ml/½ pint water*
*50-75 g/2-3 oz sugar*
*1 tablespoon rum or brandy*
**Ground hazelnuts are obtainable from health food shops. If you cannot buy the nuts ready ground, chop in a food processor. To remove the skin before grinding, roast nuts in a moderately hot oven for 10 minutes and rub away the skins – this is not essential.*

Line the base of two 20 cm/8 inch sandwich tins with rounds of greaseproof paper. Grease and flour this paper and the sides of the tins. Whisk the egg whites until very stiff, then gradually beat in the sugar. Fold in the ground hazelnuts, vinegar and vanilla essence. Divide the mixture between the tins. Bake in the centre of a moderate to moderately hot oven (180-190°C/350-375°F or Gas Mark 4-5) for 35 minutes. Turn out of the tins very carefully and peel off the paper. The cakes will be slightly sticky on the base. Allow to cool.

Fold the rum or brandy into the whipped cream. Sandwich the cakes with the flavoured cream. Gently heat together the ingredients for the sauce, allow to cool. The sauce becomes appreciably thicker when cool. Serve the gâteau with the sauce.

VARIATIONS

Omit the chocolate sauce. Top the gâteau with melted chocolate and decorate with whipped cream and whole hazelnuts.

⊛ **Raspberry Walnut Gâteau:** Use ground walnuts instead of ground hazelnuts. Sandwich the cakes with fresh raspberries and whipped cream. Decorate with whipped cream and raspberries.

## Macaroons ⊛

*2 egg whites*
*few drops almond or ratafia essence*
*150 g/5 oz ground almonds*
*150-176 g/5-6 oz caster sugar*
*rice paper*
DECORATION:
*glacé cherries*
*blanched almonds*

Whisk the egg whites until frothy, add the essence, ground almonds and sugar and form into balls. If too soft, add more ground almonds; if too dry a few drops of water. The mixture makes 12 to 18 macaroons or about 48 tiny ratafias. Put on to the rice paper on baking trays and decorate with pieces of cherry or almond. Bake for 10 to 25 minutes (depending upon size) in the centre of a moderate oven (180°C/350°F or Gas Mark 4). Cool sufficiently to handle and cut around the rice paper. Macaroons are better eaten fresh as they harden with keeping.

To produce a sticky macaroon, put a bowl of water in the oven on a shelf below the biscuits or use 75 to 100 g/3 to 4 oz ground almonds only and pipe the mixture on to the rice paper instead of rolling in balls.

## Almond and Chestnut Vacherin

MERINGUE:
*6 egg whites*
*350 g/12 oz caster sugar*
*50 g/2 oz blanched almonds, flaked*
FILLING:
*1 x 450 g/1 lb can unsweetened chestnut purée*
*50 g/2 oz butter*
*50 g/2 oz icing sugar*
*150 ml/¼ pint double cream, lightly whipped*
*nearly 150 ml/¼ pint single cream*
*25 g/1 oz flaked almonds, blanched*

Cut out three rounds of greaseproof paper 20 cm/8 inches in diameter. Oil each round very lightly and put on to flat baking trays. Whisk the egg whites until very stiff then gradually whisk in half the sugar and fold in nearly all the remaining sugar. Pipe or spread the meringue over the oiled greaseproof paper to give neat rounds. Sprinkle with the almonds and remaining sugar. Dry out the meringues for 2½ to 3 hours in a very cool oven (90-110°C/200-225°F or Gas Mark 0-¼). Lift the meringue rounds off the trays while still warm. Carefully peel away the paper, then transfer to wire cooling trays. When cold, store in an airtight tin, separating the rounds with greaseproof paper.

To make the filling: beat the chestnut purée to soften it slightly. Cream the butter and sifted sugar until soft and light, then gradually beat in the chestnut purée. Gradually blend the whipped cream with the single cream – this gives a softer mixture – but it should be sufficiently thick to pipe.

Spread the first layer of meringue with a quarter of the cream and one-third of the chestnut purée; put on the second layer of meringue and repeat the filling. Top with the final layer of meringue and spread the chestnut purée neatly over the top. Pipe a border of whipped cream and decorate with the almonds. Serve soon after preparation so the merignue does not become too soft. Serves 8.

VARIATION

**Pavlova:** Prepare a round of greaseproof paper 23 cm/9 inches in diameter and place on a baking tray. Whisk 4 egg whites, add 225 g/8 oz sugar, as above, but blended with 1½ teaspoons cornflour. Finally fold in ½ teaspoon white vinegar. Bake as above, but allow a little longer, as you have a greater depth of mixture. Cool and store in an airtight tin. Fill just before serving.

One of the nicest fillings is made by blending 350 g/12 oz lemon curd with 300 ml/½ pint whipped cream. In Australia, where this is so popular, they blend passion fruit (Grenadilla) purée with whipped cream, but other fruit purées can be used, or fill with fresh fruit, such as sweetened strawberries and whipped cream.

## Choux Pastry ⊛

*150 ml/¼ pint water*
*25 g/1 oz butter*
*pinch salt, if making savoury choux pastry or sugar for sweet choux pastry*
*75 g/3 oz plain flour*
*2 eggs, beaten well*
*part of 1 egg yolk, if necessary*

Put the water, butter and salt or sugar into a pan; heat until the butter has melted, then remove from the heat. Sift the flour, add to the pan, return to a low heat; stir well until the mixture forms a dry ball. Once again remove from the heat and gradually beat in the eggs to give a smooth sticky mixture. You may need part of the third egg yolk with this recipe.

VARIATION

A more delicate pastry is made by using 150 ml/¼ pint water; 50 g/2 oz butter, 65 g/2½ oz flour and 2 eggs.

## Cream Buns ⊛

*Ingredients as Choux Pastry above*

FILLING AND TOPPING:

*150 ml/¼ pint double cream, whipped*
*icing sugar*

Either spoon or pipe the mixture with a 1 cm/½ inch pipe into rounds of the desired size on a lightly greased baking tray. You can make 8 to 10 large buns or up to 20 small ones. Bake in the centre of a moderately hot oven (190-200°C/375-400°F or Gas Mark 5-6). Large buns take 20 to 25 minutes; small buns up to 15 minutes or until firm to the touch. If necessary, reduce the heat slightly after 10 minutes. Cool away from a draught; split and if there is any uncooked mixture inside carefully remove this. Fill with the cream and top with sifted icing sugar.

Cooked but unfilled Choux Pastry freezes for 3 months.

VARIATIONS

Use a savoury filling (see page 13).

**Croquembouche:** Make double the amount of Choux Pastry if you want an impressive pyramid. Pipe into about 40 little buns and bake as above. Cool and fill with whipped cream. Make a caramel by boiling together 150 g/5 oz sugar and 5 tablespoons water; keep warm so it does not set. Form a round with some of the filled buns, dip the next 6 or 7 buns into the caramel and press in position. Continue like this until you have a tall pyramid. Decorate with whipped cream and seasonal fruit.

⊛ **Éclairs:** Pipe or spoon the choux pastry into finger shapes; bake as for the Cream Buns above. When cold, fill with whipped cream or Créme Pâtissière (page 359). Top with Coffee or Chocolate Glacé Icing (page 352).

**Profiteroles:** Make tiny cream buns, cool and fill with cream, coat with a generous amount of Chocolate Sauce (see page 346).

## Mincemeat ✱

*100 g/4 oz cooking apples, grated*
*100 g/4 oz suet, shredded or grated or 100 g/4 oz butter, melted*
*100 g/4 oz demerara sugar*
*100 g/4 oz candied peel, finely chopped*
*225 g/8 oz currants*
*100 g/4 oz seedless raisins*
*100 g/4 oz sultanas*
*100 g/4 oz glacé cherries, finely chopped*
*100 g/4 oz blanched almonds, finely chopped*
*2 teaspoons finely grated lemon rind*
*2 tablespoons lemon juice*
*1 teaspoon mixed spice*
*½ teaspoon ground cinnamon*
*½ teaspoon grated nutmeg*
*4 tablespoons whisky, brandy or rum*

Mix all the ingredients together, put into jars; cover well. Store in a cool dry place.

✱ **To make Mince Pies:** Use puff, flaky, shortcrust or the sweet pastry in the flan (see page 322). You need a total weight of about 450 g/1 lb pastry for 12 to 18 average-sized mince pies. Roll out the pastry thinly, use just over half and cut into rounds to line fairly deep patty tins. Put in a spoonful of mincemeat but do not over-fill. Cut the remaining pastry into slightly smaller rounds as 'lids'. Damp the edges of the pastry and press the 'lids' in position. Make two slits on top with scissors. For a shiny top, brush with beaten egg or egg white.

Bake for approximately 20 minutes in the centre of the oven. Use a hot oven for puff or flaky pastry (220°C/425°F or Gas Mark 7), a moderately hot oven (200°C/400°F or Gas Mark 6) for shortcrust pastry and a slightly cooler temperature (190°C/375°F or Gas Mark 5) for the sweet pastry. Reduce the heat slightly in each case if the top pastry is over browning.

Dust with sifted icing or caster sugar before serving.

The mince pies can be prepared or cooked and frozen.

## Palmiers Glacés

*Puff Pastry, made with 225 g/8 oz flour (see page 292)*
*50 g/2 oz caster sugar*
*150 ml/¼ pint double cream, firmly whipped*
*2-3 tablespoons jam*

Make the pastry as usual, but on the sixth and seventh rollings, sprinkle the board with the sugar, so the pastry absorbs this; use up all the amount of sugar given. Finally roll out the pastry to a large oblong, the pastry should be wafer-thin. Pick up the corners of one half of the long side of the oblong and roll towards the centre, as though making a Swiss Roll; stop at the centre. Pick up the opposite corners and roll the dough towards the centre. You can have both rolls meeting in the centre or reverse one roll. Cut into slices of 5 to 8 mm/¼ to one-third inch thickness. Bake on an ungreased baking tray just above the centre of a hot oven (230°C/450°F or Gas Mark 8) for about 12 minutes; lower the heat slightly after the pastry rises if it becomes too brown. Allow to cool and sandwich two slices with the cream and jam. The filling is not essential, the pastry is delicious without this. Freeze without a filling.

VARIATION

Use flaky or rough puff pastry instead of puff.

## Brandy Snaps

*50 g/2 oz flour**
*½ teaspoon ground ginger*
*50 g/2 oz butter*
*50 g/2 oz caster sugar*
*2 level tablespoons golden syrup*
**if using Imperial weight, deduct 1 teaspoon flour*

Sift the flour with the ginger. Put the butter, sugar and golden syrup into a saucepan and heat only until the ingredients have melted; if boiled for any length of time, the mixture becomes too dry. Add the flour mixture and stir briskly to blend. Grease 2 to 3 baking trays with a little oil or melted butter. Put teaspoons of the mixture on the trays, allowing a great deal of space for the sticky mixture to spread out. Put the first tray of biscuits into the centre of a moderate oven (160°C/325°F or Gas Mark 3) and cook for 7 to 8 minutes, or until the edges of the biscuit rounds begin to set. During this time it is important not to have two trays coming out of the oven at the same time as there would be insufficient time for you to roll the biscuits before they set. While the biscuits are cooking, grease the handle of a wooden spoon.

Take the first tray of biscuits from the oven. Allow to cool for 1 minute then lift the first round off the tin with the help of a palette knife and roll around the spoon handle; hold in position for a few seconds then remove. Continue like this. If by any chance some of the biscuits begin to harden before you can remove them from the tray, then replace in the oven for 1 minute. Store in an airtight tin.

## Parisienne Biscuits

*ingredients as Brandy Snaps (see above)*
*2 tablespoons walnuts, finely chopped*
*2 tablespoons glacé cherries, finely chopped*
*2 tablespoons candied peel, finely chopped*

Make the biscuits following the Brandy Snaps above. Bake for 4 to 5 minutes only then remove from the oven, top with the nuts, cherries and peel. Return the trays to the oven and complete the baking, as Brandy Snaps but do not roll.

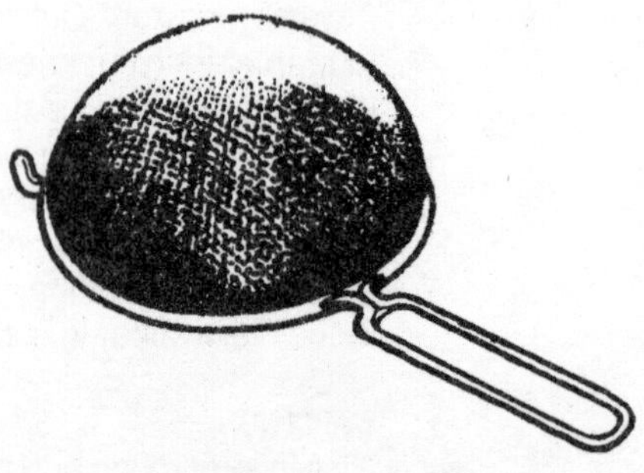

## Scotch Shortbread ⊛

*100 g/4 oz plain flour*
*50 g/2 oz rice flour or extra plain flour or cornflour*
*100 g/4 oz butter*
*50 g/2 oz caster sugar*
COATING:
*dusting of rice flour or cornflour*

Sift the flour and rice flour or cornflour into a bowl. Cut the butter into small pieces and rub into the flour mixture with the tips of your fingers. Add the sugar and knead very well until the mixture binds together. Lightly dust a shortbread mould with the rice flour or cornflour. Press in the mixture and leave for a time and then turn out onto a lightly greased baking tray. Bake in the centre of a cool to moderate oven (150-160°C/300-325°F or Gas Mark 2-3) for 30 minutes or until firm to the touch. Cool slightly, mark in sections and allow to cool on the baking tray.

Store in an airtight tin.

VARIATIONS

Dust with caster sugar immediately after cooking.

Bake on a larger flatter tray to give a thinner shortbread, bake as the recipe for Caramel Shortbread.

⊛ **Vanilla Shortbreads:** Cream together 75 g/3 oz butter, 50 g/2 oz caster sugar, a few drops vanilla essence; add 100 g/4 oz self-raising flour. Form into 12 to 18 balls, put on to an ungreased baking tray and bake in the centre of a moderate oven (160°C/325°F or Gas Mark 3) for 12 to 15 minutes. Cool on the baking tray.

## Caramel Shortbread

*Scotch Shortbread (see above)*
CARAMEL LAYER:
*100 g/4 oz butter or margarine*
*50 g/2 oz caster sugar*
*2 tablespoons golden syrup*
*1 x 175 g/6 oz can full-cream sweetened condensed milk*
CHOCOLATE TOPPING:
*100-150 g/4-5 oz plain chocolate*

Make the shortbread and bake for 25 to 30 minutes in a greased baking tin, measuring 20 x 28 x 4 cm/8 x 11 x 1½ inches; allow to cool and remain in the tin.

Put the ingredients for the caramel layer into a strong saucepan. Stir over a low heat until melted, then allow to boil steadily until golden brown. Stir continuously during this process. Cool until a spreading consistency, then spoon over the caramel.

Melt the chocolate in a basin over hot, but not boiling, water or in a microwave cooker then pour this over the caramel topping. When this is completely covered with chocolate, spread evenly and firmly with a knife so the chocolate adheres to the caramel. Finally swirl the chocolate with a fork. Allow the topping to set for several hours. Cut into about 20 fingers, lift out of the baking tin. Store in an airtight tin until ready to serve.

# My Favourite Gâteaux

## Almond and Strawberry Gâteau

*50 g/2 oz blanched almonds, finely chopped*
*2 egg whites*
*½ teaspoon vinegar*
*100 g/4 oz caster sugar*
GLAZE:
*6 tablespoons redcurrant jelly*
*1 tablespoon lemon juice*
*½ teaspoon arrowroot*
*3 tablespoons water*
TOPPING:
*450-700 g/1-1½ lb strawberries, choose uniform size if possible*
*150 ml/¼ pint double cream, whipped*

Brown the almonds under the grill or in the oven; cool. Whisk the egg whites until stiff, add the vinegar and the sugar. Line a 20 cm/8 inch sandwich tin with oiled paper or silicone paper. Spread the meringue over this and allow to set for about 1 hour in the centre of a very slow oven (130-140°C/250-275°F or Gas Mark ½-1). This gives a crisp outside but a soft centre. For a very crisp meringue that keeps well in a tin, bake for a longer period at an even lower temperature.

Put the jelly and lemon juice into a pan. Blend the arrowroot and water and add to the pan. Stir over a low heat until the jelly melts and continue stirring until clear. Allow to cool but *not* to set. Brush a little over the meringue base, top with the strawberries then the rest of the glaze. Decorate with the cream. Serves 6.

## Jamaican Gâteau ⊛

*Victoria Sandwich (see page 351)*
FILLING:
*4 tablespoons ground coffee*
*300 ml/½ pint water*
*miniature bottle rum*
*75 g/3 oz butter*
*150 g/5 oz icing sugar*
*25 g/1 oz cocoa or 50 g/2 oz chocolate powder*
DECORATION:
*300 ml/½ pint double cream, lightly whipped*
*25 g/1 oz icing sugar*
*50 g/2 oz plain chocolate, grated*
*about 12 finger-shaped meringues (see page 363)*

Make the Victoria Sponge and bake it in one 20 cm/8 inch greased and floured tin without a loose base. (If you do not have a tin without a loose base, use a soufflé dish to complete the gâteau.) To complete this recipe, allow the sponge to cool then cut into four layers horizontally.

Put a round of greaseproof paper into the tin or soufflé dish. Make the very strong coffee and add most of the rum. Beat together the butter, sugar and cocoa or chocolate powder to make the butter icing. Put the first layer of sponge in the tin, moisten with a quarter of the coffee and rum liquid; spread with one-third of the butter icing. Repeat this until all the layers of sponge are in the tin or dish; spoon the remaining coffee and rum liquid over the final round of sponge. Put a round of greaseproof paper and light weight on top; leave for 24 hours. Turn out on to a serving dish. Blend the whipped cream, sifted icing sugar and remaining rum together. Spread over the top and sides of the gâteau and decorate the top with grated chocolate. Press the meringues around the sides.

Freeze this gâteau without the meringues.

# Cooking With Yeast

I derive particular pleasure from handling a yeast dough and watching the dramatic way it rises. A good loaf of bread depends upon the right choice of flour (see page 348), handling the dough correctly and baking quickly. I have given bread based on only 450 g/1 lb flour. As soon as you become confident in your skills then I would suggest you make larger amounts and freeze the excess quantity.

## Bread ⊛

*450 g/1 lb strong or plain flour*
*1 teaspoon salt, or to taste*
*25 g/1 oz butter, margarine or cooking fat*
*15 g/½ oz fresh yeast, or 2 teaspoons dried yeast with 1 teaspoon sugar*
*300 ml/½ pint water or milk and water, at blood heat*
GLAZE:
*see under 'shaping' next page*

Sift the flour with the salt. Rub in the butter, margarine or fat (this can be omitted, but I like the slightly richer texture given). Blend the fresh yeast with the warm water or milk and water. If using dried yeast, dissolve the sugar in the warm liquid, sprinkle the dried yeast on top. Allow to stand for 10 minutes, or until frothy, then proceed as if using fresh yeast.

Blend the yeast liquid with the flour mixture and work with your hands until a smooth dough. (Makes of flour vary slightly, so if too soft add a very little extra flour, if too dry a few drops of extra warm liquid).

Turn the dough on to a lightly floured surface and knead well with the base of the palm of your hand, called the 'heel'. To test if sufficiently kneaded, press with a floured finger; if the impression comes out the dough is ready to prove (this means to rise). Either replace the dough in a large bowl and cover with polythene or a cloth or put into a lightly oiled large polythene bag and tie loosely. Put in a warm place, this can be the airing cupboard or warming drawer of the cooker. The small amount of dough given takes about 1 hour; if preferred leave at average room temperature, when it will take about 2 hours or leave 12 hours in a refrigerator. The dough is adequately proved when it has risen to twice the original size. If leaving in a refrigerator you will need to bring it out for a short time before the next stage.

Knead the dough again, test carefully to see if ready, as instructions above, then shape into the desired shape, bake as instructed, see next page.

## To Shape and Bake Bread ⊛

*Bread Dough (see page 371)*
TO GLAZE:
*a little milk or 1 egg beaten with 1 teaspoon water*

The dough made on the previous page can be shaped into one large, or two smaller loaves, or it would make 15 to 18 rolls.

A tin loaf is made by pressing out the dough to form an oblong, the width of which should be the length of the loaf tin you intend to use. The oblong length should be just three times the width of the loaf tin. Fold the dough neatly over, so it fits the tin. Grease the tin, put in the dough with the join at the bottom. You need a 900 g/2 lb loaf tin if making one loaf or two 450 g/1 lb loaf tins if dividing it into two portions.

You can make round loaves or cottage loaves. To make the latter, form two-thirds of the dough into a round, flatten it slightly. Form the other third into a smaller round to fit on top, press this on the larger round and make an indentation in the top. Put on to a greased baking tray.

Rolls can be made into rounds or any desired shapes. Allow the shaped dough to prove until almost double the original size. Brush with a little milk or beaten egg to give a shine. It is advisable to put oiled polythene lightly over the dough as it proves to prevent a hard skin forming.

Always preheat the oven thoroughly before making bread – it needs to be hot (220°C/425°F or Gas Mark 7). Bake the large loaf for approximately 40 minutes, the two smaller loaves for approximately 30 minutes in the centre of the oven; you may need to reduce the heat slightly after the first 20 minutes.

Bake rolls at the same temperature but just above the centre for approximately 12 to 15 minutes.

To test if the loaves are cooked, remove from the tray or tin(s); knock on the bottom, they should sound hollow.

## Wholemeal Bread ⊛

*Ingredients as for Bread on page 371 but use wholemeal or wheatmeal flour*

This bread can be made in exactly the same way as white bread on the previous page, except you will find the flour absorbs a little more liquid. However, I often make a very moist dough, rather more like a very thick batter. You cannot knead this by hand, you must beat it with a spoon for some minutes or knead slowly with a mixer.

Allow to prove and bake in exactly the same way as for white bread, but allow a longer cooking period. The bread keeps more moist. When wanting to shape wholemeal rolls you will need the usual consistency.

## York Mayne Bread ⊛

*4 tablespoons milk*
*4 tablespoons water*
*15g/½oz yeast*
*350g/12oz plain flour*
*225g/8oz sugar*
*1 teaspoon coriander seeds*
*1 teaspoon caraway seeds*
*3 egg yolks*
*2 teaspoons rose water (obtainable from chemists)*
*2 egg whites*

Warm the milk and water and blend in the yeast. Sift the flour, add the sugar, coriander and caraway seeds. Add the egg yolks, the rose water and the yeast liquid (there is no need to allow this to stand before blending with the flour). Mix well with a wooden spoon. As flours vary in the amount of liquid they absorb, you may find you need to add a little extra warm milk or water to give soft consistency, or it may be necessary to incorporate a small amount of flour when kneading the dough. Whisk the egg whites until stiff, fold into the mixture with a metal spoon. Turn the dough out of the bowl and knead on a floured board until smooth. Leave for approximately 1 hour to prove (see page 371). Form into either a round or a tin loaf. If forming the round, put on to a lightly greased flat baking tray and leave to prove for approximately 25 minutes. If making a tin loaf put into a lightly greased and floured 1 kg/2 lb tin and allow to rise in the same way. Bake in the centre of a moderately hot oven (190-200°C/375-400°F or Gas Mark 5-6) for approximately 25 to 30 minutes or until golden coloured and hollow when tapped on the base. Serve fresh, thickly sliced and spread with butter as a loaf, or cut thinly as a cake.

## Orange Apricot Loaf ⊛

*175g/6oz dried apricots*
*12 tablespoons orange juice*
*2 teaspoons grated orange rind*
*50g/2oz glacé cherries, chopped*
*75g/3oz halved walnuts, chopped*
*75g/3oz butter or margarine, melted*
*350g/12oz flour*
*100g/4oz caster sugar*
*2 eggs*
*1 tablespoon milk*
DECORATION:
*4 walnut halves*
*4 glacé cherries, halved*

Cut each apricot into 8 small pieces. Put into a good-sized mixing bowl. Add the orange juice and leave soaking for 12 hours. Add the remaining ingredients and mix well. Grease and flour a loaf tin measuring 12 x 23 cm/5 x 9 inches. Spoon in the mixture. Bake in the centre of a moderate oven (180°C/350°F or Gas Mark 4) for 30 minutes. Open the oven door carefully and press the walnut halves and glacé cherries on top of the partially set mixture. Reduce the heat at this time to cool (150°C/300°F or Gas Mark 2) and continue cooking for a further 1 to 1¼ hours until firm to the touch. Turn out carefully on to a wire cooling tray. Keep for at least a day before cutting. Slice thinly and spread with butter.

VARIATION

⊛ **Date Loaf:** Use dried dates instead of apricots (weight should be 175g/6oz after stoning). Soak for 1 hour only in 12 tablespoons hot water or warmed orange juice. Omit the cherries in the recipe and topping.

## Scones ⊛

*225 g/8 oz self-raising flour or plain flour with ½ teaspoon bicarbonate of soda and 1 teaspoon cream of tartar*
*pinch salt*
*25-50 g/1-2 oz fat (this can be butter, margarine, good lard or cooking fat)*
*25-50 g/1-2 oz caster or granulated sugar*
*milk to bind*

Sift the flour and salt, or the flour with the salt, bicarbonate of soda and cream of tartar, if using plain flour. Rub in the fat, add the sugar, then mix to a soft dough with the milk. Either press out with your hands on a lightly floured surface or roll until 1-1.5 cm/½-¾ inch in thickness. Cut into rounds of the desired size with a lightly floured pastry cutter, put on to an ungreased baking tray.

Bake towards the top of a hot oven (220-230°C/425-450°F or Gas Mark 7-8). Use the hotter temperature for thin scones. Lift off the baking tray and allow to cool.

VARIATIONS

⊛ **Buttermilk Scones:** Use plain flour and bicarbonate of soda, omit the cream of tartar and mix with buttermilk. These scones are particularly light.

⊛ **Cheese Scones:** Sift a good pinch salt, shake pepper, pinch dry mustard with the flour, omit the sugar. Add 50 g/2 oz finely grated Cheddar or other strongly flavoured cheese after rubbing the fat into the flour. Blend with an egg and a little milk. Put on a greased baking tray, brush with beaten egg and bake at the lower temperature given in the basic recipe, reduce heat slightly after 5 minutes.

⊛ **Fruit Scones:** These can be varied a great deal; for a basic fruit scone, add from 50 g/2 oz dried fruit, but you can add the grated rind of 1 lemon or orange to the flour then use a little fruit juice when blending the dough. Add dried fruit plus chopped candied peel or finely chopped glacé cherries.

⊛ **Honey Scones:** Add 2 tablespoons honey instead of sugar to the flour and fat mixture; black treacle or golden syrup could be used instead.

## Scotch Pancakes ⊛

*100 g/4 oz self-raising flour*
*pinch salt*
*1 egg*
*scant 150 ml/¼ pint milk*
*25 g/1 oz butter, melted (optional)*

Blend the ingredients and beat until a smooth thick batter. Preheat and grease a griddle, or base of a strong frying pan. To test the heat, drop on a teaspoon of batter; it should set within 1 minute.

Drop tablespoons or teaspoons of batter (depending on size required) on to the hot surface. Cook for 1 to 2 minutes or until the surface is covered with bubbles, turn with a knife and cook for the same time on the second side or until firm to the touch. Cover with a cloth on a wire cooling tray as the pancakes cool.

# Preserves

Over the years I have shown people how to make all kinds of preserves, but in this book I am giving you just the recipes I find most enjoyable. I like jams with a very definite flavour; where possible I make conserves that are full of large pieces of fruit, rather than smooth jams. I am afraid conserves are more extravagant, as one takes more generous helpings, so I have given variations for economical jams too. I love to watch the tiny fruits developing on my crab apple tree, for I know they will produce a delicious jelly, which makes a good alternative to redcurrant jelly. You will find Apple Jelly with others on pages 385 and 386. Jellies are equally good as part of both sweet and savoury dishes.

Remember that a correct balance of ingredients is essential for the successful making of jams, jellies and marmalade. You must have sufficient fruit to provide an adequate quantity of pectin (the ingredient that makes the preserve set). If using fruit that is low in pectin, you either use a higher proportion of the fruit to the amount of sugar, or add pectin in the form of lemon juice or acid apple or redcurrant juice.

Never over-boil preserves, for you spoil the colour, flavour and consistency. In some cases, over-boiling means that the preserve will not set, for you have passed the setting stage. The ways in which to test the preserve to ascertain whether it has reached the correct setting stage is given on the next page.

You may find it convenient to freeze fruit purées, ready to make preserves at a later date. This is very satisfactory if you remember that freezing does reduce the pectin content of fruit. To compensate for this, add additional pectin. If the standard recipe does not contain lemon juice add 1 tablespoon lemon juice to each 450 g/1 lb fruit. Where the preserve already contains lemon juice, or additional acid, use double the amount given in the recipe.

I hope you will try the rather less usual chutney and pickle recipes given in this chapter.

# Making Preserves

Always use a good-sized preserving pan, so the ingredients can boil rapidly without fear of their boiling over.

When making conserves allow the sugar and fruit to stand for several hours, so the natural juices will flow. This helps to keep the pieces of fruit firm.

Conserves never set as firmly as a jam. Allow the completed conserve to cool for a short time in the pan, stir to distribute the fruit, then put into the hot jars.

When making jam, simmer the fruit, or fruit and water slowly; this softens the fruit skins and extracts the natural pectin. Add the sugar with any acid recommended in the recipe; stir over a low heat until the sugar has dissolved then boil rapidly until setting point is reached, see below.

Spoon or pour the hot preserve into heated jars; fill to within 5 mm to 1 cm/¼ to ½ inch of the top of the jars (to exclude the maximum amount of air). Put on the waxed circles and final covers. Store in a cool dry place.

**Testing for Setting Point**

a) Put a little of the preserve on to a saucer when you think it is ready; cool then push with your finger; if the preserve wrinkles and forms a skin, it has reached setting point.

b) Stir a wooden spoon in the preserve when you think it is ready. Leave some preserve on the spoon and allow to cool. Hold the spoon over the pan; if the preserve really has set the mixture will hang on the edge of the spoon, forming a firm flake.

c) Use a sugar thermometer. Stir this round in the hot preserve. When the thermometer reaches 104°C/220°F you have a light set. For a firmer set allow the temperature to reach 105°C/222°F. The ideal temperature for jellies is 104.5°C/221°F. Always read the temperature with the thermometer IN THE PRESERVE; and do not put this on to a cold surface when removing it from the pan.

d) Check the weight of the finished preserve. From each 450 g/1 lb sugar used you should make 750 g/1¼-1½ lb. If you have made much more, then it is doubtful whether the preserve has set correctly.

**Choice of Sugar**

Special preserving sugar helps to avoid the slight scum that forms on most preserves, but loaf or granulated sugar can be used. It is extravagant to use the more expensive caster sugar. If you add 15 to 25 g/½ to 1 oz unsalted butter to the hot preserve when it reaches setting point, then stir briskly, you disperse most of the scum.

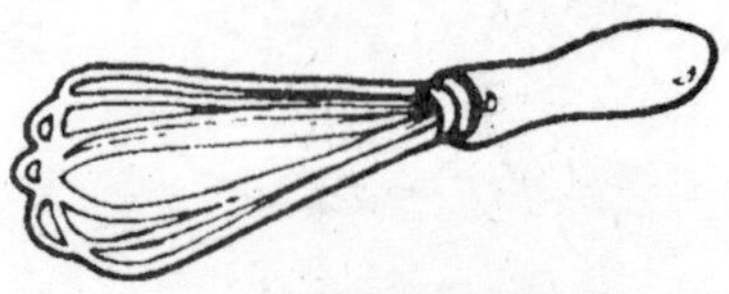

## Apricot Conserve

*450g/1 lb ripe, but firm apricots (weight when stoned)*
*2 tablespoons lemon juice*
*450g/1 lb sugar*

Halve the fruit, put into the pan and add the lemon juice and sugar. Stir well so that all the fruit is coated with lemon juice and sugar – this keeps the apricots a good colour. Leave for about 4 hours. Put the pan over a very low heat and stir until the sugar has dissolved, then boil rapidly until setting point is reached. The stones can be cracked and the kernels added to the preserve just before it sets. Spoon into hot jars.

## Apricot Jam

*450g/1 lb apricots*
*4 tablespoons water (if the fruit is under-ripe) or 2 tablespoons water (if the fruit is ripe)*
*450g/1 lb sugar*
*1 tablespoon lemon juice (if the fruit is under-ripe) or 2 tablespoons lemon juice (if the fruit is ripe)*

Put the halved fruit and water in the pan, simmer until the fruit is soft. Add the sugar and lemon juice, stir until the sugar has dissolved then boil rapidly until setting point is reached. The stones can be cracked and the kernels added to the preserve just before it sets. Spoon into hot jars.

VARIATION

**Dried Apricot Jam:** Do not despise jam made with dried fruit. The flavour is quite different from when fresh apricots are used, but you make a very rich jam, which is delicious in tarts. Soak 450g/1 lb dried apricots in 1.7 litres/3 pints cold water for 48 hours. Put into the pan and simmer very slowly until the fruit is soft. This takes about 1 hour. Add 1.35kg/3 lb sugar and 6 tablespoons lemon juice. Stir until the sugar has dissolved, then boil rapidly until setting point is reached. Spoon into hot jars.

## Blackberry and Apple Jam

*225g/8oz cooking apples (weight after peeling and coring, retain the peel and cores)*
*225g/8oz blackberries*
*450g/1 lb sugar*

Dice the apples, tie the cores and peel in a piece of muslin. Wash the blackberries in cold water. Put the fruit into the pan with the bag of peel and cores. Simmer gently until the fruit is soft. Add the sugar, stir well until dissolved (remove the bag of peel and cores) then boil rapidly until setting point is reached. The peel helps to give flavour and make the jam set. Spoon into hot jars.

VARIATION

**Elderberry and Apple Jam:** Use elderberries instead of blackberries.

## Black Cherry Jam

*450g/1 lb black cherries (weight when stoned, see method)*
*400g/14oz sugar*
*1 tablespoon lemon juice if the fruit is very ripe*

Stone the fruit over the preserving pan, so no juice is wasted. You can do this with a proper cherry stoner or with a fine hairpin. Insert the bent end of the hairpin into each cherry, move this until it goes around the stone then pull firmly. The stones can be tied in muslin and added to the pan to give more flavour to the jam. Put the fruit into the pan, with or without the stones. Simmer gently for a few minutes. Add the sugar, stir briskly until dissolved and add the lemon juice. Boil rapidly until setting point is reached. Cool slightly and remove the bag of stones. Stir the jam to distribute the fruit then spoon into hot jars.

VARIATION

**Morello Cherry Jam:** Increase the sugar to 450g/1 lb. To ensure the cherries keep whole you can follow the method for Apricot Conserve on page 377.

## Blackcurrant Jam

*450g/1 lb blackcurrants*
*300ml/½ pint water*
*560g/1¼ lb sugar*

Put the blackcurrants and water into the pan and simmer slowly until the skins are very soft. This is important for they do not soften after the sugar is added. Add the sugar, stir well until dissolved then boil rapidly until setting point is reached. Spoon into hot jars.

## Cranberry Jam

*450g/1 lb cranberries*
*150ml/¼ pint water*
*560g/1¼ lb sugar*

Cranberries make a delicious jam. Simmer the fruit and water until the cranberries are tender. Add the sugar, stir until dissolved then boil rapidly until setting point is reached. This can be served instead of Cranberry Sauce or with apples or other fruits or as a filling for tarts and sponges.

## Damson Jam

*560g/1¼ lb damsons*
*300ml/½ pint water or use 150ml/¼ pint if the fruit is very ripe*
*450g/1 lb sugar*

It is impossible to stone damsons before cooking, so I allow the extra weight to compensate for the weight of the stones. Simmer the damsons and water until the fruit is soft; remove the stones, add the sugar, stir until dissolved then boil rapidly until setting point is reached. Spoon into hot jars.

VARIATIONS

**Damson Cheese:** Simmer the fruit and water until a smooth pulp. Rub through a nylon sieve, measure the pulp and allow 450g/1 lb sugar to each scant 600ml/1 pint purée. Heat the purée, add the sugar, stir over a low heat until dissolved then boil rapidly until setting point is reached.

**Blackcurrant Cheese:** Use proportions as for jam. Simmer the fruit and water until soft, rub through a nylon sieve, then proceed as for Damson Cheese above.

## Fresh Fig Jam

*450g/1 lb fresh green or purple figs*
*450g/1 lb sugar*
*2 tablespoons lemon juice*

Halve small figs, or quarter larger ones. Put into the pan with the sugar and stir until the fruit is coated with sugar. Leave for 4 hours. Stir over a low heat until the sugar has dissolved; add the lemon juice. Boil rapidly until setting point is reached; cool slightly, stir briskly then spoon into hot jars.

VARIATION

**Dried Fig Jam:** Soak 450g/1 lb diced dried figs in 450ml/¾ pint water for 24 hours, simmer gently until soft; add 675g/1½ lb sugar and 3 tablespoons lemon juice. Stir until the sugar has dissolved, boil steadily until setting point is reached and spoon into hot jars.

## Japonica Jam

*450g/1 lb japonica fruit*
*scant 600ml/1 pint water*
*sugar (see method)*
*lemon juice (see method)*
*preserved ginger (optional, see method)*

If you are lucky enough to have japonica bushes you have lovely shrubs, plus fruit for making a most delicate flavoured jam. Halve the fruit, do not peel or core. Put into a pan with the water and simmer until soft. Rub through a nylon sieve. Measure the purée and allow 450g/1 lb sugar, 2 tablespoons lemon juice and you can also add 50g/2oz diced preserved ginger to each scant 600ml/1 pint pulp. Heat the japonica pulp, add the sugar and lemon juice and stir until the sugar has dissolved then add the ginger. Boil steadily until setting point is reached. Spoon into hot jars.

## Loganberry Jam

*450g/1 lb loganberries*
*450g/1 lb sugar*

This rich berry jam is probably my favourite of all jams. Put the fruit into the pan, crush with a wooden spoon to make the juice flow, this saves having to add water. Simmer until soft then add the sugar and stir until dissolved. Boil rapidly until setting point is reached and put into hot jars.

VARIATION

**Raspberry Jam:** Use the same proportions of fruit and sugar as Loganberry Jam, above. In order to minimize the cooking of the raspberries warm the sugar in a bowl in a very cool oven for a few minutes. Simmer the raspberries for only 3 to 4 minutes, add the warmed sugar, stir to dissolve then boil rapidly for a few minutes only until a light setting stage is reached. Spoon into hot jars.

## Strawberry Conserve

*about 100g/4oz redcurrants (to produce 4 tablespoons juice)*
*425g/15oz sugar*
*450g/1 lb small and firm strawberries*

Heat the redcurrants for a few minutes until the juice flows. Put through a jelly bag and measure out the 4 tablespoons juice. Sprinkle the sugar over the strawberries and leave in a pan for 2 hours. Stir over a low heat until the sugar has dissolved. Add the redcurrant juice and boil steadily until a light setting stage is reached. Cool slightly, stir to distribute the fruit and spoon into hot jars.

## Victoria Plum Conserve

*450 g/1 lb sugar*
*4 tablespoons water*
*450 g/1 lb Victoria plums (weight when stoned)*

Heat the sugar and water in a pan and stir until the sugar has dissolved. Halve small plums, or quarter large ones. Put the fruit into the syrup and poach gently until the plums are soft. Increase the temperature and boil steadily until setting point is reached. Cool slightly, stir to distribute the fruit, then spoon into hot jars.

VARIATIONS

The stones can be cracked and the kernels added to the preserve just before it sets.

**Greengage Conserve:** Choose greengages that are just ripe, but not over-ripe; halve and proceed as above. When the fruit is nearly tender, add 1 tablespoon lemon juice to each 450 g/1 lb fruit to aid setting.

## Quince Jam

*450 g/1 lb quinces (weight when peeled and cored)*
*150 ml/¼ pint water*
*2 teaspoons grated lemon rind*
*2 tablespoons lemon juice*
*450 g/1 lb sugar*

Peel, halve and core the fruit, then cut it into small pieces. Simmer with the water until tender. Add the grated lemon rind and juice with the sugar. Stir over a low heat until the sugar has dissolved, then boil rapidly until setting point is reached. Spoon into hot jars.

VARIATION

**Quince Marmalade:** Use the same proportions as for jam. Peel and halve the fruit, then cut the pulp into neat thin slices (the thickness of the peel in marmalade). Heat the sugar, lemon rind and water together and stir until the sugar has dissolved. Add the sliced quinces and poach gently until tender. Add the lemon juice and boil rapidly until setting point is reached. Cool until the marmalade has stiffened slightly, stir to distribute the slices, then spoon into hot jars.

## Uncooked Raspberry Jam ⊛

*450 g/1 lb sugar*
*450 g/1 lb raspberries*

This jam is only successful if the raspberries are ripe and quite perfect. Heat the sugar for a few minutes in a warm oven. Mash the fruit, add the warm sugar, stir until the sugar has dissolved. Spoon into hot jars and seal as usual. If making large stocks, put the surplus in the freezer and bring out when ready to use.

## Rhubarb Conserve

*450 g/1 lb rhubarb*
*450 g/1 lb sugar*
*100 g/4 oz seedless raisins*
*1 teaspoon grated lemon rind*
*1 teaspoon grated orange rind*
*1 tablespoon orange juice*
*2 tablespoons lemon juice*

Use autumn rhubarb for this preserve as it has more flavour and a firmer texture. Cut the rhubarb into 1 cm/½ inch pieces, sprinkle with the sugar and leave for 6 hours. Put into the pan, add the raisins, fruit rinds and orange juice. Stir over a low heat until the sugar has dissolved, then add the lemon juice and boil steadily until setting point is reached. Allow to cool slightly, stir well, then spoon into hot jars.

## Tomato Jam

*450 g/1 lb green or red tomatoes*
*3 tablespoons water if using green tomatoes*
*450 g/1 lb sugar*
*1-2 teaspoons ground ginger if using green tomatoes*
*2 tablespoons lemon juice*
*2 teaspoons grated orange rind if using red tomatoes*
*2 teaspoons grated lemon rind if using red tomatoes*

This jam is invaluable to serve with cold meats as a change from chutney. It is equally good as a filling in pastry cases. You can use either green or red tomatoes, the flavour can be varied.

Skin the tomatoes, cut into slices. If using green tomatoes, simmer with the water until a soft purée. Add the sugar, ginger and lemon juice. If using red tomatoes, omit the ginger and simmer the fruit without any water but with the finely grated fruit rinds.

When the tomatoes are soft add the sugar and lemon juice, stir until the sugar has dissolved then boil rapidly until setting point is reached. Spoon into hot jars.

## Lemon Curd

*225 g/8 oz sugar*
*3 medium lemons*
*100 g/4 oz butter*
*2 large eggs*

If using loaf sugar, rub this over the lemons until all the top part of the rind (the zest) is removed. If using granulated sugar then grate the top zest very finely; take care not to use any white pith.

Squeeze out the juice from the fruit. Put the lemon rind, juice, butter and sugar into a heatproof basin. Stand this over a pan of boiling water and heat until the butter and sugar have melted. Lower the heat, so the water is no longer boiling. Whisk the eggs, stir into the lemon mixture and cook slowly until the curd coats the back of a wooden spoon. Pour into hot jars and seal as jam.

VARIATION

**Orange Curd:** Use oranges instead of lemons.

# Making Marmalade

To most people marmalade is an essential part of a breakfast menu and good home-made marmalade is not difficult to make. This selection of recipes enables you to choose the kind of marmalade you prefer, from a rather bitter chunky type to the less usual flavours, based upon tangerines.

Traditional marmalade is made from Seville or bitter oranges, if you have not time to make the preserve when these are in season, freeze the fruit and use it later, but please do follow the advice about adding extra lemon juice on page 375.

Always simmer the peel of the fruit slowly and do not add the sugar until you are satisfied that the peel is really tender.

Marmalade is a preserve in which the setting period is very brief; if you over-boil the mixture you will pass this stage. Do read the comments about testing for setting on page 376.

The advice about the type of sugar to use and filling the jars given on page 376 is just as important when making marmalade as any other preserve.

## Orange Marmalade

*450 g/1 lb Seville or bitter oranges*
*1.7 litres/3 pints water*
*1.35 kg/3 lb sugar*
*3 tablespoons lemon juice*

Wash the oranges in cold water; halve and remove the pips and tie these in muslin. Shred or mince the peel and pulp of the oranges. Put the fruit to soak with the bag of pips, in the water for 12 hours. Tip the pulp, water and bag of pips into the pan and cover (see page 384). Simmer for 1½ hours, or until the peel is tender. Remove the bag of pips. Add the sugar and stir over a low heat until the sugar has dissolved. Add the lemon juice and boil rapidly until setting point is reached; cool until the marmalade has stiffened slightly, stir well and spoon into the hot jars.

VARIATIONS

**Sweet Orange Marmalade:** Use 450 g/1 lb sweet oranges, 1.2 litres/2 pints water, 900 g/2 lb sugar and 6 tablespoons lemon juice. Follow the method above.

**Lemon Marmalade:** Use 450 g/1 lb lemons, 1.2 litres/2 pints water, 900 g/2 lb sugar and 2 tablespoons extra lemon juice. Follow the method above.

**Mint and Lemon Marmalade:** Make the Lemon Marmalade, as above. When setting point is reached, stir in 6 tablespoons finely chopped fresh mint. Heat for 1 minute only. Cool slightly, stir and put into hot jars. Serve instead of Mint Sauce or Mint Jelly.

## Chunky Marmalade

*450 g/1 lb Seville or bitter oranges*
*scant 1.2 litres/2 pints water*
*900 g/2 lb sugar*

Wash the oranges in cold water. Put the oranges into the pan with the cold water. Cover the pan (a sheet of foil can be used to cover a preserving pan) and simmer gently for 1½ hours or until the peel is very soft. Remove the oranges from the liquid, cool sufficiently to handle then halve and remove the pips. Put these into the liquid in the pan and boil steadily for 10 minutes; strain and discard the pips, but return the liquid to the pan. Cut the halved oranges into neat small dice. Put into the liquid, heat gently, then add the sugar and stir over a low heat until dissolved. Boil rapidly until setting point is reached, cool until the marmalade has stiffened slightly, then spoon into hot jars.

## Jelly Marmalade

*450 g/1 lb Seville or bitter oranges*
*1.7 litres/3 pints water*
*1.35 kg/3 lb sugar*
*3 tablespoons lemon juice*

You can make a jelly marmalade with any of the fruits on page 383. The proportions of water, sugar and lemon juice are the same as when making thin cut marmalade.

Cut the top orange part of the rind from half the oranges, shred this very finely. Tie the pulp and pith from these oranges and the remaining halved fruit in muslin. Do not discard any pith or pips, for these are needed to give flavour and make the preserve set. Put the shredded peel into the water together with the bag of pulp, peel and pips. Soak for 12 hours. Tip all these ingredients into the pan, cover and simmer gently for 1½ hours, or until the peel is tender. Remove the bag of pips, pith and extra peel. Add the sugar, stir until dissolved then add the lemon juice; boil rapidly until setting point is reached. Cool, then stir well and spoon into hot jars.

## Tangerine Marmalade

*450 g/1 lb tangerines (see method)*
*scant 900 ml/1½ pints water*
*675 g/1½ lb sugar*
*3 tablespoons lemon juice*

Use tangerines with pips rather than the seedless variety as the pips help the marmalade to set.

If you like chunky marmalade, follow the method in the recipe above. If you prefer neatly sliced fruit follow the recipe on page 383.

Whichever method is used, add the lemon juice when the sugar has dissolved and be particularly careful to test early for the setting point, as this marmalade has an exceptionally short setting period.

# Making Jellies

A perfect jelly depends upon a good flavoured juice and the clarity of the cooked mixture. Do not increase the amount of water suggested in the recipes, for too much water produces an insipid liquid.

When straining the juice allow it to drip through the bag or muslin slowly; never squeeze the bag, for this would produce a cloudy liquid.

The stages of making jelly are simple.

a) Simmer the fruit and liquid slowly to extract the juice.

b) Strain this through a proper jelly bag (made of flannel, and obtainable from good ironmongers) or through several thicknesses of muslin placed over a nylon sieve.

c) Measure the juice and calculate the amount of sugar, or sugar and lemon juice required.

d) Heat the juice, add the sugar, stir until dissolved, then boil rapidly until setting point is reached. The comments about testing for setting, the type of sugar to use and filling the jars on page 376 are just as important when making jelly as any other preserve.

I have based the recipes on using 900 g/2 lb fruits.

## Apple Jelly

*900 g/2 lb crab apples or cooking apples*
*scant 600 ml/1 pint water*
*sugar (see method)*

Use the whole crab apples, or dice, but do not peel or core the cooking apples; put into the pan with the water. Cover and simmer gently to make a smooth purée. Put through the jelly bag. Measure the juice and to each scant 600 ml/1 pint, allow 450 g/1 lb sugar. Heat the juice, stir in the sugar, then allow the mixture to boil rapidly until setting point is reached. Pour into hot jars.

VARIATIONS

**Mint Jelly:** Allow 1 tablespoon finely chopped mint and 1 tablespoon white malt vinegar to each scant 600 ml/1 pint juice. Boil the juice and sugar until setting point is reached, stir in the mint and vinegar. Boil for 1 minute; cool slightly, stir well, then pour into hot jars.

Sage, tarragon and rosemary can be used instead of mint. Omit the vinegar for these jellies.

All these herb-flavoured sweet jellies are excellent with hot or cold meats and they can be served with curries as a change from chutney.

## Bramble Jelly

*225 g/8 oz cooking apples (see method)*
*150 ml/¼ pint water*
*900 g/2 lb blackberries*
*sugar (see method)*

Dice the apples but do not peel or core. Put into the pan with the water; cover the pan and simmer until the apples are nearly softened, then add the blackberries and continue cooking until a pulp. Put through the jelly bag. Measure the juice and allow 450 g/1 lb sugar to each scant 600 ml/1 pint. Heat the juice, add the sugar, stir until dissolved then boil rapidly until setting point is reached. Pour into hot jars.

VARIATION

Omit the apple and allow 2 tablespoons lemon juice to each scant 600 ml/1 pint blackberry juice. The blackberries should be cooked with only 4 tablespoons water

## Cucumber Jelly

*900 g/2 lb cucumbers*
*150 ml/¼ pint water*
*sugar (see method)*
*lemon juice (see method*
*ground ginger (see method)*

Chop the cucumbers into small pieces but do not remove the skin. Simmer with the water in a covered pan until a soft purée. Strain through a jelly bag. Allow 450 g/1 lb sugar, 2 tablespoons lemon juice and ½ teaspoon ground ginger to each scant 600 ml/1 pint juice. Heat the juice, add the sugar, stir until dissolved then add the lemon juice and ginger and boil rapidly until setting point is reached. Pour into hot jars. This is excellent with cold meats or fish dishes.

## Redcurrant Jelly

*900 g/2 lb redcurrants*
*150 ml/¼ pint water (if the fruit is very ripe or 300 ml/½ pint water if slightly under-ripe)*
*sugar (see method)*

Put the redcurrants and water into the pan. Cover and simmer until a soft pulp. Put through the jelly bag. Allow 450 g/1 lb sugar to each scant 600 ml/1 pint juice. Heat the juice, add the sugar and stir until dissolved, then boil rapidly until setting point is reached. Test for setting early, for redcurrants quickly pass this stage and if this happens the jelly does not set well. Pour into hot jars.

# Making Pickles

These preserves depend very much upon a good balance of flavours together with the use of vinegar to act as a preservative. Buy the best quality malt vinegar; choose white vinegar where you need to preserve a light or bright colour, but brown vinegar to darken a mixture.

When you need to make a brine, or salt the ingredients, buy household salt (sold in packs) not table salt.

Pickling spices vary in their strength; if the mixture is finely ground it is very strong, so be sparing with the amount used and shorten the cooking time, as detailed under Mustard Pickles below. Vinegar should be boiled in an aluminium or enamel pan.

Cover pickles carefully; never put metal lids next to the acid mixture, use a glass top or pad inside the metal cover with a thick layer of paper or cardboard.

## Mustard Pickles

*900 g/2 lb vegetables (include cauliflower, courgettes or marrow, cucumber, runner beans, shallots or pickling onions, tiny green tomatoes)*
*600 ml/1 pint brown malt vinegar*
*1-3 teaspoons pickling spices*
*½ tablespoon cornflour*
*1 tablespoon dry mustard powder*
*2 teaspoons turmeric*
*1-2 teaspoons ground ginger*
*50 g/2 oz sugar*
BRINE:
*50 g/2 oz salt (see above)*
*600 ml/1 pint water*

Put the salt and cold water into a large basin for the brine. Prepare the vegetables as though for cooking and divide the cauliflower into small florets; peel and dice the courgettes or marrow; dice the cucumber (this can be peeled if desired); string the runner beans and cut into bite-sized pieces; peel the shallots or onions; leave the skin on the tiny tomatoes. Put all the vegetables into the salt and water mixture and place a plate on top so they are well immersed in the solution. Leave them soaking for 12 hours. Drain the vegetables through a sieve and rinse in plenty of fresh cold water, allow to dry before proceeding further.

Boil three-quarters of the vinegar with the pickling spices. If you like a very mild flavour, bring the vinegar just to boiling point then strain. If you prefer a stronger taste, boil steadily for about 5 minutes then strain.

Blend all the remaining ingredients with the rest of the cold vinegar, add the strained hot vinegar; return to the pan and stir over a low heat until well thickened. Add the vegetables to the mustard sauce, stir to blend then simmer gently for 5 minutes only. Spoon into hot jars and seal, see introduction above.

VARIATION

**Sweet Mustard Pickle:** Increase the amount of sugar to 100-175 g/4-6 oz, according to personal taste.

## Vinegar Pickles

*900 g/2 lb mixed vegetables (as described on page 387)*
BRINE:
*50 g/2 oz salt*
*600 ml/1 pint water*
*approximately 600 ml/1 pint white or brown malt vinegar*
*1-3 teaspoons pickling spices*

Prepare the vegetables as page 387 and put into the salt and water brine, as described under Mustard Pickles. Boil the vinegar and pickling spices together as described on page 387; strain and cool. Pack the mixed vegetables into jars, cover with the cold spiced vinegar and seal the jars.

**Note:** It is essential that the vegetables are completely covered with the vinegar. The amount of vinegar given should be sufficient if the vegetables are tightly packed.

## Pickled Eggs

*12 eggs*
*600 ml/1 pint brown malt vinegar*
*1-3 teaspoons pickling spices*

These make an unusual and interesting accompaniment to an hors d'oeuvre or cold buffet menu. Hard-boil and shell the eggs. Boil the vinegar with the spices as described on page 387; strain and cool. Pack the eggs into jars, cover with the cold spiced vinegar and seal.

## Pickled Walnuts

*18 fresh walnuts*
*600 ml/1 pint brown or white malt vinegar*
*1-3 teaspoons pickling spices*
BRINE:
*50 g/2 oz salt*
*600 ml/1 pint water*

Walnuts must be picked when soft and green. Prick with a silver fork; place into the brine, made by mixing the salt and water together as described on page 387. Leave for 3 days. Lift the nuts from the brine and spread out on flat trays. Leave for 2 to 3 days, or until black in colour, turn every day. Boil the vinegar and pickling spices together, as described on page 387; strain and cool. Pack the nuts into jars; pour the cold vinegar over the nuts and seal the jars. Leave for at least one month to mature.

## Pickled Fruits

*600 ml/1 pint white malt vinegar*
*1 teaspoon pickling spices*
*450 g/1 lb sugar*
*900 g/2 lb ripe pears or peaches*

Simmer the vinegar and pickling spices as described on page 387; strain and return the vinegar to the pan. Add the sugar and stir until dissolved. Peel or skin the fruit and cut into halves or quarters. Put into the sweetened vinegar and simmer gently for 5 minutes. Lift the fruit from the vinegar with a perforated spoon and pack into jars. Boil the vinegar vigorously for 5 minutes, pour over the fruit and seal the jars.

# Making Chutney

Do not reduce the quantity of vinegar or sugar in the recipes, for these are the preservatives. Taste the chutney as you cook it and adjust the flavouring to suit your own palate.

The comments made about good vinegar and the correct covering of pickles on page 387 are equally important when making chutney.

Chutney mixtures should be cooked until they are the consistency of a thick jam. Choose an aluminium or enamel pan for cooking the mixture; do not use a brass, copper or iron pan.

## Mango Chutney

*1-2 teaspoons pickling spices*
*350 g/12 oz onions, finely chopped*
*600 ml/1 pint brown or white malt vinegar*
*900 g/2 lb mangoes, stoned and sliced*
*450 g/1 lb cooking apples (weight when peeled), sliced*
*450 g/1 lb granulated sugar*
*1-2 teaspoons ground ginger*

Now that mangoes are becoming more plentiful and less expensive, this is the chutney I prefer to make more than any other. It is a perfect partner to most curries. Tie the pickling spices in a muslin bag. Put the onions, pickling spices and half the vinegar into a pan; simmer until the onions are nearly tender. Add the remaining vinegar, mangoes and apples and cook until the fruit is soft. Stir in the sugar and ginger and boil steadily until the consistency of a thick jam. Remove the bag of spices. Spoon into hot jars and cover.

VARIATIONS

Add ½ to 1 teaspoon salt if desired.

**Sweet Tomato Chutney:** Use 900 g/2 lb skinned and chopped green tomatoes in place of mangoes; add 225 g/8 oz sultanas with the sugar and ginger. Green tomatoes make the better chutney, but red tomatoes can be substituted. Use light brown sugar.

**Spiced Tomato Chutney:** Use 1.35 kg/3 lb green tomatoes instead of mangoes; add 1 teaspoon black peppercorns and 1 teaspoon mustard seed to the pickling spices. Simmer the onions with the vinegar and spices in the above recipe, together with 2 red chilli (hot) peppers. Remove these when adding the apples and tomatoes. Continue as the above recipe. This chutney can be flavoured with 1 to 2 teaspoons salt.

**Apple Chutney:** Omit the mangoes and use 1.35 kg/3 lb cooking apples (weight when peeled). Continue as the above recipe, but use only 450 ml/¾ pint white malt vinegar. Light brown sugar makes the most pleasing colour. Add 175 g/6 oz sultanas with the sugar and ground ginger. You can omit the ginger and flavour the chutney with the grated rind and juice of 2 lemons.

## Beetroot Chutney

*350 g/12 oz onions, finely chopped*
*900 g/2 lb cooked beetroot, peeled and diced*
*350 g/12 oz cooking apples (weight when peeled), diced*
*450 ml/¾ pint white malt vinegar*
*1 teaspoon pickling spices*
*350 g/12 oz caster or granulated sugar*
*1½ teaspoons salt*

Put the onions, beetroot and apples into a pan with the vinegar. Tie the pickling spices into a muslin bag, add to the ingredients in the pan. Simmer steadily for about 30 minutes, or until the onions and apples are soft, then add the sugar. Stir well until dissolved, then boil steadily until the chutney becomes the consistency of a thick jam. Add the salt gradually during this process until the desired flavour is reached.

Remove the bag of spices and spoon the chutney into jars and seal as described on page 387.

VARIATION

**Beetroot and Horseradish Chutney:** Beetroot blends well with horseradish. Omit the pickling spices and add from 1 to 3 tablespoons grated fresh horseradish to the above recipe when adding the sugar. Add the horseradish gradually, tasting continually so that the chutney does not become too hot.

## Orange and Lemon Chutney

*3 large lemons*
*2 medium oranges*
*600 ml/1 pint white malt vinegar*
*225 g/8 oz onions, finely chopped*
*1 teaspoon pickling spices*
*1 teaspoon ground cinnamon*
*450 g/1 lb caster or granulated sugar*
*salt and pepper*

Halve the lemons and oranges; remove and discard the pips. Squeeze the fruit and put the juice on one side; then shred the peel, as though making marmalade. Put shredded peel and pulp into a bowl with the vinegar and leave to soak for 12 hours. Tip into a preserving pan and add the onions. Tie the spices in a muslin bag. Put spices, fruit juice and cinnamon into the pan.

Simmer steadily for about 1½ hours until the peel is very tender. Cover the preserving pan during this period, so the liquid does not evaporate too quickly. (If the pan has no lid, cover with a large piece of foil.) Stir in the sugar, add a little salt and pepper, then boil steadily, without covering the pan, until the mixture has the consistency of a thick jam. Remove the bag of spices and spoon the chutney into jars and seal (as described on page 387).

VARIATIONS

**Lemon Chutney:** Follow the recipe above, but use 4 large lemons instead of 3 lemons and 2 oranges.

**Grapefruit and Orange Chutney:** Follow the recipe above, but use 2 small or 1 large grapefruit and 3 oranges instead of 3 lemons and 2 oranges.

## Plum and Damson Chutney

*450 g/1 lb plums (weight when stoned), halved or quartered*
*450 g/1 lb damsons*
*450 g/1 lb cooking apples (weight when peeled), diced*
*450 g/1 lb onions, finely chopped*
*900 ml/1 ½ pints malt vinegar, white or brown*
*2 teaspoons pickling spices*
*1 to 2 teaspoons ground ginger*
*1 to 2 teaspoons salt*
*675 g/1 ½ lb granulated or caster sugar*

Put the fruits, onions and vinegar into a pan. Tie the pickling spices in a muslin bag; add to the ingredients in the pan and simmer until the mixture forms a thick purée. Remove the damson stones. Stir half the ginger and half the salt into the fruit mixture, together with the sugar. Boil the mixture steadily until it forms the consistency of a thick jam. Taste and add the rest of the ginger and salt, as desired. Remove the bag of spices and spoon the chutney into jars and seal (as described on page 387).

VARIATIONS

**Blackberry and Apple Chutney:** Follow recipe above but substitute 900 g/2 lb blackberries for the plums and damsons.

**Damson Chutney:** Follow recipe above but substitute a generous 900 g/2 lb damsons (the extra weight to compensate for the stones) for the plums and damsons.

**Rhubarb Chutney:** Follow recipe above but substitute 900 g/2 lb diced Autumn rhubarb, which has more flavour than the delicate Spring rhubarb, for the plums and damsons. The amount of ginger can be increased slightly as it blends well with rhubarb.

## Spiced Apricot Chutney

*1 large lemon*
*225 g/8 oz dried apricots, cut into thin slices*
*600 ml/1 pint white malt vinegar*
*2 teaspoons pickling spices*
*2 cloves garlic, peeled*
*350 g/12 oz cooking apples (weight when peeled), diced*
*100 g/4 oz seedless raisins*
*100 g/4 oz sultanas*
*450 g/1 lb light brown sugar*
*1 teaspspoon salt*

Grate the rind from the lemon, squeeze out the juice. Put the lemon rind, apricots, lemon juice and vinegar into a bowl and leave for several hours. Tip the mixture into a pan. Tie the pickling spices and whole garlic cloves in a muslin bag and put them into the pan containing the other ingredients. Simmer steadily for 30 minutes. Cover the pan during this period so the liquid does not evaporate too quickly. (If the pan has no lid then cover with a large piece of foil.) Add the diced apples and continue cooking for a further 30 minutes. Stir in the dried fruit, sugar and the salt. Boil the mixture steadily until it forms the consistency of a thick jam. Remove the bag of spices and garlic and spoon the chutney into jars and seal (as described on page 387).

# Ketchups and Vinegars

If you are able to obtain good supplies of tomatoes and mushrooms at a reasonable price, then it is worthwhile making your own ketchups. Ketchups should be frozen or the bottling jars sterilized, as given in the method below. Flavoured vinegar allows you to vary the flavour of salad dressing with the minimum of trouble.

## Tomato Ketchup ⊛

*2.25 kg/5 lb ripe tomatoes, chopped*
*450 g/1 lb cooking apples, cored and chopped*
*2 medium onions, finely chopped*
*scant 600 ml/1 pint white malt vinegar*
*1-2 teaspoons pickling spices*
*350 g/12 oz sugar*
*1-2 teaspoons salt*
*cayenne or white pepper to taste*

I find it better not to skin the tomatoes or peel the apples (these give flavour and colour to the sauce). Put the tomatoes, apples and onions into a pan, cover and heat gently until a purée. Rub through a nylon sieve; do this very firmly so only the skins and pips remain. You could use a food processor of liquidiser if you do not mind a slightly less smooth purée.

Bring the vinegar and pickling spices to the boil, then strain. Put the tomato purée and remaining ingredients (including the spiced vinegar) into a pan. Stir until the sugar has dissolved, then boil until a thick coating consistency. Pour the hot sauce into hot bottling jars; seal lightly as directed by the manufacturers. Stand in a pan of boiling water and allow the water to boil for 10 minutes. Remove the jars; tighten the seals.

If freezing, cool the sauce, put into small containers and freeze.

VARIATION

⊛ **Mushroom Ketchup:** Cut or break 2.25 kg/5 lb mushrooms into small pieces. Sprinkle with 75 g/3 oz salt. Leave for 24 hours. Meanwhile boil 300 ml/½ pint brown malt vinegar with 1 to 2 teaspoons pickling spices for 3 minutes then strain. Simmer the salted mushrooms, 2 finely chopped onions with the spiced vinegar in a covered pan until a thick purée. Add pepper to taste, then proceed as Tomato Ketchup above. This ketchup gives a good flavour to stews and gravy.

# Tempting Sweetmeats

I must confess that I am not a great eater of sweetmeats, although I produce them quite often, for they make delicious 'treats' and presents. Children love helping to make sweetmeats, but may I beg every adult to ensure they are never left in a kitchen with a pan of boiling sugar mixture, for nothing could cause more damaging burns if a child happened to knock against the pan and tip over the contents.

Some sweetmeats can be made without cooking the mixture and children can be left quite happily shaping these. You will find recipes on the next page; the cooked sweetmeats begin on page 395; in these the mixture must be cooked to the correct temperature to achieve the desired result. If you intend preparing an appreciable quantity of boiled sweets then it is well worthwhile investing in a sugar thermometer. These are not very expensive. There are all kinds of specialist moulds for shaping fondant and these give a very professional appearance to the completed sweets.

When boiling fudge or toffee use a really strong saucepan and one that is level on the base, so you achieve even cooking, sugar mixtures scorch easily. The recipes state whether, and when, you must stir, for continual stirring tends to lower the temperature of the mixture and could prevent it reaching the correct stage. Always stir the mixture until the sugar and fat (if used in the recipe) are adequately dissolved.

Keep a pastry brush and bowl of cold water beside the cooker, so you can brush down the inside surfaces of the saucepan, for as the sugar mixture splashes slightly during cooking it could set and become hard there; brushing down makes it softer and it drops back in the pan with the rest of the mixture.

There is a great sense of achievement in producing a good assortment of attractive looking sweetmeats. It is a form of cooking to which one easily becomes addicted and I would recommend it to those of you who have a favourite charity, for home-made sweets taste so good that you will have no problems in selling them and raising an appreciable amount of money for a good cause.

Keep toffees and sweets that become sticky when exposed to the air well wrapped after they set.

# Uncooked Sweetmeats

Royal icing and marzipan can make the basis for a whole range of sweetmeats, so that when you have either of these mixtures left over, after decorating a cake, use them for this purpose. Suggestions for using marzipan are on page 355.

## Hazelnut Creams

*Royal Icing, made with 225 g/8 oz icing sugar etc. (see page 358)*
*1 tablespoon double cream*
*few drops raspberry essence*
*few drops pink culinary colouring*
*24 to 36 hazelnuts*

Prepare the icing, as page 358, but add the cream to give a softer texture. Blend in a few drops of raspberry essence and sufficient colouring to make the mixture a delicate pale pink. The best way to measure both essence and colouring, and to avoid adding too much, is to dip a skewer into the bottle, remove this and allow the drops to fall from the skewer into the icing.

Divide the icing into 24 to 36 small portions, form each portion into a slightly rounded pyramid shape, press a hazelnut in the top of each sweetmeat. Allow to harden in the air.

If you have special fondant moulds, press the nuts into the small portions of sweetmeat, place in the mould and allow to harden.

VARIATIONS

**Peppermint Creams:** Make the Royal Icing, add the cream as in the recipe above, then work in a few drops of peppermint essence or oil of peppermint. Do this gradually, so that you do not use too much flavouring. Dust a rolling pin and board with a little sifted icing sugar, roll out the uncooked fondant, cut into tiny rounds and leave in the air to harden.

**Chocolate Fondants:** Make small shapes of the fondant (as in main recipe above) and allow to become firm. Add chopped glacé cherries or nuts to some of the small sweets. To coat remainder melt about 300 g/10 oz plain chocolate or chocolate couverture in a basin over hot, but not boiling, water. Drop one or two sweetmeats into the warm chocolate, turn with two forks or small spoons until coated, then lift out and allow the chocolate to set. Continue like this until all the sweets are covered. Decorate the chocolate-coated sweets with tiny pieces of cherry or nut.

## Vanilla Fudge

*450g/1 lb granulated sugar*
*50g/2oz butter*
*397g/14oz can full-cream sweetened condensed milk*
*150ml/¼ pint milk*
*½ to 1 teaspoon vanilla essence*

Put all the ingredients into a saucepan, stir over a low heat until the sugar and butter have dissolved, then boil steadily, stirring quite frequently, until the mixture reaches the 'soft ball' stage. This means that when a little piece is dropped into cold water it forms a ball that can be rolled, but never quite holds its shape. If using a sugar thermometer it should register 114.4°C/238°F. Take care not to exceed this temperature, otherwise the fudge will reach a stage between fudge and caramel, which does not set properly. Beat the mixture in the pan until it turns cloudy; this is important, for it gives fudge its characteristic appearance. Butter a tin about 20cm/8 inch square, pour in the mixture, allow to set, then cut into pieces with a sharp knife. Pack in a box. Fudge does not need individual wrapping.

VARIATIONS

For a firmer, and less creamy, fudge use water in place of the milk in the recipe above; for economy use skimmed condensed milk.

**Chocolate Fudge:** Add either 50g/2oz cocoa powder to the melted ingredients in the above recipe or 100g/4oz diced plain chocolate when the final stage is reached.

**Fruit and Nut Fudge:** Add approximately 75g/3oz seedless raisins or sultanas and 50 to 75g/2 to 3oz chopped blanched almonds or chopped walnuts to the fudge when it reaches the final stage.

**Extra Rich Fudge:** Use the above recipe, but substitute 150ml/¼ pint double cream for the fresh milk.

## Nougat

*50g/2oz blanched almonds*
*75g/3oz glacé cherries*
*225g/8oz granulated sugar*
*15g/½oz butter*
*4 tablespoons water*
*1 egg white*
*2 to 4 sheets rice paper*

Cut the almonds into narrow strips. Dice the cherries. Put the sugar, butter and water into a saucepan, stir until the sugar and butter have melted, and boil until the mixture reaches a 'firm ball' (see Vanilla Caramels on page 396, i.e. mixture comes to 121°C/250°F). Stir in the almonds and cherries. Whisk the egg white until stiff and fold into the nougat mixture. Place half the rice paper in a 15cm/6 inch square tin, top with the nougat then more rice paper. Allow to set, then cut into fingers or in squares. Wrap in waxed paper.

VARIATION

**Raspberry Nougat:** Add a few drops raspberry essence to the mixture before adding the almonds and cherries.

## Everton Toffee

*100 g/4 oz butter*
*225 g/8 oz granulated sugar*
*225 g/8 oz golden syrup*

Put the three ingredients into a saucepan, stir over a low heat until the butter and sugar have dissolved. Boil steadily until the mixture reaches the 'hard crack' stage, i.e. if you drop a small amount of the sugar mixture into cold water you can hear a distinct crack as this sets into a hard mixture. If you have a sugar thermometer it should register 142.5°C/290°F. Grease a 15 cm/6 inch tin with butter, pour the toffee mixture into this and allow to become nearly set, then mark into squares. When quite cold and set, wrap each piece of toffee in a small square of waxed paper.

VARIATIONS

If you like a slightly softer toffee, boil only to 137.5°C/280°F; this is known as the 'crack stage', for the toffee mixture does not become quite as brittle.

**Toffee Apples:** This toffee can be used to coat apples. Wipe small crisp eating apples, insert a wooden skewer in each one. Make the toffee as above recipe, keep warm in the pan. Dip the first apple in cold water and shake off the surplus water. Dip the apple into the toffee, turn until coated, then dip in cold water again to make the toffee set. Continue like this until all the apples are coated. To make sure the toffee keeps warm, stand the saucepan in another pan of boiling water. This amount of toffee should coat 6 small apples. Wrap each apple in waxed paper when the toffee is quite set.

**Treacle Toffee:** Use black treacle instead of golden syrup in the above recipe.

**Nut Toffee:** Stir about 100 g/4 oz chopped blanched almonds or other nuts into the toffee at the final stage.

## Vanilla Caramels

*450 g/1 lb granulated sugar*
*100 g/4 oz butter*
*397 g/14 oz can full-cream sweetened condensed milk*
*1 tablespoon golden syrup*
*2 tablespoons water*
*½ teaspoon vanilla essence*
*pinch cream of tartar*

Put all the ingredients, except the cream of tartar, into a saucepan. Stir over a low heat until the sugar and butter have melted, then allow the mixture to boil steadily until it reaches the 'firm ball' stage. This means that when a little of the mixture is dropped in cold water it forms a ball, that can be shaped quite easily. Stir from time to time. The temperature for caramels varies. If you like a very soft 'chewy' type then boil only to 121°C/250°F; but if you like a firmer caramel boil to 131°C/270°F. Add the cream of tartar, stir well to blend. Grease a 15 cm/6 inch tin with butter, pour in caramel mixture, allow to nearly set, then mark into squares. When quite set, wrap each caramel in a small square of waxed paper.

# A to Z of Cookery Terms

**Arrowroot**
A starch used for thickening sauces.

**Aspic**
A clear savoury jelly used for setting and as a garnish.

**Bain marie**
A large roasting pan half-filled with water, in which a dish of food is cooked in the oven; the water prevents the food curdling or drying.

**Bake blind**
A pastry case cooked in the oven without a filling. It is lined with greaseproof paper and dried beans or with foil while being cooked.

**Basting**
To prevent meat becoming dry while roasting, spoon over the juices and melted fat from the pan to moisten the meat.

**Blanching**
Blanching means to boil briefly to whiten certain meats such as tripe; to remove the skin from almonds; to preserve the colour of vegetables and kill enzymes before freezing; or to remove strong flavours from foods.

**Blending**
Mixing liquids or solids together.

**Boiling**
Cooking in a liquid at 100°C/212°F.

**Bouquet garni**
A small bunch of herbs tied together in muslin or bought ready-made in sachets. Used to flavour savoury dishes.

**Braising**
Food is usually browned in hot fat then cooked slowly in a covered dish with vegetables.

**Casserole**
A dish with a tightly fitting lid used to cook meat and vegetables. It can be ovenproof for oven use only, or flameproof for using on top of the cooker as well as in the oven.

**Chopping**
A sharp knife and chopping board are used to cut food into small pieces.

**Coating**
Covering food with flour, egg and crumbs or with a batter.

**Consistency**
Used to describe the texture of a mixture.

**Creaming**
Mixing ingredients, often fat and sugar, to the consistency of cream.

**Crimping**
To decorate the pastry edge of a flan or tart by giving it a fluted effect.

**Croquettes**
Mixtures of fish, meat or potatoes, formed into shapes, then coated with egg and crumbs and deep fried.

**Curdle**
When mixing or cooking foods, the ingredients separate.

**Dice**
Using a sharp knife, cut foods into small even cubes.

**Dredging**
Food is sprinkled lightly with flour or sugar.

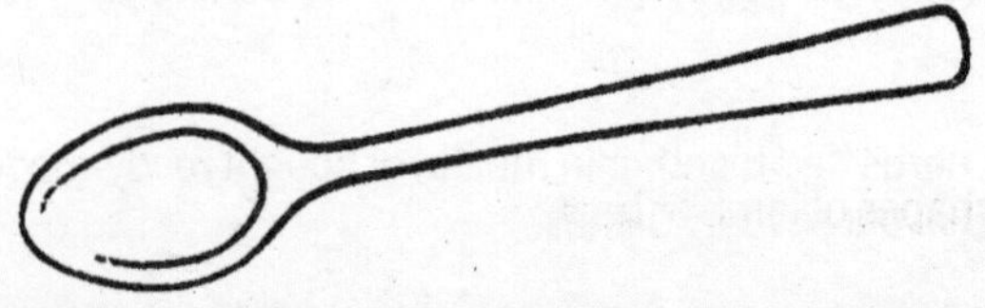

**Flaking**
To divide fish into small pieces using a fork.

**Folding in**
Incorporating one ingredient into another by very gentle folding to keep mixture as light as possible.

**Frying**
To cook in hot fat – either shallow frying in a frying pan or deep frying in a deep fat fryer.

**Glaze**
Usually beaten egg, egg white or milk brushed on to give a shine.

**Grilling**
Cooking or browning under the heat of a grill.

**Kneading**
Working a dough firmly – usually when making pastry or bread.

**Knock back**
To knead a yeast dough that has 'proved' until it has returned to its original size.

**Marinade**
A mixture of oil, wine, vinegar, herbs and spices in which meat or fish is left for a time to tenderize and flavour the food.

**Meringue**
Whisked egg whites and sugar dried in an oven until crisp.

**Mincing**
Chopping foods into very small pieces with a knife or mincer.

**Noisettes**
Trimmed round shapes of lamb or beef.

**Par-boiling**
The food is partially cooked by boiling, then finished by another method of cooking.

**Paring**
Thinly removing skin or rind from citrus fruits.

**Poaching**
To cook food slowly in simmering liquid.

**Prove**
Dough is left covered with polythene in a warm place until risen.

**Purée**
A smooth mixture which has either been sieved or liquidized in a blender or a food processor.

**Roasting**
To cook meat, poultry or vegetables in extra fat, or fat of meat, in the oven or over a rotisserie spit.

**Roux**
A mixture of fat and flour which are cooked as the basis of a sauce.

**Rubbing-in**
A method of incorporating fat into flour with the fingertips to make shortcrust pastry and some cakes.

**Sauté**
The food is cooked in fat or oil in a pan over a strong heat, shaking the pan to make the food 'sauter' or jump so that it does not stick.

**Season**
Either to add salt and pepper to a dish, or to prepare an omelette pan or wok before using for the first time.

**Sieve**
Passing an ingredient through a sieve or strainer to remove any lumps.

**Simmer**
To cook just below boiling point so that there is just an occasional bubble.

**Sponge**
Either a type of light cake, or the first stages in yeast cooking.

**Steaming**
A method of cooking food in the steam from boiling water.

**Stewing**
The food is simmered slowly in liquid in a covered container.

**Toss**
Turning a pancake to cook the other side.

**Trussing**
Tying a joint of meat or bird into a neat shape using string or skewers.

**Whip**
To beat eggs until frothy and cream until thick.

# Turn disaster into Success!

We all have those days when everything seems to go wrong – here are some ways to rescue those disasters.

**Sauces or stews with a lumpy sauce?**
Lift the meat and any vegetables from the liquid in the stew and keep them warm. Whisk the liquid or sauce well, rub through a sieve or put into a liquidizer and blend until smooth. Reheat the smooth sauce and add the meat etc.

**Sauces, stews or soups that taste too salty?**
Add 2 or 3 peeled and sliced potatoes to the liquid. Simmer for 10 minutes then remove the potatoes. If still rather salty, blend in a little milk or cream as this absorbs the flavour.

**Sauces, soups or stews that have burned?**
Do not stir – pour gently and carefully into a clean pan. Flavour with curry, chutney or mustard to camouflage the burnt flavour. If it is a sweet sauce, add vanilla or almond essence.

**Stew or casserole with too thin a sauce or gravy?**
Remove the crusts from a slice of bread (this can be spread with butter and chopped herbs or made mustard if wished). Drop into the pan or casserole. Leave for 10 minutes and then stir in briskly until blended. If preferred, blend a little cornflour with cold liquid and add to the stew or casserole.

**The meal is ready, but the joint is not really cooked?**
Slice the meat neatly and heat gently in the sauce or gravy. Or put on buttered foil on the grill pan and heat under the grill.

**The joint of meat is over-cooked?**
Cut into thick steaks to serve not neat slices.

**The meat is over-cooked in a stew?**
Quickly make toast or fried bread, lift the meat from the gravy on to the crisp base (to give a change of texture) and pour round the gravy.

**Pastry breaks badly as it is rolled out?**
Put the pastry on waxed paper, cover with waxed paper and roll out firmly.

**The pastry sticks as it is rolled out?**
Either liberally dust with flour although this does tend to spoil the basic proportions of the pastry. Or gather up the sticky dough and chill for 1 hour.

**The mayonnaise has curdled?**
Put a fresh egg yolk into a basin, gradually whisk the curdled mixture on to this and it will thicken.

**The cake or pastry has burned?**
Rub a fine grater gently over the cake or pastry or remove the burned part. Dust a cake with sieved icing sugar, a sweet pie with sieved icing sugar or caster sugar, and a savoury pie with finely grated cheese, mixed with a little chopped parsley.

**The cake has sunk in the centre?**
Cut out the centre carefully and turn the outside into a ring cake. Ice or decorate if wished. Crumble the cake from the centre and blend with an egg. Steam for 35-40 minutes and serve as a hot pudding. Or slice the cake from the centre neatly, dip in beaten egg and fry in hot butter. Sprinkle with sugar and serve as fritters.

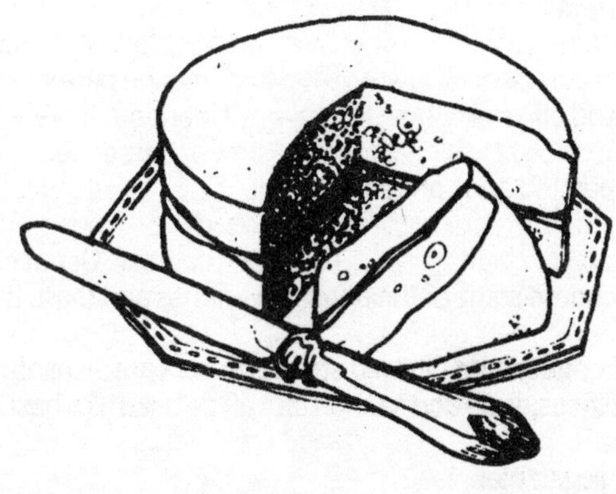

# Good Store Guide

Shopping takes a great deal of time and effort, so it is wise to have a well stocked larder, refrigerator and freezer (if you own this appliance).

**In the store cupboard**
Plain and self-raising flour
Breakfast cereals
Cornflour
Custard powder
Cake mixes
Raising agents and dried yeast
Rice – long grain for savoury dishes; short grain for puddings
Pasta – macaroni and spaghetti
Dehydrated vegetables for convenience and quickness
Dried herbs when fresh are unobtainable
Nuts – ground almonds, whole almonds and walnut halves
Sugar – granulated, caster and demerara
Bottled sauces – tomato ketchup, Worcestershire sauce etc.
Spices
Pickles and chutneys
Jams and marmalade
Vinegar
Oil – cooking oil and olive oil
Dried fruit
Milk – dried, evaporated and condensed
Tea
Coffee
Canned soups – choose some of the unusual varieties and those that could be used for sauces
Canned meats – tongue, ham, stewed steak and pork are all useful
Canned fish – sardines, tuna and salmon can all be used as a basis for interesting dishes
Canned fruit and vegetables
Root vegetables – store in a cool place
Citrus fruits – store in a cool place

**In the refrigerator**

Use your refrigerator sensibly and do not expect perishable foods to keep more than a few days. Ensure you use items such as butter and milk in the correct order; it is all too easy to bring in fresh supplies, use these first and still have the old stocks. You will probably use much of your refrigerator space for meat and fish and for left-over foods you plan to use up within a day or two, but in addition check you have:

Butter, margarine and other fats
Cheese – hard cheeses like Cheddar store well, covered
Bacon
Eggs
Salad ingredients and fresh herbs

**In the freezer**

Keep a clear record of what is in the cabinet and where it has been placed. Label packages of food clearly so there is no problem finding them and so that you can keep a good idea of your stock. In addition to cooking dishes to keep in the freezer for emergencies, these are some of the most useful frozen foods to store:

Vegetables and fruits
Meat – steaks, chops and smaller pieces of meat can be cooked from the frozen state
Fish – ready-coated for frying
Bread, cakes and scones – sliced bread can be toasted from the frozen state and rolls need just a few minutes to warm through
Ice cream – home-made or can be bought in bulk

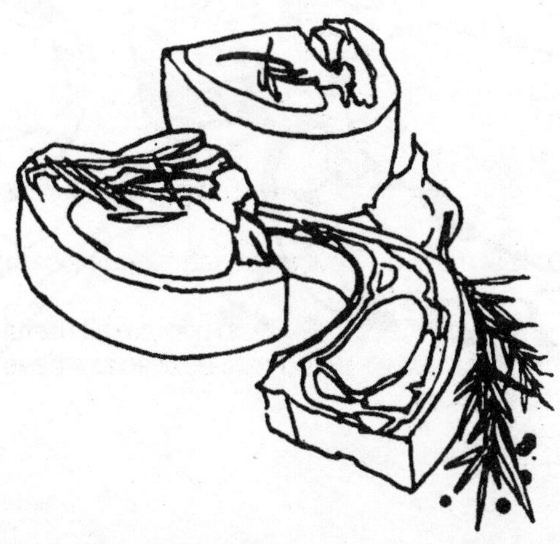

FLO

# Index

Illustrations by Mary Tomlin.